ESSAYS IN SOUND

CONTEMPORARY SOUND ARTS

ESSAYS IN SOUND
Published and edited by Contemporary Sound Arts
PO Box 1265, Darlinghurst NSW 2010, Australia

Editors: Alessio Cavallaro, Shaun Davies, Eddy Jokovich, Annemarie Jonson
Design: ARMEDIA
Contact: info@armedia.net.au

CSA was established in Australia in 1991 to facilitate an interdisciplinary approach to the critical investigation of sound, encompassing historical, political, philosophical, artistic, and technological perspectives, and to engage in and support research, and the production and distribution of various forms of print and electronic media related to sound.

ISBN 978-0-9587956-0-9

©1992, 1995, 1996, 1999. Contents copyright of Contemporary Sound Arts, and the respective authors, artists and photographers.

Republished in 2016.

IMPORTANT NOTE:

Essays In Sound was a series of four individual publications produced during the 1990s, and has been packaged here as one publication. The details contained in each publication are correct as at the respective original publication dates and have not been updated. Because of this, details of many authors are not current.

ESSAYS IN SOUND

1–1992

FIRST

CONTEMPORARY SOUND ARTS

ESSAYS IN SOUND
Published and edited by Contemporary Sound Arts
PO Box 1265, Darlinghurst NSW 2010, Australia

Editors: Shaun Davies, Annemarie Jonson, Eddy Jokovich
Design: ARMEDIA

Special thanks to W. P. Lowe

CSA was established in Australia in 1991 to facilitate an interdisciplinary approach to the critical investigation of sound, encompassing historical, political, philosophical, artistic, and technological perspectives, and to engage in and support research, and the production and distribution of various forms of print and electronic media related to sound. These concerns are also expressed in public activities such as the SOUNDcheck series of forums and other events.

©1992. Contents copyright of Contemporary Sound Arts, and the respective authors, artists and photographers.

First published in 1992. Republished in 2016.

Contents

Miniature Sound: Notes on a Soundscape for a Radio Program on Nanotechnologies *Ian Andrews*	8
Architecture and Sound: A Statement by Edgard Varèse *Translated by Phillip L. Ryan*	14
More Than Just Married: Sound and Image in Jackie McKimmie's No Problems *Trish FitzSimons*	17
Verbal Judo (Demonstration Script) *Brent Clough*	22
Circuits of the Voice: From Cosmology to Telephony *Frances Dyson*	24
Philip Glass: Collaborating with Ginsberg *Interviewed by Nicholas Zurbrugg*	36
Xenakis: Towards a Philosophy of Music *Phillip L. Ryan*	41
Found Sounds *Michael Leggett*	47
Paul DeMarinis: The Melodic Voice Box *Interviewed by Shaun Davies and Annemarie Jonson*	49
Transcription Drawings *Ruark Lewis*	58
The Acoustics of Saint John the Evangelist's Church, Camden *Brian Marland*	60
Eisenstein and Cartoon Sound *Douglas Kahn*	63
Extract from 'Modes for Listening', a Work in Progress *Ashley Scott*	69
Chris Mann: A Viewpoint on Telematics and Sound *Interviewed by Daniel Cole*	76
Towards a Phenomenological Archaeology of Sound in its Relation to Musical Experiment *Phillip L. Ryan*	82
A Note On Juan Lamilliar's *Caballos en el Jardin*[1] *Martin Harrison*	85
Radio is My Bomb *Raking the Shagpile*	92
Some Monuments for a Critical History of Music, Sound Generation and Transmission *Phillip L.Ryan*	94
Homage to John Cage	100

Notes on Contributors [1992]

Ian Andrews is a film, video and music maker based in Sydney.

Brent Clough is a writer and presenter at Radio Notional, Australian Broadcasting Corporation, Sydney.

Daniel Cole is a member of the Peel sound performance group, and a sound producer based in Sydney.

Frances Dyson is an audio artist and theorist in sound studies based in the USA.

Trish FitzSimons is a sound producer, and lecturer in Screen Production at Griffith University, Queensland.

Martin Harrison is a writer and sound producer, and lecturer in sound composition and the cultural study of sound and radio at the University of Technology, Sydney.

Douglas Kahn is an artist and writer, and associate professor in Arts and Sciences at Arizona State University West, USA.

Michael Leggett has worked with film, video and sound for many years, and is currently developing work utilising computers.

Ruark Lewis is an artist based in Sydney.

Brian Marland is a lecturer in Environmental Science with the Faculty of Architecture, University of Newcastle, and tutor in Environmental Science at the University of Sydney.

Phillip L. Ryan is a graduate in Sociology and Philosophy. He is also a writer, artist and translator.

Ashley Scott is a composer based in Sydney.

Nicholas Zurbrugg is a writer, and senior lecturer in Humanities at Griffith University, Queensland.

Editorial

<< listen >>

The known world is a noisy ball.*

Occasionally, noises assemble as scraps of speech, perhaps as a tune once forgotten, as declarative statements that can be heard plainly in the din—a mutable and plangent tableau.

This edition of *Essays In Sound* attempts to engage in the critical investigation of sound in its various modalities—ranging across fragmentary historical, technological, political and philosophical terrains. Gathered around this tenuous title, these works do not assume any univocity, nor claim any thematic or doxa. Rather, they may momentarily harmonise, echo and interweave, or clamorously compete.

This is not to suggest that any attempt to locate sound through particular readings leads ineluctably into misprision; rather, it serves to reminds us of a certain vagrancy that tends to resist acts of taxonomic registration. But theoretical 'nomadism' need not imply a disengagement or abandonment of context or place, the 'siting' of aural practices—their embodiment, literal and otherwise, in a world felt, thought or experienced. For studies in sound offer possibilities for productive engagement not yet imagined within a philosophical paradigm bedazzled by light (that of western reason). As Hannah Arendt reminds us: "...if one considers how easy it is for sight, unlike the other senses, to shut out the outside world, one may wonder why hearing did not develop into the guiding metaphor for thinking."

* From "Mystery Tapes" by Mystery laboratory, in *Sound By Artists*, edited by Don Lander and Micah Lexier, Art Metropole and Walter Phillips Gallery, 1990.

Miniature Sound: Notes on a Soundscape for a Radio Program on Nanotechnologies

Ian Andrews

> "I once read somewhere that a hermit who was watching his hour-glass without praying, heard noises that split his eardrums. He suddenly heard the catastrophe of time, in the hour glass. The tick tock of our watches is so mechanically jerky that we no longer have ears subtle enough to hear the passage of time."
>
> —Gaston Bachelard[1]

Nanotechnology is electro–chemical–biological technology of the very small, (the prefix *nano* denotes the order of ten to the minus nine). To what extent is it possible to apply notions of the miniature to theories of sound, and conversely to conceive of a soundscape which relates to microminiaturisation and the infinitesimal?

***

Sound is an alteration in pressure, particle displacement, or particle velocity which is propagated in an elastic medium (air). But sound is also the auditory sensation produced through the ear by the alterations described above.

The first port of this description belongs to the objective realm of science, while the second, requiring the presence of a subject of perception, finds its place in the domain of phenomenology. A phenomenological description of sound would consist of the knowledge that a disinterested subject, 'living among things', might acquire of the spatial relationships between objects and sounds, as well as a reflective description that seeks out underlying relationships from an ideal non-position, a pure position distinct from the situation of the object in its concrete context. But the perceptual object is, to a large extent, a cultural phenomenon which is both socially and linguistically constructed. The subject of perception has an *a priori* knowledge of things, of space, of dimension and direction, which precedes perception. This body of knowledge contributes to the formation of the phenomenological 'perceptual cogilo' which orders the passage from perceptual meaning to language meaning, from behaviour to thematisation. But there is also a prejudicative *logos* that remains hidden, veiled by language, and implicit in perception, which establishes a level at which every other experience will henceforth be situated. Merleau–Ponty calls this level "the invisible". The invisible is to the visible what the unconscious is to consciousness. For Merleau–Ponty, perception, like the unconscious, is structured like a language.

Merleau–Ponty, in *The Visible and the Invisible*, formulates a philosophy of the flesh. The flesh is the body in as much as it is the audible hearer; the equivalence of sensibility and sensible thing; the doubling up of the body into inside and outside; an intertwining of introjection and projection. Merleau–Ponty insists that we must reject the Cartesian model, which places the perceptual cogito inside the body, which is consequently placed in the world. "The body sensed and the body

Miniature Sound: Notes on a Soundscape for a Radio Program on Nanotechnologies

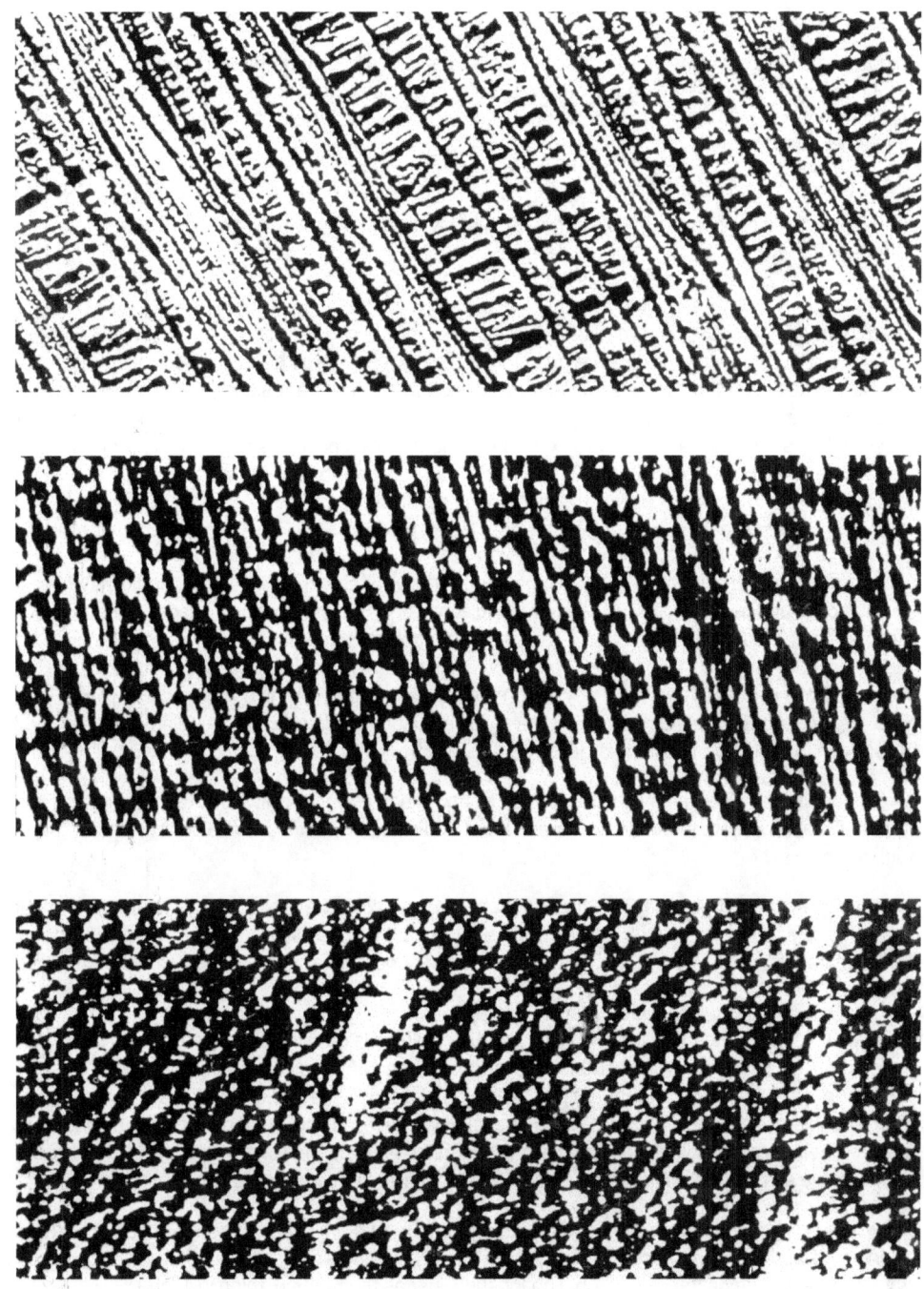

sentient are as the obverse and the reverse".[2] The flesh is not matter, not mind, not substance, but an 'element' of being; "not objects, but fields, subdued being, non-thetic being, being before being".[3]

Things become dimensions only insofar as they are received in a field, the body is this field itself; "my body is to the greatest extent what everything is".[4] The subject of perception in this case becomes not one of phenomenological interiority, but rather a complex interpenetration of outside and inside.

There is no boundary between the self and the external world. Reality is not things (dead matter) but events, fields of energy, Eros and Thanatos, libidinal cathexes, flux, bands of intensity, differentiations of the flesh.

***

The miniature, however, problematises the perception of the subject, for whom it constitutes a remoteness (for Heidegger, a *de-severance* [*enterferung*] as regards being-in-the-world) that cannot be visualised; "this knowledge still remains blind".[5] The "lived distance" which binds us to things disappears and so, in terms of perception and subjectivity, the micro and the macro present a reality that is unlivable and unbearable to anthropomorphic consciousness. The schizophrenic lives at one extreme of the Chiasm; "'I' the world" (as opposed to 'I', the other), as close as possible to matter, " ...the terribly disturbing sound of matter".[6]

***

Imagine a miniature (virtual) perception made possible with advances in nanotechnology, where we can construct self-replicating automata, and send them into microscopic spaces to gather information, to 'hear' for us with micro-miniature microphones and nanotransducers, with built-in interactive autonomous machine perception, possessing the same dynamics and frequency characteristics as the human ear. They become ears; ears ripped off the body, the body made obsolete. William Burroughs recognised the aural implications of self-replicating automata with the sudden availability of tape recorders in the 1960s.[7]

What could be described as miniature sound? Sound made by very small objects (of miniature origin)? Or small (faint) sound on the threshold of audibility, regardless of the dimensions of the originating object?

It may at first seem logical to posit the first schema, as it could be argued that a faint sound made by a large object is merely an effect of distance. But does not this assumption betray one of the fundamental problems of western metaphysics: the distinction between cause and effect, object and sound?

Christian Metz describes a "primitive substantialism" which is ingrained in the culture of the west, designating sound always as an attribute, a non-object, and ontologically privileging the visible object of emission. This undoubtedly has something to do with the subject–predicate structure of Indo–European language, which for Nietzsche, always places 'being' behind' doing'.Nietzsche argues that in language we separate the lightning from its flash and thus we duplicate the doing— we make the same phenomenon first a cause and then the effect of that cause:

Our whole science is still, in spite of its coldness, of all its freedom from passion, a dupe of the tricks of language, and has never succeeded in getting rid of that superstitious changeling 'the subject' (the atom, to give another instance of such a changeling, just as the Kantian 'thing in itself').[8]

Because western metaphysics privileges the material over the immaterial, we have the tendency to neglect the characteristics of the sound itself in favour of those of the originating 'substance'.

In Lautreamont's *Moldoror*, a spider listens:

> It listens attentively for any sound that may be moving its mandibles in the air. Allowing for its quality as an insect, it cannot do less, if it has any ambitions of adding brilliant personifications to the treasures of literature, than to attribute mandibles to sounds.[9]

With the aid of Nietzsche we can begin to recognise what at first seems strange in the logic of Loutreamont's 'spider': that which questions the cause–effect, subject–predicate oppositions of language by inverting the equation and thus making the object an attribute of a sound.

***

It becomes clear that if we consider sound as a phenomenon in itself (as a process or a becoming), and dispense with the need to establish origins, a de-materialised notion of miniature sound must extend to all that is on and below the threshold of hearing.

In an anechoic chamber hearing does not cease, but merely changes from acoustic to visceral: from consciousness 'at a distance' to self-proximity. The composer John Cage, in such a room, still hears two distinct sounds, one high, and one low. He is told that the high sound is his nervous system and that the low sound is his blood circulating. Silence, even relative, is destroyed as soon as there is a body to perceive it.

***

The smaller an object is, the less its behaviour can be understood in terms of traditional abstract geometrical localisation. The study of micro-physics reveals the condition that the spatial position of a material object cannot be exactly determined. The artificial distinction between geometrical and temporal descriptions breaks down, necessitating a phenomenalist synthesis of space and time. It is impossible to conceive of an object independently of its movement. The ontological consequences of this are that we can no longer distinguish between what is real 'now' and what will be real in some time in the future. This has lead to a shift, in physics, from a study of spatial forms of matter, to a study which re-unites energy and matter, and which is bound up with the hypergeometry of space–time. This entails that matter be thought of not as 'thing oriented' but as 'event oriented'.

Here we encounter again the problem of language, which is inherently substantialistic. As with sound we tend to think of energy as an attribute or a quality, and thus we attribute too much importance to the atom as a causal entity. We should not say that matter *has* energy, but rather that matter *is* energy and, conversely, that energy *is* matter.

Energy, like sound, is immaterial and insubstantial, it is devoid of an obvious structure, it occupies a middle ground between potential and actual, between space and time. Gaston Bachelard argues that "In its energetic unfolding the atom is *becoming* as much as it is being, motion as much as it is object".[10] He suggests that the implications of Einstein's equation $E=mc^2$ are not only transformational, but ontological: "it obliges us to ascribe existence to radiation as much as to particles, to motion as much as to matter".[11]

***

In *The Poetics of Space*, Bachelard explores the theme of the miniature in literature, in a phenomenology of the poetic imagination in which each sense has its own imaginary. Bachelard argues that the miniature worlds of the imagination provide an exercise in "metaphysical freshness", which permits the philosopher to renew his experiences of "an opening onto the world", "of entrance into the world".[12]

It is here that Bachelard introduces the "sound miniature", inviting us to hear in regions beyond perception, to hear the impossible sounds of the poet's imagination, from Poe's auditory hallucinations to the sonorous depth of being in Claudel's *L'annonce Faile a Marie*:

> VIOIAINE (who is blind): —I hear...
>
> MARA: What do you hear?
>
> VIOLAINE: Things existing with me.[13]

For Bachelard, Claudel's dialogue establishes the ontological link between the invisible and the inaudible, and the confirmation of existence through that which is audible.

Bachelard's explorations into "ultra-hearing" provide a point of departure for a phenomenology of the verb 'to listen'. Thus he speaks of a "hearing oneself seeing," and a "hearing oneself listening". But what is the relation between "hearing oneself listen" and "hearing oneself speak"?

Jacques Derrida, in questioning the phenomenological value of the voice, argues that hearing oneself speak (*s'entendre parler*) is pure auto-affection, which gives the illusion of self-presence, resulting in an apparent transcendence of the voice with regard to signification. When we speak, we hear ourselves at the same time that we speak; we hear the sounds (phonemes), and we understand and are affected by the expressive intention (the signifiers) that we produce, without a detour into the external world (as in seeing ourselves). To hear oneself speak is to hear our own presence in the self-assured certitude of consciousness, and "consciousness as meaning (*Vouloirdire*) in self-presence".[14]

***

For Derrida, this pure auto-affection, occurring in absolute proximity to self, constitutes an "absolute reduction of space in general":

> As pure auto-affection, the operation of hearing oneself speak seems to reduce even the inward surface of one's own body; in its phenomenal being it seems capable of dispensing with this exteriority within interiority, this interior space in which our experience or image of our own body is spread forth.[15]

***

What remains for a phenomenology of sound is to rescue sound from speech (*phone*), and thus from apparent transcendence and onto-theological ideality. Saussure distinguishes the sound-image, the "psychological imprint of the sound",[16] from the material sound. For Derrida, real objective sound, in the world, though indispensible to the sound-image, is radically dissimilar to it. The sound-image, the *being heard* (heard + understood) of the sound, is "*lived* and *informed* by differance".[17] Derrida assigns objective sound to external experience, to the non-phenomenal, the unheard, the inaudible, and thus neglects that which, in sound, is heterogenous to meaning and signification.

What is needed is a study of pure objective sound in language; that which is pre-predicative, the 'inarticulate cry', echolalias, rhythms, intonations, glossolalias, the musication of speech, in short, that which "produces shapes and exceeds operating consciousness".[18]

1. Gaston Bachelard, *The Poetics of Space*, trans. Maria Jolas, Beacon Press, Boston, 1969, p. 167.

2. Maurice Merleau-Ponty, *The Visible and the Invisible*, trans. Alphonso Lingis, Northwestern University Press, Evanston, 1987, p. 138.

3. ibid., p. 267.

4. ibid., p. 260.

5. Martin Heidegger, *Being and Time*, trans. John MacQuarrie & Edward Robinson, Basil Blackwell, Harper and Row, New York, 1983, p. 141.

6. Antonin Artaud, Quoted in Deleuze and Guatari, *Anti-Oedipus: Capitalism and Schizophrenia*, trans. Robert Hurley, Mork Seem, & Helen R. Lone, University Minnesota Press, Minneapolis, 1989, p. 19.

7. William Burroughs, *The Ticket that Exploded*, John Colder, London, 1985.

8. Friedrich Nietzsche, 'The Genealogy of Morals', (1, 13), *The Works Of Friedrich Nietzsche*, trans. R. J. Hallingdale, Tudor, New York, 1931.

9. Camte De Lautréamont, *Les Chants de Moldoror*, trans. Guy Wernham, New Directions, New York, 1965, p. 243.

10. Gaston Bachelard, *The New Scientific Spirit*, trans. Arthur Goldhammer, Beacon Press, Boston, 1984, p. 70.

11. ibid, p. 72.

12. Bachelard, op. cit. (note 1), p. 161.

13. ibid, p. 180.

14. Jacques Derrida, *Speech and Phenomena*, trans. David B. Allison, Northwestern University Press, Evanston, 1987, p. 147.

15. ibid., p. 79.

16. Ferdinand de Saussure, *Course in General Linguistics*, trans. Wade Baskin, McGraw-Hill, N.Y, 1959, p. 66.

17. Jacques Derrida, *Of Grammatology*, trans. Gayatri Spivak, Johns Hopkins University Press, Baltimore, 1976, p. 63.

18. Julia Kristeva, 'From One Identity to Another', in **Desire and Language**, trans. Thomas Gora, Alice Jardine, & Leon S. Roudiez, Columbia University Press, New York, 1980, p. 131.

Architecture and Sound:
A Statement by Edgard Varèse

Translated by Phillip L. Ryan

I lived in Berlin as a young man, for six years before the war of 1914. Reading the book *Aesthetic of a New Music* by Busoni made me very enthusiastic. I went to knock on his door. The scores that I submitted to him subsequently interested him. Despite the difference in age, a profound friendship was developed and established. Commenting an and dissecting his book, I asked him for certain clarifications. In turn, he posed me questions. Often our opinions diverged; otherwise, I was persuaded that it was these interviews with Busoni which helped me to crystallise, open up my ideas on the necessity of new means permitting the liberation of sound outside the limits of the tempered system of tonality, a conception of rhythm as the element of stability and the possibility of metric simultaneities without relation between them.

Arriving in America at the beginning of 1916, I soon began to narrate my credo. In one of my first interviews, which appeared in the *New York Morning Telegraph* in May 1916, I said "Our musical alphabet must be enriched; we also need new instruments capable of being adjusted to varied combinations and not to be content with scrutinising and recollecting what has already been heard. Composers must study the question with specialised engineers". And in July, 1922, in the 'Christian Science Monitor', I made it clear: "…instruments producing continuous sounds at no mailer what frequencies. Speed and synthesis are characteristic of our epoch. We need instruments of the twentieth century. Composers and electricians must cooperate". In 1922, it was still not a question of electronics.

From the first executions of my works in the United States, the critics began to get used to my expression "spatial music". In 1925, Zanotti Bianco, in the review 'The Arts', on the subject of my *Ameriques*, and *Hyperprism*, mentioned "Sound-masses molded as though in space" and "…great masses in astral space". In 1936, in a conference at the University of Albuquerque, New Mexico, I explained, in the paragraphs which I cite below, what I envisaged to be obtainable one day as spatial projection:

> *Intégrales* was conceived for a spatial projection. I constructed it for certain acoustic means which do not yet exist, but which, I know it, will be able to be realised and will be utilised sooner or later. I am going to take you to task to give you an idea of the work as I conceived it. Whilst in our musical system, we distribute quantities whose values are fixed, in the realisation which I desire, the values will be changing continually in relation to a constant. In other words, this would be like a series of variations, changes resulting from gentle alterations in the form of a function or in the transposition of one function to an other.
>
> To understand what I am doing better—for the eye is more rapid and disciplined than the ear—let us transfer this conception into the visual domain and consider the changing projection of a geometric figure on a plane, with the figure and the plane both moving in space but with each having its own speed, changing and varied, translation and rotation. The instantaneous form of

the projection is determined by the relative orientation between the figure and the plane at that moment. But by allowing the figure and the plane to have their own movements, one is capable of representing an image, which is highly complex and apparently unpredictable, with the projection. More, these qualities con be augmented ulteriorly by letting the geometric form of the figure vary as well as the speeds...

And in Paris, in 1955, in an interview at French Radio, I added: "I hope that an apparatus permitting spatial relief will be within our grasp. Even if it is only a documentary gesture, I would be interested in realising *Intégrales* as I conceived it originally". After twenty years, this term 'corporification', knocks at my imagination and induces me to conceive sound as 'living matter', apt to be treated freely outside of scholastic coercions, beyond intervallic academicisms.

A few years later, in the midst of sirens, yielding myself to experiences similar to that of Heulmnoltz, I obtained sonorous traces equivalent for me—in the visual domain—to certain parabolic and hyperbolic curves. I incorporated a siren for the first time into the orchestra of *Ameriques*, later in 1923, one into the instrumental ensemble of *Hyperprism* and in 1931 two in Ionisation (for percussion instruments). In the electronic domain, in 1934 the inventor Leon Theremin modified, to my specifications, two of his instruments for Ecuatorial. Afterwards, all the while pottering about, it was necessary for me to wait until 1954 to realise the sections of 'organised sound' to be interpolated in *Deserts*, which Pierre Boulez presented in these terms:

> ...If we return to the sonic effects of *Deserts*, it contains two irreducible elements...on the one hand, an orchestral formation, on the other, a two-track magnetic tape on which the 'organised sound' is inscribed. The orchestral formation comprises forty wind instruments (wood and brass), five percussionists and a piano employed as an element of resonance. The magnetic track, formed of two different tapes, requiring two columns of high-standing speakers, is interpolated three times into the milieu of the orchestral development; there is thus no melange of the two media but only interpolation.

Edgard Varèse at work, 1958.

On the question often posed to me of knowing whether electronics is there to dethrone and replace existing instruments—and whether it will be given to the whole world for electronic composition—I wish to be precise that for me at least, electronic means have not been imposed forever to the detriment of other vigorous means of decent descent, but that they must be accepted as additive factors. It is through a constant development and instrumental addition that our music in the West possesses a rich and varied patrimony. Our orchestra must continue its functions for the works written for it up to our time, and for those works which continue to be orchestral. I will go even further, desiring the rehabilitation of ancient instruments together, if possible, with the techniques in accord with them, in order to present the works which have been written for them, executed according to their time.

As for the composer who wishes to adopt electronic means (despite the revolutionary appearance of the latter), his problems remain fundamentally the same—in part, naturally, the problems which the new technique presents The music horizon appears to be infinitely extendible. Meanwhile, the musician must be suspicious—liberty is not licence—and must not 'envisage' electronics as a *deus ex machina* which is automatically going to compose for the musician. Science today offers a collaboration which has been impossible to foresee for a score of years, but it does create new responsibilities.

—Edgard Varèse, 1958

Discography.

There have been quite a few recordings of the music of Varèse since the advent of the LP record; however, these LP records are no longer available and there is only one compact disk of his music, conducted by Pierre Boulez: viz. *Ameriques/Arcana/Density 21.5/Ionisation/Intégrales/Offrandes*—Sony Classical CD45844.

More Than Just Married: Sound and Image in Jackie McKimmie's No Problems

Trish FitzSimons

> "I was attracted to do the film by the sound of the woman's voice. ...I knew, the minute that woman opened her mouth, what the film was going to look like... she had the most melancholy, evocative, nostalgic voice and I thought—you use this voice.
>
> She was talking with longing about all these lovely things—the fruit, the vegetables, life on the form and the animals. I knew she'd been token away and put into a home and that there had been troubles with the father and the grandfather taking off. I thought: it's such a contradiction what she's remembering, what she's allowing herself to remember, and what she wants us to remember. That out of what actually happened, this is what kept her going—these memories. I just saw it. I knew it would be images of fruit and things like that and just her voice running through it; and I knew that that there would be be no music. I didn't know at that stage I'd get her to sing—that sort of come later.
>
> So I knew the general feeling we wonted, the images and the sounds. The problem was, how were we going to make them work more than double; how were we going to do more than just marry them?"[1]

This paper will analyse the ways in which Jackie McKimmie approached her aim of getting the sound and image tracks to work in synergy in *No Problems*[2], an eleven minute documentary film subtitled: 'Mercy Steele remembers her childhood in Lowmead, Queensland, in the 1920s.'

At first glance, the film is very simply constructed. It consists of Mercy Steele's voice-over and a small amount of synchronised dialogue, all relating to her childhood. The only music used is several hymns sung *a cappella* by Mercy, their only musical accompaniment an occasional self-harmony.

Other than several still photographs seen or half-seen, and one shot of Mercy's synchronised dialogue almost at the end of the film, the image track consists entirely of footage related to, but only sometimes directly illustrative of, the rural childhood evoked by her voice-over. Yet a close textual analysis of the sound–image relations of this film is rewarding, for behind its apparent simplicity lies careful orchestration. In thinking of *No Problems*, I am reminded of Walter Murch's statement:

> Image and sound are linked together in a dance. And like in some kinds of dance, they do not always have to be clasping each other around the waist: they can go off and dance on their own, in a kind of ballet. ...Yet there is, there has to be, some kind of connection being mode, a mental connection. ...The more dissimilarity you can get between picture and sound and yet still retain a link of some sort, the more powerful the effect.[3]

Much of the power of *No Problems* derives from the disjunction of its images and sounds. In departing from the 'talking head' format that is currently conventional for films based on oral history, McKimmie has opened up a whole new area of meaning in her film. This resides in the space between the image and the sound tracks, and leaves open the possibility of myriad different interpretations, depending upon how these tracks meet with the viewer's imagination.

Because of the filmmaker's deferral of establishing synchronised dialogue, it is entirely possible that a viewer unfamiliar with the cadences of Aboriginal English could be surprised in the final minute of the film to realise that Mercy is Aboriginal. In explaining her reasons for this formal decision, McKimmie says:

> Everyone assumes that Aboriginal people can't have a life like that; that they never did. Part of what I wanted to do was to set up people's expectations that what they are listening to is one thing, whereas what it is is something quite different, with different historical connotations and everything...Why is it that people can't have pleasures in childhood synonymous with other people's pleasures? The bottom line is: the juice of a mango or the fur of a horse's feet are the same, whoever you are.[4]

In this way the film works against existing stereotypes of what it means to be Aboriginal. Christian Metz[5] has pointed out that in experiencing a sound, an audience typically 'searches' for the person or object that has produced it. In *No Problems* a clear image of the 'owner' of the voice-over is delayed sufficiently that a viewer inevitably conjures up their own image of the speaker before actually seeing her.

The sound track of the film opens with Mercy's rendition of a hymn:

> The father waits over the way,
> to prepare us a dwelling place there
> in the sweet by and by.
> We shall meet on that beautiful shore.

This is initially accompanied on the image track by a shadowy archival photograph and then by a slow pan across a rich rural morning landscape. In conjunction with the title, this appears to locate Mercy within a bastion of security. When the voice-over begins, the sense of rural plenitude is strengthened. Mercy tells us in a voice of rich presence:

> They had what they called those times 'possum season' and sometimes the possums would have little joeys, and we'd keep the joeys.

Although she is speaking of native animals being hunted, her incantatory tone bespeaks childish contentment and wonder.

McKimmie's decision to begin with a story set in an unspecific time signals to us that it is the nature of memories, rather than strict historical chronology or accuracy, that we should care about. Mercy's memories as they develop in the early part of the film contain many negative elements the death of her mother, her abandonment by her father and grandfather—but her tone and the way she tells the stories, as well as the images McKimmie uses to accompany these anecdotes, make it clear that her memories of childhood are overwhelmingly positive. The security provided by her grandmother at that time means that this period now occupies a place in her memory as a 'paradise lost', compared to the difficulties of her later life.

Mercy's sense of emotional nourishment is reflected in memories of plenitude, of a land "where anything they put in the ground grew" to provide the child with a cornucopia of pineapples, corn, peaches, guavas, sweet potatoes, pawpaws, apples, mangoes and bananas. Alongside this list, McKimmie has used not only luscious close-ups of several of these fruits and vegetables, but also a slow pan past rich, furrowed soil—suggestive of an inordinate fertility, beyond even the list-making powers of memory. The luminous clarity and resultant impact of these close-ups vindicates McKimmie's decision to shoot the film in 35mm—a luxury for documentary. The mythic quality of these memories is subtly underscored by a song in this section of the film:

> Spinning dreams of the long, long ago
> Spinning dreams of an old fashioned garden,
> and the maid with the old fashioned bow.

A little later, the camera tracks slowly through a 'chook' run of healthy hens and ground-laid eggs whilst Mercy sings:

> Yesterday, today, forever, Jesus is the same,
> All may change, but Jesus, never—
> Glory to his name.

Objects still available to her senses in the present evoke for Mercy a past unreachable through the ordinary processes of memory, because everyone she then knew has either disappeared or died.

Mercy also has access to her past through its associated sounds. Jackie McKimmie has said of her film: "I wanted there to be sound memories as well as visual memories"[6] For example, in a scene where Mercy speaks of feeding the draught horses at the local timber mill, and the images are from a child's perspective—extreme close-up shots of a draught horse eating—the sound-track is dominated by a persistent fly buzzing and an almost musically rhythmic chewing. Throughout the film the atmosphere and effects tracks are exceptionally full and present. This is made possible in many places by the relative sparseness of the voice over and songs.

By contrast, human voices other than Mercy's in the sound-track are uncommon, and, where present, are muted and distant. In one scene, Mercy describes forays down to the swimming hole accompanied by her grandmother who would sit and fish while the children played There is a single, loud, synchronised splash as an unidentified child 'bombs' into the water. Also, in brief moments, children can be heard playing and swimming. The barking of a dog (that is also mentioned) is much louder and is heard for longer periods It is as if humans can only provide mere mnemonic traces, as compared with the insistent forces of plants and animals, whose tastes, sights and sounds yield an immediate connection to Mercy's past.

The final section of *No Problems* is a shocking contrast to the pervasive natural and emotional luxuriance of the bulk of the film. Mercy has been talking of going to sleep with "contented thoughts of what might be in store for you next day". A sound-track of frogs croaking loudly accompanies this story, and the imagery is one of calm night nature—the moon, a horse, a cat, the hens, the roof.

Day dawns and Mercy's equilibrium is shattered: "There were problems in the family, families were taken away". For the first time, the film's imagery tells us unequivocally that this is an Aboriginal family we have been hearing of, and we now see clearly the still that opens the film. Over an image of clouds scudding by in fast motion, repeated from the opening section of the film, we hear that Uncle Tom has gone, though she never saw him go. Mercy is herself taken away by the police: her grandmother goes mad with grief at her loss, and dies.

It is in this section of the film that the sound-track is at its most poignant. The abundance and complexity that has been the sound-track's hallmark for much of the film is stripped away. What is most notably left is the sound of screaming curlews. These bird's calls were present earlier in the sound track, but only subtly, when Mercy described her mother's death during childbirth, and the defection of her father and grandfather. Now they predominate and function almost musically, to deepen the audience's emotional response. They are like a Greek chorus, proclaiming the fate of the protagonist. McKimmie says she chose to use these birds in this way because Mercy had told her that screaming curlews were a "harbinger of bad things" within her Aboriginal tradition.[7]

As the sound of the curlews dies down and the credits roll, we hear Mercy humming the tune of the hymn that opened the film: "In the sweet by and by, we shall meet on that beautiful shore". The music is now suggestive of the irony that is at the heart of the film's title. For if Mercy does not meet the people she loves "on that beautiful shore" they will be lost to her forever. *No Problems* may be how she thinks of her childhood, but this reflects much more the subjective processes of memory than on how outsider would view her history.

Returning to the filmmaker's stated intention of "more than just marrying" image and sound, it is interesting to know a little of the process that went into the achievement of that aim. The voice-over and songs were recorded first, in a studio, having to be taped twice to achieve the intimacy and intensify of tone that McKimmie remembered from her original research interview. Next, the images were shot and a rough cut established. Emma Hay, in an interesting departure from standard practice, both picture and sound edited *No Problems*. This allowed image and sound to continue to be cut and laid in relation to each other for much longer than would usually be the case. The picture-cut that director and editor had considered final before the voice-over was added then continued to be adjusted right up until the mix was completed.[8] McKimmie says:

> By then, we could only take things out. It was just that feeling that you are not letting any opportunity go by. I must say *No Problems* is the best experience I've ever had making a film, because I felt that there was nothing more I could have done and that was the most fantastic feeling at the end.[9]

This is unusual practice in the film industry, where the picture-cut is routinely 'locked off' before the process of sound editing begins.

I experience a kindred sense of completion in viewing *No Problems*. Its pleasures are the pleasures of poetry—it has a strong sense of rhythm, makes much use of repetition, and the meaning of the film is embodied as much in the qualify of its sounds and images, and their connotations, as in their denotative significance. This is achieved largely by manipulating the image and sound tracks separately, rather than seeing these elements as just confirmatory mirror images of each other. Robert Bresson's aphorisms: "What is for the eye must not duplicate what is for the ear" and "The noises must become music"[10] seem particularly pertinent here. McKimmie says of Bresson:

He's the only one who's ever influenced me. I tend not to be specifically influenced... but that's the book [Bresson's *Notes on Cinemotography*] I read when I get depressed about film.[11]

In eschewing the aesthetics of the verité or interview-based documentary, McKimmie has succeeded in her stated aim of "more than just marrying" image and sound, and in so doing has created a complex and intense meditation on the nature of memory and personal history.

1. Jackie McKimmie, unpublished interview with Trish FitzSimons, Paddington, Brisbane, May 6, 1992.

2. Jackie McKimmie, *No Problems*, 35mm Film in Dolby Stereo. Also available on video. Distributed by the Australian Film Institute, 1989.

3. Walter Murch, 'Sound Design: Walter Murch Interviewed by Frank Paine', in *Journal of the University Film Association* 33:4, Fall, 1981, p. 13.

4. Jackie McKimmie, op. cit. (note 1).

5. Christian Metz, 'Aural Objects', in E.Weis and J. Belton, *Film Sound: Theory and Practice*, New York: Columbia University Press, 1985.

6 Jackie McKimmie, op. cit. (note 1).

7. ibid.

8. ibid. Also Emma Hay, unpublished telephone interview with Trish FitzSimons, May 7, 1992.

9. Jackie McKimmie, op. cit. (note 1).

10. Robert Bresson, *Notes on Cinematography*, Urizen Books, New York, 1977, p. 27.

11. Jackie McKimmie, op. cit. (note 1).

Verbal Judo (Demonstration Script)

Brent Clough

Tori: ...Verbal Judo...

Uke: After George J. Thompson's exposition of 'words as force options' we are teaming up as a sort of mini-Ninja squad, deploying 'situational rhetoric' to defuse the potentially hostile expectations of an audience demanding 'performance'.

Tori: In our collaborative verbal stance, we align ourselves to the audience's direction and perspective (the initial harmony necessary) and then we work on the audience in such a way as to move or 'throw' them in the direction that we feel is right. We frequently pin their response faculties to the floorboards and administer a severe polysemantic whack to their collective consciousness.

Uke: Some of the moves we've perfected over several years of intense study in both street encounters and Media Retreats include...

Tori: The Oblique Dragon Howl...

Uke: Tori summons up tremendous energy and invents a multi-layered flourish of signifiers. After expelling air in a guttural shout he uses various 'urban alienation' tropes to terrify the assembled group, and then allows their own disarray to short-circuit any unified group action. In time his relentless howls provoke either retreat or a fascinated surrender to a subtle system of disbelief...

Lip knives...

Tori: We pivot through a series of laryngeal manoeuvres designed to make confusing any 'original' vocal moment. This sets up an inability in the audience ta make false distinctions between biography and fiction. To the accompaniment of a disorienting 'hum-drum' we execute the exacting move of the 'lip knives'. Small serrated-edge phoneme-discs are ejected from our mouths, their velocity and direction determined by the lip formations of our 'rictus-in-motion'...

Uke: The markings on the discs invariably indicate affiliations to an international Fluxomatic order or the Hokey Pokey sect of fake monks.

Tori: N.B. It is inevitable that this somewhat less-than-defensive move will produce casualties in the assembled group. Organisers are liable for all claims in the absence of warnings to patrons concerning psychic wounding to the ears, eyes or throat... the We-Are-Friends Approach ... adapted from master G. J. Thompson...[1]

Uke: Since the audience feels abused, beaten, our questions become worded in such a way that they show confidence in the group's ability to change the present situation. Questions like "Isn't there a much better word than 'art'?", "What do you think would help the situation in your workplaces?", or "Don't you think you should each take the lead in straightening the problems out?" convey the sense that the warrior-talkers are looking to the audience for direction, putting them in the position of strength in solving the problem rationally and non-violently.

Tori: It is important with such an approach to smother all anxiety with a language-silencing gesture such as the 'Gently Inclusive Smile'.

Uke: The Voice of the Sea...

We try to define the task on the spot...

Tori: We orchestrate disinterestedly the extreme perspectives and behaviours of others. Like water altering its shape to fit a container, we are malleable enough to change our approach as the situation dictates...

Uke: Much bowing, scraping, and blowing of kisses.

...Saliva Formation and Back Flip...

Tori: Spitting and flipping move, used only to control incensed and unreasonable groups.

Uke: The Tiger's Tongue...

Tori: Finally, rather than simply using a 'double phonation' and speaking as a controlling or reassuring voice for the audience, we seek to speak through a 'third voice', a voice summoned up from the combined desires of the audience and performers alike. This voice must imagine its own contours, its own origins, and mysteries.

Yet, this is a voice which is more material than any of the chimerical devices generally employed in the performative encounter...

Speech martialled in such a fashion is a powerful, persuasive force...

Uke: At certain moments this third Word-Force becomes like a Tiger padding through the forest at night. Replete after vanquishing and chewing the limbs of its enemies, the Tiger is generous to the after-dark 'world at large'. Seeking a medium in which it might best enjoy the warm evening air, the Tiger slips into a nearby lagoon. From the safety of the cool water, the Tiger sucks fragrant water-lillies and gargles mouthfuls of water for minutes at a time ... This meditative and whimsical action is the mark of a great beast now freed from its own bodily form, present only as the sounds of water bubbling over larynx, a tongue free to splash and play...

1. George J. Thompson, *Verbal Judo: Words as a Force Option*, Charles C. Thomas, Springfield, Illinois, 1983.

Circuits of the Voice:
From Cosmology to Telephony

Frances Dyson

1. THE MEANING OF THE VOICE:

While vocal communication between individuals within culture has received much attention from theoreticians, less has been given to the *meaning* of voice within different epistemological systems.'The meaning of voice'...not only indicates a difference from 'the meaning of language' but more importantly implies that speaking is not wholly reducible to the predicament of being 'spoken by language' as many post-structuralists would suggest. It also involves a surrender to the non-semantic meaning which the voice generates in speaking language: the corporeal resonances and references it continuously emits despite our best efforts to contain the cough, the sigh, the strain, the hoarseness, the wheeze, the stammer, through which the body 'speaks', as it were, to the world. This aspect of the speaking voice has been referred to as the 'groin of the voice' by writers on the subject, and has fallen prey to a fairly massive cultural schism—that between the concrete and the abstract, or body and mind. An attractive solution has been to bifurcate the voice, to eradicate the linguistic side in favour of the purely sonorous and corporeal, and to view the latter as some kind of originary voice—voice unencumbered or constrained by language, thought, intellect.[1] However, the *meaning* of the voice is not reducible to inchoate bodily utterings, for its 'grain' is also intimately connected to the sonorous emissions of the mouth, the Vibratory responses of the ear and the air circulating between them, and this phenomenal and visceral triad: voice, ear and breath, the very stuff of vocal communication, is always surrounded by a host of cultural beliefs connecting it to a symbolic system. Thus the 'originary voice', no matter how pure, is bound to a certain hermeneutics; prior to any utterance, it is already a metaphor, and already caught within particular circuits, switchboards or 'machines' which both literally and figuratively encode, transmit and give meaning to vocal acts.

This paper will examine three cosmological, mythological and epistemological systems in which the meaning of the voice is paramount: that of the Dogon; the Christian; and post-industrial, western culture. These systems reveal a common hermeneutics based not so much on what the voice says, nor what it reveals about the body, but on its transmission or flow between one space, be it physiological, phenomenal or spiritual, and another. From this perspective, the meaning of the voice lies in its *movement*; its ability to occupy different symbolic niches within different cultural/historical epochs. Perhaps the best description of this kind of flow is that which the metaphor of the circuit evokes. There are many models for circuits: the Chinese system of meridians or energy flows Circulating the body; the western neuro-physiological mapping of the nervous system; transportation networks, money markets, communication grids. The circuitry is as much metaphorical as material or technological, and represents the flows and logics of cultural proclivities as much as the movements of material phenomena. When thinking of voice transmission both as an aural phenomenon and as a symbol, one is immediately reminded of Christian theology's extremely productive and adaptable circuit, the Holy Trinity, consisting of The

Word, the Word made Flesh, and the Breath or Spirit. This of course has been modified in recent times to accommodate lesser Trinities and means of transmission, but the flow or logic remains the same, as do the consequences. For it should always be remembered that circuits generate powerful metaphors, they name deities and demons, they perpetuate myths, and their particular construction will determine the nature of social relations. At the same time they are invisible, and can often only be seen 'elsewhere'—in radically other cultures or epoches.

2. VOICE, BREATH AND EXCHANGE IN DOGON COSMOLOGY:

One such 'elsewhere' can be found in the cosmological circuit of the Dogon people who inhabit the Upper Niger in north-west Africa. Researches by ethnologists Marcel Griaule and Genevieve Calame-Griaule reveal that the Dogon regard the voice and speech as *the* original movers behind the forces of creation and the perpetuity of existence, and have based their complex systems of astronomy, calculation, anatomy, physiology, pharmacology and theology on the symbolic power of speech and 'the Word'.[2] While it is impossible to go into the vast details of Dogon cosmology here, a number of points will help clarify the significance of the triad—voice, ear and breath—within the general hermeneutic system, and provide a relief against which the meaning of the voice in western thought becomes visible. Perhaps the most salient feature of Dogon mythology is the correspondence between the metaphor of speech, speech itself, and worldly actuality. Because the symbols of speech have the value of fact, all phenomena are regulated by the passage of the voice, for the Word is always spoken and is always present in the formation and flows of being. The first words, constituting the first 'language' of the world, were:

> ... breathed sounds scarcely differentiated from one another, but nevertheless vehicles. Such as it was, this ill-defined speech sufficed for the great works of the beginning of all things. [MG:20]

They were composed of the warm vapour which both conveys and constitutes speech, which 'has sound' and which dies away. They did not originate as a singular, coherent and eternal Word (as in the Biblical myth), but rather as a vapourous' sounding'; voice but not yet speech which 'clothed' the world, inscribing, as a text, its fabric with the spiritual revelation of existence. The connection here between sound, words, language, text and cloth (textile) is important, for it implies that language, as text, is a creative, existential technology which also embraces multiplicity: the multiplicity of sounds indistinguishable as words, of sound as both aural phenomenon and water-bearing breath or vapour.

The second Word heard on earth was clearer than the first and led directly to the art and primary metaphor of weaving:

> ...the Spirit was speaking while the work proceeded... he imparted his Word by means of a technical process, so that all men could understand. By doing so he showed the identity of material actions and spiritual forces...[the words) were woven in the threads...they were the cloth and the cloth was the Word. [MG:28]

This notion of word-weaving has parallels in western idioms: we think of 'text' (from the Latin 'textere': to weave) as a weaving of words, and are familiar with expressions such as 'weaving a web' (usually of lies).'spinning a yarn', losing the 'thread' of a conversation, creating a 'fabrication', etc. However, 'the Word' of the Dogon is not a word in the usual sense—firstly because it is synonymous rather than analogous with a material thing, especially cloth which is worn because, as the Dogon sage Ogotemmeli remarks, "to be naked is to be speechless". Secondly because it is composed of water-bearing breath, water symbolising the primary cosmic and human purpose of procreation and regeneration. Thirdly because the word is also a sound—the sound of weaving with block and shuttle, which translates as "the creaking of the word".[3] The third Word develops the more materialistic aspects of existence, representing the integration of divine principles and forces with the human condition. It initiates iron founding, agriculture, grain storage, the human skeletal form, drumming and the hierarchical classification of beings within the world order, with each activity or schematic rendering becoming more complex than the last.

Within the purview of the third Word, the Dogon's hermeneutic approach to life inflects every aspect of matter and being: speech is deeply symbolic, relating both to nature, industry, and knowledge; all phenomena are considered as signs to be interpreted, all events are messages of some sort. Knowing the world is understanding its signs, given in symbols, which are synonymous with 'the word of the world', while the calling of humanity is the interpretation of existence. Because actions and words are linked together, speech symbolically represents the outcome of an action—indeed as Genevieve Calame-Griaule summarises: "action is speech transformed into matter, speech taken to its final limit".[4] But the material of speech—words and voice—is also action and sign in and of itself. As mentioned, speech is always heard: there is always an ear (even if it only be a potential ear) which will hear even the faintest whisper. When a person speaks, their inner psycho-physiological states are projected upon the listener in the form of a doppleganger or double; their words enter the listener, causing actions which have beneficial or detrimental effects.

Because water is considered the most desirable, indeed the *necessary* element within Dogon cosmology, 'fluid', easily understood speech, known as 'moist', symbolises fecundity and the 'natural' state of the universe. Speech filled with anger (the 'heated' argument) on the other hand, indicates that air and fire are predominant while earth and water are absent because the saliva, as fluidity, has dried up and the words have become incoherent or 'unearthed'. This kind of speech is antithetical to the natural order because it represents the dry season, drought and periods of infertility. In the same way that an absence of water interferes with the bearing of fruit or the ripening of the seed, hot, incoherent speech interferes with the flow of language and meaning; it is "speech without seeds", it fails to produce a response in the listener, and in extreme cases will cause infertility.[5] The generative aspects of speech create a unity and coherence between the voice of the speaker and the ear of the listener via the transmissions and movements between them. It is these movements—within the individual, between the speaker and the listener, from the inside to the outside, from above ta below—which constitute life:

> To draw up and then return what one has drawn—that is the life of the world...the Word is for everyone in this world; it must come and go and be interchanged, for it is good to give and receive the forces of life.[6]

While the voice is able to summon divine action, to call into being the person named, to emit harsh and unfruitful words or to penetrate and fertilise, it is able to do this only because, being breath and vapour, it carries the life-force; it is the bearer of the Word, indeed the Word itself.

However, the power of the life—force is dependent upon a symbolic union between the two sexual organs—the mouth and the ear. The product of this union is the literal and metaphorical conception of a 'seed', both human and divine, which may or may not manifest in birth or further speech.

There is perhaps no better example of the intricate circuit the Dogon construct to map the flows between body and mind, individual and community, nature and culture, the human and the deific, generated via the voice and the Word, nor is there a clearer warning of the perils of interrupting such circuits, than the idea of 'decoyed' speech. This describes a nasal voice with improper timbre, and a resulting speech which is caught between the nose and the throat, unable to follow the proper course of words nor fulfil its generative function. Embodying a lack of fertility the words literally 'decay', causing an unpleasant sensation in the listener not unlike a bad odour. When the Dogon speak of "a hearing smell" or use the expression "to hear the bad odour of your words is bad for me" [G.CG: 42], they are referring to the physical as well as psychical affects of 'bad speech' on the listener. In assimilating the other's speech, transforming it into water which then irrigates the internal organs, the listener's body is itself made vulnerable. The liver, for instance, as centre of the individual or object and locus of the life-force, is affected by the biochemical and spiritual ingredients within the 'food' of speech:

> The liver serves as a receptacle while speech, still in its basic water form, begins to boil. Steam accumulates. The fat in the liver supplies speech with oil, and by melting gradually lends sweetness and an unctuous quality to the words about to be said. The words boil gently and then go out in the form of a small, light stream. The uttered words are good, and have a beneficial effect.
>
> When the liver is unhappy, there is no heat to warm the fat, and the words lack charm. In anger, the heat produced is too intense, the water contained in the words comes to a boil. The oil becomes too hot, it seethes and sputters causing the words uttered to be spiteful, fiery, bitter from the bile the gall bladder pours into the liver. [G.C-G: 45]

This vulnerability to the other's speech is a necessary factor in the circulation of speech and life, for although it is true that 'bad' words cannot be repelled—"the ear cannot be made to spit"—the ear's receptivity, its bi-sexual and dualistic nature, symbolises the individual's essential openness to the world. At the same time, such openness is regulated: the pathways of speech are directed by the structure of the ear, the alchemy of interior processes is determined by organic givens, the routes of elemental and psychic forces follow a rhythm of ascent and descent within the body and through the cosmos. The circulation of life: the word, the seed, the life-force, water, knowledge and information—all these elements evolve from the interior of the individual to the exterior reality. The circuit is thus continually evolving between the spiritual and the mundane—when its flows are blocked or interrupted, death and decay will result.

3. VOICE, BREATH AND SPIRIT-FLOWS IN THE CHRISTIAN TRADITION:

To apply the model of a circuit to a culture considered by most westerners as 'other' might seem unforgivably eurocentric. However, there is no doubt that both the Dogon and Christian symbolic system share common roots in Arabic and Egyptian mysticism. Both, for instance, believe that creation proceeded from a primordial 'ward', indicating their commitment to an anthropomorphic and hermeneutic approach to existence. Both configure the word as a medium for transmutation, and consider language, itself composed of 'joints' or syntactical relations, as representing a cosmological 'text' or universal fabric, there to be unravelled and deciphered. The categories or organising principles—the very mechanics of interpretation—are also similar: four elements—two sexes and two motions, ascent and descent—constitute the basis for dichotomy and dualism.[7] Finally, the Dogon life-force or spirit ('noma') also corresponds to the Greek concept of *pneuma* and the Christian concept of grace.

That voice and sound are integral to the symbolic system of Christian culture is evidenced by the primary circuit of the Holy Trinity: the Word, the Word made flesh, and the Breath or Spirit, while the example *par excellence* of human/divine exchange is the myth of the immaculate conception, in which the Madonna is impregnated by the Word of God via her ear. As a circuit of greater complexity, this myth offers the procreative power of the word (as 'seed': semen). The efficacy of the breath, the receptivity of the ear and the notion of vocal transmission as the medium for divine transubstantiation, as 'axis' upon which movement and exchange between the heavens and the earth can occur.[8] The Word (or seed). characterised as breath, is generally thought to have been carried by a dove or a tongue of fire, representing the Holy Spirit, and in Quattrocento paintings is often depicted as being transmitted through a tube fixed between the mouth of God and the Madonna's ear, or travelling along a ray of light. The primary cosmic principle and metaphor motivating this passage from above to below is however not water ('vapour' carried by the voice) as in the Dogon system, but *soundless* air. One consequence of this difference is, as I will later elaborate, the inability of the circuit to offer an equitable exchange between the divine and the human without serious modifications to the nature, indeed the existence, of both.

Air—the element and the symbol—has a long history in hermetic thought. However it has not always been privileged over the other elements, nor considered the cardinal force. It was only with the Greek concept of *pneuma* that air began to represent the vital principle, the soul and the fertilising 'breath' of God. For Piontinus, writing in the second century AD:

> As the association of the soul with matter implies a degradation it cannot be placed in immediate contact with the body, so it makes use of a mediating element, a form of *pneuma*, in which to clothe itself and be guarded from a defiling character;... [9]

From the notion of *pneuma* as Breath/Spirit, the doctrine of the humours developed—disease by infection was thought to be carried by bad air, the *pneuma* was conceived as a regulating and nourishing principle acting directly on the body. The *pneuma* doctrine, containing all these physical, elemental and spiritual attributes, also appropriated the discovery and workings of the nervous system—Augustine, writing in the third century AD, maintained for instance that the nervous system consisted of tubes of air. This is important, because it links the idea of breath with the notion of electrical impulses which later became the trope of the nervous system. It also mirrored within the human anatomy the initial 'speaking' tube, through which God's word, as 'seed', travelled from the heavens to the Madonna's ear.

The *pneuma* doctrine corresponded with a shift from the tenor of the Old Testament, where sound featured often as a manifestation of divine presence and intervention and the voice of God thundered from above, to the Christian emphasis on the 'Word' uncontaminated by bodily voice. Also, the passage of the Word—descending on a ray of light or through an enclosed tube—ceased to involve any externalisation; in particular it did not mingle with earthly elements or atmospheres. Consequently, both the materiality of the voice, ear and breath triad, and the corporeal connection between mouth and ear, was forgotten. Viscerality and phenomenality became increasingly reduced to abstract symbols and metaphors, and the circuits of the voice were set on a path of ascent from "evil matter" (Plonitus) to divine intelligence. This symbolic journey also, it should be noted, allowed the now soundless, bodiless voice a certain immortality. Not only was the Word of God rendered anechoic—being silent Breath/Spirit, it eventually ceased to have any associations with the mortal physical body, including the breath, altogether. According to David Applebaum, by the time of Aristotle (fourth century BC) the breath had become an instrument: "in voice the breath in the Windpipe is used as an instrument to knock with against the walls of the Windpipe"[10], and as such could be viewed as a proto-technology rather than an involuntary organic process. This severed its prior attachment to the body: no longer *the* vital and necessary element, the breath was merely a means to an end—the end being the production of voice. Yet the theological voice, having already undergone the above transformations, was itself becoming fused with the inner monologue of Cartesian dualism, and the inner voice of the Christian conscience. Representing cognition on the one hand, the soul on the other, and characterised as intellectual/spiritual rather than corporeal, it had no need of bodily breath, and was therefore not subject to the condition of mortality which the breath, by its very presence, automatically signals. As Applebaum writes:

> The breath is dispelled from the mind's voice altogether. The mind does not perish like the breath. Therefore mental voice is immortal.[11]

A voice situated in the mind or soul (which of course does not breathe) would now connect with an ear similarly abstracted, and indeed in the modern era, with the institutionalisation of electricity and the telephone, the ear as receptive organ begins its prosthetic reformulation. On the one hand abstracted (deified) through technology, on the other given a new exteriority through electricity and communication grids, the ear and its associate the mouth, together with the voice, ear and breath triad, begins its metaphorical descent into the material world—to the Trinity of the nuclear family, the despiritualisation of *pneuma* as electricity, and the noise of mass communication.

4. TELEPHONY AND TELEPATHY:

It is to the telephone that the metaphor of the circuit is most readily applied, prompting certain connections with the 'transmissive' mappings of the voice and speech already described. The telephone shares with the 'elemental/theological' circuits of the Dogon and Christian cultures similar ideas and mechanisms of transference. It is constituted by a circuit: sender–operator–receiver, which allows the disembodied voice of the speaker to be electronically coded and sent via a communication network to a receiver (instrument). which then decodes or interprets the speech and amplifies it for the listener. The medium in this case is electricity. Compare this circuit to that of the Trinity and the myth of the Immaculate Conception: the word of the Father (the speaker, the initiator, the *caller*) is 'condensed' into breath and travels by the Holy Ghost, or the Spirit, to become either word, breath or seed through a process of decoding or interpretation. This process allows transubstantiation to occur—Christ is born as the word made flesh. The medium is breath or light. The Dogon circuit is similar: the creator creates a universe of signals (signs, messages) which must then be interpreted, decoded by the individual, who reads the speech of phenomena and transforms it into action, or verbal speech.[12] The medium is the lifeforce or'nama'. Common to all three systems is the belief that vocal transmission is primordially generative: creating dialogue which is not just restricted to speech, but which causes transformations within bodies, between bodies, between radically different spheres such as the heavens and the earth, and radically different forms of being—human and celestial. And these exchanges are themselves embedded within a symbolic system which endows each factor in the flow-voice, air, breath, movement, ear and mouth—with multiple metaphoric values and relational possibilities.

The nature of the symbolic system is of course integral to the functioning of the culture, and the telephone system also forms part of a wider communicational and cultural matrix, providing a link, an organisational network, between individuals in a society and directing flows of speech necessary for the society to survive. Without the telephone, one is disconnected from the larger, technological society; literally and metaphorically 'cut-off'. Yet the telephone's ambit is not purely communicational—by bringing the outside into the home and day-time into night-time, by transmitting invisible voices from the electronic ether (from the heavens) at great speed, by delivering a 'call', the telephone penetrates and transforms spatio-temporal, conceptual and cultural barriers. It transmits the voice of the 'other', but at a slightly ethereal frequency—the telephonic voice *sounds* as if it is coming from an 'elsewhere'; public and placeless and at the same time extremely intimate—a whisper from ear to ear, mind to mind. The Madonna, like the clergy of today, was thought to have received a 'calling', presumably through the 'speaking tube'. The telephone, like the voice of God, also calls the individual to answer, but to answer a voice bereft of body, of locale, of full sonorous presence—a voice caught up in some placeless communications network, subject to interference, crossed lines, and abrupt terminations.

Not that the call of God, at least in the Christian circuit, has always been direct. Indeed, the introduction of the telephone switchboard, regulated by a female operators, as a means of mass communication is analogous to another difference between the Old and New Testaments. As mentioned in the Old Testament the great prophets, Moses, Abraham etc., heard the voice of God directly, not necessarily as speech, but definitely as sound. The transmission between deity and human was therefore two-way and unmediated. With the New Testament, God's word is mediated by the body of Christ—a body which, while highly accessible, is also unquestionably human. No longer appearing in other sonic forms (as wind or whatever), God's Word does not require the same degree of interpretation. Furthermore, its message is no longer concerned with the salvation of a chosen people. Rather, the preachings of Christ are directed to the salvation of humanity at large. Christ's voice is projected at the level of mass communication, it speaks to the 'brotherhood of man', and its speaking is literally dependent upon the presence of vocal chords, upon embodiment. The latter is ultimately guaranteed by the Immaculate Conception—that Christ was 'of woman born'. The Madonna in this case is a little like an operator connecting two worlds or dimensions—the one from above to the one below. Interestingly, in the same way that the vocal transmissions of the ancient God were unmediated and two-way, the telephone proper doesn't need an operator either—between Bell and his assistant Watson there was initially a direct line—one called and the other answered. With the employment of operators, the telephone entered the age of moss communications, an age concerned not with one-to-one correspondence (Bell to Watson) but with the linking of humanity at large; the 'brotherhood of man'. At the same time, developments in the technology made the 'message' much clearer: the voice is heard as voice rather than a jumbled signal, it emits decipherable speech rather than the sounds of the wind or the murmuring waters. Thus for both the invisible voice on the telephone, and the invisible voice of God, a woman is necessary for it to become universal, that is, to depart the shallow shares of individual happenstance and assume responsibility for the absolute, indubitable connection between the caller and the called.

Telephony, however, cannot be contained within nor wholly explained by Christian mythologies, but is open to its own hermeneutics. It is not strictly theological or elemental because it appears in the 'electronic' age, and electricity is not quite an element nor a life-force or *pneuma*. Nor, in the early twentieth century, is the Trinity the main unit or model in circulation. This is, after all, the age of humanism, and is 'post-Christian' in the sense that it is often characterised as the period of when man became 'the measure of all things', and of science and technology, a credible substitute for God. However, the organisational structure or motive of modernity's theological past still resonates: in the place of God's Breath or the Spirit as the vehicle transmitting ethereal voices, lies the electronic ether; in place of the silent voice of God, or the audible preachings of Christ, the electronic voice of the telephone is installed; and in the place of the Holy Trinity stands the nuclear family. However, there are further modifications: not only does the female operator, like the Madonna, occupy a pivotal role in the 'transmissions of the word', but the bodies and the vocal apparatuses of psychic mediums—generally women, become the chief vehicle for the other-worldly channellings so popular at this time. Similarly, with the popularisation of Freudian psychoanalysis, the western hermeneutic system, while still grounded upon the 'Word of the Father', is now embodied and 'spoken' by the analyst who, in many respects taking the place of the priest, (as the priest is the 'mouthpiece' of Christ, as Christ was the 'word made flesh') interprets and translates the 'inner voice' of the unconscious.

Freud linked telepathy with telephony, viewing the latter as a medium for the transmission of the former, in the same way that psychoanalysis was the' instrument' for analysing, through interpretation, the telepathic dream, and the means by which the hidden messages of the unconscious and the ethereal could be "given a voice".[13] Through this connection, Freudian psychoanalysis becomes both the medium (metaphorically the telephone) and the interpretative method of telepathy, or thought transference. It allows the psychical to become physical... like the breath or *pneuma*, like the electrical impulse itself.[14] But these telephonic tropes are also wired with Futuristic, human-as-machine phantasies and fears, revealed by psychic disorders of the time in which patients discovered 'telephones in the head', and analysts speak of the "automatic machinery of the unconscious complexes".[15] With the analysis of schizophrenics, we find that the telephone (the unconscious) inside the head has gone awry: its voice is muffled and directionless, it lacks an operator and can only be regulated by the intercession of the analyst, who takes the place of the traditionally female operator.[16] This is interesting in light of the early telephonic experiments of Bell and Watson. Watson was intrigued with communicating with the dead via the telephone (as were Tessler and Marconi), and would attend nightly seances in Salem—the town known for its witch burning in the middle ages. Witches practised mediumship, held séances, but also, belong to the ancient tradition of alchemy. Avital Ronnel describes Watson's experiments with the telephone as 'electronic' witchery: a substitute for the 'mediumship' which was held to be a feminine ability at the time, taking place in the symbolic town of Salem.[17] His experiments with electricity, "that occult force", is another form of witchery: alchemy, the primary science of the transmutation of matter.

5. DEATH CIRCUITS AND THE ANAEROBIC VOICE IN THE MODERN PERIOD:

In the Dogon cosmological circuit, air and fire are masculine and make for "bad speech" because water is lacking. Water is also lacking in the Christian concept of the Holy Trinity which, according to Ernest Jones, replaced the eternal Mother, the feminine, symbolising water, with the Spirit—breath, air, fire, electricity. In the modern era, with the recording and transmission of disembodied voices, interest in the ethereal turned to the newly dead. Bell carried a dead ear with him on his treks to invent the telephone—the ear of a corpse becoming the first receiver. And Freud's telepathic cases, like the preoccupation of the mediumship common to the time, were most often concerned with messages from dead siblings, plugging the circuit of psychoanalysis into bad air and noise, decay and death.

The overwhelming presence of death as a founding metaphor of modernity is again linked to the evolution of the voice, both in terms of its meaning or cultural significance, and the symbolic circuitry regulating its transmission. While 'post-Christian' modifications directed the flows of voice towards the strictly human theatre of symbols, myths and meaning, at the same time they instilled in the content of vocal transmissions a distinctly human inflection. Messages of the afterlife, descending upon human ears from an immortal God, gave way to the more mundane concerns of man; the preaching and eventual crucifixion of Christ seemed more a symbol of human mortality than evidence of heavenly salvation ; the' inner voice' of the soul could be misheard as the chatterings of an irrational unconscious; and the disembodied voice (once the purview of God) appeared, in the literature on sound reproduction at the time, to be wrapped in the shroud of bodily death, even if 'resurrected' by electricity. Throughout these transformations in the circuit, the distinction between God on the one hand, and human on the other, becomes increasingly ambiguous. God, or the godly, descends somewhat to the state of electronic ether, which is eventually 'tapped' by wireless radio (a metaphor also for mediumistic channelling). Humans, through the control of electricity, ascend to the deific, and undergo a kind of reverse transubstantiation—not 'becoming God' but becoming like God through the immortality bequeathed to the machine.[18] Because electricity, or the electrical circuit (the nervous system, the flows of bodily energy, the telephonic system etc.) is, like air itself, infinite, in the transition from *pneuma* to electrical impulse, in the re-definition of the breath 'as instrument' (Aristotle), the human form, now equipped with its telephonic ear and mouth, becomes, by association, a machine-like thing for whom it makes no sense to speak of death.

Yet the voice of this new form contains something of a death rattle, for the very possibilities it offers are also signs of an irretrievable loss. Just as in the shift from the Old to the New Testament where communication with God is mediated by representation (the apostles), text (the Bible) and the finite mortal voice of Christ, in the twentieth century, communication amongst the brotherhood of man becomes similarly mediated—first by the loudspeaker and then by the telephone, with in both cases the fullness of communication being lost. The brotherhood of man demands, by its size and constitution, an amplified voice; one that will reach the many ears gathered for the purposes of audition ('audire': to hear and obey) and ultimately, of deciding who may speak for, or represent them (vote–voice). At the same time, the masses cannot be heard when the loudspeaker is introduced—the voice of any response is therefore silenced. There are personal losses also: when one speaks to another on the phone, one hears only the fullness of one's own voice, not that of the other, who's voice is always diminished, in volume, in clarity and presence. Presence truly only belongs to the 'I' of the phone call, never the 'you'. One embraces then, a pseudo-solipsistic situation; on the phone one hears mainly oneself—it's a bit like talking to the analyst—an ear hears, but a little voice responds.

Solipsism, reflected in the concept of the 'inner voice' in western metaphysics, is an attempt to shut out the corporeal or phenomenal exterior, to close the gap between the mind and its thinking. The eradication of distance between voices is also the *raison d'être* of the telephone; it is the attempt to install an anechoic vacuum, a space of no distance, an absolute space which bodies, being voluminous things, cannot occupy, but through which disembodied voices can travel. The space of the network, the 'ground' of the telephone system, is mapped again, by a reified and closed circuit, transmitting from mind to mind, without any airborne or corporeal externalisation. It is also the domain of the anaerobic voice—the voice infused with electricity, defused of breath, evacuated, that is, of anything which would signal the body. Think of the long-distance call (especially international) where dialogue is cut off because of an untimely explosion of breath—a laugh, cough or exclamation. Indeed, speech itself is reduced to an interchange of monologues communicators adopt in order to accommodate the delay, the echo, and the potential interruption of transmission inherent in spontaneous conversation. According to Applebaum:

> Breath retention and articulate voice form two sides of the compound completed by knowledge and technology... no technology of fullness exists. Technology is invented only when plenty is lost.[19]

Perhaps this is why the 'obscene' phone call is characterised by heavy breathing: the obscenity being the return of breath to the site of its elimination—the return of archaic breath, the breath of the body, to the clean and infinite topos of technology.

We remember the Dogon's distaste far decayed speech, "bad speech", speech that goes nowhere With this in mind, listen to the following:

> The phone booth is a grave in which the one buried olive is re-animated by a woman's long distance breathing: the grave opens... The poet finds that he, too, is on the phone. As he looks into the receiver at his end of the end of the call, he visualises—alongside the distance he thus traverses—the woman with whom he has conversed. In her place he accepts the charges of mourning.[20]

Mourning and loss, decay and death, are the effluents of a system where voice is caught in the throat, is repressed, stifled, and denuded of the body. In Dogon symbolism, the voice circulates primarily below the collar-bone, flowing through the body to the world and the listener outside. As a result it is always 'aired', completing an infinite cycle which connects body, mind, interior and exterior with the community, the cosmos and the elemental, phenomenal earth. In the western Christian system, the voice has become increasingly relegated to the mind, without return to the body, to earth, to mundane mailer. It travels a symbolic circuit which survives only through increasing modification, abstraction and technologisation, and during this course is stretched between two literal and metaphorical 'axes':[21] the disembodied voice of mass communications, and the non-vocal, non-sounding, anaerobic voice of the mind. With no middle ground—no 'earth' or 'water', the meaning of the voice is thus 'charged' with muting the cries of mailer.

* This article was first published in *Musicworks #53* 'Radio Phonics and other Phonies', Summer, 1992, edited by Dan lander, Toronto, Canada.

1. The phrase "the groin of the voice" was I believe, coined by Roland Barthes in his essay by the some name. See *Roland Barthes: The Responsibility of Forms*, Hill and Wong, New York, 1985. The bifurcated voice also appears in David Appelbaum: Voice, SUNY Press, 1990, and Don Ihde: *Consequences of Phenomenology*, State University of New York Press, New York, 1986.

2. See Marcel Griaule: *Conversations with Ogotemmeli*, Oxford University Press, 1970, hereafter cited as MC' and Genevieve Colome-Grioule:'Voice and the Dogon World', *Notebooks in Cultural Analysis*, Vol. 3, ed. Norman F. Cantor and Nathalia King, Duke University Press, USA, 1986, hereafter cited as G.C-G.

3. ibid., p. 73. Note that in the Dogan language the word 'soy' means garment, which clothes one with words, 'so', which recall the seventh 'soy' ancestor, who was the master of speech.

4. An example of this association would be the expression which translates as "it has now become tomorrow's speech" meaning that the works continuation will be postponed until tomorrow. G.C-G:22.

5. ibid., p. 28 passim. The body is regulated by eight spiritual principles, or "souls", associated with "nose, breath, life", because the principles move about as wind and enter the individual as s/he breathes. They may be male, female, intelligent (moving upwards) or animal (moving downwards) and as such reflect the

essential duality of an individual composed of a double soul and penetrated by opposing movements and forces. Speech characteristics are also gendered. For instance, air and fire are masculine; earth and water are feminine. Feminine speech has more oil (timbre) which, represented as a 'life force', musicates speech, giving it warmth and presence.

6. Ogotemmeli, cited in Griaule, op. cit. (note 2). pp. 108, 136.

7. Think of the opposing forces: positive and negative, life and death, upper and lower, ascent and descent, common to Dogan and Egyptian hermetic thought, and also the 22 joints in the Dogon system compared to the 22 arcana in the Quabbalistic and Egyptian occult. The four elements feature in Astrology, generally representing both matter and movement. *Air* represents thought, inspiration (in-spire), speed, ethereal vapour, the sword—insight, 'piercing the veil of matter', the eye, masculinity. *Water* represents fluidity, the feminine, fertility, green, the unconscious, the moon, the hidden or secret, the cup or vessel, blood, life flow etc. *Earth* represents materiality, stability, the pentacle, money/values, ethics, etc. *Fire* represents passion, transmutation, the wand, the phallus, the tree of life, the instrument.

8. For a lengthy and erudite analysis of this myth see 'The Madonna's Conception Through the Ear', in Ernest Jones: *Psycho-Myth, Psycho-History: Essays in Applied Psychoanalysis*, Hillstone, New York, 1974.

9. ibid., p.163.

10. Aristotle: *De Anima* 420b, cited in Appelbaum, op. cit. (note 1), p. 30.

11. ibid, p. 31.

12. Note that seed is speech in the Dogon, Word in Christianity, and a euphemism for semen: impregnation.

13. Freud writes: do not forget that it was only analysis that created the occult fact—uncovered it when it lay distorted to the point of being unrecognisable.

    And further:

    [telepathy] is a kind of psychical counterpart to wireless telegraphy... The telepathic process is supposed to consist in a mental act in one person instigating the some mental act in another person. What lies between these two mental acts may easily be a psychical process into which the mental one is transformed at one end and which is transformed bock once more into the some mental one at the other end. The analogy with other transformations, such as occur as speaking and hearing by telephone, are unmistakable... It would seem to me that psychoanalysis, by inserting the unconscious between what is physical and what was previously called psychical, has paved the way for the assumption of such processes as telepathy. Cited in Rickels, op. cit. (note 16), p. 28.

14. But the medium here, the telephone, the electrical, is both material and metaphorical—the metaphoricity almost short-circuits. With the analyst as the operator, "putting through, within the system of transference, the ultimate transfer, the transfer of the call, of that direct line to the first five years of the patient's life" as Rickels describes [p. 283], infantile associations form the basis of a symbolic structure in many ways similar to the infantile hermeneutic system which Ernest Jones regards as central to the conceptual and interpretative circuit of divinity, as expressed in the concept of *pneuma*, or divine breath, and by association voice, music all sonority. For Jones, this structure is grounded not in breath but in flatulence. Not in good, sweet sound, but in pungent noise.

15. Avital Ronnel cites a patient of Jung who retained, alongside her cryptic discourse, a coherently critical agency she called the 'telephone'. Only by taking the place of the telephone is Jung able to engage in analysis, a procedure which leads him to describe her schizophrenia as "eroding the covering of

consciousness...so that one could now see form all sides the automatic machinery of the unconscious complexes". Avital Ronell: *The Telephone Book*, University of Nebraska Press, Lincoln, 1989. p. 132.

16. Rickels suggests that the call from the Oedipalised past "tops into and outlasts telepathic lines of communication of dead siblings" thus the potential of mediumship is smothered by the re-establishment of the "home" now containing an internal and internalised "beyond", like a telephone in the head. Laurence Rickels, *Aberrations of Mourning*, Wayne State University Press, Detroit, 1988, p. 28.

17. Ronell, op. cit. (note 16), p. 247.

18. The new Spiritualism was in fact token up by Christians as a shield against the increasing agnosticism the discoveries of science and the theory of evolution (linking man with the savagery of animals) was provoking. Messages from souls in the ether proved the Christian belief in immortality, at the some time the 'occult' connotations of electricity lent a scientific, technological flavour to many Spiritualist experiments. 'Techno-spiritualism' thus conflated technological and spiritual immortality within the concept of the ether, thought of as the cohesive force of the universe, the vehicle of transmission of all energies, and the sphere within which bath telephonic, telegraphic and later wireless communications, together with messages from the 'other side', could occur. For a detailed account see Janet Oppenheim, *The Other World: Spiritualism and Psychical Research in England, 1850–1914*, Cambridge University Press, New York, 1985.

19. Applebaum, op. cit. (note 1), p. 105.

20. Rickels, op. cit. (note 16), p. 293.

Philip Glass: Collaborating with Ginsberg

Interviewed by Nicholas Zurbrugg

One of the most interesting developments in contemporary sound art is the increasing collaborative experimentation between composers, writers, dramatists and artists. In the following interview, American composer Philip Glass discusses *Hydrogen Jukebox (1990)*, a music-theatre collaboration—or 'chamber opera'—based upon the poems of veteran 'beat' poet, Allen Ginsberg.

NEW YORK, DECEMBER 12, 1991

NZ: I believe you've been working with the poet Allen Ginsberg on an opera entitled *Hydrogen Jukebox*.

PG: Yes, it's a chamber opera for six voices and a small ensemble. I had been asked to perform in a benefit to raise money for VIETCO, which is a Vietnam Veterans' theatre group. And I said, "Well, maybe I'll have my friend Allen do this with me"—I've known Allen for some time—we live in the same neighbourhood, and we run into each other all the time. They liked the idea very much and suggested I do something from *Iron Horse*, because it's about Vietnam. A week or so later I ran into Allen in St. Mark's Bookstore, and he said, "Oh, what a nice idea". He sent me a tape of *Wichita Vortex Sutra* and I worked with the tape—I wrote music for his reading and we performed that together, as a duet as it were. That turned out so well, that I said, "Let's try to do another work". So I got the idea to do this piece with Allen.

NZ: How did you put this opera together?

PG: Well, we combed through his *Collected Work*—covering a period of forty years—and picked out about twenty poems, and those became the libretto. In *Hydrogen Jukebox* there isn't much of a story there, and there's not much of an attempt to create one. In a way, we leave the poems as poems, and don't try to act them out in some way. The staging of them is done by a young woman called Ann Carlson. Jerome Sirlin also did some of the visual material.

Father Death Blues, for example, is done as an abstract staging of people in particular configurations of circles and lines. But then, some of the other pieces, like *Allah/Jaweh*, which is a poem about Israel and Palestine, are set in a way that makes you think that the subject matter of the poem is being expressed in visual terms as well. I'm not sure that that's so important. With another poem, called *The Green Automobile*, there is no green automobile. You don't see it. We thought at one point we'd have everybody sitting in a green automobile but in fact that turned out to be rather redundant since the poem describes the automobile. And what Ann did was devise a staging that explored some of the more abstract ideas of the poem, without the particular one. I think that was the most successful way to work. I think she did very well with it.

NZ: Did you find your musical settings of the poems contained or constrained by the patterns of Ginsberg's intonations?

PG: No, I didn't. What Allen had always done in previous collaborations with other composers was to take the music and retain the meter exactly as a spoken meter. So the music was a kind of a window dressing for the words. And I had no intention of doing that. In *Hydrogen Jukebox* I devised other ways of working. Sometimes the music was very different from the poems, and sometimes the music fitted the poem. I would take one aspect or image of the poem, turn that image into a musical image, and that became the setting. But it could sometimes be only one phrase of the poem. And you might have to wait through the whole poem to come across the phrase that matches you to the music. A simple example would be the poem *Aunt Rose*. He describes her as an elderly woman—she has one leg shorter than the other, and she limps. So the music was set in a five-eight rhythm, which is a kind of limping rhythm. You might not know why I picked that rhythm until at one point in the poem he mentions that she limps down the hall. And the match is there. But there's no attempt to describe anything.

There's another poem called *The Green Automobile* which is a very early poem—Allen wrote it when he was only twenty-five. The refrain is, "If I had a green automobile", and then he goes on to describe what he would do with the green automobile. What I did for that poem was write a piece of music in which a very rapid modulation that ends up in a new key becomes the image of starting the car. You may not know that that's what the intention is, but after a while this rapid series of chords finally arriving in a new key, and stabilising there, becomes a kind of musical image of the car. But the music doesn't have horn-honking or anything like that. So it's a musicalisation of one feature of a poem.

It's a very satisfying work artistically. Ann Carlson and Jerry Sirlin both made beautiful contributions to the work, and it became a kind of four-way collaboration in the end—you have the words and the music and the staging and the visualisation—the four things together. It's one of these extremely happy collaborations where each part is a kind of a unique contribution that the other contributors were not able to do—or even to imagine. I mean, I didn't have any idea what Ann Carlson would do, or how Jerome Sirlin would approach this work. It turned out to be a very successful collaboration.

NZ: What are you presently working on?

PG: I'm working with Bob Wilson on a new piece—it's called *White Raven*—and in this piece we really are equal collaborators. He does the staging and the design, and I do the music. *White Raven* is commissioned by the *Teatera S. Carlo* in Lisbon in commemoration of the ten years of discoveries between 1490 and 1500. This is the time when the Portuguese went around the Horn of Africa, went to South India, China and Japan. Later, they were in Brazil. The theme of it is basically the Portuguese discoveries, and among the main characters is an explorer that we're calling Vasco da Gama.

NZ: What is the relationship between Wilson's staging and your music? When I saw him rehearsing the Cambridge production of *Quartett* in 1988, he repeatedly modified performers' positions, perfecting gestures and lighting. It seemed to be quite a laborious and continual operation.

PG: Yes, it's very detailed.

NZ: He was presumably changing his notion of how people should be on stage. Does your music vacillate as well

PG: No, it doesn't. With *Einstein* the music was done first, and I didn't change it very much throughout the staging. But with the *CIVIL warS* he had done the staging first, and then I wrote the music, so it wasn't necessary. In this case we're doing it that way again. We conducted a workshop together in Lisbon with about twenty actors playing the parts in the opera, and we more or less made a dry opera—an opera without music. We'll do the opera 'dry' first, and then when it's staged we'll do a video-tape of all the staging. And then we'll do all the timings from the video-tape. And so, there, it's not necessary to rewrite the music, because I'm fitting it to the action that's already conceived.

NZ: Do you ever have problems in terms of the timing, or in terms of matching your music to Wilson's variously prolonged or variously accelerated actions...

PG: Not much. Not really. Things can be mode longer or shorter without too much trouble. I've now done three pieces with Bob—two *CIVIL warS* operas and *Einstein*, so this is our fourth work together. Besides that, I've seen quite a lot of his other pieces, so it's a style of work that's very familiar to me, and I know how to work with him.

NZ: Do you find that there's a substantial difference between the operas that you've directed like *1000 Airplanes*—and the effects that you like, and the effects that he likes...

PG: Oh yes, certainly. If Bob hod done *1000 Airplanes* it would have looked nothing like what I do. My own way of working as a director—though I haven't done that much—is in a certain way much more traditional than what Bob does. And one of the reasons that I like working with people like Bob or like Richard Foreman is that they are very innovative directors, and they bring something very fresh to the work. In my own field, which is composition, I can be innovative, but in the field of directing—when I do direct—I'm not inventing theatre language.

NZ: But presumably you share a very similar aesthetic, and your approach is compatible?

PG: Obviously, clearly it is. When I direct a piece it's just for my amusement—and not just that. With *1000 Airplanes* I more or less hod to direct it because that was the only way to put the words and the music in the right place. With *Hydrogen Jukebox* I was interested in finding another director—someone to bring a very fresh and different way to think about the staging. And that's what Ann Carlson did. It did not occur to me to be the director of that piece, though I've been asked to direct The *Fall of the House of Usher* in Germany, and I'd like to do that. I have ideas of how to do that, and I'd also like to direct *Akhnaten* some time. There have been three productions of it, one in Germany, one in America that went to London, and one in Sweden. But I haven't seen a production of it that is true to the music in the way that I conceive it.

NZ: What is the particular problem here?

PG: Well, it's getting a director that will do what you wont to do. And they don't. The real problem is that most directors think of themselves as collaborators with an author, but most of the time the authors are dead, so there's no one to argue the point, and they can do what they like. Then when you give them a new piece, they're quite likely to soy, "Oh I'll just do it as I like". And you'll say, "Well, I didn't write it that way". And invariably, they'll never see it your way. Which means you'll never see it your way. But if you only work with directors that are compliant, you then may not get anything that's interesting. So in order to get the interesting directors who'll bring something new to the work, very often there will be certain aspects of the work, which you've cared for, which won't appear. That ideal director that will be both completely innovative and obedient to the author—I don't think that he or she exists! So, in the end, I've always chosen to go with the director who simply doesn't pay any attention to my ideas, but follows the music in his own way, and does something quite original. In the end, I think it's been more interesting to work that way. But on a few occasions—for example, for *Akhnaten*—I would like to see the opera once done the way it was written, just in terms of following the libretto!

NZ: This suggests yet again that your interest in content, and a particular kind of mythological content evoking many things, contradicts the prevalent critical conviction that post-modern culture is somehow superficial or vacuous.

PG: Well, I don't consider myself a post-modernist, as I understand that term. You see, I have an anti-historical approach, but it's not a post-modern approach. They're different ways of leaving history behind. There's a kind of post-modernism that simply equates history and style as though the two were the same thing. Isn't that so? Historical materials are mixed very freely—that's one way of doing it. I don't believe my work is a part of that. Because I think that if you look at what I've done, I think my work—if I can be candid about it—has a real individuality to it. It's not a borrowed language. In other words, it's not a collage of other styles.

NZ: Is it possible for you to guess which direction your work will take or continue to take over the next decade?

PG: No. But I'm interested in these collaborations that I did with Ravi Shankar and Foday Muso Suso, so that's one. That's been interesting. And I have a new project with the filmmaker Godfrey Reggio, that will also involve world-music.

NZ: Do you have any new projects for video or television?

PG: No, I don't like it very much for music. It seems to me that opera is not good on close-ups, and that's what television is. Television is all about close-ups. And opera is not about closeup—it's about big-scale things. And for me, when I look at opera on television, it doesn't work very well. So I don't do it. I mean, there are plenty of opera productions an television. I don't think the lack of mine will be noticed very much. I'm not interested in documenting on television or on film in that way. I'm interested in film, but not films of music pieces—I mean films like *The Thin Blue Line* or *Powaaqatsi* or *Koyaanisqatsi* or *Mishima*—I am interested in those films But the idea of making a film out of a theatre work doesn't interest me. I think there's something, to me, jarring and fundamentally at cross-purposes about bringing these mediums together.

NZ: Very finally, could I ask what it is that you find most exciting in your work?

PG: The collaborative process is still the most exciting one. And each theatre piece I do has a different team of people. Bob Wilson is an exception, but I rarely repeat the groups exactly in the same way. For example, with *Hydrogen Jukebox*, I'm using Jerome Sirlin, but I didn't use David Hwang, and I used Allen Ginsberg as the writer. With *The Voyage*, I work with David, but not with Jerome. So—I'll work with different people.

Xenakis: Towards a Philosophy of Music

Phillip L. Ryan

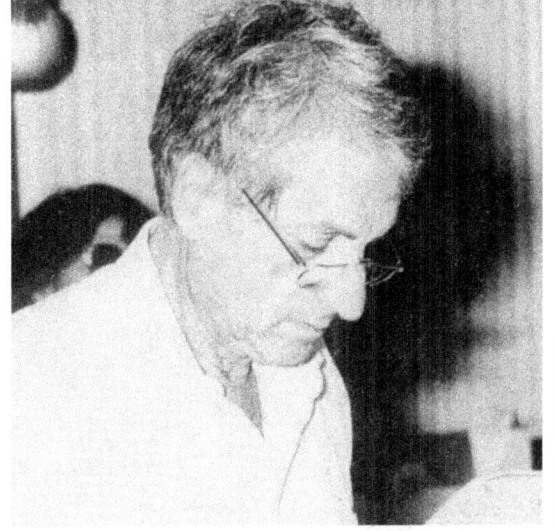

Iannis Xenakis, 1990

This paper consists of an attempt to contextualise the work of Iannis Xenakis, and present a chronology of his work such that the development of his achievements can be grasped.

> "*Our* cultural revolution cannot be envisaged as aesthetic; it is not a revolution based on culture, neither is culture its aim or motive; ...The objective and directive of our cultural revolution is to create a culture that is not an institution but a style of life; its basic distinction is the realisation of philosophy in the spirit of philosophy."
>
> —Henri Lefebvre

to introduce Iannis Xenakis—

First References:

1. Musique. Architecture—Iannis Xenakis. Casterman, 1971.

2. Arts/Sciences: Alloys—Iannis Xenakis. Pendragon, New York, 1985.

3. Formalised Music—Iannis Xenakis. Pendragon, New York, 1991.

> "In the fields of art, science, even of politics, it is alright to see things differently and to act in a different way. If you are aware of it, and you may not always be, you can really lead a fundamental life."
>
> —Iannis Xenakis, 1990

Essays In Sound

"The man of music thus arrives at the frontiers of a general and absolute *axiomatisation* of his art, which announces the epoch of a 'metamusic', enjoining science and philosophy and making the composer a 'craftsman in philosophical theses and global architectures'."

– Maurice Fleuret, 1969

Iannis Xenakis (right) with Le Corbusier (left, wearing glasses) designing the Philips Pavilion for the Brussels World Fair, 1958.

CHRONOLOGY OF THE MAJOR WORKS AND ACHIEVEMENTS OF XENAKIS

1922 born May 29 at Braila, Romania to a wealthy family of Greek ancestry;

1932 moves to Greece—secondary studies at a private Greco-English college on the island of Spetsai;

1934 decides to consecrate himself to music and the sciences;

1944 fights in the Greek Resistance movement and is seriously wounded on January 1.

View of the Philips Pavilion, Brussels World Fair, 1958.

1945 one of the leaders of student demonstrations against the Nazis;

1947 graduates from the Athens Polytechnic with an engineering diploma; exiled from Greece due to his political activities and moves to Paris where he becomes associated with the architect Le Corbusier (later, Xenakis designs major elements of the church of La Tourette, including the windows); projects with Le Corbusier include housing in Marseilles and Nantes, buildings in Chandigarh and Baghdad;

1948 works in composition with Arthur Honegger and Darius Milhaud;

1950 commences composition with Olivier Messiaen at the Paris Conservatory and participates in the course of Hermann Scherchen at Gravesano;

1953 marries Francoise, writer and heroine of the French Resistance;

1954 *Metastasis* for orchestra—a scandal later at the Days of the Donaueschingen Festival, 1955, conducted by Hans Rosboud;

1955 'The Crisis of Serial Music' published;

1956 *Pithoprakta* for 50 instruments;

1957 'Elements of Stochastic Music' published;

1958 *Achorripsis* for 21 instruments—formulating his minimal rules for composition, *Diamorphoses* for electromagnetic tape; designs the Philips Pavilion for the Brussels World Fair, music (the *Poeme Electronique* by Edgard Varèse, spectacle by Le Corbusier) augmented by his *Concret Ph*, on tape—425 speakers were used;

1959 *Duel*, game for two orchestras; *Syrmos* for 18 strings; *Analogiques A+B* for nine strings and tape;

1960 leaves Le Corbusier; *Orient–Occident*, tape music for UNESCO; member of the jury for the Paris Biennale;

1961 *Herma* for piano; invited to the *Orient–Occident* congress in Tokyo;

1962 completes his studies at the Paris Conservatory; computation of *ST/ 10-080262*, 'stochastic music', using an IBM *7090* computer; *Polio Ta Dhina* for children's chorus and orchestra; *Strategie* for two orchestras and two conductors; *Morisma–Amorisma* for four instruments; *ST/48* for orchestra; *Bohor* for tape; invited to the Festival of Contemporary Music at Varsovie;

1963 designs *Cosmic Cities*—5,000 metres in altitude Ipublished in 'Urbanisme, utopies et realities' by Francoise Choay, Ed. du Seuil, 1967); 'Farmalised Music' first published at the Editions de 10 Revue Musicale, Richard-Masse; invited by Aaron Copland to teach composition at the Berkshire Music Centre at Tanglewood, Massachusetts;

1964 *Eonta* for piano and five brass; music for 'The Suppliants' of Aeschylus;

1965 *Akrata* for 16 wind instruments; *Namos Alpha* for 'cello; Festival Xenakis in Paris; obtains French nationality;

1966 establishment of the School of Mathematical and Automatic Music (C.E.M.A.Mu.) at the Ecole Pratique des Hautes Etudes in Paris; anends 'Orchestral Space' in Tokyo; *Terretektorh* for 90 musicians spread amongst the public in the form of the spokes of a wheel; music for 'The Oresteio' of Aeschylus;

1967 'Towards a Metamusic' published; music for 'Medeo' of Seneca; *Polytope De Montreol'* at Expo'67, Montreal—light and sound event; Xenakis Days at the Museum of Modern Art, Paris; Centre of Mathematical and Automatic Music at the University of Indiana, Bloomington;

1968 'Towards a Philosophy of Music' published; *Nuits* for 12 mixed voices;

1969 *Nomos Gamma* for orchestra; *Kraanerg* for tape and orchestra; *Anaktorio* for eight instruments; *Persephassa* for percussion, with the musicians placed around the audience;

1970 member of the Centre Notional de 10 Recherche Scientifique (to 1972);

1972 *Polytope De Cluny*—light and sound event; Professor at the University of Paris I;

1974 Cendrees for chorus and orchestra; Gold medal Maurice Ravel;

1975 *Phlegra* for chamber orchestra;

1976 *Retours-Windungen* for strings; *Khoai-Xoai* for harpsichord; Doctor of Letters and Humanities, University of Paris I;

1977 awarded the Prix Beethoven; *Diatope* at the Pompidou Centre, Paris; *Upic* (Unite Polyagogique Informatique du Cemamul, a graphic system of composition, located at CNET, Issy-Ies-Moulineoux;

1979 *Pleiades* far percussion; 'In the Immediate Future', *Vogue*, Paris 11/79;

1981 *Kombui* for harpsichord and percussion;

1983 member of the French Institute;

1984 *Thallein* for 14 instruments; *Naama* for harpsichord;

1986 *Keqrops* far piano and orchestra; *A L'ile De Goree* for harpsichord and instruments; *Jalons* for instruments; *Keren* for trombone;

1987 finalisation of the music for 'The Oresteia' of Aeschylus; Grand Prix of the City of Paris; (Honorary member of several academies in the United States, Great Britain and Germany).

EXTRACT FROM "TOWARDS A PHILOSOPHY OF MUSIC"

(Revue d'Esthetique, Nos. 2–3–4, 1968, Paris).

> "Thus, applied to music, the *question* leads us to the heart of our mentality. Once and for all, and now much more precisely, modern axiomatics are disengaging the signifying paths which the post has traced on the rock of our being. These mental premisses are confirming and justifying the millions of years of accumulation and destruction of signs. But consciousness of their limitation, their closure, is forcing us to destroy them.

Brutally, it is inconceivable that the whole of humanity is developed in childhood such as to give rise no longer to its own conception of time and space (cf., the works of Jean Piaget)'. So that the base of the cove will not reflect the beings which are behind us but will be a filtering gloss which will allow us to predict that which is at the heart of the universe. It is this base which must be shattered.

Consequences:

a)   it is necessary to change the structures of the order of time and space, those of logic...

b)   art with science annexed will be able to realise this mutation.

> Let us resolve the duality Mortal–Eternal: the future is in the post and the inverse is true, the evanescence of the present is abolishing itself, it is everywhere at once. The here is also millions of light years away...On their own, the keys to the stars produced by an ambitious technology cannot liberate us from our mental chains. This is the fantastic perspective which Art–Science is opening up for us in the Pythago–Parmenidean field."

—Iannis Xenakis, Paris, 1968

> *"To be like Ulysses, in the midst of the waves..."*

—Iannis Xenakis, 1990

> *"...After all, our physics was never capable of truly understanding the Leibnizian harmony of the thousands of voices translating each other in a universal code."*

—Ilya Prigogine/Isobelle Stengers, 1982

Found Sounds
Michael Leggett

I

The Museo del Belles Artes in Mexico City is one of the classic examples of architecture of the Art Deco period, lavishly constructed from marble, limestone, copper, glass, bronze and brass. With a massive interior vestibule topped by a copper dome, balconies project from the marble staircase and form the entrances to a series of large rooms. Once the centre of cultural life in the city, the ageing building is pensioned off into providing recital space for virtuosos and allowing native painters to display their appallingly derivative work. Remarkably, several murals by Rivera and Oroczo survive in splendour alongside these decadent façades. The place is hushed; should someone cough, the sound reverberates around the interior.

Suddenly from outside, a flash, and moments later, a crack of thunder. Torrential rain beats on the copper and glass dome in a fusillade of percussion. The doors at the entrance swing and slam as the pedestrians rush for shelter. Squeals, shouts and stomping feet reach up from the base of the buildings as the tumult continues above. Museum attendants are observed carrying metal buckets up the stairs to the upper floor. They place them, apparently randomly, around the floor area and retreat in conceited confidence. The fury of the storm soon relents and reduces to a steady downpour. The first drop hits the bottom of a bucket; then the next hits another, then the next, then another, then another, then another as the rain begins to seep through the glass and copper dome with accelerating rapidity.

As the noise of the rain begins to recede, the sounds from the ensemble of unattended buckets begin to crescendo, creating complex rhythms as each bucket's respective drip speeds up and slows down according to the size of the hole in the road. Before long, the tone and reverberance emitting from each bucket alters as it fills with water which in turn alters the sound of the recital as it echoes around the building.

The rain gradually dies away and the sun streams through the windows; sometime later, not long after the last drip has landed, the attendants remove the filled buckets.

II

In the lush panelled concert hall of a provincial university, an ensemble of five brass-playing musicians in a relaxed and highly confident manner perform a repertoire of works, displaying in their professional manner the standards of excellence to which brass-players can aspire, if in doing so, their capabilities excel the qualities of the pieces selected.

As they played, something else could be heard from an indistinct distance. By turning the ear one way, it sounded as if one of the light fittings in the high ceiling was vibrating in (or out) of sympathy with a particular pitch of note. By turning the ear another way, it was as if a small insect was about to burrow into the recesses of the auditory organ itself.

This continued for several, short pieces of music, by the end of which the ear, the eye and the brain had in co-ordination explored every possible corner of the concert hall for a clue to this random accompaniment. Perhaps the fabric of the building itself was resonating in sympathy with certain notes? Images of the brass-outside-the-walls-of-Jericho myth began to expand the possibilities of the music, beyond the walls that enclosed it.

Applause marked a break in the programme and the leader of the group stepped forward to introduce the next section. Suddenly, whilst he talked, there was the sound again. From outside the building? The corridor? No, there on the stage was the culprit. The euphonium player was making some quiet alteration to the tuning of his instrument and as he did so, the sound of his tongue rasping in the fluted sides of the mouthpiece was reflected off one of the ceiling panels and heard as if only a few metres away.

Evidently, none of the rest of the audience were in the reflection zone and as the leader continued to speak, it was only one pair of ears which heard the sound of his voice superimposed with small, sporadic but perfectly clear and exclamatory raspberries...

Paul DeMarinis:
The Melodic Voice Box

Interviewed by Shaun Davies and Annemarie Jonson

Paul DeMarinis is an American electronic artist who has been creating sound, computer, performance and interactive work since 1971. Much of his recent work involves computer synthesised and processed speech.

SYDNEY, NOVEMBER 15, 1992

SD: I am interested in the performance that you did at the Museum of Contemporary Art the other night with the glove.[1] I was reading about what Merleau–Ponty had to say about gesture being a nascent form of language...that these sorts of movements, while they don't contain any semantic content, as it were, were the very things which were the precursors to spoken language. I was curious as to any ideas you may have about that...

PO: Well, yeah, an interesting thing is when I started hacking the glove together and started playing with it, I realised that with my finger controlling the pitch of the voice with the finger gesture, I could do all different accents, it just come so easily...I could make them sound really fruity, or sound really commanding. I was talking with Edward T. Hall, the anthropologist, who's very interested in body language and gesture; he's the guy who did the original research on proxemics, body distancing, and he said that it's the some area of the brain that controls the vocal chords and sa there's a natural translation of these things, whereas if you were to try to do it with your eye—blinking your eye—you couldn't create quite that analogue. The idea is that these more sensory modalities—or motor modalities, I guess you'd call them—the ones that have common evolutionary or physiological origins, almost create the analogue. Certainly the work with the pitch of the voice is less about the similarity of perception than the similarity of production, of speech, of language, and of music. I mean, people have speculated from way back ...Nietzsche wrote an extensive piece about this 'primordial language' that was somewhere between music and speech ...

AMJ: *'Ur'* language, Heideggerian *'Ur'* language ...the originary tongue... ?

PD: There's a researcher, Lieberman, at Brown University, a physiologist who's studied the evolution of the vocal tract in humans by examining skulls of Neanderthals and CroMagnons, estimating how long their vocal tracts must have been, and how many different sounds with such a vocal tract you could have mode. And his conclusion is that the real advantage that Homo Sapiens hod over Neanderthals wasn't brain power, but verbal communication. He challenges Chomsky in, I think, a very interesting way, when you look at it physiologically. Chomsky would have us think that language was born out of Adam's rib or something, as a 'whole thing': production, perception ...but physiological evidence would have that perhaps the parts of the brain that are responsible for understanding speech may have existed very early, may exist in birds or lizards ...they're already there ...to be able to take a symbol stream of that variety, and that density, thirty symbols a second and put it together into a meaningful pattern. What Lieberman says is what was slow to come was the actual physiology for producing that variety of symbols at that rate. The brain areas, to produce a symbolic communication existed, maybe, as part of something else, but the length of the vocal tract became very important. And one of his little asides that I thought was so compelling, is that in evolutionary development, the same parts of the body are used over and over again. I mean, there's no reason, as pointed out years ago, we don't fart to communicate. It evolved with this vocal tract, being the same place where we eat, and later, where animals breathe; we do three things with it now, you see, it must have had some great evolutionary advantage ...if we're doing three things through this narrow passage. I was in a restaurant the next day and I saw a poster for the Heimlich manoeuvre, and I realised, God, Lieberman's right. A million years later, you're in a restaurant and you're breathing, eating and talking. All through this one little narrow passageway. The fact that people are still choking to death *(laughter)* a million years after the evolution of speech, means that speech must be very, very important. If you buy Lieberman's thesis about the evolution of language, it looks like the brain's area for understanding speech developed, and the brain's area for producing symbols and some kind of vocalisation developed later. Then the real development, the latest development a million years ago was the development of a very mechanically variable vocal tract for actually making these symbols Then it's possible that what must have been before that, what these Neanderthals must have hod, with a limited ability to produce different, distinctive symbols, was something like song, something melismatic, where the melody, and expression of the speech would be there, but with no semantic precision. Then you would have this kind of aural language, this kind of ...something that pre-dated linguistic precision.

AMJ: I'm interested in this in relation to the Foucault quote[2] that we talked about earlier, the one you used in relation to some of your earlier voice work. Why the invocation of the theological in relation to speech?

PD: If 'divine' is never something that we see and yet it's something that we know... divinity being somehow associated, I think, with something transcendental, primordial ...It's something that's not around us. Yet ...we talk about it all the time. so: It's proximal, but out of sight.

SD: It's out of sight, but it's in the saying; it ...happens. We talk about it all the time. So, this other thing that you could call divinity or something, the other quality that we're never sure of, I think we find in music a lot. The experiencing, the belonging that you feel in music ...some kind of 'big belonging' ...when somebody plays their blaster-box, they're feeling like they're belonging...

SD: There was a fellow I was with recently... he'd had this experience of singing in a choir and wanted me to explain to him why he felt so good afterwords. And I found it a really challenging question and a really difficult one to answer. I don't know whether it's a release of endorphins in the brain from breathing very hard or something like that. But I think I know what it is he was talking about. It's a sort of accommodation of that which, like you say, is beyond ...grasp; there's a sense of controlling something that's, at the same time, uncontrollable...

AMJ: The voice and sound are often used as primary exemplars of the transcendental…

PD: Mmm …yeah, I think so, and so that quote's an anomalous quote for Foucault who doesn't deal with the notion of divinity very much. I liked that. I did an interactive installation piece with two telephone booths at the Exploratorium—which is a science museum that has artists come in and do projects—where people could talk to each other and perform computer operations on their voices to explore that region between language and music. I used that quote at the top of it.

SD: There's something about that intermediary space with telephones, between the said and the hearing, where this 'third term' comes into it. It's like a …*deus ex machina*. I wonder if you've got any thoughts on this… technical intermediary space?

PD: There are so many thoughts to have, there are so many things that have been said well. I was just re-reading Edmund Carpenter, "Oh what a blow that phantom gave me!" He's an anthropologist who spent a lot of time in New Guinea in the sixties with film and radio, dealing with the government there …*(opens book)*…

SD: It seems to me to be a large part of the TISEA[3] project, this technological 'other space' as it were

PD: …this was published in 1972. It's post-McLuhan …dealing with how the government was approaching media, and the cultural implications of this, and he starts his book with a little chapter –'Angelisation': "Electricity has made angels of all of us. Not angels in the Sunday-school sense of being good or having wings, but spirit freed from flesh, capable of instant transportation, anywhere. The moment we pick up a phone we're nowhere in space, everywhere in spirit. Nixon on TV is everywhere at once. That is Saint Augustine's definition of God, a being whose centre is everywhere, whose borders are nowhere". There's so much that's been written and said about that issue. I'd have to say it's almost like my 'grounding' rather than anything I'd like to try to expound or extend in any way.

......

SD: Just getting back to the performance the other night, I was curious about what you call a "hacked glove". I wasn't sure whether it was actually a device or just some kind of stage prop.

PD: It's a 'Mattel Power Glove'. It's a controller for the 'Nintendo' video game. It has these finger-flex controllers which is all I use, and then it has some ultra-sound things for spatial location. You're supposed to be able to play video games by using the fingers to fire the missiles or something. The design of it makes it look very cyber-prosthetic. There wasn't much use for it except for these finger-flexers, 'flex sensors', so I threw away the rest of it and made a 'hack' to get it talking to the computer directly instead of through its software. Those things are not too interesting to me as general-purpose musical controllers. They're not as interesting as, for example, a keyboard, because you can't do something very precise and repeatable. I mean, on a keyboard you can do things that are extremely precise and repeatable, and you can also do very expressive things that have a large degree of indeterminacy. So the glove doesn't afford that kind of repeatability. I mean, gestures transpose well in space. You take this gesture and add it to this gesture, and you make another gesture. You can put gestures together and create a language. The glove controller as it exists doesn't allow that kind of fluidity and it doesn't ...computer software doesn't allow any way to parse combinations, and put them together. Such a language is probably technically possible, but it hasn't been developed yet...

...I thinks it's one of the most interesting things... machine translation of human communication. I have to say, with computers, I don't deal with the idea of artificial intelligence. To my thought, the computer is an artificial memory device. It's something that stores or transmits, over time and place, inferences, signs and symbols: signs that are meaningful to the various users. The arbitrariness of computer symbols is certainly a part of their power, I mean, a certain computer number can either be an instruction that tells the central processing unit to do something, to fetch data; it could be data itself; it could be the character of a letter of a text; it could be a musical note; it can be all of these different things, and it's completely contextual. These symbols are very, very arbitrary. The computer cannot look at patterns of information, it can't re-synchronise itself with anything other than physics. That is, a hard reset: you pull this line law—all these transistors are drained of the stared charge in them, you start with a blank slate. I'm not too interested in the idea that I'm communicating with someone in the computer, some 'cyber-being'. I think I'm communicating with myself, and you have a marvellous storage device... the double is your own memory that you forgot about. Which it always is in our dreams. The double is always the things we forgot about. The wonder of dreams, the stories that we can experience—and they're still a surprise to us even though we're supposedly scripting them along—is really that we have such a vast memory, and these halls, these chambers of memory are there and we put things there and forget them and we go back and they're port of us again. I think the computer at it best is that, or it's communicating with somebody else.

······

AMJ: You mentioned earlier that precision and repetition were central to your work. I guess that reading through this stuff that you've produced, that element is very strong. What is it about repetition that...

PD: Oh, let's see ...Gee, I could go about it so many different ways ...How do you get good at playing the piano? How do you get to Heaven? How do you do any of these things? You say you prayers, and you say them better and better, or you practice the violin, or you ...make love, you know, these are all practices...

AMJ: Or you create capitalism as a 'production line'. There are obviously utopian and negative effects of repetition depending on context and reading...so:...the idea that the mare something is repeated, the less kind of...'wholesome' the product is...

PD: Well that only came about in the nineteenth century. In Siegfried Gideon's book *Mechanisation Takes Command*, he talks about the beginning of machine reproduction and how at first it was making better products than artisans could make, because it could repeat them so precisely, and then after a while that became kind of a negative quality.

SD: There's something about the weight of the number of repeated farms that causes them to collapse in on themselves. I was thinking that what I found interesting about your performance was that because what you were doing was not, in a sense, able to be repeated in the same way as you might perform something on the keyboard, it threw something over to the audience that had to be dealt with there and then. You couldn't take it away and listen to it again, and again, like an LP record. Adorno talks about that sort of thing as well...

PD: Yeah, absolutely, otherwise I wouldn't perform ...I mean it is like playing music and, say, performing it at the keyboard. You can't ever perform something in the same way at a keyboard. If there's nobody listening, even *your* ears change. If there's somebody, even one other person listening, you can't say it the same way. That's just so basic to music; music as a kind of... belonging, engaging... I dealt a lot with that in the *Edison Effect* piece[4], I've dealt a lot with the idea of the mechanical repetition and the music, you know, where music *is*.

AMJ: So what do you think of, for example, theories like those of Walter Ong's and McLuhan's, that the communality, the 'belonging' that is produced by sound, by virtue of what it is, experientially, phenomenologically, was destroyed once visual culture gained primacy, for example with the book, mechanisation of printing and so on ...you got a kind of individuation of consciousness—based on vision—that wasn't possible in oral cultures? Of course the situation has now become massively complex with the proliferation of 'sensory' technologies...

PD: I mean, I have to say about oral cultures, I don't know ...Who was it the other day that pointed out that none of us has an experience of an oral culture ...or all of us do. (long pause). I don't think it goes away, very much, really. Discourse is always about discourse, talking is always about talking—as Deleuze and Guattari say, it's always about hearsay, it's never about seeing, we don't say what we've seen. They quote somebody who denies that bees have a language, because bees can only repeat 'linguistically' what they have seen: "there are flowers at this place". A bee can't go and eavesdrop on another hive and hear this information and then go back and tell its hive about that. Deleuze and Guattari seem to hint at that as being one of the crucial qualities of language, that it's always hearsay, it's always based on what has been heard. Then how are things heard Visually? Well, you have text. Carpenter says "you can't say 'no' with images". That's a problem with pictorial images. In New Guinea, they were putting posters up, trying to get people not to steal, not to drink beer, etc., and this only promoted more because, he said, denial, negativity, in an image, is always a sub-text, a subtitle to it.' Don't do this!' assumes that you're not living in a visual world, but within a textual world. Now text is also, as is well known, an auditory modality, this is well established in brain physiology. In the brain, it goes from the visual cortex to the auditory cortex before processing as meaning. This has been really well established.

Text is sound... how about network computers? That's text... and it's completely communal, it is very communal. The people who are into it are like a bunch of hippies, who are into a kind of communal living thing. I'm not into this electronic mail stuff. People who are, are just as 'hippy-communy' as the 'touchy-feely' people were, and it's purely textual. It may be that the auditory modality that's inherent in text keeps that happening again and again. It isn't like the distant, voyeuristic scrutiny that multiple viewings of a pictorial image offer. They're always mute. That's the idea. The picture is always mute.

AMJ: So, what do you make of what are said to be the phenomenological differences between, say, visual modalities and aural modalities?

PD: I haven't thought enough about visual modalities …I think about sound and auditory phenomena in distinction to something else, but I don't quite know what that is. I've noticed that in learning computers and other things that there are people—and this is kind of folklore—who are visual, they don't have too much of a problem with computers; people who are auditory, they are excellent at computers, and people who are spatial—sculptors, architects and mathematicians who have brilliant encompassing minds—can be horrid at dealing with computers …they don't get that kind of reasoning. So there might be something other than this visual-auditory axis. It doesn't just have to do with just the eyes. A good friend of mine, a sculptor, can do these great 3D models but he couldn't write a computer programme. I could write a computer programme to do those but I couldn't make a picture of Mickey Mouse in 3D—I wouldn't know where to start. So again, this textual thing comes down to an auditory thing, but the spatial thing seems the thing apart. When I talk ta PhD mathematicians they are always waving their hands in the air, trying to elucidate what they're saying and I guess it 'does it' for them but it doesn't 'do it' for me: I don't 'get' what they're saying. They're actually locating points in space, in the multi-dimensionality inside their heads.

SD: You raised an interesting point before… about what you do with computers, about how you understand this to be a way of communicating with yourself, rather than a more communal sense of communicating. I'm interested in extending that idea a little bit, in terms of the way that use of language and sound are considered the guarantors of self-presence in western philosophy. If you view the computer as a prosthesis of your own 'internal time consciousness', I wonder if the computer might not act as a kind or means of deferral…

AMJ: …or you seem to suggest some kind of 'externalisation'? so:

PD: …externalisation of consciousness… it raises all sorts of issues. I don't know. You may be dealing with your own memory, with other people's memory, in some way, for example, the programmer who wrote Microsoft Word you' re communicating with. I think that as far as the being or the 'identity', the 'stamp' or the 'mark' or whatever that moment of being is, mechanical reproduction and recording erased forever the certainty of authorship. You could take everything else away about the machine age and art, but you'd be left with an uncertain authorship.

SD: You spoke earlier also about the advent of electricity…about, for example, the phone making us nowhere in space and everywhere in spirit…

AMJ: … Like God, the ultimate author …

PD: We put our mythology of life force onto electricity. Electricity is the most lucid medium. It's more lucid than coal, it's more lucid than authority, because authority is always contextual whereas electricity can always be changed into heat, or information. It's like an ideal currency. You can turn it on and turn it off, instantly. We like to turn things on and off, we get this great feeling of satisfaction…Switches—there's no reason to construct a switch in a particular way. These things are mechanical encodings of some kind of mythology.

AMJ: It's fairly appropriate in terms of a cultural tradition of knowledge being associated with light. To be 'lucid' is literally to do with brightness or shine, reflected light. It has to do with intelligibility, and metaphors of light have to do with the ability to construct and control a space of knowing. But what of sound?

PD: Well here's the thing: light casts shadows. From Plato on we are aware that all that we see are the shadows. I don't see you, I only see the reflected light. I talked about this in my work *The Edison Effect*. This is the effect that recording had on our way of remembering and belonging. Another aspect is the idea of uncertain authorship because Edison was such a charlatan. And another is a reference to the actual phenomenon which is the boiling off of the filament which would deposit on the light globes causing them to cast shadows instead of light. The idea is that every technology, if it's a mythical encoding, also has these shadows. And what are the shadows of mechanical recording? Indeed, they are the tune running through the head. You don't just experience the record when you are listening to the record, in fact you experience the record with such joy and delight because of the anticipation wrought by this shadow in the brain, this memory. The first time you hear a record it's no big thing, the second time it may have something that reminds you of something else, but it gets to the point where you can only enjoy a certain performance of Brahm's fourth symphony or something, maybe only the one that has the scratch in the certain place. These are the shadows that the medium costs and we 'make' those, we 'carry' them. This tune running through the head is the shadow of the medium… so it's temporal but it's not only deferred to the moment when it happens, the moment of mechanical reproduction. It's about the anticipation, you can listen to it inside your head and this can create a desire to want to hear it.

SD: It's almost as if the record needle cuts a groove in the brain.

PD: Interestingly enough there are no references to a tune running through the head before mechanical recording was invented, with the exception of Emily Dickinson talking of obsessive thoughts about her distant lover as "my mind running in its groove". This medium, like the light globe, is very much part and parcel of the experience. And to speak of it as a deferral…

SD: This quote from the SoundCulture catalogue says it all: "The needle in the groove, no less than the needle in the vein, is one symbolic emblem on the quixotic quest for a perfect moment of fulfilment." This is the some sort of thing that you're talking about?

PD: Yes, I wrote that, so…

SD: That come up in Yuji Sone's piece at the ABC[5], where the audience was asked to imagine, for example, a piece of Bartok's, and if you knew the piece, the tune ran through the head. And yet, there was no sound at all. There was already that shadow, the groove was already cut in the brain, so to speak, the rest of it just had to be filled in. But I'm wondering if the shadows are not 'long' in the sense that if there is the capacity in the brain for the recognition of certain sounds, that these grooves are not 'vestigial'. You talked earlier about the idea that a comparison, historically or archaeologically speaking, can be drawn between language and music. One's ability to recognise language must mean, therefore, that before mechanical reproduction, we must have already had something for 'scoring' 'grooves'. For example, folk music…

PD: Yes, some forms have a lot mnemonic devices such as rhythm and rhyme built in to them. A–B–A is one of the few universals in music.

SD: Just back to your performance the other night, I was interested in the woy you set yourself up as a conjurer. In a sense you were punning a musical performance. There was a real sense of tongue-in-cheek, as it were, going on throughout your performances.

AMJ: This idea seems to be strong thematically in your work. You say in your piece of writing for the TISEA performance that you are interested in the voices of "evangelists, hypnotists and salesman": shonksters, tricksters manipulators, and for the phonograph piece in SoundCulture lost year you wrote that it was about 'ancient' phonograph records which was clearly...

PD: Phoney...

AMJ: Yes, phoney

SD: Interesting pun...

PD: Well, it's not a pun. The Oxford English Dictionary says the word 'phoney' didn't show up until 1900—phoney: false, the false voice—whereas Carpenter seems to think that it comes from telephone but that doesn't make sense because there is an inherent truthfulness ...there *is* somebody there on the other end of the line in 1900.

AMJ: This interests me in relation to different modalities of sound and voice, their purported 'truth' or otherwise.

PD: Well, interestingly, when I started talking to people about this 'melody' of voice and musical content and its importance, I found that people (with the exception of George Lakoff, who seems to 'get' a lot of the ideas about sound, and living linguists) just think about texts which can be written or spoken as if it doesn't really mailer. But anthropologists, particularly Edward T. Hall, understood the difference, and the other people who understood this are salesman, 'sales engineers', who go out and sell. A lot of them have humble backgrounds doing door-to-door and they understood, they knew exactly what I was talking about. In fact several of them from different companies said: "can you make a machine that will train salesman how to sing?" There's apparently a series of books that's part of a training course that teaches salesman how to 'sing', how to say things in a convincing way. And I think a lot of people come by it honestly, that is, they come out of evangelical backgrounds in the south and become soap salesman or politicians—they come out of this school of rhetoric that's very predictable. But these are traditional encodings of the convincing voice, and these are the people who make their living by 'singing'. A lot of my material comes from tapes that I find discarded in opportunity shops from companies such as Amway. There is this one of four Amway cassettes with a 'high up' Amway salesman teaching the philosophy and methods of soles to other people, and interviews with successful salespeople from Arkansas—we just elected one of them—and you know, these voices are just marvellous. At one point this guy who must have had a high school education from Illinois or somewhere says: "It's not the words that you say, it's the music that sells the product". These voices that have to convince have a great deal of musicality in them and if you listen to a marketplace, in a place where markets are still central to the economy of a country, you'll hear a whole interplay of the rhythm of the marketplace, of the people chopping meat, the hawkers, all at once. Hall has observed with children in the playground this 'entrainment' that goes on. That marketing, that selling, that commerce and exchange are all a kind of 'symphony'. This summer I heard of a performance that Anne Carlson did. She had been studying auctioneering and did this piece standing in her bridal gown auctioning herself off and then she went into 'the evangelist' routine ...very good voice characterisations. Speaking of this 'deferral', I was staying in a YMCA in Taipei in 1971 and there were these two Baptists from Alabama, these two big fat porky guys in white suits doing faith-healing. They had an assembly hall and were doing the laying on of the hands and praying to God for the blind person or the crippled person, and then they had a translator who would translate their English to Chinese, and *that's* when the person would be healed... only when the translation was accomplished. *(laughter)*

1. Paul DeMarinis performed *The Power of Suggestion* at the Museum of Contemporary Art, Sydney, on 10 November 1992 as port of the Third International Symposium on Electronic Arts (TISEA), 9–13 November, 1992. The performance involved the use of a hacked Mattel power glove, linked to a computer in such a way as to vary the pitch and speed of the voice according to the gestures of the person wearing the glove.

2. The Foucault quote reads "God is perhaps not so much a region beyond knowledge as something prior to the sentences we speak". The quote was used in a piece of writing accompanying a work by Paul DeMarinis at the Exploratorium.

3. Third International Symposium on Electronic Arts.

4. *The Edison Effect* was an installation piece exhibited by Paul DeMarinis at The Coachhouse, The Rocks, Sydney, as part of the SoundCulture 1991 festival, presented by The Performance Space, Australian Broadcasting Corporation and the University of Technology, Sydney in October–November 1991. *The Edison Effect* forms port of DeMorinis' *Laser Disk* series of sound sculptures–electromagnetic devices which play 'ancient' phonograph records with laser beams.

5. Yuji Sone performed *Nonetheless Marinetti* at the ABC Eugene Goossens Hall on 13 November 1992 as port of TISEA.

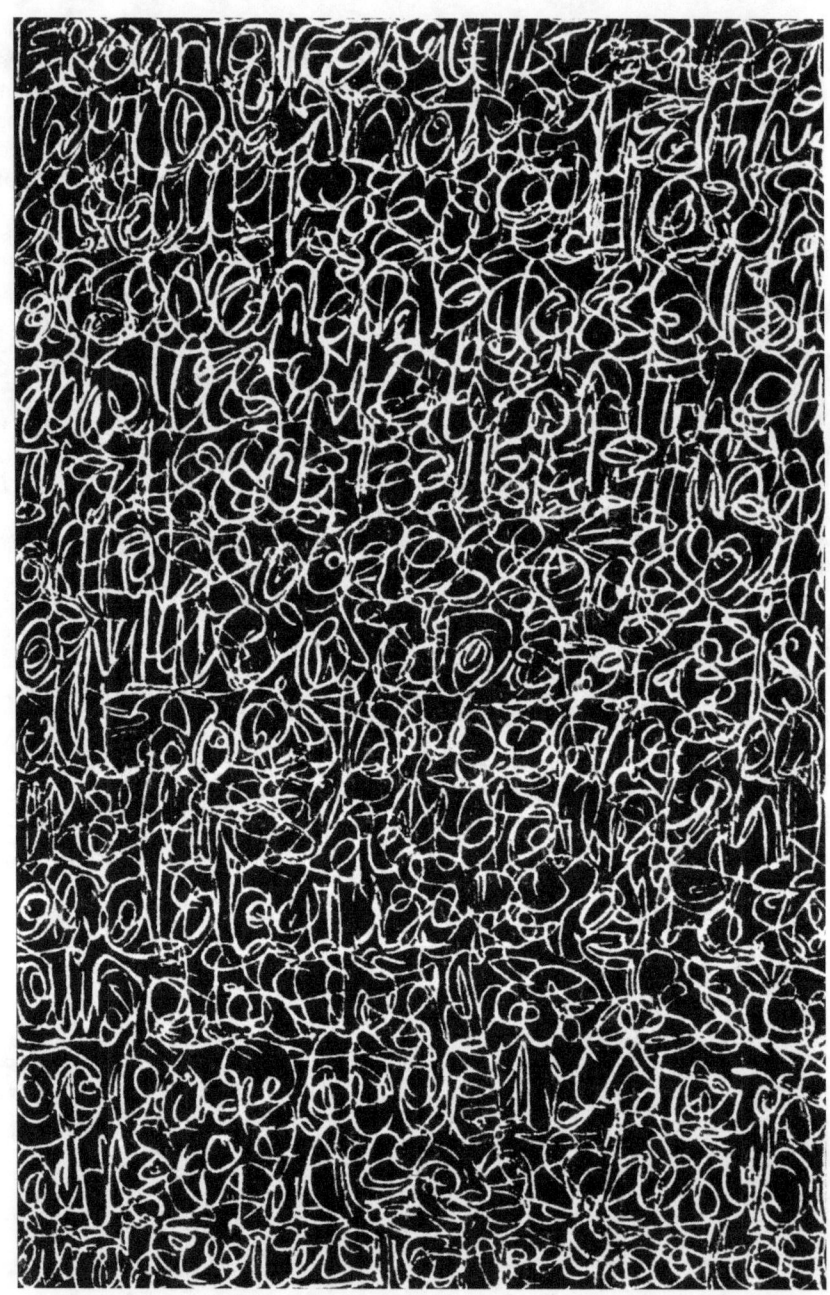

"Fragrant Kimberley Dawning; Joan Brassil". Transcription drawing, Ruark Lewis.
[pen and ink and graphite on paper. 1989. 115mm x 170mm]

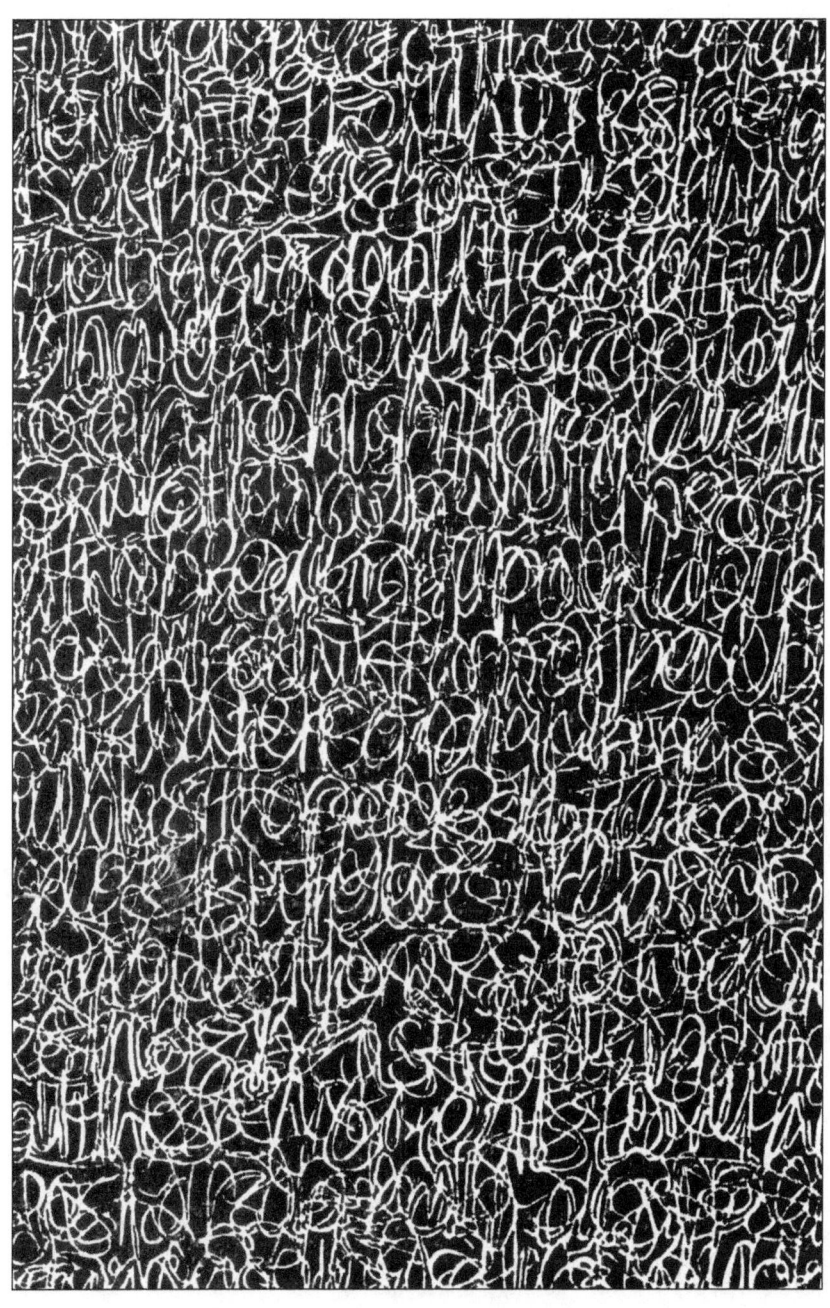

"A Gulf Trip; a radio tape composition by Andrew McLennan". Transcription drawing, Ruark Lewis.
[pen and ink and graphite on paper. 1989. 115mm x 170mm]

The Acoustics of Saint John the Evangelist's Church, Camden

Brian Marland

> O praise ye the lard, all things that give sound;
> each jubilant chard re-echo around;
> loud organs, his glory forth tell in deep tone,
> and sweet harp, the story of what he hath done.
>
> Hymn 83, v3, The Australian Hymn Book
—Henry Williams Baker 1821–1877

Church acoustics are often an amateur affair—the original pipe organ being replaced by a modern electric organ from the local music store and a pair of loudspeakers placed on either side of the nave so that the vicar can be heard. This is a far cry from the approach taken at Saint John's Anglican church in Camden, New South Wales. Here an entirely integrated approach to church acoustics is adopted.

The church of Saint John the Evangelist, an example of Victorian Gothic revival, was built during the period 1840–1849. The architect was Mortimer William Lewis.

The church has ideal acoustic qualities for music; the reverberation time is 1.95 seconds. This means, however, that the reverberation interferes with speech clarity due to the overlapping of syllables. During a normal Saint John's service, the following musical and speech demands are placed on the acoustics—from the nave; the lesson or gospel and sermon, the organ and hymns from the congregation, and from the sanctuary; choir and prayers.

The acoustics of Saint John's are remarkably successful; the organ magnifies a Victorian parish church into a cathedral, the spoken word is clear and, when appropriate during announcements and the sermon, conversational. This success can be credited to the church organist, David Johnson, whose expertise in acoustics and music has enabled an electronic system to be developed which complements, and is enhanced by, the building acoustics.

An organ was built to Johnson's specification by Johannus in Holland. The organ basically follows the standard specifications of the American Guild of Organists and the Royal College of Organists. The organ is a modified Johannus Opus 540 with a purpose-designed amplification and reproduction system. The technical qualities of the organ, amplifiers, speakers and speaker enclosures are described in "A 'pipe organ' without pipes".[1]

As a general rule, a pipe organ will naturally produce full, rich sound in the lower frequencies. Conversely, an electronic organ can more easily produce better quality sound in the higher frequency range. The production of sound at Saint John's has been designed to overcome this characteristic and to make use of the natural resonance of the building. Ten speaker enclosures, containing a total of thirty speakers, are used to produce the sound from the organ. On the left hand side of the nave are the great bass, great mid-range and great treble enclosures. On the other side are the swell bass, swell mid-range and swell treble enclosures. The choir bass and treble enclosures are placed above the choir stalls on either side of the sanctuary.

The remaining two speaker enclosures, one on each side of the nave, are 640 litre subwoofers. Each of these houses four 300 millimetre speakers, with a frequency range of 16 hertz to 4,000 hertz mounted on a massive baffle board. Sound in the frequency range 16 hertz to 128 hertz is filtered via an active cross-over unit to the sub-woofers. Unlined reflex cabinets are used; the speakers and baffle board resonate at low frequencies forcing air out of a slot at the front of the enclosure. The enclosures are designed to set in motion the entire 4,000 cubic metres of air in the church. This technology is essential in order to reproduce the qualities of a pipe organ which resonates the structure and the furniture within the structure. In this way, people both hear and feel low frequency sound. Achieving this successfully involves avoiding distortion and colouration. The length of the nave is 19.4 metres, a distance great enough to allow for low frequency sound waves to develop within it. The congregation has the experience of walking in and out of the sound while moving in the central aisle, greatly adding to the drama and dynamic quality of the sound.

The choir is present at every second Sunday morning service. The choir is trained to make effective use of the building acoustics; they are taught to enunciate clearly by accenting opening and closing consonants.

Speech in a large parish church presents a problem which results from the conflict of producing a majestic interior which, in turn, can be used to produce equally majestic organ and choral music. The problem of unassisted speech is not so severe at Saint John's that natural speech cannot be made intelligible; speaking slowly, projecting the voice and repeating important points will get the message of the sermon across to the congregation. In Victorian times, sections of services would have been sung. A medieval service would not have had a speech intelligibility problem since the entire service would have been sung in Latin, requiring little understanding from the congregation and with the aesthetics of the service playing an important role.

The message is now at least as important as the medium. Many years ago, a pair of column speakers was installed half-way along and on either side of the nave. The speakers were poor quality, with voice colouration, and with the possibility of sound from the loudspeakers reaching the congregation before the direct speech from the pulpit; a recipe for unrealistic speech reproduction.

The current speech amplification system makes use of the great mid-range and swell mid-range enclosures. Lessons are read from a lectern on the left and prayers from the prayer desk on the right-hand side of the sanctuary steps. From these positions, speech is amplified from the left and right-hand speaker enclosures respectively. The pulpit is on the right-hand side of the nave with speech amplified from the right-hand speaker enclosure; this is positioned above the pulpit. The Gradual is spoken from the communion table in the chancel, beyond the sanctuary; this is amplified equally from both the right and left-hand speaker enclosures. At each of these speaking positions there is an Audio Technica condenser microphone. These have foam wind protectors to prevent problems with explosive syllables.

Throughout the main Sunday services, the balance of speech loudness is controlled manually from a console located in the original pipe organ gallery at the back of the nave. This is under the control of Jeff Wilson who was largely responsible for setting up Saint John's public address system. In this way, allowance is made for different voice projection abilities of speakers. A good speaker, probably experienced in speaking in large spaces, may have the electronic assistance removed completely. The control console includes a graphic equaliser which is used to restrict amplification within the speech frequencies.

The combination of good quality microphones, loudspeaker enclosure placement related to the position of the speaker and the manual control of the amplified speech result in a system which creates a natural, unobtrusive presence for the voice. Saint John's church is a fine building which is elegantly situated in the town of Camden. The attention and expertise given to its acoustics makes it also a fine working building.

1. W. T. Muscio, "A pipe organ without pipes", *Electronics Australia*, June 1988, pp. 16–19.

I would tike to acknowledge the help given by David Johnson Dip Mus, LLCM; Dip Mus A; ALCM in the preparation of this article. David has played the organ in many major cathedrals and concert halls in England and USA. In Australia, he has played in the Sydney Town Hall and the Opera House. He is organist and director of music at Saint John's, Camden.

Eisenstein and Cartoon Sound

Douglas Kahn

Developing out of Soviet cinema's hothouse theoretical debates, Sergei Eisenstein's ideas on sound and cinema are a remarkable encounter of the visual cut with the suture and mix of sound, the speed at which the visual world could be comprehended with a laggard aurality not yet accelerated by the auditive mass media, the international visualist language of montage with the nationalising effects of the sound of language, the desire for an ongoing development of cinema as an independent art with the inertia of "photographed presentations of a theatrical order",[1] and a materialist experiment intent upon anti-illusionism with the increasing stultification of the Stalinist cultural order. This much is either well-known or self-evident. But what of Mickey, Bambi and Oswald the Lucky Rabbit?

These and other cartoon characters were ushered into the Russian avant-garde through its early fascination with 'American eccentrism', an appetite expressed across the entire European avantgarde for ragtime and jazz, cowboys and Indians, cops-and-robbers and Chicago gangsters, Salvation Army, for slapstick pratfalls and sight gags, Charlie Chaplin, for all that was fast, funny irreverent and overflowing with artifice. Eccentrism was discursively linked to sound film through the Russian avant-garde theatre's reaction to the simple prospects of sound cinema. In 1913 Vladimir Mayakovsky said that theatre, in the face of cinema, should give up its naturalistic copying of nature in the same way that painting had given up copying with the advent of photography.

Otherwise, theatre would be "...merely the three-dimensional photography of real life"[2] The kinetophone made this especially true because "The only distinction between [theatre] and cinema silence has been removed by Edison with his latest invention".[3] Naturalistic theatre reproduced through sound cinema was a copy of a copy of nature, twice the reason to develop 0 new theatre, an 'anti-illusionist' theatre, and this is what eccentrism provided, the performances of music hall, clowning and the circus, and the spectacle of eccentrism in general. It was this theatre where Eisenstein cut his artistic teeth and first sent forth his theories of cinema.

In 1922 Eisenstein co-wrote an essay with FEKS (Factory of the Eccentric Actor) cohort Sergei Yutkevich that pitted 'eccentrism' against cinematic illusionism and more specifically against synchronised sound cinema circa 1905 (*The Jazz Singer* was late 1927). The essay quoted the French critic Claude Blanchard who remarked, "People who visited the darkened halls in 1905–6 will of course remember the primitive imitation sounds that invariably accompanied the showing of a film (the crashing of waves, the roar of an engine, the sound of breaking crockery, etc. etc.)."[4] Blanchard himself thought little of such synchronisation because the technical imperfections were too evident: "The illusion did not work!"[5] Eisenstein and Yutkevich questioned the desire for illusion in the first place. In addition, they were puzzled why America, the wellspring of "eccentrism" had itself not overcome "the temptations of illusion"[6] in its own films. America had not only given in to temptation but it now housed the supreme trompe l'oeil artists, constructing the slums of Rio, Hindu temples or the back-alleys of San Francisco out of *papier mâché* in Hollywood studios.

Later in the decade, American cartoon characters were accommodated in the space opened up by Chaplin—all of them offspring of the bioscope who had the allegiances of both children and intellectuals. The late 1920s gave birth to Oswald the Lucky Rabbit (September 1927), Mickey Mouse (May 1928) and the 'Statement on Sound' (August 1928), written collectively by Eisenstein, Pudovkin and Alexandrov. The 'Statement' rehashed earlier Soviet arguments about cinema as an art farm separate from theatre and went on to propose that sound montage be developed along the lines of visual montage and that the two be asynchronous to one another. The 'Statement' posed this relationship through the metaphor of music: *"Only the contrapuntal use* of sound vis-a-vis the visual fragment of montage will open up new possibilities far the development and perfection of montage". The developmental process will be marked initially by "*...a sharp discord"* and ultimately lead to" ...the creation of a new *orchestral counterpoint"* between sound and visual image.[7] This play of music would diminish the role of speech enough to avoid the reduction of cinema to a 'filmed play' and to mitigate against the language-based national markets that so threatened the international position and internationalist disposition enjoyed by Soviet cinema.

In general, the 'Statement' sought a continuous line of development out of the silent cinema, instead of the dramatic disjuncture that appeared to be occurring. There is similarity here with what Disney did in the early cartoons, successfully extending the elements of silent cinema into sound under the actuality, not the metaphoricity, of music. Take, for instance, the exaggerated gestures and actions of silent film acting: they disappeared with the advent of the talkies but lived on in the cartoons. Mary Ann Doane has stated that these exaggerations were produced as a compensatory voice: "The absent voice re-emerges in gestures and the contortions of the face—it is spread over the body of the actor".[8] In early sound cartoons, voices were re/introduced along with sounds, although both had been implied through a variety of techniques. As with all silent films, music had always been there; it had just been on the outside looking in. In cartoons, the music that structured the visual dominion of gestures and actions provided the sonic device to introduce voices and sounds to any and every latency that could be heard. Thus, voices, sounds and music were spread out over the bodies of both characters and objects, whether it be a squeaking elbow joint, fly footsteps or flesh ripped off to playa rib-cage xylophone, everything that could make a sound or speak through any means did so. Any implied or compensatory sound, and many more, made themselves heard with a vengeance. Disney, in fact, ran into trouble when he tried to add sound after the fact to two unreleased silent cartoons: "The finished products reveal their origins; because the animation was not done to a specific beat, and gags were not geared to particular sound effects or songs, there is no fusion between sound and picture".[9]

In 1935, the British filmmaker John Grierson singled out the precedence of sound as the basis for Disney's success:

> Out of the possibilities of sound synchronisation a world of sound must be created, as refined in abstraction as the old silent art, if great figures like Chaplin are to come again. It is no accident that of all the comedy workers of the new regime the most attractive, by for, is the cartoonist Disney. The nature of his material forced upon him something like the right solution. *Making his sound strip first and working his animated figures in distortion and counterpoint to the beat of the sound*, he has begun to discover those ingenious combinations which will carry on the true tradition of film comedy. [10] [my emphasis]

That Grierson echoed the contrapuntal principle of the 'Statement on Sound', was no accident for he was quite familiar with Russian film and only a year earlier he had written favourably on Pudovkin's use of sound.[11] Eisenstein's first move toward applied sound cinema ran counter to giving sound precedence; it was a plan to add sound after-the-fact to *The General Line* (1929), renamed *Old and New*. Unfortunately, financing for the project promised by a London firm was withdrawn,[12] his first use coming years later with the banned *Bezhin Meadow* (1935–37) and then finally in *Alexander Nevsky* (1937–38).[13] but by that time his approach and the times had become conservative. The sound script for *Old and New*, on the other hand, was very adventurous despite the fact that the story—the efforts of a peasant woman, Marfa, to collectivise and technologise farming in her community—might seem like an unlikely vehicle for major experimentation. Eisenstein's lack of experience apparently sanctioned a wish-list freed from practicality—just as well, many ideas would have been technically difficult or impossible to realise at the time—or perhaps he was intent with his very first sound project to establish a cinematic practice commensurate in sophistication with visual montage. For whatever reasons, the script demonstrates a systematic attempt to achieve an auditive montage very much along the lines proposed in the 'Statement'. The very fact that he chose to retroactively add sound assured, again, a diminution of language. likewise, the autonomy of the sound montage was established. In fact, there could be little other response; if the quickness of the visual cutting had been paralleled with like speed in sound cutting the result would have fallen on laggard ears. Historically, there had not yet been the cumulative decodes of auditive mass media needed to produce a properly accelerated comprehension of code, such as television channel switching. Instead, Eisenstein was still relying on the cumbersome Wagnerian leitmotiv, i.e., a clichéd music or on internal construction of code.

One way Eisenstein proposed to use sound was similar to how conventional cinema uses music: to bridge the cut/s. Far example, in an early scene in *Old and New* where two brothers cut their hut down the middle and inefficiently partition their fields simply because they are separating (set as an example of irrational peasant behaviour), the sound in the script moves from a crosscut saw, to a circular saw, to the "...deformation of the saw sound (Zeitlup [slow-motion]) into sobbing,"[14]—the sobbing signaling the poverty and suffering such irrationality imposes. This ability to stretch across the cut (of the hut and montage), to meld continuously from one 'object' or entity to another, is a feature intrinsic to sound and it has had little parallel within the cinema or videography until the recent computer-based capacity for 'morphing'. Yet it was the same nonobject-like stretching that gave Disney an early success with Oswald the Lucky Rabbit just prior to *Steamboat Willie*. Oswald's selling point" ...was a rubbery kind of movement that tied into fresh and amusing gags". In *Oh, What a Knight*, Oswald wrings himself out to dry, and later, when kissing a fair maiden's hand, he pulls an endless length of arm from her sleeve in order to have more to kiss! In *Trolley Troubles* even Oswald's electric car is flexible, "widening and flattening to accommodate the unpredictable changes in the tracks beneath it".[15] There was also a phallic fascination, a morphing between flaccid and erect and back again, easily observed in the cartoon cannon and rifle barrels relaxing after each firing; itself well within Eisenstein's own field of fixations, as evidenced by his cock drawings. Eisenstein's essay on Disney has this very elasticity as the main concern, finding precedent in Lewis Carroll, the German caricaturist Walter Trier, etchings by Toyohiro, Bokusen and Hokusai, etc.[16] He calls it "plasmaticness" and considers Mickey in possession of " ...this plasmation *par excellence*".[17] He briefly entertains the idea that its secrets are held in a prenatal, even cellular memory, a standard from which to gauge the morphing of growth and shrinkage. To explain the "pre-logical attractiveness" of Disney cartoons in the United States, he says that the plasmatic "all-possible diversity of form" finds its ground as a counter to a " ...social order with such a mercilessly standardised and mechanically measured existence".[18] He then goes on at length to generalise such transformations to fire,[19] a fire "...assuming *all* possible guises"[20] in a aural-like flux where borders dissolve and things are born and die in a moment, and through fire back to music: "...herein also lies the secret of the fascination of music, for its image too is *not stable*". In fact: "'Music'—the element of Disney". But not completely. While Eisenstein revelled in the action in Disney's foreground, he thought that "Disney is amazingly blind when it comes to landscape—to *the musicality of landscape and at the same time, to the musicality of color and tone*".[21] *Bambi*, for instance, lacked the lyricism of Chinese landscape and painting " ...in its treatment of fluffy beings—monkeys or fledglings".[22]

At one point in the sound script for *Old and New* a fanfare is blurted out only to become shrill laughter, then saw sound is distorted into laughter which melds into 'animal laughter'. Eisenstein must have thought his farm animals arthritic in comparison to the transformative talents of cartoons animals and animal sounds. But the cartoon connection is actually more immediate. As preface to the script, Eisenstein lists among several categories *kinds* and *degrees* of sound. The three kinds of sound are (1) musical, (2) natural surroundings and (3) animated cartoon. The three degrees of sound are (1) slow motion, (2) animated cartoon (an exaggeration of number three above), and (3) special types of distortion of a purely acoustic sort (to be found). Eisenstein, faced with the problem of associating certain sounds to rapid visual cutting from shot to shot, uses the quick, often disjunctive sound/visual image relationships of the early sound cartoons as a means to accelerate sounds into at least some proximity of association—"Must find ecstatic gradations of timbres, corresponding to the ecstatic gradations of the shots..."[23] The difficulty he faced was inherited by his plans to add sound after-the-fact to *Old and New*. A shot in a cartoon is much longer in duration than a flurry of Eisensteinian shots; with a new film he could have geared the shooting to the exigencies of sound. Nevertheless, 'animated cartoon sound', later called 'Mickey Mousing' in filmmaking jargon, served as an example of coordinating sound and image in rhythmic, contrapuntal and timbral ways. For example, when the collective's baby bull, Fomka, grows to full size in a series of shots constructed much like the awakening stone lion sequence in *Battleship Potemkin*, then inseminates his 'bride' in one of cinema history's rare cross-species point-of-view camera shots...

> Wedding—"lyricism"—Negro chorus. Parody on
> Fomko's motif with Hawaiian guitar
> Growth of Fomko—crescendo of Fomka's leitmotiv.
> Choppy. With each jump in Fomka's growth the sound
> gets stronger. Without transition. This same figure is
> repeated in Fomka's running. There they fuse
> The "Attack"—terrifying increase
> Cow spreads her legs—complete pause. Then sound of
> gunfire and an apogee of mooing.[24]

And perhaps when animated cartoon sound existed in both kind and degree it would result in how the film's harvest time becomes a bountiful occasion for a "...whole *gamma* of sound effects".[25] Finally, Eisenstein's own drawing talents must be taken into account, not just in how they might dispose him as an inside admirer of the technical proficiency of the Disney company cartoonists, but how his penchant far graphics corresponded to an inscriptive notion of sound and sound cinema. Eisenstein's interest in things Japanese is well known, and this extended to sound cinema: "If European painting owes the origins of impressionism to the Japanese, if modern sculpture stems from the Negro plastic, the phonetic cinema will be no less indebted to the Japanese..."[26] As Harry Potomkin wrote, in an essay that moved topically from Eisenstein and japan into cartoons: "...graphic sound—the key to the sonorous film".[27] He then quotes Eisenstein, "...it is necessary to reduce to the same denominator the conceptions visual and phonetic"[28] One manifestation of this reduction was the phonographic script, i.e., sound drawn directly on the optical track, scattered throughout *Romance Sentimentale* (1930), a film attributed to Grigori Alexandrov with arguable collaboration from Eisenstein (the first sound film *by* Russian/s if not in Russia!.[29] From this perspective, the orthography of phonographic inscription, and the implications for a universal alphabetics (making a return to their initial encounter with Far East languages as the biblical lost language), make their true debut in the infantilised bodies of cartoon animals, where bent elbows squeak because they form the proper phonographic letter for a squeaking sound, one that is read as well as heard. Eisenstein's early principle of asynchronicity was criticised as dogmatic by Dziga Vertov, who said that all possible relationships of sound and visual image should be used in the pursuit of 'Pravda'. Yet in his dogma, and in his awkward attempt at conceptualising sound after the fact for a decidedly silent film, Eisenstein has proven to be more artistically provocative than his fellow Soviet filmmakers of the period. The various trajectories of Eisenstein's unrealised ideas have only rarely been attempted since. If he had achieved even his initial plans for sound experimentation it might have changed the terrain of subsequent cinema, music and sound arts.

1. Sergei Eisenstein, Vsevolod Pudovkin and Grigari Alexandrov 'Statement on Sound', *The Film Factory: Russian and Soviet Cinema in Documents, 1896–1939*, edited by Richard Taylor and Ion Christie, Harvard University Press, Cambridge, Massachusetts, 1988, pp. 234–35.

2. ibid., p. 37 Vladimir Mayakovsky, 'The Relationship Between Contemporary Theatre and Cinema and Art'.

3. ibid., p. 37 See also 'The Destruction of 'Theatre' by Cinema as a Sign of the Resurrection of Theatrical Art" p. 34–35.

4. Sergei Eisenstein and Sergei Yutkevich, 'The Eighth Art On Expressionism, America and, of course, Choplin' in *S. M. Eisenstein: Selected Works Volume 1, Writings, 1922 34*. Edited and translated by Richard Taylor BFI Publishing London, 1988, p. 29.

5. ibid, p. 29.

6. ibid., p. 30.

7. 'Statement on Sound', op. cit. (note 1). p. 234–35.

8. Mary Ann Doane, 'The Voice in the Cinema: The Articulation of Body and Space', in *Film Sound: Theory and Practice*, edited by Elisabeth Weis and John Belton, Columbia University Press, New York, 1985, p. 162.

9. Leonard Maltin, *Of Mice and Magic: A History of American Animated Cartoons*, New American library, New York, 1987, p. 35.

10. Cited in Maltin, p. 35.

11. John Grierson, 'Pudovkin on Sound', in *Cinema Quarterly*, Vol. 2, No. 2 (Winter 1933–34). pp. 106–8.

12. Jay Leyda and Zina Voynow, *Eisenstein at Work*, Pantheon Books with the Museum of Modern Art, New York, 1982, p. 38

13. The full status of *Romance Sentimentale* in this respect is outside the scope of this article.

14. *Eisenstein at Work*, op.cit. (note 12), p. 39.

15. Maltin, op.cit. (note 9). pp. 32–33.

16. Sergei Eisenstein, *Eisenstein on Disney*, edited by Joy Leyda, translated by Alan Upchurch, Methuen, London, 1988, p. 12ff.

17. ibid, p. 69.

18. ibid., p. 21.

19. ibid., pp. 24–33 and 44–47.

20. ibid., p. 41. He arrives finally at Heraclitus, Hegel on Heraclitus, and Lenin on Hegel an Heraclitus.

21. Sergei Eisenstein, *Nonindifferent Nature*, translated by Herbert Marshall, Cambridge University Press, Cambridge, 1987, p.389.

22. ibid, p. 391.

23. Leyda, op. cit. (note 12). p. 39.

24. ibid., p. 40.

25. ibid, p. 40.

26. Cited in Harry Potamkin, 'The Compound Cinema: Further Nates' (*Close Up*, April 1929). in *The Compound Cinema: The Film Writings of Harry Alan Potamkin*, edited by Lewis Jacobs, Teachers College Press, Columbia University, New York, 1977, p. 9.

27. ibid., p. 9.

28. ibid., p. 9.

29. cf. Harry Potamkin, 'Playing with Sound', ibid., pp. 86–88.

Extract from 'Modes for Listening', a Work in Progress

Ashley Scott

The initial aim of this essay is to elaborate a semiotics which is adapted to the study of sound texts—their constitution, transmission and interpretation. The eventual aim is ta develop a theory of sonic types and the means for their classification—but this is only possible through first addressing the processes of sound perception and the constitution of auditory knowledge and context, for which a meta-language (a semiotics of audibility) can be proposed.

We shall define theoretical objects which have at least some concrete (material, vibratory) reality and functions which connect and structure them, according to various kinds of necessity (conventional, creative). In a sense, this is to overstep the boundaries of semiotics (because it involves much study of the referent and relations other than those of 'semiosis') in the interest of establishing the conditions of denotation in the perception and classification of sounds.

1.

The Situation of Hearing: There are, on reflection, three non-metaphysical sites through which one can define the process which leads to the 'hearing of a sound'. Even though these fall into different genres of address in language (one is a real object, one an event, one an activity of consciousness!), there can be no relevant abjections to considering them upon the same level, once one demonstrates their connectedness. They are:

a) an EMITTER (ER): a material object, machine or agent which, due to some form of excitation or work, transmits energy as audible vibrations. The ER is the sound source, or 'sounding object'. It belongs in the order of action or motion.

b) an EMISSION (EN): what is given off, produced by the emitter due to some action. The EN is often characterised as a material (especially in a recorded, spatial state), but let us characterise it as an articulation of sound waves, to distinguish it from the 'stronger' force involved with the ER.

c) a LISTENING SUBJECT (SU) the subject is here dealt with as the site of perception, interpretations and judgement. These are the vital interior functions which will enter the account. For the SU, one can say that there exists an order of aspects which describes the subject's interrogation of the EN.

This constitutes what will be taken as a fundamental case, even though it is but one of a number of action/signal/perceptual chains which might be invented to study the transmission of sound sequences. The above chain plots the itinerary of 'a sound event' from source to its 'final destination': someone's ear.

The divisions of this itinerary are demonstrated in phonetics, where the vocal apparatus constitutes an articulatory stage (ER); the sound waves, an acoustic stage (EN); and the hearing apparatus, an auditory stage (SU).

2.

All this seems intuitively plausible: what are its characteristics? It is causal: according to the conditions of audibility (distance, loudness, frequency angle the chain describes the production of sounds, their dispersal and perception. The concern here is for the immediate sonic situation, such as might be taken from a 'random sampling' of any instant.

It is simplified: the chain ignores the mediations and additional processes through which the EN may have passed, in order to present it as an entity or actant in a tripartite situation—instead of it being dissolved into a relation between, for instance, the two halves of emitter (speaker) and subject (listener)

It is irreversible: it describes an itinerary of that which is heard, literally, at the speed of sound. Apart from the causal relations of the chain, which are fixed, the EN reveals a unique temporal ordering integral to it: it initially belongs to an irreversible order of duration.

These principles are based upon the practicalities of listening—for example, a listener's interrogation of the EN reverses the chain in order to 'find' the ER (i.e., to source 'that sound'). The activities of thought don't always match the physical necessities governing its objects (they have nothing to do with a knowledge of acoustics as science or the just-mentioned irreversibility). However, it is important to define the objective situation which governs the activity of hearing, and this is essentially the background which acoustic science takes for itself, in order to concentrate upon the practical or interesting characteristics of the chain.[1]

3.

Having proposed this Signal chain, it is (as above) typically validated for each individual by the very act of imaginatively reversing its flow, from audition back to action (encompassing the activities of identification and location): the subject 'envelopes' or absorbs the EN in a recorded, repeated or memorised form and seeks to identify the ER through this perception and to map aspects of the sound to the mechanical elements of the ER, or to a temporal sequence which it seems to present.[2]

Taken literally, the connection EN to SU is the condition of hearing, degree zero. Of course, the EN and ER are known in a different form to the listener than those relevant in acoustics: the EN must be provisionally accounted for as the perceived articulations of some kind of sonorous 'matter'. The ER is usually known as a referent, a technical artefact or some natural event, but it is only an object of auditory knowledge through some sort of action, leading to an emission.

This perception of 'sounds', audible entities, is assumed to constitute as valid an object of knowledge as the decomposed set of relations which describe the acoustic physics specific to any situation in correspondence to general laws. Musical knowledge can be assumed to follow the same outline and is in fact functionally complete (as is one's knowledge of the native sound-world). in reference to its own practice prior to science.

Extract from 'Modes for Listening', a Work in Progress

4.

Some comments are in order regarding the artificiality of this chain. Common auditory experience, which is not separated from all other sorts of perception, is contextualised before the fact by the listener's expectation of environment[3] The above situation would seem to describe the subject of an experiment, kidnapped by musical psychologists and placed in a 'neutral' environment, where stimuli are rarefied (the audiometrics lab, a soundproof room or headphones) and expectation is 'surprised'.

In the context of 'listening to the radio' or walking through a park 'hearing various soap-box orators', the subject's sound world is determined by their intentions and the probabilities of what emissions are offered.

These situations immediately plunge one into the world of what can be naively called 'forms', and the necessity of explaining how we perceive or derive 'contents' (as meaning) as well as providing a multiplicity of emissions not necessarily tailored for hearing. These are complex sound worlds, both in concrete and formal terms, although absolutely typical of real experience. But the first act is to make basic separations amongst the 'stimuli', and the world of SOUND (as the 'field' of potential sound events, which assumes metaphysical proportions) is swiftly reduced to a set of 'sounds' (defined occasions).[4]

This context of isolation is commonly used in psychology experiments, but the aim here is different: not reactions to stimuli from a wider environment, but response to and constitution of sound. This context differs from the above 'natural' situation in the loss of the subject's choice and focus upon a sound environment as a lived continuum, expressed as the listener's intention.

The 'signal chain' is proposed so one might examine the determination or definition of forms which the isolated subject engages in. The common factor within all instances of audition is that no matter what the subject derives from hearing (alerts, sensible and meaningful information), it is all derived from vibrations in the air, that is, it has a concrete basis.

A 'body' of interpretation, which constitutes a phenomenology of form, is at work, consciously or not, within the hearing of any individual. It is for this reason that the auditory field (which is thus much more than just 'the auditory mechanism') is characterised by acts of hearing: there is no virtual concept of 'SOUND' worth positing, but articulated sonic forms, perceived and re-formed in the hearing of…[5]

The dialectic of the experience of form and of time is mediated, but not at all resolved through the functions of memory and those of recording and notation. This will be dealt with later, but 'form' must come first.

Let us say that a subject perceives an EN of which they have no prior experience or information (the 'unheard', the 'lost chord', etc.)—something for which there is no immediate comparison or meaning, no reference and thus no code or causality.

The following chain applies: (ER)   (EN–SU)

The ER is struck out of the chain as inaccessible (although it may be sourced later). The crucial relation is EN–SU.

It seems plausible that the listener will deal with this sound-event in a way which highlights its unfolding as an 'object', a sort of audible 'substance' (whereas before, it was more likely to be subsumed into the never-ending flaw of phenomena). The following preliminary stages of getting to know this isolated object (essentially, calculating its dimensions and composition) seem possible:

SEGMENTATION (analysis of the perceived energy flow): is the sound discrete or continuous according to the acoustic parameter of amplitude? Are there recurrent features, oscillations in the intensity of the event, which suggest the breaking up of the flow into units which could be called 'audible segments'?

This is a purely mental operation—the sound is unaffected—but its trace in the listener's consideration is marked according to the criteria of what Pierre Schaeffer has called stress articulation' (the points of intensity or gaps which reveal the modular nature of a sound-chain; the gaps between words and attacks of consonants in speech, etc., best demonstrated in the breaking up of O poem into syllables thus rendering an energetic profile of the object and its separation from the chain or flow of sounds within which it is usually located. This stage which seems primary—because it is a matter of form over time—reveals the 'beginning' and 'end' of the object (its 'length') as well as giving an impression of its execution, whether it is discrete and singular, or one cycle of a repetitious sound.[6]

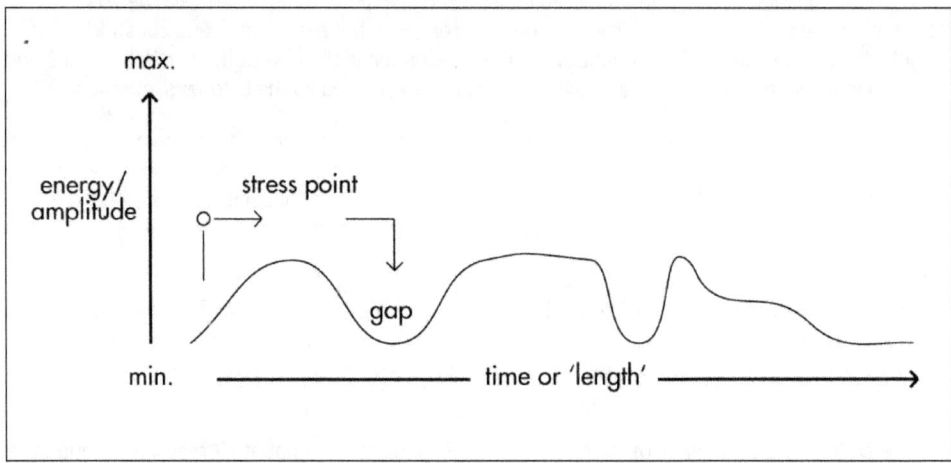

Figure 1: 'stress-articulation'.

This practice represents the first stage in the 'abandonment' of the temporal flow towards a static consideration of a sonic 'substance',[7] which is as yet undefined.

CHARACTERISATION (delimitation of components): firstly, what within this segment is 'of the sound' and what is added by the environment, as reverberation, resonance, reinforcement and other 'distortions'? In attempting to separate the ER and EN as received, one loses the neat distinction between 'that sound' and the effects of the acoustic environment (an emitter is usually portable and its 'true sound' is known). The ramifications of taking the EN as the starting point must be accepted: acoustic 'colouration' is part of the EN (although, in terms of recognition, a

Extract from 'Modes for Listening', a Work in Progress

listener may be able to define the environment in more detail than the emitter!

More importantly, the basic morphology of the object can be defined:

Simple objects: a fused or single perceptible sonic form, with clear start and finish, basically discrete.

Compound objects: "consisting of objects which have more or less merged at the same instant into a single outline"[8] in the manner of a chord. An entity with 'layers' or components.

Composite objects: composed of elements which overlap or succeed each other in the length of the segment, in the manner of a melody.

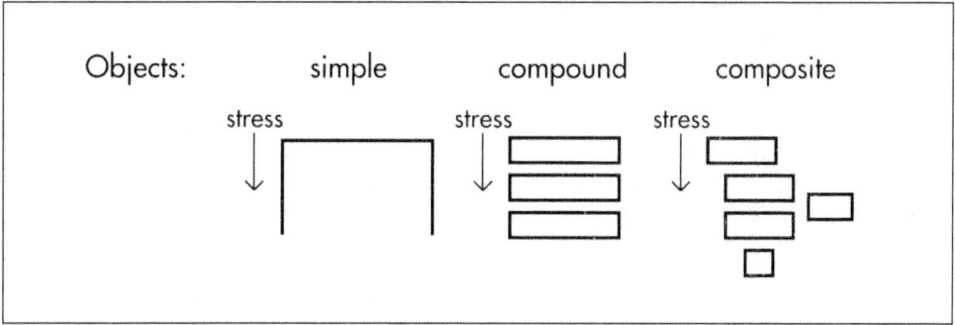

Figure 2.

Two themes emerge—that time is necessarily abstracted into memory, or a graphism, which parameterises time as one of the axes of a sonic representation and, that as 'segmentation', focused upon the global unity of 'that sound', 'characterisation' traces and splits this unity into the components of the whole object. Indeed, there is no other justification for these concerns, except that these components strike one as formations, identities in themselves.

QUALIFICATION (componential analysis): firstly, what the listener might have seized upon immediately—impressions of motion, solidity, friction, hardness, softness, etc.—what are called sonic 'allures' which, like a vapour or type of luminance, radiate from the object. These comparisons are admissible, because by 'allure' is meant the immediate and synaesthesic sensuality of the sound, over and above reference and what might be mistaken as the connotative aspects of the sound, which tends to be too narrow.

These qualities are the ones most readily described in ordinary language (or rather, approximated); they belong to the immediacy of perception and do not 'need to be thought'. A parallel might be drawn with the 'direct' or onomatopoeic aspects of pronunciation and language.

This Qualification stage is also, within the analytic lineage outlined, a closer characterisation of the sonic components which make up the object, which will tend to lead even further into a temporality, graphism and to a certain extent, acoustics. There is insufficient basis to begin to define this so far, so it must be left for the moment.

The three procedures of segmenting, characterising and qualifying are operations through which the listener might define the perception, by operating upon it imaginatively and graphically. They cannot be called 'levels' (of some comprehensive theory) as there is as yet no plausible context for their deployment: we have not defined any sort of systematic procedure leading to the definition of 'sonic types'.

What has been gained from this dissection is a sense of complication—that knowledge stems from the contexts and constraints imposed upon perception. The everyday participation in the decoding of sound texts, or rather, known sound media, which is essentially a social practice, is thus relegated to one category of sonic experience which depends upon a plenitude of phenomena and pre-existing codes or protocols.

The sound 'substance'—which supports whatever derivations the listener makes of perception, as signifying, aesthetic, pertaining to natural environments, whatever—is not defined, but seems to be a necessary hypostatisation of what are only ripples in air-molecules in order to state that:'sound may become an object of knowledge outside of so-called 'structures' and thus constituted, may be dealt with, even, as abstracted from temporality (its essential basis), according to criteria derived from the analysis of nothing but other sound-events'. This has become possible through the technological fact of sound recording, which radically improves access to a) the concrete sound as a plastic item encoded an a spatial carrier-medium, and b) the repetition of the emission allowing a more concentrated hearing of 'that sound', or sufficient re-audition.

It is thus a rather complex environment within which this analysis can take place, crossing media boundaries (actual 'sound as recorded', 'sound as graphed or written') and requiring new expertise: that of hearing and judgement according to 'sound as emission' (not as bound to a source or instrument). A great revision of our judgement and sensibilities is obviously required, in order to come to terms with this.[9]

5.

The operations described created abstracted (consciously derived) identities (sound identities) according to criteria which are auditory (they did not require measuring instruments). The above stages were carried out in some order as acts not in an acoustic sphere, but by the 'ear and its brain'—the auditory apparatus—a representation of a concrete sound entity.

An instance of' sound' was experienced: a segment of the world of 'SOUND' which is the total acoustic substance which might be articulated (formed) as communicative utterances or significative alerts.[10] The aim was to try and experience by proxy—in writing—on un-named but real occasion: all the abstract, informative or meaningful characteristics of sound, intentionally formed or not, are derived from the concrete, purely physical features which were described in a preliminary manner above. This is assumed to be true through all the hierarchies which a system using sound waves as its carrier or medium might exhibit. Likewise, a means of designating sound events will be similarly constituted. The preceding pages constitute the initial terms prefacing a study of sound perception through the terms of information theory and semiotics, proceeding to discussion of Pierre Schaeffer's proposals of 'reduced hearing'.

Extract from 'Modes for Listening', a Work in Progress

1. Phenomenological knowledge is thus distinguished from that of science, developmentally—first hand observation would usually precede the learning of explanatory discourses.

2. For instance, the sound of plucked guitar strings is one thing, the squeak of the fingers on the wound strings or a topping upon the body of the instrument are other events, immediately distinguishable; each of these betrays certain characteristics of the source or ER, that is a' strong, wooden resonant body'.

3. Perhaps the listener feels most 'present in the world' when their expectations are fulfilled—when consciousness finds an 'answer' to its call, as poets or philosophers imagine that the world speaks. This is more rationally approached through defining repertoires corresponding to location and thinking of emissions as determined by statistical laws (i.e., what is one most likely to hear in a park, in a concert hall at a particular time and date?).

4. When Don Ihde states that 'the shape of sound is round' he means literally that the field of hearing corresponds to real points or directions; personal (left, right, etc.) local geography (north, south) and so on. (Don Ihde, 'Parmenideon Meditations' in *Sense and Significance*, Duquesne University Press, Pittsburgh, 1973.) Through this empiric monitoring of sounds, reaching the ears from any direction (or being felt as vibration—very overrated area of perception unless one is deaf-like the percussionist Evelyn Gleny). this potential directionality establishes a 'round' or spherical field which surrounds the subject.

5. An 'inherent' phenomenology of form may be token as developmental—as one learns to interpret the repertory of natural sounds and especially to refine the one's expertise with photic-linguistic systems. Or it may be given a quasi-genetic status, as with Gestalt perception in the separation of 'figure' and 'ground'.

6. This succession of qualifications, characterisations, etc. is based upon Schaeffer. (Pierre Schaeffer, *Solfege de l'objet sonore*, Editions du Seuil, Paris, 1967.)

7. This most closely corresponds to the concept of the 'substance of expression' in linguistics or semiotics (after Hjelmslev) the carrier entity or object upon which the functional or systematic 'form of expression' rests.

8. Schaeffer, op. cit. (note 6). 77.4

9. This is exactly what Pierre Schaeffer has tried to expound since the late 1940s with variable success. It is also obvious that it requires more than this revision or 'dawning' on the port of the composer or artist. Sound recording, in the technical and concrete sense, is close to a century old and there seems to be little interest in renovating our notions of sound perception, which extend to concepts such as 'authenticity', 'fidelity' and a reliance upon the referent which emits ...

10. This distinction between SOUND and sounds. is maintained to differentiate between the 'total acoustic' encompassing all possible articulations of audible vibrations and the actual instances which are perceivable. Just as there is no pure philosophical 'mailer' which is capable of being experienced—only formed manifestations—it seems even more so when dealing with sound. SOUND is an abstraction of these concrete instances; it is less a metaphysical label than a crutch for thought—as what addresses the 'faculty' of hearing.

Chris Mann: A Viewpoint on Telematics and Sound

Interviewed by Daniel Cole

> "Sound is an unanalytical model of sense. It is a collaborator with no loyalties, no implications. Sound is true imperialism. Composers push it around as if their careers depend on it. When I grow up I wanna be a fact of life."
>
> – Chris Mann, *Changing The Subject*, Machine for Making Sense

Chris Mann is a writer of conceptually-based, polemical, semi-Dadaist fiction, as well as a visual artist oriented toward a text-based format. He has worked on a number of telematic art projects, and is a member of Machine for Making Sense, a collaborative sound and performance group.

SYDNEY, MAY 3, 1992

DC: In recent years your work has involved a community-based notion of telematics. The notion of telematics—can you elaborate?

CM: ...There are several forms of telematics. On the one hand, there is a form of telematics which is informed by cybernetics, which is in turn informed by expert systems...

DC: ...what would be an example of an expert system? A basic programme, perhaps...a digital delay?

CM: An expert system is a factory, where the first thing that the worker on a factory floor does is produce themselves...after that, reproduce themselves...so that's what an expert system is; a system that merely reproduces itself...and the marketing arm of expert systems is called 'virtual reality'...which from my understanding is basically an American boy's game for a very labour-intensive way of generating metaphors...it's a high-tech metaphor...

DC: From what I've heard that seems to be so...from NASA...the boys from NASA...

CM: NASA is actually doing more interesting work than anybody else...where they're actually going is directly into the eyeball now...they have given away all the monitors, the headgear stuff and all that crap and they're putting lasers directly through the eyeball... they're somewhat embarrassed by the manual override system that humans employ...which is called 'blinking'.

DC: It's like *A Clockwork Orange*...that scene where the eyes are...

CM: I'm afraid I haven't seen that... not only have I not seen *The Sound Of Music* I haven't seen *A Clockwork Orange*.

DC: It is frightening though…that it's all just a metaphor…for what reality?

CM: Well… or for being something else…but the Americans have never been very good at metaphors because the Americans are into Nominalisation…American English is superficially and structurally German, so they turn everything into nouns—which is that whole thing about 'commodification'.

DC: You link the noun to 'commodity'?

CM: It's that old 'born again' notion that if you can name it you have power. Power consists of various things; one aspect is that you can price something…and the other aspect is that you can tell someone with power because they don't have to decide anything…they're actually immune to decisions and employ other people to make decisions for them and are *immune* to which way decision-making folds out… So a bureaucracy is mapped negatively; one assumes that most people are employed to say no…but the demarcation is a negative portrait in which they have no power…so, that's the cybernetic version of telematics …

DC: …and the telematics which interests you…?

CM: I'm interested in cybernetics and the form of linguistics which is now consistently referred to as compositional linguistics…which tends to be informed by cybernetics and second-order cybernetics. So it's about constructing systems…how you would set up a system to construct.

DC: Do you mean 'compositional' as composing within a musical framework?

CM: That which would not have happened otherwise…a composer is that which is required for something to happen …

DC: This comes back to the question …

CM: Well, yes…the question is whether the question has manners… and then the question is to ask why and how…but, I produced a piece for radio called the *Blue Moon Project*—basically a musical progression, and the chord structure for *Blue Moon* is basically the model chord structure for 70 percent of all subsequent popular musics…it's the classic. I was very interested in the fact that many art composers—serious, academic, avant-garde art composers—were at one stage or other, cocktail pianists…Stockhausen, Kenneth Gaburo, Don Banks, Milton Abbot, Keith Humble—so the idea was at the same time, in Melbourne at five-to-eight, we would have a rendition of *Blue Moon*. So we learn more about the way a composer deals with anything by having something to throw it against. On Monday we had Elvis doing it, on Tuesday, Col Chaterby and so-on and so-forth. It was a conceptual drone, and it was a contradictory necrophilia, during a breakfast programme … so it was a consistent loop, and we had a hundred versions of it. Except that it became a cult number where the people would go into a jazz club and request *Blue Moon*. All the musicians in Melbourne hated me—portable moments of time—so that's what I think we do with radio.

DC: Can you explain the connection between cybernetic structure/data field and a concept of music …

CM: I've been interested for a number of years in the relationship, of what the job description of the arts is—in my case most specifically music—what the job description of music is in the economy as a whole. Fifteen years ago music was the second-largest industry in the world, now it's ranked about eighth or tenth and going down—the economic clout which used to be reversed for music is now occupied by drugs. The question then arises:'what's the difference?' So what is the traditional role of music? What is music supposed to do... what has been its job description...music is a modelling environment...

DC: As a framework?

CM: I'm stuck on the orchestra; this is the model, the model factory.

DC: Yes, you have 'slave violinists' ...

CM: ...but this is what is; historically this is the case, this is not a metaphor, this is a description.

DC: We have the pictures to prove it.

CM: I know—I was there! In the 1950s, 1960s, 1970s, if you wanted to find out what your inter-continental ballistic missile systems were capable of, you would be put into a music school—not in an airborne fashion into a music school (!)—the computer was taken out and delivered to a music school and the students and composers used these programmes to generate pieces ...so you find out what the computational capacity of that computer is ...

what systems it will allow...where its dysfunctions are...what structures and strategies it's capable of complementing.

DC: All this through the application to a musical framework... there are whole areas of pyscho-acoustics which have been legislated about, there are whole groups of frequencies which you are not allowed to use.

DC: Such as sub-sonics?

CM: Yes, and within audible range—for example, if you use 76 cycles per second for any period of time. There was a lot of modelling done in music schools in the 1950s, 1960s, and 1970s for music synthesis, music scheduling events in time...this is now used by Ford and Toyota, in a manufacturing process called 'Just In Time' ; it is the standard manufacturing ethos in most factories these days. It was around in the 1970s.

DC: So, certain structures and motifs have been used in music to increase productivity, outputs?

CM: Yes, but this is what the job description of what music is... to investigate structures, to model structures and then extrapolate and employ wherever ...this is not a peculiar argument. Jacques Attali has exactly the same argument. Music is a modelling environment, a harmless modelling environment.

DC: You speak of music as a totality, as a particular structure—what sort of music is it; are there examples of that 'cold-war' music you describe—produced from the defence computer models? There was a lot of that type of work being done. It's not my favourite time—go through any American computer composer list from the 1950s.

DC: Nevertheless it still comes under the ambit of Music.

CM: That's the relationship between music and cybernetics.

DC: Is that when it first started?

CM: No, I would not agree with that, because there are series of sacred musics, such as Balinese and Gamalan, that are all mathematically-based and incredibly precise; they are modelled on the movement of the heavens, all sorts of metaphysical and physical correspondents are there.

DC: Are you working within a model of cybernetics which is not the NASA model but a concept that goes back further?

CM: Traditionally, the military have modelled their developments for industry

DC: Where would we be without them?

CM: That's their job description, they're the research arm of industry, they model all sorts of things. Safeways is designed the way it is because of the work that the military did in Vietnam—it's a real connection. The aisles are the width they ore, shelves are the height they are, the amount of information that you take in is what is, the check-out is what it is. All of this was modelled in Vietnam ...

DC: So does it come down to an efficiency as a general aim?

CM: This is what you can get humans to do, how efficiently you can get them to exploit themselves. It's just a modelling, that has really been its job description. So I've been interested in cultural expressions like music. The big crisis in the economy at the moment is in management. Certain sectors of the economy have increased their productivity tenfold...the only sector not to increase its productivity in Australia since the 1950s is management—and management is in deep shit.

DC: But there are schools which encourage and teach management as a process.

CM: Yes, so the point of this is that managers now have computers on their desks—but they have not increased their productivity because most managers of course can't type!

DC: Survival is perhaps something you hope to bring to these managers.

CM: Yes, I've been spending a bit of time with the Graduate School of Management of Monash University talking about these issues—how you can use music in relation to the organisation/corporation/school—as a medium—in the sense of media; a medium like radio, television, the print media, or the voice ...

DC: How can the orchestra or music help business achieve their aims and productivity?

CM: Peter Drucker, the manager guru, constantly talks about conductors and orchestras... Attali is more interesting, he wrote a book called 'Noise'[1]; he was Mitterand's economic adviser, and is now head of the 'Bank of Europe'.

DC: Now, going off the track...do you see mapping fitting in to this?

CM: The first requirement of the map is that it is more portable than the terrain. The American military used 300 different computer languages, which was embarrassing. So they developed a single language called AIDA. It is such an incredible language that it could not be modelled—only implemented. So there was no way to test run it.

DC: Sounds rather dangerous...

CM: Well, there was a period of a couple of weeks where the world could have blown up. It still may happen—possibly—it has already happened—we may indeed be parenthetic. So the idea of a modelling is in fact an implementation. In the *Machine for Making Sense*, I was talking about when a model is its own experiment—I use modelling in preference to mapping because I'm interested in what hasn't happened.

DC: The example I had in mind was that—page 26 from my street directory was missing, and it was essential to get here...

CM: That's an argument for narrative... 1953 was a more or less interesting place to visit but I would not like to live there. If I wanted to live there I would listen to the radio—the radio is, by and large, a consistent portrait of 1953.

DC: You are specific about the year, before or after?

CM: We can as meaningfully talk about the nineteenth century and the most attractive thing about the nineteenth century is that it has finished...we *don't* need to do it again.

DC: A lot of people would disagree with you there! But perhaps via maps we can find our way back there.

CM: Yes, there is a lot of that. Maybe the distinction we're establishing here is that models are preoccupied with 'not yets'. Maps are invariably nostalgic—which really makes them a job description for Romanticism.

DC: And telematics—how would this connect to your model?

CM: 'Telematic' automatically means that it is not space sensitive, it's not sensitive to geography, and it may in fact be something that you can exploit...

DC: Exploit?

CM: You can farm space... people talk to one another over the phone differently than they do face to face; people are much more likely to agree over the phone. If you are going to have a telematic office for example, people don't fight about 'no smoking in here' or, 'I can't see the window'—office politics takes on a completely different nature.

DC: 'Don't look at me in that tone of voice'...

CM: Which is why video conferencing will never work or why video phones will never work.

DC: And back to the original concept of the phone.

CM: I'm convinced that they will try again and they will foil again. As part of the PABX network, we will actually get an increase in voice quality because on telephones, there is an incredible compression—voice is a much more efficient way of communicating information than sight, and you learn much more by listening to intonation than you do by looking at somebody—and this is getting back to lying; they found out that people—specifically in business—object to video-phones because its very hard to lie ...

DC: ...listening to the voice ...

CM: ...listening is forming data; listening is a cultural expression of how you determine information—this side of town and that side of town have got different acoustics—you listen for different things, you hear different things. Meaning has no consistency. This is one of the strengths of Australia–Sydney less so than Melbourne. Melbourne is more cosmopolitan which means the acoustic environment is more sophisticated—much, much more sophisticated than Manhattan for example. In Manhattan you don't get Lebanese talking to Vietnamese; it's a series of Villages and ghettos. Merely for this reason Melbourne is more cosmopolitan. So there are sounds that will only enter the language when you get Lebanese and Vietnamese talking together...there are logics that can only enter language if you have that intersection; grammars, structures only enter language that way—there are well formed compositions that can only enter that way—there are whole series of 'not yets'.

DC: Perhaps now to an idea of maps and telematics... transcending gaps; what you are essentially talking about are gaps ...

CM: ...and how we can amplify gaps. Gaps are traditionally about disability—a moment of time—but gaps are things to be amplified. A gap is an access to structure, not a simple negation or simple absence. It is an access—something to be explored.

DC: A side effect or residual?

CM: Of course, if it's not doing double duty, it has no potential for feedback and if it has no potential for feedback, it starts to smudge into what I call 'pornography'. That is, without any redeeming social importance. It has structural significance in that it is redundant, in other words, it has an in-built obsolescence.

DC: It sounds rather dangerous that all these gaps are going to be heard all of a sudden.

CM: But they always have been...

1. Jacques Attali, *Noise: The Political Economy of Music*, Manchester University Press, Manchester, 1985.

Towards a Phenomenological Archaeology of Sound in its Relation to Musical Experiment

Phillip L. Ryan

"Whatever else art is, (it is) at a very simple level...a way of making."

—Robert Morris

Let us begin with a definition of sound:

> A mechanical disturbance from a state of equilibrium that propagates through an elastic material medium.
>
> Calibration: speed of sound (1986)
>
>   1) in dry air
>   2) temperature – 0° celsius
>   3) at sea level pressure – 1,013.25 millibars
>   = 331.29 metres per second
>   = 33,129 centimetres per second
>
> A mechanical disturbance (in most solids, liquids and gasses of ordinary experience) will consist in a sudden increase in pressure at some point. The compression is not permanent, thus the compressed region will rebound, but then compress an adjacent region. The result of this cycle repeating itself is a compression wave, followed by a rarefaction wave. These waves are longitudinal, in the direction of wave motion. The waves thus generated travel through the medium at a speed that is a function of the equilibrium pressure and density of the material and, to various extents, of the specific heat (of a gas), the elasticity (of liquids and solids), and the temperature of the medium and the frequency of the wave. Regular sounds are characterised by periodic, dominant frequencies, or pitch. Sounds increase in complexity from a pure tone to those whose overtones render a sound 'white'. loudness of a sound is essentially 'subjective' and is measured only in relation ta a standard reference sound under specified conditions. Sound waves can be reflected, refracted, diffracted and scattered, differences reflecting differences in wavelengths.

—*Encyclopaedia Brittanica*, 1987

ON THE NATURE OF ARCHAEOLOGICAL ANALYSIS:

The epistemological and aesthetico-productive significance of 'archaeology' was introduced and exploited primarily by the French thinker, Michel Foucault. In his *Archaeology of Knowledge*, he makes the functioning of archaealogical analysis explicit:

> If archaeology brings...discourse closer to a number of practices, it is in order to discover ... far mare direct relations than those of a causality communicated through the consciousness of the speaking subjects. It wishes to show not how political practice has determined the meaning and forms of. discourse, but how and in what farm it takes part in its conditions of emergence, insertion and functioning...It is not a question then of showing how the political practice of a given society constituted or modified the...concepts and theoretical structure; but how...discourse as a practice concerned with a particular field of objects...is articulated on practices that are external to it and which are not themselves of a discursive order. If in this analysis archaeology suspends... casual analysis, if it wishes to avoid the necessary connection through the speaking subject, it is not in order to discover the domain of existence and functioning of a discursive practice. In other words, the archaeological description of discourses is deployed in the dimension of a general history; it seeks to discover that whole domain of institutions, economic processes and social relations on which a discursive formation can be articulated; it tries to show how the autonomy of discourse and its specificity nevertheless do not give it the status of pure ideality and total historical independence; what it wishes to uncover is the particular level in which history can give place to definite types of discourse, which have their own type of historicity and which are related to a whole set of various historicities. (pp. 163–165)

Thus—

Questions and Consequences—

1) Given the *insertion* of discursive formulations, political practices and necessities into the domain of the 'factual', i.e.' Production' in to the domain of 'Nature', what is the nature of 'experiment' with sound, the nature and role of composition ('Composition'), the *aesthetic* significance of these insertions; how do they 'reflect' their 'times', is there a utopia or are there utopias, finality/ finalities whose 'ambiguity' leads us' away'?

2) In what way is there a 'productive contradiction' between' Production' and 'Nature'—can such a split be healed ('musically'), according to the dream of Hegel–Marx, for example?

3) What is the Being of sound as mediated by humankind? Since the 'thing' cannot be forgotten (I yotard), how can there be Forgetfulness of Being (the Thing) (Heidegger)?

THE ANALYSIS OF THE AESTHETIC EXPERIENCE BY MIKEL DUFRENNE:

a) The work of art is not automatically an aesthetic object;

b) It becomes so only when it is 'present' as a *phenomenon*;

c) Its distinguishing characteristic is found in its gestalt or inner unity—its unity of 'for-itself' and 'in itself' making it a quasi-subject, a unique type of 'ambiguity', even self-contradiction;

d) Aesthetic perception contains three aspects—the presence as mediated by the senses, representation, and reflection;

e) Representation mediates presence and reflection as imagination;

f) The understanding directs imagination, leading to a 'response' of our being to the perceived aesthetic object;

g) This 'response' is 'sentiment', revealing Being not only as reality but as depth, 'measureless' content beneath our grasp;

h) Sentiment is the experience in which the depth of our own experience answers to the depth of the object.

Sound as disturbance—the archaeology of the insertion of discursive formations—the aesthetic response to inserted disturbances; and yet—

> Through all the tones there sounds
> In earth's many-coloured dream
> One soft, long drawn-out note
> For him who listens intently.
>
> —Friedrich Von Schlegel

A Note On Juan Lamilliar's
Caballos en el Jardin[1]

Martin Harrison

What is it, in terms of sound, that occurs on first reading Juan Lamillar's poem? We may say of it that it is written in an unfamiliar or at best partly familiar language, and yet something occurs on first contact with this text, whether this is no more than recognising a set of shared typographic conventions ('it looks like a poem') or a stumbling attempt to sound it out according to a common notion of script. The poem is never, indeed, a completely undecipherable text because, as soon as there is any idea of reading, we make an assumption about a mutual linguistic context which negates the possibility of an innocent, unknowing moment of discovery. Regardless of how distinct, no two languages simply hold mirrors up to each other, casting back to each party in the transaction a reflexive image of only 'our' language's identity. We have no option but to deal with how the unfamiliar text works, how it deals with figural space, how it indicates behaviours to a potential voice and how it organises metaphorically and historically a 'place'' in which it originated. The degree to which reading is immediately immersed in this matrix of assumed, shared practices is a moment of disclosure, literally of 'opening out', which renders inoperative the claim that there is a level of opaque materiality between the 'here' of our immersion in our own language and the poem's immersion in *its* language. Though we may not understand a word of it, we deal here neither with mirrors nor walls.

Do we then deal with a window[2] That is, with a view into, an opening out into, another language's organisation? Not necessarily. For that moment of disclosure takes so much for granted which has yet to be corroborated: this first contact is no moment of exchange, any more than it automatically implies a way to take over the foreign text. Besides, in this matter of hearing the sound, we have yet to clarify differences between a reading of the poem (to work with its meanings) and a listening to the poem (to work with its sounds) Thus, for instance, it is clear that the poem *qua* text is 'silent' until we voice it, delivering it over into *our* voices, those very same voices which hesitantly seek to acquire a Spanish accent. At exactly the moment of first contact where we might have been able to 'uncover' the sounds which are *there* in the text or perhaps mirror-wise reflect an unfamiliar language's organisation, we hear our own voices reciting something which has not yet been heard before: "De piedra en el olvido, en el silencio..." Banal little detail of the text's operation, it is worth recalling that to recite the text is not to imitate it but to sound it out according to a series of contextual practices which it is solely our reading which guarantees. Nor, it should be stressed, is the nature of this reciting changed if we are reciting not an unfamiliar piece of print but, say, an unfamiliar *spoken* moment in a foreign language—as might be the circumstance on meeting someone whose language you do not know and who does not speak yours. Here, too, capturing the hitherto unheard sounds of this 'first contact' speech (that beachside moment, Colombus-style) we do not imitate or mirror in any simply echolalic fashion: if we choose to give voice to what we hear, we recite what is at once constituted as 'spoken text'. If repeating the unknown or unfamiliar language was only to mimic it—putting, as it were, innocent sounds into unknowing air—then we would have no measure for the accuracy of rendition, nor for its inevitable inaccuracies. Mimicry presupposes that there is no 'other' person taking part in the transaction. In brief, that 'no-one' is speaking.

Thus, to sound out *Caballos en el Jardin* is to sound it *outwards*, to sound it *from* a text: to sound it away. Unlike mimics, we do not naively and unconsciously pin its sounds down to some already given set of pre-existing sounds, some 'something' just heard, just posited, 'within' the text. Whether made into sound from a subvocal, in-the-head experience or actually spoken aloud, sounding-out is to sound the poem out into the air our bodies breathe, and into our own hearing. In this sense, there are no sounds ever to be captured between a 'here' and a 'there', transiting in some imaginary atmospheric space between the foreigner's mouth (perhaps the Sevillian poet, Juan Lamillar's) and a reader's tracking ear. Instead, one recites within a larger, performative structure which must, in a logically necessary way, subsume the other voice whether this means what literary critics used to call the 'poetic voice' or the still unmeasured syllables of someone whose language is completely unfamiliar to us. To suppose a transit between a 'here' and a 'there' (the issue concerns not physics but audition) is to endow sounds with a materiality which they do not possess or, more exactly, which they do not possess *unless they have been graphed, written, as a further and different kind of textual instance*. This might, for example, be through sound recording or some other type of circumstantial documentation. But placing a 'here' and a 'there' in merely naturalistic terms within the process of meeting, reading and listening is to confuse the atmospheric properties of sound with its communicative properties. After all, what can be heard, what can be voiced, may never be any kind of physical event at all. By the same token, sounds do not necessarily have to be predicated within real-time 'geographies' of distance, position, transit and so on.

Descriptively, then, two different means of defining sound within a transmissive situation have to be separated out from each other. Firstly, we must not confuse environing, atmospheric sound and its behaviours with the more limited notion of sound within that communicative situation. And secondly, we must not confuse the experience of sound within that communicative situation with any further kind of textuality predicated as a 'sound-object' over there, back there, somehow subtextually set' in' the text. A proper object—definition of the sounds we recite, the sound of Lamillar's poem, require that we remember *how* those sounds occur as transitory, moving sounds.

These sounds, whether vocal, sub-vocal or simply sounds 'in mind' occur as part of our voices. Deceptive formulation: they exist temporally as what we hear. Not located yet as any clearly definable text, they tend towards, they move towards, a location this side of the transaction with Lamillar's poem and are not exclusively predicated on any further, already existing sound—text which could be said to be Lamillar's. Perhaps only 'I' 'hear' this voice, this reciting voice. By putting it like this, what one wants to do is not lose a sense of the immediacy, the *this-ness* of this primary experience of the sounds of the unfamiliar Spanish poem and to remember how this experience is 'sited' in time.

When reading this poem's unfamiliar language, all such projections of a further 'sonic' textuality *within* the language-experience are deeply equivocal and, it needs to be said, far too knowing. For it is as if we deal with a sleight-of-hand by which a third 'reading position' is brought into the transaction between poem and reciter—namely, that of an already historical, panoptic presence which tells us that we can somehow make a transfer *at the level of sound alone* between an originary voice and a voice which we sound outwards as our own voice's reciting of the Spanish versification. But do voices ever speak just sound? And is this 'third reading' dealing with voice or sound? Heard only by a panoptic presence, a universalist of language who seemingly but how?—holds in his ear both our own performance of the text and 'another' equivalent, unheard performance (a 'Spanish' reading), even a stuttering phoneme (*is* the twelfth syllable of line eight a 'they' or a 'say' or perhaps a sound with the final modificatory 'e' of the trump card, an 'ace'?) must already have been written as a superior text available only to this obscured third reading. It is a third reading imposed, geographically speaking, always from 'our' side of the transaction: surely the deepest denial of what precisely the poem, way beyond the universalist's desire to visibilise and materialise this thing called 'sound', communicates.

In short, this 'third reading' is the typical modernist chimera of an interlinking, tangibly utterable 'sound' which somehow takes off from language as we know it (from any given example of a text) as if marking a space 'between' informants and, accordingly, a neutral zone between language worlds. Not surprisingly, this 'third reading' usually assumes a probabilistic relationship between what is heard (concomitantly, what is uttered) and what is lived (what occurs). The phoneme, isolated from any network of actual occurrence, is taken literally, is read at 'face value'. Because = itself intervenient, such reading invents an intermediary zone, a world of sonic 'as if' or a fantasised' place' where there is no *arbitrium* or measure: there is quite visibly, in other wards, no demarcation, including that of the poem's sequenced phonemes themselves, laid upon a ground whose intimacy Lamillar's sculpted horses protect ("los jardines íntimos que guardan"). Coming-inbetween, this 'third reading's' text comes to operate as a writing never completed, always (not to say, plangently) in the process of *being written*. This is, for instance, the 'sound' of Dadaist work, of Joycean collage and wordplay and even of more architectonic approaches to vocalic documentation in the bricolage of huge modernist texts such as Pound's Cantos. Indeed, what such texts equivocate over is a key issue in the theorisation of sound—namely, the difference between 'script' (the representation of sound) and sound's temporal moment. A 'third reading' exposes a text full of illusory participations, over-marked 'voices-off' and quoted energies. It is, above all, the text of collage, of 'sounds': the text of double hearing (*double entendre*).

Against a temptation to suppose this intermediary area in which somehow language as 'sound' has a type of spatial reality, one has to insist on real-time features of translatability and recitability. One has to remember that sound is temporal, that it comes and goes always within a 'moment' of experiential passing. This is why to sound Lamillar's poem is to sound-out. Further, if there is any kind of 'sounding moment' in language, then it is here alone (within a non-imitative account of reciting) that a reader might, at least on first contact with the text, discover something tantamount to a 'pure' sound whose graphic form does not require instant location: possibly, here, experiencing a sounding-out which, though it can never be innocent of meaning, may for a split second be possessed of innocuous meanings not addressed to any listener ("las inmutables llamas acrecidas"). So different from the collagist sense of it, this is sound's moment, so to speak, in occurrence. As such it is a moment of pleasure far the tongue alone, where voice can uninhibitedly glide' on' the phonemic mobility of the words being recited and where, free of referential meaning, the ear hears no more than rhythmic structure, a tonality, a musical variance within a group of word-sounds.

Clearly (and, again, this is why sounding-out cannot be treated as if it is an exact replication) there is no way to mark this auditory experience in graphic form. To put diacritical marks on a text is to do precisely that, namely, to write in a substitutive reading and thereby invent a new element in a restraining text. Thus, to mark the just quoted line as follows:

    y quebró el a >> bandóno sus válero >> sas crínes

may suggest some provisional system for greater and lesser rhythmic emphasis but fails to capture the lyric quality of temporal ease and flexibility just described. All that has happened is that more instructions have been provided for a supposedly more 'proper' reading within the performative structures of modern Castillian Spanish. Why not indeed mark a substitutive reading which identifies similar vowel sounds:

> y >> quèbro° èl obondo°no° sus volèro°sas cri " nès

or key consonants or phonemic maps and so on. Each new text (some may, for other purposes, even be useful) misses the only mark which cannot be put there—which is to say, each new substitutive reading misses the flexibility of a transient, auditory mark. Each misses the airy mark of what has in fact occurred, a sounding-out neither achieved through mimicking language nor re-presentable through any other reader's imitation of the heard sounds.

Sounds within a reciting are, so to speak, already off and away. Momentarily, Lamillar's poem possesses a lyricism not beyond, but extended from, its Spanish: a moment of cantilever out into sounding space. Akin perhaps to Barthes' notion of a 'rustling' language in which meanings are tentative possibilities selected solely by our experience of the well-functioned working of articulation, this extended lyricism does not posit any Barthesian horizon, any susurration or murmur ('rustle') beneath or beyond what is vocally made and hearable as such. Rather, this lyricism is directly predicated on breath, rhythm and extension—not unlike certain extended vocal techniques in song. It could continue for ever, but does not. It could express with maximum subtlety every nuance available in the experience of sounding language, yet is almost mechanically committed to the specific pattern of vowels and consonants which compose Lamillar's poem. The body which speaks it, which throats it, is like a body in energised traverse, a body charged with an undetermined gift of flying. Possessed of a truth which cannot be gainsaid, weightless because constituted only of what ancient writers of rhetoric used to call 'measure', such a lyricism places the burden of truth elsewhere this singing does not, in any proper sense, know what it is saying. Beautifully proportioned in relation to each other—and how could they not be?—these sounds shoot forward as if nearly free of gravity. It seems that their recitation alone is sufficient to capture a speaking presence, neither of the poem nor of the reciter. In short, this momentary recitation of the poem is not dissimilar to Heidegger's comment about how we 'reach what is' by letting language do the work for us, albeit unknowingly. For Heidegger:

> When we go to the well, when we go through the woods, we are already going through the word 'well'', through the word 'words', even if we do not speak the words and do not think of anything relating to language.[2]

But how might these words 'well' and 'woods' be hearable if not as precisely this kind of half subliminal lyricism? How (and by whom?) could they be sounded if not in this kind of imaginary flight? This, Heidegger says, is the primary task of the poet, what after Rilke's formulation he calls 'to dare language'.

For Heidegger, this sense of language (and poetry) leads him to desire a "more primal elucidation of the nature of subjectness"[3] and to consider what that earlier mentioned 'third reading' dumbly prohibits i.e. an investigation, in relation to sound, of the boundaries between the material and the non-material, between the visible and the non-visible. For we must keep on asking what is this sounding, this hearing which occurs.

A sounding-outward, it nonetheless requires a degree of literal competence, in this case with a printed text but in all cases with something uttered as a text. Far from being based on any intermediate materiality as 'sound', this competence is interpretive, sensitive and pragmatic: it is based in short on a knowledge of limited operational elements within Lamillar's text, aspects of the unfamiliar language's morphology and phonetics. This sounding-out can, in other words, be both corrected and deepened by a knowledge of, dare one say it, another' locution of the text, another' presence. Thus one might learn a 'new' 'sound' for the 'ge' of 'fingen' (1.6) or one might come to position compatible tonalities derived from other Spanish poems, in this case from Jimenez and Quevedo, which set up resonant echoes within the musicality of Lamillar's verse. To do so is to start reclaiming (calling back) a sounding-out which hovers transiently in its own temporal fall, rehearing a series of writings and readings based within Lamillar's printed text. It is to bring back a moment of potentially subliminal release into the boundedness of a more fully cultural, and therefore, translatable 'reading'.

This, of course, is not to deny the pleasure of what was earlier referred to as an almost 'pure' audition, nor the facility of a gliding encounter with a language which does not yet *need* to be located. It is simply to say that this glide implies a downward-looking and upward-gazing regard (a verticality) not unlike Lamillar's horses who, on their pedestal, pretend disdain (downwards) while knowing their (upwords) superior certainty: downwards, that is to say, towards a semantic ground and upwards into the skiey space of hearing. As we recite we know how reciting, far from being an imitation of an intermediate event, will ultimately 'place' the sounds which compose it within a lexicon, even if it defers that moment as long as it can maintain a musicality pertinent to an unfamiliar Spanish poem.

Though to recite may well defer a lexical kind of placement, it does not necessarily invoke any kind of neutral zone between familiar and unfamiliar word-sounds: it does not invent a corridor along a 'frontier' between languages. The very idea of a traceable space, or geographical gap, in which 'sound' alone is transacted is an illusion. To recite ('recitar') is no neutral activity but a way of marking and meeting a different language. It obliges us to deal with the paradoxically subsumed position of an 'other' voice. We begin, as it were, to keep our date ('la cita') with a larger understanding of Spanish—who knows, perhaps this way beginning a longlasting affair with Lamillar's poem. Capable of unbounded lyricism—is it in our voices or is it in the language we meet?—not to know the poem further would be mere frustration: a hang-up, a disappointment. Reciting, repeating these sounds, they have not become ours, but they have got into our mouths, onto our breaths. We hear ourselves say things we did not dream of. Besides, the poem's manner of measuring sounds has implicated us in a 'music' which, not starting with us, does not end with us. It is precisely the continuum of this music and its variedness which holds our voices in equilibrium as the poem metes out each line's three-part cadence across its dominant twelve syllable length and, thereby, builds up a sense of blocks and surges. These rhythmic spaces (partly cadential, partly conceptual) are not 'around' the poem, they are temporal divisions (cuts and flows) which are inseparable from the sounding-text. So, for example, is the interrogative tonality of the poem's final moments. Does it address us, or have we, reciting it, taken its question on board? And if that interrogativeness is a matter of interest, then so is the accumulated, prepared weight of the sounded language which has gone before. Something is being said. Something is being pointed to. Objects, newly signalled, come into view, buried up to their flanks in the undergrowth, swallowed by it ("Golpeó la maleza sus ijares").

In thinking about the sounds of *Caballos en el Jardin*, the shift required conceptually is highly pertinent to the whole matter of theorising sounds. It is a shift from a model which places the main weight upon declarative models for sound (sounds exchanged from palate to palate) and one which considers more closely the question of hearing, of audition. To hear is to take up a position, both literally and conceptually, in relation to sound: to hear is both to position that sound and be positioned in relation to it. It is to find, to have found, a place: in this case, a place of potential release from the productive aspects of the poetic text e.g. it's conversion of musical language-sound into meanings. And this opens up to us the ways in which the some 'sound occurrence' is not heard in univocal ways, though it may be declared (enunciated) by a single textual voice, occurring in a singular space. listening to our reciting of the poem, we take up many different positions in relation to the sounds we 'hear'. These positions cannot be marked visibly in the visible world. Perhaps, indeed, one could imagine a text, which far from containing overlapping textual levels (interplays), contains overlapping 'hearings', rather like ears nested inside ears. This would be the writing of a deeper hearing, a hearing which already goes on during its recitation: a text already heard before it is recited. Within hearing, posited as an element of the 'heard', we would experience a sound marking and tracking its traverse, non-visible and immaterial, indicated as a possibility or a gap beyond any textual evidence (realised sound) but not itself ever rendered at the level of known, tangible utterance: a voice beyond all voicing.

To invent a 'third' abstract reading (to collage) is to withdraw into a state of permanent misprision. This may be willed as a device to hold only our own 'sound' up to ourselves, or it may, worse, be the inevitable result of an incompetence. For though the horses are weak guardians, their incontrovertible strategy is that what they guard is not necessarily the territory which appears at first sight, or rather not what is available to only a spatial sense of the figural text. Stone moving into forgetting, into silence, Lamillar's horses guard the answer to the question they pose. Neglect broke their manes, and yet the image is of something already broken, something fallen apart before the verb was retrospectively applied, something abandoned slowly. Neglect 'broke' them? Neglect 'smashed' them? Yes. No. Provisionality here is not of sounds in relation to meanings, but of meanings in relation to each other: that is to say, of a series of interlinked meanings made provisional in the move back and forth across Spanish and English. The horses, yes, those valorised signs, stand/stood in an untended garden. Or in one of the melancholy, autumnal gardens of Aranjuez: there, by the entrance to a small grove off an alley. Yet, hiding time, they are not cabals or cavils. Shhh! valorous crimes! Nor were/are *their* intimate gardens Time's siftings. Only by abandoning such word-play do things no less provisional than sounds become more clear.

CABALLOS EN EL JARDIN

De piedra en el olvido, en el silencio,
vislumbran los caballos la eternidad,
los inmutables llamas acrecidas,
el pequeño diluvio que sucede
en los jardines intimos que guardan.
Desde su pedestal fingen desdenes
y saben superior su certidumbre.
Solitario el jardín desde hace décadas,
golpeó la maleza sus ijares
y quebró el abandono sus volerosas crines.
Tras la criba deltiempo prevalecen.
En su reducto mágico y ruinoso
¿que eternidad contemplan los caballos?

HORSES IN THE GARDEN
(after the Spanish of Juan Lamillar)

    Stone horses, they catch
    A lost glimpse
    Towards silent infinitude,

    Whether a fixed flame's
    Bright increase
    Or moment of tiny downpour,

    Frozen on a pathway
    More lost than
    Their intimate guard.

    On a pedestal, they hold
    Aloft pure certitude,
    While they feign disdain.

    For no-one's visited them
    Year after year.
    Dense shrubs, outsprouting them,

    Have swallowed their flonks,
    Proud manes
    Now broken by neglect.

    Time's passage sieved them,
    Sifting them
    Into this overcoming:

    Reduction of winged horses,
    What eternity
    Do they, abandoned, gaze at?

1. Juan lamillar, *El Paisaje Infinito*, Renacimiento, Sevillo, 1992, p. 27.

2. Martin Heidegger, *Poetry, Language, Thought*, trans. Albert Hofstadter, Harper & Row, New York, 1971, p. 132.

3. ibid., p. 134.

Radio is My Bomb

Raking the Shagpile

This document come out of a radio class in the BA (Communication), University of Technology, Sydney as a guideline for an on-going radio programme which would showcase work not only from within the university but also serve as a bit of a clearing house for audio works from Sydney, from the rest of Australia, from ...the world! Rather than being a 'how to' about a live radio programme, it's hoped that this document will give some clues to future programme groups or current, casual readers as to the spirit of the show when it was first created. People who are not involved in the show either might want to be, might want to listen or might just find this a good read.

RAKING THE SHAGPILE or HOW TO MAKE RADIO GO OFF LIKE A BOMB

The most successful explosive devices have a rigid casing that safely contains the deadly mixture of volatile components until they reach their maximum explosive power either through impact or temperature.

One part of the casing of each programme is a theme which can be approached in a variety of ways from the banal to the extreme, and which hopefully addresses listening and radio making as cultural activities. *Raking the Shagpile* is at the barriers of traditional nations of passive radio consumption and tosses a few missives at the boundaries between who produces and who consumes.

The human content of each casing is unpredictable. An on-going group co-ordinates the show, but sub-groups are formed around each programme. There is no set membership of these groups. Once the sub-groups are formed, it is the shameless application of subjectivity and energy that will gaudily decorate the casing of the bomb. The ears that are to the ground in the casing of *RS92* will always belong to a range of sets of cultural, sexual, political and aural experience and in each programme those differences are promoted in all their glorious or inglorious clashing. *Raking the Shagpile* is not ashamed.

The radio programme, like the bomb, must go out live and smoking; when it's blown it's gone. Of course, another bomb can easily be made, but it is never exactly the same as the one before. Hopefully, they are quite different. 'Live' can vary from a carefully timed, edited and scripted mayhem, to a free-for-all construction. On-location targets could make the sparks fly. Interaction with the listeners an the phone either through talk-back, or receiving listener-recorded material down the phone line, ensures that the listener becomes an active producer. But hell—radio makers are listeners too! What exactly are the ingredients of these bombs—are we talking of a mix of voice, sounds and atmosphere? Well of course, but our scientists are examining ways of making sound and atmosphere more than background to the voice, that is, to aurally attack the hierarchy of voice over sound. Then, once this order has been thoroughly dismembered, it must be reconstructed in a way that is not elitist or inaccessible either mentally or physically, yet it must still take stands, nudge a few great monuments in radio and hit current issues without the gluggy objectivity and imaginative presentation so proudly claimed by the journalism profession.

RS92 has no illusions of neutrality—but it is slightly disillusioned as to how to adequately provide access to people from outside the university arena. How to encourage people from a range of cultural, sexual preference, age, ability, political groups who maybe have never considered radio to be involved in the programme. But then, how to deal with tokenism—people need to be involved for a reason. We must play devil's advocate to our own opinions and prejudices and avoid preciousness. But is demystifying radio and promoting diversity an easy excuse to let anyone do whatever they want?

While we will always set our ears to the ground and rake around in our own urban shagpile for those sounds that make up our space, *RS92* wants to look globally—not to Europe, the revered home of Great Shagpile Art, but to our place, to south-east Asia and the Pacific for the sound of our region. Already we have links established with an artist in Japan, and we are spreading the rake further through people involved in SoundCulture[1] and the Pegasus network.[2]

All of this is part of a series of explosions that spread their lethal contents on 2SER-FM and other sympathetic public broadcasters. The first two programmes were detonated in May and June 1992 on 2SER-FM and new programmes continue to detonate sporadically.

We live in a Radio Major which is situated in a minefield of unexploded works, safely stored underground on Broadway, Sydney. *Raking the Shagpile* or *RS92* can be contacted via the Radio Area of the School of Humanities at University of Technology, Sydney, Box 123 Broadway 2007 phone (02) 330 1053/4 fax (02) 330 1041.

>Sue Anderson, Dennis Archer, Mel Boyle, Jason Crawford, Abby Duruz, Daniel Grahon, Natalie Kestecher, Fiona McKenzie, Paul Mason, Kate Stuart, Annabel Tiernon, Liz Willis.

1. SoundCulture 1991, an international festival of sound art was staged by The Performance Space, ABC Radio and the University of Technology, Sydney, in October–November 1991.

2. Pegasus Networks is an Australian-based communications system enabling transfer and shoring of information via electronic mail, and 'gateways' into other computer systems across Australia, and globally.

Some Monuments for a Critical History of Music, Sound Generation and Transmission

Phillip L. Ryan

Music as Possibility

natura naturans...

> "Here, this intonational, rhythmic...' instinctual' breakthrough is situated at the most intense place of naming...They continue to upset commonplace logical order by setting in motion the most active, insurgent, modern practices... These have found their most fruitful ground in music: Cage, La Monte Young, Kagel, and Stockhausen ...
>
> —Julia Kristeva

> "The total rationality of music is its total organisation. By means of organisation, liberated music seeks to reconstitute the lost totality—the lost power and the responsibly binding force of Beethoven."
>
> —Theodor W. Adorno

> "The word 'experimental' is apt, providing it is understood not as descriptive of an act to be later judged in terms of success or failure, but simply as of an act the outcome of which is unknown."
>
> —John Cage

Le Printemps – Claude Le Jeune, 1603.
Claudio Monteverdi: 'new music' in Venice, c. 1610.
Musurgio Universalis – Athanasius Kircher, 1650.
'Battle of Harmony and Melody' – Jean-Philippe Rameau and Jean-Jacques Rousseau, c. 1750.
A Musical Dice Game – Wolfgang Amadeus Mozart, c. 1780.
'*Choral*', *Symphony No. 9* – Ludwig van Beethoven, 1825.
Prelude Omnitonique (manuscript lost) – Franz Liszt, c. 1835
A Faust Symphony (introductory bars) – Franz Liszt, 1857.
Prelude to *Tristan und Isolde* ('Tristan chord') – Richard Wagner, 1859.
'On the Sensations of Tone' – Hermann von Helmoltz, 1862.
Invention of the 'musical telegraph' – Elisha Gray, 1874.
Invention of the phonograph – Charles Cros/ Thomas Edison, 1877.
Bagatelle without tonality – Franz Liszt, 1885.
Invention of radio telegraphy – Guglielmo Marconi, 1896.
Invention of the 'Singing Arc' – William Duddell, 1899.

Some Monuments for a Critical History of Music, Sound Generation and Transmission

"My ambition is to hurl a lance as for as possible into the boundless realm of the future."

—Franz Liszt

"One pays heavily for being one of Wagner's disciples."

—Friederich Nietzsche

Invention of the Telharmonium, 1906.
'Sketch of a New Aesthetic of Music' – Ferruccio Busoni, 1907.
Five Pieces for Orchestra – Arnold Schoenburg, 1909.
Six Pieces for Orchestra – Anton Webern, 1909.
Work (dance) of Loie Fuller, Maud Allen, Isadora Duncan, c.1910.
Furniture Music – Erik Satie, c. 1910
Invention of the Dynaphone, – René Bertrand, c. 1910.
Promethée, Poème du Feu – Alexander Scriabin, 1910.
Allegro Barbaro – Béla Bartók, 1911.
The Rite of Spring – Igor Stravinsky, 1912.
Jeux – Cia ude Debussy, 1912.
Victory over the Sun – Mikhail Matyushin, 1913.
Musica Futurista – Francesco Pratella, 1913.
'The Art of Noise' – Luigi Russolo, 1913.
Futurist performance: *Intonarumoris* – Luigi Russolo, 1913.
Musical Erratum – Marcel Duchamp, 1913.
Piano Concerto No. 1 – Cyril Scott, 1914.
Parade – Erik Satie/Pablo Picasso, 1916.
Symphony No. 4 – Charles Ives, 1916.
Establishment of Dodo – Hugo Boll (Music – Hans Heusser), 1916.
L'Homme et son desir – Darius Milhaud, 1918.
Work of Josef Hauer, c. 1920.
Work of Nikolai Roslovets, c. 1920.
Ameriques – Edgard Varèse, 1921.
Futurist performance: *Bruiteur*, 1921.
Pacific 231 – Arthur Honegger, 1923.
Relache – Erik Satie/Francis Picabia, 1924.
Symphony No. 2 – Sergei Prokofiev, 1925.
Ursonate – Kurt Schwitters, 1925.
The Age of Steel – Sergei Prokofiev, 1925
Work of Nicholai Obuchov, c. 1926.
Presentation of the first moving picture with sound, 1927.
Invention of the onedes martenot – Maurice Martenot, 1928.

The Iron Foundry – Alexander Mossolov, 1 928.
The Mother – Alois Hobo, 1929.
Opus Clavicembalisticum – Kaikhosru Sorabji, 1930.
Invention of the Theremin, c. 1930.
'New Musical Resources' – Henry Cowell, 1930.
Ionisation – Edgard Varèse, 1931.
Invention of the rhythmicon – Henry Cowell/Leon Theremin, 1932.
Suntreader – Carl Ruggles, 1932.
Mana – Andre Jolivet, 1935.
Introduction of the Hammond organ, 1935.

"Sometimes one sees so for that expression refuses to follow as though it were afraid."

—Edgard Varèse

"At first only a faint echo of these melodies will penetrate the spheres of human endeavour, and the music of the next few decades can only be, as it were, a prelude to what will follow."

—Cyril Scott

Work of Lou Harrison, c. 1938.
Invention of the prepared piano – John Cage, 1938.
Imaginary Landscape No. 1 – John Cage, 1939.
Turangalila Symphonie – Olivier Messiaen, 1948.
Symphonie pour un homme seul – Pierre Schaeffer, 1948.
Initiation of 'musique concrete' and the first works of electronic music.
Introduction of the magnetic tape recorder, c.1950.
Free Music – Percy Grainger, c. 1950.
Work of Harry Partch, c. 1950.
Symphony, The Harmony of the World – Paul Hindemith, 1951.
4'33" – John Cage, 1952.
Symphony No. 6 – Karl Amadeus Hartmann, 1953.
Metastasis – Iannis Xenakis, 1954.
Deserts – Edgard Varèse, 1954.
'Experimental Music', (two papers) – John Cage, 1955 and 1957.
Gruppen for three orchestras – Karlheinz Stockhausen, 1957.
'Bewusstsein und maschinen: eine metaphysik der kybernetik' – Gotthard Gunther,
Le Poeme electronique – Edgard Varèse, 1958
'Moving Pictures and Electronic Music' – John Whitney, 1960.

Kontakte – Karlheinz Stockhausen, 1960.
'Programmierung des schonen' – Max Bense, 1960.
Threnody to the Victims of Hiroshima – Krystof Penderecki, 1960.
Symphonie Monoton-Silence – Yves Klein, 1961.
Compositions 1961 – La Monte Young, 1961.
Instigation of the work of *Fluxus* – George Maciunas, c. 1961.
Epitaph for Aikichi Kuboyama – Herbert Eimert, 1962.
Siberian Symphony – Joseph Beuys, 1963.
The Theatre of Eternal Music – La Monte Young/ Marion Zazeela, 1963/-.
Poeme symphonique – Gyorgy ligeti, 1964.
The Well-tuned Piano – La Monte Young, 1964/-.
Robot K–456 – Nam June Paik, 1965.
Work of Conlon Nancarrow, c.1965
The Flicker (film) – Tony Conrad, 1965.
'Happenings' and 'Events' continue through the decode.
Nine Evenings: Theatre and Engineering, New York, 1966.
Experiments in Art and Technology, established 1966.
'World Music': *Telemusik* – Karlheinz Stockhausen, 1965.
Hymnen – Karlheinz Stockhausen, 1967.
Acustica – Mauricio Kogel, 1968/-.
Dialectical Counterpoint for the Mind – Luigi Nono, 1968.
Charlotte Moorman/New Yark – Festivals of the Avant-Garde continue
HPSCHD – John Cage, 1969.
Invention of the Moog Synthesizer – Robert Moog, c. 1969.
Work of Max Neuhaus, c. 1970.
A Rainbow in Curved Air – Terry Riley, 1970.
For Times to Come – Karlheinz Stockhausen, 'intuitive music', 1970.
Work of Henri Pousseur, c. 1970.
Pavilion (E.A.T.), 1970.
Work of Luciano Berio/Cathy Berberian, c. 1970.
Soundtrack (film) – Barry Spinello, 1970.
Appearance of live electronic music – Sonic Arts Union, AMM, Musica Elettronica Vivo, Ensemble Stockhausen, etc., c. 1970.
Work of Cornelius Cardew, c. 1970.
Universe – Alexander Scriabin/ Alexander Nemtin, 1914–1972.
TV Bra for living sculpture – Nam June Paik, 1973.

> "All the while accompanied by a John Cage-inspiring symphonic masterpiece—the majestic silence of eternally regenerative cosmic integrity."
>
> —Richard Buckminster Fuller

Music for 18 Musicians – Steve Reich, 1976.
Bread and Roses – Christian Wolff, 1976.
'Introduction to the Sociology of Music' – Theodor W. Adorno, 1962–1976.
'Noise' – Jacques Attali, 1977.
UPIC, graphic system of composition – Iannis Xenakis, 1977.
Institut de Recherche et de Coordination Acoustique/Musique – Pierre Boulez, 1977.
'The Tuning of the World' – R. Murray Schafer, 1979.
Automatic Writing – Robert Ashley, 1979.
Work of Philip Corner, c. 1980.
'Revolutions per Minute (The Art Record)', 1982.
Harmanika – Helmut Lachenmann, 1983.
The Harp of New Albion – Terry Riley, 1984.
The Desert Music – Steve Reich, 1984.
Horizons – Dick Higgins, 1984.
Thallein – Iannis Xenakis, 1985.
Prometeo – Luigi Nona, 1985.
'The Ear of the Other' – Jacques Derrida, 1985.

> "Everything comes down to the ear you are able to hear me with."
>
> —Jacques Derrida

Eve's Magic – Karlheinz Stockhausen, 1986.
Chess Piece – John Cage, 1986.
Musical notation – Bernard Tschumi, 'deconstructive' architect, 1987.
Pluton – Philippe Manoury, 1988.
Europerae – John Cage, continued 1988.
'The Listening Self' – David Levin, 1989
The Cave – Steve Reich, proposed 1992.
Completion of *Light* – Karlheinz Stockhausen, projected 2002.

Some Monuments for a Critical History of Music, Sound Generation and Transmission

"And this ordering in our musical expression means a house, indeed a crystal, but one derived from our future freedom; a star, but one that will be a new earth."

—Ernst Bloch

Natura Naturans …

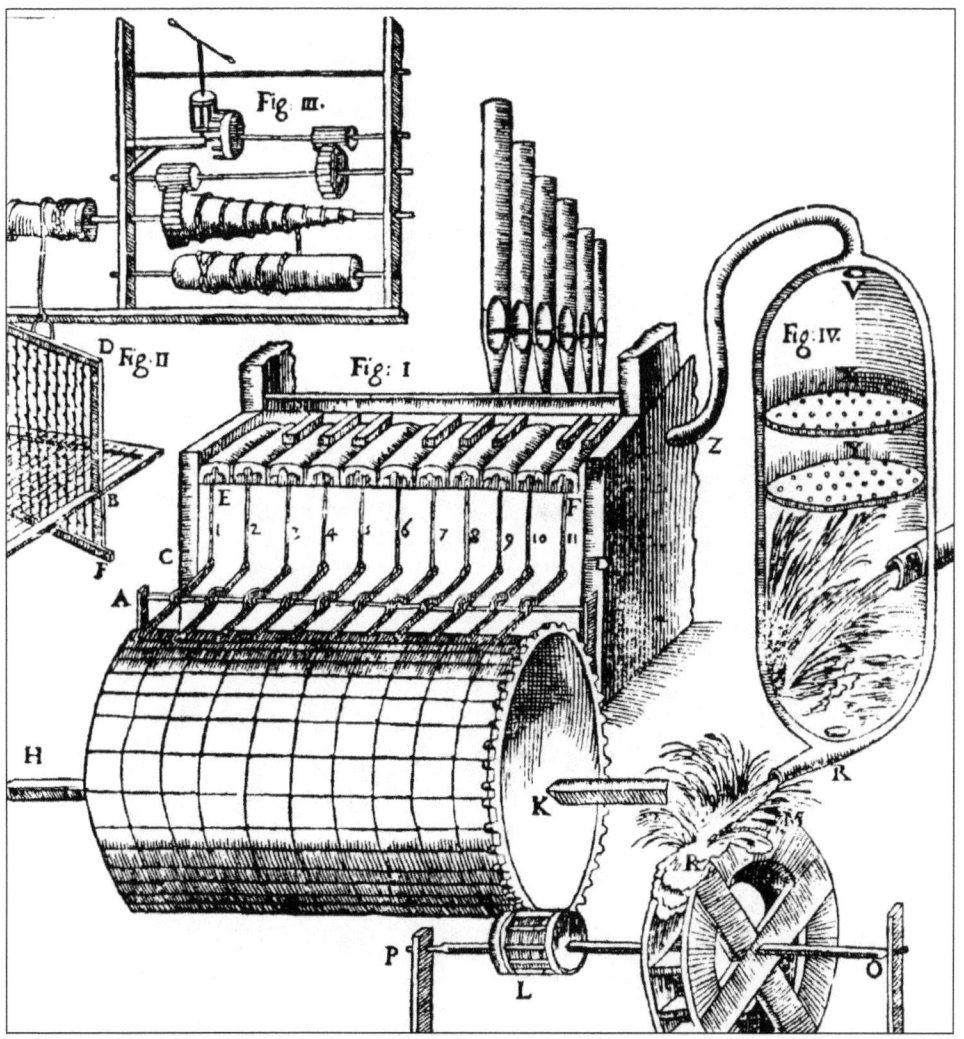

Organum hydraulicum automatum, from *Musurgia universalis sive ars magna consoni et dissoni*, Tome II, by Athanasius Kircher, Rome, 1650.

Homage to John Cage

"That which is one is one. That which is not one is also one."

—Chang-Tzu

        Water music
        Concert for piano and orchestra
        Fontana mix
        Reunion
        Bird Cage
        A Dip in the Lake
        Thirty Pieces for Five Orchestras
        Europeras

"Only that day dawns to which we are awake."

—Henry David Thoreau

...carrying a shoe in his hand he went home quietly, without ceremony (Ch'an lin Lei Chu, 1307).

 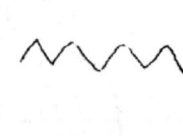

"Zen is your everyday thought, it all depends on the adjustment of the hinge, whether the door opens in or opens out."

—Joshu

"My deepest desire regarding contemporary music is to hear it all, not successively, but all at once, at the same time. Everything together!"

—John Cage (1912–1992)

ESSAYS IN SOUND

2-1995

TECHNOPHONIA

CONTEMPORARY SOUND ARTS

ESSAYS IN SOUND
Published and edited by Contemporary Sound Arts
PO Box 1265, Darlinghurst NSW 2010, Australia

Editors: Alessio Cavallaro, Shaun Davies, Annemarie Jonson
Founding editors: Shaun Davies, Eddy Jokovich, Annemarie Jonson
Design: ARMEDIA

Thanks to W. P. Lowe; the Australian Centre for Photography; the Art Gallery of New South Wales; the Contemporary Music Events Company; Sonia Leber; Modern Image Makers Association; the Museum of Contemporary Art; and all contributing authors and artists.

We gratefully acknowledge the financial assistance of the Research Centre for Artistic Exchange and Innovation, Faculty of Creative Arts, University of Wollongong.

This project has been assisted by the Commonwealth Government through the Australia Council, its arts funding and advisory body.

With special thanks to the Hybrid Arts Committee (now the New Media Fund) of the Australia Council.

CSA was established in Australia in 1991 to facilitate an interdisciplinary approach to the critical investigation of sound, encompassing historical, political, philosophical, artistic, and technological perspectives, and to engage in and support research, and the production and distribution of various forms of print and electronic media related to sound. These concerns are also expressed in public activities such as the SOUNDcheck series of forums and other events.

©1995. Contents copyright of Contemporary Sound Arts, and the respective authors, artists and photographers.

First published in 1995. Republished in 2016.

Contents

Introduction   109
Annemarie Jonson

Notes Towards Sound Ecology in the Garden of Listening   112
Virginia Madsen

Schizochronia: Time in Digital Sound   117
John Potts

RAFT   123
Ruark Lewis and Paul Carter; Alexandra Pitsis

Erotic Nostalgia and the Inscription of Desire   126
Allen S. Weiss

Lost in Space   133
Shaun Davies

Nothing Here but the Recording: Derrida and Phonography   138
Frances Dyson

Cellular Phones: Corporeal Communication Technologies in William S. Burroughs and L. Ron Hubbard   144
Douglas Kahn

Naum Gabo's Linear Constructions   151
Densil Cabrera

Before the Beep: A Short History of Voice Mail   156
Thomas Y. Levin

Exhibitions   164
Joan Brassil
Sherre DeLys/Joan Grounds
Nigel Helyer
Joyce Hinterding
Herb Jercher
Derek Kreckler
Iain Mott
Ion Pearce
Jodi Rose
Julaine Stephenson
Anna Sabiel
Deborah Vaughan

Please, Please—Identify Me! 176
Yuji Sone: Works, Texts and Commentaries
Colin Hood

Who was that Masked Maus? 181
Norie Neumark

The Sound of a Dream 187
Niall Lucy

Soundsite 191

Notes on Contributors [1995]

Joan Brassil is an installation artist based in Sydney. Her work often incorporates already existing sounds ('found sounds') and electronics to explore 'the phenomenology of landscape'.

Densil Cabrera is a Sydney based sound artist.

Paul Carter lives in Melbourne and is a fellow at the Australian Centre. He has written extensively for radio, especially ABC FM's *The Listening Room*. His most recent books are *The Sound In Between* (1992), and *Baroque Memories* (1994).

Shaun Davies is a writer and art critic and a founding member of Contemporary Sound Arts.

Sherre DeLys and **Joan Grounds** investigate intermedia and temporal processes. They are collaborating to implicate their work in architectural contexts from public spaces to intimate environments such as living areas and domestic gardens.

Frances Dyson is an artist and writer specialising in sound and new media. She currently teaches in the Faculty of Creative Arts, University of Wollongong.

Nigel Helyer currently lectures in the Sculpture, Performance and Installation Studio at the University of Sydney College of the Arts. His major gallery-based sculptural installations employ a diverse range of construction processes.

Joyce Hinterding is a Sydney based installation artist whose works frequently highlight sound phenomena.

Colin Hood writes regularly on performance, visual arts and new media.

Herb Jercher is a Melbourne based artist who is active as a sound sculptor, composer, musician, performance artist, sonic consultant, and educator.

Annemarie Jonson writes on the arts and is a founding member of Contemporary Sound Arts.

Douglas Kahn, an artist and writer living on the South Coast of New South Wales, is the coeditor of *Wireless Imagination: Sound, Radio and the Avant-Garde* (MIT Press, 1992) and an international editor for *Leonardo* journal.

Derek Kreckler is currently a guest lecturer and researcher at the Western Australia Academy of Performing Arts. His work encompasses installation and sound art, performance and theatre.

Thomas Y. Levin is from the Department of Germanic Languages and Literatures at Princeton University and is an editor of *Musical Quarterly*. His most recent publication is a volume of Weimar Essays by Siegfried Kracauer entitled *The Mass Ornament* which he translated and edited with an introduction for Harvard University Press, 1995.

Ruark Lewis is a Sydney based visual artist and writer closely involved in radio, audio arts and performance events. He was curator of *Writers in Recital* for the Art Gallery of New South Wales from 1985–1990.

Niall Lucy teaches in the School of Humanities at Murdoch University, Perth, and is the author of *Debating Derrida* (Melbourne University Press, 1995).

Virginia Madsen is an independent radio maker and writer.

Iain Mott makes interactive sound sculpture and writes music for film and television. Marc Raszewski works as an architect and is a designer of interactive sculpture and theatre sets. Tim Barrass is a visual artist working with computers and a multimedia programmer.

Norie Neumark is a radio/sound producer and senior lecturer in the Faculty of Humanities, University of Technology, Sydney.

Ion Pearce is a composer and sound artist based in Sydney. His compositions involve the design and construction of sound objects and machines, and an exploration of the movement (carriage) of sound between such objects, the human body, and their environs.

Alexandra Pitsis is a writer living in Sydney.

John Potts is an audio artist who lectures in media at Macquarie University. His digital audio works *3.27 pm*, *5.06 am* and *Midnight Noon* explore aspects of time and memory.

Jodi Rose is founder of The Cult of the Mad Genius ArtStar.

Anna Sabiel is a Sydney based performance artist. The interaction between the body/movement and the production of sound is a major concern of her work. Relationships between installation, sound and performance are explored to present a dynamic 'vessel' of physical memory and conceptual space.

Julaine Stephenson is a domestic artist based in Sydney.

Deborah Vaughan is a Sydney based artist whose recent work is concerned with the use of sound and metaphor: the tranferring/tranference of the analytic process.

Alan S. Weiss is a writer based in New York. He is most recently author of *Perverse Desire and the Ambiguous Icon* (SUNY Press, 1994); *Phantasmatic Radio* (Duke University Press, 1995). He is currently editing a special issue of *The Drama Review* on experimental radio (1996).

Introduction
Annemarie Jonson

This second issue of *Essays in Sound*, 'Technophonia', coincides with an historical moment of intense interest in sound art and theory in Australia. The Museum of Contemporary Art in Sydney has recently concluded a major exhibition of Australian sound art (*Sound in Space*, 26 May–22 August 1995). Another national sound art event, 'Earwitness', the sound component of *Experimenta '94*, was held in Melbourne in November 1994. As this journal is launched, a number of Australian sound writers and artists are preparing presentations on sound related topics for the International Symposium on Electronic Art in Montreal, maintaining the strong antipodean presence at recent ISEAs. The System X collective, a Sydney and Perth based group of sound artists and writers, has recently established the first site dedicated exclusively to sound art and criticism—Soundsite—on world wide web. (*Essays in Sound* will also be available on Soundsite http://sysx.apana.org.au/soundsite/)

This journal is situated in this field. Its themes—and its title—reflect more generally the concerns which preoccupy criticism, theory and sound art practices in the final decade of the millenium: critical confrontations with information and communications technologies (digital audio, voice mail, analogue recording); conceptions of acoustic ecology; interrogations of the spatio-temporal aspects of sound; notions of sonic inscription from the philosophical to the subcellular; theorisations of the voice; 'sculptural' and performative sound art practices; and the notion of sound art itself.

A major feature of this issue is its focus on artists' work. Ruark Lewis and Paul Carter present images from their sound installation, *RAFT*, exhibited at the Art Gallery of New South Wales in early 1995, reproduced here with a text by writer Alexandra Pitsis. Densil Cabrera presents a lucid exposition of the acoustic inferences in the linear constructions of Russian sculptor Naum Gabo. Colin Hood evocatively appraises the work of Yuji Sone, a Japanese performance artist resident in Australia, whose practice enagages questions of linguistic difference, orientalism and alterity. A series of artist's pages documents work by sound and performance artists represented in 'Earwitness', *Sound in Space* and other recent sound art exhibitions.

Shaun Davies develops an agonistic assessment of *Sound in Space* as it is represented in its accompanying catalogue essay by Rebecca Coyle. Davies underscores the labile conceptions of sound and sound art which frame the event, and which are more broadly emblematic of discourse on sound: sound art as an artform which defies categorisation versus sound art as the product of 'distinct and particular practices and histories'; sound as a 'natural', 'ever-present' phenonenom versus technologically reproduced sound as a cultural construct; the aesthetic status of sound as a 'thing in its own right' versus conceptions of the sound object as preeminently synaesthetic. Davies' essay, in traversing these polarities, illuminates and problematises the already polemical and fluid discursive field in which the exhibition was situated, and which *Essays in Sound* takes, in part, as its focus.

The reproblematisation of nature and 'natural' sound as 'alterity' is taken up by Virginia Madsen who pursues the theme of sound ecology as theorised by, amongst others, R. Murray Schafer in his World Soundscape Project. Madsen eloquently polemicises the overdetermined rhetoric played out in the discourse and practice of acoustic ecology—a genre which opposes a pristine nature to a vitiated culture. Eschewing naive dualism—the desire to preserve and idealise nature against the encroachmnents of the cultural and the technological—Madsen advocates (after Guattari) an 'eco-sophical' practice of listening which negotiates the always shifting and littoral space where environment, socio-political concerns, and the subject interact. In such a space and time ('the *durée* of listening'), suggests Madsen, we might produce an 'intensive listening' alert to the chimerical condition of a *fin de siècle* moment which increasingly couples—as it indetermines the boundaries between—the technological, the 'virtual' and the natural.

Questions of technology and temporality are related to the relatively new field of digital audio production in John Potts' essay. Potts revisits Henri Bergson's critique of the tendency of the 'mechanistic' intellect to spatialise and to visualise time—to divide temporality into isolable instants—and thus to render redundant duration as apprehended by 'creative intuition'. Potts evinces that precisely this process—discrete time sampling conceived as the 'essence of digital audio'—opens up fecund possibilities for the creative manipulation of sonic material as a preeminently temporal phenomenon.

Norie Neumark presents a more skeptical and perhaps dystopian appraisal of a new communications technology—the CD ROM. Neumark's analysis of the CD version of Art Spiegelman's *Maus* novel traces the experiential contours of this new form in the light of the coextant print media version, throwing into question the effects of the re-purposing. Interestingly, Neumark notes that the low grade quality of the CD ROM's voice track— the noisy grain of technology—hyperbolises the voice's affective qualities, at the same time undermining the CD's claim to pure, unadulterated informational and authorial integrity. On the other hand Neumark shows that while Spiegelman's novelistic *Maus* deploys, as a central trope, the mask—in its genealogical richness as a device for a *play* of unstable personae—the CD ROM version, with its plenary archive, its voice-over, and its talking heads, claims for itself the ground of univocal identity and singular truth, traditionally the realm of documentary. Neumark ultimately throws into question claims that the ostensibly innovative interactive, non-linear CD ROM form necessarily promotes access to multiple and contested textual readings.

Frances Dyson returns us to a critique of the philosophical appropriation of an earlier technology. In a reading of Jacques Derrida's *Cinders* and *Ulysses Gramophone*, Dyson critically evaluates Derrida's recuperative analysis of voice which posits the phonographic voice—always-already-written speech—as a deferral of the ontological presence grounded in the silent voice of soliloquy. In these texts, Derrida's answer to the interior and silent voice of metaphysics is an appeal to a technology which will amplify and prosthetise the soliloquy—the tape recorder. In Dyson's estimation, Derrida's recourse to the phonographed voice is not unproblematic. The acorporeal voice of technology comes to substitute for the interlocutor's presence; at the same time, it supplements the solipsistic, silent voice of consciousness. The price paid for this simultaneous 'evacuation and restoration' of inner voice, Dyson shows, is precisely that of embodied sonority: in this schema, the voice as a function of corporeality is, in an archetypical philosophical gesture, effaced. In a complex and rigorous reading Dyson demonstrates that Derrida's reliance on an old inscriptional metaphor is far from revolutionary, and ultimately conventionally intrametaphysical.

Douglas Kahn also turns to inscriptional motifs in a highly idiosyncratic reading of William S. Burroughs' dictum 'language is a virus', refracted through L. Ron Hubbard's Dianetic 'engram' and the General Semantics of Count Alfred Korzybski. Kahn adroitly elucidates the early genealogy of the tropes of binary code or trace—in the human organism as genetic information, in computers and in viruses—which preoccupy many contemporary artists and theorists. Here, metaphysics' notion of inner voice is refigured as Burroughs' 'resisting organism'—the viral word.

The word, as it is inscribed by the technologies of sound storage, transmission and reproduction which predate voice mail, is the subject of Thomas Levin's scholarly ur-historiography of the analogue to digitial paradigm shift. Levin's archaeology of the acoustic trace illuminates such fantastical instruments as Giovanni Battista Porta's 'speaking tube' of 1589 and the apocryphal indigenous Australian 'sound sponge' (subject of an anonymous seventeenth century report in the Bibliotheque Nationale); Levin ultimately demonstrates the persistence of the inscriptive trope.

Allen S. Weiss' rich meditation—which also broaches the inscriptional—ranges through fragmentary reflections on, amongst many others things, Charles Cros' desire to fix time and sound in the 'paleograph', a sound recording device conceived in the same year as the phonograph (1877); Villiers de l'Isle-Adam's 'glory machine' which would mechanise the *claque* (the hired clappers), transforming auditoria into enormous sounding machines which literally 'bring the house down'; Mallarmé on Wagner and poetry; Valéry's nostalgia for revivification of the voice which haunts the dead letter of the inscribed poetic text; and the relation between the orgiastic sounds emanating from Sadean chateaux and the necropolitan space of circulating radiophonic voices. Weiss' reading traces Dionysian and Apollonian, erotic and thanatic motifs in these instances of sounding, technology and inscription. The essay culminates in a memorium for friends lost to thanatos in the cataclysm of AIDS. Weiss sets his moving, final fragment against the acoustic backdrop of the confluent sounds of live, feverish Dionysian sex and the disembodied voices of the monster/horror film soundtrack in the conventionally Apollonian space of the cinema—a space reconfigured in the second-run movie houses or 'scatological "*maisons ouvertes*"' of 1960s Paris as a site for anonymous erotic activity.

Niall Lucy's *The Sound of a Dream* concludes 'Technophonia' with a melancholy reverie on the oneiric qualities of sound. Sound, for Lucy, can be understood as both corporeal and dream-like: it is thus, he suggests, susceptible to 'accidental effects' (as are the dreamer or the conscious subject), and indeed bears an intimate relation to the ultimate accident—death. The recording studio becomes, Lucy suggests, a topos in which the body's death, the liminal site of passage to a 'dimension beyond the conscious self', is both experienced and externalised in the voice's (recorded) trace, a reliquary of 'living presence'. We might suggest that the studio also becomes, perhaps, one of the many prosthetic, technological, inscriptional and acoustic spaces of 'technophonia' explored herein.

Notes Towards Sound Ecology in the Garden of Listening

Virginia Madsen

> As soon as I heard my own voice I couldn't make the piece. It was a truly shocking experience. I had come to view these recording experiences as a type of connection to the environmental sound. [By speaking] I was violating that connection which I was trying to make with the sound. It makes me feel quite emotional to think about it even now. But this had happened and I didn't know it had happened.
>
> —Les Gilbert, sound designer, reflecting on the making of his *Kakadu* soundscape, 1990.

Go into any music shop these days and you are likely to be confronted with a whole host of CDs, cassettes and videos all aiming to soothe and nourish the soul with hour upon hour of healing 'natural' soundscapes. Nature appears in the form of these 'natural symphonies' (also the name of an Australian CD label)—recordings of specific ecosystems. It has also innocently entered (via the digital) the subcultural realm of techno dance and trance music, as evidenced in the extraordinary success of the *Deep Forest* series.

Prior to this, and concurrent with it, has been the sonic exploration into the natural sound world by all manner of composers, sound artists, radio soundscapists and sound designers.[1] Natural sound environments around the globe increasingly are being recorded, explored and 'tuned' using the hi fidelity technology at our disposal. All sorts of sound windows 'appear' to be opening onto a pristine and undisturbed Nature. Les Gilbert remarks:

> I don't know whether we're replicating natural environments, or re-creating or simulating them. All these words are wrong to me because as soon as we do the sort of things we do, we are re-depicting, we are creating something entirely new.[2]

Natural soundscapes or sonic eco-architectures are in effect being grafted as 'virtual realities' onto the flesh of Culture. Les Gilbert's soundscapes, for example, were used as an integral part of the San Diego Zoo in California. Here, through an interactive computer sound system, various complex recordings from 'the wild' were re-located and 're-depicted' for the benefit of human and particularly (one imagines) animal ears. Through a sonic 'virtual reality' grafting process animals were able to hear the sounds from their original habitats and interact with them. The already virtual space of the zoological garden with its artificial pools, mountains, vistas, etc., was given a second degree of actualisation by embedding the animals in this sonic environment. Here 'the wild' meets its lost shadow or echo (memory): a new time-space comes into existence which may well serve to confound our preconceived notions of the 'natural' and the 'cultural'.

Much of this genre of sound design is rooted in the field of acoustic ecology, which finds its inspiration in the 'sound design' philosophy of Canadian composer R. Murray Schafer, particularly through his book *The Tuning of the World*.[3] Here Schafer outlines his 'World Soundscape Project' which, he states, 'will begin to lay the foundations of a new inter-discipline—acoustic design'.[4] For Schafer, acoustic design begins with a particular ecological ear. His research enters the realm of ecology proper by 'collecting sounds threatened with extinction'[5] and by analysing a sound environment (that is, an acoustic ecosystem of interrelations of sounds which in turn reflect interrelations in the bio- and technospheres) in order to 'decide which sounds to preserve, encourage, multiply...'.[6] Almost like weeds, '[b]oring or destructive sounds will in this process become obvious and we will know why we must eliminate them'.[7] Schafer is not only referring here to nature as separate from culture but specifically is discussing the lo-fi soundscape he believes we are fast approaching everywhere. For Schafer, this essentially is a homogenising, polluted, and 'disturbed' environment where noise (equated with poorly designed acoustic technology) is the parasite that consumes its host.[8]

As Schafer outlines it, any ecosystem or environment has a sonic character which comes from the particular economy of sounds which bestow upon this system its 'signature tune'. When the sounds of an environment lose their definition they tend toward white noise. And white noise, as Schafer hears it, is the dominant key of the lo-fi soundscape.

The influence of Schafer's thinking can be heard in the work of Australian writer and radiophonic artist Paul Carter, who has worked in association with Gilbert. He writes:

> What the musical richness conveys is information about the health of the environment, about the integrity of its spaces, dimensions and distances. Degraded environments will be sparsely orchestrated and badly tuned, while relatively undisturbed habitats will be harmonically subtler and rhythmically more various. These are the precise meanings that the music of the bush communicates. The musical signature of a natural environment may be essential to its survival.[9]

Gilbert's labour of listening, recording, and tuning such an environment is of course a cultural practice and a specifically compositional one, but it is above all to be heard within a larger ecological/conservationist practice. The perspective of listening opened by the microphone is 'scientific' and bio-acoustic in spirit, as well as musical. But it is the precision instruments of microphone and its hi-fi 'pick-up' via low noise analogue and now digital recording technology, which gives this practice its epistemological and ecological foundations. Through hi-fi, sound presents itself as the distilled spirit of the real—its vibration, its invisible presence.

Noise, then, is the enemy of high fidelity, as in Schafer's lo-fi soundscape, where noise becomes the parasite which threatens to dominate the environment in the same way as weeds choke a vacant block. Lo-fi, like the eco-system degradation it refers to, amounts to a 'sound sewer' or a 'screen of white noise'.[10] Beyond this, it contributes to the loss of the 'sacred' (in Schafer's terms), the loss of resonant wildernesses. One of these neglected sacred spaces worth reconsidering, according to Schafer, is the space of listening. To this I would add the lived time or *durée* of listening.

Listening lies at the heart of what we might now define as a sound ecology—an ecology which implicates listener and environment, sound and acoustic space. In this reckoning it is not just the sounds of an environment that are threatened with extinction but our ability to listen to them, to distinguish a tune, to extend ourselves through *technè* into sonorous space and to open ourselves to a more 'germinative thinking'.[11]

Just as there are a variety of ecologies and eco-sophical[12] positions, however, we should be wary of one all-encompassing sound ecology which seeks to dwell outside of an engagement with culture. It is time to open up sound ecologies, to explore what in fact is an eco-sophical, heterogenous field where the subject is not a given, and is as susceptible to the loss of place (bewilderment) as to the possibilities opened up through 'machinic'[13] mutation and cultivation. In an urban intellectual environment 'cultivation' has acquired the taint of soil erosion and factory farming—of exploitation. But 'cultivation', in the sense of gardening, may still hold the key to a re-enchanted sense of nature. And perhaps this re-enchantment will stem from the space opened up by the relative slowness of an open and tactful listening, a listening which is aware of its presence, is alert, solicitous, and open to the possibility of interpenetration and mutation. Listening is not only an action born of the desire to know and to acquire; one cannot strain too much to hear. Sounds must be allowed to settle and to resound.

If listening is to be recognised as playing a key role in the development of what we might call an eco-sophical practice (a practice that impinges on the environment, the socio-political as well as on a rethinking of subjectivity[14]) then the ear might lead us away from dialectical oppositions between subject and object, nature and culture. Listening as an eco-sophical practice would abandon a passive positionality of the ear and become actively charged. The ear is only passive to the extent that it is not lent or cultivated.

Schafer suggested in his essay 'Radical Radio', that we might

> put microphones in remote locations uninhabited by humans and broadcast what ever might be happening out there; the sounds of wind and rain, the cries of birds and animals—all the uneventful events of the natural landscape transmitted without editing into the hearts of the cities.[15]

Here, he was proposing an acoustic ecology which relied for its effect on the magical and healing properties of high fidelity radio and recording technologies. But the key to new and more productive hybrid forms may in fact lie in an ancient gardening (cultivating) practice, that of grafting. Schafer adds: 'It seem[s]...that since man has been pumping his affairs out into the natural soundscape, a little natural wisdom might be a useful antidote'. In this he is echoing an almost shamanistic belief that nature's forces (through sound) could be gathered up and channelled by a medium, by a healer, and brought to bear on the sick body (traumas) of the patient. The patient was in need of being touched by nature's voices and of being infused with their healing power. Here that patient is culture. But in Schafer's vision, we are bound by the essential dualism of the western metaphysical tradition. In these terms culture is as distinctly separate and distant from nature as is the occidental trope of wilderness.

What Schafer touches on here turns out to be a central trope of what we might call the 'culture of nature'—the trope of innocent nature versus corrupting culture. Many writers have critiqued this simplistic schema. Donna Harraway, writing about the repressed 'fictions of science' pervading scientific discourse, suggests:

> Nature is such a potent symbol of innocence partly because 'she' is imagined to be without technology. Man is not *in* nature partly because he is *not* seen, is not the spectacle.[16]

The easy elision made between innocent nature and, for example, Pygmy culture (the sampled singing in the *Deep Forest* recordings) should concern us for the same reasons as Woman being equated with nature concerns Harraway and other expressly feminist readings. Nature, wilderness, and the forest have long been at play within cultures and carry diverse meanings.[17] Neither the 'deep forest' nor Woman exist outside history, outside cultivation. Nature, woman, and all kinds of cultures are not to be seen as threatened 'acted-upon' reserves. As long as we see ourselves and our tools outside of nature's reserve (or try to conceal them, even if in the name of ecological protection), we set up an impossible ecology beyond the reach of history or politics, an ecology that will always consider 'us' (those with tools, technology) as exiles inhabiting an 'offworld', a kind of 'spaceship earth', where survival becomes a matter of regular reconnaissance trips to nature (hunting trips?) in order to re-infuse sick culture with nature's healing spirit. In this light, the 'New Age' appears naively unaware of history. Women, 'noble savages', children, animals and nature are often reduced to the realm of the bewildered, the speechless, the static, even when removed to the magical and high-definitional realm of high fidelity. That other nature we call culture (coming from agriculture, cultivation) is simply edited out. Cultivation now 'appears' to leave no traces, no history, just as the sound designer, in faithfully recording the wilderness (and representing it to the public) seeks to silence all noises of his passing, particularly the excessive rustle of his history-writing-in-sound.

Let's address Les Gilbert's bewilderment upon hearing his own voice while trying to create a soundpiece in Kakadu National Park. This loss of speech and subsequent trauma speaks as a wound speaks—of a subject, a place, a time. It came only after he had been intensively listening to the sounds around him via digital longplay technology. He writes:

> At the time I was using a PCMF1 digital [audio tape] recorder which for the first time allowed me to make complete two hour uninterrupted recordings of an environment. That becomes a process then of the observation of the environment—lizards walk over your feet, things which wouldn't happen in the normal course of events happen. In this type of recording, you have to sit in this place, totally still for two hours. I then realized this was an amazing *meditative* experience which provided a real sense of connectedness to what I was doing; so when I'm recreating these things [as sound documents] I'm recreating, to myself, the essence of those experiences. I'm totally convinced that somehow or other the power of those things allows something to be transferred.[18]

Gilbert's trauma[19] at hearing his own voice coming back to him in the wilderness is the trauma opened up by the noise of language, of self consciousness, of cultivation—that which separates him definitively from nature. This leads him onto the path of silence and into the garden of an intensive listening.

The paradox of course is that Gilbert, through his high fidelity sound recording technologies, and Schafer, with his version of a radical radio where no editing occurs—
no cuts, no wounds—*are* present *in* nature as never before. It is through tools of cultivation that the sound ecologist is able to call up neglected 'wild sound'[20] and 'sew' it as a virtual presence onto the flesh of culture—and give it new prominence as a player rather than as a background. This is the type of 'magic' Gilbert performs when he grafts his wild sounds onto cultural sites such as the museum, the gallery, the zoo. To Gilbert, authenticity comes only from the *relation* he has to the sounds, a relation established in the *durée* of listening. He enacts the suturing of virtual sound flesh, alleged bearer of a transcendental presence, onto the cultured listening spaces of second nature.

What we hear are the wild gardens shaped by the cultivating machinic listening of the sound ecologist. Gardens which are not the simple transport of nature, or wilderness, into culture, but which involve the graft; that liminal and transformative space which is the turbulent border zone of the culture of nature. In this space, this *durée*, we could go on producing purely ornamental cultivars or, instead, labour in a place where we might respond creatively to intensive listening, raise hybrid forms where even noise might lose its parasitical nature and instead be turned towards the reinvigoration of neglected grounds.

1. For instance, *Wild Soundtracks* by Jane and Phillip Ulman was featured at the recent Brisbane Biennial. Musical consultant to the Biennial and composer Jonathon Mills is now a senior research fellow on the Acoustic Environment at the Royal Melbourne Institute of Technology's Faculty of Environmental Design and Construction. Soundscapes and radiophonic art based on sounds recorded in 'the wild' make up a large proportion of the work broadcast on the Ausralian Broadcasting Corporation's (ABC) audio arts program, *The Listening Room*. CD and 'wilderness' cassette magazines add to this proliferation.
2. Les Gilbert interviewed by Tony MacGregor, ABC Radio, for the 'Second Nature' series, broadcast on *The Listening Room*, ABC FM, 1990. Gilbert was then Director of Melbourne's Sound Design Studio (now defunct). The company's work principally involved the production of large-scale computer interactive sound designs, using a vast collection of recorded soundscapes from many different eco-systems.
3. R. Murray Schafer, *The Tuning of the World*, Philadelphia: University of Pennsylvania Press, 1980.
4. ibid., p. 4.
5. ibid., p. 4.
6. ibid., p. 205.
7. ibid.
8. Robert Pogue Harrison takes on philosopher Michel Serres' idea of the parasite when he says: 'More precisely, we are beginning to appear to ourselves as a species of parasite which threatens to destroy the hosting organism as a whole'. See *Forests: The Shadow of Civilisation*, Chicago: University of Chicago Press, 1992, p. 199. I have in fact drawn on Serres' use of the word 'noise' which in French also comes to mean noise in the system, the parasite. (See Serres' *The Parasite*, Baltimore: Johns Hopkins University Press, 1982.) It goes without saying that noise, as the parasite-in-the system, cannot be completely excised. Communication can never be a pure pathway to Truth; noise is part of its message. Noise is both parasite—interference to communication—and the possibility, through chaos, of rejuvenation and mutation.
9. Paul Carter, sleeve notes from the CD *Gone Bush* by Les Gilbert, Natural Symphonies, Camden, Australia, 1992.
10. Schafer, op. cit., p. 98.
11. See on this point Gemma Corradi Fiumara, *The Other Side of Language, A Philosophy of Listening*, London: Routledge, p. 60. Fiumara consistently uses ecological metaphors.
12. I have borrowed this term from Felix Guattari. See *Chaosmose*, Paris: Éditions Galilée, 1992, and *Les Trois Écologies*, Paris: Éditions Galilée, 1990.
13. Guattari ties his eco-sophical thinking to the need for not only an ecology of the natural, of the environmental, but for an ecology of the virtual spaces opened up through the coupling of humans and machines.
14. See Guattari, *Les Trois Ecologies*, op. cit., p. 12.
15. R. Murray Schafer, 'Radical Radio', in *EAR Magazine*, 1987.
16. Donna Harraway, *Primate Visions*, London: Routledge, 1989, p. 54.
17. This is not to say that the natural world is a fully cultured subject; humans have language and the world continually slips out of language's net as an excess. As Harrison remarks: 'Language is a differential, a standing-outside of nature, an *ecstasis* that opens a space of intelligibility within nature's closure...Language is the ultimate 'place' of human habitation...We do not inhabit the earth but inhabit our excess of the earth'. Robert Pogue Harrison, op. cit., p. 201.
18. Gilbert interview, op. cit.
19. Trauma, from the Greek, originally means any wound.
20. 'Wild' sound is used to refer to 'actuality' or background ambience in film/video production. It is always 'collected' by the sound recordist in order to make the audio-visual scene sound natural.

Schizochronia: Time in Digital Sound
John Potts

You are sitting at a digital work station. You press a key and watch as the cursor moves through the waveform. You hear the sound at the same time as you see it traversed by the cursor. You decide to retrieve a sample, which you've stored in the computer. It's located way up ahead of the present waveform: in a few seconds you've scrolled forward, claimed the sample, and positioned it next to the waveform. You magnify the image, to get a better 'look' at the sound. You decide to insert the sample into the waveform, trying various positions. If you change your mind, nothing is lost: this is, after all, non-destructive editing.

'Our writing instruments contribute to our thoughts.'[1] Nietzsche wrote this in 1882; as usual, his aphorism is prescient of profound developments in twentieth century culture. Nietzsche was writing—or typing—about the typewriter, but his idea has been tested—and contested—in the context of succeeding generations of mechanical and electronic technologies. That the properties of a medium can contribute at least in part to the nature of the transmitted message is a familiar idea in the late twentieth century. That the technology of that medium affects the cognitive functions of those who use it is a more radical re-voicing of the same idea, and one consequently more likely to be resisted. But the concept is explicit in Nietzsche's statement; it has been pursued in far greater detail by several theorists in the second half of the twentieth century. It has been expressed most famously in the work of McLuhan; more recently, writers such as Kittler, Ong, Meyrowitz, Virilio and Levy have elaborated this in a more scholarly fashion.

This article examines digital audio technology in the wake of this concept. Digital audio—including sampling, editing and mixing—is considered as an 'intellectual technology' which, in Pierre Levy's words, modifies the 'cognitive ecology' into which it is introduced.[2] Digital audio shares the properties of other digital technologies: it is founded on the immaterial (information); this information is endlessly manipulable. These properties form the basis of an emerging intellectual economy, in which familiar epistemological categories—including intellectual property and the codes of realism—are challenged. Digital audio adds to these general properties its distinctive re-alignment of the technological reproduction of sound. The digital audio user works with sound in a specific manner, particularly with regard to time. The focus of this article is on the consequent refiguring of our conceptualisation of sound, in terms of time.

MATHEMATICAL TIME

Digital audio is fundamentally a numerical technology. Unlike analogue audio, which creates an analogue of the waveform in various media (voltage control, deviations in a groove, magnetic patterns on tape), digital audio represents a sound event as a set of numerical values. This binary data is processed and stored—as information—to be reconverted to the original waveform at the point of output. The most cited advantages of the digital process are its lack of degradation in copying, its ability to error-correct, and its flexibility in editing. All these advantages derive from the fact that digital audio works with an immaterial stream of data—with numbers.

Discrete time sampling has been called 'the essence of digital audio'.[3] This technique encodes the analogue wave form into infinitessimal pieces of information. Each slice is discrete in time; the standard 44.1 kHz sampling rate means that 44,100 time-samples per second are taken of the waveform. An analogy used to describe this process is the technique of cinema:[4] the 24 discrete frames per second of film merge to reproduce images of movement. Digital audio takes 44,100 discrete snaps per second, to reproduce variations of sound in time.

Such a description of this technology invokes Bergson's philosophical treatment of time. Writing at the beginning of the century, Bergson drew a distinction between time as constructed by the intellect, and duration as glimpsed by intuition. The former, which he variously termed scientific or mathematical time, is a succession of instants divided by the pragmatic faculty of intellect. In a famous analogy, he likened the workings of intellect—cutting up movement into discrete moments—to the cinema apparatus, taking 'snapshots...of the passing reality'.[5] Each frame represents a static point, isolated from the flow of movement: this is the 'cinematographic illusion' perpetrated by intellect. It is only through intuition that this illusion can be overcome, that 'the infinite multiplicity of becomings'[6] can be grasped.

Yet in his *Cinema 1: The Movement-Image*, Deleuze salvages the cinema from Bergson's 'rather overhasty critique'[7] appraising the twentieth century art-form in Bergsonian terms. At the same time, he deploys cinema as a mode of thought, with its own concepts. In the same way, digital audio may be approached, from a Bergsonian perspective, in more than one way. The very basis of digital audio—its 'essence'—is founded on the binary number system developed by Leibniz—whose thought is a cornerstone of the 'universal mechanism' assailed by Bergson. Mechanistic science, as characterised by Bergson, took 'time as an independent variable', to be measured, to be divided into ever smaller intervals: 'as great a number of moments as we wish in the interval of time it considers'. As a result, according to Bergson, something profound is lost: 'real time, regarded as a flux...as the very mobility of being, escapes the hold of scientific knowledge'.[8]

Yet digital audio, despite its high-speed dissection of time into immobile cuts, need not be dismissed as the sterile operation of mechanistic intellect. Its principles are mathematical, its mode is extreme precision. But its properties offer a vast array of potentials for creative use. Time in digital editing is infinitely supple. All of the analogue audio techniques—cutting, fading, mixing, looping, delay, reversing—are honed with greater precision and control in the digital domain. Some techniques, such as vari-speed and delay, benefit from the greater accuracy available, affording more creative scope. Digital editing and delay permit the tiniest fraction of a sound to be repeated indefinitely, as if that sonic material is frozen in time. The digital sampler, pioneered by the Australian Fairlight company in 1979, and widely available since the mid-eighties, has added another range of manipulations of sound in time. When played on a sampler keyboard, any sound can be detuned, elongated, looped or sped up, while retaining its basic properties; that is, a sound can be reshaped in time, yet remain recognisable. The sampler plays sounds as if they were musical instruments, inserting their specific sonic profiles into the flow of music in time.

Digital audio presents us with a range of paradoxes. Its high precision encourages non-linear editing, in which material can be retrieved and assembled in any order. Its mathematical nature offers an infinite number of choices in non-destructive editing. It is based on tiny slivers of frozen time, yet it offers inexhaustible means to explore the ambiguities and flux of time. These paradoxes proceed from its central concept, which comprises the greatest paradox. Its stuff is numerical information, yet that stuff is a non-stuff, manipulable to an unprecedented degree. Its binary language is brutally simple, but the ways it invites us to think and create are unfathomably complex.

VISUAL SOUND

The first experience of digital editing, for those accustomed to analogue sound, has a startling effect. The sense ratios are altered: instead of the tactile/aural configuration of working with magnetic tape, there is a visual/aural alignment. You *see* the sound, in the form of a spectrograph, a visual representation of the waveform. Or, whole sequences of sound are displayed in visual terms as rectangular shapes, stretches of recorded time waiting to be accessed. On demand, a cursor moves through the sound-as-image: this cursor represents the 'now', the present moment of the displayed sound which we hear as we watch it move across the screen.

There are several consequences of this digital conceptualisation of time. For Bergson, the 'fundamental illusion'[9] about time is to consider it in terms of space: we visualise time, most often represented by a line or an arrow in space. Digital audio, prevalent since the 1980s, has constructed a representation of time in these very terms. Sequences of recorded sound are visualised; they move from left to right across a screen occupying pictorial space within the computer monitor. Yet once again we are presented with paradoxes. Digital editing allows the user to see the whole project as it is being edited—all components, all sequences visualised as stretches of time. Unlike a digital watch, which merely shows the viewer a numerical representation of the present moment—a time sample—the visual display of a digital audio system allows all items of recorded sound to be present. These sounds—their temporal identity transposed to the spatial domain—are situated in any order within the visual display, either behind the cursor or ahead of it. The user can see the past and the future (in relation to the cursor, which represents the present); but the positions of these sequences can be re-arranged at will. Time for the user is full of possibilities. It can be reshuffled with ease. It can be intuited in an infinite number of permutations.

R. Murray Schafer coined the term 'schizophonia' in the 1970s to describe the effect of sound recording technology in splitting a sound from its source, preserving the sound in recorded form.[10] But such a technology also splits a sound from its time: it is 'schizochronic'. In recording a sound, we preserve its flow in time. The recording represents a past sequence of time, which when played, returns to occupy the present. Any recording is a past waiting to return to the present. The replayed sound is ontologically distinct from the original, since it is a recorded version displaced in both time and space. Its return at a later time is a form of difference: the sound is marked by both the technological intervention and the displacement in time. Incorporating these markings of future difference, the sound once recorded is re-constituted: it is split across time, imbued with the potential of re-emergence in time.

Digital audio technology adds a further dimension to the schizochronic aspect of recorded sound. The visualisation of sound components displays an array of recordings waiting to be retrieved, re-assembled, shuffled with others in the register of time. The cursor—in some systems referred to as 'now-time'—represents a mobile present; jumping forwards and backwards, bringing into the present whichever waveform it lands upon. Time becomes fluid, continually realigned by the mobile cursor. As well, the system permits a rapid shifting of the time-scale. The cursor may be observed sweeping through individual sounds, or, from a much larger perspective, the entire project may be represented on the screen. At the moment of looking, the user sees the whole time-scale of the project in question. The past and future of the project are apprehended—or rather, a profusion of possible pasts and futures, waiting to be assembled. There is made possible an intuitive grasp of a project's shape in time.

This digital visualisation of sound takes its place in a history of such technological developments. Edison's phonograph of 1877 was intended by its inventor primarily for 'letter-writing and all kinds of dictation';[11] it was, as its name suggested, designed for 'sound-writing'. Both Attali and McLuhan have commented on the birth of sound recording technology in the nineteenth century, in an age culturally dominated by the visual medium of print. Ironically, the phonograph, along with its predecessors and rivals such as the phonautograph and gramophone (*gramma* = letters), shared the aim of printing: 'to transform sound into writing'.[12] So dominant was the concept of mechanical writing in 'the Gutenberg era with its smooth, uniform lines of type and organisation',[13] that the inventors could not conceive of their sound recording devices except in terms of inscription. This predisposition to the written word was also, of course, a bias towards the visual; for McLuhan its influence was not supplanted until the 1950s with the emergence of hi-fi and the availability of the tape recorder. The emphases of this electric era were tactility and acoustic space, representatives of an episteme vastly different from that of only a half-century before, in which the 'graphophone' needle was conceptualised as a type of pen to write sound.[14]

The age of digital sound, commencing three decades later, problematises these relations in a new way. The binary code of digital information has been construed as 'a kind of writing',[15] yet such interpretations betray a hermeneutic directive founded on the graphic—the 'grammatological'—as an organising and privileged metaphor. It is equally possible to undermine the metaphor of 'digital writing' by celebrating 'the loss of inscription' in the removal of 'the trace [by] acts of erasure'.[16] Such debates, however, are based on the articulation of sound, in the nineteenth century manner, in terms of writing.

It is less contentious, and more fruitful, to focus on the contribution of digital audio to our conceptualisation and experience of sound. Certainly, the visual display of sound constructs the user's experience in ways absorbed from earlier media, including print. The role of vision is privileged. We read, or perhaps scan, the information from left to right (in the same way that Western music notation borrowed this convention from print). We are encouraged to consider sound items in linear terms, as stretches of time, visually represented. Yet there are complicating factors. The experience of digital audio is a visual-aural synchronisation: the visual is privileged, but not pre-eminent. The linear movement of items in the visual display is subsumed into a greater whole within digital editing; non-linear editing, as already discussed, incorporates movement from right to left, as well as the testing of unlimited versions of the edited sequence.

In addition, the visual display of multitrack mixing adds the element of vertical movement, as sections from one track may be moved up or down to another track. Digital mixing represents the multilinear in visual terms; it is a visualisation of the 'all-at-onceness' of multitrack mixing, in which complex combinations of sounds can be grasped in visual terms—as they are heard, or, indeed, before they are heard. There is a complicated and rapid interplay between the visual and aural senses in digital editing/mixing. The visual display is not merely a representation of sound in spatial terms; it has a temporal dimension as well. It affords an intimation of elaborate sound constructions before they are heard. The eye, in combination with the ear, builds complex layers of sound in time.

The digital age of convergence renders all information—audio, video, text—into streams of numerical data. Multimedia formats meld previously discrete media forms into new amalgams. Technological sound now has a visual component; it is capable of both great precision and great subtlety. Digital audio incorporates contrasting facets of time. Founded on the rationalist principles of time-dissection, it nevertheless affords enormous scope for the creative manipulation of sound in time.

1. Friedrich Kittler, 'The Mechanized Philosopher', in *Looking After Nietzsche*, ed. Laurence A. Rickels, Albany: State University of New York Press, 1990, p. 195.
2. Pierre Levy, 'Toward Superlanguage', in *ISEA 94* catalogue, Helsinki: University of Art & Design, 1994, p. 10.
3. Ken C. Pohlmann, *Principles Of Digital Audio*, Indiana: SAMS, 1992, p. 40.
4. ibid., p. 42.
5. Henri Bergson, *Creative Evolution*, London: MacMillan, First Edition, 1911, p. 322.
6. ibid., p. 321.
7. Gilles Deleuze, *Cinema 1: The Movement-Image*, Minneapolis: University of Minnesota Press, 1993, p. xiv.
8. Bergson, op. cit., p. 355.
9. Genevieve Lloyd, *Being in Time*, London: Routledge, 1993, p. 101.
10. R. Murray Schafer, *The Tuning of the World*, Philadelphia: University of Pennsylvania Press, 1980, p. 90.
11. Jacques Attali, *Noise: The Political Economy of Music*, Minneapolis: University of Minnesota Press, 1985, p. 93.
12. ibid., p. 91.
13. Marshall McLuhan, *Understanding Media*, London: Abacus, 1974, p. 297.
14. ibid., p. 293.
15. Friedrich Kittler, 'Gramophone, Film, Typewriter', in *October* 41, Summer 1987, p. 117.
16. Marcos Novak, 'Liquid Architectures and The Loss of Inscription', in *Non-Located On Line*, Knowbotic Research, January 1995.

RAFT

Essays In Sound

I couldn't cast the *RAFT* aside, even after I had finished with it. In a way it had become my casket as well. First it carried me to blind safety and of course it took me beyond places most would understand. I was drowning in the desert and the *RAFT*, that which was my safety, became the words that I drifted so aimlessly over. As one language merged with another so did our paths. Our journeys in time became the same, to seek refuge and to know one another. To know my actions were guided by faith no longer consoles me. *I too, went in search of you and found nothing.* Or, I too, went in search of you and found only my memory. I had been making my measurements harshly against infinity and now I wonder, was I too hard on myself and those

RAFT signals the epitaph on Carl Strehlow's gravestone: 'by faith we perceive that the universe was fashioned by the word of God'. Strehlow (1871–1922) was pastor at the Lutheran mission at Hermannsburg when he died tragically on the Finke River at Horseshoe Bend. Among the first to transcribe Aranda and Loritja poetry, song, myth and traditions, his work appeared in German as *Die Aranda—und Loritja—Stamme in Zentral Australien*, Vols 1–5, 1907–1920, Frankfurt am Maim. Strehlow also helped translate the Bible into the Aboriginal languages of Dieri and Aranda. *RAFT* commemorates the coexistence of two marginalised cultural groups—one indigenous and one non-indigenous—in Anglo-Saxon Australian culture.

around me? For it was instilled in me that I was on the right path but the rightness of that path was itself obscured to me like the stars were by the clouds. Another backdrop to what? To forgiveness, for in this act I absolve time and language. That I still suffer yet forgive. I felt your footsteps on my path, the path that would become my grave, the path that would become myself. To merge with your path, to lose yourself in the process of becoming that which can only be read by others. And yet your footsteps were to cross my heart and bleed me again into the infinite arms of God. And then to be cast out into that which I know now: 'Weeping without cease, I went in quest of you. Unknown I would forget everything...'.[1]   *Alexandra Pitsis*

1. Quoted by O. Clement, *L'Essor du christianisme oriental*, Paris: Presses Universitaires de France, 1964, pp. 25–26.

Paul Carter and Ruark Lewis, Art Gallery of New South Wales, April–May 1995. Raft comprises: a 43 minute sound/voice archival and reflective composition in real time with environmental recordings from the Lira Beinta in Central Australia. A verandah-like or platform structure, 8.5m x 4.8m, inscribed with approximately 22,500 characters of the alphabet drawn in graphite pencil, takes up the majority of the floorspace. The text is taken from St Paul in the Acts of the Apostles, books 27–28, and appears in six languages: Greek; Vulgate Latin; High German; Dieri, English and Aranda. The entire work is framed by silk drapery, 20m x 5.5m.

photo: Babette Griep

Erotic Nostalgia and the Inscription of Desire

Allen S. Weiss

> The *deus ex machina* took the place of metaphysical comfort.
>
> —Friedrich Nietzsche, *The Birth of Tragedy*

Sacred love is often transmuted into profane desire, as when Monteverdi surreptitiously transformed Ariadne's lament into that of the Virgin at the foot of the cross (*Lamento d'Ariane abandonée*). Towards the end of 1885, Charles Cros and Villiers de l'Isle-Adam together possessed a scruffy fox terrier they named Satan, which they paraded around Paris, claiming that the dog was the receptacle of Baudelaire's soul. Yet given Villiers' technological fantasies and Cros' inventions, this gesture was decidedly anachronistic. Where, today, do we dare place Baudelaire's spirit, or, for that matter, the spirits of those we desire, or love?

*

In 1874, indignant about the failure of his play *La révolte*, Villiers de l'Isle-Adam wrote one of his *Contes cruels*, entitled 'La machine à gloire', dedicated to Stéphane Mallarmé. This sardonic diatribe against modernity ironically presents what may be deemed a prototypical manifestation of the theatre of cruelty. Villiers suggests that in the theatre, the *claque*, the hired clappers, constitutes a deception necessary to the success, indeed to the very existence, of the production. The *claque* is deemed an artform, manifesting the entire gamut of expressivity. Beyond the varied types of clapping, there is also a myriad of vocal effects: the initial, basic *bravo* is soon transformed into *brao*; one then passes on to the paroxysmic *Oua-Ouaou*, which finally evolves into the definitive scream, *Bra-oua-ouaou*— nearly a bark. But, in fact, these are still only the most basic effects; there is an entire range of special effects of which the *claque* is capable, including such refinements as:

> Screams of frightened women, choked Sobs, truly communicative Tears, little brusque Laughs… Howls, Chokings, Encore!, Recalls, silent Tears, Threats, Recalls with additional Howls, Pounding of approbation, uttered Opinions, Wreaths, Principles, Convictions, moral Tendencies, epileptic Attacks, Childbirth, Insults, Suicides, Noises of discussions (Art-for-art's-sake, Form and Idea), etc.[1]

The final word of this art is when the *claque* itself shouts, 'Down with the *claque*!', and then applauds the piece as if they were the real public. As Villiers explains, 'The *claque* is to dramatic glory what the Mourners are to Suffering.'

Even so, this is but mere art; Villiers suggests the possibility of eliminating the aleatory effects of the *claque* by mechanising the process. This is the 'Glory Machine', which will be constituted by the auditorium itself, where the entire audience will surreptitiously be transformed into the *claque*. In this apparatus, the sound effects are perfected by multiplying the presence of gilded angels and caryatids, whose mouths bear phonographic speakers to emit the appropriate sounds at critical moments; the pipes that supply the lamps with gas are augmented by others to introduce laughing gas and tear gas into the auditorium; the balconies are equipped with mechanisms to hurl bouquets and wreaths onstage; spring-operated canes are hidden in the feet of the chairs, so as to reinforce the ovations with their striking. In fact, the apparatus is so powerful that it can, literally, bring down the house, such that the theatre would be totally destroyed!

In this masterpiece of *ressentiment*, Villiers manages to eradicate the need for actor, scenario and scene. All is reduced to audience reaction, in what is not quite a conceptual theatre, but rather a purely sensual stagecraft. This ironic, unwittingly modernist event creates the immediate yet ephemeral inscription of sensation directly on the spectator's body—an iconoclastic technique of theatreless theatre which effects a counter-memory, counter-spectacle, and counter-symbolic.

This technique is consistent with physiological experimentation and theorisation of the 19th century, which understood perception to be possible in a non-referential manner, as in demonstrations which reveal how impressions of light may be produced without any visual stimuli whatsoever, by mechanical, electrical, and chemical means.[2] To seek the aesthetic limits of such techniques would be to theorise not the sublime but the countersublime, where temporality is reflexively closed in upon physiological rhythms and thresholds; where consciousness, subsumed by pure presence, eschews all transcendence; where the imagination exists in direct proportion to somatisation; and where, purged of language, the symbolic code is abolished. Narration is obliterated, time nullified, and the psychic mechanism thrust into a solipsism rivalling that of the mystics, inaugurating the oxymoron of an innate apocalyptic sublime. In what would appear to be an ultimate extrapolation of Baudelaire's utopia of an 'artificial paradise', the Romantic sensibility merges with a nascent scientific positivism to indicate a major trajectory of modernist performance.

*

The first book of Charles Cros' collection of poetry, *Le Collier de griffes* [*The Necklace of Claws*], is entitled *Visions*, of which the introductory poem, 'Inscription', simultaneously describes Cros' scientific discoveries and his erotic nostalgia:

> I wanted the tones, the grace,
> Everything reflected in a mirror,
> The drunkenness of an opera ball,
> Ruby evenings and green shadow
> To be fixed on the inert plate.
> I wished it, so shall it be.
> Like the features on a cameo
> I wanted the beloved voice
> To remain a keepsake, forever cherished,
> Repeating the musical
> Dream of an hour too brief;
> Time wishes to flee, I master it.

Cros experimented with two techniques to stop and fix time—color photography and sound recording—having conceived of the 'paleograph', a sound recording device, in 1877, the same year as Edison's invention of the phonograph. This machine established the possibility of eternally fixing and reproducing the sonorous spectacle. Thus, in antithesis to the radical ephemera of Villiers' 'glory machine', the paleograph would inscribe a past become infinitely representable and malleable. Immortality would be achieved at the cost of disassociation, decomposition and decorporealisation—beyond any possible resurrection of the body. No longer, as in his early poem, 'La dame en pierre' ['The Woman in Stone'] would Cros' amorous nostalgia need suffer the stultifying, melancholic effects of petrification:

> Death hasn't touched beauty.
>   The perverse flesh is killed,
> Yet the form, upon a tomb,
>   Is perpetuated.

Henceforth, a new relic is offered to the serendipitous modalities of a lover's discourse.

*

Such phantasies had their metaphysical correlates. In 1881, Nietzsche—seeking that atmospheric electricity which he hoped would cure his varied ills—travelled to Sils-Maria, where he received the intuition of the Eternal Return. Its motivation is expressed in *Thus Spoke Zarathustra*:

> That time does not run backwards, that is his wrath. Revenge is the will's ill will against time and its 'it was'. 'It was'—that is the name of the will's gnashing of teeth and most secret melancholy. The will cannot will backwards; and that he cannot break time and time's covetousness, that is the will's loneliest melancholy. To redeem those who lived in the past and to recreate all 'it was' into a 'thus I willed it'—that alone should I call redemption. All 'it was' is a fragment, a riddle, a dreadful accident—until the creative will says to it, 'But thus I willed it'.[3]

The elimination of temporality is a manifestation of the revenge of a strong poetic will. Within this context, which implies a shift in the classic rhetorical order and the origin of a new ontology, the figure of *hysteron proteron* emblematises a reversal of Western metaphysics, heretofore ruled by ancient dreams of temporal reversal and time travel. Of all the arts, it is precisely those based upon recording technologies, permitting a radical plasticity of time, that most vividly meet these paradoxical conditions of renewal and creativity, reversal and transmutation.[4]

*

While Villiers' glory machine offered the minimal aesthetic model of an imageless realm of pure affect, the l9th century valorised its antithesis: the totalising presumptions and effects of the *Gesamtkunstwerk* of Wagnerian opera.[5] The architectural constitution of the 'mystical abyss' separates spectator from proscenium and real from ideal, creating the conditions whereby a distant dream vision arises. Theodor Adorno, in a passage concerning *Tannhäuser*, illustrates the intimate relations between memory and technology in Wagnerian aesthetics:

> The standing-still of time and the complete occultation of nature by means of phantasmagoria are

thus brought together in the memory of a pristine age where time is guaranteed only by the stars. Time is the all-important element of production that phantasmagoria, the mirage of eternity, obscures.[6]

Wagner rejoiced in the aesthetic paradox of eternalisation through the ephemeral, not unlike the ontogenetic perpetuation of myths within the dream-work. On a decidedly less mythic level, he wished that The Ring be performed but three times, and that afterwards the libretto, scenery and even the theatre itself be destroyed by fire—a veritable glory machine.

The opposition between the purely imageless, iconophobic, physical intoxication of Villiers' glory machine with the dreamlike, imagistic phantasmagoria of Wagnerian opera is delineated by Nietzsche's aesthetic paradigm of the distinction between the Dionysian and the Apollonian. The Apollonian is the world of pure form and dreams; to the contrary, the Dionysian exists emotively, through intoxication, without images, where

> the entire symbolism of the body is called into play…the other symbolic powers suddenly press forward, particularly those of music, in rhythmics, dynamics, harmony.[7]

Dionysus is the body marked by difference, disorder, disintegration, forgetting, madness; Apollo is the body traced by identity, order, the Gestalt of good form, memory, reason. It is precisely the function of opera to transfigure Dionysian intoxication into Apollonian vision, to transform libido into sign.[8]

*

Mallarmé well understood the relation between sound and image in Wagner. In his celebratory text, 'Richard Wagner—Rêverie d'un poëte français', Mallarmé writes of the sublime, generative aspect of Wagner's music: 'an audience would have the feeling that, if the orchestra were to cease exercising its control, the mime would immediately become a statue'.[9] This inversion of the myth of Galatea is telling. Rameau's *Pygmalion* offers the scenarisation of an ontological category error transformed, through wish-fulfilment, into aesthetic delight. Here, passion is projected as beauty, in the form of a statue animated by the artist's desire. And this desire is choreographed: the statue of Galatea takes her very first steps to the sound of music, as the three Graces teach her to dance.

Yet Mallarmé, arch Apollonian, had no need of music to animate his verse: the *musication* of his poetry sufficed. This is a musicality radically divorced from expression. Though he claims that 'every soul is a melody, which must be renewed',[10] and 'every soul is a rhythmic knot',[11] considerations of the soul were in fact anathema for Mallarmé. Rather, he sought a poetics where

> the pure work implies the elocutionary disappearance of the poet, who cedes the initiative to words… replacing the perceptible respiration of the ancient lyrical breath or the personal enthusiastic direction of the sentence.[12]

Unlike that Nietzschean 'blissful ecstasy' which results from the Dionysian collapse of the *Principium individuationis*,[13] the Mallarméan disappearance of the author occurs by virtue of the absorption of lyrical voice within the text. And unlike Cros—whose lyricism was but the shadow of a dreamt reconciliation between voice and image, body and memory—Mallarmé would not valorise the disincarnate voice.

*

Paul Valéry—who defined the poem as 'that prolonged hesitation between sound and sense'[14]—finds in Mallarmé a limit of the poetic art. Only for Valéry 'The delicate point of poetry is the procurement of the voice. The voice defines pure poetry'.[15] In an updated 'muse theory' of creativity, Valéry offered an aural version of Galatea: 'The most beautiful poetry bears the voice of an ideal woman, Mademoiselle Soul'.[16] Valéry's narrow and quite traditional symbol of poetic inspiration suggests a melodic 'rhythmic knot' that is now gendered, following the lineaments of Valery's desire. From the Romantic nightmare of Poe's 'The Oval Portrait' to the Symbolist tragedy of Villiers' *The Future Eve*, the simulacrum of the beloved remains both the allegory of art and the sign of death incarnate. Yet for Valéry, a poem written but unrecited—instantiating Mallarmé's dismissal of 'the ancient lyrical breath'—would be but a dead letter. Is it the imagined voice, or rather its recorded reproduction, that shall be the vehicle of erotic nostalgia?

Though verse is fashioned by voice, there is a distinct futility in Valéry's claim that 'If we better understood this true relation we would know what Racine's voice was like'.[17] Is it any more likely that Valéry could reconstitute Racine's voice through phonological analysis, than that professor in Salomo Freidlaender's tale, 'Goethe Speaks into the Gramophone', could capture Goethe's voice by digging up the poet's skeleton, reconstructing the larynx, and wiring it to a microphone in order to recapture those vocal vibrations which, though weakened by time, could not have totally disappeared?[18] Valéry confuses desire with its object, as is evident in his hypothesis of a *besoin-phénix* (phoenix-impulse), where memory would maintain a constant renascence of desire: 'the more I have you, the more I want you'.[19] This need reveals a darker, unregenerative side of Eros, as Pierre Saint-Amand, in another context, so eloquently explains:

> This imaginary incorporation of the other into the self is invasive, even fatal. It can lead to death, which is at once deliverance, exorcism, and out-fascination. Death is the outcome of desire exhausted, and the outermost limit of confrontation with the other obstacle. Such is the madness of seduction.[20]

Seduction as unregenerative incorporation operates in chiastic intertwining with that poetisation of nostalgia common to the work of mourning. It is precisely because of the mimetic factor in Eros, its narcissistic component, that the phantasmatic origins of recording are so closely linked with amorous nostalgia.

*

The linguistic, poetic and rhetorical effects of sound recording transformed both poetical and metaphysical categories. The effects of amplification, repetition, reversal, projection, broadcast, disassociation, and disembodiment equalled those of the most profound theological phantasies. Sound recording inaugurated a new dimension to necrophilia and necrotopias, resuscitating the rhetorical figure of *prosopopoeia*, manifesting the hallucinatory, paranoid, supernatural or schizophrenic presence of invisible, deceased, ghoulish, demonic or divine beings. These disembodies demand a new phantasmatic topography, one which will find its theorisation alluded to in Gaston Bachelard's *The Poetics of Space*, where he celebrates the topophilia of 'felicitous space', all the while recognising the disquieting existence of its antithesis, what he terms 'oneirically incomplete' dwellings.[21] Here, we enter the realm of topophobia, of the architectural counter-sublime, the corporeal correlate of which would be the oneirically incomplete body: a condition manifested in the *diasparagmos* of the gods, the dismemberments regulated by schizophrenic deliria, the sado-masochistic extremes of erotic fantasy, and the acousmetric condition of the impossible radiophonic body.

The antithetical yet complementary limits of such an unrepresentable architectural dystopia mark the limits of modernism: from its anti-Enlightenment inauguration in the secret chambers of Sadean chateaux, to its closure in the vast cosmic expanses of radiophony. Both are realms of forgetting, of counter-memory: Sade's inner chambers are the sites of invisible orgies and unimaginable tortures, beyond the scope of narrative visuality, offering evidence only through the horrifying sounds emitted; parallely, the infinite expanses of radio compose a terrifying necropolis where the voices of people, both living and long dead, continue to circulate, all the while disintegrating and mixing with each other in a promiscuous auditory montage.[22] The inner chambers of Sade's chateaux shroud the most scandalous erotic liaisons. These unexpressed activities constitute a textual supplement which would totalise the erotic combinatory, if such totalisation were possible. Both chateau and radio proffer spaces obscene, because haunted by death; sites fascinating, because ruled by pure metamorphosis, juxtaposition and combination; scenes of excess, because they necessarily extend beyond the limits of any single imagination; realms of seduction, because they permit that phantasmatic projection which is the very ground of mimetic spectatorship; theatres of pornography, because of an unspeakable promiscuity; domains of transgression, because symbolic articulation is no longer possible.[23]

*

During the 1960s there existed numerous second- and third-run cinemas in Paris, specialising in monster and horror films. In the wings, one could witness, or even participate in, provocative scenes of intense, often anonymous, erotic activity. Here, the spectators became the spectacle, and the eroticised body became the scene. Several of these sites—such as *Le Brady* at Chateau d'Eau and *Le Mexico* near Clichy—offered a peculiar architectural feature, insofar as the bathrooms (where the private scenarios usually culminated) were located behind the movie screen. Thus, within these scatological *maisons ouvertes* (to ironically coin a phrase), the caresses and couplings of rapid love were dubbed with the inarticulate, inhuman, and disembodied screams of monsters and mutants, vampires and ghouls.

Can we not see in such erotic scenarios an example of the rare confluence of antithetical oneiric spaces, where the intimacy of the closed chamber and the presence of the distant, disembodied, recorded voice combine to create an oneirically *overdetermined* architecture? Such is a site where both detached, Apollonian spectatorship *and* participatory Dionysian drunkenness coexist and coalesce. At the end of the 18th century, the sublime was corporealised through libertinage, demonised by the Terror, and finally interiorised by Romanticism. Now, during the cataclysm of AIDS, the ideals and pragmatics of Eros differ vastly.[24] I offer this text in memorium for friends lost; with nostalgia for an eroticism transformed; and as a lament for a terrible new appearance of Thanatos. Given these epochal shifts, what, today, can be the difference between the sublime and the uncanny?[25]

1. Villiers de l'Isle-Adam, 'La machine à gloire', in *Contes cruels* (1874), Paris: Gallimard, 1983, p. 108.
2. See Jonathan Crary, *Techniques of the Observer*, Cambridge, Massachusetts: MIT Press, 1992, pp. 89–92.
3. Friedrich Nietzsche, *Thus Spoke Zarathustra*, Part II, section: 'On Redemption', trans. Walter Kaufmann, in *The Portable Nietzsche*, New York: Penguin Books, 1980, pp. 249–254ff. The present citation is a loose condensation of Nietzsche's text. The notion of the Eternal Return was first expressed in 1882, in *The Gay Science*.
4. On the use of this trope in cinema, see Annette Michelson, 'Dr. Crase and Mr. Clair', in *October* 11, 1979, pp. 31–53ff.
5. In 1869, Cros dedicated the journal publication of his early poem, 'L'orgue', 'A Richard Wagner, musicien allemand.' See Louis Forester, *Charles Cros: L'homme et l'oeuvre*, Paris: Minard, 1969, p. 350.
6. Theodor Adorno, *In Search of Wagner*, trans. Rodney Livingston, London: Verso, 1985, p. 87.
7. Friedrich Nietzsche, *The Birth of Tragedy* (1872), trans. Walter Kaufmann, New York: Vintage, 1967, p. 40.
8. See Allen S. Weiss, 'Possession Trance and Dramatic Perversity', in *The Aesthetics of Excess*, Albany: State University of New York Press, 1989, pp. 3–11ff.
9. Stéphane Mallarmé, 'Richard Wagner—Rêverie d'un poëte français' (1885), in *Oeuvres complètes*, Paris: Gallimard/La Pleiade, 1945, p. 543.
10. Stéphane Mallarmé, 'Variations sur un sujet', in *Oeuvres complètes*, Paris: Gallimard/La Pleiade, 1945, p. 363.
11. Stéphane Mallarmé, 'La musique et les lettres', in *Oeuvres complètes*, Paris: Gallimard/La Pleiade, 1945, p. 644.
12. Stéphane Mallarmé, 'Variations sur un sujet', op. cit., p. 366.
13. Friedrich Nietzsche, *The Birth of Tragedy*, op. cit., p. 36.
14. Paul Valéry, 'Poésie', in *Ego scriptor et Petits poèmes abstraits*, Paris: Gallimard, 1992, p. 73. This citation comes from his diary of 1912.
15. ibid., p. 85.
16. ibid., p. 84.
17. ibid., p. 102.
18. This 1916 tale is cited in Friedrich Kittler, *Discourse Networks: 1800/1900*, trans. Michael Metteer with Chris Cullens, Stanford: Stanford University Press, 1990, pp. 230–231.
19. Paul Valéry, op. cit., p. 144.
20. Pierre Saint-Amand, *The Libertine's Progress: Seduction in the Eighteenth-Century French Novel*, trans. Jennifer Curtis Gage, Hanover, New Haven: Brown University Press/New England University Press, 1994, p. 13.
21. Gaston Bachelard, *The Poetics of Space*, trans. Maria Jolas, New York: Beacon Press, 1969, p. 26. Such constructions are perhaps best instantiated by Frederick Kiesler's projects, notably the 1959 model for the *Endless House*. See Lisa Phillips, *Frederick Kiesler*, New York: The Whitney Museum/W.W. Norton & Co., 1989.
22. The secret chambers must be distinguished from the *salon d'assemblée* in the Chateau de Silling of *The 120 Days of Sodom*, insofar as the latter constitutes a more classic theatric space, though one where the audience of libertines, inflamed by the narratrices' tales, soon become actors as they act out their passions. See Anthony Vidler, 'Asylums of Libertinage', in *The Writing of the Walls*, New York: Princeton Architectural Press, 1987, pp. 103–109ff.
23. See Gregory Whitehead, 'Out of the Dark: Notes on the Nobodies of Radio Art', in Douglas Kahn and Gregory Whitehead, eds., *Wireless Imagination: Sound, Radio and the Avant-Garde*, Cambridge, Massachusetts: MIT Press, 1992, pp. 253–263; Marcel Henaff, *Sade: L'invention du corps libertin*, Paris: P.U.F., 1978, pp. 88–93; Allen S. Weiss, 'Structures of Exchange, Acts of Transgression', in David Allison, Mark Roberts, Allen S. Weiss, eds., *Sade and the Narrative of Transgression*, Cambridge: Cambridge University Press, 1995.
24. See Douglas Crimp, 'Mourning and Militancy', in *October* 51, 1989, pp. 3–18ff.
25. It was suggested to me that the relations between technology and poetics sketched out in this paper might appear to be too teleological. I would answer by evoking Maurice Merleau-Ponty's claim that there are inevitably dead-ends in the historical—and certainly also the art historical—dialectic. To situate the aesthetic ideal with which this paper concludes in the toilets of a seedy, third-rate Parisian movie theatre would indeed seem to suggest such an impasse, where dialectic dissipates into excess. But hasn't the avant-garde always been precisely what hovers about, or creates, such felicitous spaces?

Lost In Space: Sound in Space: Adventures in Australian Sound Art[1]

Shaun Davies

> That dialogue may happen
> Ask first
> Then listen
>
> —Antonio Machado

In the accompanying exhibition catalogue essay,[2] the Museum of Contemporary Art's (MCA) guest curator Rebecca Coyle situates *Sound in Space* in an indecisive and problematic relation to the historical avant-garde and the visual arts generally, claiming 'sound art defies categorisation by virtue of its multiple histories' (SIS, 11). It could perhaps be argued that a lack of curatorial clarity might only exemplify some of the ironies and difficulties encountered in attempting to fulfil what MCA director Leon Paroissien has described as the museum's function in 'addressing some of the most challenging developments in contemporary art' (SIS, 4). But *hindsight,* as we know, is a wonderful thing.

To problematise sound art's origins (its 'more general roots' [SIS, 11]) and to make various claims—specious or otherwise—regarding sound's ontological status (that it is 'a thing in its own right' [SIS, 8]) seems only to preclude the possibility of asking more difficult and even obvious kinds of questions, those, for instance, genuinely concerned with the future development of sound art theories and practices. If it seems somewhat odd, therefore, that the curator should lament the 'dearth of serious critical writing' on the subject, then her complaint that the 'commonly accepted way' (i.e. 'philosophical theory') of discussing sound art tends only to 'mystify' and so discourage access 'to a broad general public' (SIS, 15) not only presents a manifest contradiction, but an even greater oddity, especially given the suggestion that *Sound in Space* might or should, in fact, present a challenge. It seems, however, that the only 'challenge' actually presented to the 'broad general public' (not to mention sound theorists) was to make some sense out of the plethora of propositions presented in the essay, and to discriminate between particular sounds made in the exhibition—given that the individual works often competed with one another for air and space, and so also for the listener's attention—not that the fault lay, here, with the exhibiting artists. In *Sound in Space* the museum space was transformed, literally, into an audition space, sometimes ironically offering only visual cues to guide the 'public' through it, and from one piece to the next. Perhaps a less farcical challenge might have involved actually addressing some of the fundamental philosophical and art-historical problems relating to sound-art, and attending to some of the acoustical problems which might have been anticipated *before* the show went up. If anything is to be learned from this experience, and any criticism given a fair hearing, then the precise relation of the museum and its surrogates to the development and representation of sound art histories, practices and theories, and the value of this relationship, should undergo rigorous analysis and deep questioning.

If there is nothing terribly new in raising questions regarding the role of the institution in determining arts practices and theories and the (re-)writing of their histories, then it seems strange that this relation should not have been mentioned by the curator. Given that this kind of relationship has long been recognised as a historiographical index, and that 'the avant-garde art movements of the twentieth century' supply but one of the 'multiple' historical nodal points (the 'range of sources, histories and technologies' [SIS, 15]) around which the curator strains to anchor an allegedly vague and indeterminate set of sound-art practices (those which defy 'categorisation'), it again seems odd—if not a little subreptitious—that this elision should have occurred.

The question of the lack of clear definition of what actually constitutes sound art has by now become a well worn cliché, perhaps having even become the very emblem of sound art. In *Sound in Space* it is claimed, therefore, in more florid curatorial leaps, that almost anything at all might constitute and be claimed as sound art, so long as *some* kind of sound is produced, even, say, those emanating from 'Sydney's central transport point, Circular Quay...' (SIS, 9), situated right on the MCA's front doorstep. The exhibition strains to expand far beyond the physical peripheries bounded by the sandstone walls of the museum, and sometimes even outside the bounds of the most extravagant curatorial assertions. To begin, there is an audio work at each of the museum's entrances and exits: Derek Kreckler's *boo!* on the western side with Panos Couros'/Wayne Stamp's *A Noise of Worms* on the eastern aspect. The latter continue the theme of extension by incorporating the museum's grassy surrounds, with the relatively nearby Royal Botanic Gardens Tropical Centre (housing the work of Sherre DeLys and Joan Grounds: *Ceci n'est pas une pipe)* representing, in a sense, the outermost limits of this, the museum's 'front lawn'. Site specificity becomes the keyword here; although 'site' may be connected to 'space' in respect of the title *Sound in Space*, there are many other 'sites' claimed by the exhibition's curator, ranging from the radiophonic,[3] sculptural and experimental to the 'indigenous' (SIS, 11). Although sometimes paradoxically delimiting sound-space to a simplistic notion of geographical, environmental terrain, this almost totalising gesture also reflects a perception of sound as an unbounded and uncontained 'medium' capable of accommodating a 'multiplicity of...ideas and practices' (SIS, 11), thereby inviting and perfectly justifying an unrestricted curatorial and 'conceptual' acquisitiveness. *Sound in Space* is, after all, the curator admits, 'inclusive and expansive' (SIS, 13). That the reader could become completely confused, however, when reminded of the earlier, almost opposite assertion: 'sound art [has] a distinct and particular set of practices with specific histories...' (SIS, 5) should come as no surprise.

The representation of a terrain as that which is explored and investigated by a marginalised, 'avant-garde' minority ('much of the exhibition and performance of sound artworks has been marginal...' [SIS, 5]) also seems, questionably, to depend upon the setting up of numerous—perhaps false—problems and premises, not least concerning this 'avant-garde' and Cagean lineage.[4] Having raised the question of blood-line and categorical definition, together with the problem of 'over-emphasis' on the mystifying propensities of avant-garde and philosophical references (dragging an improbable 'public' in along the way), the whole box and dice is then, unchallengingly, thrown into the too-hard basket.

Anxiety is often expressed in the form of sound's difference from visual media or other forms, i.e., what sound art is *not*, or in terms of its synaesthetic coupling with other sensory faculties ('It is the interconnection between the senses that is important' [SIS, 14]). In other words, the aesthetic status of sound, despite the desire to flesh out its meaning on its 'own terms', as it is sometimes put, seems linked in an ambiguous relation with various other media. On the one hand, affirmation of this differential relationship is often maintained ('Any discussion of the visual over the audio is spurious...' [SIS, 13]), but on the other, the struggle to 'free' sound from what is often posited as its purely ancillary and subordinate relation to the visual has sometimes become the sound artist's catch-cry (where sound is posited as 'a thing in its own right' [SIS, 8]). But it is this negational manouevering which has provided, in fact, the very means by which sound art has been able to be curated and museologised here, and the very thing which has maintained the field's dubiously determined 'marginal' status.

The avoidance of raising from the outset the kinds of questions which might offer some interesting new directions and freshness only thwarts any attempt to think clearly about what might constitute a sound arts practice, and is one of the conceits by which certain 'problems' (lineage/definition) are able to be maintained and seen to represent a 'challenge'. As it is represented here, sound art's very future seems to actually depend upon its being immersed in these muddy and confused waters, clouded *not* by asking questions of a fundamental and philosophical nature, but by denying that even raising them has any validity. The raising of false problems, on the other hand, manages to avoid the responsibility of engaging with more pressing and difficult tasks by throwing out the stillborn baby with the murky bathwater.

If it is the case that sound artists, theorists and curators prefer to grope about in relative obscurity, and strive to place sound art on an equal footing with any other plastic art ('discussion of the visual as distinct from the audio is spurious...', and 'All definitions of sound art...presuppose a pre-existing definition of art' [SIS, 12]), then long may they continue to agglomerate and calcify in the visual art museum's penumbra. Under quite different curatorial circumstances, however, the critical possibilities afforded by the involvement of a better advised and informed museum could offer great potential for the field and work towards the cultivation and development of more appreciative *audiences*. Obscurantism is not real status.

This desire to raise sound to the status of the plastic, visual arts, and to provide an ontological and epistemological enframing of sound, also seems tied into a preoccupation with reification, or the recovery of some notion pure, original experience or with ostensive demonstration. This is variously expressed in the essay by way of references to 'original or "live" sound' (even as an 'original "virtual" medium'!) which both has 'roots', is 'ever-present' and is an 'entity', and by linking it to manifestly plastic art objects such as Densil Cabrera's and Robert Britton's *Pipes and Bells*, Deborah Vaughan's *Dora's Feet*, and other works. Also, a preoccupation with inserting sound art—sometimes almost sideways—into already well established and documented art histories, and the placing of general 'historical' readings over sound, establishes the credentials by which sound art may be *viewed* as itself a valid form of arts practice. In *Sound in Space* this anxiety over the recovery of 'historical' and 'primary' experience, coupled with notions of substantiality (as we are told when entering the exhibition '...sound...has a substance') is quite apparent, and the relationship between these anxieties and the desire to conserve and encase these notions within institutional or museological parameters is also quite clear. In the process, one could argue, more curly questions regarding the nature of this relationship are often bypassed, with the result that the phenomenal/art status of sound becomes concatenated with a purely museologically determined 'epistemology'. After having accrued certain exchange value, sound, of course, takes on other properties and uses, serving, perhaps, a more utilitarian *function*; perhaps the curator's reference to 'the cocktail party effect' in the essay may in fact reveal another preoccupation of hers altogether?

'History'—whether in reference to a relationship with 'avant-garde' arts practice or as a continuation of the spirit of technological reproduction—represents but one of the means for validating and retrospectively inserting sound art into the canons of established practice. The other preoccupation is with reference to 'nature', in respect of the transformation, transubstantiation or reproduction of the 'primary' raw material of 'sound', whether this is articulated as earthly, environmental sound, or as a form of ambience, a term which lends itself to a number of interpretations and possibilities: 'the sound ever-present in the enfolding spaces of the body...' (SIS, 9), etc. In this show, however, it seems that simple reference to 'bodies' suffices to justify and bolster certain art practices, as if mere incorporation of the term 'body' into 'theory' takes full account of the complex subject of bodily representation generally.

In Joan Grounds' and Sherre DeLys' *Ceci n'est pas une pipe*, an installation housed in the Sydney Tropical Centre at the Royal Botanic Gardens, a number of inferences can be drawn with respect to the relation between the conservatory and the museum experience. Tropical plants housed here represent a metonymic contraction of an exotic world existing well beyond the confines of the centre's shapely glasshouses; various species of plants relocated here, for the well-being of a nature-loving urban public, thrive in an artificially produced atmosphere. Domestic and constructed objects placed amongst the plants, and the sounds emanating from them, either mimic 'natural' forms or contrast with them, both reduplicating the effect of artificiality whilst at the same time commenting upon the very contrivance of the public space and the problematic of origins and originality. Vocal and other mimicry mimics mimicry; a system of labyrinthine referentiality is established which on the one hand presses the listener to suspend auditory disbelief onto an even more tenuous level, to move beyond the disruptive predicament of the revelation of this nature/culture distinction and to seek refuge in some exotic, represented ideal 'space'. (Mimicry, as we know, functions to both attract and repel.) Like Magritte's painting of a pipe, the reference never settles precisely upon a concrete object as such, and even if it seems to, the very process of referencing, given the title of this work, is at the same time ironised. On the other hand, by tracing sound back to some material source, imagined or not, 'present' or 'absent', one may seek to reify the listening experience and ground it in some notion of embodied or natural 'reality'. But this sign-play interestingly indicates the reificational preoccupations of sound art in *Sound in Space,* its anxiety over the establishment of historical and material credentials, and the grounding of listening into some idealistic notion of 'real experience'.

In the absence of some such signifieds, then, the experience of listening may, in a sense, run in proximity to a loss. This, as stated, raises an interesting problem regarding the very possibility of sourcing sound along historical or natural axes. If, as Coyle states in the catalogue essay, 'recorded sound...cannot reproduce sound as it actually occurs in space' and 'technology used for sound storage and reproduction is [not] culturally neutral' (SIS, 8), then this implies that sound 'as it occurs in space', i.e. 'natural sound' *is,* as such. Of course, the very projection onto 'nature' of the *idea* of nature, or the very consideration of 'nature', is always from the outset a philosophically and historically locatable cultural activity. In other words, there can in no sense be a natural 'raw material' such as sound. The enculturation of sound, 'historically' or 'naturally' may thus be seen to be the function of a retrospective conceptual grasp, and an attempt to situate an already cultural product within an even more highly delimiting institutional apparatus. In a similar kind of way, sound installations, housed in the museum space as they are in *Sound in Space*, are positioned as if they are the collected specimens of exotic arts practices, displaying vaguely blue-blood lineages, examples of the activities of certain cultural species which take place 'over there' somewhere, but which have been taxonomised and metonymically *contracted* into museological practice and parlance. But in a quite disingenuous tone, perhaps in an attempt to raise another fog, the curator claims the contrary: 'Sound art defies categorisation', and then, in a paradoxical and revealingly 'naturalistic' phrase, goes on to list the historical 'roots' from which it nevertheless 'stems': 'electronic music; sound/concrete poetry, art installations and sculpture, sound design, radio art and performance' (SIS, 11). If, however, this material and historical tracing is exposed as simply an anxious attempt to locate any putative ground(s) in which sound art can be embedded, then even the museum's role must be seen, in the end, as merely—regrettably—ancillary. In the MCA, we *see* the works on display, and sound is channelled through them in an almost auxiliary role. In a most revealing comment towards the end of the essay, Coyle proclaims: 'Sound in Space *focuses* on carving out a more positive *vision* for sound art' (SIS, 15) (my emphases). One might ask if after this exhibition any sound will have been left unprivatised, enough of it left over for the development of more finely-tuned and disciplined kinds of listening experiences, for the articulation and generation of more authentically challenging and exciting ideas, and for the enculturation and development of audiences.

Paradoxically, however, the show does remain something of a curate's egg: if stock is taken of the fact that the exhibition disappoints, and fails the artists, and serious thought is given as to the many and complex reasons why, then the development of the field nevertheless remains a distinct and exciting possibility. One might say, ironically, that *Sound in Space* was the exhibition we had to have.

With thanks, for discussions, to Daniel Cole.

1. An exhibition held at the Museum of Contemporary Art (MCA), Sydney, from 26 May–22 August, 1995, incorporating performances, installations, audiothèque, film screenings, radio broadcasts, and artists' talks.
2. 'Sound in Space: a Curatorial Perspective' in *Sound in Space: Adventures in Australian Sound Art,* Sydney: Museum of Contemporary Art, 1995. Hereafter cited as SIS.
3. From 1–29 May, the Australian Broadcasting Commission's *The Listening Room* broadcast a number of works by various artists; 2SER FM's *Audiodaze* featured items from and about *Sound in Space*.
4. See Douglas Kahn, 'Yodelling in Space', in *The Sydney Review,* July 1995, p. 13.

Nothing Here but the Recording: Derrida and Phonography[1]

Frances Dyson

On the phonograph record *Minutes* it is possible to hear—along with W.S. Burroughs, Jean Cocteau and other luminaries—the voice of Jacques Derrida discoursing on death and deconstruction. Derrida's voice appears as an excerpt from a discussion that, we learn from the liner notes, took place after the *Linguistics of Writing* conference in Glasgow, 1986. On death, Derrida suggests that the desire for presence is not necessarily a bad desire, just unfulfillable, because its fulfilment would mean death. On deconstruction, Colin MacCabe responds by pointing out its failure to account for the way that new communications technologies have questioned the whole relation between speech and writing enshrined within the dominant literary tradition. Deconstruction, he argues, has been used not to open up the literary curriculum but as a last way of going back and *saving* that curriculum.[2]

Regardless of the perspicuity of MacCabe's point, what is interesting is the fact that it is not heard on the excerpt chosen for the *Minutes* record—which, by the way, is copyrighted by Derrida. We learn of MacCabe's contribution only from a brief passage in the book that was produced from the proceedings of the conference, which presumably originated—via transcripts—from audio recordings of the conference. In this confusing mediamatic configuration, the presence of MacCabe's point regarding the relationship between speech and writing which new technologies have torn asunder, moves in and out of both visibility and audibility, between one medium and the next.

Derrida would probably be delighted at this sort of confluence, but not delighted about MacCabe, whose criticism is quite misplaced, particularly as Derrida's recent writing embraces technologies of communication such as the tape recorder, the phonograph and the telephone, and particularly as Derrida is more concerned with saving himself than saving the literary curriculum. In fact, salvation comes for Derrida *via* the recording, through which he is saved from having to hear this criticism along with his own voice which, furthermore, is also saved for posterity. But more than this, the phonographed voice defers the possibility of full presence—which for Derrida would mean death—by instituting the disembodied voice of technology. Through the prosthetic subjectivity that the disembodied voice grants, Derridean deconstruction is saved from being mute in the face of Western metaphysics—which Derrida refers to as a metaphysics of presence, constructed from the so-called presence of an inner and silent voice.

Against the silence and absoluteness of the inner, metaphysical voice, Derrida poses the concept of the trace. The trace is a mark of a presence which is never fully present, and an absence which is never entirely absent, and is associated with a Derridean tropology of inscription. The trace is revealed not through speech, but through writing (écriture), which allows the difference, the absence, the other inherent in discourse, to appear. As a 'writing-before-speech', écriture has no associations with either the inner voice of metaphysics, or the romanticised voice of primary orality. However it does share with western metaphysics the element of silence: the trace reveals, and is revealed by, the space, or spacing, of writing—be it the gap between letters on the page or the silence which differentiates phonemes in speech.[3] An associated concept, *differance*, operates through the silence of the phoneme 'a' which can be seen written on the page, but cannot be heard in speech. According to Derrida, this oscillation between hearing and seeing, between speech and writing, which is revealed through a silence, absence or gap, provides a way of articulating the mechanisms or logics which constitute metaphysical presence and at the same time *interrupt* those mechanisms.[4] Derrida's appeal to silence as an instrument of rupture is, however, always veering towards the inner and silent voice of western metaphysics. Perhaps this is why he turns to the metaphor of gramophony to sonorise his inscriptive schematic—his 'science of writing'.

For Derrida, the gramophone interprets (reads) the phonographic voice as form of writing, a writing-before-speech, and by doing so deconstructs the myth of presence and origin upon which metaphysics relies. At the same time, the possibilities for a non-philosophy, or philosophy of difference, are made audible through what he calls the 'phonographic act'. In the 'Prologue' to *Cinders* (1987)[5] Derrida writes that for some ten years he had been thinking about the sentence 'cinders there are (*il y a là cendre*)'. Like the *a* of *differance*, the accent on the *là* of *il y a là cendre* is silent, marking a tension between writing and speech which is reflected in the text itself. In the same text, Derrida re-names the trace as the 'cinder', and describes *Cinders*, the book, as a 'writing apparatus' which 'calls' to the unheard voice/s rumbling through the authorial text of metaphysics. The key question Derrida asks in the 'Prologue' is '...how can this fatally silent call that speaks before its own voice be made audible?' (C, 22). That is, how can the call which precedes the voice, which is only emitted through writing, be made audible? How can the silence of which the accent on the *là* speaks be made to sound?[6] Derrida acknowledges that since the polylogue is written and therefore 'destined for the eye' it 'corresponds only to an interior voice, an absolutely low voice' (C, 22). So how can it be amplified? Derrida finds the answer in sound technology: 'Then one day came the possibility, I should say the chance of making a tape-recording of this' (C, 22–23).

In *Cinders* the tape recorder appears at the moment when this 'almost' silence is given a voice— the moment when Word becomes flesh, when the thundering heavens are given to utterance:

> For that it is necessary that you take the word into your mouth, when you breathe, whence the cinder comes to the vocable, which disappears from sight, like burning semen...Cinder is only a word. But what a word for consuming itself all the way to its support (the tape-recorded voice or strip of paper, self-destruction of the impossible emission once the order is given)...And you can also receive semen through the ear (C, 71–73).

It is interesting that Derrida inserts a tape recorder at the the site of the Immaculate Conception, especially given that in quattrocento paintings the Madonna's impregnation by the Word is often depicted by a tube stretching from the mouth of God to the ear of the Madonna. Being the 'support' of the word, the tape recorder produces the voice as an analogue to the originary inscription/emission of the Judaic Torah, which is a set of ciphers both forming the name of God, and providing the circuit from which, and within which, writing and discourse can proceed. The Torah is a writing-before-speech, because the voice of an incorporeal God could not be terrestrial, that is, sonorous. However, while the Judaic Word might seem to be a static object, it is animated by the vitalism of the cinder. Inscribed but also broadcast, the word is a seed, a palimpsest, which contains and generates all possible writing (note that 'broadcast' is originally an agrarian term, referring to the spreading of the seed in planting). Gershom Scholem writes that, to Jewish mystics

> the Torah is...a living organism animated by a secret life which streams and pulsates below the crust of its literal meaning...[It] does not consist merely of chapters, phrases and words; rather it is to be regarded as the living incarnation of the divine wisdom which eternally sends out new rays of light.[7]

Routed through Derrida's notion of the cinder and écriture, the Judaic 'Word' is never originary, since every word signifies another in an endless chain which neither ends nor begins with a first cause, or unitary God. Yet while escaping the myth of origin, the word is still caught in a potential silence. According to Moshe Idel, with the emergence of Jewish philosophy the Biblical verse 'Moses spoke and God answered him with a voice' was re-interpreted, the speech and the hearing now belonging only to Moses, while God's message was delivered through 'the instrument of *spiritual speech* addressed to the soul, whereafter the soul itself transforms this...into speech which another human being is able to hear'.[8] The instrument of the soul is, in Derrida's phonographically inspired science of writing, an analogue of the tape recorder or amplification device; it transmits and makes audible a message from elsewhere.

If the cinder is always already inscribed, it cannot be originary. But still, how does it avoid the silence of 'spiritual speech', or the anechoic space of traditional metaphysics? In the recording, the word 'self-destructs' in the temporality of sound, consuming itself as a cinder, while the voice, which for Derrida also represents 'sound in general' becomes literally a trace—the phonograph's grooves, the tape's magnetic configurations, the cipher of the 'impossible emission'. So the aurality of the recording, by creating an 'aural-trace', a vocal-writing, represents the always-already-inscribed, but also the always-potentially-audible nature of the cinder. The gramophonic recording is therefore a trace of a trace, a trace which makes pure difference— Being itself—finally audible and which, through the operations of technology, can be made to sound.[9]

What then, does the cinder make audible through the recording? Derrida writes:

> ...the spoken 'recorded' voice makes a reservoir of writing readable, its tonal and phonic drives, the waves (neither cry nor speech) which are knotted or unknotted in the unique vociferation, the singular range of another voice (C, 25).

Technology amplifies writing at the same time that it sonorises the 'interior voice', the 'absolutely low voice' which, as Derrida says, is 'destined for the eye' (C, 22). But how does the interior voice reach its ocular destination? While the cinder might be amplified by the tape recorder, it is also transmitted. Radiating outwards, the cinder passes from one metaphysical and symbolic space to another; like the 'speaking tube' present at both the immaculate conception and the invention of phonography, it becomes a vehicle for carrying and transmitting the silent seed, the Word, in much the same way as a telephone. Appropriating this transmissional technology, Derrida now supplements gramophony with the spatiality and movement of telephony. Gramophony becomes 'telegramophony', a concept which also hinges on a barely audible, barley legible silence. In *Ulysses Gramophone* Derrida introduces the telephonic metaphor anecdotally, as an occasion which prompted a chance decision concerning the title of the talk he would give on James Joyce. Glancing at a page of notes Derrida reads '*hear say yes in Joyce*' as a kind of 'telegraphic' order, 'irresistible' in its brevity:

> So, you are receiving me, Joyce's saying *yes* but also the saying or the *yes* that is heard, the *saying yes* that travels round like a quotation or a rumour circulating, circumnavigating via the ear's labyrinth, that which we know only by hearsay (*oui-dire*).

Because 'hear say yes' and 'hearsay' are homonymous in French (l'oui dire), differing only by an umlaut on the 'i' of hearsay, Derrida concludes:

> ...*Yes* in *Ulysses* can only be a mark at once written and spoken, vocalized as a grapheme and written as a phoneme, yes, *in a word, gramophoned*.[10]

In sympathy with the meaning of 'tele' as transmission over a distance, a telephonic 'hearsay' travels, as does rumour, through spatial and social networks, often spreading from ear to ear like wildfire, carried by the multiple voices of a Heraclitean style hearing/saying. But if the '*yes*' in *Ulysses* travels via the rumourology of the telephone, then being described as 'gramophoned' it connotes the old style telephone system, which sent electronic signals via the mechanical actions of the predominantly women operators. The mechanical connotation of the metaphor refers us to the telephone's introduction, that era when electricity was still a new and barely understood phenomenon, compared to the commonsensical operations of machines like the gramophone. It also refers us to an older mode sociality, where the telephone was the province of extended rumour-ing amongst women, and short, to the point, almost telegraphic brevity in message sending and receiving amongst men.

Derrida continues this masculine mode of communication, by translating *entendre*, meaning to hear/understand, as 'receiving', thus situating hearsay and 'yes' within the metaphoric circuits of telephony. The first phone call in *Ulysses*, which Derrida reads as a call to Israel from God, takes place 'in the offices of *The Telegraph* newspaper (and not *The Tetragram*)' (UG, 269–70). The tetragram comprises the four letters spelling God's name in the Kabbalistic tradition, a tradition which, according to Scholem, is 'both historically and metaphysically...a masculine doctrine, made for men and by men'.[11] The phone call, containing the 'yes' of *differance* and the cinder, put through by women operators in the feminine sphere of rumour and 'hear/say', nonetheless 'takes place' in the vicinity of the silent cipher of the tetragram, site of an originary 'emission'. In other words, rumour occurs within the sphere of a silent deciphering—metaphysics itself; *differance* is already contained by technology, be it writing, phonography or telephony.

For Derrida, writing is now 'a telegramophonic obsession', concerned with receiving a certain call; the call 'between God...and Israel', which occurs in the mode of a recording.[12] The prayer is now a telephone call—or the call is a prayer—caught in the grooves of a phonograph. But the obsession is also with receiving (*entendre*) the untranslatable. Through telegramophony this dialogue with the other is amplified and transmitted. It moves from the 'almost silence' of the 'writing-before-speech', to the uncanny circulations, rumourological networks and crossed wires of the telephone call.[13] And through this movement the tension between writing and speech, and on a deeper level, between presence and absence, begins to resonate and resolve into audibility.

A kind of sonorous presence takes the place of the 'almost silence' of the trace, renamed as cinder:

> ...the cinder is...the name of the being that...remains beyond everything that is...remains unpronounceable in order to make saying possible although it is nothing (C, 73).

The cinder radiates from a centre, and in that radiation expresses the becoming of aurality and fire alike. Like the 'sound object' of recording and some sound art discourses, the cinder waits to be amplified, broadcast, transmitted by the prosthesis of the stylus, be it the phonograph needle, the recording head of the tape recorder, or the nib of the pen. Amplification is culturally connected to notions of synaesthesia, of technologically transforming the sensorium such that hearing becomes feeling and feeling is experienced as the cosmic vibration of life emitted from all things both animate and inanimate. Amplification both detects and transmits this vibration, supplying the listener with a prosthetically induced access to the plenitude of an otherwise inaudible phenomenal life and metaphysical Being. In Derridean terms, amplification or the 'phonographic act' makes the call, the prayer, the cinder, the 'yes', finally audible.

Through the 'phonographic act' the recorded voice seems at first to dislodge metaphysics because it is inscribed, written rather than spoken, and therefore does not ensure the present presence of the speaker. However, the present presence of the speaker is replaced by the disembodied voice of technology, which substitutes for the silent voice of the mind. Rather than making audible the *differance* which aurality—like fire—represents, the phonograph restores and at the same time evacuates the inner voice and origin of Western metaphysics. What is lost in this process is the sonority of sound and hearing, the corporeality of noise and rumour, corporeality itself. In Derridean deconstruction, rumour is untranslatable, it cannot be heard but only read 'with the eyes'. And while the feminised ear hears hearsay amidst a labyrinth, the eye, through the glance or the rapid scan, reads the 'irresistibly brief', 'telegraphic order': hear say 'yes'. Following this order, Derrida deems the *là* of the cinder silent and says 'yes' to a philosophical era which has represented sound as other, and otherness as a reservoir which will always provide a hidden, silent ground. What is heard in gramophonic écriture is this scratching of the unpresentable, the hidden, the trace, represented through the metaphoric circuitry of a masculinised technology. It is not surprising that for Derrida hearsay is 'gramophoned', and by the end of *Ulysses Gramophone*, the telephone is situated 'in the head', providing as he says, a 'telephonic interiority', a 'mental telephony' which 'inscribes remoteness, distance, differance' (UG, 272).

In *Speech and Phenomena* Derrida first likens the *a* of *differance* to the silence and secrecy of a tomb, and it is from this silence that all others in his non-philosophy follow. The tomb is the home of the cadaver, the place where the noise of the body has ceased, where silence can finally 'be'. In order to hear that absolute silence one must be already dead. But to hear an 'almost silence' it is only necessary to be prostheticised—to have an electronically or mechanically aided hearing. Disembodiment belongs to the telephonic ear or phonographic voice, for which there is no split between seeing and hearing, nor speech and writing. And through this refigured subjectivity, death is displaced.

Which returns us to the recorded salvation which began this paper. Contra Colin MacCabe, it is Derridean deconstruction itself, and not the literary curriculum, which is saved by gramophony.

But it is saved only by recourse to fairly old, mechanical, primarily inscriptive technologies and metaphors which in the contemporary cene are far from revolutionary. And far from revolutionary is the slight shift from the absolute to the 'almost' silence of the voice, from the absolute to the almost inaudibility of the rumours of the other.

1. This paper was first presented at the Lab Gallery, San Francisco, in 1992.
2. Jacques Derrida, 'Some questions and responses', from *The Linguistics of Writing* conference, Strathclyde University, 4–6 July, 1986, published as *The Linguistics of Writing*, eds. Nigel Fabb, Derek Attridge, Alan Durant, Colin MacCabe, Manchester: Manchester University Press, 1987, pp. 260–61.
3. 'The difference that brings out phonemes and lets them be heard and understood (*entendre*) itself remains inaudible.' Jacques Derrida, 'Differance', in *Speech and Phenomena*, Evanston: Northwestern University Press, 1973, p. 133.
4. ibid., p. 130. 'This differance belongs neither to the voice nor to writing in the ordinary sense, and it takes place...between speech and writing.' ibid., p. 134.
5. Jacques Derrida, *Cinders*, trans. Ned Lukacher, Lincoln: University of Nebraska Press, 1987. Hereafter cited as C.
6. 'But how can this fatally silent call that speaks before its own voice be made audible? How could it be kept waiting any longer?' (C, 22) 'How can the accent on the *là* of *il y a là cendre* be pronounced "on two *incompatible* registers"—speech and writing?' (C, 24).
7. Gershom G. Scholem, *Major Trends in Jewish Mysticism*, New York: Schocken Books, 1941.
8. Moshe Idel, *The Mystical Experience in Abraham Abulafia*, Albany: State University of New York Press, 1988, p. 84.
9. In *Early Greek Thinking* Heidegger refers to language as 'the house of Being'. In *Cinders* Derrida states: 'There are cinders only insofar as there is the hearth, the fireplace, some fire or place. Cinder as the house of being' op. cit., p. 41.
10. Jacques Derrida, 'Ulysses Gramophone', in *Acts of Literature*, New York: Routledge, 1992, p. 267. Hereafter cited as UG.
11. Scholem, op. cit. p. 37.
12. '...he had somewhat mechanically repeated this prayer, the most serious of all prayers for a Jew, the one that should never be allowed to become mechanical, to be gramophoned.' (UG, 269).
13. The telephone appears in relation to chance, specifically the chance meeting between Derrida and Jean-Michel Rabate: 'we later said...that this coincidence must have been "telephoned"...' (UG, 267). The uncanniness of this crossing makes the telephone, as Freud had mused, 'telepathic', that is, psychoanalytic. Chance, the uncanny coincidence, perhaps the uncanny *per se*, is made audible through the telephone, which in this case is Derrida himself. Thinking back to Heidegger, the 'call' is always to *Dasein*, and heard through uncanniness, when one is in the mode of 'hearkening attunement'. Re-routed through Derrida, does the call become audible only when one is in the state of being-a-telephone?

Cellular Phones: Corporeal Communications Technologies in William S. Burroughs and L. Ron Hubbard

Douglas Kahn

To better understand what William S. Burroughs might have had in mind with the phrase 'language is a virus' let us begin with the well known passage from his novel *The Ticket That Exploded* (1962):

> The 'Other Half' is the word. The 'Other Half' is an organism. Word is an organism. The presence of the 'Other Half' a separate organism attached to your nervous system on an air line of words can now be demonstrated experimentally. One of the most common 'hallucinations' of subjects during sense withdrawal is the feeling of another body sprawled through the subject's body at an angle...yes quite an angle it is the 'Other Half' worked quite some years on a symbiotic basis. From symbiosis to parasitism is a short step. The word is now a virus. The flu virus may once have been a healthy lung cell. It is now a parasitic organism that invades and damages the lungs. The word may once have been a healthy neural cell. It is now a parasitic organism that invades and damages the central nervous system. Modern man has lost the option of silence. Try halting your sub-vocal speech. Try to achieve even ten seconds of inner silence. You will encounter a resisting organism that forces you to talk. That organism is the word.[1]

Secondly, here is a passage from *Nova Express* (1964), 'Technical Deposition of the Virus Power', written with the assistance of Ian Sommerville, describing a new technological habitat of the virus in which subatomic radiation of a cyclotron is focused upon a virus made of computer code 'developed by the information theorists' containing 'our own image':

> It was found that the binary information could be written at the molecular level...However, it was found that these information molecules were not dead matter but exhibited a capacity for life which is found elsewhere in the form of virus.[2]

Thus, over thirty years ago Burroughs had developed viral tropes of genetic mutation, genetic algorithms, binary code as genetic information of the human organism, computers and viruses, i.e., concerns of present-day artists, many of whom have Laurie Anderson's contagious ditty running through their heads: 'language is a virus, oooooo'. Although the old man of the Beats seems to grow younger against an increasingly pervasive backdrop of viral tropes and technological rhetoric, it is best to temper thoughts of prophecy when listening to Anderson's pop praise song because it just so happens to be a paean to L. Ron Hubbard, the founder of Dianetics and the Church of Scientology.

Burroughs' notion of the virus had developed through his engagement with a series of organismic theories, the first one being the General Semantics of Count Alfred Korzybski, the second the orgone theories of Wilhelm Reich, and the third the Dianetics of Hubbard. The first two theories were an important source for the uncanny bodies familiar to Burroughs' readers, bodies capable of amoeba-like osmotic ingestion of other bodies as though their entire surface had become orifice, bodies with the gelatinous consistency of protoplasm, entire bodies, in other words, that mimicked cells. Culminating with *Naked Lunch*, these goo bodies were the culture in which Burroughs' first variety of virus grew, what I call the *usurper* virus, one that overtakes completely through the pathologising of Burroughs' self-described gay erotics of becoming one and the same, through the monomaniacal drives of junk and sex, through an association with the global metaphors of cancer, or through incorporative operations of metaphoricity itself.[3] Dianetics, on the other hand, influenced the virus' first major mutation in his writings immediately following *Naked Lunch*, creating a new virus that shifted from its formerly crass amoeboid behaviour to a differentiated and technically sophisticated entity and, most importantly, to something that functioned so similarly to language that it became language.

This capacity for and of language was a product of the combined effect of Hubbard's engrams and the Dianetic demon, namely, of inscription and voice. Furthermore, it was fused at every point with communications technologies which recorded absolutely everything into the core of cells, took over the internal broadcasts prefiguring the voice, and rendered people inveterate senders or receivers. On an evolving historical backdrop of twentieth century psychotechnologies (in the non-Cartesian framework of organismic theories, psychophysiological), the movement from Burroughs' usurper virus to its mutation is repeated in the transformation of Korzybski's psychogalvanic tests, used to assert the existence of psychosomatic responses, to Scientology's E-meter, something akin to a lie detector used to 'clear' the 'aberee' of engrams. In the same manner Reich's atmospheric orgone energy became intermixed in the post-war period with both the mutative background radiation of above-ground atomic testing and the mind-control transmissions of telecommunications.

In addition, the functional inscriptive and transmissional attributes of actual viruses—their organic-inorganic threshold status mimicking the requirements of writing to find a living host in order to reproduce, the biolinguistic segmentations of genetic code with syntax and phonetics, and the sociality produced by their communicability—came to find their technologies within Burroughs' practices (with Brion Gysin) of literary cut-ups and tape recorder experiments, attempts at recording sub-vocal speech, and the tech specs in his writings afforded by wiz-kid lover Ian Sommerville.[4] Indeed, Burroughs occupies a place of historical importance with his insistence that the endophasic and mnemonic psychotechnologies of modernism be practically realised. That this occurred at the same time that other concurrences of language and technology lodged at the cellular level moved from being couched in organismic theories to those of genetics, also places Hubbard and Burroughs at the heart of the historical shift from mechanics, with its modernist surface-rendered cuts and wounds and sutures, to a mechanistic genetics and all it can grow, engineer, communicate or infect.

By the time Burroughs read L. Ron Hubbard's *Dianetics*,[5] it must have seemed very familiar, for here was not only the third in a sequence of influential organismic theories, but one obviously influenced by his first love—Korzybski's General Semantics. It was also a theory whose pathological sphere was practically limitless, eagerly ascribing all those areas to which Korzybski granted a benign existence a veritable plague of evil agency: the 'engram', an entity highly conducive to the (fallen) personifications that constituted Burrough's character studies and equally susceptible to the heroics of a correspondingly expanded therapeutic that constituted the cornerstone of Hubbard's pretentiousness and popularity.

For Hubbard, the engram is, most simply, an injurious or otherwise painful moment literally recorded, not as memory, but into the cell as a 'definite and permanent trace left by a stimulus on the protoplasm of a tissue' (D, 87). The recording is done within the cells themselves and 'is not a memory; *it is a cellular trace of recordings impinged deeply into the very structure of the body itself*'. The recordings themselves contain absolutely everything and would be very much 'like phonograph records or motion pictures, if these contained all perceptions of sight, sound, smell, taste, organic sensation, etc.' (D, 87). If these engrams stay in place and are not 'discharged' through therapeutic means, they will predispose the individual to psychosomatic illnesses, mental disorders and always something less than complete psychophysiological sanity. The therapeutic process basically entails discovering these recordings and playing them back over and over again until these lose their power, become boring and are shifted out of the reactive mind into regular memory banks where they will do no harm. When Burroughs first read *Dianetics* he wrote to Ginsberg that therapy was a way to 'simply run the tape back and forth until the trauma is wiped off. It works'.[6]

Hubbard secured the term 'engram' from Richard Wolfgang Semon's idea of the *mneme*, developed early this century.[7] His *mnemic principle* is based upon how stimuli produce a 'permanent record...written or engraved on the irritable substance', i.e., upon cellular material energistically predisposed to such inscription...(M, 24). The resulting 'mnemic trace' (or 'engram') can be revivified when an element resembling a component of the original complex of stimuli is encountered. Thus, Semon recounts how the smell of Italian cooking oil invoked 'most vividly the optic engram of Capri' (M, 92) from a trip years before. It did not invoke 'the melody of the barrel-organ, the heat of the sun, the discomfort of the boots' which were equally part of the original engram complex, but this does not rule out that sometime in the future a pair of tight boots might revivify Capri. The complete engram complex of the entire organism is thereby effectively reproducible from small units anywhere throughout the organism. Cut-up planaria, hydra, stentors, and begonias provided ample evidence for mnemic dispersal and regeneration from pieces approaching the size of 'germ-cells'. But Semon ran into difficulty when confronted with the evidence for cortical localisation of memory in vertebrates, for how could it be reconciled with a capacity for cellular recording and reproduction of stimuli throughout the organism?

Semon found evidence in the way that different parts of the body relate to each other involuntarily, such as 'reflex spasms, co-movements, sensory radiations' to infer distribution of 'engraphic influence' (M, 123). He also took inventive recourse to phonography, the mneme machine, to explain the uneven distribution and revivification of engrams. Here, each phonograph represents a primary site of excitation that privileges its immediate vicinity yet nevertheless contains fainter impressions of the entire orchestra, the organism. Thus, 'tight shoes' might invoke walking to Capri but the smell of cooking would be weaker:

> Let us imagine that in an opera house of the usual construction a great number of very similar phonographic recording machines are distributed in different parts of the building, among the boxes, the stalls, the dress and upper circles, on and behind the stage, and also in the orchestra between the seats of the players. In the separate reproductions of the various records made during the playing of the orchestra it will be found that no two of the records are alike, despite the similarities of the machines. According to the location of the machines, it will be possible to distinguish differences of clearness and power in the reproduction of the music. Among the instruments distributed in the orchestra itself, those in the vicinity of the basses will reproduce the renderings of

the bass parts out of all proportion to the designed effect of the total production. The phonographs placed between the 'cellos will in their reproduction give us the impression that during the performance the 'cellos played the leading part, and that the rest of the instruments provided merely a pianissimo accompaniment. So, with the records made by the other machines, there would be differences of emphasis according to their position (M, 125).

Although Semon explicitly warned against following this model too closely because the relationship of an engram to a phonogram was the same as 'a horse pulling a carriage to a locomotive propelling one' (M, 124), his qualification was based upon the complete sensory register of the engram—'photic, thermal, and electric influences, that is, with stimuli belonging to all possible kinds of energies' (M, 125)—versus the singular acoustics of the phonograph. In other words, he would have been perfectly happy to compare his engram with some more advanced, multisensory technology; it was not recording technology *per se* or its prosthetic applicability to the *organism* that bothered him. What at the time besides the phonograph, with its historic displacement of the voice, could disperse a sense of mind and memory throughout the entire organism to decentralise cortical localisation?

Similar to his disposition toward Korzybski, Hubbard transformed what Semon considered functionally neutral into something intrinsically pathogenic. Hubbard's engram was first and foremost inscribed as a record of trauma, the most unadulterated cases being those instances where the individual/organism is abused while in an unconscious state resulting from accident, anaesthesia or some other means. The cells are recording these physical and verbal abuses while the usual mechanism of the conscious self, the 'analytic mind' which would otherwise be recording absolutely everything, is completely shut down for pure survival reasons. However, if engrams were created only by the exceptional traumatic circumstances Hubbard initially describes, then few people would have need for therapy. Therefore, he retains the unconsciousness of severe trauma for its rhetorical clout while extending the capacity for engram formation to any degree of reduced consciousness. In other words, any shortfall of complete, lucid consciousness on the part of the analytic mind will be met with a proportionate degree of 'unconsciousness' and with it a recording of engrams. In fact, much of Hubbard's *Dianetics* is concerned with describing means by which engrams proliferate. For instance, we are alerted to the fact that foetuses are busy accumulating engrams not just by the underestimated frequency of attempted abortions but seemingly by any little bump or jostle. Furthermore, motherly love is a cruel hoax: the act of leaving that prenatal hell of a womb creates another slew of engrams in both baby and mother and continues to do so as the baby's voice invokes within the mother the trauma of childbirth and as the engramic production of this 'revivification' itself finds its way back to the baby, and so forth in a truly vicious cycle. Since 'zygote, embryo, foetus, infant, child, adult: these are all the same person' (D, 188)—there will never be any shortage of therapy required.

The accumulated bank of these recorded and stored engrams produce the 'combined cellular intelligence' constituting the 'reactive mind', the mind of a coalesced trauma body, an evil phantom double to the 'analytic mind', the intrinsically good and perfectly running calculating machine that is always recording everything as a matter of consciousness and storing it in the 'standard memory banks' (D, 185). During any prolonged suspension or minute lapse of consciousness, from trauma to picnolepsy, the reactive mind is busy doing its own recording, causing further problems for the analytic mind. Assuming that anything short of epiphany has a dose of dim-wittedness about it, then it is clear that the reactive mind is likely to be ever-present.

This evil phantom is the 'Other Half' from *The Ticket That Exploded* passage cited above. The Other Half could, of course, be language itself as an entity preceding any one individual, dictating its own conditions upon an individual's fundamental ability to exist socially, acquired contagiously in youth long before any prophylactic possibility of critical self-consciousness. Most persuasively, language is a virus in that both are dead until they find life within a human host: '...the evilest of them all are the viruses...So bone lazy they aren't even hardly alive yet. Fuckin' transitional bastards'.[8] But language in this sense has no body, nor is it solipsistically bounded by a single body. The Other Half could also be the hallucinated body set askew during sensory deprivation, the kinaesthetic body, the astral body, the imago, the phantom body that makes its appearance felt when limbs are amputated, but none of these bodies have language and none have the agency, let alone a subaltern one, that could work the line between symbiosis and parasitism, let alone take over the whole show. The reactive mind has both a concrete corporeal existence and language. The Other Half mimics the submerged presence of the reactive mind in the modulated symmetry of consciousness and unconsciousness, as both exist in order to record. With respect to agency, that both record experience into their respective banks (as though in a proprietary ritual of capitalism) should account for the move to parasitism and beyond.

The reactive mind meets the virus in Hubbard's assertion that 'it is fairly well accepted in these times that life in all forms evolved from the basic building blocks: the virus and the cell' (D, 73). Viruses may in fact have played a part in the electrical and cognitive functioning of an individual because 'even neurons exist in embryo in the zygote, and neurons do not themselves divide but are like organisms (and may have the virus as their basic building block)' (D, 185). Burroughs' version simply reverses the order; neurons do not have a virus in their collective past but instead the healthy neural cell mutates into the virus that is language. The evolutionary development toward language proposed by Burroughs was aided by Hubbard in at least two ways: first, the reactive mind was already equipped with its own voice engramically recorded and played back—the Dianetic demon—and second, there was a radio station available to transmit the recordings.

Hubbard, through a very familiar process, derived his demon by pathologising the Socratic dæmon which in contrast more resembles a best friend. In fact, what looks like premonition of 'language as a virus' by Burroughs in 1955—'It's almost like automatic writing produced by a hostile, independent entity who is saying in effect, "I will write what I please"'[9]—is actually a melding of traditional muse, Surrealist automatism and Socratic dæmon, and is too beneficial for Burroughs, too insufficiently pathogenic, to be Dianetic and viral. The Dianetic demon is, according to Hubbard, a demon 'who gives thoughts voice or echoes the spoken word interiorly or who gives all sorts of complicated advice like a real, live voice exteriorly'; yet it should not be confused with psychotic voices: '(People who hear voices have exterior vocal demons—circuits have tied up their imagination circuits)' (D, 126). Hubbard equates its form and function:

> A *Dianetic demon is a parasitic circuit*. It has an action in the mind which approximates another entity than self. And it is derived entirely from words contained in engrams (D, 124).

This other-entity-than-self is wired in between an individual's analytical consciousness and the standard data banks of memory. When the consciousness asks for data pure and simple, an exchange that usually transpires in silence, it is given some other data by a voice. That voice eventually insinuates itself more and more until it effectively takes over, leaving the '"I" on a tiny and forlorn shelf' (D, 125). This is not a hydraulic condition caused by what Korzybski would call a 'semantogenic blockage'; instead it is a electronic flow redirected within circuitry fed with a nefarious source of countermanding engramic voice from the coexistent body of mind which is the reactive mind. Here, Hubbard gives wiring instructions; the 'analyser' belongs to the analytical mind of consciousness and self-identification and 'got to listen to me, by God' are words, in this case, inscribed as an engram:

> An electronics engineer can set up demons in a radio circuit to his heart's content. In human terms, it is as if one ran a line from the standard banks toward the analyser but before it got there he put in a speaker and a microphone and then continued the line to the plane of consciousness. Between the speaker and the microphone would be a section of the analyser which was an ordinary, working section but compartmented off from the remainder of the analyser. 'I' on a conscious plane wants data. It should come straight from the standard bank, compute on a sublevel and arrive just as data. Not spoken data. Just data.
>
> With the portion of the analyser compartmented off and the speaker-microphone installation and the engram containing the above words 'got to listen to me, by God' in chronic restimulation, another thing happens. The 'I' in the upper-level attention units wants data. He starts to scan the standard banks with a sublevel. The data comes to him *spoken*. Like a voice inside his head (D, 124–125).

It might sound a bit disconcerting (although you know where to get help) that something as commonplace as inner speech might constitute an aberration caused by *other voices* interceding upon the self-contained self, yet

> It is a safe assumption that almost every aberree contains a demon circuit… A Clear does not have any 'mental voices'! He does not think vocally. He thinks without articulation of his thoughts and his thoughts are not in voice terms (D, 125).

Of course, this inner biologic is what Burroughs describes above in his rhetorical imperative to 'Try halting your sub-vocal speech. Try to achieve even ten seconds of inner silence. You will encounter a resisting organism that forces you to talk'. This resisting organism—the virus, word, language—has become widespread and naturalised by not calling untoward attention to itself and by not destroying its host, although it has the capability to exile the self to a 'tiny and forlorn shelf'; thus, bearing the strategical acumen of other viruses, the word virus joins both Hubbard and Burroughs who also extol the existential role of *survival*. For Hubbard, survival is no less than the Goal of Man, and for Burroughs, 'I am primarily concerned with the question of survival—with Nova conspiracies, Nova criminals, and Nova police. A new mythology is possible in the Space Age'.[10]

1. William S. Burroughs, *The Ticket That Exploded*, New York: Grove Press, 1962, pp. 49–50.
2. William S. Burroughs, *Nova Express*, New York: Grove Press, 1964, pp. 48–49.
3. The following passage best typifies the usurper virus: 'The end result of complete cellular representation is cancer. Democracy is cancerous, and bureaus are its cancer. A bureau takes root anywhere in the state, turns malignant like the Narcotic Bureau, and grows and grows, always reproducing more of its own kind, until it chokes the host if not controlled or excised. Bureaus cannot live without a host, being true parasitic organisms…Bureaucracy is wrong as a cancer, a turning away from the human evolutionary direction of infinite potentials and differentiation and independent spontaneous action, to the complete parasitism of a virus.' William S. Burroughs, *Naked Lunch*, New York: Grove Press, 1959, pp. 133–134.

4. On Burroughs' audiotape experiments see Robin Lydenberg, 'Sound Identity Fading Out: William Burroughs' Tape Experiments', in *Wireless Imagination: Sound, Radio and the Avant-garde*, eds. Douglas Kahn and Gregory Whitehead, Cambridge, Massachusetts: MIT Press, 1992, pp. 409–437.

5. Early mention (7 October 1959) of *Dianetics* in *The Letters of William S. Burroughs: 1945–1959*, ed. Oliver Harris, New York: Viking Penguin, 1993, p. 429. This edition was L. Ron Hubbard, *Dianetics*, New York: Hermitage House, 1950. Henceforth cited as D.

6. Letter to Allen Ginsberg (27 October 1959), *Letters*, ibid., p. 431.

7. Richard Semon, *The Mneme*, London: George Allen & Unwin, 1921. Henceforth cited as M.

8. Letter to Allen Ginsberg (13 October 1956), *Letters*, op. cit., p. 335.

9. Letter to Allen Ginsberg (7 February 1955), ibid., p. 262. The Socratic dæmon relates also to Burroughs' suspicious attitude toward the Buddhist attempts of some of his peers to quell the inner voice, such as Ginsberg, who sought to rid the voice by vibrating his brain pan with chant. Such attempts might, after all, create a 'cured writer'. *Naked Lunch*, op. cit., p. 138.

10. Victor Bockris, *A Report from the Bunker with William Burroughs*, London: Vermillion, 1982, p. 2.

Naum Gabo's Linear Constructions
Densil Cabrera

Some sound theorists defensively construct an opposition between visual and auditory fields, hoping to liberate their ideas from 'visualist' tendencies. Sound space is especially susceptible in this respect because of the otherwise common reductive association of vision with space and audition with time. In certain sculptural works of Naum Gabo, however, we see reflections of contemporaneous icons of sound space.[1] His taut line constructions following the mid 1930s pre-empted Iannis Xenakis' 'music-architecture' (e.g. *Philips Pavilion, Polytope de Montreal*),[2] had some parallels with Edgard Varèse's image of sound space,[3] and were appropriated from time to time in the early marketing of stereophony.[4] Even in his earliest works there are acoustic inferences; the resonant porosity of the *Constructed Heads* (from 1915) gives a sound-like communication between interior and exterior, and the *Kinetic Construction* (1920)—a standing wave—embodies sound as it claims space. Yet Gabo's space was highly visual.

The sound spaces of Xenakis, Varèse, and early stereophony shared Gabo's aim of expressing spatiality for itself: they were modernist descendants of an abstract and non-figurative musical space. Modernist sound space introduced emphases on the concrete and on continuous forms. There was an interest in sound as a physical entity in a dynamic space that was partly acoustic, partly auditory, and partly imagined.

Gabo's interest in sound was peripheral, essentially a by-product of his fundamentalist approach to sculpture and space. Like many artists of his time his space was shaped by emerging mathematical and physical models, many works adopting their techniques, processes and forms.[5] His *Constructed Heads* applied the engineering technique of stereometric construction, the *Construction in Space-Crystal* (1937) closely resembled a mathematical model, and the *Spheric Theme* (1936) also had mathematical precedents.[6] Nevertheless his space remained phenomenal; he always sought to capture visual space, as he saw it, in sculpture.

The twisted surfaces that characterised much of his work following the mid 1930s satisfied a long quest for a means of expressing his vision of space. Gabo strove for sensations of continuity, surroundedness, dynamism, self-sufficiency, and of force as much as mass. These works are formations of complex surfaces of double curvature, often made up of innumerable threads or wires, strung on a frame which is sometimes a heavy counterpoint to the lines, sometimes transparent and empty. The multiple layers of lines found in many of these constructions give a heightened sense of movement as the viewer circumnavigates the work. These works are primarily about engaging with space.

The *Linear Constructions* verge on audibility in a number of ways. The hundreds of taut threads form a vibrant mass, the sculpture becoming an incredible harp. Were this harp to sound, it may well approach Xenakis' stochastic music.[7] A musical potential also exists in the stave-like image of ruled lines, but a stave exploding in the spirit of modernity. Or, as Xenakis shows in *Metastasis* and *Concret PH*, the lines can be trajectories in musical space.

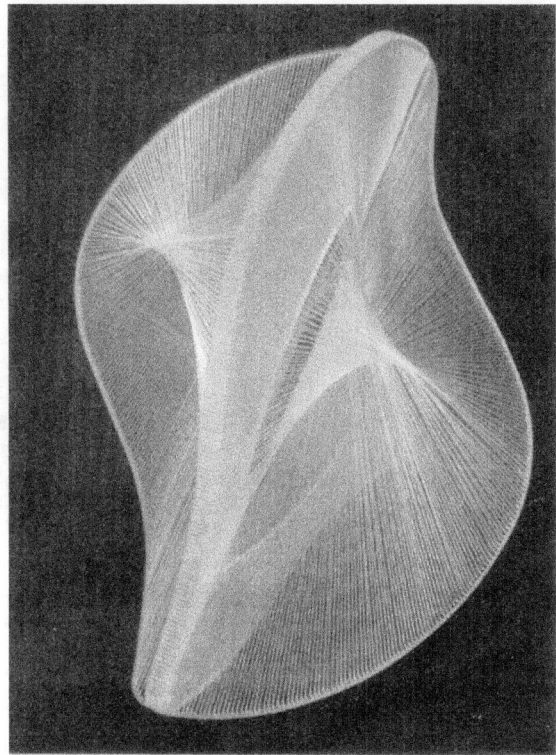

Naum Gabo: Linear Construction in Space No. 2 (1949/circa 1976)

The ruled lines also draw on two images of abstract visual space: the Cartesian grid and lines of ruled perspective. These interpretations are compelling in an art that concerns itself with revealing and mapping spatiality. In the first instance, the lines form distorted surfaces—Euclidean planes but for the work's internal forces. Indeed this tension between a simple and strongly articulated geometry and the curvilinear form gives a sense of instability, again contributing to its dynamism. As lines of perspective, the image is complicated, suggesting multiple viewpoints, multiple depths, and higher dimensionality. Space recedes and expands in several directions at once; the sculpture represents a multi-stable[8] and shifting space even as it exists in real space.

Gabo's visual space is not the angular space of Euclid or that of ruled perspective; it is continuous and surrounding. In psychology there have been a number of attempts to formalise such a model of visual space, a notable one being that of Rudolf Luneburg and his successors.[9] Patrick Heelan has reinterpreted Luneburg's model and proposed a 'quasi-stable', 'hermeneutic visual space'.[10] This model recognises that a viewer is inevitably well-versed in Euclidean spatial models, and is likely to interpret visual space in such terms when Euclidean structures are the focus of vision. The model also recognises a natural visual space surrounding the viewer. Here the size and shape of objects varies depending on their position in visual space—unlike Euclidean space, where dimensions are constant. In the far zone, depth is compressed and objects are flattened onto the visual horizon. Space is limited in extent: the stars are *on* the sky, not *in* the infinite cosmos. In the near zone, depth is expanded and objects bulge towards the viewer. There is an area between these extremes where Euclidean space is approximated. These phenomena are commonly experienced in 'uncarpeted' environments: in the open sea, for example, the water curves up to the horizon. Space envelops this embodied viewer through a heightened sensitivity to depth. Following Luneburg, this subjective visual space is mapped to approximate a Riemannian hyperbolic space.[11]

This space has also been observed in phenomenology. Maurice Merleau-Ponty invokes depth, not as the third dimension, but as the single dimension of a visual body-centred space.[12] Depth is the vertigo-like sensation of space receding around oneself, or the sensation that occurs in intense darkness of space pressing up against the skin. He describes night as 'pure depth' because of the darkness' cohesion and its intimate, even invasive, contact with the body.[13] Euclidean space is the space of measurement; a depth-based space is the space of the body.

Gabo's *Linear Constructions* sensitise the viewer to depth by vibrating between Euclidean motifs and surrounding space. The simplicity, singularity and precision of the lines speak of a measured and ruled space. Yet even as they accumulate the forms of advanced geometry, the constructions become elusive except as algorithms: one can see how the surfaces are made, but the surface itself is difficult to grasp as a geometric entity. The overall wave-like form, however, is readily appreciated as shifting depth. This is partly a function of the subtle curvature itself, but also of the representational aspect of the ruled surfaces. Their sometimes hyperbolic contours (especially in Xenakis' hyperbolic paraboloids) are an apt cue for a perception of hyperbolic space.

Gabo-like constructions are primarily purist expressions of space: non-figurative, with a strong abstract theme, but also compellingly concrete. To claim them as images of sound space is partly arbitrary; after all, how could one find a definitive visual representation of an auditory phenomenon? Their use also reflects a shared ideology about the nature of space, space being a thing in itself, expressed substantially through insubstantial forces and sounds. The spaces have general qualities in common such as a vibration between extension and depth, but specific forms suggest an idealised mathematical sound space. But even when these spaces are constructed in a scientific or mathematical imagination, they must speak through perception. For Varèse the use of hyperbolic and parabolic trajectories represented a break from the established discrete space of musical proportions, heralding a new, continuous sound space grounded on the physicality of sound. Xenakis imagined a geometric space, where sound particles and trajectories might be precisely defined, but which was experienced in performance on a non-mathematical level. In the case of early stereophony Gabo-like images lent a pseudo-scientific aura (reminiscent of relativity) to the technology that promised to bring sound space into the home. Sound space was partly imaginary.

Merleau-Ponty's night becomes a sound space: much more than for vision, sound surrounds and invades the listener. It is scarcely possible to imagine an auditory Euclidean world. The depth apparent in the *Linear Constructions* is the same depth as that discussed by many sound theorists (especially from the fields of psychology and music), often as the distinguishing and overwhelming feature of auditory space.[14] Depth might be found in music, in surround-sound installations, in reverberation and resonance, and in synaesthetic sensations of sound.

The strong counterpoint of geometry and depth in the *Linear Constructions* parallels one of the major projects of modernist sound—the expansion of the frequency range to the extremes, wherein audition is most physical. At the high extreme, acoustics often approximates optics, wavelengths being short with respect to their environment. A geometric or ray model of sound propagation can be applied, and sound is often heard as directional and discrete. Wavelengths of deep sound are large, and sound propagates more like a fluid. There is often a sensation of immersion, as the body is caught up in vibration. While both extremes can give a sensation of proximity, high frequencies tend towards immediacy, while low frequencies are more intimate. The comparable juxtaposition of spatial extremes in Gabo's work may have held some attraction to proponents of modernist sound space.

The multi-stable effect of the *Linear Constructions* is also reflected in modernist sound space, where space is often loosely defined, or defined in a number of overlapping ways. Thus there might be a formal musical space (traditionally pitch, loudness and time); an acoustic three dimensional space; and an auditory space transcending the musical and physical (such as Varèse's sense of 'projection').[15] This laxity in the definition of sound space reflects ambiguous spatial factors in hearing, exploited by the imposition of a number of *a priori* models. Spaces coexist and overlap; there are spaces in spaces. Gabo's works begin to approach this as they play between real, represented, measured and surrounding spaces.

1. Naum Gabo was born in Russia in 1890. His first constructions date from 1915, when he was living in Norway. He returned to Russia in 1917 and published *The Realistic Manifesto* in 1920 which was co-signed by his artist brother Antoine Pevsner. He has become known as a major artist in the Constructivist movement, and he pursued the ideals of his manifesto throughout his long career. He left Russia in 1922, moving to Berlin, then England, and finally the United States. He died in 1976. A good general reference text is *Naum Gabo: Sixty Years of Constructivism*, eds. S. Nash and J. Merkert, Munich: Prestel-Verlag, 1985.
2. See I. Xenakis, *Musique, Architecture*, Tournai: Casterman, 1976.
3. Such parallels include a vision of hyperbolic and parabolic contours (in sound space), a sense of 'projection' and depth, a multi-dimensional space perceived in several ways, and a fundamental commitment to spatiality. See G. Charbonnier, *Entretiens avec Edgard Varèse*, Paris: Editions Pierre Belfond, 1970, and *Contemporary Composers on Contemporary Music*, eds. E. Schwartz and B. Childs, New York: Holt, Rinehart & Winston, 1967.
4. D. Cabrera, *Sound Space and Edgard Varèse's Poème Electronique*, unpublished MA thesis, University of Technology, Sydney, 1994.
5. See for example M. Corrada, 'On Some Vistas Disclosed by Mathematics to the Russian Avant-Garde: Geometry, El Lissitzky and Gabo', in *Leonardo* 25 (3/4), 1992, p. 377–384.
6. L. Relin, 'Two Pioneering Sculptures by Balla and Depero, 1915', *Gazette des Beaux-Arts*, 107, February 1986, pp. 81–85; and A. Hill, 'Constructivism—The European Phenomenon', in *Studio International*, 178 (914), September 1969, pp. 140–147.
7. See I. Xenakis, *Formalized Music*, Bloomington: Indiana University Press, 1971.
8. 'Multi-stable' is used by the phenomenologist Don Ihde to describe the perception of an optical illusion, where an image can have more than one stable spatial interpretation.

9. See, for instance, A. Blank, 'The Luneburg Theory of Binocular Space Perception', in *Psychology: A Study of Science*, ed. S. Koch, New York: McGraw-Hill, 1959, Volume 1, pp. 395–426. Based at Princeton University, Luneburg published his *Mathematical Analysis of Binocular Vision* in 1947 shortly before his death. It was based largely on experiments from early in the century employing isolated points of light in a darkroom to show that visual depth perception is not Euclidean.

10. P. Heelan, *Space Perception and the Philosophy of Science*, Berkeley: University of California Press, 1983. Heelan is a New York based philosopher of science.

11. Riemann, a major figure in nineteenth century geometry, proposed that there are three possible spaces of constant curvature: Euclidean space (with zero curvature); elliptical space (with positive curvature); and hyperbolic space (with negative curvature). The latter space can be mapped to a trumpet-like flare or double flare. A simple and elegant introduction to these concepts can be found in D. Hilbert and S. Cohn-Vossen: *Geometry and the Imagination*, New York: Chelsea Publishing Company, 1952.

12. M. Merleau-Ponty, 'Eye and Mind', in *The Primacy of Perception*, ed. J. Edie, Evanston: Northwestern University Press, 1964, p.180.

13. M. Merleau-Ponty, *Phenomenology of Perception*, trans. C. Smith, London: Routledge & Kegan Paul, 1962, p. 283.

14. D. Cabrera, op. cit., pp. 67–72. Such theorists include William James, Jon Frederickson, Martin Nass, Victor Zuckerkandl, arguably Peter Strawson, Edward Lippman, Don Ihde, and others.

15. D. Cabrera, op. cit., pp. 50–67.

Before the Beep: A Short History of Voice Mail

Thomas Y. Levin

> We shall deal here with humble things, things not usually granted earnest consideration, or at least not valued for their historical import. But no more in history than in painting is it the impressiveness of the subject that matters. The sun is mirrored even in a coffee spoon.
>
> In their aggregate, the humble objects of which we shall speak have shaken our mode of living to its very roots. Modest things of daily life, they accumulate into forces acting upon whoever moves within the orbit of our civilisation.
>
> —Siegfried Giedion[1]

BEFORE THE BEEP

A dramatic advance in voice storage, processing and retrieval technologies has taken place during the last few years, a transformation that has already begun to show up in appliances that have suddenly begun to 'talk', announcing with uninvited familiarity that 'you have twenty three messages' or reminding one, as a rented car did recently in an annoyingly insistent manner, to fasten one's seatbelt. In America the futuristic thrill of navigating a complex of touch-tone menus in order to avoid an interminable hold and the resulting musak migraine is by now a commonplace. Prompted by pre-recorded, synthetic voices, we are increasingly encountering and exploiting all sorts of interactive, remote controlled, intelligent data processing machines. What I am referring to, of course, is the conjunction of affordable, high speed computing power and sophisticated, as well as affordable, AD (analogue to digital) and DA (digital to analogue) conversion devices, i.e. contraptions that translate sound into digital information and vice-versa. Among the more visible of the various products that this alliance has produced in conjunction with the telephone, for example, is the phenomenon of voice mail, i.e. the step beyond the (still largely) electro-magnetic answering machine to the digitalised storage of analogue traces which can be retrieved (re-analogised) upon command. Even more state-of-the-art is voice email. Transmitted via the already widespread networks for electronic mail, voice email allows one to 1) play back email as acoustic information, 2) transmit voice messages via a computer network (send someone a greeting that they will 'hear' when they 'read' their 'mail', 3) verbally annotate a file as it scrolls by on somebody else's screen, and 4)—this is still in its very initial stages—speak data into the computer rather than typing it.

Sound is thus slowly breaking into the domain of digital information processing systems, expanding a computer age still largely dominated by text (i.e. data and word processing) and (increasingly) image (autocad, etc.). As an unabashedly logocentrist author in *PC Magazine* puts it, rehearsing a litany of phonocentrist clichés:

> Why would you want to hear voices over your network? Because, as humans, we used verbal expressions years before we began writing, and for many people verbalising is easier and more satisfying than jotting thoughts down on paper. Speaking potentially evokes greater emotion, conveys greater sincerity, and promotes a higher level of trust than writing. What this means is that, most likely, in the years to come people will be using more and more voice in their 'documents', including, of course, dispatches of electronic voice mail. The computer is becoming a site of tele-phony, a sending of the voice as data. But...for your voice to be sent, it must...be translated into a form that can be stored, transported and reproduced; it too must, in other words, become writing.²

However strange the idea of writing with sound, I think most people do have some memory of a primitive voice mail experience, probably that now charmingly anachronistic use of the post to send friends recorded 'letters' (acoustic epistles) on audiocassette tape, or, depending upon your age, on records recorded in booths specially outfitted for that purpose. I describe these as primitive, of course, only because of the dramatic discrepancy between the speed and quality of the recording and the much slower rate of their subsequent transmission, a frustrating inequality that may well be one of the reasons for their ultimate failure.³ Nevertheless, it is just this sort of rather literal voice mail or acoustic sendings that concern me here, that is, voice mail understood as the inscription, storage and retrieval of acoustic traces on material media physically sent to a destination. For this sort of seemingly retrograde voice transmission may well explain a lot about the more sophisticated voice mail systems that so many of us increasingly revel in, resist and/or resent. What follows, then, is a provisional archaeology of this sort of voice mail, a history that culminates with the beep of that currently most widespread type of voice mail technology: the answering machine.

The answering machine itself, however, is hardly as 'completely modern' as most people assume. Indeed, this now so widespread domestic technology was in fact invented in 1898 by the Danish physicist and engineer Valdemar Poulsen (1869–1942), pioneer of wireless or radio telegraphy and the man who broke the Marconi monopoly in the British Empire. Poulsen first presented his device to the public at the Paris Exhibition in 1900, officially divulging the details of his discovery in the 22 September 1900 issue of *Scientific American*,⁴ the same year Freud published *The Interpretation of Dreams*. And yet this late nineteenth century contraption—known variously as the 'recording telephone' the telegraphone, the telegraphophone or the telephonograph—did not differ in any fundamental technical way from our contemporary answering machines. Patented in 1899 as a means of 'storing up speech or signals by magnetic influence', the telegraphone employed a steel wire or band (and soon thereafter a steel disc) instead of the now ubiquitous magnetic tape, recording acoustic information in the form of electro-magnetic impulses and allowing for the indefinite storage or subsequent obliteration of these inscriptions on a medium whose inscribability was in no way compromised by being erased. In fact, the quality of the recordings were lauded by contemporary science writers as being significantly better than those of the phonograph. Even the employment of this device was from the start hardly different from that of today. But why, if the answering machine was effectively invented in the nineteenth century, did it take so long to get developed? Why, for example, did it take thirty years before an article in the *New York Times* of 27 June 1931 announced the impending marketing of the first telegraphone in the US with the headline 'Phone Messages to be Recorded'?

Of crucial concern here is the fact that the invention of the answering machine marks an important shift in the voice mail paradigm, belonging to a technological episteme in which the voice itself travels *per* telephone and activates a remote inscription device. Here, in other words, the sending, the epistellein of the epistle, the materiality of the transmission, appears to have been dramatically transformed, having become as rapid as the act of recording. Despite this seeming instantaneity, however, I would suggest that it is a mistake to succumb to the temptation of considering telephonic or digital voice mail as no longer material, since—as anybody who has had a 'bad' telephone connection knows—the media of such inscriptions must still be understood as having a materiality, albeit one whose phenomenality is of a very different order, i.e. is no longer tangible. In other words, the missives of telephonic and digital voice mail still get lost, misdirected, damaged, delayed, etc., just as did their more primitive predecessors. What the newer forms allow one to overlook, however, is the very fact of that materiality and the practice of inscription which is their condition of possibility. The ur-history of that materiality, of the longstanding dream of voice mail, will hopefully make clear that the history of voice mail cannot be understood apart from the history of the attempts to capture the acoustic, to render sound as writing, the history of the *graphe* or *gramme* of *phone*, which is to say, the history of the phonograph and gramophone.

The vision of voice mail is a motif that dates back not three decades, as one might expect, but almost three centuries.[5] According to some accounts, this rather long history of voice mail begins in China during the reign of K'ang-hsi in the seventeenth century. A device, invented by Chiang Shun-hsin of Hui-chou, which became known as the 'thousand-mile speaker' allowed a sender to speak into a wooden cylinder which was then sealed and sent sometimes thousands of miles. On arrival, the recipient broke open the seal and the voice message re-sounded. Basically, the idea here is that since sound is a spatial phenomenon (a vibrating mass of air), if you could capture that vibrating air mass in some sort of container, you could liberate it from its tie to the body, to presence. A similar image of sound conserved in tubes recurs on a number of occasions, such as the seemingly well-known speaking-tube described in the Greek scholar Giovanni Battista Porta's *Magia Naturalis* of 1589. The primitive model of physical conservation here is given a subtle (and literal) twist by J. J. Becher's 1682 description of the stentrophonium which this adviser to Prince Ruprecht of Pfalz is reported to have discovered in the workshop of a Nuremberg optician and mechanical artisan named F. Grundel. This machine, so Becher claims, was capable of 'catching many words as an echo by means of a spiral line within a bottle in such a way that one could carry it for almost an hour over land' and then, upon opening, the words would sound anew. Even Becher describes the idea as fantastic, but notes that one ought not fail to attempt to make it a reality (note here the invocation of another important proto-gramophonic form: the spiral).

Or take the following example from 1632. In the Bibliotheque Nationale there is a thin little book with the title 'Le Courrier Veritable' (the true mail!): no author, no publisher but just a note indicating the date of publication to be 23 April 1632. In this mysterious document the anonymous author—someone researching Australia—tells the story of a land of people with bluish-black skin which has no art and no science nor any written exchange. Nature has, however, given them a marvellous alternative means of communication, providing them with sponges that soak up all sounds and human language as well. People simply speak into the sponges and then send them to the person for whom the message is destined; they in turn lightly press on the sponge in order to hear the words they contain.

The sponge-model of voice mail assumes that the materiality of the acoustic is somehow liquid: sound is something that can be soaked up. A similar liquidity of sound informs another proto-voice mail fantasy: storage by means of freezing and reproduction by subsequent thawing. Perhaps the most famous version of this rather widespread sixteenth century folkloric topos, besides the one by Munchhausen, is the rather amusing episode in Rabelais' *Gargantua and*

Pantagruel, Chapter LVI, Book IV, in which a battle takes place during a winter so cold that the sounds of battle freeze and fall to the ground, only to thaw in the spring:

> [Pantagruel] threw on the deck before us whole handfuls of frozen words, which looked like crystallised sweets of different colours. We saw some words gules, or gay quips, some vert, some azure, some sable and some or. When we warmed them a little between our hands, they melted like snow, and we actually heard them, though we did not understand them, for they were in a barbarous language. There was one exception, however, a fairly big one. This, when Friar John picked it up, made a noise like a chestnut that has been thrown on the embers without being pricked. It was an explosion, and made us all start with fear. 'That', said Friar John, 'was a cannon shot in its day'.[6]

Even more amazing is the Moon book described by Cyrano de Bergerac in 1656 in his *Histoire comique des états et empires de la lune*. Recounting his arrival on the moon, Cyrano tells of being given two strange books which one did not read but, instead, listened to. Each contained a complex of watch-like gears and the pages had no letters. One read them 'with one's ears', he explains.[7] In order to grasp the contents one simply placed a needle on the desired chapter and—as if spoken by a human voice—one would hear it, loud and clear, albeit in the lunar language, of course.

The crucial step that moved voice mail from the domain of fiction to that of experiment was made, surprisingly enough, in the context of German Romantic physics, still abuzz with the aphorist and researcher Georg Christoph Lichtenberg's 1777 findings that tiny metal particles formed distinct figures on positively or negatively charged fields: here the mysterious phenomenon of electricity had finally become palpable, that is, electrical force had been translated into a visible, i.e. readable medium![8] An even more dramatic breakthrough of a very similar sort was the discovery in 1787 by Ernst Florens Friedrich Chladni—now considered the father of acoustics—of the visual patterns produced by acoustic waves. Chladni's experiment consisted in spreading quartz dust on glass plates that were then made to vibrate. Depending on the rate of the vibration, the sand distributed itself into lines, curves and hyperbolas, gathering in those areas that were free of movement. Here, for the first time, one could associate acoustic phenomena with specific graphic figures which, most importantly, were 'drawn' by the sounds themselves! These 'tone figures', as Chladni explained in *Die Akustik* (1802), were not arbitrary but rather in some sort of a 'necessary'—indexical—relation to the sounds. In the graphic traces of these 'script-like ur-images of sound' one could see, what another German physicist, Johann Wilhelm Ritter, called 'the notation of that tone which it has written by itself'.

Barely a generation later, there begin a series of attempts to translate this idea of sound writing itself into a practical technology. Consider, for example, the apparatus that measures the vibrations of sounding bodies described by Thomas Young in his 1807 Course of lectures on natural philosophy and mechanical arts: here Young takes a tuning fork made to sound by bowing, and affixes to it a pen that draws the wave form corresponding to the pitch on a rotating cylinder. The same basic translation of sound into graphic traces also informs the appropriately named 'phonautograph' invented by the typographer Leon Scott of Martinville in 1858. In the mid 1850s Scott replaced the tuning fork with a sensitive membrane and a horn, rendering his device capable of capturing the acoustic waves in the air produced by various types of sound and translating them into wiggly lines inscribed on a charcoal-blackened paper mounted on a turning cylinder. Crucial here is to note that this apparatus was—true to its name—only an autograph, a self-writing as traces of sound. This is, of course, only the realisation of the first part of the tube voice mail fantasy: the capturing of the sounds as potentially transportable and then potentially readable inscription.

With the invention of photography the realisation of the essential second stage of voice mail—the restoration or retranslation of these traces back into sound—begin to proliferate. Typical in this regard was how Nadar himself in 1856 came up with the idea of a *daguerreotype acoustique* which would faithfully record and reproduce sounds with a fidelity comparable to that of the photograph. In 1864 he again mused:

One of these days it will come to pass that someone will present us with the daguerreotype of sound—the phonograph—something like a box within which melodies would be fixed and retained, the way the camera surprises and fixes images. To such an effect that a family, I imagine, finding itself prevented from attending the opening of a Force del destino or an Afrique, or whatever, would only have to delegate one of its members, armed with the phonograph in question, to go there. And upon his return: 'How was the overture?' 'Like this!' 'Too fast?' 'There!' 'And the quintet?' 'Don't you think the tenor screeches a bit?'[9]

It was not Nadar, however, but another Frenchman, Charles Cros, a brilliant French poet, artist, and scientist (author of the first two-colour photographic process), who took Scott's idea and pushed it one step further, proposing in a dossier deposited at the Paris Academy of Sciences on 30 April 1877 that one replace the charcoal paper with a wax cylinder onto which a needle would engrave the traces transmitted to it by the sensitive membrane. This is a major step, for by incising these waves, they could subsequently be retraced by another needle—or another stylus— which could translate them back into an acoustic event. Here was the principle for a machine— the paleophone—that accomplished both inscription and subsequent reproduction. The only problem was that the poor poet Cros—a friend of Verlaine's, and favorite son of the Surrealists— was just that: poor. He thus did not have the money to actually build his device, which he christened the Parliophone. Then, to Cros' dismay, the 17 November 1877 issue of *Scientific American* announced that work was being done in Menlo Park on the bold and original idea of recording the human voice upon a strip of paper, from which at any subsequent time, it might automatically be redelivered with all the vocal characteristics of the original speaker accurately reproduced. Fearing—and rightly so—that he would not be credited as having been the first to propose such a device, Cros demanded that his dossier be opened and read at the Academy, which it finally was on 5 December 1877. Two weeks later Edison, who had been able to actually build a working model of his phonograph, applied for a patent.

What is crucial here is to consider for a moment the consequences already anticipated by Scott's 'phonautograph' which was an attempt to produce, as the machine's subtitle explained, an 'Apparatus for the Self-Registering of the Vibrations of Sound'. The resulting 'natural stenography' would, in turn, be sound writing itself.[10] Similarly, during the first half of the nineteenth century, phonography—understood as 'a system of phonetic shorthand invented by Isaac Pitman in 1837' (OED)—was heralded as a 'natural method of writing' and was arduously defended by worker's groups as a means of making writing more widely accessible.[11] But in what sense could the gramophone function as a 'natural stenography', as a type of 'phonography' in the Pitmanian sense?

To answer this question it is crucial to recall that one of the most popular—but forgotten—uses of the early phonographs was to record one's own voice. Through the use of the gramophone, illiteracy would be eliminated by substituting listening and speaking for reading and writing—for the first generation of gramophones could both play and record. They not only played pre-recorded music, but could also be 'erased' and re-inscribed with new music or a spoken message. The most widespread commercialisation of this capability, of course, occurred in dictating machines, such as Dr. Seward's phonograph diary in Bram Stoker's *Dracula*, and in gramophones customised for learning languages. The use of gramophones as domestic music machines was only a much later development. During both the initial and the later phases however, there were also attempts to market the new read/write talking machines (as they were called) for other purposes, among them postal correspondence. Despite the fact that the phonograph would eventually become almost exclusively a playback technology for musical entertainment, Edison himself had conceived the device first and foremost as a tool for business correspondence:

> The main utility of the phonograph, [is] for the purpose of letter writing and other forms of dictation, the design is made with a view to its utility for that purpose.[12]

Edison envisioned that 'phonogram' sheets containing as much as four thousand words each would eventually become the primary epistolary form. What we have here is nothing less than the first, literal, voice mail, the birth of what elsewhere would come to be known as the phonopostal.

The 'phono-post' speaking postcards which one could record and send through the mail has made writing superfluous, a fact stressed by advertisements which invited potential users to drop their dictionaries and 'Speak! Don't write any more! Listen!' The ambivalent political consequences of what is effectively a vision of instantaneous universal literacy—similar in this regard to the esperantist discourse surrounding the advent of cinema—are quite dramatic. Advertisements frequently staged the figure of the young woman or girl juxtaposed with the dictionary-toting, bespectacled old man, clearly casting her as the figure of the paradigmatically disenfranchised—that class of illiterates or semi-literates excluded from the privilege of correspondence by their inability to read and write. Indeed, women do become the primary users of the new dictation technology, marking, as Friedrich Kittler has pointed out, a dramatic shift in the gender of the previously male scribe class, with the proviso that, while women now do largely dominate the material production of writing, it is most often the writing of a male voice. Female secretaries take dictation, translating voice into writing, phone into graphemes. Thus it is hardly surprising that woman not only becomes identified with the phonographic correspondence, but actually becomes the figure for the phonographic technology itself, as in the logo of the Phonographische Zeitschrift, where the device that translates the acoustic into writing is nothing other than a woman's body.

Unlike the cylinder phonographs used for dictation machines, the phono-post apparatuses were often disc machines, a flat medium—based on the gramophone model developed by Emil Berliner in Washington in 1887—preferable less because of its resemblance to traditional writing surfaces than for the ease with which it could be mailed. The apparatuses marketed especially for this purpose included the Phonopostal, a small, rather low quality machine, and Pathi's Pathipost machine introduced in 1908 and sold in limited quantities through WWI after which its name was changed to Pathigraph. The phono-post, effectively the first not merely fantasmatic but actually functional voice mail, unfortunately had problems: the inferior quality of the phonographs produced recordings that were difficult to understand (to which it must be added that few people knew the proper way to speak into the horn in order to get the maximum clarity); and the recording medium itself was quite fragile.

The subsequent history of phono-post is short-lived, voice mail having to wait for the advent of the next popularly available read/write technology: the tape deck. In the meantime, a commercialised variant of phono-post appeared; the largely gimmick-oriented fad in the late 1940s and 1950s for gramophonic postcards—images that one could play on a phonograph. These curious artifacts—fascinating in that the two systems of their doubly inscribed surfaces (photographic and gramophonic) in no way interfere with each other despite the exponential increase in the density of information—are not acoustic epistles in the same sense, for here sound (and image) are pre-fabricated, leaving only the traditional obverse space of the postcard for a penned missive. However, as a transportable materialisation of sound they are nevertheless part of the tradition of postally transmitted acoustic inscriptions.

The late 1950s saw the birth of yet another type of sendable acoustic data—the first acoustic news magazine: *Sonorama*. This complex artifact, comprised of image, text and 33rpm discs to be 'read with the ear', effectively adds, so we read in the premier issue of October 1958, a new sensory dimension to print media, giving radio news a memory trace; a duration that exceeds its transmission. Spiral bound and punctured in the middle with a hole, one turns the pages of this journal, reading articles and then placing the entire object on the gramophone, in order to listen to the acoustic documents, music and interviews that make up the other 'pages'. Made possible by the development of high quality record pressing on very thin vinyl (flexidisks), the multimedia journal *Sonorama*, which continued well into the 1960s, never provoked the dramatic revolution in the history of the press that its founders anticipated. In its juxtaposition of text, image and sound, in its insistence on the status of sound as text, it did, however, make an important point about the condition of possibility of the material storage, transmission and reproduction of sound, namely that it too is, in an important sense, writing. The proximity of the photographic, textual and gramophonic traces in *Sonorama* only served to foreground their semiotic heterogeneity. Unlike the photographs and articles which usually can be read by means of our 'built in' apparatus (along with the necessary technological supplements such as glasses, etc.), the acoustic 'texts' usually did require an external interface in order to be read (indeed one that— through its spinning—momentarily rendered the others unreadable). Even the latter condition seems only contingent, if one is to take seriously the case of Tim Wilson, a 33 year old Englishman who made the rounds of British and American talkshows in 1985 demonstrating his particular ability to 'read' unlabeled records simply by looking at them, ostensibly reading the patterns of the grooves with his eyes! Alas, this rather hilarious confirmation of Moholy-Nagy's vision of a gramophonic 'groove-script' remains unavailable to most people for whom the phonograph 'pages' remain undecipherable without the required technical prosthesis. Although recognisable as inscriptions in their concentric spiral form, it is these very traces that are being obliterated and/or reconfigured in the pop-cultural practice of scratch.

AFTER THE BEEP

What then can one learn in the school of scratch? Many things, surely, but among them, a lesson about the historicity of the inscriptional status of sound, a point also explored by contemporary work on the gramophone by artists such as Stuart Sherman or Maurizio Kagel. For with the elimination of the literal grooviness of sound, acoustic writing has entered a new episteme, a new paradigm called the digital. Today sound, image and text are all 'written' in the same digital language, a language whose 'fidelity' and 'longevity' depends—as voice mail always has—on the particular qualities of its mode of inscription. What we see here in this field of pure difference—which is to say the condition of writing as such—is also, of course, sound as writing, but it is an inscription of a significantly different sort. No longer an indexical trace, this digital code has abandoned the order of the analogue which characterised both the photograph and the gramophone, revealing the hidden semiotic solidarity between the two elements of the gramophonic postcards: a now anachronistic indexicality. If both the photo- and the phono-graphs bore some sort of existential semiotic relation to the information they contained—this being their analogic character—digital code is a writing that forsakes that economy entirely, providing us with reliability of transmission by transforming analogy into information, a sampling of the acoustic curve approximately 44,100 times per second which is then translated into 14, 16 or 18 digit strings of zeroes and ones. It is this that allows us, with contemporary voice mail systems, to not only record, revise and/or erase a message remotely, but also to literally send it elsewhere and to multiple addresses.

This is not the place to explore in detail the semiotic specificity of digital sound. Rather, the more modest goal of this meditation has been to establish that for sound to travel—across distance and time—it must first be translated into something else that is the condition of possibility of that transmission. Indeed, as the voice and sound in general becomes increasingly transmitted, as phonetic inscription seems to displace the practice of writing, the history of phono-post reminds us—as does the auratic indexicality in contemporary hip-hop culture's practice of scratching—that, before the voice can be mailed, it must first be written. Voice mail, in other words, reveals speaking as inscription, as translation, as writing.

1. Siegfried Giedion, *Mechanization Takes Command*, New York: W.W. Norton, 1948, p. 3.
2. Frank J. Derfler, Jr., 'Voice E-Mail: Building Workgroup Solutions', in *PC Magazine*, July 1990, p. 13.
3. To get a sense of just what sort of memory demands we are talking about here, it might be helpful to point out that while the file size of a spoken text depends both on the sampling rate of the AD (analogue to digital) converter and the speech rate of the person speaking, for email it is circa 100k/minute; the higher the sound quality, the more memory it takes.
4. 'Poulsen's Telegraphone', in *Scientific American*, 22 September 1900, p. 178.
5. On the pre-history of the gramophone, see Eugéne H. Weiss, *Phonographes et Musique mécanique*, Paris: Hachette, 1930, and W. Weiss-Strauffacher, *Mechanische Musikinstrumente und Musikautomaten*, Zurich: Orel Füssli Verlag, 1975.
6. François Rabelais, *The Histories of Gargantua and Pantagruel*, trans. J. M. Cohen, Harmondsworth: Penguin, 1955, p. 569.
7. Cyrano de Bergerac, *Voyages to the Moon and the Sun*, trans. R. Aldington, New York: The Orion Press, 1962, p. 136.
8. On the details of Lichtenberg's discovery see Walter D. Wetzels and Johann W. Ritter, *Physik im Wirkungsfeld der deutschen Romantik*, Berlin/New York: Walter de Gruyter, 1973, p. 88ff.
9. F. Nadar, *Les Mémoires du géant*, Paris: 1964, p. 1, cited in Jacques Perriault, *Mémoires de l'ombre et du son: une archéologie de l'audio-visuel*, Paris: Flammarion, 1981, pp. 133–34.
10. Edouard-Leon Scott de Martinville, *Le Probleme de la parole s'ecrivant elle-meme*, Paris: La France, l'Amerique (chez l'aute), 1878. In 1849 Scott had published a study of stenography entitled *Histoire de la Stenographie depuis les temps anciens jusqu'a nos jours*.
11. See the Pitman's 1840 Treatise *Phonography* or *Writing by Sound; Being a Natural Method of Writing, Applicable to All Languages, and a Complete System of Shorthand*, London: S. Bagster and Sons.
12. Thomas A. Edison, 'The Phonograph and Its Future', in *North American Review*, June 1878.

Essays In Sound

JOAN BRASSIL

Randomly Now and Then Campbelltown City Art Gallery, 1991, and *Sound in Space*, Museum of Contemporary Art, Sydney, 1995

Eight diorite cores randomly resonated throughout the installation by the use of transducers vibrating the rocks, each to its own resonant frequency. 'Listen to the sound of a million years singing'.

photo: John Baird

SHERRE DeLYS and JOAN GROUNDS

Ceci n'est pas une pipe *Sound In Space*, Museum of Contemporary Art, and the Royal Botanic Gardens, Sydney, 1995

'**Ceci n'est pas une pipe** by Sherre DeLys and Joan Grounds…is a wonderful metamorphosis of René Magritte's not-pipe into Leonara Carrington's hearing trumpet, mapped onto sound and mythology. If it wasn't for Grounds' objects, you might think it was similar to those attempts to make zoos more lifelike—humane is it?—by adding environmental sounds. But the birds you hear in this cultured nature are at least twice cultured: not only are they recorded and not-*live*, they are all imitations made by humans (does this preclude humans imitating birds mimicking other birds?). In other words, these not-birds have larynxes not syrinxes. Even the virtuoso gum leaf player from Malaysia imitating a turtle dove has simply found a prosthetic larynx, much like Leonardo's laryngeal flute, among the birds in the trees. […in the work…] the relations of seduction and destruction, the losses pertaining to simulation and the species connectedness practiced through mimicry, among natures and cultures and territories…become vertiginously provocative.'
—Douglas Kahn, in *Real Time* 8, August–September 1995, p. 13.

photo (studio): Joan Grounds

Essays In Sound

NIGEL HELYER

Oracle *Sound in Space*, Museum of Contemporary Art, Sydney, 1995

Oracle inhabits the nexus between the body and architectural space by proposing the voice as the carrier of both prophesy and of ideological imperative. In this fusion of *corpus* and *polis* the sound field simultaneously operates as actuality, as virtuality and as metaphor—Architecture unfrozen!

photo: Heidrun Löhr

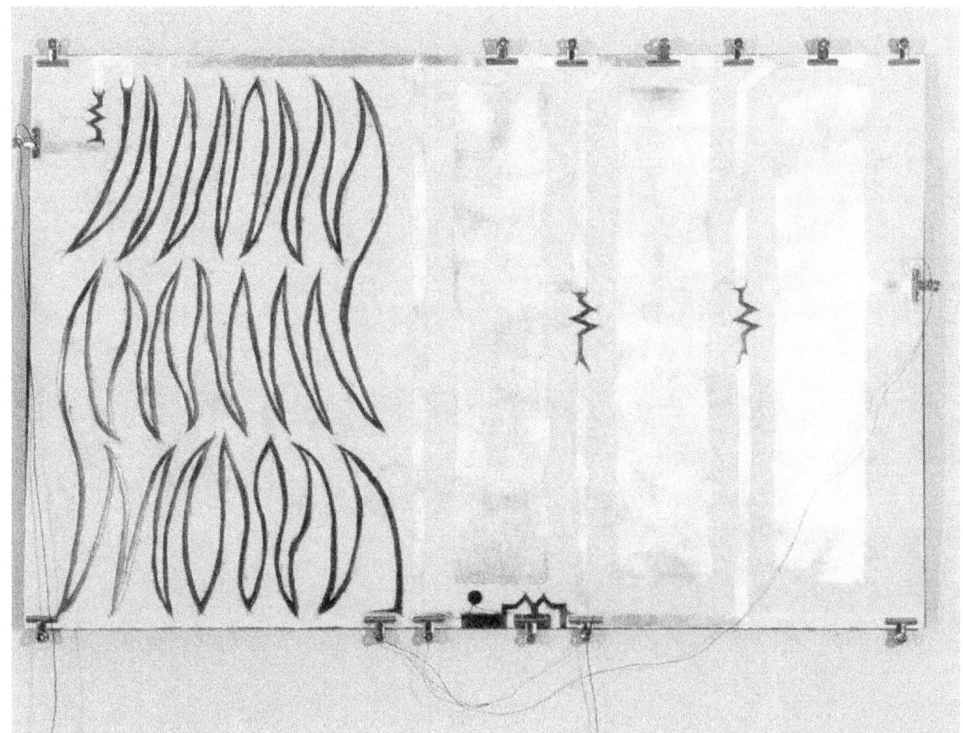

JOYCE HINTERDING

The Oscillators (detail) *Sound in Space*, Museum of Contemporary Art, Sydney, 1995

Comprised of conventional art materials—pencil (graphite), paper, and silver leaf—these drawings are functioning interpretations of the circuit diagram of the electronic device: the phase shift oscillator. Electricity generated by the solar panel is fed directly into the drawing. Each component of the drawing, the pencil marks, silver and paper are used to conduct, impede and collect electricity. The need for regular electronic componentry has been reduced to one transistor and a small piezo speaker on each drawing. The sound produced by this circuit is generated by controlled electrical feedback, and the frequency and sound quality are determined by the size and unique characteristics of the drawn components.

photo: Ian Hobbs

Essays In Sound

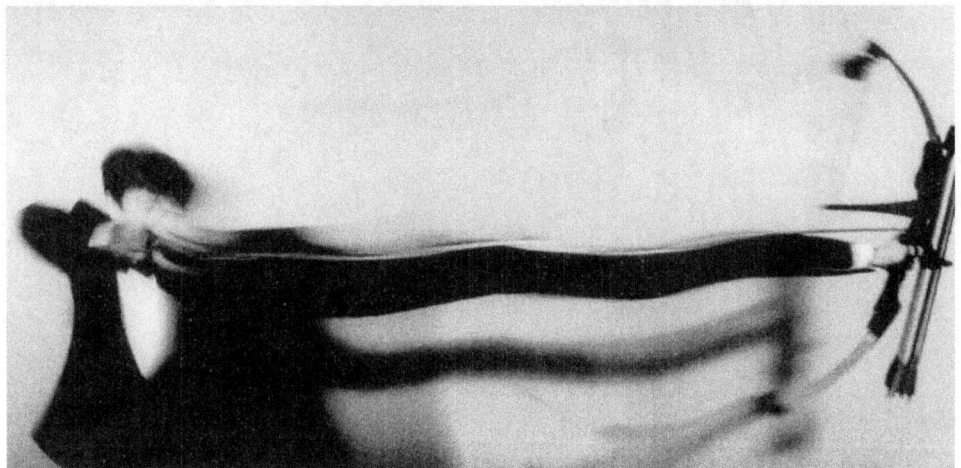

HERB JERCHER

Stealth Cycle (performance) 'Earwitness', *Experimenta '94**, The Gasworks, Melbourne, 1994

Matching sensory mechanisms allow artificial and natural rhythms of vibration to evolve super-sense-sound-sharing deception strategies.

Constructing a performance with sound sculptures is akin to stealth dancing with acoustic instruments that choreograph one's sonic physique. The ear becomes the primary sensory perceptive mechanism for movement, whilst the eye supports perceptions of time. It is an exercise of releasing energy in silence whilst coping with survival rituals and sound deceptions. Aural fascinations occur during balance phases in transition. The reality of consciousness dominates, terminating an otherwise effortless song of silent authorship. Yet, to believe that the 'fauna caller' would ever have been able to endure without performing, forsakes the quarry's call, inverts the action and renders the participants to a vicarious curfew.
—Herb Jercher, *Experimenta '94* catalogue, p. 45.

photo: Ross Bird

* *Experimenta* is a biennial survey of Australian and international experimental film, video, electronic, and sound art presented by the Modern Image Makers Association.

DEREK KRECKLER

How to Discipline a Tree/boo! 'Earwitness', *Experimenta '94*, the Australian Centre for Contemporary Art, Melbourne, 1994

An installation of compressed newspapers in the form of a buttress root. An audio speaker is attached to a wall near the installation; every 90 seconds the word 'boo!' is heard.

Essays In Sound

IAIN MOTT, MARC RASZWESKI and TIM BARRASS

Iain Mott concept and composition, Marc Raszweski design and sculpture, Tim Barrass animation
Squeezebox (sound sculpture) 'Earwitness', *Experimenta '94*, ether ohnetitel, Melbourne, 1994

Squeezebox is a public interactive artwork. Participants push down on pneumatic hands to alter the timbre and spatial location of sound above the sculpture, in addition to shaping a centrally located graphic image. Sound and image are presented as an integrated plastic object, a form to be squeezed and moulded by participants.

photo: Ross Bird

ION PEARCE

mobile-without-mobility *Sound in Space*, Museum of Contemporary Art, Sydney, 1995

In **mobile-without-mobility** the pursuit of classical forms represented by the piano keyboard and the family ensemble (in the photograph) is troped by the truncation of the keyboard and its juxtaposition with a railway crossing bell. In this still and therefore repetitious composition the reasons for movement have been forgotten and what remains is the primal rite of the playing gesture only, now devoid of signification.

photo: Heidrun Löhr

Essays In Sound

JODI ROSE

Song to Dissolve the World *Sound in Space* audiothéque (selection of tape-based sound art), Museum of Contemporary Art, Sydney, 1995

An investigation of the sonic properties of the city, as the decoding of an alternative language; one other than the purely pragmatic and visual experience of architecture. The city has become our temple; electronic networks our religion; the inaudible vibrations of the bridge cables are the voice of the divine. The word of the universe soaks through my cochlea into the nerve centres. I am wired to god.

photo: Jodi Rose

ANNA SABIEL

Internalised Cities *Sound in Space* (performance programme), Artspace, Sydney, 1995

Internalised Cities is a performance piece incorporating a dynamic installation. Within this installation, time based media such as video, and amplification techniques are utilised to explore the concept of the internalised city: of physical memory, gesture and the human condition. The project is a collaboration between performance/sound artists Anna Sabiel and installation/multimedia artist Sarah Waterson. Sound engineer/ acoustician Shane Fahey is also involved in developing amplification techniques and measuring appropriate resonances of the installation.

photo: Heidrun Löhr

JULAINE STEPHENSON

Dust The Performance Space, Sydney, 1995

Dust toys with the concepts surrounding mainstream sound producers' preoccupation with 'clean sound' juxtaposed with the redundancy of domestic analogue technology. The cracks in the gallery floorboards become the 'groove' of the record, played by a sharpened fork prong stylus and gramophone soundbox, acoustically amplifying the dust in the 'grooves'. A reverse dust bug is dusting, spreading vacuum cleaner dirt over the record/floor.

photo: Julaine Stephenson

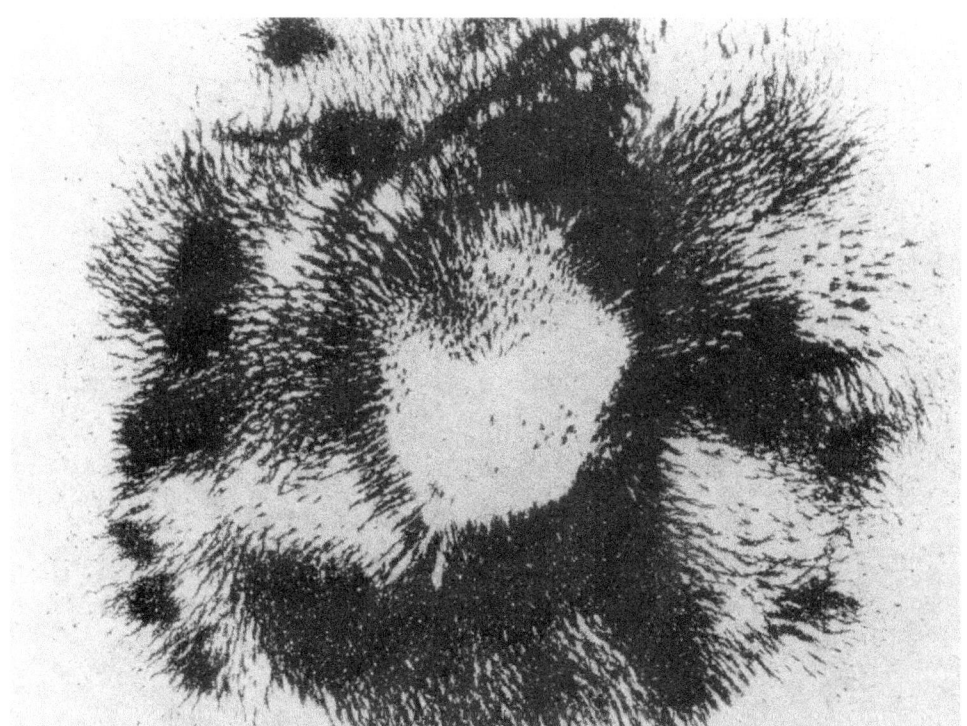

DEBORAH VAUGHAN

Dora's Feet *Sound in Space*, Museum of Contemporary Art, Sydney, 1995

'Psychoanalysis is said to be "speaking on the field of the other" which linked in my mind to magnetic fields and the polarities of self and other. Clearing my throat? Spit disturbing the centredness that makes for things to exist.'

Examining vocalisation and inscription as ways of determining and separating self and the vibratory field of self and other are recurring themes in Deborah Vaughan's work. Present also is the performative quality as she records the repetition of her body involved in certain activities.

photo: Deborah Vaughan

Please, Please—Identify Me!
Yuji Sone: Works, Texts and Commentaries

Colin Hood

> Thus we grasp everything—we cling to everything—we are anxious about time, place, people, things, all that is and will be; we are ourselves but the least part of ourselves. We spread ourselves, so to speak, over the whole world, and all this vast expanse becomes sensitive.
>
> —Jean-Jacques Rousseau, *Emile*

We sat together in the large auditorium watching the words flash by on the electronic billboard. There was nothing particularly modern about the experience at all. I felt—for a moment—like a Florentine choir boy pressed into a collective reading of the psaltery. My voice, frozen into one of Della Robbia's low reliefs, soon melted into the audible appreciation of the scripted humour.

> Now for this part I was going to use phrases from Beckett's *Waiting For Godot*. However I did not ask the publisher's permission. Therefore, I cannot use them. What I would like to do now is ask you to imagine a scene in Act 2 of *Waiting for Godot* and put the image onto what you are seeing now. Those who don't know the book, ask a person next to you, or please refer to the book later in order to complete this part of my performance.

Switching one's gaze across the small platform, a man's body appeared lying prostrate before a fuzzy TV set, openly mimicking—or so it appeared to this member of the audience—the actions of Vito Acconci's heard but not seen masturbatory antics from a 1972 performance *Seedbed* in New York's Sonnabend Gallery. A voice—which seemed to issue from the TV set—wound up the techno-body collage/performance to a climax of pop song titles with erotic/romantic nuances.

> Imagine the Rolling Stones' *I Can't Get No Satisfaction*...Imagine the Beach Boys' *Good Vibrations*... Imagine Carol King's *You've Got a Friend*...Chicago's *If You Leave Me Now*...The Doobie Brothers' *Minute by Minute*...Madonna's...*Justify My Love*...

Yuji Sone's *Nonetheless Marinetti* was first performed at the Third International Symposium of Electronic Art (TISEA) in November 1992, and again for Melbourne's *Experimenta* performance program. It belongs to a series of intertextual, 'intercultural' performance works developed over the seven years of his Australian residency.

> The emphasis in my work is on defamiliarising an audience in a performative situation, not to create a seamless hybrid or a fixed perspective. Thus my focus is on 'simultaneity' and to make the topos of heterogeneity visible in order to reveal the problem of frozen knowledge, the categories of art, culture and the body.

Yet there was more to impress in the piece than the simple disjunction between textual devices, mechanical voice and appropriated modernist transgression. For Sone played out the *faux-naiveté* of an immigrant struggling with the language, a bizarre ritual of auto-didacticism shading into a comically aggressive scene of linguistic and cultural pedagogy.

In an earlier work, *Nonetheless Duchamp*, Sone works the frustration of learning a second language into the performance context. For Sone, the commodity art stratagem of Duchamp (which is ultimately sublated as acceptable fine art within the dialectic of avant-gardes) becomes analogous to an opaque (but ultimately effective) teaching strategy. For perhaps the audience/class is as dumbstruck by the foreign sounds as an art lover may be by a bottlerack or a urinal.

> As an application of Duchamp's readymade, I taught Japanese with a language teaching method called 'Direct Method', in which only the target language is spoken by the teacher.

In a number of Sone's works, performance, as the activity of 'true visual communication',[1] is substituted by an impure vocabulary of the rebus, installing delay, static and repetition in the space of 'uncontaminated' communicative exchange.

> In relation to [their] textual materiality, a division between 'reading' and 'seeing' becomes ambiguous. The very act of both 'reading' and 'seeing' is a structured procedure in which one of the many levels inherent in textuality is thematically focused while others remain as undifferentiated background.

Sone's references to masturbation and communicative (in)competence produce what Thierry de Duve has described as a mode of aesthetic questioning, the insistence on 'the enunciation of a contract' rather the 'proper' consumption of communicative or artistic praxis.[2] This splitting of the artistic ego born under the sign of painting, performance and the inspirational 'other' of modernist orientalism is also enhanced by Sone's utilisation of discourses on the technological and ethnographic hybrid.

Sone undertook his early theatrical training with Shuji Terayama's Tenjosajiki Theatre Laboratory followed by two years of full-time performance with the Banyu-Inroku Theatre Company. Sone describes the work and rehearsal schedules as gruelling, requiring typical Japanese dedication and discipline. Departing from family-approved career paths, many of these budding avant-garde performers supported themselves with fish market and sex industry occupations.

> My very first performance in Australia was in 1987. I wore a white kimono, and a white wig, and used lots of candles. The reason for the use of typical traditional Japanese imagery was that I had never used this material when I was in Japan. I was in an experimental theatre company which used mostly western imagery as opposed to Butoh or traditional Japanese theatre. When I left Japan, I wanted to explore different areas unavailable to me in the Japanese experimental context. Butoh imagery was one of them.

Scratch the surface of Butoh and you'll find a complex historical, cultural and generic patchwork. A 1968 film of Tatsumi Hijikata's *Revolt of the Flesh* clearly reveals the citational origins of this style of dance/performance. Within the frenzied mix of fur, sun-shade, G-string and The Beatles' *Oh Darling, Please Believe Me*, Hijikata played out of role of midwife to a later Butoh style rooted in history and a Japanese culture of the earth.[3]

The naturalisation of Butoh (the masking of the heterogeneity of its origins) illuminates other aspects of Japanese cultural identity. The incorporation and parodic assimilation of other cultures and languages (where even the thoughts of a cartoon rabbit or infant are expressed in a foreign alphabet) threatens the idea of a culture being defined by its 'natural' language. According to the music critic Shuhei Hosokawa, those import cultures parodied in the *Ur*-Butoh of the late sixties and on the streets of Japan's alphabet cities, are ultimately constrained through the gestural micro-politics of Shinto and a re-affirmation of the 'superiority' of the spoken Japanese language.[4]

The export culture of 'traditional' Butoh performance becomes an early target of Sone's work. Set against this simulacrum of traditionalism and a western desire for the physicality of Butoh movement (as well as Tadashi Suzuki's stomping method), Sone's performances have developed as a kind of 'inverse Butohism', moving from the Butoh parodies and guerilla pieces of the late eighties into fractured and sonorous appropriations of cultures, languages and image repertoires.

> My [early] guerilla performances were meant to be phantasms of a modernist avant-garde—appropriated and fetishised versions.

The word 'phantasm' also evokes the fictional circuitry of cultural dialogue as opposed to the originary seduction (mutual or aggressive) of western cultural imperialism. The effect—in his later work—is one of an unstable inscription of cultural or media identity, a space of enunciation where art history, orientalism, the Beckett of *Krapp's Last Tape*, the work and writings of Duchamp and Trinh T. Min-ha (to name just a few of his 'referees') are all left suspended in live quotations and footnoted program notes (the textual supplement to all of Sone's later performances).

For Sone, the rupture between semantic space and physical space, the encounter between one language user and an 'other' has to be maintained (at the performative level) as a dynamic and heterogeneous event. Sone remains wary of the 'symbolic topography' of the contact event, the performative model of exchange which Paul Carter (in *Living in a New Country*) counterposes to the levelling discourse of a theatricalising historiography.

> The problem I have with his [Carter's] argument is his emphasis of the poetic structure of a contact event. For whom is it poetic? To identify a contact event with the western notion of the poem may be another trap for taming the Other.

In 'Voice of the Masked Other', Sone performs a theoretical intervention into the debate around alterity and the levelling of linguistic difference through the globalisation of information and media technologies. The work consists of a series of taped voices sourced ambiguously to both a live performer (a mime punctuating the vocal patchwork with scare-quotes and rhetorical emphasis) and a TV screen filled with static.

> As a performed paper, it not only presents my analysis of the Western notion of the Other, it also demonstrates the [linguistic] problematics accompanying them. In other words, it presents the enunciation as an enunciation, not as an enunciated. It juxtaposes an electronically manipulated female voice through a TV monitor with a Japanese body...The performance set-up reveals the gap between preconceived cultural images and gestural vocabulary, dislocating the system of ordinary enunciation.

There are two dominant narratives for understanding and/or subsuming cultural difference. The first analyses morphological similarities in kinship, language and art; the other unites cultural differences (which are also internal to any culture) back to a higher, level of understanding either mythic or transcendental. Drawing on the writing of Naoki Sakai, Sone creates his own performative model of the crisscrossing of 'different' voices, comparing the slippage from 'I' to 'you' (through the arbitrariness of pronomial attachment) to lived scenarios of cultural and linguistic difference.

When Sone performs his 'difficulty' with the English language, sampling the range of linguistic and postcolonial critiques of culture, identity and language, he reveals irregularities both within and between languages and genres.

> I have used the irregularities as 'noises' against the purity of language based on linguistic correctness. The 'performance' of migration between genres, reveals the heterogeneity within established art categories that are, after all, 'languages'.

For Deleuze, the slippages and anomalies within language reveal the collective condition of enunciation, an energetic, transformative process within and without the 'mother tongue'. There is a kind of unnatural and unpredictable coupling between the breast which animates the thought and the sounds—intelligible or otherwise—that emerge. Not a hiccough, or a stuttering—the standard Deleuzian trope of entropic causality—but the burst of laughter caused by a bad joke on speech disorders: 'I meant to say, "Pass the cornflakes honey" but instead I said, "You fucking bitch, you ruined my life!"'. Jokes and their relation to molecular sonority—now there's a topic for future discussion. Sone's performative 'I' detached from expression and returning to the body in brief moments of gestural emphasis (scare quotes, mood indicators and the like), speaks frankly, but the frankness points only to the anonymity of what Brian Massumi describes as a 'transpersonal agency'[5] rather than the true confessions of a male Japanese performance artist working and living in Australia.

> I wonder if the reason why I love my girlfriend, who is a white woman, is because she has white skin, or, simply because she is a white woman...This is not true. I am lying. These are nothing but the statements of a mask. But to say this is already a mask. Then this last statement itself is a mask. Then another mask, then more...

The telos of language will always fall short of that mutual understanding which co-ordinates 'appropriate' social action. Language, like an 'endless high school', conceals the anonymity of what—we thought—she said—he did. The 'marginalised', communalised performance event, the language class, the 'white-anting' at yesterday's staff meeting—they all have in common this 'unsaid doing of a saying'.[6]

> Thus I will remain suspicious of any euphemistic phrases regarding cross-cultural communications...Well I am tired...All of these statements are too schematic...
>
> When you are silent, it speaks
> When you speak, it is silent...

John Cage once claimed that it was the unframed 'noise' of reading which challenged the dominant conventions of sound performance. This is in keeping with Carla Zecha's remark regarding musical composition: 'that in the absence of noise, which is a by-product of notation, the [written] work would cease to exist.'[7]

In Sone's most recent performance, 'This is Sound Art', the noise is composed of gestural, pictorial and textual indicators. Sone, the virtuoso mime artist, plays the smartly dressed conductor, stenographer and unplugged keyboard player. The audience is being asked the question 'What is Sound Art?'. Noise and sound are invited to appear—as if in a séance: the prestidigitator raises his hands; keys are struck; slide images—cartoons, questions, audience cue cards, musical notation of the joys of sex—blend in glissandi of images and in the clicking of the apparatus. Not an invitation—as Cage would have it—to a listening to ambient or environmental noise. No, my attention holds firmly to the question—another thought balloon slowly filling with air. Will it finally burst and make a noise which mouths the words which brings yet another question to mind: 'Who can tell?'?

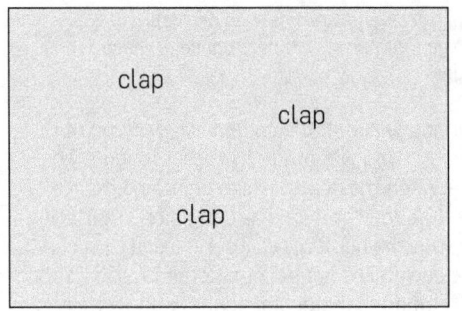

From Yuji Sone, **This is Sound Art** *Sound in Space (*performance programme*)*, Artspace, Sydney, 1995

1. Liberation from the (fine) art work offered 'the possibility of moving toward an art in which the idea would dominate. Performance, like Conceptual art, would enable the artist to shun mere pictorial values in favour of true visual communication: art as a vehicle for ideas and action', Robert Nickas, 'Introduction', in *The Art of Performance: A Critical Anthology*, eds. Gregory Battcock, Robert Nickas, New York: Dutton, 1984, p. xi.
2. Thierry De Duve, *Pictorial Nominalism: on Marcel Duchamp's Passage from Painting to the Readymade*, trans. Dana Polan, Minneapolis: University of Minnesota Press, 1991, p. 98.
3. Mark Holborn, 'Tatsumi Hijikata and the Origins of Butoh', in *Butoh: Dance of the Dark Soul*, New York: Aperture, 1987, p. 8.
4. Shuhei Hosokowa, 'On Tokyo-go: Pidgin Japanese', in *Against Nature: Japanese Art in the Eighties*, New York: Grey Art Gallery, New York University, 1989, pp. 35–38.
5. Brian Massumi, *A User's Guide to Capitalism and Schizophrenia: Deviations from Deleuze and Guattari*, Cambridge, Massachusetts: MIT Press, 1992, p. 33.
6. ibid.
7. Carla Zecher, 'Reading the Noise: Performance and Textuality', in *Criticism: a Quarterly for Literature and the Arts*, 32/2, Spring 1991, pp. 159–173.

Who was that Masked Maus?[1]
Norie Neumark

I thought there was some masquerade occurring with interactives. Something in the very name. How could this experience, which offers only choices set up by the producer, get hailed as interactive? How could this form, which offers only low quality sound, usually subordinate to low quality video, and slick ad-like graphics, masquerade as a new medium? Why would something like *Maus*, an innovative, radical, disturbing graphic (or comix) novel, a pleasure to hold in your hands and read the words and images, come out on one of the proliferating numbers of infotainment CD ROMs? *The Complete Maus* on CD ROM seemed like a good place to start a tracking of voice, sound and interactives.

In the *Maus* novel, woven within a genealogy including ancient Greek and Roman plays, commedia dell'arte and Hollywood animation, Art Spiegelman masks the Jews as mice and the Nazis as cats. The masks in *Maus* serve not to masquerade but to reveal something of their characters and to tell the story of Vladek Spiegelman, a holocaust survivor, and his relationship with his son, Art, the artist/writer. But is it the *true* story, or even history, or is it a story? In the graphic novel, it is a story with Art masked, more or less self-consciously/evidently. It is a story flowing through voice and memory, the recordings of interviews in or through which we see the Art character performing with the Vladek character. But the voice is not the Voice of truth or origin; it's the voice of story telling. What the CD ROM, *The Complete Maus*, offers and invites, however, are quite different configurations of sound and voice and story and history. It masquerades as access to the *real* story, the *real* Art and the *real* Vladek, because now we can see them unmasked and hear them speak their own words.

The CD ROM offers, then, not story or history but a compilation of film, video and aural truth—constructed as Truth, not just via a (limited) documentary tradition but now compounded by the ideology of information. An Archive as database to be accessed. Even Art was seduced by the 'illusion' that it could contain 'zillions of things'. Or so he says.[2] CD ROM, not just as a repository of truth through access to 'originals' (sketches, photos, interviews), but through provision of quantity. CD ROMs offer an ersatz archive, refigured within the 'Mode of Information' where information *per se* is 'privileged' and the '*configuration* of information exchange' is not questioned. With this fetishisation of information, quantity consumes quality[3]—and masquerades as transparency and completeness of meaning. All we can see and hear on the CD ROM is information, organised as infotainment; the complex story/history of the novel turned into empiricist History. We scamper around amongst data, rather than lingering on 'the work'. We have bought 'interaction' as choices in accessing information rather than working through history and reading the work—all of which takes time and contemplation, which are not, after all, experiences encouraged for speed addicted, itchy-fingered users of digital technology.[4] Speed cuts across/cuts out time and space as memory, and replaces it with instantaneity.

Maus' storytelling voices of history and memory, on the other hand, are voices which are locatable, contextual, voices with duration. Voices which have a materiality through their graphicness and occupation of time and space even though they are not sounded. They resound in the quiet despite their 'silence' and are too intense to pin down.[5] *The Complete Maus'* Voices of History and Authority, which are sounded, are in some ways less material and vivid. These extradiegetic authors and movers allow the user limited questions, connections, perceptions, positions, subjectivities, as if they are a full choice. Now that we can hear them, we can know them—or recognize them as ones who know.

The blurb on the back of the CD ROM box promises '2 hours of the original audio interviews between Art and Vladek Spiegelman' and 'Hundreds of sketches and family photos that have never been seen before'. Never seen, *original* audio. It's an invitation, a kindling of a desire to bring back the Author, the originator, whose true essence is recognisable through the Voice. The sound in the CD ROM ties us into an originary narrative, via Voice. Now we have Art unmasked, as never before seen, telling us, in his own voice, what his intentions were, his relationship to 'the Art character' in the book and to Vladek. And we hear (and can see transcribed) Vladek's 'original' interviews. We can measure how well Art rendered him. Or, as Art says:

> So that rather than having me always win in my discussions with Vladek of how something's going to be presented, to be able to let him have the last word and to actually have it be a heard word.[6]

'Last word' suggests first word; 'heard word' bespeaks recognised word—a tying again of sound and voice to origins and authority. *The Complete Maus*—total, complete, final, last words.

Under the sign of presence of the original, this CD ROM version of voice and sound sits within the illusory limits of 'faithful reproduction', rather than radical reproduction or the possibilities of representation.[7] So despite the claims of CD ROMs to radical non-narrativity, it takes narrativity to another dimension, to the ultimate ontological narrative: who Art and Vladek really are; what meaning they intend for the work. A work of Art rather than a work of art. And what is 'the work' now? Is it within a new medium, opening the way to new perceptions[8] or a conglomeration of low quality versions of existing media masquerading as a new medium? Which is not to say that new media do not draw on the existing, but to draw on is different from just accumulating. And without the sensuality of the earlier drawings. To access *Maus* in *The Complete Maus* is not only to miss the visual pleasures of the novel, but also to lack some new visual experiences and pleasures appropriate to a new medium, with new forms and new genres. It is also to lose the impact and pleasure of the novel's narrative pull, under the alibi that linear narrative is somehow by definition bad—a delusion which also neglects the radical and innovative form/content of the graphic novel with its play of masks.

Masks. Masks enable and carry a different sonic history of voice than the CD ROM has accessed. In the traditions of sound in ancient Greek and Roman drama, commedia dell'arte and Hollywood animation, voice and sound through masks play differing but always provocative roles. In a short essay, I can only scurry past a complex history and controversies of interpretation...and present a version of this genealogy, a version which reveals the possibilities rather than the limits of sound. In ancient Greek and Roman drama the mask with its (sometimes) protuberant mouth was about sound, *for* sound—'*per sona*', *persona*—a technology used by a player to enable the voice to carry to the back of the amphitheatre as well as a surface on which to depict stock character traits.[9] A play between character and character, so that what is *revealed* by the technology and techniques of the mask is the persona of the character, not some true essence of an individual. In commedia dell'arte, with its half masks and (often animal) characters, there was a play by the actors between character and character, and between mask and mouth—the character already written on the mask, and the character played by the speaking mouth. But neither is 'true' nor originary nor essential. In animation, some different mouse trails can be followed. Those of 'mickey mousing', for instance—the term for the particular animation synching of music to image, which renders the sound and image inseparable and equal and undoes the subordination of sound to image. Indeed there is an elasticity, a 'multimorphic' quality of sound (and image) in terms of space, event, object, voice: 'The "distorted" voices of cartoon characters are analogous to their "distorted" and "elastic" bodies'.[10] There is also a disruption of body, voice and sound: 'voices, sounds and music [are] spread out over the bodies of both characters and objects'.[11]

Not by chance, in animation (as compared to live action) there has been space for different performances and modalities of sound—sound that can function iconically and analogously, rather than indexically and literally; image that can perform in '*distortion* and *counterpoint*' to the sound.[12] Rather than drawing on this genealogy, *The Complete Maus* instead promises reproduction and Original Truth, not just through the Voice, as I have argued, but also through sound and music. With archival material, talking heads, voice-over narration, the sound says 'documentary' and Truth. And the sound is anchored, held down, limited by the image. The CD ROM is vision-driven: both vision-centred and driven not to linger and decay in time and space. Rather than the animation line of Mickey Mouse's graphic 'movement' in space as a 'dynamic process', the CD ROM is driven by a different sort of mouse, running with a different sort of speed in a different sort of space.[13] It does not have a sound which roams around or maps out space because of the way space (and time) are eliminated by a digital imperative and kinaesthetics. Not surprisingly, given the relation of sound to bodies, although users are sped up, they are also tied down by this digital documentary sonic realism.

But of course there was no sound in *Maus*, beyond the reader's turning of pages and perhaps the quiet dropping of tears. So isn't the CD ROM also giving us access to a sensual pleasure we couldn't have with *Maus*? Well, yes, and that's where I lose track of the simple story I had intended to tell here about voice, sound and CD ROMs. True, the sound quality is unnecessarily and infuriatingly limited (you'll never convince me it is technically impossible to do better—or different—not, at least, until it is culturally possible to expect something different or better). True, sound as bait for the trap of resurrecting the Author and an 'aura' can be retrograde, and at least contradict the hype about a radical new medium. And yet. And yet...

And yet you can hear a body in Vladek's voice, a rhythm, an accent, intensities. So the historical embodied voice, the voice of the body and of culture, works against the Voice of the soul, of the Author. Vladek as storyteller, not fountain of truth; a survivor of the holocaust as something to be worked through—through storytelling—not as something singularly transcendental (personally or historically) in meaning. And you can also hear the sound of the technology: the poor quality tape recorders whose 'noise' speaks of the everyday, contingent, mobile quality of the recording events; the sound of the exercycle Vladek rode during some recording sessions;

and even the difficulty of making out his words. This sound of the technology, trace of the event and context, is still more a squeak than a bark—it is not encouraged, or perhaps even allowed, to be insistent—you can choose to read a transcript at the same time, thereby directing attention to the words and the transcription (correct meaning and accuracy) rather than the speaking, material, historically located voice. And yet this 'noise' hasn't been eliminated in total subservience to 'information' as digital modes usually require.[14] And so the intense and cultural quality of the voice also somehow escapes the narrow intentions and even imperatives of the CD ROM form, thanks, ironically, to the technological/aesthetic lack of attention to sound quality (and ideological concern with authenticity). Vladek's voice is not quite there—so if you do want to listen, you have to listen carefully.

And Art? True, he's there to satisfy the need (re)created by the CD ROM form to know about the Author, his every sketch, his every intention, rather than to read his work. His own voice confirms this, telling, for instance, that he was unhappy with the way some people read 'the Art character' in the novel as him.[15] The CD ROM intends to re-dress the character, to take off his mask. And yet...

And yet there is a tension between the trajectory of the CD ROM form (and its deadly serious and derivative invocations of sound and image) and the trajectory of the New York Jewish humour and its ironic (re)presentations of the self in *Maus*, a tension and an excess present in Art's voice and performance, which makes *The Complete Maus* less complete but more full. Art escapes the imperatives of Truth, Archive, and the CD ROM way, thanks to his irony, his raw edge, and his perception. Even at the moments when Art explains himself, he not only blows the breath of life back into the balloon of 'Author' but at the same time pricks it with knife edge humour:

> Vladek was a very good story teller...And unlike certain survivors was not reluctant to talk about it although unlike certain other survivors he had no specific need to bear witness. What he had a need for was for his son to hang out and be around and about the only way I could arrange for that to happen was with a microphone holding him at bay. And so he was glad that I was there and he was willing to talk about this stuff.[16]

And so there is a creative role for sound in their relationship that escapes the confines of the vision-driven CD ROM. And if your desire is sound you can find pleasure sniffing through the pages via the 'Find Art audio' or the 'Find Vladek audio'. And you can even play them together, varying their volumes and start times—a sort of mix, and a mix up of the transcendent realities that the form implies. That's where you can finally get lost in the sound, where the inbuilt impetus to move with the vision, to speed through dataspace, faded. You fade Vladek and Art in and out of each other, playing with their relationship, understanding the play of their relationship—not fixed in meaning, despite the heavy weight of the holocaust and despite the heavy weight of the form (as an archive of information, so 'complete', so final).

Fading. The faded quality of the recordings of Vladek are part of their appeal. A feeling of ephemerality, not fully there (not complete). Difficult to grasp. Nibbling at the ear. Exceeding the authenticating role assigned to them by the CD ROM form. So, perhaps, it is in the sound, which is so limited, that a whiff of the possibilities of something new in the form emerges. But just a squeak and not as hyped and despite the promise. Perhaps this is sensed more easily when *The Complete Maus* is read not against the graphic novel *Maus* but heard across an interactive sound event that created a very different listening/speaking space. A tasty morsel for light relief from digital fingerfood.

'Expresso', broadcast (as part of 'Food for Thought' on *Sideshow*, Radio 2SER FM) in Sydney in June 1995, invited listeners, via 'talkback' facilities, to participate in a partly scripted play and take it where they wanted. The responses were not what the writers/actors had anticipated and planned for. The actors' gasps (surprise, delight, confusion) expressed and took place in a suspended moment (momentary silence) not of speed but real interaction. Significantly, this sort of interactive sound was possible on radio without the distractions and masquerades of vision.

A radio *listener* is moved by a different aesthetics and kinaesthetics than that which constructs a CD ROM *user*. Pinned to their seat by the monitor, a user plays the CD ROM with twitchy mouse fingers, eager to move, so much to see and do. But maybe, yet again, more is less. Driven by the valorisation of speed as a pleasure (addiction) and as a technique in multimedia interactives, users experience less and less time for listening/contemplation. They feel less and less time for sound, with its capacity for a different sort of movement—past the interface, through time, and into their bodies. And with this movement, a different sort of imaginative contact—speaking directly and viscerally to the imagination. But in ROMland, why wouldn't you scamper about, when there is no irony of form to stop you in your tracks, and when there is no production (of a new medium) to engage your attention? There is instead a loud and glaring absence of any new genres and forms, of new ways of performing, recording, directing and designing. There is an absence in *The Complete Maus* of a form that *fits Maus* at the same time as writing and sounding it for a new medium.

Instead, the CD ROM imperative to Archive and to gain legitimacy and 'aura' through the Voice of the Author propels producers to agglomerate existing videos of performance with documentary interviews. This overrides a new medium's concern with developing its own genres, aesthetics and politics of production. What production for/in this new medium might be is still an open question, I would argue, in part because the tendency to treat it as defined by questions of the technology rather than to question the technology and work on and through questions of aesthetics and politics. And when the desire for sound is there, it will be possible. Possible to hear whether there is a new medium in CD ROMs. Meanwhile the masquerades are concealing the lack of this desire and inhibiting the development of it.

Thanks to Maria Miranda for discussions about comix, animation, and CD ROMs.

1. Maus, the German word for mouse, is phonetically the same.
2. Art Spiegelman, 'Introduction—Why a CD ROM', in *The Complete Maus, a Survivor's Tale*, New York: Voyager, 1994.
3. Mark Poster, *The Mode of Information: Poststructuralism and Social Context*, Cambridge: Polity Press, 1990, pp. 5–8.
4. Norie Neumark, 'Diagnosing the Computer User: Addicted, Infected, or Technophiliac?', in *Media Information Australia*, No. 69, August 1993, pp. 80–81.
5. Art Spiegelman, cited in Graham Smith, 'From Mickey to Maus: Recalling the Genocide through Cartoon', in *Oral History Journal*, Vol. 15, No. 1, Spring 1987, p. 30.
6. 'Art audio', in 'Maus Part One', in *The Complete Maus*, op. cit., p. 1.
7. On representation as compared to reproduction, see Rick Altman, 'The Material Heterogeneity of Recorded Sound', in *Sound Theory, Sound Practice*, ed. Rick Altman, New York: Routledge, 1992, p. 29. On reproduction and 'aura' (discussed below) see Walter Benjamin, 'The Work of Art in the Age of Mechanical Reproduction', in his *Illuminations*, ed. Hannah Arendt, trans. Harry Zohn, New York: Schocken Books, 1969, p. 220.

8. Benjamin, op. cit., p. 222.
9. Thanks to Arnie Goldman, Suzanne MacAlister and Richard Green for etymological discussions of masks.
10. Scott Curtis, 'The Sound of the Early Warner Bros. Cartoons', in ed. Rick Altman, op. cit. p. 202. 'Multimorphic' is Norman Klein's term. The full citation is: 'The entire inanimate world is alive and Mickey is its shepherd. One can see how sound assists in the squashing and the stretching of Iwerks' silly protoplasm. Linear movement, with an essentially sketched background, is replaced by a *multimorphic* style, which dominates the cartoon world for two generations.' Norman M. Klein, *Seven Minutes: The Life and Death of the American Animated Cartoon*, London: Verso, 1993, p. 11 (emphasis his).
11. Douglas Kahn, 'Eisenstein and Cartoon Sound', in *Essays in Sound*, eds. Shaun Davies, Annemarie Jonson, Eddy Jokovich, Sydney: Contemporary Sound Arts, 1992, p. 70. See also Norman Klein, op. cit., p. 8ff.
12. John Grierson in Douglas Kahn, op. cit., p. 70. Kahn's emphasis. See also Scott Curtis, op. cit., pp. 200–202.
13. 'Eisenstein on Mickey', cited in Norman Klein, op. cit., p. 7. On the anchoring of sound in documentary, see Jeffrey K. Ruoff, 'Conventions of Sound in Documentary', in ed. Rick Altman, op. cit., p. 221.
14. Frances Dyson, 'The Genealogy of the Radio Voice', in eds. Daina Augaitis and Dan Lander, *Radio Rethink: Art, Sound, Transmission*, Banff: Walter Phillips Gallery, 1994, p. 183. See also Mark Poster, op. cit., p. 7.
15. 'Art audio', in 'Maus Part One', in *The Complete Maus*, op. cit., p. 147.
16. 'Making Maus: Interviewing Vladek', in 'Introduction', in *The Complete Maus*, op. cit.

The Sound of a Dream

Niall Lucy

Sounds are never simply something we just hear; we never just listen to sounds. We don't just listen, because there are no sonic objects for listening to. There are only sonic events.

That sounds can be transmitted across space and recorded over time is no proof at all of an object-value for sound. Like the objectifiable written word, the sound-object is a theoretical convenience: the one is always subject to event-ualities of being read, the other to being heard. In this way it may be possible to hear the sound of one hand clapping, on the model of narrating the event of a dream.

Dreams aren't nothing, on say the model of a square triangle, but what they are has no materiality beyond so many electrical impulses in the brain. Yet dreams are not reducible to these impulses, any more than sounds can be reduced to precise configurations of pitch, tone, frequency and other variables. No less than dreams, sounds are irreducible to what they're made of. But what each is made of, neurological and sonic impulses, lends them a certain object-status insofar as these impulses are able to be recorded, even though it would be absurd to suppose that an EEG read-out of a dream was actually a record of the dream itself.

Imagine if I took along one of my dreams in the form of a neurological chart to a psychoanalyst and expected him or her to read it for symbolic content, as if the shape of this peak meant that I wanted to sleep with my mother and the shape of that trough that I wanted to kill my father. Dreamwork isn't palmistry, in other words. But still it's worth noting that, for psychoanalysis, the form of the dream that is of least professional interest is in fact the form that is most objectifiable. Every other form will do, including a lie. So dream analysis is, in principle, able to be carried out on a drawing or a photograph or a theatrical performance of a dream, but not on a chart of neurological activity—and it would not matter to the analytical process (although of course it would to the analysis) if any of these forms were deliberately misleading.

Contrary to an earlier remark, then, it would seem that dreams are in fact *not* dissimilar from square triangles, except that the latter can have absolutely no material form whatsoever. A square triangle can exist only in the form of a desire for it to exist, and this is of a slightly different order of being from that of a dream. While dreams might *express* desires, it is precisely in this sense that the dream acts as a carrier of meaning and can to such extent be understood as semiotic. One might therefore be tempted to say that dreaming is a cultural achievement, that dreams are no more 'of' the natural world than butter or plastic.

But to suppose from this that somebody could choose to stop dreaming would be as preposterous as thinking that someone who chose to live on a desert island had escaped culture. The choice, in both cases, is simply unavailable. This is not to deny that dreaming, while it is clearly at some level involuntary, is perhaps still a cultural practice, no less than writing or kissing (which may also be involuntary).

Unlike writing, though, dreams (so far as we yet know) don't leave behind traces of themselves, except in a form of degree zero semiosis that's effectively unreadable. To the extent that dreams are unrecordable, but nevertheless still 'real' or 'actual', they are more like events than texts (at least insofar as 'text' describes a cultural object that requires reading and which can circulate, precisely *as* an object, independently of its producer). But dreams can of course be turned into such texts, by means of some form of inscription—and it's at this point that the dream-event becomes, like a page torn out of a diary, something to be scrutinised at a distance.

However, a page from a diary is not just any page of writing: it isn't like a legal document, or a newspaper column, or even a poem. Ideally, diary entries are personal and spontaneous; their ideal genre is that they don't have one, and their ideal reader is the writer him- or herself. They are in fact like dreams, in other words. Precisely that: *in other words*.

It is only in the form of other words (other pictures, etc.), as text, that dreams are able to be recorded. These other words, ideally, are a transparent textual form of a memory-event. Once again it is important to note that such texts cannot be produced from a neurological chart (though other texts can), which cannot act as a memorial substitute. Memory can be supplemented only by writing. Whatever memory is, in other words, it can be known only via forms of supplementation, forms of writing, whether verbal or inscriptive. And to the extent that memory is writing-dependent, we can say that memory *is* writing (and writing, memory) insofar as it is never available in some pure, whole and original form outside writing. Nor is there an outside-writing form of the dream, a square triangle, or the sound of one hand clapping.

Insofar as this is true for remembering, I think it is also true for listening, despite the fact that sound is recordable and therefore, in its textual form, plastic, able to be cut up and played backwards. But plasticity is of the nature of texts, of writing in general, and cannot be confined to sonic texts as a special feature of their aurality (or their orality) based on the object-value ascribed to them by virtue of recording practices and mechanisms. A sound is no more plastic than a memory or a dream, and this is certainly no less true for the object-value lent to sound by being able to be recorded.

Sound's recordability, then, which appears to be the condition of its reversibility and hence its plasticity, is not in my view its most interesting feature. It isn't what appears to be the essence of sound that makes sound interesting, in other words. So instead of coming at a theory of sound from the inside, as it were, I prefer (no doubt perversely and cautiously at the same time) to approach the matter from an outside, in a form of the dream.

Dreams are as insubstantial as square triangles, while also being different. If dreams never quite just 'are,' at least they can be said to happen; but not even this can be said of a square triangle. And I think the same is true of sounds as it is of dreams: sounds and dreams are event-like, by which I mean *they happen*, but without ever coming into being as objects. Sounds, like dreams, are never capturable by technology; so that any sound recording is in fact of the same ontological status as a photograph of a ghost, which one might liken to a photograph of a square triangle, or indeed of a dream.

And so we arrive at a continuum—of sounds, dreams, square triangles, and ghosts. Strangely, of these it would seem that it's only sounds that must always remain unable to be photographed—if it were to be believed that ghosts are real; that somehow a square triangle could exist outside a desire for it to exist or beyond the present limits of human cognition (in which case it would already exist, unbeknown to anyone); or that in the future it will be possible to photograph our dreams. Each of these events is at least able to be imagined: I have a sense, for example, of what a photograph of one of my dreams would look like, etc. But the idea of photographing a sound seems to make no sense at all.

This is not simply because sounds can't be seen to be photographed, since I do not believe that ghosts or dreams or square triangles can be seen either. But they can be imagined in this way, and that's the crux.

So what if we began to think of aurality in terms of visuality: what might this produce? What would sounds 'look' like as a consequence of such thinking? By the same token, what would the visual 'sound' like if we began to think the specular in terms of the sonic?

I'm not asking these questions in order to inspire new forms of avant-garde practice in relation to sight and sound. Instead, what I'm suggesting is that sounds are heard through the body, that they resonate corporeally and not only on the tympanum. Certainly I think this is true of the sounds that I make myself, especially through my voice. My voice, I think, no less than my imagination, while it is able to be prosthetised, exists in such relation with my body that prevents it from being an effect of the operations of some part of my body alone. This is why a recording of my voice, coming to me from outside my body, always has the quality of a prosthetic device: just as if I were to write a novel—that might be a kind of prosthetics of my imagination.

For this reason, then, I prefer to think of a corporeality rather than a pure aurality of sound, insofar as this allows for sounds to be seen and felt, as well as simply heard. One may even go so far as to postulate an olfactory sense of sound. In such a way sound is able to be thought in terms of a different set of codifications, which doesn't rely on the relation of a hearing subject to a sonic object (a thing to be listened to) but rather can begin to develop an understanding of sound in terms of a corporeity that is always in the process of arriving at its own eventuality.

The body is never able to be thought in terms of a completion, that is to say, but always insofar as it decays and develops—entropically, intellectually, psychically, physiologically, etc. There is never a moment at which the body is fully realised or finally formed, a point at which the processes of its own internal densities come to rest. No such moment short of death, when still the body carries on towards the point of a passing through into some other dimension beyond reach of a conscious 'self'.

And so for living bodies, the recording studio marks a space in which it might be said that the body can experience its own death—externalising itself as a prosthetic trace that memorialises a living presence no less assuredly than a gravestone. A recorded voice is always, then, a voice from the grave, from beyond the body, even though it reaches the body as an event to be actualised (where there is both loss and acquisition) through a kind of endless corporeal receptivity. This is of course especially true of one's own recorded voice, which arrives in a form of the self as other, but is perhaps no less true of the recorded voice in general insofar as this must always take the form of a lost and open detachment, like a page torn out of someone else's diary.

No less than a dream, in other words, a sound is a corporeal event. This does not mean that sounds eventuate in terms of a sort of private interiority, either in a psychoanalytic or an existential sense. For this might be to suppose that dreams are the expression of an unacculturated unconscious or of an individual's essential alientation. Dreams, although they happen in the body, do not occur outside culture.

This is why it seems to me that we can think the sound of a dream, on the model of being able to dream a sound. And there is no way of knowing whether the sound of a dream might be different from so-called other sounds that occur in our bodies while awake. But if sound can indeed be thought this way, as corporeal and dream-like, then it may be that as a medium (and I'm thinking here especially of sound-usage with regard to radio) sound can be understood in terms of accidental effects, to which it is no less prone than a body dreaming or awake.

Every body is an accident, waiting for the ultimate accident to occur—death. This, too, is part of our corporeality, so that perhaps in every dream and sound that eventuates in our living bodies we are reminded of that accident that remains to become, at the moment of our unbecoming, crossing to an afterlife like switching to another channel.

Soundsite

Soundsite is a world wide web publication for sound artists, practitioners and theorists. Soundsite deals with the cultural, theoretical and practical aspects of sound as manifest in:

language and discourse; voice; poetics; psycho-acoustics; perception and sensory experience; hearing vs. listening; aurality and corporeality; post-musics; sound geographies; philosophies of sound; film, video and tv soundtrack; sound art and sound by artists; sound and noise; virtual systems; human-computer interface; communication and technological systems; low fidelity sound; space and architecture; radio and radiophonic art; acoustics; performance; recording; composition; aesthetics; art.

This list is not exhaustive!

We are looking for contributors. Our first issue is a broad overview of the field. We expect subsequent issues will be themed to special topics. We are also very interested in artists' descriptions of sound works they have recently exhibited, or critical analysis of such works.

People who wish to participate in any way are also welcome to respond.

Please respond to: soundsite@sysx.apana.org.au

http://sysx.apana.org.au/soundsite/

Soundsite
PO Box A2253
Sydney South
NSW 2000
Australia
tel: Jason (+61 2) 368 0210
tel: Scot (015) 95 7414

ESSAYS IN SOUND

3–1996

DIFFRACTIONS

CONTEMPORARY SOUND ARTS

ESSAYS IN SOUND
Published and edited by Contemporary Sound Arts
PO Box 1265, Darlinghurst NSW 2010, Australia

Editors: Alessio Cavallaro, Shaun Davies, Annemarie Jonson
Founding editors: Shaun Davies, Eddy Jokovich, Annemarie Jonson
Design: ARMEDIA

Thanks to W. P. Lowe; the Women's Research Centre, the Department of Music, Faculty of Visual and Performing Arts, and the Research Projects Unit, the University of Western Sydney, Nepean; Dr Paul Redding, Department of General Philosophy, The University of Sydney; Victoria Lynn, The Art Gallery of New South Wales; Shimoda Nobuhisa, Xebec Corporation, Kobe, Japan; and all contributing authors and artists.

CSA gratefully acknowledges the sponsorship of Counterpoint Sound and Megaphon Acoustic Design.

This project has been assisted by the Commonwealth Government through the Australia Council, its arts funding and advisory body.

With special thanks to the Hybrid Arts Committee (now the New Media Fund) of the Australia Council.

CSA was established in Australia in 1991 to facilitate an interdisciplinary approach to the critical investigation of sound, encompassing historical, political, philosophical, artistic, and technological perspectives, and to engage in and support research, and the production and distribution of various forms of print and electronic media related to sound. These concerns are also expressed in public activities such as the SOUNDcheck series of forums and other events.

©1996. Contents copyright of Contemporary Sound Arts, and the respective authors, artists and photographers.

First published in 1996. Republished in 2016.

Contents

Introduction	198
Video Installation and the Neo-Classical Soundtrack *Sean Cubitt*	199
Towards a History of Listening *Martin Harrison*	211
Aggressive Listening *Robin Rimbaud (aka Scanner)*	222
Sonogram *Ashley Scott*	224
Sound Theory, Sound Art: Same Theory, Same Art *Ian Andrews*	225
Foundations…(a Response to Ian Andrews) *Scot Art*	227
Creaking Grounds: Tectonics and SoundCulture 96 *Ed Osborn*	230
Silence: 'Unhearable' Sound Between Us *Yuji Sone*	238
Sonic Architecture: An Interview with Nigel Helyer *John Potts*	245
Ere and Bele Chose: The Wife of Bath's Deafness *Louise D'Arcens*	251
His Master's Voice: Derrida and Vocal-Writing *Robert Sinnerbrink*	257
Nietzsche's Recovery of Primary Acoustical Experience: The Birth of Tragedy out of the Spirit of Music as 'Fundamental Ontology' *P. Christopher Smith*	263
Second-Hand Emotions: Constructions of Interiority in Music *Susan McClary*	273
Virtuoso of Vox: An Interview with Diamanda Galas *Nicholas Zurbrugg*	285
Des Funken Sprunkling Globus *Joyce Hinterding*	292
Booth. Special Delivery *Kathryn Bird*	296

Notes on Contributors [1996]

Ian Andrews is an experimental filmmaker and video artist, and a producer of electronic music and experimental radio. He has written several essays on music and sound theory.

Scot Art is a composer and producer, editor of Soundsite, and a member of Clan Analogue.

Kathryn Bird and co-producers **James Verdon** and **Grant Hilliard**, with sound consultant Andrew Howie, are MutleyMedia, a cross-state collaboration of new media artists.
email: mutley@magna.com.au

Sean Cubitt is Reader in Video and Media Studies, and route leader in Screen Studies at Liverpool John Moores University. A member of the editorial boards of *Third Text* and *Screen*, he is the author of *Timeshift: On Video Culture* and *Videography: Video Media as Art and Culture*, and has published widely in the arts, media and contemporary culture. email: s.cubitt@livjm.ac.uk

Louise D'Arcens is currently completing a PhD dissertation at the English Department, The University of Sydney, on gender and literary authority in the late Middle Ages.

Martin Harrison's next book is a collection of poems, *The Kangaroo Farm*, which will be published by Paper Bark Press early in 1997. He is currently at work on a collection of essays, *Ancient Noise: Hearing the End of Theory*, to do with poetics, sound and hearing.

Joyce Hinterding is a Sydney based installation artist whose works frequently highlight sound phenomena.

Susan McClary is Professor of Musicology at UCLA. She has published numerous books including *Georges Bizet: Carmen*, Cambridge Opera Handbook (Cambridge University Press, 1992); and *Feminine Endings: Music, Gender and Sexuality* (University of Minnesota Press, 1991). Books in progress include *De-Tonations: Narrative and Signification in 'Absolute' Music* (under contract for Wesleyan University Press).

Ed Osborn is a sound artist who has worked in a variety of formats including video, installation, and performance, and has exhibited throughout the USA, Canada, Europe, and South America. He has held various residencies including at the Banff Centre for the Arts in Canada, and taught sound studies at various institutions throughout the USA. He was the director of SoundCulture 96.

John Potts is a Sydney based sound artist and theorist, and a lecturer in Media Studies at Macquarie University.

Robin Rimbaud (aka **Scanner**)—musician, writer, media critic, cultural engineer—is a telephone terrorist, a techno-data pirate whose scavenging of the electronic communications highways provides the raw materials for his aural collages of electronic music and found conversations. email: robinr@easynet.co.uk

Ashley Scott is a Sydney based sound artist and composer.

Robert Sinnerbrink is undertaking a PhD in philosophy at The University of Sydney.

P. Christopher Smith is Professor of Philosophy at the University of Massachusetts Lowell. He has published numerous books including three translations, with introduction and commentary, of Gadamer's hermeneutical studies on Hegel and Ancient Philosophy (Yale University Press); and *Hermeneutics and Human Finitude: Toward a Theory of Ethical Understanding* (Fordham University Press, 1991).

Yuji Sone is a Sydney based performance artist whose recent works investigate an intersubjective mediated exchange between different cultures at the close of the twentieth century.

Nicholas Zurbrugg is Professor of English and Cultural Studies, and Head of the Department of English, Media and Cultural Studies, The School of Humanities, De Montfort University, Leicester. His publications include *Beckett and Proust* (1988), *The Parameters of Postmodernism* (1993), and *Positively Postmodern: The Multimedia Muse in America: Interviews with the Contemporary Avant-Garde* (Maison Neuve Press, forthcoming).

Introduction

Shaun Davies

This third edition of *Essays in Sound* arrives in the wake of the third in the series of trans-Pacific sound arts festivals, SoundCulture 96, an event exploring sound in its various artistic and cultural manifestations, ranging from performance to sculpture through to radio broadcast, telephonic, and installation works. It also arrives at a time when the current interest in sound can be shown to not lie exclusively in the domain of the fine arts, nor to have been exhausted by it, but to range across a diversity of fields and disciplines covering a broad philosophical, historical, musicological and technological spectrum. *Essays in Sound* has sought to not only represent this diversity and to display it in all its contrasting/complementing accents and tones, but also to acknowledge a form of archaeological questing now taking place. Though no doubt in part due to, and motivated by, the recent emergence of sound arts discourse, this current excavation, if it may be called that, reveals the existence of an abiding interest in sound as a cultural and also a phenomenological and intellectual object—an interest far antedating its more modern construction and appraisal. As the distance existing between these archaic and contemporary assessments becomes increasingly critical, where they face each other off, a kind of reverberative, susurrating field of affects is produced which informs, vitalises and contextualises our current purchase on sound, and which affirms that the present stands in part or complete reciprocity with its historical antecedents. However the voices of the present may subtend and qualify any understanding of the past, each echo of the past nevertheless resonates with, and enriches the tone of the present. Where diffractions in any case occur, the consequences may nonetheless (re)produce a different or archaic (that is, simply forgotten) kind of listening, one yielding presently unavailable and unassessable results.

All of this is not to say that there are no shared areas of interest among the writers represented here. In making these selections—essays and smaller, fugitive pieces—the editors have aimed to emphasise as much. Individual works have sometimes been brought into sharp relief, resulting—not unexpectedly—in the positive accentuation of some of their more significant and distinctive features.

The results, we hope, will promote and sustain the reader's interest for some time to come.

December, 1996

Video Installation and the Neo-classical Soundtrack

Sean Cubitt

Videos have soundtracks. Galleries don't. In the museum, sound, music, even speech are invasive. They are also elements of a new audiovisual art, which has important implications for the cinema.

A few years ago there was a major retrospective of European video installation at the Kölnischer Kunstverein. One installation is perhaps manageable, but more than one soundspace in a gallery not only wrecks the fictive silence of contemplation; they appear to interfere with each others' autonomy. No pure work, but mélange, spillage, mess. The curatorial solution: to equip visitors with headsets tuned to trip from one soundtrack to another as you moved from piece to piece. This temporary and temporising restoration of a suitably contemplative subjectivity in the audience produced uproar among the artists involved. Sound in installation, they argued, defines a space, as sculpture and architecture do. To restrict sound to this Cartesian solipsism, anchored to the ears rather than the whole, resonant body, and focused at the mystical seat of mental governance midway between the ears, this is to erase the sculptural specificity of sound. Recounting this anecdote at a conference,[1] I argued further that the Cartesian headset militated against the sociality of moving through sound.

I was thinking about John Cage, and about his discovery that music is less a mode of composition than a mode of listening:

> ...one may give up the desire to control sound, clear his mind of music, and set about discovering means to let sound[s] be themselves rather than vehicles for man-made theories or expressions of human sentiments.[2]

For Cage, music was not merely durational, not merely non-linear ('NO BEGINNING, MIDDLE, OR END (PROCESS, NOT OBJECT)'),[3] it could also be considered spatial:

> Rehearsals have shown that this new music, whether for tape or instruments, is more clearly heard when the several loudspeakers or performers are separated in space rather than grouped closely together...Where do we go from here? Towards theater.[4]

Like most people who have come across Cage's works and writings, I was entranced, found myself turning off the refrigerator the better to hear the winds and tides competing over the estuary waves fifty yards from my window. I re-read Rick Altman's essay on playback,[5] prowling about the room listening to how my body altered its acoustic. I heard distant record players and traffic hum. I woke up to duets between the garden robin and airliners. I held my breath to hear my lover's breathing.

When I was writing up that piece, I came across an essay that disquieted this Elysian renewal of perception, a brilliant critique by Douglas Kahn of the musicalisation of noise:

> The main avant-garde strategy in music from Russolo to Cage quite evidently relied upon notions of noise and worldly sound as 'extra-musical'; what was outside musical materiality was then progressively brought back into the fold in order to rejuvenate musical practice...But for a sound to be 'musicalised' in this strategy, it had to conform materially to ideas of sonicity, that is, ideas of a sound stripped of its associative attributes, a minimally coded sound existing in close proximity to 'pure' perception and distant from the contaminating effects of the world.[6]

I began to have second thoughts. These are they.

THE MONTAGE OF EFFECTS

You could cherish, in the dialogue film, a Derridean reversal of the ostensible primacy of speech. Not only is the soundtrack subordinated, in the classical Hollywood film bien fait, to the image, but the soundtrack, dominated by dialogue, serves to make explicit or audible a written script that predates and pre-empts it. The script of *The Maltese Falcon* is the fabula which cinematic syuzhet and style devote themselves to unearthing. Script-driven soundtracks dominated the producer system of the studio period as they dominated radio from its beginnings achieving their apogee in the military-information societies of Nazi Germany and wartime Britain. The script is efficiency, the basic tool of budgetary administration, the armature of employment. Efficiency rules not only the production but also the delivery of dialogue films. They aim to provide information, if necessary to the point of redundancy, visual data repeated as sound effect, musical accompaniment and dialogue. ('Babba-ba-boom. Bang! Thud! "He's a gonner".') If, as Bordwell argues, 'The mystery film, with its resolved enigma at the end, is only the most apparent instance of the tendency of the classical syuzhet to develop toward full and adequate knowledge. Whether a protagonist learns a moral lesson or only the spectator knows the whole story, the classical film moves steadily toward a growing awareness of absolute truth',[7] its climax and closure arrives at the moment of fullest match between dialogue and image, a point explored in Kaja Silverman's analysis of the making audible (and comprehensible) of women's speech.[8]

This classical, dialogue-driven, information-led soundtrack tells what the image shows, and its relation to the image is narrational: a series of witholdings and red herrings finally brought to realisation in the coincidence of showing and telling. It is, despite the redundancy, massively efficient. To listen to *Some Like It Hot* with a studious audience is to become almost painfully aware of the pauses in dialogue left by Wilder to allow for laughter without spoiling the clarity of delivery. These pauses, like the redundancy of telling and showing, are not inefficient: they belong to the aesthetic of 'No-one ever lost money underestimating the public', an aesthetic that at its zenith turns the catchphrases and choruses of music hall and burlesque into a form of branding, replicating in their iconic status the lost fantasias provided by the absent dialogue of the silent screen.

The classical soundtrack subordinates everything to clarity of dialogue, even long after the technical limitations of microphony had been overcome, and the 'phonogenic' voice was no longer a technical requisite.[9] Dynamics, expression, realism in vocal delivery were all sacrificed long after they had to be. Sound effects remained throughout completely tied to the action, and music was delivered over to atmospherics and the banalities of melodramatic realism. As Adorno and Eisler argued, one of the most widespread prejudices in the motion-picture industry is the premise that the spectator should not be conscious of the music. The philosophy behind this belief is a vague notion that music should have a subordinate role in relation to the picture. As a rule, the motion picture represents action with dialogue. Financial considerations and technical interest are concentrated on the actor; anything that might overshadow him is considered disturbing.[10] But even they succumb to the thesis that 'The musical material must be perfectly subordinated to the given dramatic task'.[11] When they complain of Hollywood's failure to appreciate the dynamic and dramatic properties of modern 'objective' (post-Schönbergian) music, they go so far as to argue for a specific analogy between dissonance and the classical paradigm: sound is robbed of its static quality and made dynamic by the ever-present-factor of the 'unresolved'. The new language is dramatic even prior to the 'conflict', the thematic development with its explicit antagonisms. A similar feature is inherent in the motion picture. The principle of tension is latently so active even in the weakest productions that incidents which of themselves are credited with no importance whatsoever appear like scattered fragments of a meaning that the whole is intended to clarify and that transcend themselves. The new musical language is particularly well-suited to do justice to this element of the motion picture.[12] The work of George Antheil, Bernard Herrmann and Louis and Bebe Barron, among others, shows that, at least within generic boundaries, Hollywood was not averse to dissonance.[13] But these examples show that even while contrasting the use of new 'objective' musical resources to music which 'is supposed to be inconspicuous in the same sense as are selections from *La Bohème* played in a restaurant',[14] drama according to the classical paradigm remains the raison d'être of the film, and serialism was incapable of regenerating the Hollywood soundtrack.

To the extent that it is premised on the gradual revelation of information, the classical soundtrack is linear. The subordination of music and sound effects to dialogue is a process of unification, in which the disparate tracks, sync and post-synch, sourced and unsourced, can be brought into a single experience, itself subordinated to the image and the whole organised along its temporal axis. The classical soundtrack transmits information in a linear, hierarchically unified temporality in which sound effects, music and dialogue are unified in their subordination to the restrained yet total revelation of absolute truth, the whole directed towards narrative conclusion. In the neo-classical tendency of recent decades, however, the soundtrack is musicalised in Kahn's sense, so that the delivery of dialogue becomes as interesting for its sonic qualities ('Here's Johnny'; 'Hasta la vista, baby') as for its narrative reference, and in which melodies are converted into sound effects. This is the case, for example, in *Pulp Fiction*, where all the music is sourced in the film's fictional world, down to the acoustic quality of the playback systems, qualities accentuated by Tarantino's well-known dislike of CD.

Neo-classical cinema is emergent. There are few, perhaps no, pure examples of the kind of film I mean. Narrative and script still hold sway over the Hollywood mode of reproduction. Neo-classicism has roots in the art cinema, and enters the mainstream in part through the cult status of European- and Japanese-influenced directors like Tarantino, Scorsese, Lynch and more homegrown realist-oriented filmmakers like Jim Jarmusch and Spike Lee. Neo-classicism's key indicator is the relative downgrading of narrative in favour of the exploration of (fictional) worlds. *Goodfellas*, *Blue Velvet*, *Pulp Fiction*, *Do the Right Thing* and *Down by Law* share with Wenders' road movies, Leone's westerns, Ozu's family melodramas and Kitasone's atmospheric yakuza pix a sense that story is merely a device for uncovering a world. Deep focus and mobile camerawork (like the entry into the nightclub via basement corridors and kitchens in *Goodfellas*, or the arrival at Trader Jack's in *Pulp Fiction*) are its visual hallmarks; indeed, in films like *Fatal Attraction*, they become its clichés. The interest of *Twin Peaks: Fire Walk with Me* and *Do the Right Thing* lies in their communities, their worlds, their interactions. Diegesis is at least as important as narration. Like Altman's *The Player* and, even more so, *Short Cuts*, the neo-classical film appropriates the communitarian stylistics of European and North American popular front filmmaking for the purposes of entertainment.

Nor is neo-classicism restricted to the marginal box-office of arthouse success. If the script was the best proof against loss in a vertically-integrated studio era, the synergetic corporations of late capitalism's infotainment industries are geared towards sharing profit across a raft of product lines, among which a feature film release will function as much as a core marketing device as it is a core profit centre. No-one remembers a *Batman* plot; but everyone remembers Gotham City. Like the universes of *Star Wars* and *Star Trek*, Gotham can be the site of endless rewriting and remaking, in every medium, from comics and talking books to computer games and theme park rides. This is the cynical reading. A more sympathetic one might note that this is an evolution of audience engagement with stars as vehicles of fantasy. In exploiting the diegesis over the actor, however, contemporary studios can spread the risks of stardom, and at the same time create fantasy scenarios in which identification is less important than the polyvalent modes of fantasy which D. N. Rodowick characterises as 'the activity of reading as difference'.[15] Arriving at such fantasy scenarios through the gentle substitution of diegeses for stars may well be the source of that 'coldness' noted by many critics of the new action film, from *Dirty Harry* to *Thelma and Louise*, where we are invited to place ourselves in a mythic domain, not to play the protagonist.

Mag-sound prints for exhibition, multitrack stereo digital recording, and Dolby and THX theatre sound designed to compete with home hi-fi systems are the technical base on which the neo-classical soundtrack evolves in parallel with this modification of hegemonic imaging. In the classical soundtrack, temporal, linear unification is narrativised by two processes which parallel Laura Mulvey's analysis of scopophilic pleasure.[16] The phonophiliac equivalent to voyeurism is eavesdropping, whose narrativisation is accomplished by exploiting the desire to discover the source of a sound (a sense caught in Elizabeth Weis' analysis of sound in *The Birds*[17] and in Metz's essay 'Aural Objects'[18]); the equivalent to fetishism is the anchorage of voice in the synchronised soundtrack. Both involve a disavowal of the search for origin, the lack at the source, the silence in the centre of aural communication, especially of recording. Both, crucially, involve the reduction of perceptual awareness of extra-diegetic voiceovers, incidental music and sound effects to preconscious levels (rather at odds with the cognitive model of ideal audience activity. Moments of unification of sound and image operate the familiarly paradoxical hiding and revealing of fetishistic disavowal to produce a 'spectacularisation' of sound as closure. Alternation between the two modes produces a rhythmic structure, akin to that produced in the oscillations between spectacle and narration in the visual field. This rhythm is the unity of the classical soundtrack.

The evolution of new soundtrack techniques endangered classical unity. Digital playback necessitated new recordings: the old libraries of archived gunshots and gallops were inadequate for the new, spectacularised theatrical playback.[19] The arts of the Foley stage, multitracking and soundscaping were faced with a new problematic: how to reunify soundtracks in danger of falling apart (a facet of new recording technology celebrated, for example, in Frank Zappa and Tony Palmer's *200 Motels* and Peter Watkins' *Edvard Munch*). One solution is marked by the career of John Williams, who anchored so many of the Spielberg and Lucas films of the '70s and '80s with Oscar-winning pastiches of Eric Korngold. Here Williams faced the early institutionalisation of the montage of affects—film as a series of set-piece FX sequences whose narrative thread was of marginal interest to its target audiences. His response was the leitmotif. The sub-Wagnerian motifs that dominate films like *Jaws* and the *Indiana Jones* series, in the absence of narrational devices of more than picaresque complexity, operate, like the TV sports soundtracks described by

Rick Altman,[20] as cues for reinvested attention in a spectacular effect (dum-de-dum-dum dum-de-dum: Harrison Ford is derring-doing). As such, they lose their previously linear functions, and begin to operate as markers in diegetic space. This is the function of pop music mixed into the soundtrack of *Goodfellas*: each song marks a moment in time as an environment for exploration, songs operating as motifs to demarcate an era as affect.

In this soundscape, Chion's 'superfield',[21] the audio innovations of Renoir, Welles and Mizoguchi become common currency. The effective evocation of a world always depends less on the underpinning of character psychology through music, and far more on the humble atmos track.

Ambient sound becomes, after Cage, the arena for sound design at its highest bent. This, rather than any pursuit of narrative goals or Bazinian realism, explains why spaceships in vacuo make deep rumbles in *Star Wars* (rather than Strauss waltzes as in *2001: A Space Odyssey*): these designed sounds give mass and scale to miniatures. They express the occupation of space. In a film like *Se7en*, technoir visually reduced to sepia disgust and resigned misanthropy, only the soundtrack (and, one has to admit, the title sequence, worthy of the best graphic novel work of Bill Sienkiewicz or David McKean) establishes the vital, (a)moral core of the film, the typicality of its serial moralist. *Se7en* persists in memory as the endless grievings and grievances of its sound design, a world given space at the expense of history.

The momentary foregrounding of incidental music in *2001* was a transitional point, playing on the paradoxical conjuncture of scientific futurity and nineteenth-century masked balls. It is interesting that it should have been a science fiction film, and one apparently deliberately emptied of psychological interest in the casting and direction of Keir Dullea, that marked this turn. The potential for silence in space operas, as in desert films, is marked by musical codes acting to represent silence. In the fully-fledged neo-classical film, still a rare creature, even music becomes a sound effect, replacing connotation with denotation, anchored in the movie's world, as it is, in another key film, by the radio receivers of *American Graffiti*. Music, since Russolo and Cage, colonises noise. In neo-classical Hollywood, melodic music itself becomes a mode of noise, a point on a continuum between sound and silence, ready to be reassimilated into a Cagean listening.

Russolo's experiments with industrial noise, an obligation forced upon him by the logic of his futurist manifesto commitment to the acceleration of modernity, instigate the hegemony of music as the dominant auditory technology of the century, more effectively even than Elvis. To register the sonorous as musical is to accommodate to music's self-enfolding quietism, its inspiration towards silence in its immoderate race to the solution of its internal dialectic. Sound is dragged by the avant-garde into the finality of music's fading to silence. Ironically, in the cinema's espousal of dialogue in the classical period (and in the radio of the same period) we can descry a certain resistance to this finality. Much of the beauty of the classical cinema derives from the dialectical relationship, not between sound and image, but between dialogue and music, at its height in the classical musical, but also audible in works like the Korngold-scored *Adventures of Robin Hood* and Max Steiner's scoring of *Hanover* Square.[22] Perhaps one might characterise the earlier sound film as premised on a dialectic of music and noise, with dialogue as synthesis. In the neo-classical soundtrack, the dialogue-music dialectic is resolved through the synthesis of music and noise, with dialogue reduced to an instance of this unified soundscape/superfield.

The limitation of the neo-classical synthesis is its very spatialisation of the soundtrack. Dialogue film's dependence on closure excludes it from history: soundscaped film's architecsonics[23] debar it from geography. Classical and neo-classical share their autonomy from the social world, an autonomy marked most of all by the silencing of the audience, first by narrative curiosity, and later by spectacularised sonic effects. The design of Dolby and THX cinemas for optimal acoustics is based in the same aesthetics as the Cartesian headset: the structuring of soundspace in which the two ears are acoustically engineered to receive sound, as information or orientation, as at an ideal point of (hyper)individuation. In sum, the imagination of the neo-filmic world as a zone of freeplay for quasi-narrative fantasy independent of protagonists is a point of identification with the playworld of the synergetic corporation, the ineffective, amoral industrialisation of the carnivalesque.

ABERRANT ENCODING

Though in some ways a less influential figure than Cage, Karlheinz Stockhausen produces more by way of openings and entry points to a new aural space. His very megalomania makes it not only possible but imperative to escape the musical, in a crucial example by tuning radios to random, often dead wavebands: to hear what any ear can hear. But even Stockhausen, in his explorations of the purity of timbre, rhythm and the rest, immerses himself and his audience in pure perception. The meticulous acoustic attention he gives to concert performances is in its own way an emanation of the Cartesian headset, a construction of the auditor as central individual. But the use of radio intrudes on this contemplative subjectivity, introducing the dependency of listening on the mediation that makes it possible.

Sound theory introduces major problems for the concept of realism, and especially for the familiar problematic of representation. Recording is no more an innocent or transparent replication of real, pro-phonographic sound than the photograph is of the pro-filmic. It has its own techniques of framing and selection, its entrenched aesthetics, its practices of erasing the marks of its making. The advent of tape recording allowed for a burgeoning practice of beautifying sound through splicing different takes, and if necessary different artists, to approximate an ideal, studio-perfect rendition. In certain aspects, the kinds of recording attacked by Glenn Gould are themselves locked into an endless dialectic of the delirious pursuit of an inaudibly perfect and authenticated score. The problem for realism and the critique of representation is not simply that music, however defined, is non-referential, but that the more perfect a recording, the less it refers to a pre-existing sound. The craft of contemporary sound design is rich in technique to the point at which its devotion to the revelation of reality has to be doubted. This might be both a Bazinian criticism of film sound, and a critique of the idealising tendencies of representational theory. It is also the problematic in which much of the most interesting new work in audiovisual practice is being undertaken. In the work of electronic composers like Pierre Schaeffer, Stockhausen and Michel Chion (as indeed in some of Cage's tape pieces), the medium of recording is brought into the foreground, a modernist solution: but what is required is a way of delinking pro-filmic and filmic in the interests of reintegrating film into the history and geography of the post-filmic. A key to this is to shift emphasis from the study of representation to the study of mediation.

In a recent installation, *Killing Time* (1994), Sam Taylor-Wood uses an opera recording as soundtrack. On each of four screens is projected images of anonymous friends of the artist who have memorised the sung parts of one of the opera's characters, by rote. The camera is still, as are its subjects, and there is no visible editing as they wait, listening, and then sing their parts, utterly deadpan. The gallery soundtrack is of the source recording, eliminating the specific acoustics of the depicted living rooms and the voices of the performers, who appear to lip-synch. The piece succeeds as an eerie contemplation of a null point of cultural incomprehension based in the distance between operatic melodrama and the banality of contemporary daily life, a disturbance of Gorbman's principle that 'Soundtrack music may set specific moods and emphasise particular emotions suggested in the narrative...but first and foremost, it is a signifier of emotion itself'.[24] As installed in the Spring of 1996 at the Cornerhouse Gallery, Manchester, for the British Art Show 4, the soundtrack flooded out of its dedicated gallery into the offices beside, the restaurant below and the next gallery upstairs, careless of boundaries, and creating as an almost casual side-effect an architectural disruption demanding a visit to the piece to satisfy that spatial curiosity that was earlier allied to cinematic voyeurism. But where in film the fetishistic match of sound and image which comes to satisfy this longing presents itself as a completion—discovery of the fictive source of the sound presented as origin—this installation baffles that search with its patent inauthenticity.

Taylor-Wood dislikes being pigeonholed as a film/video artist. In common with many of her generation, she is more interested in the content than the medium-specificity of the work. Yet this interest provides a certain test for the notion of art as mediation. To some extent, all art is a work of aberrant encoding, an interference in the habitual means of communication. In terms of recording, this interference occurs in the mismatch between installation sound and what one would normally expect of playback. While the use of the original recording directly in the gallery is to some extent a technical solution to the problem of synching four videotape sources, it produces too a disturbance at the level of perception, so that auditors are aware of the disjunction between the ideal sound of the CD and the acoustic signatures of rerecording in materially heterogenous living rooms. At the same time, it debars the assumption that vision be the authenticating perception in which the origin of sound, especially of the voice, can be determined. Such indeterminacy then becomes a part of a dialectical yearning which can be situated not in the opposition of screen and sound, but within the soundtrack itself, between the ideality of operatic recording, the erasure of re-recording, and the sculptural volume of the installation in situ. Central to this dialectic is the factor of movement, especially of the movement of the audience into and through the soundspace of the piece, an effect that might have been enhanced by using four synched CD players rather than one, but which at least opens the door to a more complex mode of listening than that offered in the idealisation of the cinema auditor. It would be easy enough to read the on-screen performers, never leaving their frames, as parodic allegories of just that enframed listener of classical recording. On the other hand, their nonchalant performances of their parts can also indicate another aspect of the gallery as soundspace: its vulnerability to any audience sound. Except in cases in which volume is used to drown out extraneous noise (as in some recent works by Bill Viola and Thierry Kuntzel), sound installations tend to make you more aware of the absence of silence in the soundless areas of the museum. By inference, they may also make us aware of the sounds of the cinema auditorium, in the sense caught by Jean-Christophe Royoux: 'If cinema has rendered theatre silent by transposing its text into the sound-image relation of montage, the plastic arts have reinvested the procedures of montage in a stage space where the spectator becomes the actor'.[25]

In another installation in the same show, Mat Collishaw's *Song Cycle* (1994), the sound is of eight budgerigars in a large aviary, whose song is tape-recorded and played back on a delay. At times the budgies respond to their reel-to-reel doppelgangers, while at others they ignore them. The reproduction quality is good enough to fool most visitors at first. The parallel between cage and recording is, however, easily apparent; and the sense of the caging of the birds in both auditory and material space is a subtle commentary on the freedom of the visitor:

> In all the things I do there is this scenario being played out before you. There's no beginning and no end. It's continuous: it's going on before you arrived and it will continue after you leave. If it works, it will put you in a position where you are made to feel quite comfortable, because you are looking at something in a position that's less comfortable than your own. They're trapped, and you're on the outside. You're there to experience it for as long as you want—10 seconds or 10 minutes. And then you can go away and you know you are leaving this thing to this situation: it's condemned there.[26]

Like *Killing Time*, *Song Cycle*'s title refers to the durational aspect of the piece, in this instance the fractured and uncertain feedback loop between birds and recordings (and between the current audience murmur and that recorded from a previous time). In this case, it is not so much movement in and through the space that alters one's perception, but the act of leaving, tinged by Collishaw with the difficult ethical betrayal that it represents. It is this betrayal which is the real concern of the work, not its imprisoned birds, not least because budgies are bred to be imprisoned. The work engenders discomfort about a society of asociality, an ethic founded on walking away. That regret belongs with the live sound/recording/playback process in which the past becomes a strange country, a world of actions for which we no longer need take responsibility. The difference between this fatalism and that of *Se7en* is that it depicts this abnegation of responsibility as regrettable, not inevitable.

The pre-existing record of an opera shapes the duration of *Killing Time*, but it does not function as the revealable absolute of a narrative strategy. Its function is closer to that of melody in the superfield of neo-classical cinema: the definition of lived spaces. But the space which it identifies for exploration is no longer that of the hors-champ of cinema, but of the architectural space of the gallery. *Song Cycle*'s departure from even this kind of scripting, and its use of live songbirds, might appear to reintroduce the Bazinian ideal of a dramaturgy of nature. Yet this nature is already very clearly a construct, and part of the piece's impact derives from the denaturing of birdsong and the cognate denaturing of our twinned reactions to the birds and their recording that allows us to recognise it as 'just' art, and so ripe for abandonment. Such deconstructive turns are visible in recent installations by the Canadian Stan Douglas. *Pursuit, Fear, Catastrophe: Ruskin BC* (1993) plays a complex of micro-narratives against a player-piano version of Schönberg's *Begleitmusik zu einer Lichtspielszene* (*Accompaniment to a Cinematic Scene*, 1929–30), evoking an analytic history of incidental music. In *Hors-champ* (1992), two video projections on the recto and verso of a screen recreate the style of ORTF jazz documentaries of the '60s, one near-perfect, the other including all the edited-out shakes and movements from a two-camera set-up, allying studio technique to the recreation of a moment of diaspora when New Thing jazzers found a welcome for Black nationalist-inspired improvisation in Paris. In both, music becomes a zone of concentrated attention, a hermeneutic moment in which, as Douglas has said, 'the way one understands the music is based on what we see on the screen, and how we inhabit the space'.[27] Pursuit seems to find analogous histories of the fate of democracy in the cooperative origins of the town of Ruskin that later slid into racist incarceration, and the slide of anti-hierarchical twelve-tone serialism into programme music subordinated to images. *Hors-champ* suggests something of the historical blindness of nationalisms in the working through of Albert Aylers' 1966 *Spirits Rejoice*, with its echoes of revolutionary anthems of France and the USA. In Douglas' work, we have a further sense of the possibilities of sound freed from the Cartesian model of contemplation, or the cognitive model of ideal audition. Those possibilities revolve around the historicisation of the moment of hearing as a specific duration within the synchrony of the half-heard inattentive listening encouraged by the hegemony of spectacle and the spectacularisation of music. As Attali observes, 'when Cage opens the door to the concert hall to let the noise of street in, he is regenerating all of music...But the musician does not have many ways of practicing this kind of music within the existing networks: the great spectacle of noise is only a spectacle, even if it is blasphemous'.[28] Aberrant encoding, the subversion of existing networks—the institutions, discourses and technologies that frame sound reproduction—has from this standpoint to be overcome in the interests of radical recoding, involving not resistance but, as Benjamin argues a remaking of the apparatus.[29]

* * *

Contemporary theme park rides, central to the emergence of new screen technologies, have been at pains to individualise the experience of sound, for example by bedding directional speakers in the headrests of attractions like Space Mountain at Disneyland Paris. Here the effect of travel through a soundscape is simulated within earshot of the Cartesian subject. This individuation of the aural experience is a further solution to the problem of dispersal between tracks instigated by theatre stereo sound. In Belton's account:

> Audiences, at least in certain CinemaScope and Todd-AO films, were repeatedly 'distracted' by the dialogue, which travelled from one position to another behind the screen, and were overwhelmed by sound effects on the fourth track…The myth inspiring its evolution may have been the quest for 'greater realism', but that demand was already being satisfied, it would seem, by existing sound technologies—in particular, by monaural optical sound. Instead, it satisfied other demands—the need for spectacle and the desire for and fascination with technological display.[30]

The solution of spectacularisation involves moving the focus of playback from its apparent on-screen source to the individuated spectator in the audience, and in doing so to remove spectator and spectacle into the fantastic realm of display, that fantasia of the synergetic playworld. Though immersive audiovisual environments, such as virtual reality kits and themed attractions, may appear to have something in common with installation work, in fact they are far closer to an evolving cinematic model than to the sculptural/architectural and perhaps finally theatrical model suggested by our examples. By assuming the spectator into a spectacular world, such attractions disembody, and so disemplace and dehistoricise the experience as subjectivity. What I would argue of the Taylor-Wood, Collishaw and Douglas installations is that they work in counter-directions, among other things questioning this tendency of the cinematic to become merely playful.

In a new installation, *The Garden of A– – – –* (1996), Pervaiz Khan and Felix de Rooy move these problematics in a particularly fruitful direction. A light-trapped labyrinth leads to two installation points. The first, a VDU in a mirrored recess whose home screen metamorphoses between a Star of David and an arabesque, picked up in the geometric reflections of its shelf, reacts to a single viewer's selections by running a flickeringly fast, randomised montage of clichéd images from a database of orientalist themes in packaging, postcards, advertising and other sources, while the soundtrack, ostensibly sourced behind the screen, plays displaced collages of music and sound. In the second, larger space, a pyramid of monitors runs a pattern of found materials comparing orientalist cinema and news coverage of the Gulf War, while projected on the floor are treated images of desert sands. In this second space are two more sound sources, also playing complex mixes of found, sampled and musical effects produced in consultation with the artists by Trevor Matthison of Black Audio Film Collective.[31] The whole piece works as an extensive archaeology of the orientalist mediations of Desert Storm coverage and audiovisual rhetoric. Like the digital drift applied to the images in both segments, the treatment of sounds in the audio mix operates as spatial effect and spatial metaphor. Movement towards any one of the image areas brings you closer to the sound of a single source, rendering audible its samples of belligerent speeches, the wailing of the bereaved, the scratched elements of films like *Kismet* and *The Garden of Allah*, and in doing so at times bringing sound and image into synch. But at no point can you be unaware of the interference of other sources, nor of the complexity of the mix in each source, especially their rhythmic beats and looped and modulated quasi-electronic textures. The logic of *The Garden of A– – – –* is the logic of dispersal, not of focus. As a whole, the work acts as critique of the process of identity-formation which produces the Oriental as its shadow. Matthison's soundtracks therefore direct attention outwards and away from the possibility of either linear duration or focused spatiality, in the interests of reconstituting the possibilities of history and geography. The installation does not posit a true Orient behind the veils of Western orientalism, but shatters, in its dispersal of orientalist sound and image, the very notion of a coherent Western subjectivity from which, historically, such an identity has become conceivable.

To this extent, its problematic is not one of transmission (how are orientalist modes of thought communicated?) but one of translation (what are the conditions for understanding the Orient as oriental?). In part, that translational issue is explored through the translations between sound and image: the fleeting synchronisation, the falling apart and the drifting together, the fortuitous and the compelling. It demands, too, not so much an effort of adequation on the part of the audience to the work, but a series of approximations, in which the processes of misunderstanding and understanding can be seen for what they are, negotiations between spaces and times of recording and playback, sound and image, artists and audiences. The subjectivity it evokes in this process of mediation is one of scattering, the root sense of both diaspora and broadcast: a granular fluidity of the psyche that recognises both its pattern-making gestalt and its capacity for that hybridity which makes intercultural hybridity not a desirable goal, but the actuality on which any contemporary humanity is based.

The Garden of A– – – – premises its critique of individuation on a prior critique of identity, itself founded on a critique of the usage of the 'cultures' in the plural. As Jonathan Friedman argues:

> From the global point of view, culture is a typical product of Western modernity that consists in transforming difference into essence...Culture as the anthropological textualisation of otherness... does not correctly represent the way in which the specificity of otherness is generated and maintained. It consists merely in the translation of the identification of specificity into the specification of identity and ultimately the speciation of identity...In global terms, the culturalization of the world is about how a certain group of professionals located at central positions identify the larger world and order it according to a central scheme of things...the concept remains logically predicated on the notion of culture as text, as substance.[32]

In common with other globalisation theorists, Friedman doubts the political or analytic purposes of the hypostatisation of any way of life as whole or autonomous, insisting instead that there is no unified and protectable culture to inhabit. Yet the ideological drift of classical and neo-classical cinema alike has been to produce just such a concept, even as it struggles to maintain an impossible unity within its very technical means, the soundtrack and the image-sound relation. It is in this sense that installation work like this is radical, not for subverting the dominant, but for operating within an other problematic.

That problematic is the ground of diaspora, in which geography and history are lived as the experience of distance and movement. Another recent work, Bashir Makhoul and Richard Hylton's *Yo-yo Yo-yo* (1996) continues this exploration through an outdoors installation (premiered at the Bath Festival) which uses recycled home-movie footage made by Hylton's Jamaican father on a trip to Kenya in the 1960s, accompanied by the sound of foetal heartbeats. The installation preserves the traces of Kenyan dust on the emulsion of the negative, and this physical contact between recording and recorded is preserved in the use of a contact mike to pick up the vibrations of the maternal body and its passenger. That sending out of sound is the child's first transmission to a world, a traffic of meaning which is one-directional: it transmits, we translate. From infancy, we are irreducibly the source of rhythms, patterns and behaviours that will radiate out into other lives, whatever silence, as tourists wary of cultural difference, we might wish to keep along the way. Despite the swiftness with which raw images flow inward to the Western metropolis, and processed images flow outward to the colonised, even the private collections of images we keep in our family albums broadcast their yearning through difficult and circuitous routes back into the global circuits of humanity. The rendering of time into the arbitrary 24 frames per second of the movies is not, as perhaps the clock was, an imposition on the world of an administrative grid, but a process of projection through which the constituent elements of movement and change are uprooted from the limitations of the local, broadcast through space and time to join the nomadism to which the media arts return us. Like Douglas' double-sided screen, *Yo-yo Yo-yo* asks that we move as the images move, demanding motion, change, a nomadic audience. The allusive translation of Africa to Somerset, of the domestic memoir to the public park; the substitution of equestrian statue with video installation; the reflected and scattered light of projection: all of these take up the promise of the recorded and broadcast world—that the audiovisual, the definitive art of distance, is the art of diaspora, returning, transfigured, the immanent freedom of migration and communication.

This paper was initially given at the Screen Conference, University of Glasgow, July 1996, organised by the editors of the journal Screen *and the John Logie Baird Centre at the University of Glasgow and Strathclyde.*

1. Sean Cubitt, 'Sound: The Distances', in *Definitions of Visual Culture II: Modernist Utopias—Post-Formalism and Pure Visuality (Conférences et Colloques* 4), ed. Chantal Charbonneau, Montréal: Musée d'Art Contemporain de Montréal, 1996, pp. 97–111.
2. John Cage, 'Experimental Music', Music Teachers National Association, Chicago, Winter 1957; reprinted in liner notes to *The 25-Year Retrospective Concert of the Music of John Cage*; Mainz: Wergo Schallplatten, 1958, p. 8.
3. John Cage, 'themes and variations', in *Composition in Retrospect*, Cambridge MA: Exact Change, 1993, p. 57.
4. John Cage, 1958, op. cit., pp. 11–12.
5. Rick Altman, 'The Material Heterogeneity of Recorded Sound', in *Sound Theory, Sound Practice*, ed. Rick Altman, London: Routledge, 1992.
6. Douglas Kahn, 'Introduction: Histories of Sound Once Removed', in *Wireless Imagination: Sound, Radio and the Avant-Garde*, eds. Douglas Kahn and Gregory Whitehead, Cambridge MA: MIT Press, 1992, p. 3.
7. David Bordwell, *Narration and the Fiction Film*, London: Routledge, 1985, pp. 158–159.
8. Kaja Silverman, *The Acoustic Mirror: The Female Voice in Psychoanalysis and Cinema*, Bloomington: Indiana University Press, 1988. See also Amy Lawrence, *Echo and Narcissus: Women's Voices in Classical Hollywood Cinema*, Berkeley: California University Press, 1991.
9. Michel Chion, *Audio-Vision: Sound on Screen*, ed. and trans. Claudia Gorbman, New York: Columbia University Press, 1994, pp. 101–104.
10. Theodor W. Adorno and Hans Eisler, *Composing for the Films*, New York: Oxford University Press, 1947, p. 9; London: Athlone Press, 1994.
11. ibid., p. 33.

12. ibid., p. 41.
13. David Bordwell, Janet Staiger and Kristin Thompson, *The Classical Hollywood Cinema: Film Style and Mode of Production to 1960*, London: Routledge Kegan Paul, 1985, p. 72.
14. Adorno and Eisler, op. cit., p. 10.
15. D. N. Rodowick, *The Difficulty of Difference: Psychoanalysis, Sexual Difference and Film Theory*, London: Routledge, 1991, p. 94. See also the whole of Chapter 4.
16. Laura Mulvey, 'Visual Pleasure and Narrative Cinema', in *Screen,* Vol. 16 No. 3, Autumn 1975; reprinted in Laura Mulvey, *Visual and Other Pleasures*, London: Macmillan, 1988.
17. Elisabeth Weis, *The Silent Scream: Alfred Hitchcock's Sound Track*, Rutherford: Farleigh Dickinson University Press, 1982, especially pp. 110–111.
18. Christian Metz, 'Aural Objects', trans. Georgia Gurrieri, in *Cinema/Sound*, ed. Rick Altman (*Yale French Studies* No. 60), New Haven: Yale University Press, 1980.
19. Vincent Lo Brutto, *Sound-On-Film: Interviews with Creators of Film Sound,* New York: Praeger, 1994. See interview with Ben Burtt.
20. Rick Altman, 'Television/Sound', in *Studies in Entertainment: Critical Approaches to Mass Culture*, ed. Tania Modleski, Bloomington: Indiana University Press, 1986.
21. Chion, 1994, op. cit., pp. 144–154.
22. Claudia Gorbman, *Unheard Melodies: Narrative Film Music*, London: BFI, 1987, pp. 70–98.
23. Philip Brophy, 'The Architecsonic Subject', in *Culture, Technology and Creativity*, ed. Philip Hayward, London: John Libby/Arts Council, 1991.
24. Gorbman, 1987, op. cit., p. 73.
25. Jean-Christophe Royoux, 'The Conflict of Communications', in *Stan Douglas*, ed. Christine van Assche, Paris: Centre Georges Pompidou, 1993, p. 68.
26. Mat Collishaw, artist's statement, The British Art Show 4, exhibition guide, London: South Bank Centre, 1996.
27. Interview with Douglas in Jean-Yves Bosseur, *Sound and the Visual Arts: Intersections between Music and Plastic Arts Today*, trans. Brian Holmes and Peter Carrier, Paris: Dis Voir, 1993, p. 153.
28. Jacques Attali, *Noise: The Political Economy of Music*, trans. Brian Massumi, Manchester: Manchester University Press, 1985, pp. 136–137.
29. Walter Benjamin, *Understanding Brecht*, trans. Anna Bostock, London: New Left Books, 1973, p. 98.
30. John Belton, *Widescreen Cinema*, Cambridge, MA: Harvard University Press, 1992, p. 206.
31. A discussion of BAFC's audio work is included in Sean Cubitt, 'Footprints in the Air: Mechanical Perception, the Media Arts, Diaspora and Sound', in *Art & Design: Film and Art*, (*A&D* profile 47), 1996, pp. 72–79.
32. Jonathan Friedman, in *Global Modernities*, eds. Mike Featherstone, Scott Lash and Roland Robertson, London: Sage, 1995, pp. 80–82.

Towards a History of Listening
Martin Harrison

Seeing has its own history. Art historians, anthropologists of art and, increasingly, intellectual historians have all concerned themselves with what can be understood from studying the differences between different cultures' and different historical periods' ways of depicting and visualising experience. Whether we are considering issues to do with the Renaissance invention of perspective, or the importance of the picturesque in eighteenth- and nineteenth-century painting or the differences between, say, the iconic system of a Desert-school painter compared with his or her European counterpart, an assumption can be made that the historical function of the modality of seeing varies in alignment with the documents which represent that seeing. We have no problem in agreeing with the claim that we see the world as a Turner or a Michelangelo or a Namatjira saw it, not because we see it in the same way but (at least in part) because of the way Turner and Michelangelo and Namatjira saw it. The eye, in other words, has been constantly influenced by the objects and media systems which specifically reflect and extend its seeing—principally paintings, films, theatre designs, communication technologies and architectural spaces. Framed within a broad history of subjectivity, these and similar forms of visualisation have a dynamic, often semiotic relationship with the modality of vision. Differences in the ways things have been seen can be legitimately said to represent differences in the psychology of the historical subject, no less than in the subject's views and philosophies.

A similarly historical and relativising approach, however, is not so keenly evidenced in the case of listening. Here, the tacit assumption is that listening has been a more or less unvarying kind of modality, operating on a stylistic continuum. If, for instance, problems in the relation between listening and broader, more modal changes in sensibility are raised—and they sometimes are, for example, in the study of music or in otiatrics—then the normative assumption favours a style of auditory transparency according to which the behaviour of the ear is said to be measurable as a steady reference in relation to which it is only paradigms, theories, scientific study, etc which change. Listening itself does not change. That is to say, listening is treated as a given natural event in relation to the philosophical discourses which value it or the scientific and medical theories which explore it, whether those of neurological discrimination or speech recognition or tonal value. Listening is framed, in other words, within a much more narrowly conceived approach to subjectivity than seeing is. True to its traditional identification with aspects of the psyche such as intuition, innerness and attentiveness, listening's immutability is the immutability of the core, or of the essence. Yet no less true to its intangibility as a behaviour, and the discreetness of its position in relation to utterance, listening is also treated as being too subordinated to its objects for it to be constituted as a separable and culturally determined mode of perception. Both ways—that is, whether identified as an aspect of human psychology or subordinated to an objective code—listening is denied the status of being a true form of historical regime. It is refused the position of an epistemological economy whose habits can be studied in an historical manner. It is treated, in other words, as if it is a pure faculty, much like the great ear in Nietzsche's fable, which, 'as big as a man', dwarfs the body on which it is situated. As such, listening ceases to be a behaviour prone to cultural contingencies. It is no longer conceivable as a modality modified by a series of historical inflections and discordances.

Contingencies, inflections and discordant zones are exactly the matters which any attempt at a history of listening would have to explore. This would necessarily be a history not only of cultural and technical modifications to listening, but also a history of its mythologies and of the varying placements and emphases given to the so-called subjectivity of listening. And it would trace evolutionary shifts in the discourses which seemingly manifest a concern for listening. Such a history would in that sense be a history of listening's 'reach', quite literally of where it goes, where it is seen, how it is spoken of and how far it can be tracked. Thus, one could imagine, first off, a genuinely fabulous history of listening which proceeds, much in the manner of a symbology, by gathering together significant examples of where things are heard differently, of where the description of listening undergoes major changes and of where listening seems to take on an historically changed position within the modal construction of self and psyche.

Unemployable in any traditionally conceived school of media studies, such a historian of listening would be something like Italo Calvino's Marco Polo: this historian would be a raconteur of exotic life patterns and bizarre modal interlinkages. Whereas Calvino's Marco Polo recounts to his Great Khan the multiplicity of urban designs and cityscapes he has visited, our auditory historian's work would be to collect specimens of the dwellings and living-spaces of listening and to pay particular attention to the many different kinds of auditory information which human beings are capable of receiving. Further, such a history would then attempt to demonstrate the emergence of coherent structures within the auditory modality and a set of historically traceable links between, for example, hearing and language-theory, between hearing and movement, between hearing and the design of communication systems. These exotic 'listening cities', whether traceable only as a past archaeology or visitable across cultural frontiers, would be not so much instances of a social architecture but instances of Heideggerian stopping-places. They would be places where language and meaning had momentarily become particularly hearable, particularly structured within the listening modality, as sites of convergence between linguistic practice and metaphysical systems. They would be the cultural and historical sites where, to adopt Heidegger's phrase, we might begin to be able to 'rid ourselves of the habit of only hearing what we already understand'.[1]

Admittedly, a contemporary literature of this kind is not entirely lacking. Thus, for instance, the works of an anthropologist such as James Weiner who studies the relationship between living space, linguistic structure and the auditory field of the Foi people of Papua New Guinea might be a key text in such a history. Focusing equally on speech sound-patterning and the function of metaphor in song-form, Weiner traces a set of connections between location (sense of place) and utterance (lexical and syntactic form) which clearly delimit a divergent form of listening modality. Listening is not, it must be said, Weiner's primary concern, but the scope of his phenomenological approach is such that issues to do with listening are inevitably nuanced strongly in an account of a non-European modelling of living space and of lived time. A culturally relativised sense of listening follows automatically from his methodological commitment to a view of language, derived largely from Merleau-Ponty, that 'speech as a kinetic activity models and is modelled by such spatial and temporal configurations'.[2] It opens up the prospect that the syntactical and semantic preference in Foi discourse for stressing proximity and farness as key determinants of meaning-discrimination is not only a facet of a language's logic but also of its auditory geography. In particular his study of body language, the positioning of speakers and listeners in relation to each other, and his attention to the homology between phonological root-structures and geographical features are revealing. For Weiner's representation of a Foi landscape of both language and topography is also a mapping of the community of the Foi ear.

Similarly, anthropologist Stephen Feld's work on the intermix between morphological form and musical form in Kaluli song and performance offers a comparable kind of projection of the situatedness of listening in repertoires both of custom and of topography, highlighting key differential areas of subjectivity. Here, to take one of many examples, morphological structuring 'pivots' (if my precis can be permitted) a coherent referencing of water sounds in order to produce a sense of what Feld terms the 'inside dimension' of poetic utterance. According to Feld, a key metalinguistic concept of 'inner speaking' relates both lexically and through acoustic symbolism to images to do with waterfalls and water sounds: thus, this

> Kaluli metalinguistic-poetic concept is *sa-salan* 'inner speaking' or 'meaning inside speaking'. *Sa* is found in two semantic fields: waterfalls and sound. Used alone, it means waterfall, and as a prefix to other water terms indicates parts of waterfalls. As a prefix to verbs of soundmaking, it indicates the addition of text 'inside' the sound.[3]

A little later Feld talks about the sound symbolism, or more properly the phonesthesia, of Kaluli, demonstrating how overt symmetries and disymmetries of vowel sound refer directly to phenomena such as rain sprinkling, trees changing with the season, earth-tremors, echo-effects, proximal and distant relations of movement and so on. Sound values in utterance have, so to speak, an overt and conscious role to play in the production of meaning. The sound-web of poetic language does not sink transparently into the weft and warp of textual significance: sound is not, in this regard, pure affect. Listening operates differentially in terms not only of what is to be discriminated but how language is 'sited' environmentally in relation to the whole auditory compass of the sound world, whether this means the world of waterfalls and bird-cries or the world of human voices and dead, ancestral voices.

Both Weiner and Feld are deeply indebted to phenomenology as a tool of philosophical analysis. It might be argued, indeed, that our Marco Polo of listening's history will always have to transcend the role of raconteur by taking on, to some degree, the role of a phenomenological traveller. This historian's work will, in other words, always have to be grounded in a philosophical poetics, since such work will necessarily require the organisation of multiple strata within the history of an epistemology and not just an empirical account of listening per se. If such a statement sounds, at this stage, somewhat vague and hortatory, that is because such history still has to define the symbolic order in which the modality operates. Thus, this type of historical approach to listening would be also a history of subjectivity or, more precisely, a history of the differently constructed sensoria which can operate in the relationship between 'subject' and 'world'. Similarly, a history of listening is one which principally traces, if I may put it like this, the situatedness of listening within the theorisation of the subject no less than within a set of technological and communicative practices or a set of historical relations between self and other. This is why, as anthropologists, Weiner and Feld are able to write about how aspects of the natural and cultural world link up with listening in ways which may not be familiar to us and which accordingly illuminate how listening maps not just empirically defined 'other' cultures but maps core elements within the notion of culture itself.

For listening's history is inevitably a history of how representation itself is made cultural. It is a history of the modal acculturation of a concept of language, action, listening and self. Perhaps indeed by virtue of being situated outside the European context—that is to say, by virtue of its Marco Polo format—such anthropological study offers a momentary backward glance on the seeming transparency of the connection between meaning and hearing. It is as if an apparently indivisible layering between the two can suddenly be prised apart and thought about. What is revealed is that different sounds, and different kinds of attentiveness to sound, may not just be indices of different needs and social uses, but can reach profoundly into the way classificatory systems operate, the way grammatical norms are fixed and concepts are recognised as concepts.

* * *

Preliminary explorations are as far as the future historian of listening is able to go. Audible cultural memory can reach back only as far as the late 1870s. The earliest surviving documents of audibility are, besides, only fragments and shards. Most obviously, they are the fragmentary recordings of famous writers and statesmen made by the first phonograph manufacturers' sales teams; or they are the crackling records of late nineteenth-century ethnographic expeditions. Similarly, audibility's first literature is constituted by early attempts of writers and theorists to deal with the impact of a broad array of new communication technologies, where again the response to listening is fragmentary and limited, given that it is only one element of a much wider set of reactions to new technologies of representation. Mostly, indeed, this literature is secreted in quasi-futurist fantasy and anecdotes of invention. A hundred or so years later, it is still the case that listening occupies the place of shadow-effect in relation to a much more fully developed historical theorisation of cinema and visual communication, where image, sign and symbol offer the primary tools for understanding changes in the subjective circuitry of seeing and hearing is secondary. The study of modernist and late-modernist painting, the study of iconic systems such as TV and photography, the study of place and body speak to each other across, as it were, an already constituted planar projection of thought and mind. Fully established as part of an historiographical commitment to 'world-picture' approaches to social life, customs and manners of the past, such writing provides the ground for the deployment of specialist critical analysis of conscious and unconscious tendencies within perception.

A key problem, I would suggest, is the problem of belatedness where the technologies of listening are concerned—namely, that whereas regimes of the visual have over centuries possessed the techniques and the technologies which objectify sight we have only recently acquired the means of objectifying sounds. Listening's belatedness, in short, is already intrinsic to the project of European intellectual history, which from the start is a history of the mind's visibility. The establishment of European philosophy and scientific study after Descartes on the principle of the certainty of the visible world—its externality, its spaciousness, its measurability—has provided a long tradition not only of analyses of seeing and of light, but also an abundance of metaphoric extensions of the visible into descriptions of logical form and epistemology. 'We are thus faced', as Gemma Corradi Fiumara asserts, 'with a system of knowledge that tends to ignore listening processes'.[4]

If for instance we adopt Derrida's contention that all philosophical language has what he terms an intrinsic 'white mythology' of underlying metaphoric projection onto the world by which the theorist is captured, it is clear that the *principium* of that mythologising metaphor within the rational-scientific model is visual. Time and again, philosophical treatises offer a full archaeology of the way that the seeing eye has thought about the world, including Derrida's own critique of the audible presence of voice. Visible, extension-filling angels hover on the point of the scholastics' pin-head, not auditory ones. In the same way the diagrammatising, visualising tendency of Western thought has provided a wealth of testimony about how thought is laid out visually (Ramus), how objects are seen (Locke), how they relate to space and optics (Berkeley), how the mind visualises its own structures of perception (Kant), how language and mind relate to the historical project of sublime visibility (Hegel), how senses of presence-to-self are conceived in ocular terms (Merleau-Ponty) and so on. When searching for non-visual evidence, the historian of listening must find traces of the listening modality in interstices or in guess-work or in rare dissenting voices, such as Dewey's or Heidegger's. Or, even more daunting, such a historian must re-establish lost philosophical traditions, patching together areas of study which have been pushed out of the mainstream of the history of ideas such as the mid-nineteenth-century tradition of the philosophy of music and the hidden stream of modal theories to do with acoustics in early twentieth-century German philosophy.

The problem of belatedness is tied, in other words, to a much deeper issue: namely, the emphasis on representation. Together with a number of contemporary critics and historians of sight and sound, we may ask David Levin's question: 'What is left today of the rational vision of the Enlightenment?'[5]—but this does not automatically bring into play any clear path for the study of listening as a perceptual regime. The character of dominant vision may change without listening being privileged. For if the primary subject matter of the historian of listening acquires a truly representative status with the arrival of sound recording in the 1870s, then this arrival itself can only be conceptualised within a larger visualist enterprise. In fact, it is only when sounds can be written (subliminally visualised) in a way which frees them from the limits of the real-time acoustic world that listening acquires its own traceable modal form. Sound recording allows a first visual glimpse of reversibility, a first visual projection of raw sound as writing. Sounds, in other words, are no longer artefactual and expressive in the way that the sounds of musical instruments are; instead, they become representations of themselves, measurable in relation to an already implied source or authentic starting-point. But if this claim is correct, then it follows that it is only as an extension of a visualising regime that unconscious subject matter at last starts to inhabit the representation of sounds in a manner which is already familiar in equivalent literary, painterly and cinematic forms.

My point here, however, is not to play over the logical conundrum of interrelated modalities. It is simply to state that the belatedness of listening is both visual and literal. Quite literally (as marks), the sounds which Edison and Cros and others were mapping on the lamp-blackened, shellacked surfaces of cylinders and discs are the first hearable sounds to transcend acoustics and arrive at a fully formed status as representations of sound. This fact was not lost on those contemporaries who peered into the wavering, pinprick lines of early discs as if they could possibly see there some form of proto-language which might ultimately be readable for itself—that is to say, without the assistance of phonographs to decode them. Others saw these patterns (especially the patterns generated by non-reproducing phonautographs) as somehow offering insight into general waveform patterning in colour, in topography, in botany and the structure of crystals. Similarly, it is well known that the early listeners to radio waves linked their listening to a representative proto-listening, an etheric listening which seemed indistinguishable from listening to the 'other side' or to mantic voices derived from Ouija and mediums. Charles Grivel comments on this prevalent morbid aspect which inhabits the early imaginary of the phonograph, claiming that the phonograph had the effect of emphasising the listener's self in what he terms 'the lack of subject'. To early listeners, the phonogram produced not only an irremediable impression of death but also opened up the auditory equivalent of an endless mirror chamber, an inherently immeasurable dimensionality, in which 'a voice comes from a voice comes from a voice. Generic transmission'.[6]

During the latter part of the nineteenth century, listening became incorporated so firmly within a regime of representation that 'to listen' could for the first time be conceived as analogous to other forms of perceiving, to other aspects of subjective experience, or to the experience of other voices and sounds. Thus, we can puzzle in an anecdotal manner about the oddity of the fact that so many early pioneers of radio, like Lodge or Fiske or the founders of 2GB, were spiritualists and Rosicrucians, but the connection is not so much from an unconscious recognition of a hidden voice or a hidden truth already at work in recorded sound or radio sound, but rather from the fact that radio sound (in particular) achieved the status of objectifying a modality already linked in with unconscious and sub-audial aspects of the psyche. Radio set up sounds, heard and half-heard sounds, on a representative plane. Together with phonography, it did for sound what painting and photography had long before done for seeing: namely it externalised a subjective position in relation to a modality. Interestingly, it expressed that relationship primarily as a frisson, as a shudder, as a ghost and as spiritism.

* * *

The challenge to the historian of listening lies at the heart of this historiography of technology. What I mean here is that historians of technology habitually prioritise the discursive structures (the ideas and the contexts of those ideas) which lead to inventions and their introduction together with their consequences on customs, living patterns and the development of later systems. They study these discursive forms first. Such technological history explores and expands the thought-systems implicit within technological innovation. It talks about origins and outcomes, and it offers a classification system of periods and breakthroughs. So, for example, a pioneer sound historian and critic such as Douglas Kahn's tripartite division of avant-garde, modernist sound into three predominant, though not mutually exclusive, figures of 'vibration', 'inscription' and 'transmission' may usefully distance practice from technological format, but this discursive division remains a taxonomy of creative practice and intention.[7] The figures form, in essence, a type of discursive expansion. There is still the underpinning of an essentially technocratic account of sound's release from acoustic experience into a storable format, which then hybridises into a wider array of long-distance communication systems.

In this way, the *motus diabolus* of the transforming relation between differently 'figured' practices—whether inscriptive, vibratory or transmissive—remains at heart the change occurring between the ways in which sounds can be transported and relayed: namely, these changes reflect differences between a relay across time (the disc) or across place (radio waves) or out of time and place (writing). Discursive shifts in technological format 'explain' changes in sound. Yet though this undoubtedly tells us something about changes in listening, listening is reduced to being the interlinking space for the articulation of these different historically projected relations between sounds and places. Modality is readable only in an analogic fashion, as if it is directly constructed by inventions or interfaces and as if the primary documents which the historian of listening needs to study come principally, or exclusively, from the history of technological design. Kahn himself comments how from the beginning of what he terms the modern artistic 'fixation' on sound—which means from the beginning of modernism itself—this fixation has constantly emphasised the connectedness of sound and technology as artistic themes. Here a future historian of listening might respond that it is precisely the insistence and emphasis given to the making of this connection—and the belatedness of the documentation associated with it—which constitute a key problematic. It cannot be taken for granted as a starting point.

For one difficulty with such a techno-historical view is that the link between technological sound and technological system is often not evidenced in many early modern references to sound and hearing just as many times as it is. What is, however, extremely clearly evidenced is an overwhelming preoccupation at the beginning of the century with various aspects of audiovisuality. Radiophony, vanguardism and sound are only one theme within a larger historical repertoire which seems, broadly speaking, to be more focused on the interlinking of the two modalities of sight and sound than on sound per se. This is as true, for instance, of Cubist pictures—with their vocal newspaper collages and many-sided depictions of musical instruments—as it is of Futurist images with their speed lines and calligraphic notations of auditory experiences. It is as true of the spiritual polyphonies of a Klee or a Kandinsky as it is of the early experiments in multimedia assemblages of a Vertov or an Eisenstein. Sound technology and auditory form do not line up in these instances in an analogous fashion. What is suggested constantly is the articulation of a captured, freeze-framed moment where hearing and seeing coalesce in a concretised, 'objective' percept. Indeed, listening's self-reflexive appearance on the historical scene is inextricably involved in this still largely unstudied intersection between synaesthetic experience and an increased sense of the interiorisation of subjective space. Accordingly, the listening modality has to be treated within a broad array of issues to do with what might be termed the internal theatricalisation of the sensorium and across divergent modal regimes and different technologies.

There is a very clear example of what I am referring to in a recent study of the history of photography and cinema by Jonathan Crary. In his *Techniques of the Observer*, Crary studies a variety of pre-cinematic visual technologies, including many types of camera obscura used by painters.[8] Most interesting for my purposes, he studies the importance and range, especially during the 1820s, '30s and '40s, of scientific enquiries into the function of the visual after-images together with the popularity and extensive influence of the many inventions (thaumatropes, phenakistoscopes, kaleidoscopes and stereoscopes) associated with after-image technology. A provocative instance of not taking at face value the received continuities of invention, Crary argues that it is principally after-image technology and research which offer the initial conceptual and experiential form in which foundational aspects of classical optics break down. The instantaneity, the objectivity, of the visual object is threatened. The aesthetic assumption of simultaneity between the camera obscura image and its exterior image had previously, he writes, remained unquestioned. Following on from Goethe, the study of the retinal trace and its mechanisation constitute a theoretical and technological moment in which, as he puts it, 'observation is increasingly tied to the body...[and] temporality and vision become inseparable'. For Crary,

> the problem of the afterimage and the temporality of subjective vision is lodged within larger epistemological issues in the nineteenth century. On the one hand the attention given to the afterimage by Goethe and others parallels contemporary philosophical discourses that describe perception and cognition as essentially temporal processes dependent on a dynamic amalgamation of past and present.[9]

Tracing the intersection of these philosophical and technological discourses, Crary argues that there is not one unifying history of invention which leads from painting to photography and then to cinema, but rather that nineteenth-century visual technologies offer two quite distinct and competitive notions of technological 'seeing'—namely, three-dimensional, stereoscopic seeing and, opposed to it, kinetic and, later, filmic seeing. Further, he argues that kinetic seeing—the analysis and fragmentation of movement which leads to filmstrip's moving image—is for most of the century the less dominant form of technological image making. Indeed, for Crary photography and cinematics only become dominant forms because of their implicitly 'phantasmagoric' nature; that is to say, cinema and photography reconstruct the naturalism of the camera obscura by virtue of their phantasmic ability to map what they depict as once again the classicist's desire for a timeless mirror of the real world.

Against conventional film history Crary argues the critical importance of the stereoscope's capacity to provide three-dimensional, in-depth, present-to-life images. Notions such as authenticity, standing-out, depth, static look-alikeness and fidelity cluster around our nineteenth-century ancestors' fascination with the stereoscope, no less than with the landscape or the portrait. In particular, key elements of perception foregrounded in stereoscopic vision are tangibility (an image is made to seem so real it could be touched) and the metonymic relations established between the viewer's experience, the machine and the object seen. Transparency is broken down: to 'see' the in-depth image stereoscopically seems to require a particular kind of subjective participation and a conscious awareness that the image is not just being seen 'out there' but is being constructed as a reality-effect largely within the subject's own experience of seeing. Unlike looking at a photograph, which illusionistically conceals the way in which it is being seen, it is only a 'stereoscopic' seeing which can see things stereoscopically. Stereoscopic and afterimage theory, accordingly, produce a form of seeing constituted equally by localisation and disjunction, in which

> stereoscopic relief or depth has no unifying logic or order. If [eg Renaissance] perspective implied a homogeneous and potentially metric space, the stereoscope discloses a fundamentally disunified and aggregate field of disjunct elements.[10]

In other words, in its very pursuit of an authentic tangibility, stereoscopy immediately dislocates and nostalgises up-front experiences of seeing. It creates a dislocated sense of the relative, participatory role of the viewer. It raises questions of the image's origin and of its relation to its source. It immediately creates a sense of the duration of the experience's occurrence and of its 'over-tangible' intangibility.

The point of this excursus into Crary's work on stereoscopy may be starting to be clear. Though Crary does not develop this idea, the historian of listening might start to recognise a different kind of continuity which over-rides the deletion of technologies and which glances past the logic of the history of inventions. For another modal linkage with stereoscopy is sound recording, a technology of listening (developed in the high-tide period of stereoscopic imaging and speculation) which similarly emphasises dimensionality, authenticity, depth in relation to background, truth-to-lifeness and an acoustic attention to ghostly presencing which nineteenth-century consumers of sensory technology experienced first as a visual form of presence and nostalgia in the stereoscope. It must be stressed that this link is modal and epistemological, and not necessarily conveyed through a literal account of historical invention. It would, for example, be interesting to draw an epistemological analogy between the visual patterns of acoustic waves which Chladni (and others working in the early 1800s) were mapping on trays of quartz dust when vibrated by sounds and the abstract retinal after-image shapes which researchers such as Purkinje were producing some twenty years later: the link, however, is epistemic. What is common to both is the notion of after-effect and the discovery of a certain level of autonomy within the structuring of modal regimes.

For all that, however, a historian of listening could argue for the persistence of this perceptual mode, accordingly studying the way it intersects across a variety of inventions and a variety of periods. Perhaps indeed it would be possible to propose that these days every home possesses a latter-day model of the many versions of the mechanical stereoscope which a hundred and thirty years ago were being produced in their thousands, virtually as furniture items for Victorian households. 'Stereoscopic' listening was already implicitly structured within an equivalent set of metonymic relations created by the interplay of listener, apparatus and early acoustic recording's reality-effect. The modern hi-fi system with its balance button, its tone control, its re-creation of a picturesque room-space for sound, the phasing and the room-plan of its sound projection still inhabits a similar technological imaginary. The latest emanations of this consistent pressure towards presence and dimensionality within the technologisation of the ear are to be found in contemporary film editing and film sound techniques which emphasise proximity of the image-surface and wrap-around, stereophonic presentation of the sound-track. Recent films such as *The Piano* or *Dangerous Liaisons* do this, for example, making use of the THX multiphonic sound system. The modal preoccupation with the ghostly shudder hidden in Grivel's voice from a voice from a voice keeps on recurring.

If we return for a moment to that curious, often quite eerie, sense of 'extra-dimensionality' which seems to haunt the early technological literature of sound and listening, its spiritism and ghostliness start to make more sense as a modal preoccupation of which the technologisation of listening is only one, albeit a significant, factor. The spookiness in Bell's accounts of his first experiments with a telephone voice, hearing it coming like a ghost's from a room downstairs, is part of a more generalised discovery of how from henceforth a displaced 'presence' would occur in a virtual space which automatically brings with it a heightened, over-verified sense of dimension. The many contemporary accounts of shock (even to the point of fainting) and the often expressed anxiety about its potential magic and diabolism with which some listeners heard the displaced mimicry of a phonograph playing a human voice are similarly symptomatic evidence of a quasi-virtual, fantasy place where hearing is starting to reside. No less, the still visceral sense of melancholy, the gut-sense of presence and nostalgia, which haunts early acoustic forms of sound recording can still give us some sense of this broadly experienced modal moment. This moment is one where listening has to reckon with its own presence, and where hearing is transformed into an externalised image. In a psychoanalytic sense, the ear has to start recognising itself in a symbolic order. As equipment, listening achieved what the eye had long before accustomed itself to: listening became part of an imaginary, a part of an 'Other'.

For, right from the beginning, the stereoscopic room of listening was under construction. Nearly a hundred years later in the mid-1970s, Barthes, describing the experience of listening to a performance of Schumann's *Kreisleriana*, is still 'living out' this modal space in one of literature's fullest accounts of the internalisation of a sense of heightened auditory dimensionality. In his essay, *Rasch*, his listening is an account of an ear which has totally subsumed this space as inside-the-body space. Interestingly, the essay leaves unclear whether this listening is a listening to a recording, a listening to a live performance by another pianist or possibly a moment of reflection while Barthes himself plays the piece. Perhaps Barthes' sense of auditory dimensionality is so uppermost that the importance of suggesting any 'framing' of the technologised experience has disappeared: the music itself floats, as it were, in an already constituted auditory space, and it is seemingly no longer necessary to discriminate between the space of the mind, the space of real-time or the space of a high-fidelity recording. For this internalised, high-fidelity space is one which, for him, proliferates what he calls 'somathemes' or fragmentary, pneumatic bodies which respond to the beating and pulsing of the performed music. This ear is now hearing sounds as more embodied, more true-to-life, than the listener's actual body:

> I actually hear no note, no theme, no contour, no grammar, no meaning, nothing which would permit me to reconstruct an intelligible structure of the work. No, what I hear are blows: I hear what beats in the body...I hear this body which beats.[11]

Barthes' essay is a justly famous instance of a post-technological integration achievable between auditory dimension and embodiment. Together with his essay on what he terms the grain of a singer's voice (where similar themes are related specifically to listening to high-fidelity recordings of the 1960s), the account of listening given in *Rasch* is unusual in being one of the few pieces of writing which consciously sets out to reflect upon the listener's experience of the positioning of that listening-moment between subject and technology. Yet the history of listening had in fact already anticipated Barthes' localised, metonymic, fleshly articulation of its central theme.

A hundred years earlier, Edison had given a newspaper interview, perhaps deliberately self-mythologising, about a similar 'fleshy' moment when he realised how to solve the problem of converting the marks laid on the wax cylinder back into audible sound. For some twenty years, phonautographs had been able to lay a distinctive track of needle-marks in response to air pressure wobbling a diaphragm and needle in response to an emitted sound. But no working model had been able to play those sounds back as versions of the original. The moment of breakthrough was, Edison said, the moment when fiddling around with a diaphragm of a telephone, it accidentally pierced his finger:

> I was singing...to the mouthpiece of a telephone, when the vibrations of the wire sent the fine steel point into my finger. That set me to thinking. If I could record the actions of the point, and then send the print over the same surface afterwards, I saw no reason why the thing would not talk.[12]

It was this (in every sense) incisive experience which made him understand that playing the needle again over the grooves of a recording track ('I tried the experiment first on a strip of telegraph paper, and found that the point made an alphabet')[13] would reduplicate the vibrations of the original sound sufficiently to enable an audible sound to be emitted. Not a moment of ocular reasoning, but a moment of fleshly presence, Edison's embodied ear situated itself objectively, via his finger, within an externalised modality. Within a modality, that is to say, which already possessed virtual dimensions. For the first time, listening could listen to itself metonymically. And accordingly it could take place as an historically changing modality within an historical style of subjectivity.

* * *

A history of listening is a history of a modality. As such, it cannot be conceived as being synonymous with a history of a particular technology's reception, nor with a progressivist history of invention. As I have been at pains to show, a historian of listening will often be at odds with such histories. The figures by which listening is historically determined are not exclusively held by a singular strand of media. Accordingly, the periodisations of listening will follow a logic which reflects the history of epistemological change just as much as it searches for consolidated modal 'figures' by which listening is changed, trained, and re-situated as a concept and a practice.

Likewise, the types of documentation which this history will depend on will be very varied, drawn from many diverse sorts of writing and technological artefact. If, for example, one wanted to study further the themes of dimensionality and otherness which appear to characterise a late nineteenth-century listening, it might be just as useful to go to poems such as Hardy's where he repeatedly hears voices (like tape recordings) emitted from various churchyard graves as to consider Edison's claim that a major selling point for the phonograph will be that it will allow us to play over to ourselves the pre-recorded voices of loved ones after they have died. Both poem and recording-usage are symptomatic of a listening with which we are no longer familiar, but which inflected still largely unaccounted-for areas of the early modern psyche. Following the history of a modality and not that of a literary form or a technology, such an historical approach to listening might then link up these documents with, say, the recurrence of the telephone as a key metaphoric zone inhabited by early-modern ideas of the unconscious. The telephone, for example, speaks the unconscious for both Freud and Proust while, as unconscious angelic herald, it haunts even more recent anthropological study of the ways in which communication technologies are perceived. In a similar way, radio and sound recording appear to operate as the symbolic framework for literary techniques (such as stream of consciousness) which present fragmentary senses of self and, more grandly, fragmentary senses of a collapsing culture.

No less interestingly, the modernist period's preoccupation with synaesthetic experience cannot be separated out from its ghosts, its spirits, its sense of a listening whose technological articulation is both as 'shudder' and as voice from beyond. Both forms break modal boundaries, situating the self's fragmentation at that point where, once having separated out parts of the sensorium (the sub-audial, the visual, the tactile, the auditory) the moment of 'breakage' can be transgressed in a subliminal move which, by definition, can neither be 'seen' nor 'heard' nor 'touched'. Together, both the 'shudder'—literally, a shaking apart—and the beyond-voice continue to form the territory of a persistently utopic claim for an absolute re-integration of modal experience in the latest hyper-technologies. The super-reality of interfacial logics in current multimedia is symptomatic of this utopic drive towards integration, no less than is the otherwise inexplicable continuance of virtually magic claims about the transmutability of sound-form, the 'livableness' of virtual systems, the valorisation of intermediate cultural zones and so on. As the anthropological examples given earlier demonstrated, neither a naturalistic nor a techno-historical approach will be able to ask adequate questions of these latter-day formations. Only a historian of listening is at heart engaged on a history which must proceed through a series of historical definitions of ontology, of senses of world, of situatedness and the re-ordering of subjectivity.

Such and similar matters would be the province of a history of listening just as much as any specific study of sound. Indeed, the study of the emergence of the notion 'sound' (so often simply taken for granted in modern critical literature) would itself be a part of the task of such a history, for it would have to explain how that term is consolidated, how it comes to be experienced particularly in the inter-war years, and how it takes on its current role as an endlessly permutable *materia*. My hunch is that such a history would trace the increasingly detailed externalisation of listening and its fragmentation into various sub-modes: the musical, the psychoanalytic, the intuitive, the spiritual, the authenticating, the geomantic, etc. It would show, too, how belatedness is a permanent condition of listening not just in relation to its own technologies but also in relation to seeing during the course of this century. And it would study how this mismatch has often been experienced as a moment of crisis in the history of subjectivity. What I mean by this is that whereas ocular senses have increasingly been subsumed within the invention of more and more new interfaces—cinemascope, TV, computer imaging, electronic writing systems, teleconferencing, etc—listening has yet to deal with the full impact of the modal restructuring of linkages between sound, spirit and psyche. The image-world has become largely de-spiritualised and communicative. But the ghosts of sound continue to haunt a house of virtual dimensions. The history of how they have been heard has not yet been written.

A version of this essay was given as a paper at the 1996 Australasian Sound Recording Association Conference, National Film, Radio and Sound Archive, Canberra.

1. Martin Heidegger, *On the Way to Language*, trans. Peter D. Hertz, San Francisco: Harper, 1971, p. 58.
2. James E. Weiner, *The Empty Place: Poetry, Space and Being Among the Foi of Papua New Guinea*, Bloomington: Indiana University Press, 1991, p. 71.
3. Stephen Feld, *Sound and Sentiment: Birds, Weeping, Poetics and Song in Kaluli Expression*, Philadelphia, 1982, p. 193.
4. Gemma Corradi Fiumara, *The Other Side of Language: A Philosophy of Listening*, trans. Charles Lambert, London and New York: Routledge, 1990, p. 1.
5. David Michael Levin, ed., *Modernity and the Hegemony of Vision*, Berkeley: University of California Press, 1993, p. 3.
6. Charles Grivel, 'The Phonograph's Horned Mouth', trans. Stephen Sartarelli, in *Wireless Imagination: Sound, Radio and the Avant-Garde*, eds. Douglas Kahn and Gregory Whitehead, Cambridge MA: MIT Press, 1992, p. 33.
7. Douglas Kahn, 'Introduction: Histories of Sound Once Removed', in ibid., pp. 14 ff.
8. Jonathon Crary, *Techniques of the Observer: On Vision and Modernity in the 19th Century*, Cambridge MA: MIT Press, 1990.
9. ibid., p. 98.
10. ibid., p. 125.
11. Roland Barthes, *The Responsibility of Forms*, trans. Richard Howard, New York: Hill and Wang, 1985, p. 299.
12. Thomas A. Edison, *Scientific American*, Vol. xxxix, July 1878, p. 20.
13. Edison, ibid., p. 20.

Aggressive Listening

Robin Rimbaud (aka Scanner)

> Manipulation or reorganisation or pre-recorded images and sounds is like the process of thinking. Thus editing becomes the superimposition of consciousness or the intelligent structuring of this recorded experience.
>
> —Bill Viola

The Scanner series of recordings features the intercepted cellular phone conversations of unsuspecting talkers, edited into minimalist musical settings as if they were instruments.

Scanner is a means of mapping the city, where the scanner device itself—a handheld radio receiver—provides an anonymous window into reality, cutting and pasting information to structure an alternative vernacular. It's an opportunity to record experience and highlight the threads of desire and interior narrative that we weave into our everyday lives. Whether it's eavesdropping on an illicit affair, a liaison with a prostitute, a drug deal or a simple discussion of 'What's for dinner?', all exist within an indiscriminate ocean of digital signals flying overhead, but not beyond our reach. Every live performance, recording, or mix is in some sense a true representation of that moment in time and in that way relates to performance art in the temporality of its data, a sound Polaroid of interception.

The work constantly shifts its parameters; it is nomadic in its style. Sometimes the high frequency of cellular noise pervades the atmosphere, at other junctures it erupts into words and melts down to radio hiss. Intercepting the data stream, transmissions blend, the voices blur and drift, rupturing the light, audio transparencies of dreamy, cool ambience.

I am interested in the envelope of space, the environment in which we consume sound and music. How does one define the spaces between music and sound? When we listen to a Walkman how do we distinguish between that which is intended—the sound carrier—and that which is incidental: passing traffic, the roar of a plane, the screech of a train door, your own footsteps? Whether creator or listener we set up a virtual space in which we are each free to explore the sonorous and acoustic strata of what is an intimate yet global expression of space, a simple translation of the social transformations wrought by new technologies.

Digital technology has enabled a shift in focus. My work utilises what might be called the aural debris of the ether. With the easy accessibility of digital tools it has become even more straightforward to manipulate the tiniest details; processes now exist that will dissolve your ex-partner from your honeymoon photos; *National Geographic* magazine, the bastion of global reportage, allegedly moved the pyramids closer together to improve the balance of an image; radio and television reports are constantly digitally manipulated to suit an editor's political agenda. We now have the technology to peel open virtually any zone of information and consume the contents: personal video documents, sound recordings, phone scans, modem and net intercepts—highly personalised and voyeuristic forms of grazing for info foods. My recordings zoom in on the spaces between—between language and understanding, between the digital fallout of binary ones and zeroes, between the redundant and undesired flotsam and jetsam of environmental acoustic space.

The motivating force behind the work emerged from a fascination with the way we communicate. In 1865 it took twelve days for news of Lincoln's assassination to reach London compared to the immediacy of watching the 'live' coverage of the bombing of Baghdad during the Gulf War. The Victorian postal service handled 76 million letters per year, now there are 13 billion. More information is estimated to have been produced in the last fifteen years than in the whole of history. We live in a time of highly contrasting and confused communication, where people communicate not with others but with technology—utterings they consume largely for its own sake. Scanner sets out to take tiny fragments from this debris, to try to make some sense of it. We enact the role of the voyeur, observing the unobserved at the game of metrofictions.

Fusing the voyeuristic with a barrage of field recordings, textures and interference spotlights the controversial issue of privacy. What is private space, and what is public space? Video cameras cover our every movement in the streets, on the Underground, the buses, in shops. We are all featured on countless home videos without our consent. Consider the trend for real-murder TV, the O. J. Simpson case, commercially available police surveillance videos, amateur pornography magazines. These phenomena are, in a sense, an illustration of the illusion of privacy.

The Columbia Encyclopaedia notes that:

> The inception of...visual documents of personal and public history engendered vast changes in people's perception of history, of time and of themselves. The concept of privacy was greatly altered as cameras were used to record most areas of human life. The ubiquitous presence of photographic machinery eventually changed humankind's sense of what was suitable for observation.

Opening up these issues—in the aural as well as the visual sphere—is a way to encourage interaction and a return to real communication.

Scanner toured Australia in October 1996 as part of the Virogenesis project co-ordinated by the Australian Network for Art and Technology (ANAT), and hosted in NSW by Artspace and The Performance Space.

Essays In Sound

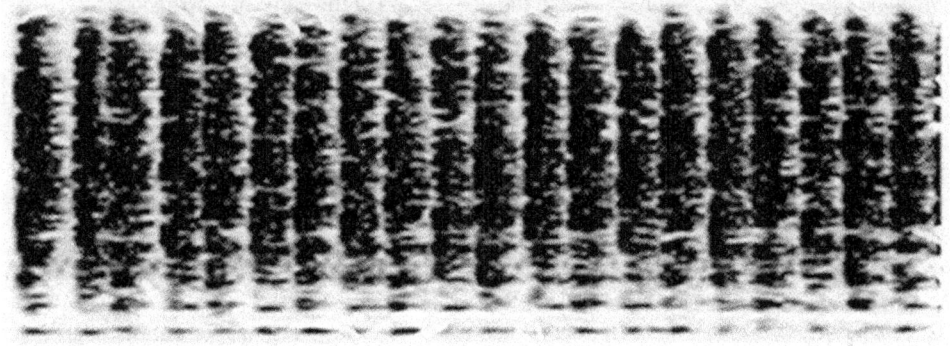

ASHLEY SCOTT
Sonogram 1996

Sound Theory, Sound Art: Same Theory, Same Art[1]

Ian Andrews

To: Scot Art <philosound@sysx.apana.org.au>

From: Ian Andrews <ian@cream.ebom.com.au>

Is sound theory a cross-disciplinary area encompassing branches of musicology, acoustic science, linguistics, cultural studies, philosophy, film theory, anthropology and history, or does it occupy, or seek to occupy, a position in the gaps between these disciplines? Like the non-objective and dynamic nature of sound itself, sound theory seems to permeate a multitude of disciplines without reference to a single parent discipline or to a genealogical or taxonomic structure. In other words, would it be equally valid to argue that sound theory is a subset of musicology, as it would be to argue that sound theory is a subset of film theory or philosophy? The sound theorist, who is very rarely merely a sound theorist, works in the way of a bricoleur, extracting knowledge from a diverse range of disciplines. This could be why sound theory seems to suffer from an insecurity regarding its own position in relation to other disciplines, which - in order to define itself in stricter terms—leads to a tendency for a reduction of its scope, or a tendency towards a perceived purity or essential idea. I find this direction (which seems to have occurred over the last couple of years) not only limiting but dangerous.

This position, however, seems perfectly understandable when large amounts of money are spent on conferences and festivals (such as SoundCulture) in the name of sound art, and when sound studies strands are becoming familiar fare in humanities courses. It is quite predictable that questions arise such as: 'What are the concepts of a pedagogy of sound?'. Sound theory gets too big for its boots and begins to exhibit the pretension of being a discipline unto itself. It is at this stage that we begin to see sharp divisions being drawn between theories of music and theories of sound, between cultural criticism and sound theory, etc. The more cynical among us could say that sound theorists/curators/publishers/artists, harbouring a deep insecurity about their discipline, have opted for an isolationist policy that seals off the borders, demarcates the territory, fortifies the limits and ultimately looks inward. Sound theory becomes an ivory tower housing a small elite of theoretical purists who constantly reinvent the wheel, as a consequence of their isolation from other disciplines. This tendency to seal off the territory of sound theory often results in a dramatic interiorisation, a search for the 'missing essence' of sound, for the lost power that resides in the sonic unconscious: ontotheology, religion.

The problem becomes even more pronounced when we move from theory to practice. In a post-Cagean world, if sound art is 'performed' in front of an audience it can too easily be perceived as music or theatre. If sound art happens on radio it becomes radiophonics or, again, music. So sound art ends up in the culturally over-coded environment of the art gallery. But even that is not enough. Sound art finds that it needs to be tied to an object (so that it can be visually documented, given a monetary value, attributed authenticity and singularity, etc). In other words, it once again became enslaved to a regime of the visual. While it is not true that all sound art pieces are dominated by the visual, the pieces which attain the position of highest importance in the art hierarchy usually command a strong visual presence. Disembodied works, on the other hand, existing in the same context, only as sound on tape or CD, are often marginalised.

It would be unfair to lay the blame squarely on the practitioners of sound theory/art. The problem can equally be attributed to the growing institutionalisation/commercialisation of this area, the gallery/high art system, and even the selfish and paranoid intellectual climate of the '90s.

Rather than seeking to define the essential values of sound theory we should celebrate its very non-position. We should celebrate the anarchic freedom, and renewed perspective which this position brings. Surely the greatest value of sound theory lies in its challenge to a philosophical world-view based on the domination of the visual, and not in the search for founding principles, aural essences, or techno-mysticism. However, the re-examination of philosophical values from the perspective of sound should not require the establishment of a new set of immutable founding concepts based on sound. We need to tread much more lightly in this area. Sound theory should be a movement from one body of knowledge to another, constantly plundering, rearranging and juxtaposing different disciplines.

1. This text was written, and placed on the philosound list on the web, in response to an article on SoundCulture 96 by Nicholas Gebhardt, 'Can you hear me? What is sound art?' in *RealTime* No. 13, 1996. Gebhardt's article raises some of the issues and encapsulates some of the dominant themes of sound theory that have been worrying me for some time.

Foundations...
(a Response to Ian Andrews)

Scot Art

To: Ian Andrews <ian@cream.ebom.com.au>

From: Scot Art <philosound@sysx.apana.org.au>

It's true that the tendencies documented by Ian do exist in modern sound theory. It's not really a discipline on its own, and it really could be a sub-discipline of philosophy, musicology, film criticism and/or cultural theory. Perhaps it would be better classified as a 'cross-disciplinary field' and left at that. But, as Ian points out, this isn't enough for at least some academics working in the area: they desperately want it to be a discipline in and of itself. And sound art is nowadays almost completely subjugated to the sound-emitting visual object; it's not there until it is seen.

My answer to the questions Ian raises can only be to supply my personal perspective, for example why we started Soundsite, and the list philosound.[1]

For me, sound studies is properly termed the philosophy of sound (hence the name of the list, philosound). Thus, if pressed to supply a concise definition, I would say it is primarily a sub-specialisation of philosophy, with strong cross-disciplinary currents. A more comprehensive definition would take several paragraphs. However, the Soundsite web page might suffice.

On this page you might notice that musicology is one area which is almost entirely excluded from Soundsite's definition. Musicology is the one area I have some problems relating to (in terms of sound studies): it is too obsessed with reasoning with/about the musical structure of sounds, how these are connected, primarily through emotions, with human subjects without saying too much about subjectivity in general. It also tends to set up the classic sound/music/noise distinction, privileging of course the music category. It is true to say that post-Cage, the category of music has expanded somewhat to include things previously lumped into sound or noise. But it is not true to say that these categories are abolished; rather they are strengthened considerably. I am sure that even Cage himself had at least something he would put into the generally negative category of noise (despite *4'33"*, which simply announces 'sound and noise can be music', and not that all noise *is* music).

This music-noise division is the only one about which I can accurately say that a sharp distinction is drawn between sound theory and musicology. This is not to say that all musicology falls sharply on the 'other side' of the border, as some of it obviously doesn't. But there is definitely a line which, once crossed, places certain types of study definitively into the territory of musicology. The other borders which are placed between sound theory, and say, cultural studies, aren't so clear cut, and there I agree with Ian's critique. However this opposition (to musicology) is one of the primary motivators in starting and continuing Soundsite: so much academic discussion of sound on the internet never does rise above mere analysis of music (or sound-as-music if you will).

If, then, sound studies is a sub-discipline of philosophy, the only question which I feel is foundational in this regard is the following: Is it possible to imagine (or live) an ontology of sound, and what does an epistemology of sound 'look' like? This is the question which in my opinion makes sound studies part of philosophy. However, to be broader, the philosophy of sound is perhaps merely philosophy as it is applied to a singular object of study - sound. It is part phenomenological, psychological, social and, yes, musical (and lots more besides).

However, I feel I should address Ian's assertion that 'This tendency to seal off the territory of sound theory often results in a dramatic interiorisation, a search for the "missing essence" of sound, a search for the lost power that resides in the sonic unconscious: ontotheology, religion'.

My perspective on this is that by theorising an 'ontology of sound' we're (well, at least, *I'm*) not trying to find sound's 'lost power' or to locate a 'sonic unconscious', but addressing a certain post-Enlightenment philosophical tendency toward a merely visual ontology, a merely visual epistemology, which privileges the seen over other sensory material, specifically, the heard. This philosophy (that I'm resisting) can be thought of as synonymous with Renaissance linear perspective painting.

So for me, the philosophy of sound is a way of resisting, deconstructing if you like, the Age of Reason which still holds us in its rational (read: visual) sway. This is the 'purpose' of such a theorisation. Thus I, like Ian, cannot brook the Balkanisation of sound theory into its own discipline with myriad sub-specialities; it isn't any such thing. Rather it's a cross-disciplinary branch of philosophy (and maybe all related disciplines), and its primary object of study is sound rather than, say, logic or social systems or cinema. Note that I think it perfectly reasonable that you can study any of those three (and more besides) and their relationship to sound. In fact I think that considering sound studies as a philosophical pursuit serves its academic pretensions rather well: labelled philosophy, it inherits the great weight of intellectual respectability that the study of philosophy affords. It also accounts for the fact that you find artists, cultural theorists, musicologists, philosophers, film critics and dedicated non-specialists all engaged with its study. As well, I find the appellation 'philosophy' an easy way to explain it to people who are not humanities academics or related specialists, and I find such 'plain English' explanations more helpful than many people will admit.

As for practice, I intended to add a whole new section but instead, let me be as brief as possible. I know I've gotten into serious trouble on mailing lists by arguing that the techno-music I make isn't 'art'; I know that in this postmodern age I'm not supposed to devalue the popular and valorise 'inaccessible' high art. But, still, as an artist I think it's right of me to nominate which bits of my output are art, or not. Then again, maybe not. I do think, however, that there is a certain qualitative difference between my work in techno and my work in other audio spheres. As a sound artist I work with radio, spoken word, music, computer media, and performance, sometimes all at once, at other times separately. This is no attempt to invalidate my music *as music* - it still *is* music. The category of sound artist is just an easy way to label the *sum* of these practices. However, I don't know if any of these individual practices actually *is* sound art.

Perhaps there is a neat (perhaps too neat) parallel here with the state of play in theory. Maybe sound art, together with sound theory, form a totality: a cross-disciplinary theoretical field and a multi-disciplinary practice. Maybe that's what makes our chosen field different from most others, and perhaps we ought to accept our status of non-specialist outsiders in the fields of artistic and intellectual endeavour. This notion appeals to me; we can bring fresh perspective to a number of areas. As Ian writes:

'the greatest value of sound theory lies in its challenge to a philosophical world-view based on the domination of the visual, and not in the search for founding principles, aural essences, or techno-mysticism. However, the re-examination of philosophical values from the perspective of sound should not require the establishment of a new set of immutable founding concepts based on sound. We need to tread much more lightly in this area. Sound theory should be a movement from one body of knowledge to another, constantly plundering, rearranging and juxtaposing different disciplines'.

I think this sums it up; our field should be like the phenomena we study: immaterial, vibratory, shimmering, difficult to pinpoint. Just as sound dies once in stasis, so will its theorisation.

However, I must disagree on the issue of 'founding principles', because that's what we're arguing for anyway. The statements (by both of us) *are* founding principles regardless of what we might say. Just because we might agree, firstly, that our thinking is based on an opposition to the primary visualist tendency in Western philosophy, and secondly, that we don't want a new set of immutable concepts to take the place of the old ones, that doesn't mean that that's not a foundation. After all, foundational issues never die, they just intermittently regress into crisis (just ask any mathematician).

1. See the System-X web page Soundsite on: http://sysx.apana.org.au/soundsite/about.html and philosound@sysx.apana.org.au

Creaking Grounds: Tectonics and SoundCulture 96

Ed Osborn

Kazue Mizushima Eve of the Future 1996. Performance.

SoundCulture 96, the third in a series of trans-Pacific sonic art festivals, took place in the San Francisco Bay Area during the first part of April of this year. The festival included 17 exhibitions, 10 panel discussions, and 55 performances and other events held at 33 sites throughout the region. Co-presented by 32 arts and culture organisations, and including the work of 228 artists from the US, Canada, Japan, Australia, and New Zealand, SoundCulture 96 was easily the largest sound art event ever held in the United States. Focused on the creative use of sound outside of the field of music by practitioners based in the Pacific region, the festival included representations of a number of differing areas of sound practice: sound sculpture and installation, radio and telephonic works, performance, acoustic ecology, noise, cultural theory, appropriation, high- and low-tech activities, educational events for kids, homemade sound instruments, sound works for public space, sound for film, and so on.

As the director and one of the participating artists, I dispensed with objectivity about SoundCulture 96 long ago; this is an overview of the event from someone who knows far more about it than is good for anyone's health. Covered here are some of the broader themes that emerged from the festival illustrated by a few of the many events that occurred over the course of 11 days last April.

One aspect of the festival that received much comment was the wide diversity of work represented. What has been common knowledge to practitioners in the field was made clear to even casual observers here: sonic art work by its nature doesn't fit well into established categories of art or artistic practice, hence artists working with sound employ a wide variety of strategies in using it. While advances in sound work have often been facilitated by technological progress, and the development of sound art can be read as a mini-history of electronic innovation, these advances have left a rich trail of methods and practices of harnessing sound, and many of these were in evidence in the festival. While Ron Kuivila worked with the latest in surveillance cameras, crackling wires, and custom digital signal processing, and Negativland employed a cryptic array of subversive electronics in conjunction with a pair of techno DJs, Julaine Stephenson rewired a washing machine to play clean a seven-inch vinyl disk and Phil Dadson drew sound out of hand-operated stones, some of which dated back to the Paleolithic era. And where Ian Pollack and Janet Silk's *Museum of the Future* was driven by computer and heard over telephone lines, Kazue Mizushima's *Eve of the Future* employed silk thread and paper cups to deploy a vast array of string telephones across an outdoor lawn space in which she performed by stroking, scraping and occasionally breaking the threads. This wide array of work was matched by the variety of circumstances in which the work was found. It was possible to find SoundCulture events in museums, universities, non-profit and commercial galleries, performance spaces, warehouses, on a beach, on radio waves, in a shopping mall, in a harbour, in a cinema, on a public transit bus, on the internet, and in nightclubs.

Where broadcasts from KPFA-FM in Berkeley brought SoundCulture to anyone who tuned in and served to give a sense of unified presence to the festival, the spatial dimension of radio was illustrated on a much more local scale by Kathy Kennedy's *SoundWalk* performed in an outdoor shopping mall north of San Francisco. Working with a small transmitter and dozens of performers accompanied by radios scattered throughout the mall, she broadcast a spare soundscore to be augmented by the improvisations of the performers; the audience was free to wander the walkways catching bits and pieces of the work from different sites. For half an hour or so the space of the mall was gently transformed from a place of commerce into a place of social engagement and contemplation; the bounds of that space were articulated by the range of the transmitter, deftly illustrating radio's twin aspects of locality and omnipresence.

Given that the geographic scope of SoundCulture is centred on the Pacific's 'Ring of Fire', it was no surprise that fire showed up literally and metaphorically in a number of works. Scot Jenerik gave an energetic performance in which he pummelled a pair of flaming wood and metal structures wired for sound. Tony MacGregor and Virginia Madsen's *Cantata of Fire* broadcast on KPFA explored the audio culture of the siege at Waco, Texas and the fire that concluded it. In Richard Lerman's *Changing States*, a tiny flame was used to heat metal strips attached to contact microphones. As the metal deformed in slow and unpredictable ways under the heat, its eerie transformations were heard greatly amplified. Evoking at once the micro-world of the grain of metal and the macro-reality of plate tectonics, the piece served as an allegory for the process of generating sound itself: sound, like fire, is simply an artifact of the transfer of one form of energy into another, expended in an instant and then gone. Later in the evening, Lerman showed a videotape of a swarm of desert ants crawling over a pair of microphones. The high gain on the recording devices again reversed the micro and macro, and as these tiny creatures produced enormous sounds their energetic activities seemed to be asking us to consider how much these microphones were in service of our intentions and how much we instead worked to fulfill theirs.

Several events highlighted the functions of sound as it plays out in a social landscape. Don Wherry's *Harbor Symphony*, played on the horns of a number of boats moored in the Port of Oakland, kicked off the festival with a noontime performance for an intrigued audience of tourists, office workers, and SoundCulture participants. Kazue Mizushima's outdoor performance brought automobile traffic on a nearby road to a crawl, and Kathy Kennedys piece mentioned above gently undid a shopping mall. Ann Wettrich's *Aviary Commute* took over an unsuspecting mass transit bus with a flock of performers equipped with tape players and recordings of bird calls. While most of the audience of regular commuters took it in stride, the imposition of these sounds into this mobile public space apparently upset the normal order of authority: the bus driver repeatedly threatened to eject all the participants unless they turned off their recordings. Fortunately for all concerned, everyone arrived at their destination before the situation reached the breaking point.

Later that day in an old and now-converted military building north of San Francisco which houses the Headlands Center for the Arts, a panel session on the subject of acoustic ecology touched on some of the issues raised in Wettrich's piece: control of social space, preservation of quiet, the harnessing of natural sounds for artistic and commercial purposes. Hildegard Westerkamp, one of the foremost figures in the field of soundscape studies, gave an eloquent talk on listening, sound, and silence in relation to personal, local, and global well-being that provided an encompassing view of the way soundscapes can be used to monitor engagement with, and connection to, our surroundings. Her talk provided a refreshing and well-considered perspective in an area that is often marked by simplistic cultural assumptions about our relation to nature; the spirited discussion that followed the panel presentation centred around these issues.

The acoustic ecology event was only one of many panels on aural culture presented over the course of the festival. Other presentations focused on the relationships between sound and literature, the use of sound in scientific practice, legal issues around sound and copyright, sound in architecture and public space, and sound as it is used to identify social and cultural location. Kent Howie's *Non-Native Species* was a comparison of the altered soundscape of San Francisco's Mission district due to a population of feral parakeets and the cultural changes brought about there by the growing Hispanic community. Negativland's Don Joyce discussed some of the legal and ethical issues surrounding the practice of audio appropriation and some of the well-publicised problems his group has encountered with the commercial recording industry. Architects John Randolph and Bruce Tomb talked about the utilisation of sound in their large-scale works, Douglas Kahn traced the use of sound in William Burroughs' writings, and Frances Dyson presented a detailed meditation on the psychological and cultural effects of sound recording. In the midst of much reconsidering, recasting, and recoding of auditory experience often in terms derived from visual culture, it was fascinating to find the reverse described in Michael Buckingham's research into visual imaging in underwater environments by using the behaviour of sound as a model for data acquisition (*Acoustic Daylight*). As can be gathered here, most of the panels had a rather academic slant to them. While the occasionally opaque language used in some of the papers undoubtedly lost some listeners, the underlying ideas and issues being dealt with were rich with insight and invention. The fact that a detailed investigation of the sonic life of such a wide variety of cultural practices could be made speaks to the relevance of the sonic arts to current critical discourse and to the larger social fabric from which that discourse is derived.

The presence of noise artists—another part of the audio continuum—was very apparent in SoundCulture. Several local warehouse spaces served as performance venues for high-volume and high-energy performances from Hijo Kadian, C.C.C.C., Crawl Unit, and others. Trading mostly in aural texture and sheer sonic impact, these events were either exhilarating or alienating—but rarely anywhere in between. These were the only performances in SoundCulture that contained the kind of numb macho posturing so often found in more standard musical or visual art contexts; their presence served as a clear contrast to the relief at its absence elsewhere in the festival. While the noise events seemed at first to have little in common with nature-sound and soundscape activities, their side-by-side placement in SoundCulture revealed more shared ground than might otherwise be assumed. The search for natural quiet and the pursuit of immersion in overwhelming sound are each a response to living in a machine-deafened culture; enough time spent in either area results in a change of consciousness, and the desire to lose oneself in a sonic environment is exactly the same.

At several points during the festival, discussion among the participants turned to finding the components of the Pacific sensibility that informed the work presented in SoundCulture. Though no definite answers emerged, it seemed to have to do with existing on a number of physical and cultural margins, the presence of those margins being central to a particular geographic psychology (that the field of sound art also occupies a marginal space goes without saying). Whether found in the illusion of instant communication to the future or past across the international date line, the constant consciousness of the distance between here and somewhere not here, or the (fading) presence of a string of natural paradises along the Ring of Fire, the pleasures and tensions that are shared among Auckland, Sydney, Hong Kong, Kyoto, Vancouver, San Francisco, and the islands in between, have to do with the concurrent experiences of splendour and impending displacement. In California the presence (and promise) of Silicon Valley and Hollywood isn't enough to completely mask the strain of infrastructure decay, rapid cultural and economic change, and—of course—seismic peril. The constant seduction of the Next Big Thing combined with a very short collective memory here ensures that there is no end to the (re)building of highways for data, automobiles, and everything else: new space for old accidents.

A possible glimpse into this state of mind was offered in Paul DeMarinis' work, *Chaotic Jump Rope*, shown at the San Francisco Art Commission Gallery. In it, a latex tube is connected horizontally between the shafts of two small motors running off the same electric current. As the speed of the each motor varies slightly, the tube is sent into a shifting and alluringly unsteady oscillation as it tries to compensate for the difference in revolutions-per-minute; the system only briefly succeeds in stabilising before faltering again. The resulting fluctuations in motor speed are used to generate a series of tones that vary in tandem with changes in the rates of rotation. Pleasurable on both intellectual and sensory levels, hypnotising and perpetually uncertain, the piece seems to contain much of the Pacific sensibility without settling in any one part of it: instability and intrinsic beauty, technological acuity and hazard, border space and physical force.

These themes were further articulated in Wang Po Shu's installation, *Hidden Music of the Golden Gate Bridge*, in which a small gong tuned to one of the overtones of the natural resonant period of the bridge is placed to the north and in sight of the bridge itself. Currently undergoing a substantial seismic retrofit, the bridge will, in a few years, have an entirely different natural resonant period and, presumably, remain in place when the earth shifts beneath it. As it stands now, an earthquake of sufficient strength and correct periodicity—the pitch of the gong transposed down a half-dozen octaves—will vibrate the bridge right into the bay. Quietly illustrating the relative scales of the structural, geologic, and social resonances of the Golden Gate, the piece evokes both an unsettling reminder of the natural forces under our feet and a sense of uncertain technical advance mixed with approaching loss (the gong's tuning will be meaningless once the retrofit is done and, retrofitted or not, one day that bridge will fail).

A trip to Oakland across a different bridge (one that partially collapsed when the earth rumbled several years ago) found a pair of Julaine Stephenson's repurposed home appliances at the Pro Arts Gallery. In *TV Dinner Scratch-O-Matic* a distressed fork serves as a stylus that bumps along a cooker lid set on a revolving microwave turntable producing a set of scrannel metallic tones as it goes. Across the room a washing machine-turned-turntable agitates a small vinyl record under a stylus; the futility of attempting to make the record clean again is heard through a speaker placed inside the machine's water hose. Elsewhere in the gallery, Tracey Cockrell's language based-sculpture explores the slippage between words and meaning, sound and body. A series of molds taken from the inside of the artist's mouth as she pronounces various phonemes and arranged inside a velvet-lined case, the piece makes solid the shape of words as it alludes to a common and cryptic taxonomy of physical language. And Eiko DoEspírito-Santo's interactive audio installation designed for people of varying physical abilities was notable for its smart interfaces of polyps, pendulums, and pattable tables. Further into the East Bay, Ellen Band's installation at Walnut Creek's Bedford Gallery focused on subtle, psychoacoustic trickery: specially blended sheets of pink noise evoked either the intended auditory hallucinations or the occasional unintended physical distress in listeners.

At the Catherine Clark Gallery (the only commercial space brave enough to join forces with SoundCulture), Jack Ox presented her stunning visual score derived from Kurt Schwitters' influential text-sound work *Ursonate*. A dynamic live performance of one section of the piece from a late-arriving Miguel Frasconi during the opening reception for the show demonstrated the continuing strength of the performance version as well as an unusually clear and powerful connection between sound and image found in Ox's interpretation of the piece. It was later reported that at least one member of the audience there had some sort of life-changing epiphany during the performance.

The largest SoundCulture event in terms of audience size was Negativland's performance at the Trocadero, a San Francisco nightclub known for its weekly Bondage A Go Go soirées. Drawing close to one thousand clubgoers and other nightcrawlers (the usual SoundCulture crowd was in short supply that evening, probably due to attending concurrent events), the group performed with the Hardkiss Brothers (a pair of turntable wizards) under a projected-image environment provided by filmmaker Craig Baldwin. Known for their free-form radio shows and theatrical gigs, this performance was somewhat subdued by comparison. Although all three elements of the evening's proceedings displayed an expected and voracious appetite for appropriation and culture-jamming, the Hardkiss Brothers' techno orientation never quite gelled with Negativland's grab-bag knobs-and-sliders approach—and neither of them could match the inventiveness of Baldwin's visuals. Perhaps it was an off night for the performers or maybe it was an experiment that looked better on paper than it sounded in the flesh, but the performance served as a reminder that, for all its currency, the cut-and-paste strategy only works as well as the brains and instinct controlling the scissors, mouse, or needle in the groove, and that a room full of appropriators doesn't necessarily make for a brotherhood of thieves.

Ron Kuivila's installation, *Parsable*, shown at the LAB's funky and cavernous Mission district gallery, created a space in which the movements of visitors were tracked by a surveillance camera mounted high overhead and registered by a set of servo-controlled sunglasses that followed any nearby activity. Motions were also translated into sound via a set of pivoting ultrasound sensors and their signals modified in part by the video feed from the surveillance camera. Elsewhere bare wires sparked intermittently and wall-mounted sheets of foil shuffled at random. Visitors were held in limbo as the tenor of the piece shifted around them from an engaging you-don't-have-to-be-a-star-to-be-in-my-show ambience to an uneasy feeling of being caught in the crosshairs of an unknown technological assailant. The performance version of the piece in which Kuivila activated various parts of the installation and performed on an auxiliary set of custom electronics was notable for its rapidly changing audio contours and the high technical and conceptual quality of his relentlessly hacked sounds. Recalling both the aural textures and compositional strategies of David Tudor (the piece was, in part, an homage to the soon-to-be-late composer), the performance demonstrated a clear sense both of the history that informed it (specifically the pre-computer era of electronic music) and of the marks that that history has left on contemporary sound practice—even as that practice spirals and morphs into new guises.

Among the many other noteworthy exhibits in the festival was Nigel Helyer's *Silent Forest*, shown at the San Francisco Art Institute. An installation comprising beautiful sound horns modelled on the air raid sirens mounted on the Saigon opera house and glycerin-immersed bonsai arrangements, the piece drew parallels between the use of dioxin defoliants during the Vietnam conflict and the culturally defoliating history of French colonial rule there. Deployed in a set of carousel formations, the horns broadcast distended abstracts of opera music and were among the most visually striking elements of the entire festival. New Langton Arts presented *PHFFFT*, a large installation by Trimpin in which sound was generated by computer-controlled bursts of air through specially tuned pipes. The piece was both visually and sonically engaging but, given the context of the festival, it had surprisingly conservative musical aspirations. My own work, *Parabolica*, was shown at the Center for the Arts at Yerba Buena Gardens. In it, a model train engine circled a suspended, serpentine track while dragging a rolling speaker behind it. Constantly varying its course across many possible routes as it went, the train illustrated with its motion the statistical form of the bell curve as it broadcast sounds referring to individual determination, confidence, and certainty.

The performance component of SoundCulture also had many rewards in it. Brenda Hutchinson's *Every Dream Has Its Number* elegantly blended a half-spoken, half-sung narrative about her mother's penchant for gambling with a delicate, audio-verité soundscore and fragments of melodies played on her Giant Music Box (an enormous version of the device often found under tiny twirling ballerinas and bears). By turns touching and painful (her mother was a handful, to say the least), the performance revealed an exceptionally rich, personal, and clearly articulated artistic vision that was free from the sentimentality that usually marks pieces built from such private histories. Local group Citizen Band presented a surprisingly stately performance using a blend of old and homemade electronics mixed with incidental parts for acoustic instruments. Employing a focused and unhurried approach, they rewarded close listening by shaping a slowly evolving mix of sound that was at once both languorous and grimy. New Zealand's Phil Dadson performed at New Langton Arts where (among other things) he managed to draw a wide variety of sounds out of manually-operated pairs of stones. A careful exercise in attentive listening and corporeal engagement with materials (literally) at hand, the performance brought to mind the recurring truth that for all the wonderful gizmos found throughout the sound world (and

Ed Osborn *Parabolica* Center for the Arts, San Francisco, 1996. Mixed media, sound.

Nigel Helyer **Silent Forest** San Francisco Art Institute, SoundCulture 96. Mixed media installation with sound.

certainly present in SoundCulture), it's difficult to top the skillful striking of one object against another.

At the Pacific Film Archive, a series of events examining sound in film included (among other events) an evening of sound works by film makers played entirely in the dark, a lecture by Douglas Kahn on sound and audio art relating to film in the first half of the twentieth century, and an illustrated talk on the development of film sound by Robert Gitt of the UCLA Film and Television Archive. A listening room located in the San Francisco Art Commission Gallery gave visitors a chance to hear a wide variety of recorded sound work from around the Pacific.

Locally, the festival has resulted in an improved profile for the sonic arts among presenters and audiences; most of the events sold out completely and the exhibitions were uniformly well attended. In addition, the chance for so many organisations to work together (something normally difficult to arrange in these parts) was welcomed because the context of the festival provided a good chance to generate new audiences; in the current (abysmal) funding climate it may prove to be a workable (if labour-intensive) model for future events of this size. Already in its wake have come several smaller sound-oriented events, usually based around the audience-drawing noise end of the spectrum. The festival also generated the curious sight of a number of local visual artists and musicians quickly trying to recontextualise themselves as sound artists. Press coverage for the festival was uneven at best. All but ignored by the local dailies (no surprise there, although one large article appeared in the Bay Guardian, an entertainment-oriented weekly), SoundCulture 96 generated coverage in elsewhere in the United States and in Canada, Europe, and Japan. Reviews have also appeared in the nationally-distributed magazines *Artforum* (New York), *Sculpture* (Washington, DC), *Art Papers* (Atlanta), and *P-Form* (Chicago); the West Coast's monthly visual arts trade paper, *Artweek*, devoted the August issue to sound art—a topic it has never covered before in such depth.

The scope of the festival greatly belies the size of its resources. Working with a minuscule budget, no office, a volunteer staff, and a great deal of goodwill from everyone involved, SoundCulture 96 managed to flourish under extremely difficult conditions. However, with the small amount of funding that exists for the arts in the United States dwindling quickly, it is unlikely that an event of this size based around a lesser-known field like sound art will occur here again in the foreseeable future. Nonetheless, SoundCulture 96 provided a detailed and varied look at and a listen to some of the activity that is taking place in the fertile area of the sonic arts. It demonstrated the strength, influence, and viability of the field and served notice that in all its forms, sonic art warrants the same kind of attention normally reserved for more established art and culture practices.

SoundCulture 96 took place 3–13 April 1996, in the San Francisco Bay Area. An earlier version of this article was published in SoundArts, *Vol. 8, Summer, 1996 (Xebec Corporation, Kobe, Japan).*

Silence: 'Unhearable' Sound Between Us

Yuji Sone

This is NOT
a Western academic
paper presentation

I don't present
a linear argument

Because I believe in
contradictions or pluralism
in oneself

My task as a
NON-WHITE PERFORMANCE ARTIST
is to
stimulate the audience

I leave the tedious task of theorisation to
Western academic professionals

Life's TOO SHORT for that

* * *

This presentation is about some thoughts I had after being at SoundCulture 96.[1] It moves in *a circle* around different cultural experiences of sound, with the notion of silence at the core. My purpose is to add a different perspective to the current reading of sound art events from the position of a non-European, non-English speaking, Asian (Japanese, that is). The presentation is not about tired avant-gardism, but about locating sound art practices in the international—including non-European—context.

> The third trans-pacific festival of contemporary sound practices, including...*experimental* and *indigenous* music...(My emphasis.)

The above is an excerpt from the SoundCulture 96 brochure: it contains an interesting juxtaposition between the two terms 'experimental' and 'indigenous'. This labelling gave me the impression that either indigenous music is a simple genre, or that the whole issue of cultural differences of sound is put into a box called 'indigenous music'. This also gave me the impression that the festival was not keen to deal with the different cultural experiences of sound.

In this post-colonial climate, 'the Other sound' should be dealt with in more interesting ways. Some questions may be asked, such as: 'Is there such a thing as a sound art in non-Western countries?'; 'If not, can we say that they are "under-developed"?'; 'If their notions of art are historically and traditionally different from those of the West, how can one approach them?'; 'Are there stronger connections between theatre, dance, and music in their traditions?'; 'Is it right to separate a sound element from its original ritual function, as a music, for example "chanting"?'; 'Isn't that silencing its original meaning and power and merely fetishising or commodifying it?'; 'After all, isn't the notion of sound art a Western concept?'.

These questions should not be considered moral and ethical accusations; rather, they should be seen as offering profound provocations in current, post-colonial discourse. Delicate and sensitive issues need to be considered, otherwise 'Other sound' will continue to be 'silenced'. As it is, when different cultural experiences of sound are discussed, they are simply amplified and absorbed by Western audiences. This is the same danger that Hal Foster[2] and Homi Bhabha[3] point out, but in a visual arts context. Such was the case in 'The Magicians of the Earth' exhibition staged at the Pompidou Centre, Paris, in 1989. This exhibition aimed to focus on different cultures at the same time, but only 'cultural pluralism with its spurious egalitarianism' was in fact displayed. Another example was 'The Primitivism Show', MOMA, New York, 1984, which was based on 'different cultural temporalities in the same "universal" space'. In both cases, culturally different representations were replaced by representations of cultural difference.

> The original text is
> always already
> an impossible translation
> that renders
> translation impossible.[4]

There have been many scholars working on the notions of 'Orientalism',[5] 'Primitivism', or 'Nativism',[6] concepts which are deeply rooted in the Western psyche. As you probably know, people like Edward Said or Homi Bhabha are analysing historical and philosophical constructions of these notions in Western civilisation.

I would like to approach these issues in a completely different way. This is an attempt to look at cross-cultural discourse with cognitive science. That is to say that we inherit our biases toward the Other as a result of our perceptional systems.

BIAS IN OUR PECEPTIONAL SYSTEMS

From birth, our brain renders into memory certain visual and aural signals, which, in their next encounter, are automatically registered. In the case of sound, therefore, all other, unnecessary sound is 'silenced'. One still receives signals, but selects from amongst them consciously and unconsciously. We only 'pick up' certain sounds when our brain recognises them, or when we want to hear the sounds that are available to us.

SILENCE DOES EXIST

Since John Cage, we have been taught that silence is a myth. But is it possible to detect 'silence', not as 'no-sound', but as the *unhearable* sound between different cultures? This type of 'silence' can be found in linguistic translations. For example, it is said that the Japanese have a problem distinguishing between 'r' and 'l', because in Japanese 'r' and 'l' share the same sound: thus, they cannot differentiate between the two. But equally, English speakers cannot hear and pronounce the Japanese sound which exists between 'r' and 'l'. It would be 'translated' by the English brain as either 'r' or 'l'.

Another interesting example is onomatopoeia. In Japanese, for instance, the sound of a rooster is 'kokke-kokko', but in English it is 'cock-a-doodle-doo'. We hear the sound of the rooster in relation to each onomatopoeia. Unless people have knowledge of these two different onomatopoeia, they probably would not realise that both represent the same, original sound. For each language, the other sound does not exist.

How about spellings? For instance, I will use the title of the Japanese cult movie *Godzilla*. The original, Japanese pronunciation is 'Gojila', but because the English translation of the film is 'Godzilla', people pronounce it accordingly. For English speakers 'Godzilla' is normal, but not 'Gojila'.

SOUND ITSELF?

Another famous Cagean project was to focus on sound itself, and to free sound from its objects. But can we really focus on sound itself in a cross-cultural context? Don't we all have some degree of sound/image association? Doesn't the appearance of a performer and/or a musical instrument affect our appreciation of the sound performance? Don't we read/interpret a work according to its background information, such as, for example, where that person comes from, or the kind of music background she or he has?

'MAKING UP' FUNCTION

Paul Churchland argues:

> The way an object is perceived is not determined solely by the external stimulus it presents to our senses. It is determined, at least sometimes and at least in part, by the antecedent cognitive state, educational background, or frame of mind of the perceiver.[7]

In the field of sound perception, important consideration should be given to the brain's ability to 'make up' meaning, or to elicit necessary information out of scattered signals. A biological being needs to detect meaningful signals from its visual and sonic environment. The ear detects sound, and sends nerve impulses to the brain. But it is the brain that interprets these sounds. We do our best to find some meaning—any meaning—from the sounds of the world around us. If one has a conversation in a noisy place, one does not have to hear every word to make sense of it: one fills in the gaps.

An interesting example of this is phone sex. According to Allucquere Rosanne Stone, in phone sex

> [t]he client uncompresses [verbal tokens expressed by the provider] and constructs a dense, complex interactional image. In a Lacanian interpretation of these interactions, client and provider mobilise erotic tension by taking advantage of lack—filling in missing information with idealised information. In this circumstance desire, theorised as response to perceived lack, arises as a product of the tension between embodied reality and the emptiness of the token, in the forces that maintain the pre-existing codes by which the token is constituted. The client mobilises expectations and pre-existing codes for body in the modes of experience, such as smell and taste, that are absent from the token.[8]

Silence: 'Unhearable' Sound Between Us

The same principle can apply to the case of cross-cultural communication, where one tries one's best to understand unfamiliar concepts or languages, or incorrect grammar or words, and so on. But the meaning we find isn't always the meaning intended by the speaker. All we can do is read the Other to the best of our capabilities or from within our interests. Occasionally, we may go outside of our own territory, but we tame and distort the differences through our interpretations, analyses, or categorisations. Otherwise, as for sonic perception, we regard unfamiliar sound as just noise, or we simply cannot hear it. As Cage argued, silence is 'unintended' noise.[9]

So, can we really focus on
sound itself or neutral sound?

Because of our linguistically, psychologically and physiologically complicated perceptional and cognitive systems, it is difficult, especially for grown ups, to hear a 'neutral sound'.

ONE HAND CLAPPING

Zen Buddhism has an interesting attitude toward sound. According to the late Shunryu Suzuki, a Japanese Zen master who lived in the USA,

> Usually the sound of clapping is made with two hands, and we think that clapping with one hand makes no sound at all. But actually, one hand is sound. Even though you do not hear it, there is sound. If you clap with two hands, you can hear the sound. But if sound did not already exist before you clapped, you could not make the sound. Before you make it, there is sound. Because there is sound, you can make it, and you can hear it. Sound is everywhere. If you just practice it, there is sound. Do not try to listen to it. If you do not listen to it, the sound is all over. Because you try to hear it, sometimes there is sound, and sometimes there is no sound.[10]

Are we ever able to hear the sound
of one hand clapping?

REASONABLE APPROACH 1: NOT TREAT SILENCE AS SPECIAL

The questions about whether we can hear a neutral sound or the sound of one hand clapping can lead to a search for the impossible, timeless/idealised moment. Our perceptions change in time and space. Our perceptions are influenced by linguistic, psychological, and physiological factors. One should not idealise 'neutral sound' as a concrete concept because sound moves in time, and so do our perceptions. According to Susan Sontag

> Silence is a metaphor for a cleaned, non-interfering vision, appropriate to artworks that are unresponsive before being seen, unviolable in their essential integrity by human scrutiny.[11]

We should not see 'silence' and/or 'noise' as negative, nor as positive, idealised, alternative concepts. It is important to realise that they are always already around us, and that only our hearkening towards silence and/or noise is that which changes.

REASONABLE APPROACH 2: DIFFERENT MEANINGS OF 'SILENCE' IN HUMAN COMMUNICATION

To be mute in the West usually carries a negative connotation; one may, for example, be considered 'dumb', 'incompetent', or 'defeated'. In Japan, however, 'silence' may be regarded as 'honourable', or even 'eloquent'.

Japanese common proverbs on silence (this writer's literal translation)

– 241 –

- Silence is gold
- The wordy means vulgar
- Mouth is a gate of misfortune
- Not saying is flowery
- A skillful hawk hides its claws ('Still waters run deep') (semantic translation)

Traditionally, Japanese society is based on the notion of modesty. Thus, muteness may be regarded as a sign of modesty, elegance or sophistication, and carries quite the opposite meaning to that given in the West.

Let me tell you about another story, one John Cage often referred to. There was another Japanese Zen monk—Daisetsu Suzuki—who, in the '50s, attended a philosophy conference in the USA. He didn't say a word for three days. At the end of the conference, he was asked why. He replied:

> I have nothing to say and I am saying it.[12]

A certain aspect of Japanese culture is that people mistrust words. This might have resulted from Zen Buddhism. Zen communication emphasises elements of the paralinguistic or the unspeakable. Ito Jinsai, an eighteenth-century Japanese scholar, once said:

> What is called good cannot be postulated in a definitive shape. One should not admonish it in language.[13]

Isn't this similar to what Susan Sontag referred to when saying that some contemporary artists express the ineffable through the aesthetics of silence? She explains this by contrasting poets with prose writers:

> Poetry, being an art, should have quite different aims: to express an experience which is essentially ineffable; using language to express muteness. In contrast to prose writers, poets are engaged in subverting their own instrument and seeking to pass beyond it.[14]

One, I guess, emphasises 'ordinary silence' while the other stresses 'heightened silence'.

> When you speak, it is silent.
> When you are silent, it speaks.[15]

REASONABLE APPROACH 3: SOCIAL INFLUENCES IN PERCEPTION

One should never forget that there is always an imbalance in communication between the West and the non-West because of the existence of both historical influences and political, economical and cultural forces deriving from the West. In this sense, how do you perceive an 'ethnic' sound in an event like SoundCulture? Either:

1) You are fascinated by its exotic element, but you suppress your fascination to avoid being seen as a naive, uncool Orientalist. Thus you dismiss it as naive folk music.

2) You see it as the most cool, postmodern, post-colonial product, the expropriation of Western appropriation.

3) You quickly find out how other people come to regard it so you can then follow the general opinion.

REASONABLE APPROACH 4: FUTURE OF CROSS-CULTURAL 'SOUND' COMMUNICATION?

It might be important to ask the questions below:

1) For younger generations, how is the difference in sound/music between West and non-West different from that of previous generations?

A country like Japan is a good example of a culture as an ongoing process. Shuhei Hosokawa writes about some aspects of Japanese popular music in the 1980s:

> Japan has nothing but a counterfeit, fake culture, but that fake is fantastic because it does not claim any authority to be the 'real thing', but multiplies 'democratically' in the sense that it is unauthorised: a temporary because makeshift, outward show, is appreciated and consumed for only a moment.[16]

The Japanese borrowed, appropriated and fetishised the elements, not only from Western cultures, but also from their own traditions.

2) How would a second generation migrant perceive sound culturally?

Children are interesting. They are both becoming us, and becoming the other—until they are made aware of differences by the polity.

What is my answer?

I don't have an answer

I question rather than answer.
In fact, I DON'T want an answer

A question hides answers.
An answer hides questions

We shouldn't enunciate it in language

This is a scripted version of the same-titled performance presented at the forum SOUNDcheck.one—SoundCulture 1996: critical distance, reverberant, presented at the Art Gallery of New South Wales, 3 August 1996.

1. The third 'trans-Pacific festival of contemporary sonic art', Bay Area, San Francisco, USA, 3–13 April 1996.
2. Hal Foster, 'The Primitive Unconscious of Modern Art, or White Skin Black Masks', in *Recodings—Art, Spectacle, Cultural Politics*, Port Townsend, Washington: Bay Press, 1985, pp. l81–208.
3. Homi Bhabha, *The Location of Culture*, London and New York: Routledge, 1994, p. 245.
4. Barbara Johnson in Trinh T. Minh-ha's 1989 film *Surname Viet, Given Name Nam*, from *Framer, Framed*, by Trinh T. Minh-ha, New York and London: Routledge, 1992, p. 80.
5. Edward W. Said, *Orientalism: Western Conceptions of the Orient*, Harmondsworth: Penguin, 1991.
6. The term used by Trinh T. Minh-ha in *Woman, Native, Other: Writing, Post-coloniality and Feminism*, Bloomington and Indianapolis: Indiana University Press, 1989.

7. Paul Churchland, *The Engine of Reason, the Seat of the Soul: A Philosophical Journey into the Brain*, Cambridge, MA and London: MIT Press, 1995, p. 108.
8. Allucquere Rosanne Stone, *The War of Desire and Technology at the Close of the Mechanical Age*, Cambridge, MA & London: MIT Press, 1995, p. 95.
9. John Cage quoted in Carla Zecher's 'Reading the Noise: Performance and Textuality', *A Quarterly for Literature and the Arts*, Vol. xxxiii, No. 2, Spring 1991, pp. 159–171.
10. Shunryu Suzuki, *Zen Mind, Beginner's Mind*, New York and Tokyo: Weatherhill, 1970.
11. Susan Sontag, 'The Aesthetics of Silence', in *Styles of Radical Will*, New York: Farrar, Straus and Giroux, 1969, p. 16.
12. Quoted in the video documentary 'American Masters—John Cage', dir. Allan Miller, The Music Project for Television Inc. and American Masters, dist. R. M. Assoc., 1990.
13. Cited in Naoki Sakai, *Voices of the Past: The Status of Language in Eighteenth-Century Japanese Discourse*, Ithaca and London, 1991, p. 82.
14. Sontag, op. cit., p. 30.
15. Trinh T. Minh-ha, *Woman, Native, Other*, op. cit., p. 96.
16. Shuhei Hosokawa, 'Fake, Fame, Folk', *Art & Text* 40, September 1991, pp. 78–81.

Sonic Architecture: An Interview with Nigel Helyer

John Potts

Nigel Helyer La Zona del Silencio Mapimi Desert, Mexico, 1992. Broadcast performance.

Nigel Helyer's works operate in a zone somewhere between sound art and sculpture. His installations are hybrid media constructs that work on many levels, with sound always in a privileged position. His works display the sculptor's grasp of sound's physical properties, while their complexity traces historical connections between sound and power. *Oracle*, an installation at Sydney's Museum of Contemporary Art as part of *Sound in Space* in 1995, ranged in its conceptual ambit from the walls of Jericho to the role of contemporary media. *Silent Forest*, exhibited as part of SoundCulture 96 in San Francisco, linked the wartime destruction of native Vietnamese forest with the colonial process exemplified by the French-built Hanoi Opera House. This latter work forms part of the *Silent Zone* series, comprising *Big Bell Beta* (1989), *An UnRequited Space* (1992), and *La Zona del Silencio* (1992). These and other works are multifaceted sounding-boards of history and culture.

* * *

John Potts: How do you define sonic architecture, with reference to your own work?

Nigel Helyer: Sound is as much a material as any dense object. Architecture in particular gives sound a texture and an identity. We think of sound as that which comes from a dynamic event in the material world, but what we tend to overlook is that that always happens within a context, and the source of the sound is imprinted with the dimensions and qualities of that context. I'm thinking of the spatialisation of the sonic event, not so much as a formal architecture, but as a kind of envelope in which the sound is propagated.

My interest has been in the kind of works which generate and transmit, and where you have a physical presence. I've always been interested in the analogue side of sound, as much as the digital, in that it's always connected back to the palpable, sensible world. I've been heavily involved not simply in sound as a kind of text, but in sound as something that's generated by these particular architectures, objects or structures. The interesting thing about sound is that it's a phenomenon and a representation of something. It's both a concrete thing and a sign. It's that doubling of sound that makes it very attractive, to me anyway.

JP: *It's both a symbol and a physical presence.*

NH: They're co-substantial. It's rather like listening to someone on the phone. The voice in a telephone transmission is highly compressed, so much that you can barely recognise who it is. The intelligibility of the message is carried in the upper part of the frequency, and the identity of the person in the lower part of the frequency. We come to believe that the electronic voice we hear is co-substantial with the voice of our friend, and happening in more or less real time, mapped onto itself. It's a kind of magical process that we do on a day-to-day basis; it's a bizarre experience, talking to someone's voice on the phone. It's a suspension of disbelief.

JP: *The relation between sound and power is continually probed in your works.*

NH: In general I've approached this issue from the reverse side, of silence belying that process. It works on a quite literal equation of industrial or military power, which is highly dynamic, with highly noisy processes. In the urban soundscape, cities are generally dominated by high-speed percussive events, usually motors. That sound is monotone and tends to blanket flora and fauna sounds, which tend to be more discreet, with greater dynamic ranges. Our urban experience is one of a literal form of power, a sonic blanket, the sounds which can eliminate other sounds, the human voice, for example, in industry.

Going back to the idea that all sounds come from a dynamic source, where you locate null points, where you locate silence, there's obviously some breakage or cessation, or smothering of these activities. In *Silent Forest*, there is the idea of a total silence because there is no flora and fauna left. If you're navigating on the high seas and you're using a radio direction finder, you listen for silence. When you listen for radio beacons, you listen for the minimum signals, you scan until you find the space where the station disappears, then you're at right angles to it. That's a metaphor for scanning social or political or environmental situations for the points where sound drops away. I have the hunch that when that happens there's a kind of breakage, a rupture. Usually it can be traced back to some form of incursion into that system or space. The more I think about it, sound works as a kind of chain system, a resonant system. There are ecologies of sound, even in industrial cultures, and when they become degraded, silence is one of the most obvious results.

JP: *How do you position your work in relation to R. Murray Schafer and the school of sound ecology?*

NH: It's a very interesting subject. I'm a bit dismayed by the way the sound area has been split down the middle between high art and theory on one side, and sound ecology and the noise abatement people on the other. To me that's a very artificial distinction. I'm fluent with the theoretical and high art side of sound art, but I'm also interested in soundscape and environmental sound. I don't see a fundamental difference; they're different aspects of the same thing. Both of the poles of that axis could learn a huge amount from each other. The people involved in the high art, theory end are totally blind to the material of the sound world, I don't think they hear it. And the people at the 'Laura Ashley' acoustic ecology end have some oxymoronic positions. I think the two positions could be usefully brought together, and I don't think the area of sound research will develop without this happening.

JP: *Regarding the formal construction of your works and their presentation, how do you balance the conceptual force with the aesthetic properties of the works? Does one jeopardise the other?*

NH: I've always thought in some ways you can have your cake and eat it too. There's no reason why something can't have a utilitarian function and a semantic function at the same time. It's the fusion of those two things in an effective metaphoric way that makes the work sing, literally. In a museum context, people spend a few seconds in front of each painting, like a drive-by viewing. If you're working with sound sculpture or sound installation, where with *Silent Forest* for instance there's a soundtrack that's 74 minutes long, a few seconds isn't going to get you even into the front door. There is an element of show business, if you like, of manipulating people's perceptual attractors, and holding their attention by making works multilayered. It's a kind of open network. I always try to make my works visceral in some way, to draw people in. They can be visually focused on an object, but bathed in a soundtrack from nearby. I'm very conscious of manipulating aesthetic devices to allow people to experience sound for relatively long durations, to allow them to stay with the sound. It's actually quite hard to do.

JP: *Do you use the visual components of the works in a secondary way, as a lure?*

NH: Absolutely. In some works the visual, physical elements are there as a servant to a sound or vibrational experience. While all the components are commensurate, for me there is a subordination to the sound experience.

JP: *Do you see any contradiction between exploring relations of sound and power, as in* Silent Forest's *reference to colonial power, and the aesthetic pleasures that derive from your work?*

NH: No, pleasure is the operative word. You can have the best of both worlds, and it's a puritanism that would deny you that pleasure. This is another reason for the manipulation of the visual field. It's always important to give something, at whatever level, so the work should be open on multiple levels. I like looking at kids in my installations. If they respond to it, I know there's something okay about it. Children respond in a direct, physical way, even though they don't necessarily get the intellectual component. That visceral level is important. If you can hold interest there, it's possible to stay with the work, to come back multiple times. Then other things start to appear. Duration is important: it's like reading a novel. You can slowly build up an experience of the site. If the work is well made, its quality will endure. It's a problem with a lot of contemporary work, which is made in a way that isn't very generous. It doesn't stand the test of multiple viewings, even a second viewing. I think it's a crisis of confidence to do that to an audience.

JP: Referring to individual works, Oracle *relates in part to the power of the human voice.*

NH: In the Book of Joshua, it's not the trumpet that brings down the wall of Jericho but a 'great shout' from the people. In this context, vocalisation may be the originary projectile. I've done a lot of work on the propaganda use of sounds, and how these sounds could be recuperated to the cultural sphere. Obviously the notion of an enclosed architectural space that Jericho brings up, the walled city, is different to the contemporary city. But if you think about the Nazis' use of radio broadcasting, and some of the military uses of sound broadcasting in villages in south-east Asia, the voice becomes incredibly pervasive as a controlling device. I thought of the voice as an analogue of thought, and as a precursor of action. It's also our instrument, the thing by which we reach out in projecting agency. So the Joshua metaphor is one in which that potential of agency through the voice is actually turned into physical violence which affects architecture.

With *Oracle*, the people in the gallery were in the place of citizenry, and in an Orwellian sense, the uses of sound and surveillance technology are projected back onto that citizenry. It's rather like the obverse of Jericho: you're not protected by the wall but contained by it, and washed over by its messages. A video image of moving lips draws people in, and people did wedge themselves into the sound wave-guides. They're then repulsed by a huge low frequency sound, a very visceral sound. The video sound came out from a tiny speaker, which draws people in to hear it, but then you're pushed back by the visceral sound, literally pushed out of the work. The push-pull mechanism worked between head and stomach, and that tension is at once contemporary and archaic.

JP: Silent Forest *forms part of a series of works called* The Silent Zone. *How are silence and space explored in these other works?*

NH: They don't form part of a central thesis, but they have a touchstone from which they develop. The *Big Bell Beta* piece is concerned with the visible wealth in Perth, and its disingenuous relation to labour. I found a ghost town 700 kilometres into the centre called Big Bell. It was one of the biggest gold mines in Australia, that closed in about 1955. I made a conceptual bridge between two sound works, one running continually in the desert, the other in the PICA gallery in Perth. It was about an economic motor that had been silenced, and the rural basis of wealth which is silenced in the city itself.

An UnRequited Space was done in a dead, never-used tunnel in Sydney. Again there was an inversion, a public space that's hidden. The timing was at midnight, the space between one day and another. The public arena was the broadcast space, which in a sense is the most populous public space, but is participated in in private. So public space in contemporary culture is silenced: they are transit spaces, between private space and corporate space. You can't do anything politically or creatively in these public spaces. Even the transport system, for example, is so noisy that it silences anything else.

La Zona del Silencio, co-produced with Tony MacGregor, was very much to do with repression. It was about the 500th anniversary of Columbus day, and the problem was not so much of silence, but of volume. The year before [1991], there were 600 books published on Columbus; there was a replica of the fleet in New York harbour: how could you speak in that cacophony? We were stumped until we came across the place called the Zone of Silence in the Mapimi Desert, Mexico, in which we made a non-functional radio broadcast. This zone is an electro-magnetic vortex caused by a meteorite, an exclusion zone where no radio transmission can enter or leave. The idea was that there had been 500 years of non-dialogue, of non-speech, a history not being enunciated. The

Sonic Architecture: An Interview with Nigel Helyer

Nigel Helyer **La Zona del Silencio**
Biennale of Sydney, 1992.
Installation detail.

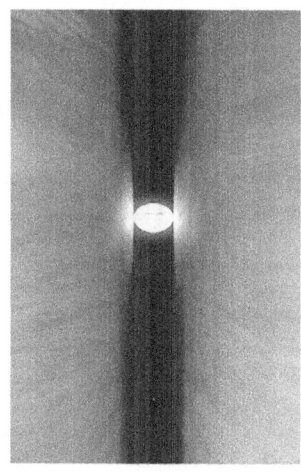

Nigel Helyer **Oracle**
Sound in Space Museum of Contemporary Art, Sydney,
1995. Installation detail.

Nigel Helyer **Big Bell Beta**
Perth Institute of Contemporary Art, 1989.
Installation detail.

Nigel Helyer **An UnRequited Space** *Working in Public* Sydney, 1992.
Performance and ABC Radio broadcast.

history that was being enunciated on Columbus Day was a North American version of world history, so we transmitted to Mexico 24 hours of the ringing of ships' bells, as if we were ringing the watch of European ships from this desert which had once been an ocean. Of course, this transmission never left the zone, it was silenced. This silent centrepiece was included in radio works and installations based on our non-transmission.

JP: *In* Silent Forest, *you make a parallel between the silencing of the forest in Vietnam through dioxin defoliants, and the imposition of one culture upon another through the Hanoi Opera.*

NH: That's the silencing of the traditional musical culture. That parallel is the core of the piece. The forest section contains dysfunctional bonsais, a visual metaphor in which nature becomes cultural, and diminished. The sound component has nine bands to it, making a continuous sound field, including Western music, sirens and Vietnamese music, while the forest recordings were made from old 78s. These were digitally reprocessed so that much of the signal was stripped out and the noise left. So the crackle and hissing of an extinct technology stands in for the idea of an extinct environment. There's a double silencing, a double repression.

JP: *Why are you drawn, in your work, to these silent or negative spaces?*

NH: Silent spaces are interstitial spaces, ruptures. We think of messages as seamless, without entry points. The media presents to the public a view of the world which we can't really have any effect on. But at the point where that barrage of sound and vision shows a crack, there is a possibility of getting a crowbar or a key in there, and start to open it up. We then see it isn't a monolithic structure, it is a construct put together and held up. And behind that, it's just structure. It's like working on a computer: behind the interface, there's just lots of code. If you jump back behind the interface and re-write the code, the interface is changed. I think sound is a great way of getting behind things.

Ere and Bele Chose: The Wife of Bath's Deafness

Louise D'Arcens

> She, a dumb virgin with lips closed, occasionally receives the favor of a word, which she must bring into the world in the shape of a child of God...(s)uch would be her participation in the incarnation, death, and resurrection of the word...This is her cross in life, the double closure of her lips...
> —Luce Irigaray, *The Marine Lover of Friedrich Nietzsche*[1]

In describing the Annunciation as the originary Christian effacement of the feminine, Luce Irigaray deploys her familiar anatomical trope of sealed lips. Evoking the link between feminine speech and sexuality, this trope locates the twofold compliance of the Virgin in her silence and her virginal motherhood.

Irigaray's doubly sealed Virgin provides an interesting counterpoint from which to examine Chaucer's Wife of Bath. For just as the Virgin's obedience to the Word is marked through her sympathetically sealed lips, the Wife's textual *dis*obedience is marked through the more uneasy association between her unsealed mouth and vagina and her damaged, sealed 'ere'.

Of the motley company encountered in the General Prologue (hereafter, GP) to *The Canterbury Tales*, the Wife of Bath is among the most famous. Gap-toothed, large-hipped, sitting astride her 'amblere' in ostentatiously unfashionable attire, this well-travelled pilgrim has not only had five husbands, but is also, interestingly, deaf.

This deafness is brought to our immediate attention in the introductory portrait:

> A good WIF was ther of biside BATHE
> But she was somdel deef, and that was scathe. (GP: ll. 445–446)[2]

Appearing alongside the aforementioned details, this deafness strikes the modern realist reader as a comic quirk in an idiosyncratic 'character'. However, while this is indeed one of its descriptive effects, the Wife's deafness is arguably of greater significance than its initial comic appearance would suggest.

The meaning of the Wife's deafness is largely passed over in Chaucerian scholarship,[3] possibly because the answer is provided throughout her Prologue by the Wife herself (hereafter, WBP). She informs her audience that she was deafened by her fifth husband, the clerk Jankyn, after she tore out either one (WBP: l. 635) or three (WBP: l. 790) pages[4] of his anthology on wicked wives:

> By God! He smoot me ones on the lyst
> For that I rente out of his book a leef,
> That of the strook myn ere wax al deef. (WBP: ll. 634–636)

These lines describe the *narrative event* of her deafening. What remains to be examined is whether any *necessary discursive* connection might exist between the Wife's sexual vigour, so wilfully expressed throughout her Prologue, her destruction of Jankyn's book, and her deafness. Here the dual provenance of the Wife's deafness needs to be emphasised. At the narrative level, she is deafened by Jankyn. At the discursive level, however, it is Chaucer who deafens her. The Wife of Bath, then, despite all her ribald immediacy as a feminine voice, remains the creation of a male author of late fourteenth-century England.

While this point would seem self-evident, it is still worth stressing in light of the numerous accounts in which the Wife is cited as a proto-feminist *female* voice from late medieval England.[5] Most commonly cited in such revisionist accounts is her famous indictment

> Who peynted the leon, tel me who?
> By God! if womman hadde writen stories,
> As clerkes han withinne hire oratories,
> They wolde han writen of men moore wikkednesse
> Than al the mark of Adam may redresse (WBP: ll. 688–696)

These lines indeed stand out as an untimely commentary on the misogynist bias of medieval discourses on women. However, rather than isolating them as a guarantee of the Wife's proto-feminism, it is important not only to remember that they are placed in her mouth by a male author, but that they function within the rather less celebratory context of this author's deafening of the Wife as speaker of these lines.

In exploring the discursive significance of the Wife's deafness, I am responding to a creative hermeneutic tendency that resists the careful contextualisation of *The Canterbury Tales* within the socio-historical conditions of its production. Such treatments, while resulting in perceptive and innovative readings of the internal dynamics of the *Tales*, can also result in detaching them from the field of meanings in which they were produced. In considering the significance of the Wife's deafness, then, it is important to examine the broader medieval notions informing it, beginning with the centrality of the ear, and the sense of hearing, within medieval ideas regarding education and literacy.

The Latinate literacy virtually exclusive to members of the clergy up to the late Middle Ages is referred to as 'eye' literacy, as it involved the visual consumption of texts.[6] However, alongside the eye-literate *literati* was a vast majority of *illiterati*, consisting of two groups. First, there were those who could not read Latin, but were able to read vernacular texts. Second, there were those who were unable to read at all, but who possessed a substantial *functional* or 'ear' literacy[7]—a familiarity with authoritative texts gained through hearing them read by spiritual advisors or husbands, and through church sermons. The relation between 'eye' and 'ear' literacy was not one of mutual exclusion, as virtually all reading practices in the Middle Ages involved some aural component, with the *literati* reading aloud to others and even to themselves.[8] The ear, then, had a fundamental importance as the locus of the reception of authoritative knowledge.

Returning to the Prologue, we see that the Wife is deafened after tearing out the pages of Jankyn's compilation of authoritative misogynist texts. It should be noted that when her earlier husbands verbally condemn women, she merely repeats their abuse, throwing it back at them, 'quit(ting) hem word for word' (WBP: l. 422), and even when the clerkly Jankyn 'preches' to her about feminine vice, she says

> ...I set noght an hawe
> Of his proverbes n'of his olde sawe. (WBP: ll. 659–660)

Yet when the same matter is *read* to her, and attached to authoritative texts, the Wife defiantly destroys the book. This suggests that the reception of knowledge specifically through *written* texts renders previously unheeded *heard* material intolerable. One explanation for the Wife's antipathy to written authority may be located earlier in the Prologue, in the Wife's statements regarding her own sexual freedom, such as the resolute 'For sothe, I wol nat kepe me chaast in al' (WBP: l. 46). For it may be contended that her rejection of chastity violates the medieval conditions of access to knowledge for women, and thus disqualifies the Wife from possessing even that layperson's 'ear' literacy which she displays in discussing the theology surrounding the issues of chastity and marriage.

To better explain this, it is necessary to explore the crucial connection in the Middle Ages between female education, literacy, and virtue. The authority of St. Paul's[9] prohibitions on women's reception and dissemination of knowledge ensured the circumscription of their access to authoritative knowledge, and its organisation into a system of masculine and institutional mediation. This denial of access to textual literacy resulted in the vast majority of women receiving no formal education.[10]

There were, in spite of this general prohibition, women who sought an education, such as the prodigiously educated Hildegard of Bingen, or her younger contemporary, Heloise. Whether educated at home or in a convent, however, the consistent injunction within literature written either for women, or on the subject of women and education, was that literacy be directly linked to the cultivation of *virtue*. Jerome, in his famous letter to Laeta on the subject of her daughter Paula's education, advocates an education of the soul, saying 'let reading follow prayer with her, and prayer again succeed to reading'.[11] In the twelfth century, Abelard, discussing nuns' education, cites Jerome's maxim 'love knowledge of letters and you will not love the vices of the flesh'.[12] Vincent de Beauvais, in his *De eruditione*, says of noble women '[t]hey should be instructed in letters…because often they will shun harmful thoughts to follow this honourable occupation, and avoid carnal lusts and vanities'.[13]

Of course, in the Middle Ages the attainment of virtue was emphasised in education for men as well as women. It was, nevertheless, more urgent to stress this with women, whose very nature was considered to be corporeal, as opposed to the more spiritual nature of men. As women were defined in terms of their sexual status as virgins, wives or widows, and as they were considered to be the very embodiment of carnal lust, the orientation of their virtue was toward *chastity*. In order to strengthen the connection between literacy and chastity, it was necessary that women's reading matter be limited to edifying material. Records of book ownership in fourteenth- and fifteenth-century England indicate the success of this restriction, as the bulk of books owned by laywomen were of a devotional nature, such as prayer books and Books of Hours.[14]

Into this tradition, then, comes Chaucer's Wife of Bath, whose functional literacy and knowledge of authoritative writings is *not* brought into the service of chastity, but, rather, is appropriated by her for the purpose of actually sanctioning her sexual enthusiasm and frequent remarriage. She relies, significantly, upon the authority of Jerome, and particularly the word of the Gospels, to buttress her argument, saying, for instance, on the subject of procreation:

> Men may devyne and glosen, up and doun,
> But well I woot, expres, withoute lye,
> God bade us wexe and multiplye;
> That gentil text kan I wel understonde. (WBP: ll. 24–29)

or, with regard to the issue of chastity and sexual activity

> Th'apostel, whan that he speketh of maydenhede,
> He seyde that precept therof hadde he noon.
> Men may conseille a womman to been oon,
> But conseillyng is no comandement.
> He putte it in oure owene juggement. (WBP: ll. 64–68)

The Wife's crime, then, is her severing of the link between the reception of knowledge and chastity; and for this her male author must have her deafened by a clerk, that is, he must ensure that her capacity to acquire knowledge and to marshal orthodox texts into an argument upholding sexual *un*orthodoxy is reduced.

Now I shall turn to Chaucer's use of Marian tradition to de-authorise the Wife's voice. As the figure most often held up as the *exemplum* of feminine chastity in the Middle Ages, Mary's virginal state was crucial to her eligibility to be impregnated with the divine Word. From the twelfth century on,[15] Marian devotion grew in importance, with laywomen's Books of Hours containing numerous representations of Mary, particularly of the Annunciation scene. Moreover, in many of these Annunciation scenes Mary holds a book or scroll, rather than her more traditional distaff.[16] The text Mary reads is Isaiah's prophesy of the Virgin Birth, so the configuration of virginity and literacy is present. These frequent Annunciation images functioned to remind women that the desired outcome of their reading was the chastity and humility captured in the Virgin's words 'be it done unto me according to thy word'. Much was said throughout the medieval period on the fertility of virgins, whose obedience to God was believed to allow them to bear spiritual children, in the form of holy acts and words. Such children, like Christ, will never die, unlike the sinful children borne by wives.[17] It is thus that Mary functions as a figure to be emulated by female readers.

This belief in the Virgin's reception of the Word was itself a fertile area for theologians, and much debate took place concerning how Mary could conceive and remain a virgin. One of the theological interpretations emerging out of this concern was the theology of the *conceptio per aurem*. This mainly Western theology, elaborated by such early theologians as Irenaeus, Tertullian and Augustine, grew out of a desire not only to explain the retention of Mary's virginity during and after conception, but also to elaborate the concept of Mary as typologically parallel to Eve. Eve's sin and Mary's redemption of humanity were both located in the sense of hearing; as Eve listened to the words of the serpent, so did Mary listen to the words of the angel.[18] The *conceptio per aurem* also resulted from the Vulgate translation of the Greek word *Logos*—word, knowledge, truth, wisdom, breath or spirit—into the more limited and concrete Latin word *verbum*, or 'word',[19] so that it came to be believed that the entrance of the Word of God carried by the angel impregnated her. In pictorial representations, this was variously represented as a scroll issuing from Gabriel to Mary's ear, or a tube between her ear and God's mouth.[20]

The ear, in this doctrine, functioned as a metonymic representation of the vagina, as the orifice in which the Word is implanted, thus maintaining the intactness of the vagina. This theology permeated popular theology for many centuries. Marina Warner[21] cites an English dancing song from a century before Chaucer which mentions the *conceptio per aurem*. Closer to Chaucer's time, it is found in the Towneley play of the Annunciation, in God's lines to Gabriel, 'She shall conceyf my derling/Thrugh thy word and hyr heryng'.[22] Other examples range from the Vernon MS poem 'Blessed be, Lady, thy riht ere' to the 'with thyne ere conceyvinge' of a fifteenth-century anchoritic hymn to the Virgin.[23]

Not only would this theology be known to Chaucer, then, but his writing of the Wife of Bath's deafening at the scene of the reception of knowledge can be interpreted as a *comic reversal* of this notion of conception through the ear. For in advocating marriage the Wife is disqualified by Chaucer from the spiritual fertility made possible by practising the feminine ideal of chastity. Hence Chaucer metonymically renders her infertile by damaging the orifice of the ear. In the first recounting of the deafening, the Wife says of Jankyn

> He nolde suffre nothyng of my list
> By God! he smoot me ones on the lyst...(WBP: ll. 633–634)

Her 'list', or sexual desire, and her destruction of the book, are mentioned together to account for Jankyn's disdain for her, and as the two conditions resulting in his assault upon her ear ('lyst') as metonymic vagina. Interesting in this context is the pun on the words 'list' (lust, desire) and 'lyst' (ear), a pun which, coincidentally, is most fully realised when spoken, that is, when received aurally. It is even more interesting to consider this in the light of the very same pun being used in two Middle English poems to the Virgin, in the lines 'Hayle! Thow conceyved all with lyst' and 'That concevuedsy him al with lyst'.[24] In reinforcing the connection between hearing and desire, these poems emphasise that this desire should be the chaste, obedient desire for God's will, rather than the wilful desire for 'sovereynetee' or 'maistre' that the Wife articulates as the utimate desire of women in her *Tale*. It is, finally, also interesting that the two parts of the Wife's body most often mentioned in her Prologue are her ear (her 'lyst' or 'ere') and her genitals (her 'bele chose', 'queynte', 'quoniam', 'privee place', and 'chamber of Venus'). The Wife's Prologue, then, registers both linguistic and discursive metonymy between the Wife's 'ere/lyst' and her 'bele chose' as the seat of her 'list'.

Considering all of the above, one might call the Wife of Bath's Prologue a narrative of the *abortive scene of the reception of knowledge*. It is interesting that for all the Wife's insistence upon the command to 'wexe and multiplye' (WBP: l. 28), there is no mention in her Prologue of any offspring from any of her marriages, so that the spiritual sterility of the woman who has failed to yoke her reception of texts to virtue is figured quite literally by her.

The volatile context in which Chaucer wrote *The Canterbury Tales* also contributes to an explanation of the Wife's deafness; for Chaucer's England was encountering the insurgence of the Lollard heresy, with its interrogation of exclusive clerical access to authoritative texts. Scholars have pointed out that within Lollardy women played a more active part than within orthodoxy, assisting in the oral dissemination of scripture, and even in preaching,[25] and have suggested that the Wife herself is a Lollard.[26] Her championing of marriage is consistent with the familial orientation of the Lollards, as is her contempt for 'glosers', interpreters of doctrine, and her insistence upon the 'expres' word of scripture.[27] The suggestion of the Wife's Lollardy might account also for her relative indifference to spoken invective, and her violent reaction to the same invective in written form, which conforms to the well-known Lollard esteem for books. Jankyn, as a member of the minor clergy, may thus be seen in his punishment of the Wife to represent the Church's retribution of the Lollards.

In spite of this evidence, the Wife's frequent pilgrimages and tendency to swear oaths suggest that she is in fact orthodox. Furthermore, in Chaucer's time women were not yet prominent within Lollardy, which was, at this stage, essentially a learned and bookish heresy. Nevertheless, it is true that any woman in the late Middle Ages who refused to accept virtue and obedience as the goal of learning courted ecclesiastical disapproval and suppression.

Something had to be sacrificed, then: 'ere', or 'bele chose'. As a male writer engaging with an orthodox discursive tradition, Chaucer, having deprived the Wife of chastity, also deprives her of the only other bodily capacity, as a non-reader, that would ensure her spiritual fertility and salvation: her hearing. So, despite the audacious humour and exegetical competence of the voice Chaucer gives her, the theological outcome of the Wife of Bath's Prologue ensures that this text is not necessarily the proto-feminist endeavour it is often claimed to be. Rather, what we see in the Wife of Bath's Prologue is Chaucer's use of the tradition of the Annunciation in such a way as to effectively de-authorise and disqualify the Wife's voice from textual tradition, relegating her to a place of 'noon auctoritee' (WBP: l. 1).

1. Luce Irigaray, *The Marine Lover of Friedrich Nietzsche*, trans. Gillian C. Gill, New York: Columbia University Press, 1991, p. 166.
2. The text used here is the third edition of *The Riverside Chaucer*, ed. Larry D. Benson, Oxford: Oxford University Press, 1988.
3. An astrological explanation is offered in W. C. Curry's *Chaucer and the Mediaeval Sciences*, New York, 1926, and a feminist one in Elaine Tuttle Hanson, 'The Wife of Bath and the Mark of Adam', *Women's Studies*, Vol. 15, No. 4, 1988, p. 405.
4. This inconsistency is difficult to interpret. One possibility is that it is a Trinitarian metaphor: the Wife literally rips God—the Trinitarian Unity—from the text.
5. Hanson, op. cit., discusses complaints against what is seen as a 'seemingly incurable tendency to overly lifelike readings of the Wife of Bath', pp. 399–400. Hanson provides a substantial bibliography of treatments of the wife as proto-feminist.
6. See Susan Schibanoff, 'The New Reader and Female Textuality in Two Early Commentaries on Chaucer', *Studies in the Age of Chaucer*, Vol. 10, 1988, p. 76; also Brian Stock, *The Implications of Literacy*, New Jersey: Princeton University Press, 1983, Part II, 'Textual Communities'.
7. Stock, ibid., pp. 88–92. Schibanoff refers to this as 'ear' literacy.
8. See Mary Carruthers, *The Book of Memory,* Cambridge: Cambridge University Press, 1990, Chapter 5, 'Memory and the Ethics of Reading'.
9. I Corinthians 14.34,35.
10. See, for example, Joan M. Ferrante, 'The Education of Women in the Middle Ages in Theory, Fact and Fantasy', in Patricia Labalme, *Beyond Their Sex: Learned Women of the European Past*, New York: New York University Press, 1980, pp. 9–42.
11. Jerome, Letter CVII, 'To Laeta', from *The Nicene and Post-Nicene Fathers*, Second Series, Vol. VI, *Jerome*, trans. W. H. Fremantle, Michigan: Erdman's, 1979, p. 193.
12. Letter 7, *The Letters of Abelard and Heloise*, trans. Betty Radice, London: Penguin, 1974, p. 264.
13. Vincent de Beauvais, *De eruditione*, XLIII, 5–7, cited in E. J. Brill, *Major Emphases in Renaissance Educational Theory*, Netherlands, 1976, p. 137.
14. See Susan Groag Bell, 'Medieval Women Book Owners', in *Sisters and Workers in the Middle Ages,* eds. Judith M. Bennett et al, Chicago and London: University of Chicago Press, 1989, pp. 135–161.
15. See Hilda Graef, *Mary: A History of Doctrine and Devotion*, New York: Sheed and Ward, 1963; Marina Warner, *Alone of All Her Sex: The Myth and Cult of the Virgin Mary*, London: Weidenfeld and Nicholson, 1976; Mary Clayton, *The Cult of the Virgin Mary in Anglo-Saxon England*, Cambridge: Cambridge University Press, 1990.
16. Bell, op. cit., p. 154, and Clayton, op. cit., pp. 142–178.
17. Letter 4, 'Abelard to Heloise', in Radice, op. cit., p. 150.
18. See Clayton, pp. 5–15 for references to the Eva-Ave reversal between Mary and Eve.
19. This is Leo Steinberg's argument in '"How Shall This Be?" Reflections on Filippo Lippi's *Annunciation* in London', Part I, in *Artibus et Historiae*, 1991, p. 28. However, 'verbum', as it is rendered in Luke's account, is translated from the more concrete 'rema' rather than from Logos. Nonetheless, the fact that 'verbum' conflated 'Logos' and 'rema' explains why Mary's reception of the 'verbum' implies a reception of the Spirit or Logos of God.
20. See Gertrud Schiller, *Iconography of Christian Art*, two volumes, trans. Janet Seligman, Greenwich, Connecticut: New York Graphic Society, 1971, Vol. I, figs. 85, 105.
21. Marina Warner, op. cit., p. 37.
22. A. C. Cawley, ed., *The Towneley Plays*, EETS, 1994, p. 94, ll. 69–70.
23. See Joannes Vriend *The Blessed Virgin Mary in the Medieval Drama of England*, Purmerend: J. Muusses, 1928, pp. 150–160. The anchoress' hymn is in Alexandra Barratt, *Women's Writing in Middle English*, London and New York: Longman, 1992, p. 277.
24. Vriend, pp. 155–156.
25. See Claire Cross, 'Great Reasoners in Scripture: The Activities of Women Lollards 1380–1530', from *Medieval Women*, ed. Derek Baker, Oxford: Basil Blackwell, 1978, pp. 359–380, and Margaret Aston, Chapter 2, 'Lollard Women Priests?', in *Lollards and Reformers*, Britain: Hambledon Press, 1984, pp. 49–70.
26. See Alcuin Blamires, 'The Wife of Bath and Lollardy', *Mediun Aevum*, 1989, Vol. 58 No. 2, pp. 224–242.
27. ibid., pp. 228–229. See Anne Hudson's *Lollards and their Books*, London: Hambledon, 1985, esp. pp. 171–172.

His Master's Voice: Derrida and Vocal-Writing

Robert Sinnerbrink

Jacques Derrida made his first 'live' Australian appearance in September of this year, beamed via satellite from Paris and screened, as they say, before a 'live' audience. The silver-haired philosopher sat calmly, reading selections from a text to be delivered in New York for an exhibition on Antonin Artaud. Along with his gestures, it was the melodic lilt of his voice which captured the audience's attention. His viewers listened with care, straining to decipher Derrida's resonant, French-accented English. Most intriguing, however, was the fact that the Sydney audience actually heard an edited English translation of Derrida's French text, written for a performance that was yet to take place. Derrida's anticipatory mime, translated before its 'proper' performance, was rehearsed, 'live' via satellite, before a distant audience. With this intriguing event in view, I offer the following reflections on writing, voice and technology in Derrida.

Frances Dyson has recently also written on the question of the voice, writing, and communication technologies.[1] She explores their relations in regard to Derrida's *Cinders*,[2] a text which incorporates a tape recording of different voices—male and female—reciting aloud the multiple 'voices' of a written polylogue. Dyson attempts to subvert Derrida's 'interpretive experiment' in *Cinders*, the use of the 'double medium' of printed page and tape recording (C, 23), by suggesting that deconstruction itself relies upon a 'metaphorics' of communication technology. This strategy of appropriating the 'transmissional technology (EiS, 43) of tape recorder, gramophone and telephone, Dyson argues, is similarly played out in 'Ulysses Gramophone'.[3] Derrida attempts, in the latter text, to show that the 'yes' in Joyce's *Ulysses* can be read as another mark, both graphic and vocal, affirmative and non-communicable, of the movement of *différance*. Since the untranslatable play in French between 'hear say yes' and 'hearsay' (l'oui-dire and l'ouï-dire) can be both heard and read, the 'yes' in the Joycean text can, for Derrida, 'only be a mark at once written and spoken, vocalised as a grapheme and written as a phoneme, yes, in a word, gramophoned'. (UG, 267).

Nonetheless, for Dyson, Derrida's deployment of the metaphorics of gramophony (the inscription and transmission of a pre-recorded voice), and of telephony (the transmission over distance of a speaker's voice to a listener), points towards his assumption of a 'masculine mode of communication' (EiS, 43). Such communication is coded 'masculine', Dyson argues, in its instrumental and informational use of technology; in the 'short, to the point, almost telegraphic brevity in message sending and receiving amongst men'. This is contrasted with the meandering pleasure of an older mode of sociality, that of 'extended rumour-ing amongst women', which is taken as a 'feminine' use of communication technology (EiS, 43). 'Hear Say Yes in Joyce', the pithy sub-title of 'Ulysses Gramophone' (which Derrida serendipitously found by casting his eyes across a page of Joyce), is thus taken, by Dyson, to evince the telegraphic brevity of 'masculine' communication, the privileging of visual scan over oral rumour, of silent meaning over bodily expression.

Dyson seeks, in short, to 'deconstruct' deconstruction's dependence, both concrete and metaphoric, on technology. First, she attempts to show Derrida's reliance upon a 'metaphorics' of technology which is at once obsolete and masculine, claiming that such 'fairly old, mechanical, primarily inscriptive technologies and metaphors' (EiS, 45)—tape recorder, gramophone, telephone—are increasingly outmoded today. And secondly, she goes on to claim that Derrida's recourse to this metaphorics simply reinstates the primacy of an 'almost' silent, disembodied voice requiring amplification and transmission in order to be heard or read at all—the very voice of the metaphysics of presence which deconstruction seeks to displace. The result, Dyson claims, is that although the recorded voice seems to 'dislodge metaphysics'—by the inscription and reiteration of a voice released from its origin in living speech—it is rather the 'disembodied voice of technology' which is substituted for the 'silent voice of the mind' (EiS, 44). Derrida attempts to undermine the concept of a metaphysical origin of meaning in the self-presence of speech, but in doing so, Dyson claims, he has recourse to technological metaphors of vocal inscription. Dyson's deconstruction of Derrida, in short, amounts to the claim that '*différance* is already contained by technology, be it writing, phonography or telephony' (EiS, 44).

Certain questions, however, impose themselves at this point. The foremost of these is the question of technology itself, which, as Heidegger sought to show, cannot be thought simply in terms of available technical equipment. The essence of technology, that in accordance with which it orders and reveals the world, is not to be confused with technology itself.[4] To claim that '*différance* is already contained by technology', is to presuppose that we already grasp what technology, as the *logos* of *techne*, is.[5] Is technology determinable into three modes, 'be it writing, phonography or telephony'? Is writing—in the Derridean sense of a general writing—reducible to a species of technology? Dyson's claim that technology already 'contains' *différance* seems, moreover, tautological. *Différance*, for Derrida, names that which designates the possibility of conceptuality and systematicity, the movement by which language or any system of reference in general is differentially constituted.[6] Hence within the system of language, we must already presuppose *différance* in order to account for the use of the term and concept of 'technology' at all. If, however, we take 'technology' to designate different forms of systematised communicability, as Dyson seems to suggest, then to say such that such systems 'contain' *différance* is just to say that these systems also presuppose it. In either case, nothing is claimed by Dyson which would conflict with Derrida's claims concerning *différance*, conceptuality, systematicity and language.

Dyson's criticism of Derrida is interesting, however, in that it raises the issue of 'technology', the relation of general writing not only to spoken utterance but to the recorded and transmitted voice. Is the mode of communication attributed to Derrida, the metaphorics of 'transmissional technology', irreducibly 'masculine'? Dyson's observations concerning the predominance of 'women operators' in the early days of telecommunications (EiS, 43) still do not support the charge that the instrumental use of technology is therefore 'masculine', nor that the subversive pleasures of rumour need only be 'feminine'. The current feminist interest in information technologies and virtual reality would seem to suggest otherwise. In any case, Derrida distinguishes the 'metaphorics' of technology from technology itself. Indeed the metaphor of writing as 'technology' is itself part of the logocentric tradition which remains in need of deconstruction.[7] But even so, does Derrida really have recourse, as Dyson suggests, to technological tropes simply in order to 'save' the silent and disembodied voice attributed to logocentric metaphysics?

This question returns us to Derrida's 'interpretive experiment' in *Cinders*, which interweaves, but also separates, the written text and recorded voice. The term 'cinder' is taken by Derrida to mark another link in the chain of differential terms which mark the open ended movement of *différance*. As the condition of meaning and intelligibility, *différance* cannot itself be both stated and accounted for within the system of meaning that it makes possible. But *différance* can nonetheless be shown to be operative in every text which articulates those fundamental metaphysical dichotomies that still operate within philosophical, literary and ordinary language. The *aporias* which emerge when a text both attempts to state and account for its own conditions of intelligibility can be rigorously shown, Derrida claims, with regard to certain 'undecidable', marginal terms within a given text: *pharmakon* in Plato, *supplement* in Rousseau, *parergon* in Kant, and so on. The novelty of *Cinders*, however, consists in the fact that Derrida performs this deconstructive interpretation—with all the caveats one might expect—on some of his own texts. Here the undecidable term that provides the moment of rupture within the text is cinder: that which still glows, remains incandescent, after what has consumed itself is expended; but also that which remains as residue, as spent ash. Derrida assembles quotations from various texts (*Dissemination*, *Glas*, *The Post Card*), all of which involve allusions to the motif of cinders, and then weaves around this theme a series of questioning remarks, attributable to various 'authorial' and 'non-authorial' voices, concerning the self-consuming character of speech and writing.

The problem which arises, however, in Derrida's self-deconstructing polylogue, is that of marking those differences in grammar and articulation which remain untranslatable between speech and writing. These include the gender of the voices, marked grammatically when written, but not when spoken. The result is a 'certain indecision between writing and voice, an indecision already risked by the word *là*, with or without the accent, in "cinders *there are*"[il y a là cendre]' (C, 22). This indecision between speech and writing, 'this vibration of grammar in the voice', becomes, for Derrida, one of the polylogue's major themes. The written polylogue seems 'destined for the eye', to be read in silence; it corresponds to a silent reading, an 'interior voice, an absolutely low voice' (C, 22)—the one in which you, presumably, are now reading these words. It is precisely this tension between the visual scan and the interior voice which Derrida attempts to investigate.

Nevertheless, the question remains as to how the tension between silent and vocalised reading can not only be shown, but maintained in its conflict and difference. The specific *significatory* qualities of vocalisation, what Barthes called the 'grain of the voice'[8]—its tonalities, timbre, inflections and rhythms—are to be brought into productive tension with the grammatical, semantic and stylistic possibilities of the written text. The opportunity to show precisely these tensions between voice and writing came, for Derrida, with 'the chance of making a tape recording' of *Cinders* (C, 23). The result was a dual text and recording, 'a sort of research laboratory, a studio of vocal writing, in which an interpretive experiment becomes possible' (C, 23)—one which explores how the difference between speech and writing can itself be made to sound, given that it can be silently marked in writing. Yet it is here, Dyson claims, that Derrida slides back into the very metaphysics of the silent, self-present voice which deconstruction aims to subvert and reinscribe.

Dyson's critique hinges on the claim that Derrida relies on technology to both amplify writing and sonorise the 'interior voice' of reading. (EiS, 43). Derrida has recourse to the tape recorded voice in order to capture the 'inaudible' difference between speech and writing, that is, to amplify those aspects of the written text which can be seen but not heard, and conversely, to transmit those aspects of the 'grain' of the voice which can be heard but not seen. Moreover, this is supposed to evince his substitution of the 'disembodied voice of technology' for the 'silent voice of the mind' (EiS, 44). While the recorded voice appears to subvert the self-presence of speech, thereby making *différance* audible, Dyson argues, the phonograph in fact only restores 'the inner voice and origin of Western metaphysics' (EiS, 44). That is, the recorded voice, as a disembodied phantom, merely *simulates* the embodied character of living speech: 'What is lost in this process', Dyson contends, 'is the sonority of sound and hearing, the corporeality of noise and rumour, corporeality itself' (EiS, 44). Derrida's blindness, or rather, deafness to this loss of 'corporeality itself', for Dyson, is explicable by the disembodied character of 'masculinised' communication. The latter privileges vision—'the glance or rapid scan'—that is, silent reading, over listening, the labyrinthine hearsay of the 'feminised ear' (EiS, 44). What Derrida lacks, so to speak, is the ear of the other—an embodied hearing, an ear for rumour. Instead, the masculine eye, the silent scan, we are told, reduces the difference between speech and writing to silence, to a merely visible, rather than sonorous, mark—*là cendre*, *différance*. Deconstruction thus unwittingly says 'yes', Dyson concludes, 'to a philosophical era which has represented sound as other, and otherness as a reservoir which will always provide a hidden, silent ground' (EiS, 44). Far from deconstructing metaphysics, Derridean *écriture* is rather its technologically amplified accomplice; the unwitting envoy of a metaphysically silenced ground, transmitted 'through the metaphoric circuitry of a masculinised technology' (EiS, 44).

As I remarked earlier, however, Dyson's provocative critique would require us to think what is meant by technology itself; whether it merely indicates forms of technical apparatus (tape recorder, gramophone), or else a metaphorical system of communication (the 'metaphoric circuitry of masculinised technology')—or otherwise to show how the assumed transition between these distinct senses is to be understood. To slide between the particular and generalised senses of 'technology', as Dyson does, is to obliterate the sense of general writing—encompassing both speech and writing in the narrow sense—and to thereby reduce it to an ambiguously construed 'technology'. It is to remain caught within the received speech/writing dichotomy and those other metaphysical dichotomies (sensible/intelligible, and so on) to which it remains bound. Derrida attempts to thwart precisely this confusion by deconstructively showing the eventual collapse and the mutual implication of any rigid distinction between the spoken voice and written word, between the interior origin and external transmission of meaning (whether or not such meaning is technically or metaphorically 'amplified'). Those aspects of the written text which can only be seen rather than heard can nonetheless be recorded; those aspects of the recorded voice which can be heard but not seen refer nonetheless to a written text. Yet a difference remains, one which opens up an interpretive space of possibility—an 'interpretive experiment' wherein voice and writing can be replayed. This double movement between recorded voice and written text thus forms a polyphonous space, a space of writing in which the polylogue of *Cinders* not only unfolds but consumes itself in this unfolding.

So what does Derrida's vocal-writing experiment involve? It is the making legible and audible of the cinder. The cinder is a figure of the self-consuming character of writing and of speech, a figure naming the self-consuming movement of meaning from which nothing figurable remains. Cinder, Derrida writes, is 'a word for consuming itself all the way to its support (the tape-recorded voice or strip of paper, self-destruction of the impossible emission once the order is given)' (C, 73).[9] The word as a vocable emission consumes itself in its temporal sonority, while the recorded voice is consumed in its transcription—whether on the grooves of a phonograph or the magnetic configurations of a tape. What is at stake in this experiment, for Derrida, is the character of the phonographic act itself: how 'the spoken "recorded" voice makes a reservoir of writing readable, its tonal and phonic drives, the waves (neither cry nor speech) which are knotted or unknotted in the unique vociferation, the singular range of another voice' (C, 25). It is the legible character of the grain of the voice, as a form of writing, which this experiment aims to capture; each 'recording' of a voice being both a singular interpretation of the written text, in the musical and textual senses, as well as an incursion into a graphic or written space open to multiple readings and recitations. Moreover, the 'recorded' voice can in nowise be taken, *contra* Dyson, to be simply 'disembodied', a spectral phantom of the corporeal subject in its bodily presence. On the contrary, vocal-writing is the corporeality of writing itself. As Barthes describes, the grain of the voice, as heard in a song, is not merely timbre, but rather the significance opened by the friction between the music and the particular vocal, melodic and grammatical qualities of the language being sung. 'The song must speak, must write—for what is produced at the level of the phenosong is finally writing.'[10] The language of song can only be heard and read in the song of language.

Indeed the very notion of a 'disembodied voice', for Derrida, presupposes a rigid distinction between speech and writing in the narrow—and metaphysically problematic—sense. That is, we can speak of a 'disembodied voice' only if we take the incorporeal intelligibility of speech to be metaphysically opposed to the corporeal significance of writing. Moreover, the act of reading is never purely 'disembodied', nor is it without history. Augustine's description in *Confessions* (VI, 3) of his teacher Ambrose reading *in silence* indicates the rarity of silent as opposed to audible reading in late antiquity: 'As he read, his eyes scanned the pages and his heart searched out the meaning, but his voice and tongue were silent. Often when we were present...we saw him reading that way and never in the other'.[11] Augustine's description lucidly renders, according to Mary Carruthers, the distinction the two reading methods taught and practiced in antiquity: silent reading (*meditatio*) and audible reading (*lectio*).[12] Augustine's description of Ambrose using his 'heart' to search out the text's meaning refers to his memory; the metaphoric use of 'heart' for 'memory' was encoded, Carruthers observes, in the Latin verb *recordari*, meaning 'to recollect'. The etymology of this verb is from *revocare* 'to call back' and *cor* 'heart'.[13] Our use of the verb 'to record' points to a recollection from the heart, as when we speak of reciting a poem 'by heart'. One could say, then, that the term 'record' derives from 'heart' as a metaphor for memory; 'recording' points to memory and recollection. To 'record' a voice thus indicates a form of recollection, both to make and to recall, that is, to replay a memory of the voice.

In this sense, the 'recorded'—recollected and memorialised—voice belongs both to speech and writing. It is a *vocal-writing*, which makes the 'grain' of the voice both legible and audible, that is, *interpretable*. The silent *a* of *différance* is not simply the dead silence of an incorporeal voice, of a masculinised and disembodied technology. It points rather to the embodied grain of vocal-writing, the differential play which nonetheless generates the 'transcendental illusion'[14] of an intractable opposition between the intelligibility of self-present speech on the one hand, and the sensuous signification of writing on the other. To show this constitutive difference between speech and writing, yet without presupposing the logical, semantic or expressive priority of one over the other, is precisely what *Cinders* attempts to do. Vocal-writing presents a kind of gramophony, a written grain, 'which records writing in the liveliest voice' (UG, 276). Gramophony responds both to the dream of preserving the living truth of the voice in a recording, and to the possibility of parody and the reiterative transformation of the voice as text (one need only think here, for example, of sampling and mixing techniques). Similarly, a verbally 'recorded' text, that is, the recitation of a text 'by heart', can present both a recollection from memory, and a reiterated rehearsal or performance.

To return to my opening anecdote, Derrida's 'gramophoned' performance in Sydney this year exhibited just this duplicity of the written voice and spoken text. Derrida's appearance was both a 'live' performance and a rehearsed mime. One could thus say that parody is the silent shadow of sincerity; which is why one could also, ironically, say 'yes' to Dyson's charge that deconstruction 'is saved by gramophony', by old-fashioned 'inscriptive technologies and metaphors' which fall far short of the 'revolutionary' technology (and metaphors?) of today (EiS, 45). Not because deconstruction relapses into the metaphysics of a disembodied, technologically mediated, voice; but rather because deconstruction saves or records, that is, memorialises and replays, the embodied interpretability of vocal-writing. Deconstruction is saved, and thereby open to reiteration and reinterpretation, by what Derrida calls the 'gramophone effect', the affirmation of memory: 'Yes must preserve itself, and thus reiterate itself, archive its voice in order to allow it once again to be heard' (UG, 276). Vocal-writing is saved, yes, memorialised, for further writing and thinking.

Many thanks to Louise D'Arcens for comments and suggestions.

1. Frances Dyson, 'Nothing Here but the Recording: Derrida and Phonography', *Essays in Sound 2: Technophonia*, Sydney: Contemporary Sound Arts, 1995, pp. 40–46. Cited hereafter as EiS.
2. Jacques Derrida, *Cinders*, trans. Ned Lukacher, Lincoln: University of Nebraska Press, 1991. Cited hereafter as C.
3. Jacques Derrida, 'Ulysses Gramophone: Hear Say Yes in Joyce', in *Acts Of Literature*, ed. Derek Attridge, New York: Routledge, 1992, pp. 256–309. Cited hereafter as UG.
4. Martin Heidegger, *The Question Concerning Technology*, trans. William Lovitt, New York: Harper and Row, 1977, p. 4.
5. Heidegger interprets the essence of technology as that mode of revealing the real as a 'standing-reserve', that is, the 'en-framing' of nature as a totality of resources to be ordered and commanded as available for use.
6. Derrida, 'Différance', in *Writing and Difference*, trans. Alan Bass, Chicago: Chicago University Press, 1978, pp. 11–12.
7. Derrida writes: 'This logocentrism, the *epoch* of full speech, has placed in parenthesis, *suspended*, and suppressed for essential reasons, all free reflection on the origin and status of writing, all science of writing which was not *technology* and the *history of a technique*, itself leaning upon a mythology and a metaphor of a natural writing'. Derrida, *Of Grammatology*, trans. Gayatri Chakravorty Spivak, Baltimore: Johns Hopkins University Press, 1974, p. 43.
8. The 'grain', for Barthes, is the significatory aspect of embodied gesture and expression; the 'body in the voice as it sings, the hand as it writes, the limb as it performs'. Roland Barthes, *Image, Music, Text*, trans. Stephen Heath, New York: Noonday Press, 1977, p. 188.
9. Translator Ned Lukacher notes the resonance in French of *l'emission impossible*' with the TV series *Mission: Impossible*.
10. Barthes, op. cit., p. 185.
11. Augustine, *Confessions* (VI, 3), quoted in Mary Carruthers, *The Book of Memory: A Study of Memory in Medieval Culture*, Cambridge: Cambridge University Press, 1990, p. 170.
12. ibid., p. 171.
13. ibid., pp. 48–49.
14. 'Transcendental illusion', for Kant, refers to the inevitable illusion generated by misapplying the categories of the understanding beyond the limits of experience; such illusion rests on subjective principles which foist themselves upon us as objective. Transcendental illusion remains inseparable from human reason, and cannot be dispelled by criticism. Rather, it continues 'to play tricks with reason and continually entrap it into momentary aberrations ever and again calling for correction'. Kant, *Critique of Pure Reason*, trans. Norman Kemp Smith, London: Macmillan, 1929, B352–B355.

Nietzsche's Recovery of Primary Acoustical Experience: The Birth of Tragedy out of the Spirit of Music as 'Fundamental Ontology'

P. Christopher Smith

> Um dies zu begreifen, müssen wir jenes kunstvolle Gebäude der apollinischen Kultur gleichsam Stein um Stein abtragen, bis wir die Fundamente erblicken, auf die es begründet ist.[1]

> Der Philosoph sucht den Gesamtklang der Welt in sich nachtönen zu lassen and ihn aus sich herausstellen in Begriffen.[2]

In his Marburg lectures of the summer of 1924, 'Basic Concepts of Aristotelian Philosophy', Martin Heidegger elaborates his project of the *Destruktion* of the metaphysical tradition in an appropriation of Aristotle's *Rhetoric*.[3] As in *Being and Time*'s exposition three years later of our being 'there' 'in the world' 'with others' and of our employment of tools, 'ready at hand', to take care of things in going about the practical tasks of day to day life,[4] Heidegger's strategy in these earlier lectures too is, first, to 'lay bare' our primary way of existing by taking away the layers of abstractions subsequently superimposed upon it and, second, to 'lay out' hermeneutically or interpretively our primary way of existing as this is now uncovered and disclosed beneath the abstractions that have been removed. In this way, the 'metaphysical' world of statically present beings given to a theoretical observer, say, Descartes' quantifiable extended things just lying about 'on hand', is shown to be 'founded' on another, primary world of temporal being, from which theoretical 'metaphysics' had abstracted and which it had obscured from our view. In the *Basic Concepts* lectures, however, this strategy of *Destruktion* and 'fundamental ontology' is applied specifically to speech and argument (*Sprache, logos*).[5] Using Aristotle's *Rhetoric*, Heidegger would display, first, that science's demonstration or proof, the *apodeixis*, is an abstraction founded in *dialegesthai* or 'talking things through' by 'topics' or the natural lines of reasoning given in natural speech, and, second, that this dialectic's still disengaged, theoretical *sun-logismos* or combination of spoken assertions (*logoi*) is, in turn, an abstraction to be founded in rhetoric's engaged, practical *en-thumêmê* or the convincing combination of spoken assertions that would move someone in his or her *thumos*, the 'heart' or 'gut', to resolve on a course of action. Rhetoric, as well as Aristotle's treatise on it, Heidegger would show, is thus not of marginal philosophical interest; rather it concerns the primary way we speak to each other when taking care of practical tasks in the temporal world and, hence, lies at the crux of our concern.

In returning to Nietzsche, who is the unacknowledged father of much of Heidegger's 'fundamental ontological' project, we will try here to go a step further than Heidegger does in the *Destruktion* of 'metaphysical' abstractions and to 'lay bare' and 'lay out' hermeneutically the *acoustical* ground and foundation of speech. Nietzsche, in ultimately scuttling the idea of founding altogether, will call this ground and foundation the *Hintergrund*, *Unterground*, and even *Abgrund*, that is, the background, underground, and non-ground or abyss. Contrary to Derrida and with Nietzsche, it will be maintained here that there is no deconstruction of 'metaphysics'' timeless, tenseless, static presence as long as one has not penetrated behind envisioned, written and read word-signs, and penetrated to the primary acoustical experience of spoken and heard word-names that tell narratively what happens to happen over time.[6] Indeed, it is not difficult to show that the history of 'metaphysics' begins with the abstraction and withdrawal from acoustical experience of temporal being and with a turn to an optical supervision and overview of static spatialised being, a turn coincident with the turn from *phasis*, or saying something out loud, to *graphê*, or written marks, or, in the language of Eric Havelock, the turn from orality to writing.[7]

THE SHIFT FROM ACOUSTICS TO OPTICS IN PLATO AND ARISTOTLE

This withdrawal and turn begins at least with Plato's rejection of epic and tragic *mimêsis*, the *mimêsis* of the rhapsode and the *hupokritês* or dramatic actor (see the *Ion* 533c–536d, *Republic* 392d–398b, 595a–608b), with his consequent rejection of the continuing concern with these forms of *mimêsis* in rhetoric's treatment of *hupokrisis* or delivery, and with his turn to the envisioning (*thea*) and contemplation (*theôria*) of the ideas or *eidê*, which is to say, of the visual 'looks' that things have about them. Exemplary here is Plato's conversion of the acoustical musical experience of hearing the *melos*, into the theoretical science of harmony (see *Republic* 530c–531c): *harmonia*, after all, comes from *harma*, the chariot, and has to do with joining and pegging parts into a visual, spatial whole. In the hands of Pythagorians, from whom Plato takes it over, the science of harmony becomes the science of *logoi*—*logoi*, of course, no longer as voiced utterances but once again as enumerable mathematic proportions, ratios, of what 'fits' together spatially.[8] These ratios are not heard but seen and 'read'. The one who has been taught the science of harmony no longer hears the melody but, much like someone who takes the score along to read during a musical performance, he or she envisions, instead, a graphic distribution of different components in the spatial *sustasis* or com-position 'placing' them in relation 'with' each other.

So, too, rhetoric becomes for Plato the theoretical, logical science of dialectical com-position: what we hear in time, as it comes over us and transforms us who undergo its effect, is abandoned. To be sure, the word '*sumphonein*', or 'to be con*sonant* with', that Plato uses in the *Phaedo* to characterise the combinative logic of each of the visible *eidê* or 'looks' of things with the others, say of 'three' with 'odd' but not with 'even', still perpetuates an earlier phonic and vocal background understanding of speech (see 100a, 104c). However, in the end the envisionable, spatialised lattice-work of *genos* and *eidê*, say, of the *Phaedrus*' genus 'madness' in its sinister/left forms or species of 'gluttony', 'dipsomania', and '*skaios erôs*' or 'left love', placed over against its rectitudinous/right forms or species of 'prophecy', 'lyric musicality', 'cathartic healing' and 'divine love', a lattice-work that we are to see arrayed before us, becomes the new focus of our redirected attention, and the phonetic and acoustical origins of speech fall into oblivion (see *Phaedrus* 264c–266c). As in the Pythagorean reconversion of *logos* from 'speech' back to its original mathematical sense of ratio, here too the *logos* of *dialegesthai* or 'talking something through' vocally in time is converted into the *logos* of a 'dialectical' spatial organisation that we see and read. And, analogously, even tragedy, we learn, would no longer consist in the communication of affects by its sound but in its envisionable 'spatial' com-position: '...as if', writes Plato, one were to think that the tragedy is anything other that the proper composition (*sustasis*) of these [parts] placed (*sunistamenen*) in relation to one another and the whole (*Phaedrus* 268d).

Now though in some ways Aristotle manages to recover things buried in Plato—after all, he writes a *Rhetoric* whose third part is devoted, if halfheartedly, to spoken style, and a *Poetics* in which a *mimêsis* or imitation is partially rehabilitated that involves the audience's participation in musical re-enactment of an action and which achieves, thereby, a catharsis of excessive affects—we must say that in the end Aristotle only perpetuates and solidifies the Platonic 'metaphysical', 'theoretical', 'scientific' withdrawal and turn away from the acoustical and to the optical.

For even if his *Rhetoric* will devote ten quite extraordinary chapters to a phenomenological exposition of the affects intrinsic to rhetorical conviction (bk. II, chapts. 2–11), affects that can only be communicated acoustically, which is to say, by voiced intonation, phrasing, cadence, tempo, rhythm, and the like, it still sees rhetoric primarily as the counterpart to dialectic, in which the affects play no role at all. And thus Aristotle says right from the start that ideally rhetoric, like dialectic, should be concerned not with the affects—and, consequently, not with the *hupokrisis*, the audible delivery that communicates them to hearers—but with the *logos*, namely the syllogistic argument. *Logos* is thus severed from *pathos* after all, speech and reasoning from affect, and, consequently, the logically envisionable is severed from the acoustical and voiced. This split, in the dichotomy of the cognitive and emotive, will go unchallenged until, and except for, Nietzsche's radical destruction of the 'theoretical' and 'scientific' and his reduction of these to acoustical art and of acoustical art, in turn, to bodily life.

Correspondingly, in Aristotle's *Poetics* we find that in the end the tragedy will achieve its catharsis, not bodily by the acoustical experience of the *melos* undergone by the audience (*hoi akouontes*), who are drawn into the dance and gesture of the imitative re-enactment, but cognitively by spectators (*theôretes*) who, in grasping the logic of the organically composed overseeable whole with its beginning, middle and end fitted together harmoniously, are purified of the influence of any affect exceeding the mean that would keep it subordinate to rational limitation. The making of melodies, *melopoia*, is, it turns out, only a matter of pleasant adornment, *hedusma*, and not intrinsic to the art of tragedy at all (see 1450b 16). On the contrary, the intrinsic essence of tragedy is said to lie in its overseeable, logical unity. The *sustasis* or composition, says Aristotle, 'is the primary and most important element of the tragedy' (1450b 22):

> It has now been established for us, then, that the tragedy is the imitation of a complete and whole action having a certain size. ... A whole is what has a beginning, middle and end. A beginning is what does not necessarily *exist* after something else, but after which something else either *exists* or *comes to pass* naturally. The end, in contrast, is what itself naturally *exists*, either of necessity or for the most part, after something else, but after which nothing else *exists*. A middle is what itself both *exists* after something else and also after which something else *exists*. Accordingly, it is necessary that well composed stories (*tous sunestotas eu muthous*) neither just happen to begin nor just happen to end somewhere or other, rather that they have made use of the ideas we have mentioned (1450b 24–34: emphasis added).

We note here the first indications of Aristotle's tendency to abstract from the temporal sequence of narrative-historical tale or *muthos* as it is told and heard—'Once upon a time this came to pass, and then this, and then this...'—and his tendency to abstract to what Nietzsche will call a 'logical schematism'. The temporal *gigignesthai*, or 'coming to pass', already starts to give way here to a timeless logical *einai*, or 'to exist', and, correspondingly, the timeless logical connections of one thing 'following', not after another temporally, but from another logically 'for the most part' (*epi to polu*) and even 'of necessity' (*ex anagkes*), have insinuated themselves into the account of tragedy. What matters now is that the composition of the components, beginning, middle and end, be overseeable and comprehensible logically, that one event be seen to follow logically from another and not merely, as in the singing of a tale, heard to follow it temporally. Extending this spatialisation and visualisation of tragedy, Aristotle thus continues:

> Furthermore, the beautiful in a living being and in any thing that is composed of certain parts consists not only in these parts having been arranged but also in a thing's having a specific size and not one that just happens by chance to hold for it. For the beautiful consists in size. Hence neither a tiny nor a huge living thing comes to be beautiful. For when the thing is tiny our viewing of it (*hê theôria*) is confused, the time for this being nearly imperceptible. And when the thing is huge our viewing of it cannot occur all at once; rather, the unity and whole of the thing escapes the envisioning of the onlookers (*oichetai tois theôrousi...ek tês theôrias*) as when a living being were to be ten thousand stadia long. Consequently, just as it is necessary for bodies and living beings to have size and necessary that this size be easily envisionable as a whole (*eusunopton*), so too must stories have a length, this being what is easily remembered (1450b 34–1451a 5).

Here too we note Aristotle's insistence on translating the acoustical and temporal into the optical and spatial.[9]

NIETZSCHE'S DESTRUKTION OF THE OPTICAL TURN

It is only Nietzsche who, after two millennia of its predominance, will call this canon of envisionable organic unity and logical consequentiality into question, and, most important for us, he does so in rehabilitating the acoustical, specifically music. In fragments from the fall of l869 he writes, 'The requirement of unity, unjustified, as we saw, is the source of all perversions in the opera and in the song';[10] 'The piece of music: it is a mistake to talk here about the architectonics of the whole and similarly with drama. Where are the laws of sequentiality?' (KSA 7, 1 [53]). It falls to Nietzsche, in other words, to overthrow the dominant Platonic-Aristotlelian 'historical effect' and to reverse the 'metaphysical' withdrawal and turn from the acoustical to the optical. This overthrow and reversal, as we will now see, finds its clearest execution in his *The Birth of Tragedy out of the Spirit of Music*, all the inadequacies of this inchoate study not withstanding. For Nietzsche's 'fundamental ontological' project in that work is to display the tragedy of Aeschylus and Sophocles as the repenetration and suffusion of the visual, three-dimensional spatial Apollonian world of the epicist Homer by the Dionysian sonic temporal world of the folk poet Archilochus and, thereby, to reduce the Apollonian as such to the Dionysian musical and acoustical *fundamentum* out of which it originates and by which it is sustained. To be sure, there was musical accompaniment to the rhapsodist's singing of Homer, the accompaniment of the lyre or cithara. But tragedy reflects the influence of another music of Archilochean heritage, Nietzsche contends, namely the music of the flute and Pindar's dithyrambic hymns (GdT §6, 49).

Nietzsche's own 'fundamental-ontological' task, accordingly, is to found the beautiful Apollonian dream pictures, conjured up in all vividness before our eyes by Homer's tales, on the *fundamentum* of another, primary experience, an experience from the very pain and contradiction of which these dream pictures release us in the first place. The Apollonian, namely, is to be grounded in its background, underground and non-ground of the Dionysian ecstatic rush that dissolves individuality and fuses us with each other and with all things but which, in shattering acoustically the optical-spatial, logical distinctions of 'this here' as opposed to 'that there', reveals to us the underlying insignificance of any and all significance that we had assigned to 'looks' of things. Thus the Apollonian dream images we see before us are to be resolved into an undifferentiated flow of time not observed but experienced physically, somatically, acoustically, as it comes over us and we undergo it, and which can be communicated only in music. It is the chant and dance of the chorus, therefore, which must be seen as the core of the tragedy, not the thought, not the action, not story, not the composition and least of all the dialogue: 'The Greek chorus', writes Nietzsche in the fall of 1869,

> is, first, the live soundingboard and second the megaphon through which the actor cries out colosally his feeling to the spectators, and, thirdly, it is the passionate, singing spectator, become lyrical, who has found in it his voice (KSA 7, 1 [4]).

'Speech', Nietzsche observes in the spring of 1870,

> arose out of the cry with its accompanying gesture; here by the intonation, the volume, the rhythm, the essence of the thing is expressed and, by the gesture of the mouth, the accompanying image of the essence, the appearance (KSA 7, 3 [15]).[11]

On Nietzsche's understanding there are, accordingly, four stages to be elaborated in the birth and the death of tragedy. First comes the 'iron age' with its battle of the Titans and its 'bitter folk philosophy', and second, the stage of the so-called naive artist Homer, whose 'naiveté', contrary to Rousseau and Schiller, can only be understood against the prior experience of the titanic realm, on whose chaos it superimposes an ordering, but only by suppressing, with 'forceful manic mirror images' and 'pleasurable illusions', a 'terrible depth in the way one sees the world' and 'a hypersensitive capacity for suffering' (see GdT §4, 41–44). Homeric naiveté is thus only to be grasped as 'the perfect victory of the Apollonian illusion' (GdT §3, 37). But this 'naively beautiful' Homeric world must, in turn, yield to the third stage, in which the 'stream of the Dionysian' 'breaks in upon it' and it is 'swallowed up' (GdT §4, 41). With that tragedy is born, but only to decay and die in stage four, the 'stiff majesty' of Doric art (GdT§ 4, 41–42) and the Euripidean post-tragedy based on 'Socratic' cognizance and logic and, now in complete disjunction from this cognizance and logic, extraneous stimulation of the affects (see GdT §§ 11–15).

Thus Nietzsche's radical question is this: What if 'for us the period reached last, that of Doric art, ought not to count as the culmination and aim of those art-drives [the Apollonian and Dionysian]' but rather the 'sublime and exalted artwork of Attic tragedy' (GdT §4, 42)? In other words, what if the verdict of Platonic and Aristotelian metaphysics were to be undone and the supposed 'culmination' in conscious knowledge of what is statically present in view were shown to be a degenerate abstraction from the primary experience of hearing over time the voiced tones of the *melos*?

Let us review Nietzsche's distinction between the Apollonian and the Dionysian 'drives', as he calls them: the Apollonian drive produces the realm of *Schein*, the sheen of appearance shining forth (GdT §1, 26), for Apollo is the 'shining one', 'the light divinity', the god of all 'picture making powers and plasticity [*bildnerische Kräfte*]' (GdT §1, 27). Hence, the Apollonian artist 'likes to *look* at these things closely (*sieht gern und genau zu*), for out of these pictures he interprets life for himself' (GdT §1, 27) (emphasis added); and in this way, in 'freedom from the wilder stimulations', he makes life 'possible and worth of living' (GdT §1, 27–28). But his is the 'reality' of dream and appearance, and as such it is subject to disruptions. To the horror (*Grausen*) of the dreamer, these disruptions, these intrusions of the real 'reality' beneath the dream, arrive as suspensions of the *Satz vom Grund* (GdT §1, 28)—*nihil est sine ratione* or 'nothing exists without a rational account'. Implied here is that the logical underpinnings of our conscious, systematised world of differences and relations are suddenly knocked out from beneath it: the 'laws' of non-contradiction, ~(A and ~A), and self-identity, A=A, which alone preserve its unified logical composition and make rational accounts possible, lose their validity.

But this horror is at the same time its own contradiction, namely *Rausch*, the rush of intoxication that overcomes us when individuation dissolves and we, 'singing and dancing' experience a 'festival of reconciliation' (GdT §1, 29). And now we experience the underlying realm of Dionysius, the primary acoustical realm of rhythm and tone, the realm of music. The optical world of shining pictures and three-dimensional images has been absorbed back into the primary acoustical experience from which they originated. 'By Dionysian', writes Nietzsche in early l871,

> I understand, first, all art that is not the appearance of an appearance but the appearance of being, the mirroring of the primary One, and hence, second, our entire empirical world, which, form the vantage point of the primary One is a Dionysian artwork, or, from our standpoint, music (KSA 7 [126]).

Music here is not the Doric 'architectonics in tones, but in tones only hinted at, like those of the cithara' (GdT §2, 33), for this latter 'tone' is far removed from the 'shattering force of the tone, the unitary stream of the *melos*', that characterises Dionysian music, far removed from the dithyramb, 'a bodily symbolics not just of the mouth, the face, the word, but of full blown dance gestures that set all limbs in rhythmical motion' (GdT §2, 33–34). Hence, while in the Apollonian realm we looked on tranquilly as visions loomed up before us, we now find ourselves undergoing and feeling physically what the primal sounds we hear do with us.

With this in mind we can see now why Euripedes' tragedy by consciousness, cognition (*Erkenntnis*), and thought thus emerges as tragedy uprooted from its ground. This Euripedes, namely, whom Aristotle finds the consummate tragedian, had sought to 'correct' the unclarity and impenetrability attaching itself to the works of Aeschylus and Sophocles: 'With all the brightness and facility of his critical thinking', writes Nietzsche in the *Birth of Tragedy*,

> Euripedes had sat in the theater and strained to recognize in the masterpieces of his predecessors, as if these were paintings darkened over, each and every trait, each and every line. And here there now confronted him something that ought not to be unexpected for anyone initiated into the deeper secrets of Aeschylean tragedy: he perceived something incommensurable in every trait and every line, a certain deceptive determinacy, but at the same time, a puzzling depth, yes, even infinity of the background. The clearest figure still had something of a comet's tail about it that seemed to point into an uncertainty upon which no light could be shed (GdT §11, 80–81).

In order to make sense of tragedy, to bring all of it within thought's purview and comprehension, Euripedes was thus constrained to wage war on its incomprehensible Dionysian underground. That which is incommensurable with logic's principles of non-contradiction and self-identity, and which by nature keeps to itself and eludes any rational overview and explanation, was to be eliminated. But in thereby eradicating the Dionysian acoustical root of the Apollonian visual dream, he cut the latter off from its source and found himself left with only a dessicated, empty form: tragedy now as a 'game of chess', mere 'cool thoughts' into which he then imported 'fiery affects', say, in Medea's gruesome violence.[12]

Hence, just as in Socrates and the subsequent tradition where conscious cognizance and thought is severed from its ground in affect and feeling and then degenerates into ancillary means of rhetorical persuasion and pleasant ornamentation, so too in tragedy the musical and acoustical, which communicates affect and feeling, becomes a mere secondary stimulant—the greatest of the *hêdusmata*, or pleasantries, as Aristotle puts it. And having been displaced by an abstract theoretical optics, the primary acoustical experience thus falls into oblivion. When Nietzsche argues that Euripedes brought the spectator onto the stage, the *theôretês, der theoretischer Mensch*, namely Euripedes himself and Socrates (GdT §§11–12), we should make no mistake about what this means for the former audience of tragedy, an audience that in hearing the *melos* had itself once been drawn into the choral dithyrambic chants and dance and, like early Christians in their mimetic re-enactment of the Eucharist, seen the reincarnate deity arise on the scene before them out of the midst of their original acoustical experience. In Euripedes the audience that hears and then sings and dances with the chorus has now become a mere onlooker with an overview of the whole. As Nietzsche put it in l869:

> Long before Socrates was alive Socrates was the element in the tragedy that dissolved it. The lack of music and, on the other hand, the exaggerated monological development of feeling, necessitated that dialectic come to the fore. The musical *pathos* is missing in dialogue (KSA 7, 1 [15]).

> In Socrates the principle of science moves in; and with that [comes] the battle with the unconscious and its annihilation (KSA 7, 1 [27]).

> Euripedes introduced dialectic, the tone of the courtroom, into the dialogue. We see the vexing consequence here: if one separates feeling and understanding, music and deed, intellect and will, unnaturally from each other, each separated part shrivels up (KSA 7, 1 [49]).

With Euripedes, says Nietzsche, 'dialectic penetrates the heroes of the stage, and they die of a superfetation of the logical' (KSA 7, 1 [7]); 'Music is the mother of tragedy' (KSA 7, 1 [7]); 'The music drama is the high point; it is dissolved by expanded reflection' (KSA7, 1 [28]).

The remarkable and radical feature of Nietzsche's argument is its inversion of the Platonic-Aristotelian 'metaphysical' priorities we have observed, an inversion too radical, in fact, even for Heidegger: on Nietzsche's account, the ordered world of sights is neither higher than, nor prior to, the non-ordered experience of sounds, and the experience of sounds is thus not, as in Pythagorean doctrines of harmony, a fallen version of the world of envisionable ratios; it is, rather, the reverse. In support of this thesis Nietzsche takes, as an example, Schiller's account of the poetic experience: 'He [Schiller] allows, namely, that as the condition preparatory to the poetic act, he did not have before him and in his possession some sequence of images ordered causally in his thoughts but, on the contrary, [found himself undergoing] a musical mood or voicing (*eine musikalische Stimmung*)' (GdT §5, 43).[13] Or, as Nietzsche restates this, 'The "I" of the lyricist is thus intoned (*tönt*) out of the groundlessness of being' (*Abgrund des Seins*) (GdT §5, 44). Put another way, 'The plastic artist, just as the epicist who is related to him, has sunk into the pure viewing of pictures. The Dionysian musician, without any picture, is himself only primal pain and the primal resonance (*Urwiderklang*) of this pain' (GdT §5, 44).

Let us say, then, that here in the original poetic experience *logos* is still embedded in *pathos*, speech still embedded in a 'feel' or affective tone to things as this is undergone, *epathen*, in the primary experience of voice and melody beneath any overseeable system of differences and relations among significations—a primary acoustical experience where the principle of sufficient reason, *nihil est sine ratione*, and the logical 'laws' of non-contradiction and self-identity propping it up, have yet to obtain. Thus in Nietzsche, as opposed to Derrida, the *pharmakon*, the

Hexentrank (GdT §2, 32) and *Zaubertrank* (GdT §3, 35 and §13, 90), as Nietzsche calls it, that subverts and shatters the ordered realm, is not 'writing' or *graphê*; it is not visual, readable markings in *space* signifying another differentiated visual order of significations some *place* else, *ad infinitum*, but rather the temporal rising and falling tone of *phonê* and *melos* that we hear, feel and undergo physically—*paschomen somatikôs*—for the *time* it reverberates and resonates in us and with us. Voice is the anarchic, unfathomable, bottomless underground, not on which the logical rests, but in which it floats precariously. When the props fall out, as they do in the primary Dionysian experience of music, *graphê* collapses into *phonê*, writing into voice, not vice versa.

'Music', writes Nietzsche in the winter of 1870,

> is a language that is capable of an unending clarification of meaning. Language makes its meaning clear only by concepts; hence feeling what someone else feels occurs in language through the medium of thought, and this sets limits to language. But that holds only for objective, written language. The spoken, intoned word rings; and the intervals, the rhythms, the tempi, the volume and emphasis, are all symbolic for the content of feeling that is to be represented. All this belongs to music too. The great mass of feeling, however, does not express itself by words. And the word too merely points in its direction. *The word is the surface of an agitated sea storming in its depths.* (KSA 7, 2 [10]; emphasis added).

> Music, however, says out loud the soul of the dramatic action. Words, after all, are the most deficient indices (KSA 7, 2 [12]).

CONCLUSION

Nietzsche the musician thus alerts us to an earlier, pre-metaphysical dimension of speech that remains inaccessible to Derrida's deconstruction and Heidegger's *Destruktion*, both of which, unlike Nietzsche's radical genealogy, cannot get behind visible, readable signification to its origins in vocal naming, both of which, this is to say, cannot get behind Plato's and Aristotle's literary *semainein* to Homer's oral *onomazein* and behind that, to the genesis of vocal naming in the primary reverberations of acoustical, musical experience. The origin and starting place here is the lyrical-poetic event of *onomatopoiein*, naming according to the sound of a thing that we hear, say, 'smooth' and, by metaphor or 'carry-over', naming other sensuous-somatic 'feels' to something as in a 'smooth' surface or taste. This metaphorical proliferation is enhanced by metonymy, or the transfer of the name for a part to the whole or vice versa, and the carrying over into other parts of speech as in the transformation of the adjective 'smooth' to the verb 'to smooth out', or, what would be better in Nietzsche's case, *Rausch*, for instance, to *rauschend* and *berauschen*.[14] It is important to note that these words, though eventually in*scribing* an envisionable system of differences and relations, continue even then to in*voke* their origins in the experience of voicing of things. It is this primary acoustical experience that Nietzsche alone recovers for us, not Derrida, and not even Heidegger, despite his evocation of '*Stimmung*'.

The consequences of this recovery of the acoustical for our understanding of speech and language are far reaching. For one thing, it would mean the recovery of an earlier, rhetorical understanding of translation. Translations of Biblical language, for instance, which try only to render accurately the cognitive content of the original Hebrew and Greek texts would be seen to have deleted the major dimension of their communication. For as is in fact the case with most contemporary translations, they provide texts that are impossible to make sound, texts with no tone, no 'voicing' audible left underneath them. Consequently the communication can no longer be the original visceral communication of the affective ground and *fundamentum* of these texts, the *melos* from which the thought arises and back into which it continues to resonate, but only the cerebral communication of information, data, facts, from one eviscerated, disembodied mind to another. Thus even for someone with ears—'Let him who has ears hear' (Luke 14:35)—there is no longer any message to be heard.

Not that the early Nietzsche of *The Birth of Tragedy out of the Spirit of Music* was entirely clear or consistent about these things, as the later Nietzsche of the *Versuch einer Selbstkritik (Attempt at Self-Criticism)* (1886) (KSA 1, pp. 11–22) acknowledges. Here Nietzsche credits his early work with recognising that 'the problem of science (*Wissenschaft*) cannot be recognised on the ground and basis (*Boden*) of science' and that science in fact has its ground and basis in art, but it was crippled in its efforts to elaborate this thesis, and having established that science must be viewed within the optics of art, it could not reach the insight that art, in turn, must be viewed within the optics of life and living (*Leben*) (§2, 13–14), which life and living is indissociable from body (*Leib*) (§4, 16). For one thing, it was, of course, held back by its inability to *affirm* life and body, by its 'romanticism of 1830 under the mask of the pessimism of 1850' (§7, 21), and by its 'artist-metaphysics' (§2, 13) and entanglement in German music (§6, 20). Hence it could not learn the art of earthly consolation, 'on this side', instead of the art of the consolation of the 'beyond'; it could not say 'to the devil with all metaphysical consolations and, first off, with metaphysics' (§7, 22) (quoting from *Also sprach Zarathustra*).

But it suffered from another constraint that is of more interest to us here: it was—as is this study (!)—still in the form of a scientific treatise and thus unable to break cleanly with science's 'logic and logicising of the world', with the tendency, born of 'physiological fatigue' to go on being ever 'more scientific (*wissenschaftlicher*)' (§4, 16). It could not, that is to say, find the form of speech in which to render its discoveries. To have really penetrated to the ground and basis of science 'It should have sung, this "new soul" ', says Nietzsche, 'and not have talked' (§3, 15), for, 'it is one who knows (*ein Wissender*) who is [still] talking there' (§4, 15). In the end, then, Nietzsche realised that his destruction of metaphysics required a language that was more than signs to be read silently; it required a language of onomatopoetics to be heard spoken out loud.

1. 'To grasp this we must take away the artful structure of Apollonian culture stone by stone, as it were, until we catch sight of the foundations on which it is based.' Friedrich Nietzsche, *Die Geburt der Tragödie aus dem Geiste der Musik (The Birth of Tragedy out of the Spirit of Music)* in *Nietzsche; Kritische Studienausgabe 1*, Munich: de Gruyter, 1988, §3, p. 34. Hereafter cited as GdT. Translations of German and Greek throughout this study are my own except where noted.
2. 'The philosopher tries to let the collective ring of the universe resonate in himself and to reproduce it out of himself in concepts.' Nietzsche, 'Die Philosophie im Tragischen Zeitalter der Griechen' ('Philosophy in the Tragic Age of the Greeks'), in *Nietzsche; Kritische Studienausgabe I*, p. 817.
3. *Grundbegriffe der Aristotelischen Philosophie*'. Hereafter cited as GBAPh. What I say here is based on the typescript of these lectures in the Marcuse-Archiv in the Stadtsbibliotek in Frankfurt a. M. It was Theodore Kisiel who alerted me to the existence and importance of this remarkable text. For an analysis of its place in the development of Heidegger's thought see T. Kisiel, *The Genesis of Heidegger's Being and Time*, Berkeley: 1993, pp. 286–301 and 558 n. 19.
4. See Heidegger, *Sein und Zeit*, Tübingen: Niemeyer, 1960, pp. 63–166. Hereafter cited as SZ.
5. Compare SZ §34, 'Being-there and speech (*Rede*). Language (*Sprache*)', pp. 160–166.
6. I want to emphasise here that Heidegger's word '*Geschichtlichkeit*' not only implies the temporality and 'historicity' which Heidegger underscores but also the 'narrativity' of a story or *Geschichte* told and sung out loud to listeners.
7. See in particular Havelock's most philosophically (ontologically) interesting work, *Preface to Plato*, Cambridge, MA: Harvard University Press, 1963, in particular chapter VII, 'The Oral Sources of the Hellenic Intelligence' (pp. 115–133) and VIII, 'The Homeric State of Mind' (pp. 134–44).

8. The original sense of *logos* is not 'spoken utterance' but 'computation'. Hence, when Heraclitus says τοῦ δὲ λόγου τοῦδ ἐόντος ἀεὶ ἀξύνετοι γίνονται ἄνθρωποι καὶ πρόσθεν ἢ ἀκοῦσαι καὶ ἀκούσαντες τὸ πρῶτον (Of the *logos*, this being what it is, human beings are always uncomprehending both before having heard it and once they have heard it) (Fr. 1), and οὐκ ἐμοῦ ἀλλὰ τοῦ λόγου ἀκούσαντας ὁμολοειν σοφόν ἐστιν ἓν πάντα εἶναι (Having heard not me but the *logos*, it is wise to agree that all things are one.) (Fr. 50), he is already thinking of something calculable and envisionable even if he still expects his audience to hear and not read silently what he has to say about it. Once, as in Plato's *dialogos* and Aristotle's *sullogismos*, '*logos*' has displaced '*rhêma*' in thinking of spoken utterances—and, accordingly, once logic has displaced rhetoric—the abstraction from the fundamental and primary acoustical experience of voice (*phônê*) has begun. It is important to note that Heidegger, in focusing on *logos* as 'collection', never recognises the shift from the acoustical to the optical which attention to this word implies. In just this regard Nietzsche, as we will see, is more radical and better.

9. For an extended analysis of the *Poetics'* abstraction from the acoustical see my 'From Acoustics to Optics: The Rise of the Metaphysical and Demise of the Musical in Aristotle's Poetics', to appear in *Sites of Vision*, ed. David Michael Levin, Cambridge, MA: MIT. Press, l997.

10. *Nietzsche, Nachgelassene Fragmente 1869–1874, Kritische Studienausgabe 7*, Munich: de Gruyter, l988, 1 [49]. Hereafter cited as KSA 7.

11. We might add in support of Nietzsche's argument, that as much as the chorus, say, of the Argive Elders, it is, for example, Aeschylus' Cassandra whose antiphonal speech, embedded as it is in the original cry, lets us hear this indefinite and indeterminate Dionysian acoustical underground from which the vision of the actions on the *skênê* or stage arises and back into which it is resolved (see Nietzsche's own reference to Cassandra at GdT §4, 42). 'Ὀτοτοτοτοῖ πόποι δᾶ' she cries out, 'oh oh oh oh, ouch ouch, ah'; 'ἒ ἒ, παπαῖ παπαῖ' 'aye, aye, ouch, ouch'; 'ἰοὺ ἰού ὦ ὦ κα κά' 'ohoh, ohoh, oh oh, shit' (*Agamemnon* 1072, 1114, 1215), all of which provide the tonal background, underground and non-ground for her own version of the wisdom of Silenus that it would be best never to have been born at all, and if born, to die early: 'Alas, poor men, their destiny. When all goes well shadow will overthrow it. If it be unkind one stroke of a wet sponge wipes all the picture out; and that is far the most unhappy thing of all' (1326–1330) (Lattimore).

12. We note that unlike Aechylus' Dionysian chorus of Furies, Euripedes' Medea comes not from the underground chaos preceding Greek Olympian order, but is rather an alien brought in from the exotic East.

13. Is this use of *Stimmung* the source for Heidegger's appropriation of the word in *Being and Time* (see SZ §29)? What Heidegger failed to note, in any event, is that *Stimmung*, which contains *Stimme* or voice, is experienced acoustically: it is not so much a 'mood' as a 'voicing', a tonality and tenor that provide the acoustical background and underground for all our experience, as when we say, for instance, 'That does not *sound* good!'.

14. As Nietzsche puts it, '…every concept is a metonymy and cognition proceeds in concepts'; and, he continues:

> Logical thought, little practiced by the Ionians, develops very slowly. Logically invalid conclusions we might better comprehend as metonymies, comprehended, that is, rhetorically, poetically. All rhetorical figures, i.e., the essence of speech and language, are logically invalid conclusions. It is with these that reason begins! (KSA 7, 19 [215]).

Second-Hand Emotions: Constructions of Interiority in Music

Susan McClary

My title pays homage, of course, to Tina Turner, who sings in 'What's Love Got To Do With It?': 'What's love but a second-hand emotion?'.[1] She dismisses romantic ideology as a kind of false consciousness masking baser instincts, but also as a force that can inflict genuine pain if one is gullible enough to have internalised its mythology: 'Who needs a heart when a heart can be broken?'. The lyrics of the song yearn to seal off that imaginary space—the heart—so as to present only a tough, impervious exterior to the world. Yet all the while, the vocal inflections in Turner's performance bear witness to what we are invited to hear as inner suffering.

In this, Turner's song reproduces a subjective structure of outside/inside that has long circulated within Western culture, and has consolidated into something like reality. We often conceive of our subjectivities in such terms—as split between the veneer we present to the public eye and the authentic Self of intense feeling, which is hidden from view but which guarantees continuity and centred identity. And music is often embraced as the cultural medium best able to express the elusive fluctuations of this inner life. As a register sensitive enough to capture in sound feelings as they are actually experienced, music presents for our delectation what appear to be second-hand emotions.

Yet I would like to argue that music does not function *merely* as a means for representing a stable inner reality, but rather that it (along with other cultural media) teaches us how to experience our own emotions. In other words, we might understand our own feelings not as hard-wired in, but as phenomena modelled to some degree after patterns articulated in and disseminated throughout the social sphere. Indeed, it is not only the feelings themselves that come to be shaped by cultural practices, but also the very notion that we possess an 'interiority' in counterdistinction to the Self that performs its various roles in public.[2]

Those who take their reactions to music as their own genuine feelings are understandably resistant to considering music as a heavily mediated set of cultural constructs. How much more reluctant they would be to accept those presumably authentic feelings likewise as culture-specific! Yet it can be demonstrated that particular feeling-types have histories, and, moreover, that the notions surrounding emotions—including most prominently the very idea of interiority—themselves change radically over time and among cultures.[3]

My project in this essay is to examine relationships between music and emotions at various moments in Western history. I will not look for universals or trans-historical practices; quite the opposite, I will be most interested in the very different ways in which 'emotion' or 'self' are shaped at different times within musical discourses.[4] Moreover, I will argue that the history of musical formal procedure can be understood in part as a by-product of the broader cultural agendas in which music participates.

Yet I will also suggest that music does not merely reflect, but actually influences the ways we experience ourselves *as selves*. I am not claiming anything especially radical here: this belief underlies all attempts at policing music—from Plato's *Republic* to Stalin's state censors to Bob Dole's presidential bid—and at using music for therapy or mood-alteration.[5] My project differs from theirs largely because I want to examine and understand the cultural practices that have the power to produce the effects sought after or feared by so many others.

* * *

I will begin with the sixteenth century, for it is only at that moment that Western music explicitly becomes involved with the enterprises both of representing emotion and also of moving the passions by means of rhetorical devices. This is not to suggest that music produced no affective responses before this time, for we have extensive evidence that it did: essays by Greek philosophers and theorists deal in detail with the ethical properties of particular modes of music; the Bible bears witness to the effect of music on listeners; and Saint Augustine's confessions testify that music often so overwhelmed him that he no longer paid proper attention to the scriptural texts the music was designed to accompany. Yet because we have access to none of the music to which these tantalising documents refer, we cannot reconstruct the sounds that triggered such powerful reactions from these historical listeners.

Several very different cultural concerns coincided in the early sixteenth century to induce musicians to involve themselves with emotional representation and rhetoric. First, the recovery of ancient sources testifying to the ethical qualities of Greek music encouraged humanists to seek ways of emulating that power. In a cultural world increasingly given to rhetorical prowess, Hellenistic descriptions of music curing disease, arousing erotic thoughts, or inciting violence proved enormously suggestive. Renaissance music theorists began to include sections in their speculative treatises on the ethical properties of modes, and neo-Platonic musicians sought to create music that would rival the magic of classical models.[6]

Second, as Steven Greenblatt has argued in *Renaissance Self-Fashioning*,[7] this period saw the emergence of subjectivity as a self-conscious construct. The split between a public, rhetorical Self who seeks to persuade in the political realm and an inner, feeling Self come into play at this time in poetry, as well as in music. Greenblatt's term 'inwardness' refers to this new location: a site no sooner called into being than it became colonised by cultural concepts of how that inner self ought to be arranged and furnished.

Finally, the continent-wide circulation of all these concepts—Greek learning, 'inwardness', and music as a medium for both representation and arousal of emotions—depended on the technologies and industries associated with the printing press. In other words, the new ideologies of private interiority relied on a form of public transmission that reproduced knowledge and structures of feeling far more effectively than any medium in history.[8] And although music printing began as a means of preserving and disseminating the 'classics' of composers such as Josquin, it soon inspired the writing of very different kinds of music: music that could take full advantage of this new commercial enterprise.

Among the first of the genres that developed in tandem with printing and its markets was the Italian madrigal. And not coincidentally, the madrigal was among the first musical genres concerned with producing self-conscious images of emotions and constructions of the Self. Within the context of the madrigal, composers sought to invent a musical vocabulary for simulating—and stimulating—the passions. Along with its other constructs, the madrigal produced the earliest explicit musical representations in the West of desire and pleasure, all spelled out in lavish detail. Then, as now, sex sells, and even the earliest of the madrigalists worked to devise ways of articulating in music the feelings associated with erotic experience.

The first and biggest all-time hit of the madrigal repertory was Jacques Arcadelt's *Il bianco e dolce cigno*, published in 1539 but still being reprinted regularly as a Golden Oldie one hundred years later. As the most popular piece in the new genre, this madrigal helped establish the terms for representing emotions in sixteenth-century music. I will focus in my discussion on two of Arcadelt's strategies.

Il bianco e dolce cigno	The white and gentle swan
cantando more et io	dies singing, and I,
piangendo giung' al fin del viver mio.	weeping, approach the end of my life.
Stron' e diversa sorte,	Strange and diverse fates,
ch'ei more sconsolate	that he dies disconsolate
ed io moro beato.	and I die happy.
Morte che nel morire	Death, that in the [act of] dying
m'empie di gioia tutto e di desire.	fills me wholly with joy and desire.
Se nel morir' altro dolor non sento	If in dying I feel no other pain
di mille mort' il di sarei contento.	I would be content to die
	a thousand times a day.

The first of these occurs first in the setting of the word 'piangendo' in line three. Up until that point, the madrigal had unfolded in a decorous diatonic fashion: that is, its pitches all belong to the F-ionian scale without any chromatic alterations, and all its moves—including the moment of affective intensification on the word 'more' ('dies')—can be accounted for as standard practice. But when 'piangendo' appears, the voices plunge into a darker domain, marked by a lowered seventh degree, E^b, first in bass and alto, then spreading its contagion to the canto. Diatonic normality soon returns and perseveres as far as the cadence. But Arcadelt chooses to underscore this moment of the text by repeating the line concerning the Self, and the E^b returns as a musical sign of weeping

The poetic text itself sets up a dichotomy between the swan and the Self: the swan dies singing, while I, weeping, approach the end of my life. Arcadelt responds with restrained poignancy to the line about the swan, then veers into the realm of the theoretically irrational for 'weeping'. His breaking of the rules of modal propriety, compounded by his purposeful reiteration of the offending line, shifts the attention away from the swan and to the speaking subject—the 'I' of the text. And musicologists usually justify this violation by interpreting it as a deliberate depiction of emotional expression.

But what kind of depiction is it? How does a mere E^b represent emotion, and which emotion is it meant to signal? As the madrigal unfolds, we learn that this 'weeping' is not (as we might have thought initially) an expression of grief, but rather a response to the experience of sexual ecstasy. In other words, it stands simultaneously for intense pain and intense pleasure. For Arcadelt has little interest in drawing distinctions among emotional types in his madrigal; he seeks rather to register the fact of emotion per se. And within the economy of this opening gambit, he defines 'emotion' as that which stands in excess of mere speech, that which disrupts the rational order.

Accordingly, he offers us a model of subjectivity that combines an outside, public façade that orates and an inner, private core that experiences feelings so strong that they threaten to seep through and topple the controlled discourse of the speaker.

I am not suggesting here that this model of outside/inside, speaking/feeling is somehow true or universal. Quite the opposite: I wish to emphasise its appearance at a certain moment in cultural history and to interrogate the ways in which the medium of music was marshalled to articulate such a construction. Later in this essay, other constructions—based on significantly different premises and different notions of selfhood—will be examined in their turn. But for now, back to Arcadelt.

Most of Arcadelt's madrigal maintains a homophonic style of delivery: that is, all four voices declaim the text at the same time to produce the image of a single speaking subject.[9] Although homophony counts as one of several common modes of deploying voices in Renaissance music, Arcadelt enlists it to stand in contrast to another common device: staggered entries among the voices. Stylistically, he does nothing unusual in alternating such textures; indeed, one could easily write off this aspect of his piece as generic practice. But again, the economy of this piece—its specific relationships between music and text, its particular succession of events—invite the listener to hear this set of alternations as highly significant.

The most spectacular moment of staggered entrances occurs at the conclusion of the madrigal. After the settings of three lines that restore the homophonic dignity of the opening, we reach the moment of truth: 'If in dying I feel no other pain *I would be content to die a thousand times a day*'. The voices that had been held together so tensely up until this point suddenly split apart; each in turn peaks, then cascades downward. The parts enter at spaced time intervals, such that the centred subject now dissolves into multiple overlapping attempts at climax and closure. Each line seeks desperately the sweetness of the cadence, yet their phased superimposition causes them to cancel each other out: every moment of would-be conclusion is swept along in the delicious flood of release, until gradually they all subside—rocking to a point of repose under what sounds like a sustained and pious 'Amen'.

Throughout the madrigal, Arcadelt offers us occasional glimpses of interiority (through those E^b frissons, through non-simultaneous declamation), held in check by the speaking subject until the end, when this emotionality overflows in torrents. Irrational disruptions of speakerly decorum—and a mixture of desire for and fear of that disruption—are at stake, rather than the constitution of any particular emotional type. This final passage brings us to fully satisfying formal closure, even as it dissolves the ego-boundaries that had been so carefully guarded up until this point.

So far as I know, Arcadelt offers here the first graphic simulation in music of orgasm. The device he uses to produce this image, however, was common imitative counterpoint: a fugal technique practiced by composers since Guillaume Dufay in the mid-1400s. Needless to say, not all points of imitation in Renaissance music intend to represent sexual transport; indeed, the device appears most often in the austere sacred music of the Flemish School, and it is usually regarded as evidence of intellectual complexity. But Arcadelt did not have to invent from nothing all his compositional techniques for simulating emotions and passions. He seems to have detected sensual power in the music of, say, Josquin and harnessed Josquin's devices for his own very different purposes. Only the poetic text in *Il bianco e dolce cigno* makes explicit the erotic connotations of its musical imagery: without the words, the concluding sequence counts only as an extended point of imitation. With the words, however, Arcadelt's madrigal becomes a paradigm of emotional expressivity: emotions understood as that which stands in excess of normative standards of reason.[10]

* * *

As familiar as this model of emotional expression may seem in the wake of the rebellions of the 1960s, it is not the only one to have reigned since the Renaissance. By the end of the seventeenth century another model—quite different in its fundamental premises—had begun to underlie the representation of emotions in music and the other arts. Not without cause was this period known as the Age of Reason, for this era celebrated the self-sufficient processes of human rationality in all domains of culture. This is not to suggest that emotions were ignored or denied during the eighteenth century. On the contrary, the power of reason to shed light into the darkest recesses of the human mind counted as one of its greatest triumphs. No longer the Other of order, emotion as it appeared represented through shared signs revealed the ability of rationality to control even this dimension of experience, formerly understood as ineffable.

We can point to several indications of this radical change in structures of feeling over the course of the seventeenth and eighteenth centuries. First, Descartes' model of psychology sought to chart and account systematically for the passions. His success in this endeavour led theorists and practitioners in several of the arts to expand upon and to implement his ideas. Witness the increasing concern of musicians of the German Enlightenment with what they called the *Affektenlehre*—the doctrine of affections, or an attempt at producing finite lexicons for the musical representation of the whole range of emotional types.[11]

Second, the musical procedures that emerge during the 1600s were designed to perform the tenets of rationality on all levels. Pre-set formal schemata come to organise much music: the ABB and ABA structures of arias, the binary shapes regulating dances and then sonatas have the effect of containing in advance whatever occurs within the piece. More important, standard tonality guarantees that all relationships within the music, whether chord-to-chord or long range, will be harnessed under an hierarchical logic. Tonality allows for extravagant expansion of musical means, but it also requires that every detail be related back to the generative centre.

By means of these various elements, music in the eighteenth century can appear to delineate the most extreme emotional states (identifiable through rationalised codes) and still secure the control of reason over anything that transpires within a movement. This is a moment of supreme confidence in human rationality and its social contracts, even though Michel Foucault and Norbert Elias warn us of how its agendas sought to penetrate and colonise the most private dimensions of human life.[12] Eventually, the Romantics will perceive Enlightenment ideology as oppressive and will rebel against its strictures and lies. But during the period in which the principle of rationality regulated the arts, an entirely different set of compositional and representational priorities come to the fore.

* * *

Let us take as an example Alceste's jealousy aria from George Frideric Handel's *Admeto*, II scene 7 (1727). In the first act of the opera, Alceste had sacrificed her life for that of her husband, Admeto, when she agreed to die in his place. Ercole (Hercules) descended into the Underworld and has succeeded in bringing her back for Admeto. But Alceste now suspects that Admeto has not remained true to her memory and insists on putting on the disguise of a warrior in order to spy for a while on his habits as a widower. As it turns out, Admeto is indeed involved with another woman, though his affections remain painfully divided between her and his memory of Alceste; when Alceste risks sacrificing herself a second time to save Admeto from an assassination attempt, she drops her disguise and is reconciled with him.

Alceste performs the aria in question right after her return from Hades. Following an extensive conversation in which she explains her plan, Ercole exits, and Alceste lingers on stage to deliver a soliloquy concerning her motives for spying on Admeto. But before she begins to sing, the orchestra presents an introduction or ritornello (ie, a unit of music that returns for purposes of structural articulation). And without the assistance of words, the ritornello already announces this as a 'rage' aria: one of several affective types that became particularly popular within opera seria. It inscribes rage through several signs conventionally associated by 1727 with that emotion: minor mode, imperious rhythmic gestures, and seething coloratura that seeks constantly to overflow its context.

When Alceste enters, her music repeats much of what has already been heard, but with words that make the situation far more explicit. She labels the emotion in question 'jealousy', but its musical representation reveals this affect as a subset of 'rage'. And in keeping with the Cartesian notion of passions as forces that overwhelm the passive subject, she claims that the rage she experiences and that guides her actions invaded her during her furlong in Hades. 'She' is quite literally possessed by this emotion; yet she strives to maintain in her verbal imagery a distinction between the Self being acted upon and the passion that consumes her without her consent.

Gelosia spietata Aletto	Jealousy, ruthless Fury,
Meco uscisti dall'inferno	You came out with me from Hell
E m'entrasti a forza in petto	And forcibly entered my bosom
Per affligger questo cor	In order to afflict this heart.
Ti vorrei scacciar dal seno	I want to expel you from my breast
Ma non ho vigore bastante.	But I do not have enough strength.
Chi non prova il tuo veleno	Whoever has not felt your poison
no, non sa, che cosa e amor.	No, does not know what Love is.

Musicologists often repeat the old Romantic critiques of opera seria and the *Affektenlehre* by complaining that eighteenth-century musicians relied on reified versions of emotional types. That they worked to standardise affective expression seems clear enough, but their rationales for doing so must be put within the context of eighteenth-century thought. For if musicians can successfully delineate rage in a ritornello or in a Vivaldi concerto,[13] then this unruly emotion no longer resides outside the cultural domain: the fact that it can be represented and publicly recognised from its representations extends the power of discourse to the extremes of human experience. Rage comes under the umbrella of the universal; instead of marking a limit to the power of reason, its domestication within cultural encoding qualifies as a triumph of civilisation.

A specifically eighteenth-century version of rationality also controls the way Alceste's aria unfolds through time. For all its gestures of defiance and overflow, the aria conforms to—indeed, acquires its power from—tonal logic. On the surface, the harmonic syntax serves always to confirm stable key areas or to indicate motion to another. Up against this framework, Handel can produce images of dynamic struggle, and even flirt with moments of rational collapse. On the background, the aria traces a progression from a prolonged G minor to B^b (a more positive key in affective implication), and back to G minor, with a slight diversion into C minor along the way. Despite Alceste's testimony that this emotion has overwhelmed her, her aria goes through the paces of most minor-mode tonal pieces of the eighteenth century and beyond.

Only the Romantics, ever squeamish of conventions, require that we apologise for Handel's choosing this standard pattern, for it allows him dynamic motion, a powerful linear structure, the freedom to delineate emotional fluctuations as he pleases. It also produces a snapshot of an affect that has essentially the same frame as the aria/snapshots of all the other affects; the content shifts, but the form remains constant and under the firm control of reason. Moreover, within this framework, Handel can make any number of extremely significant choices: when Alceste arrives after much effort at her cadence in B^b (seconded by the ritornello that confirms this new key), she immediately turns her back on the false security offered by that key and plunges right back into the 'reality' of G minor. This abrupt pivot tells us much about Alceste as a character: she is not easily distracted—not even by her own dreams—and she dismisses this ray of hope as though it were a mirage.

Although Alceste uses words to particularise its affect—tilting the all-purpose emotional type 'rage' into the more specific 'jealousy'—she deploys a scant four lines of text in the sixty-three bars of the A section of the aria. Without question, the text Handel set provides him with much of the imagery he exploits over the course of the aria: words such as 'm'entrasti' and 'affligger' invite and receive extravagant gestures. Yet structurally the aria unfolds as a piece of tonal music. It could be performed by the string ensemble alone, without the singer, and it still would make perfectly good sense: listeners acquainted with eighteenth-century style could follow its feints and dodges, its affective manoeuvring, without knowing the words. In other words, Alceste's interiority, even in its outraged condition, traces the same rational structure as all other tonal pieces of the time. It is thereby rendered transparent and entirely comprehensible—indeed, 'universal'.

But the cultural pendulum soon swung in the opposite direction. As Reason began to be construed as instrumental reason, the artists who identified themselves as Romantics resisted the affirmativity of eighteenth-century tonal structures; they regarded such performances of rationality as manifestations of false consciousness and even oppression. Consequently, they turned increasingly to aspects of experience that counted as unrepresentable within the economy of Enlightenment conventions. At this moment, a still-fundamental ambiguity arose with respect to musical expression, for 'unrepresentable' implies both not capable of being represented (ie, ineffable), and also prohibited ideologically from being represented.

Artists in all media, but particularly musicians, sought to articulate emotions that were treasured precisely because they refused the optimistic procedures of the preceding generation. The ruptured, convoluted surfaces of Beethoven's late quartets, the harmonic slippage that produces images of an idiosyncratic interiority in Schubert, the cycles constructed of obliquely related fragments in Schumann: all these bear witness to a massive change in cultural notions of the emotional self. Just as the Renaissance madrigalists cannibalised the premises of their inherited syntax in order to present images of greater and greater emotional intensity, so nineteenth-century composers eroded the certainties of tonality until Schönberg's atonality seemed the obvious next step. The biggest unasked question of twentieth-century modernism concerns the significance of atonal procedures: are we to hear it as maintaining an unrelenting extreme in affective expression? or should we believe its proponents, who insist that this music no longer has any truck with emotions?

*　*　*

Such differences in concepts of the Self and emotions are not restricted to classical music.[14] Indeed, the ideological poles of today's popular music operate according to a split similar to the one discussed above between emotions as rationally encoded and emotions as phenomena that escape encoding. Not surprisingly, the different camps of popular-music genres often castigate one another as cheaply manipulative, on the one hand, and unskilled noise on the other.[15]

I want to examine a tune by Boyz II Men, 'I'll Make Love to You', that dominated the charts and airwaves in 1994–95.[16] If ever a song lent itself to the age-old charge that music effeminises culture, this is it. With its depiction of the 'sensitive' male of the '90s, it seems to address itself exclusively to a female audience, and the latter-day Platos of rock criticism took turns ridiculing the song, hoping to shame listeners into recognising its fatuity.

The reason usually given for the success of 'I'll Make Love to You' is that 'chicks dig it'—a catch-phrase that nervous pop musicians offer each other as their excuse for edging over into the apparently terrifying terrain of ballads. Clearly, its lyrics (which speak of yielding to a woman's desires) contribute to its effect. Yet sitting there in the liner notes, this poetry remains pretty banal—scarcely words to sell millions of albums, let alone influence widespread ideals of romance. As set to music by songwriter Babyface and sung by Boyz II Men, however, it has precipitated a minor cultural crisis in what gets to count as masculinity.

Let me point out a few of elements that combine to construct this song's version of erotic male subjectivity. 'I'll Make Love To You' appeals strongly to tradition—specifically to gospel-tinged doo-wop groups of the '50s, now seen as a far more innocent moment in history. Among the accoutrements of doo-wop borrowed here is the convention of using four voices to produce the illusion of a single self—much as in Arcadelt's madrigal. It is not by accident that 'realistic' representations of centred masculinity in 'authentic' rock often involve solo voices (such as Kurt Cobain's or Eddie Vedder's) that rail in alienation against an uncomprehending universe. By contrast, ensembles such as Boyz II Men display an open, multifaceted sense of self that combines the utter dependability of the bass voice, the lyrical seductiveness of the middle-range singers, and the ecstatic moans of the falsettist, who departs from the words to deliver evidence of ineffable feeling. Co-ordinating these parts requires an eroticised give-and-take process among the singers; they enact a kind of dialogic homosocial bonding rendered 'safe' only by repeated, explicit insistence on their heterosexual intentions.

Babyface also took his musical procedures from the doo-wop legacy: its favourite chord progression and rhythmic groove, which still rule on nostalgia stations.[17] The chords (which music theorists would label I–vi–IV–V–I) produce in their syntax something of that same blend of reliability and vulnerability already performed in the mix of voices: the opening sonority—the tonic—gives us our home base, but when it gives way to a minor triad, it sounds as though we have fallen inward to a space of unguarded tenderness; the harmony drops yet further, then turns and leads us back confidently to the tonic, at which point the process repeats—again and again, for the duration of the song. This cyclic process structures a secure, continuous space with those periodic flickers of vulnerability embedded within absolute certainty. All this is supported by a slow harmonic rhythm, animated slightly by triplet subdivisions: a combination that invites slow dancing (at the very least).

When Babyface chose to use this pattern for 'I'll Make Love to You', he knew he could count on reactions guaranteed by forty years of radio play, but he also provided some new twists. For instance, the reliable harmonic formula gets thrown into crisis with a sudden collapse to the lowered seventh degree on the words 'and I will not let go till you tell me to', requiring what sounds like a negotiated settlement for the return to the tonic. Boyz II Men, unlike all those earlier doo-wop groups that took their pleasure for granted, perform a moment of intense insecurity (coincidentally, the same harmony Arcadelt employed for 'piangendo') before proceeding back to expected stability. During the bridge, this crisis leads out onto a whole episode that seems to depart very far from the frame of reference. It is as if the tiny window of vulnerability represented by the vi chord suddenly opens onto a whole vista of anguished interior feeling before leading back inevitably (through what musicians call a circle of fifths) to desired reconsolidation.

Clearly, not everyone responded to this song in the way it seems to intend. Some chicks did not, in fact, dig it (many heard its histrionic performance of sincere male emotions as a cheesy ploy to enhance female susceptibility); most critics hated it; and many other very different constructions of erotic subjectivity circulated simultaneously with this one in pop music. Yet its success tells us much not only about Babyface's talent as a songwriter and Boyz II Men's skills as performers, but also about the prevalence today of certain cultural fantasies concerning romance, sexuality, gender, the Self, and emotions.

* * *

Alongside such constructions exist the inheritors of Romanticism's concept of 'authenticity': those who embrace the ideal of unmediated, unencodable emotional expression. As musicians in the 1960s transformed the raison d'être of rock music from party entertainment to cultural criticism, they turned to the noisy, the idiosyncratic, even the ugly as ways of avoiding the very appearance of feel-good affirmation. We can trace this strand of rock from the late '60s protest music to '70s punk and contemporary grunge and 'alternative' genres. None of these would be caught dead producing the carefully groomed emotional states composed by Babyface. Their sense of expressivity comes, rather, from the sheer intensity of gesture that revels in its apparent inarticulateness.

Needless to say, most of the practitioners of this kind of music are male—as are most of the musicians we remember in Western cultural history. But many women musicians also excel in this kind of music: the bands of the Riot Grrrl movement, and also artists such as P.J. Harvey, Alanis Morrisette, and Courtney Love. In a culture that still wants to perceive women as pretty objects, this music sounds multiply transgressive, for it not only violates norms of orderly, rational musical process, but it also gives voice to the taboo of female rage—a brand of rage, however, that differs radically from that of Handel's Alceste.[18]

In 'Violet', the first song on Hole's album *Live Through This* (1994),[19] Courtney Love presents what sounds like raw, unmediated emotion, as she alternately mutters and screams over a background of grunge guitars and frenetic drumming. The emotional intensity of the song comes in large part from volume, distorted timbres, and pitch inflections that sound like impudent refusals to sing in tune. Even more important are the sudden shifts in affect between ominous quiet (the opening cliché-ridden description of a romantic evening sky) and shouts of sarcastic defiance ('You should learn how to say NO!'; 'Go on, take everything, take everything, I want you to!'). Because these affects—especially the vocal ones—resemble the utterances of enraged people in their explosiveness and passion, they seem not to require the expertise of music theorists. The song 'speaks for itself' by holding to an uncompromising 'artlessness' that invites listeners to perceive its anger as Love's own authentic emotions.

Yet this song, no less than Babyface's, relies on certain conventions that allow the initiated to hear it as transparent. No one acquainted with this style fails to anticipate the explosion that occurs on the fourth line: the distorted guitars, even though played in an artificially quiet fashion, had already forecast the noise that must dominate the song for it to pass muster among its fans. Thus when Love jumps an octave and explodes 'You should learn how to say NO!', the informed listener may be surprised but is more likely to feel gratified because the song finally meets the expectations of the genre.

Similarly, the bass line, in insisting on a half-step interval above its lowest pitch, suggests the phrygian scale, which has been associated since the Renaissance with the most extreme of emotional conditions. This connection between scale steps and affect is not arbitrary: because the 'normal' (read: rational) whole step above the tonic is unavailable in this mode, phrygian structures are deprived of conventional tonal motion and thereby sound trapped or paralysed. This characteristic feature of phrygian can be exploited to great effect; it is the mode favoured by thrash-metal groups such as Metallica, where mayhem meets entrapment head-on, and it even occurs in late Beethoven as a provocation for heroic violence.[20] In the context of 'Violet', these phrygian qualities underscore the quality of unsettled, irrational emotion that characterises the vocals, especially on the earlier presentations of the refrain 'Go on, take everything'.[21] If we detect an echo here of Billie Holiday's classic torch song 'All of Me', we also have to recognise the enormous difference in available emotional vocabularies—especially for women—between Holiday's slightly ironic delivery and Love's grunge-flavoured nihilism.

But the song does not dwell exclusively on phrygian angst: Love's sardonic refrain—'They get what they want, and they never want it again'—steps briefly outside the noise of the song to make use of traditionally 'sweet' harmonies, especially with the insistent major third on the closing word, 'again'. Needless to say, however, this coy presentation of the warning all mothers give daughters concerning predatory males demands another octave leap and the outburst 'Go on, take everything...'

There are, in other words, ways of tracing the elements of this unruly song to conventions that circulate within punk, metal, grunge, and an even longer history of expressive codes in Western music. Unlike Boyz II Men, who try to persuade the listener of the sincerity of their emotions through their smooth, intricate harmonic moves (all of which reinforce a social contract of trust and certainty), Hole draws on strategies marked as dissonant, irrational, erratic, transgressive, and deliberately uncivilised—a version of the emotional Self that defies all signs of sociality. All signs, that is, except the ones that unite as a social group the fans who identify with the emotions and version of 'authentic' subjectivity Hole presents here.

I hope to have demonstrated that it is not just the musical dimension of these emotional representations that changes over time, but also basic concepts concerning selves and their feelings. When we consider music and emotions both as culturally constituted, we lose the bedrock certainty a simple reflection model offers. But, of course, to suggest that something is culturally constituted makes it no less real: we experience our feelings—however shaped they might be by novels, movies, or music—no less intensely than if they were somehow innate and idiosyncratic. Moreover, we acquire a deeper understanding both of historical difference and of our own subjectivities when we acknowledge the cultural work performed by music in consolidating shared notions of the Self.

In his last book, *The Germans*, the late Norbert Elias comments on the vast (though often overlooked except by feminist historians) change in normative behaviours for women in this century: before World War I, women remained under the control of their parents until they were married off under conditions of tight family control, whereas a large percentage of women now live relatively independent existences and choose their sexual partners. He argues, moreover, that this process of 'informalisation' does not constitute a breakdown of culture, as is often claimed in the press; it represents the extension of social agency to a category of individuals formerly deprived of authority over their own lives.[22] Surely popular literature, cinema, and music have contributed immeasurably to the rapid spread of new mores, new structures of feeling, new versions of subjectivity. If a sixteenth-century love lyric set by Arcadelt differs enormously from one we might hear on MTV sung by Courtney Love, it is not just because Arcadelt was working within a different style: neither the musical procedures nor the emotions qualify as universals.

Yet to the very great extent that we go to music to experience 'our own emotions', we allow it to shape, to impose culturally shared order on the relatively inchoate sensations we actually feel. If according to this model 'our own emotions' become less clearly unique than the centred subject of bourgeois mythology might prefer, we gain insights into the efficacy of cultural forms to influence our all-too-mutable Selves. To return to Tina Turner: it's not just love that's a second-hand emotion. Rather, all emotions are always already second-hand.

This paper was first presented at the Word, Voice, Sound: Interactions Around Musics conference, 7–8 July 1996, Artspace, Sydney, convened by the Women's Research Centre, the University of Western Sydney Nepean Research Office, and the Faculty of Visual and Performing Arts through the Music Department of the University of Western Sydney, Nepean.

1. Tina Turner, *What's Love Got To Do With It?*, *Private Dancer*, Capitol Records, 1983.
2. For other studies concerning music and constructions of subjectivity, see Robert Walser, 'Deep Jazz: Notes of Interiority, Race and Criticism', in *Inventing the Psychological: Towards a Cultural History of Emotional Life in America*, ed. Joel Pfister and Nancy Schnog, New Haven: Yale University Press, forthcoming, and my 'Narratives of Bourgeois Subjectivity in Mozart's "Prague" Symphony', in *Understanding Narrative*, eds. Peter Rabinowitz and James Phelan, Columbus: Ohio State University Press, 1994, pp. 65–98.
3. This is not to deny recent neurological studies that show how emotional states are centred in particular parts of the brain. See, for instance, Antonio R. Damasio, *Descartes' Error: Emotion, Reason, and the Human Brain*, New York: Avon Books, 1994. Yet even if emotional types might be shown to be trans-historical, our ways of understanding them have varied radically, largely as a function of cultural mediation.
4. My project owes a great deal to the historical critiques of autonomous, centred subjectivity by Michel Foucault and by the cultural studies and feminist theorists who have developed his ideas, often in directions he might not have recognised.
5. For a discussion of music censorship since Plato, see my 'Same As It Ever Was: Youth Culture and Music', in *Microphone Fiends: Youth Music and Youth Culture*, ed. Andrew Ross and Tricia Rose, New York and London: Routledge, 1994, pp. 29–40.
6. Gary Tomlinson, *Music in Renaissance Magic*, Chicago: University of Chicago Press, 1993.

7. Stephen Greenblatt, *Renaissance Self-Fashioning from More to Shakespeare*, Chicago: University of Chicago Press, 1980.
8. Besides Greenblatt, see also Walter J. Ong, *Orality and Literacy: The Technologizing of the Word*, London: Methuen, 1982; Boorman (see below); and Friedrich Kittler's *Discourse Networks 1800/1900*, Stanford: Stanford University Press, 1990. For an overview of work being done on music-printing in the sixteenth century, see Stanley Boorman, 'What Bibliography Can Do: Music Printing and the Early Madrigal', *Music & Letters* 72/2, May 1991, pp. 236–58.
9. This convention of multiple voices representing a single 'I' should not seem too alien to us today, for it occurs also in many doo-wop and soul groups. See the discussion later in this essay of Boyz II Men's 'I'll Make Love to You'.
10. Musicologists often balk at extending their discussions beyond 'the music itself', as though linking formal procedures with cultural agendas somehow devalued the art they seek to understand. It seems to me that investigating the power of musical imagery to represent and even shape human experience only elevates its importance.
11. See, for instance, Johann Mattheson, *Der vollkommene Kapellmeister*, Hamburg, 1739, trans. Ernest Harriss, Ann Arbor: UMI, 1981. Although they were concerned with representing interiority, most of these emotional images were understood fundamentally in terms of the body and its movements. Thus sorrow was represented by musical analogues to the body as it suffers grief, with slow, drooping motions; anger was recognised by its angular, aggressive gestures; anguish by its painful dissonances; happiness by rising, ebullient qualities; and so forth. For a superb account of the centrality of body metaphors in epistemology, see Mark Johnson, *The Body in the Mind: The Bodily Basis of Meaning, Imagination, and Reason*, Chicago: University of Chicago Press, 1987.
12. See, for instance, Norbert Elias, *The Court Society,* trans. Edmund Jephcott, New York: Pantheon, 1983, and Michel Foucault, *Discipline and Punish: The Birth of the Prison*, trans. Alan Sheridan, New York: Vintage Books, 1979.
13. The same affective signs operate in the concertos of Antonio Vivaldi. Compare this aria, for instance, with the first movement of his Concerto in A Minor, Op. 3, No. 8.
14. For a discussion of how one prominent genre of popular music negotiates these same tensions, see Robert Walser, *Running With the Devil: Power, Gender, and Madness in Heavy Metal Music*, Hanover: Wesleyan University Press, 1993.
15. Critical dismissals of lyric ballads appear everywhere, but the opposite position shows up only rarely. In a recent interview with the Fugees, however, lead singer Lauryn states: 'They were calling us this "alternative" group. And alternative, from where we come from, means no skills—or some other shit you don't really want to fuck with'. *Vibe* 4/5, June/July 1996, p. 76.
16. Written by Babyface, recorded by Boyz II Men, *Boyz II Men*, Motown, 1994.
17. The following songs, for instance, follow this pattern: 'Heart and Soul', 'In the Still of the Night', 'Stand By Me', 'When a Man Loves a Woman', and 'Earth Angel'. More recent songs that recycle this pattern include Bon Jovi's 'I'll Be There For You' and Madonna's 'True Blue'.
18. See the interviews in *Angry Women in Rock*, Vol. 1, ed. Andrea Juno, New York: Juno Books, 1996.
19. Hole, *Live Through This*, Geffen Records, 1994.
20. See, for instance, Beethoven's String Quartet Op. 59, No. 2 in E Minor.
21. Later in 'Violet', this refrain comes to be reharmonised in such a way as to cadence decisively: the E that had sounded earlier like a phrygian final becomes a dominant leading to A. The phrygian flavour nonetheless prevails throughout most of the song.
22. Elias, *The Germans,* trans. Michael Schroter, New York: Columbia University Press, 1996, pp. 42–43.

Virtuoso of Vox: An Interview with Diamanda Galas

Nicholas Zurbrugg

The American performance diva Diamanda Galas is justly regarded as one of the most forceful 'sound' artists of the '80s and '90s. Best known for such LPs as *The Litanies of Satan*, *The Divine Punishment*, *You Must be Certain of the Devil*, and *Plague Mass* (all on Mute), Galas' mixture of poetry, biblical quotation, multilingual song, and high velocity screech offers a terrifyingly expressionistic alternative to the user-friendly *sotto voce* monologues of other New Yorkers such as Laurie Anderson and Robert Ashley. As Galas remarks, hers is not a minimal, conceptual or defeatist art. 'There is this stupid concept that electronics have us evolving to this unfeeling human state. I dominate my electronics. When the equipment is not working, I keep trying, doing it. I get angry. I do not put myself to sleep with music. I hate minimal crap. My music is maximal. I hate that dead shit!' In the following interview Galas discusses her most recent quadraphonic installation/performance: *Schrei X*, following its presentation in New York. Galas' lyrics are collected in *The Shit of God*, London and New York: High Risk Books/Serpent's Tail, 1996. The following interview took place in New York, 24 February 1996.

Nicholas Zurbrugg: Critical responses to your work often refer to the unusual quality of your voice and the ways in which your work ranges across such different genres as gospel, rock, avant-garde music and extended voice techniques. How do you like to be described as an artist?

Diamanda Galas: Whereas I think it's accurate to describe me as a virtuoso—or in such relatively neutral terms as a 'composer-virtuoso', or whatever—I find references to myself as 'a virtuoso singer with a three and a half octave range' absolutely mindless, because if one octave isn't interesting, who the hell cares about the next two and a half? I mean, Carmen Macrae used primarily one octave, and she sang more than most people sing in their whole life, in one octave, so that isn't really a relevant issue. As Kenneth Gaburo said to me a long time ago, 'The most important thing in composing is being able to fulfil in that exploration what it is you intended to do'. And if someone can say that he or she does not agree with what you intend to do, and finds it tasteless, uninteresting, boring or whatever, that really is just a personal, unimportant observation at the end of the day. And so what I have intended to do demands a very large technical ability on the part of the voice, because it's free-composition work, it's also improvisional work, but it also uses this artillery of timbre, of vocal range, of sound-making, of vocal-signal processing elements—which includes the spatial manipulation of the voice, and uses works in different languages by my blood-brothers, Baudelaire, Corbière and so on, to say most articulately what it is that I wish to say about the world, or what I think I know about the world, or whatever is any particular fascination. I took two composition classes from Gaburo, and the second time I was in my car and I practically had a car accident because he got me so angry. We had this discussion about my work, and he mentioned something that was quite true to do with having the largest palette available to you as a painter. What he said was, 'You've chosen this one direction in the use of the voice, but are you aware that that certain direction is repetitive in a certain way?', and I immediately thought, 'Son of a bitch!—I'm never going to see him again!', and almost crashed into a car. But of course he was completely right, and at that point, more than ever, I realised that as a painter you really have to know how to paint, you have to be a good craftsman, in order to do your work. It's not *just* that 'Picasso was a great craftsman!'. But on the other hand, he wouldn't have been a great painter if he *hadn't* been a great craftsman—he would have just been locked into what he was technically capable of doing. That is my feeling, and that is something that most New York artists don't know anything about.

NZ: *What have been the most difficult challenges that you've encountered within your chosen area of performance?*

DG: The next project that I'm working on is *Insekta*. It's a piece that's performed in a very large cage, and which we have not yet been able to spend much time rehearsing, for financial reasons. *Insekta* refers to things invisible to the naked eye, something unseen, unknown, anonymous, something that is available for biochemical, biological research—the kind carried out on prison populations after their families have signed that they are available for experimentation. The piece is very difficult because it involves solo voice, and a lot of text that I've written, texts from the Book of Job, and also from the *Apocalypse* in Greek and Latin written by John of Patmos. The most interesting thing about it is the tape-work that [sound engineer] Blaise Dupuy and I did with a combination of a lot of my vocal samples and with electronic manipulations of that. It's a very large, difficult piece. I haven't used the word 'multimedia' in my work because I've never known exactly what it means, or whether it refers to an earlier tradition of performance, or whatever. But if you think of avant-garde theatre or even avant-garde opera, it is by definition multimedia, and in this case it's very visible. I have two microphones strapped on a breastplate, so there's freedom to move really quickly through the space. It's a real rough piece, and I discuss it now because I have not had the opportunity to really work on it because it's expensive, it's dangerous—in one of the performances the cage almost ripped apart—and it's one of those things that you have to really rehearse, or it becomes your last show! After this project I want to work on something dealing with the Salem witch trials, so I'll be using more of these texts from Apocalyptic Revelations. I continue to work on Job because that's one of the most interesting texts. It's really an obscene paradigm—an absolutely untenable paradigm. When you talk to people who are sick and you read something like Job it's really like a card game between God and Satan, seeing how well God's servant Job will respond when everything but his life is taken from him. So for me it's a paradigm of torture, because if you kill the person then he's no longer available for torture—the basic de Sadean principle. My declaration of the text and the part of the work that appears to be non-verbal are not two separate things—they're very much linked through the text, and that's something that I'm doing more and more that I find very interesting.

NZ: *Are you working with pre-recorded samples? Is it a mixture of live work and pre-recorded materials?*

DG: *Insekta* is. The piece you saw last night, *Schrei X* is all live.

NZ: *That's a kind of one-person quartet in a way, isn't it? You're jumping around in microphonic space, using the four different microphones to project sound from different directions in different registers.*

DG: That's exactly right.

NZ: *It's very dense and condensed.*

DG: It's very dense—and it's as spatial choreography that I always think of it. Blaise is working with live signal-processing, with ring modulation, sound distortions and different delay times—we work very carefully together changing the processing for each section of the piece. Often very subtle changes are made, and because of the way that I sing it's often difficult for people to distinguish the vocal sounds from the processed vocal work, because of the subtlety of the processing and of the way that Blaise works as an accompanist.

NZ: *Is he playing samples and to some extent performing a duet with you, somewhat as your songs with former Led Zeppelin bass player John Paul Jones have been described as a kind of duet in which your voice 'became an electric guitar' playing along with Jones' bass line?*

DG: To some extent there is a correlation there, but it's quite different because John's playing a different part and I'm doing my part. Obviously it has that accompanimental feature, but Blaise is actually using electronics to shape an interface between my voice and his processing.

NZ: *Is he shaping it in real time? He's modifying your live voice?*

DG: Precisely—so that's quite different. In *Schrei X* he doesn't use any samples, but those are used in *Insekta*.

NZ: *Presumably, it's a very close collaboration?*

DG: Yes, when I worked on *Vena Cava* I worked very closely with Eric Liljestrand who is another great engineer and musician. The thing is, the people that I work with are always great musicians—it's not just a person who's an engineer and is just sitting there and doing some sort of abstract technical work that has nothing to do with the music, and occasionally there's an interface. But most people don't know that—it's an extremely musical process, and I appreciate it because I've been working with these people for twenty years—and you always know if somebody isn't good!

NZ: *Well, Warren Burt, whom you said you'd known in San Diego, has now done a great many collaborative performances with Chris Mann and other poets in Australia, sampling or modifying their work in real time. Chris Mann will read something, Warren will instantly sample it, and start playing it, and Chris will then improvise against that, so there seems to be a certain parallel there between your work with Blaise Dupuy.*

DG: There is, you're right. There is a mutual improvisation that takes place, especially in rehearsals, and then both parties decide upon a fixed setting. In a way, it's the way choreographers work with dancers: 'This works, try this; that works, try that'. But then, in the case of somebody like Blaise, who is so familiar with technology, he'll try something as I'm improvising, and then I'll stop and say, '*That* works, and that works and that works'. But with *Schrei X*, I wanted to do extensive work with ring modulation and distortion, because I wanted it to be an interface between the voice and the electric chair—the voice and this type of electronics. Do you know the story of Leon Theremin, the scientist who invented the instrument, the theremin? It was used for the very high sounds in a lot of horror films. He was a Russian, working in this country doing all these avant-garde compositions with the theremin, and he was kidnapped and brought back to Russia to work in factories because they said: 'This research that you're doing, it's most important for the execution of traitors to the government—don't waste your time on silliness like electronic music'. There's something very interesting about the interface of this absolute technology to kill man, and then the vulnerability of the voice. I see it as the charring of flesh, in a way, and that's what I wanted to work with. In each piece, I experimented with a different range of vocabulary, not just with the signal processing, but also working with whoever was doing the lighting. It was very important to do this piece in darkness—but it's not complete darkness, because I still need to see the text. At some point, maybe if I'm capable of memorising it, we won't have any light at all. The reason why I want to be in complete darkness is because then I will be as alone as possible, just a medium for the work. It's a sort of sensory deprivation which allows me to get closer to a certain point that blind people know.

NZ: *So it's perhaps a deprivation of superficial reality, in order to make contact with a deeper area of the self?*

DG: Exactly, in this case, yes. But as someone doing electronic music, I also enjoy the idea that the audience has nothing to look at, because I think that audiences have been getting away with having things to look at for quite some time now, and should learn to use their ears. People like Gaburo—a perfect example—and people who are real composers, like Iannis Xenakis, compose music that really is somewhat gruesome for a lot of people, and all too often the visual element detracts from the severe concentration which is needed to attend to such work.

NZ: *When you look back to earlier days in San Diego, are you surprised that you're now working on this kind of performance? Could you tell me a little bit about how you got started?*

DG: Well, in the 1970s I was working at the Center for Music Experiments in San Diego, working with my friend Richard Vonna, who's another composer, a wonderful composer, in quadraphonic space—working then as now with the four or five microphones, but at that time only working with incremental changes in reverberation, with very simple electronics. From that point on I started to develop two things, as far as my vocal techniques and technology were concerned. What most people don't understand is that my vocal technique uses technology and uses quadraphonic space, using all sorts of processing devices for the voice. I started to use a lot of tape, because you get all sorts of orchestral possibilities. For example, I would take vocal timbres and lay them so thickly, that it would just be like rock formations. You wouldn't ever think of it as being vocal sound, and that's very interesting. And now, with certain processes involving computer engineering, you can do that live and get a much better resolution than using tape. That's part of what we're going to try to do. When we take performances of *Insekta* and place it in more of a live space, that's more interesting to me. But I started out initially with no amplification, with my back to the audience, wearing all black just to be as invisible as possible. This was in a lot of different places. The Living Theater suggested I perform [with them] in mental hospitals and then I performed in a couple of art spaces. But in the '70s the art world did not like me at all because they were more interested in cold, conceptual stagings.

NZ: *And that wasn't your thing?*

DG: Hardly! They'd go, 'Oh my God, that woman's screaming!'. Eleanor Antin, I have to say, was one of the only people in San Diego who was extremely supportive, and later her husband David Antin, as well. So I just started to do solo performances, after working on the torture piece—the opera *Un Jour Comme Une Autre* by the Yugoslavian composer, Vinko Globokar, at the Festival d'Avignon in 1979. Other people—theatre people—saw me, and they said 'Do you have solo work? We'd like to invite you', and in 1980 I was invited to this cabaret in Saint-Denis, which was outside of Paris, and performed in a basement theatre. There was a Henry James play upstairs, and people came downstairs afterwards, thinking they were going to have an evening of French cabaret music, and instead I would do *Wild Women With Steak Knives*. At that time there were between three and 20 people in the audience, and the people writing about it were mainly from publications like *Libération*, but not the main papers.

NZ: All this was after your San Diego time?

DG: Oh yes. I went back and forth to San Diego because my parents lived there and because my singing teachers—and my major singing teacher—lived there. I worked very hard with him. At that time, back in Paris, I also met Iannis Xenakis and performed his work, but in San Diego, when I was doing stuff at the university, I was accepted as a piano student in the Master's programme, and then I switched to experimental vocal performance. That was quite a shock for everyone, but I just felt that what I heard in vocal performance was going a distance further than what I heard on the piano, so I didn't feel that I had much choice about it. Interestingly enough, that was the place that would have encouraged that type of work at that time, because you had a visual arts department that was interested in performance art, and the music department was interested in electronic music and avant-garde vocal music, and so I think that somehow I slipped by!

NZ: Well, it was probably the right place to be—it sounds like a rich crossroads of interests.

DG: I think so. There were a lot of very, very sharp people at San Diego. Warren Burt was there, Chris Mann visited, Dick Moore worked in the computer department, Roger Reynolds was there. I was still at that time seen as a sort of renegade who was not really excelling in the music programme, but excelling in what I was doing.

NZ: But that's pretty exciting, because I'd have thought there might have been a danger that a really live student might have been sucked into a particular orthodoxy and wouldn't have developed their own thing.

DG: Not me!

NZ: What seems so interesting is that you had these contacts with Xenakis, cabaret in Paris, the Yugoslavian composer Globokar, the Living Theater—lots of different stimulants, in the best sense.

DG: In the best sense—it's true. I worked with these people, because people would say, 'With that voice, this is what these composers are looking for', and so I thought, 'Iannis Xenakis is a hero of the Greek people, and so I'm going to work with him'. And Globokar pushed music to the limits, he pushed the limits of the instruments, and I thought, 'That's a challenge!', because his pieces had ruined two or three singers before me, just ruined them—he destroyed their voices. So I took his challenges. And then I decided that if I was going to take it as far as I was taking it, then I should do it for myself, in my own compositions, because that was more interesting to me. I played all the piano stuff, whatever the avant-garde piano stuff was, but I failed all the dictation classes—I couldn't do any of that traditional stuff. I was really miserable, and even when I did a class of extended vocal technique I got a C- because I couldn't write a paper about vocal techniques, because I couldn't give a fuck about writing a paper about vocal techniques—I just wanted to do them.

NZ: Presumably your early work was also influenced by rock music and by jazz as well?

DG: Well that comes through my father, who directed a gospel choir when I was younger. He had a black gospel choir that did all those things—'Swing Low Sweet Chariot'—and I would always hear this and play piano with them sometimes, and then play piano in his New Orleans band. And that led to listening very carefully to Albert Ayler, Ornette Coleman and Cecil Taylor—these people were real heroes to me. And then studying with some very great white be-bop pianists in San Diego who were just really great underpaid musicians that taught me a lot. So I think that my influences are quite numerous. But you know Gaburo—I keep talking about Gaburo—one of the last times I saw him, he was playing piano, playing stride piano and Errol Garner kind of stuff! It was very good! It was very good!

NZ: What about New York influences? Did you find it another ball-game here?

DG: Well, I'll tell you, the biggest New York influence is walking down the streets in New York City every day, especially at 5.00 pm yesterday, when I'm trying to get home before the show, and I can't get home, and I'm walking in Chinatown with crowds everywhere—just the sound and the noise and the speaking and the crashing into people—you can build up this real frenzy! I'm not afraid in New York—I get annoyed, not afraid! I was afraid in San Diego, I would be afraid of isolated spaces and of being on the streets by myself there. This place doesn't make me afraid, it's a kind of celebratory atmosphere, but it's a very loud and frenetic one, as if the phone lines are always taken up! So it has a different swing to it and a different language.

NZ: Have you come across any other performance work that you particularly like which seems to engage with this kind of momentum?

DG: Elizabeth Streb, the dancer—who's also managed by the same people who manage me—she's someone who's wanted to defy certain gravitational principles. She believes that dancers can fly, she has people doing things that are very, very dangerous. You should see her work—I don't think that I can describe it as well as I'd like to, but I feel it to be very kindred in spirit.

NZ: Well the impression I get from your work is that it's taking risks with energy and urgency, that you're working with great integrity to break through the limits of your gravity there.

DG: Yes—and that's what she does with her dancers. It's physically very dangerous, her work, it's very dangerous, and I really like that. I also get a lot of inspiration from sports.

NZ: I think you've mentioned boxing, and Mike Tyson.

DG: Well, not Mike Tyson any more—that son of a bitch! But you know what I mean—certain levels of vigour that are demanded in order to execute the idea. To be at one with the idea—that's interesting to me, because it really means that you have to take whatever the concept is and put it into a physical reality, which is very hard. It's something that unfortunately Artaud was not able to do, not enough, and that's what drove him crazy, among other things. He was not able to extrovert that energy and put it in a physical realm, in a physical space, and so he had all these magnificent ideas, and he was writing them down, but he couldn't breathe, he was asphyxiated by these claustrophobic spaces. This is a very dangerous thing—they're beautiful things to be learned from him, and then they're things to be sharp-eyed about as well.

NZ: Does your work frighten you sometimes? Do you feel you're pushing yourself into dangerous spaces?

DG: If I'm doing my work then I feel happier than anyone could possibly be. If I'm not hot, then it's kind of a bad thing. When you get that adrenalin surge—for any reason whatsoever, usually fear—it's a big motivator, it's very exciting. But then when you come down from it, it's quite depressing, and things look very, very bleak. So I have to keep performing so that I can keep a clear sense of how things are [otherwise] I'd just go fucking crazy because my spirit, metaphorically speaking, would be very much inside the body and I'd feel encroached upon.

NZ: Well, it's interesting that you're emphasising the physical articulation of this thing, and yet you're doing it—and I don't think it's at all paradoxical—via technology. As you said in one of your early interviews in Art Com, *you 'dominate' your technology, and it seems so obvious to me that artists can work with technology on their own terms, and make things happen.*

DG: That's right!

NZ: Whereas a lot of cultural theorists look at mass technologies and say that our culture is neutralised by their impact.

DG: If you're not strong enough to interface with the technology, then it'll come out in the wash, and everyone will hear it. I mean, a lot of sound groups that I know on the road who work for Motorhead and bands like that, they say the following: 'Shit in! Shit out!'. It'll give you what you put into it. That's it, you know. That's it. And I'm not an electronic genius. As I say, I have to work with people. I mean, I know what I want, but I still have to work with people who are masters—sound engineers who are masters of the work.

NZ: That leads to something else that I find very, very interesting. You're working with virtuosos—or fellow virtuosos—of high tech, but you're also working with contemplative writers from other centuries, even back to the Old Testament. So there are historical continuities and contemporary continuities across your work, and I think that interface probably leads to a rich potential of adventure and creativity.

DG: I think so. I really think so too. I like to say that I'm writing a liturgy for the dispossessed—not just the dispossessed, because that's a little obvious—but I'm writing an anti-liturgy, a mass, as I've said before, for people with AIDS, for people who are isolated or kept aside by their mainstream society. And it's a very complicated question, because we never know exactly what the mainstream of society is.

Des Funken Sprunkling Globus
Joyce Hinterding

Ich Phoenix, Ein Kunstereignis
Gasometer, Oberhausen, Germany, May–November 1996

Ich Phoenix took place in one of the largest Gasometers in Germany, situated in Oberhausen in the Ruhr valley, an hour from the borders of the Netherlands and Belgium. Built during 1928–29 for the coal and steel industries, the Gasometer is a giant hollow steel cylinder, 117 metres high and 67 metres in diameter.

In former times a steel floor would rise and fall like a piston plate, transforming the entire building into a machine, but having undergone some renovation it is now possible to enter this space. A rare experience of the mysterious inner space of industry—the industry that produced the infamous acid rain, the weapons of World War II, and the finest steel, knives and tools in the world—the Gasometer is now a cultural centre, a special exhibition space with a glass lift, lights and walkways. However, the vast interior space is preserved, and it remains a giant poisonous breathing machine—and a most extraordinary acoustic space. The sound bounces off 110-metre high curved walls, covered in a black, wet-looking bitumen-type substance. Visitors and workers can only remain inside the building for four hours at a time.

Ich Phoenix, Eine Kunstereignis (*Phoenix Am I: An Arts Event*), was conceived of as an exhibition that would reflect the transformation taking place in part of one of Germany's heaviest industrial regions. Attempting to articulate and embody the desired movement from an industrially-based society to an information-based one, it was the second large scale event to take place in this Gasometer, the first being an historical exhibition titled *Feuer und Flame*, which focused on the steel and mining industries of the area.

Fourteen international artists and groups of artists participated in *Ich Phoenix*. The works were created specifically for this location and situation, and ranged from a series of large scale photographic works to five dynamic installations which employed the internet, computer animation, laser, light, sound, solar energy, high voltage and video projection. In addition to the exhibition, a series of performances for fire, music and large scale projection were staged in and around the Gasometer.

My installation entitled *Koronatron: The twenty-four winds of the sparkling globe* was a solar powered high voltage sound and light work which was situated in the ceiling and on the roof of the Gasometer, 110 metres in the air.

Des Funken Sprunkling Globus

Gasometer, Oberhausen, Germany

Koronatron 1996, from 100-metre high platform

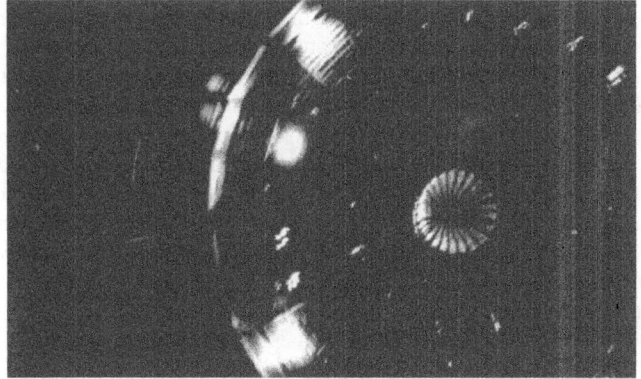
1996, from ground level

Photos: Brigitte Kraemer

> Now miners divide each quarter of the earth into six divisions; and by this method they apportion the earth into twenty four directions, which they divide into two parts of twelve each...Now miners reckon as many points as the sailors do in reckoning up the number of winds. Not only is this done to-day in this country, but it was done by the Romans who borrowed from the Greeks. Any miner who pleases may therefore call the directions of the veins by the names of the winds.[1]

The correlation between the 24 sides of the building, the internal roof structure and the system of the 24 winds used in the sixteenth century by early European miners for identifying and naming mineral veins, provided a metaphorical touchstone for this work. The notion of the wind as an invisible, unpredictable, directional force was used within the work to reference a mostly forgotten history, and at the same time explore the notion of energetic force rather than the wind itself. Thus the vast interior of the Gasometer had become a platform for addressing the dynamic nature of air.

The work drew energy from the visible light portion of the electromagnetic spectrum through a system of 24 solar panels, and translated this into electrical discharges that were both visible and audible. These were the electromagnetic winds, the winds in translation, the burning of air and the streamings of energetic exchange. From the visible to the invisible and back again, these white-hot sparks could be thought of as the mischievous offspring of the sun brought in from the outside to inhabit the interior of the roof. Host to a gathering machine, the Gasometer transformed the benevolent sunlight of summer into untempered high voltage. This metamorphosis of 12 volts to 25,000 volts was achieved by a design which reconfigured television components as part of its assemblage. It could be described as a kind of solar powered television that burns the air, a hardware hack that realises the extraordinary potential for energy from sunlight.

Initially, the event manifested mysteriously overhead: a range of intermittent and indeterminate cracks and fizzing sounds resonated from the ceiling. The sparking was small, bright and fast, and the structure and source of this sound and light were almost indiscernible in the dim vast depths of the space towering above. A glass lift elevated the 'audience' to a viewing platform where, from 100 metres in the air, the structure and the source of the sound became apparent: electricity was jumping a small gap between 24 pairs of large aluminium balls (600mm diameter) which were suspended on eight-metre aluminium poles. Standing on the edge of the enormous black space, the proximity, vertigo and unpredictability left one strangely mesmerised, caught in the moment of expectation, watching and waiting. The work appeared cold and severe, reminiscent of testing equipment, and the title *Koronatron* evoked an imaginative connection to the cyclotrons and synchrotrons of early atomic research. The 24 names on the walls were puzzling, recalling a theatre of magic or the pneumatic memory temples of ancient Greece. One had a sense that they had entered the tower of the winds, a place of histories and secrets, or a capturing machine, a place where things get trapped. Voices and sounds echoed then fell apart, becoming whisperings or strange clinking and sucking sounds which resonated throughout the building. A space of invocation, it provoked all who entered to explore the acoustic nature of the space by screaming, whistling, yelling, or banging on the steel floor. Everyone and everything in this exhibition stood in counterpoint to the acoustic anomaly of the space.

The mode of sound production in *Koronatron* was not unlike that of the sonic boom generated by objects which travel faster than the speed of sound. But this work employed a system that radically transformed the very matrix that allows us to experience sound. It was the changing state of the air itself that provided the source of activity, initiating the resulting zones of rarefied and pressurised air that bounced around the interior. As the 24 high-voltage generators produced a static charge, the surrounding air became ionised and was transformed from an insulating substance into a conducting fluid. This deformation of air from a gas to a plasma provided the conduit for electrical exchange; excited air molecules stripped of electrons leapt from charged to uncharged sphere faster than the speed of sound, thereby breaking the sound barrier. The resulting cracks and hissing sounds were sonic booms created by fast moving air molecules. Trapped inside a gas chamber, reverberating and echoing with unusual longevity, these sonic winds howled hissing and fizzing, at times cracking in rapid fire. Subvesperus sang as Vulturnus burned.

A work of sensations and contradictions, the technology used was an aberrant off-shoot of contemporary media, a monster child of television. The comfort zone of information space was challenged as the work escaped the screen to evoke another type of time and space, that of the 'outside'. This gathering of unstable forces, aroused uncanny associations with the night sky: in the brightness of day, tiny lights and echoes...

A brittle wind resonating from the Aurora at the top of the sun chamber. Volatile air of the world.

The work was designed and prototyped in Australia with assistance from Mr. Snow, Rob Largent at the University of New South Wales Centre for Photovoltaic Devices and Systems, and the CSIRO Division of Applied Physics. It was manufactured in Germany by local industries and apprentices at the trade school, then installed and maintained by the local electronics company Jost Electrotechnik.

1. Georgius Agricola (1556), Book III *De Re Metallica*, New York: Dover Publishers, 1950, pp. 56–58

Booth. Special Delivery

Kathryn Bird

THE CONCERNS

Multimedia rhetoric makes for itself a whole new set of concerns around which to fret, and none more serious than the Delivery Issues. These are those which require the maker to think simultaneously of the great possibilities of the massive workstation on which the work is being produced and the great limitations of all the archaic computers on which this work might finally be 'screened'.

Of course, it's rarely a bad thing for producers, artworkers, and designers to remind themselves that they might want to be thinking about the circumstances, conditions and actual boxes in which their work will finally appear. But in all the worry over the configuration of the computer belonging to the End User in the gallery and/or home entertainment setting, 'what will it sound like?' seems to sneak in last, like the least of our worries.

Sound designers working for multimedia are often faced with a nasty repeat of how all their careful, nuanced work fares in the other great delivery systems of the twentieth century—television and the cinema. THX notwithstanding, in the histories of the preparation of film sound for exhibition, sound is often literally treated as an 'optical element', literally allocated a slice of the image strip.

Booth began with the premise that it would be a fine and provocative thing to switch the priorities here.

Booth is a tiny, touring coin-operated cinema, purpose-built for screening interactives. Modelled deliberately on the clunky, pre-digital technologies of the black and white photobooth, *Booth* is a cinema for one which is configured to overvalue sound against image in the context of exhibition. Not an AV computer transplanted into an exhibition context, *Booth* is a box you can sit in, a gleaming aluminium wonder, a controllable sound environment which surrounds and moves around its single audience member. And the booth itself moves out to new audiences; it's a touring unit, a single AV vending machine designed to land at festivals and galleries and airports around the country. It has a companion Boothsite on the Web, showing a broadcast-delayed feed of the passage of *Booth* visitors, wherever the booth itself may be. From the visitors' stool, you can edit together the sound and image works in various improvisatory ways, access a growing visitors' soundscape, and view QuickTime video postcards of the booth's current realworld location, submitted direct to *Booth* via a VHS contributions slot. Naturally, it also spits out a take-away photo-strip souvenir of the entire experience.

Out to break the deadlock around the exhibition and distribution of short time-based artworks in Australia, *Booth* also structures an ongoing call-for-entries for work to show and sound within itself. And in distinct contrast to the customary dilemmas of short 'filmmaking', where artists are producing work for contexts of exhibition and distribution which they cannot anticipate, *Booth* asks its contributors to examine what happens to their practice when they can riff around specifics—this particular distance between viewer and screen, this particular screen resolution, and this degree of audio controllability...For this reason, we don't want anyone's 15-minute, never-before-screened thing. It has been MutleyMedia's insistence that it should be very tricky for contributors who are themselves involved in customising work for the advantages of the booth environment to only think of sound as an afterthought.

With characteristic precision, Hollis Frampton was able to locate the moment of reception which defined his production process: 'This is exactly what I'm interested in: the moment when one begins to watch oneself watching the thing'.

Booth sets out to augment the circumstances where one might begin to hear oneself hearing the thing.

Listen up.

THE THING: THE BOOTH'S SOUND CONFIGURATION (A LITTLE INTRO FOR CONTRIBUTORS)

As a tiny venue customised especially for the purpose of screening digitised short films, AV material and interactives, the booth couples a 15-inch touch screen monitor to a tweaked sound system.

And as an prompt towards dynamic approaches to mixing and sound design by contributors, *Booth* offers two sound systems: one in the 'interior' of the booth directed at the occupant, and the other sealed away in the 'cavity' located amongst the booth's mechanical guts. Both provide full bandwidth reproduction, and speaker/amplifier combinations capable of high sound levels.

The interior of the booth recesses two mid-range speakers to the side and behind the head of the viewer. The front panel facing the viewer holds two high frequency speakers either side of the screen and a low frequency speaker at shin level.

The business-end cavity is fitted out with one mid-range speaker and a sub-woofer.

The separation of these two sound spaces sets up the possibility for contributors to provide the booth itself—the free-standing, photo-producing, web-connected entity— with a soundtrack, in addition to the standard counterpoint possibilities of sound and image in any particular 'film' screening. All sound will be digitised and reproduced at 44.1Khz/16bit with the possible exception of some interactives (given memory and performance requirements). At present there will only be the facility for two channels of sound (being output from an AV Macintosh).

Given the two output channels, we're offering one standard speaker configuration, and the possibility of a second.

In the standard configuration, the left channel of the CPU output feeds the speakers in the booth cavity, and the right is fed to the booth's interior or audience space. Although the interior sound is mono this configuration allows contributors to explore sound design that imagines and incorporates a 'behind screen' space.

Further grist for sound designers and mixers is the relative proximity and wide frequency/dynamic range of the interior speaker system. The distance of the woofer and the closeness of the mid-range speakers to the listener's head will be balanced so that a loud volume level can be achieved in the bass frequencies without producing an uncomfortable level in the upper frequencies. This balance of low and higher frequency speakers will mean that a soft sound containing only high frequencies will appear close to the listener's head; a sound that contains a relatively full bandwidth will seem to encompass the listener; and a loud sound with low frequencies only will hit the listener in the seat of the pants.

In the serial/MIDI switchable two speaker system, a controllable switching device would enable the incorporation of a stereo field into the 'interior' listening environment. The switcher re-routes the stereo output from the CPU from one amplifier/speaker configuration to a second amplifier/speaker configuration. Essentially, this switches between the mono interior/cavity system as described and an interior-only stereo configuration. This would require the contributors to provide time-code references on their short films or MIDI cues on their interactives to trigger the switching between the two speaker configurations. Of course, any particular contributor might opt for one speaker configuration or another (for either the stereo interior sound environment or the mono cavity/interior sound environment). This option allows for contributors to work within one of the two sound environments only, nominating the speaker configuration their work was designed for in the submission process, and disregarding the need to provide MIDI/time code cues.

In each case, we're looking for contributors who like the idea of working with a home-made THX-y kinda thang. You imagine new possibilities for the set-up, and we'll bat them back and fro with you: email: mutley@magna.com.au

MUTLEYMEDIA
Booth 1996

ESSAYS IN SOUND

4–1999

FINAL

CONTEMPORARY SOUND ARTS

ESSAYS IN SOUND
Published and edited by Contemporary Sound Arts
PO Box 1265, Darlinghurst NSW 2010, Australia

Editors: Alessio Cavallaro, Shaun Davies, Annemarie Jonson
Founding editors: Shaun Davies, Eddy Jokovich, Annemarie Jonson
Sub-editors: Aurelia Armstrong, Tom Gibson
Design: ARMEDIA

Thanks to Julie Dixon and the REPIDU team; Sharon Hancock; W. P. Lowe; Michelle McHugh; Scot McPhee and system X for soundsite (soundsite@sysx.apana.org.au); and all contributing authors and artists.

CSA gratefully acknowledges the sponsorship of Counterpoint Sound and Megaphon Acoustic Design.

This project has been assisted by the Commonwealth Government through the Australia Council, its arts funding and advisory body.

CSA was established in Australia in 1991 to facilitate an interdisciplinary approach to the critical investigation of sound, encompassing historical, political, philosophical, artistic, and technological perspectives, and to engage in and support research, and the production and distribution of various forms of print and electronic media related to sound. These concerns are also expressed in public activities such as the SOUNDcheck series of forums and other events.

©1999. Contents copyright of Contemporary Sound Arts, and the respective authors, artists and photographers.

First published in 1999. Republished in 2016.

Contents

Authenticating The Real: Dawn on Red Lily Lagoon, 1948 *Tony MacGregor*	307
The Psychology of Terra Nullius in Australian Composition *Carolyn Minchin*	321
Back to a Sonic Future *John Potts*	328
Where are we now? Sound in Computer Interactives *Bronwyn Coupe*	331
A Shock in the Ear: Re-Sounding the Body, Mapping the Space of Shock Aesthetics *Norie Neumark*	338
Metamorphoses *Nigel Helyer*	346
On Humming *Paul Thom*	348
The Birds: The Triumph of Noise over Music *Philip Brophy*	357
Further Moments for a Critical History of Music, Sound Generation and Transmission *Phillip L. Ryan*	365
Death's Murmur *Allen S. Weiss*	383
The Moon in Front of the Window: Reflections on the Radio of Kate Mortley *Virginia Madsen*	397
The Sound of the Crowd Watching *John Conomos*	405
Measuring Sound Art *Densil Cabrera*	409

Notes on Contributors [1999]

Philip Brophy lectures in Audio Visual Concepts and Soundtrack Production in Media Arts at RMIT University, Melbourne. He is also director of the CINESONIC International Conference on Film Scores and Sound Design.

Densil Cabrera is undertaking a PhD in applied psychoacoustics at the Faculty of Architecture, The University of Sydney.

John Conomos is a media artist, theorist and critic who lectures at Sydney College of the Arts, The University of Sydney. His latest video work, *Autumn Song*, won an award at Berlin's *Transmediale 98* festival. He is currently working on a critical history of Australian electronic art for Craftsman House, due for publication in late 1999/early 2000.

Bronwyn Coupe works in film, video and multimedia and at the Department of Communications, Information Technology and the Arts, Canberra, when she is not being a mother.

Nigel Helyer is Senior Lecturer, Sculpture, in the Performance and Installation studio, The University of Sydney. His methodological practices have converged to form a pluri-discipline which synthesises sculpture with architectural/environmental sites and combines performed soundscapes (textual, musical or electronic) with radio broadcast.

Tony MacGregor is a writer, sound designer and radio producer with ABC Radio's acoustic arts program *The Listening Room*. A version of this essay was presented at *After The Big Bang* conference, Artspace, Sydney, August 1998.

Virginia Madsen is a writer and independent radio maker. She is currently devising a major radiophonic 'opera' for ABC Radio Drama, and completing a DCA at the University of Technology, Sydney.

Carolyn Minchin has worked on public radio production, studied sound and radio at the University of Technology, Sydney, and music at the University of Western Sydney.
She is currently based in Canberra in order to spend time at the Aboriginal Tent Embassy.

Norie Neumark is a sound/radio and new media artist, and lecturer in Sound and Cultural Studies at the University of Technology, Sydney. Her recent new media art work, *Shock in the Ear*, was funded by the New Media Arts Fund of the Australia Council and as a stand-alone CD ROM by the Australian Film Commission.

John Potts lectures in Media Studies and Audio Production at Macquarie University, Sydney. He has produced several commissioned audio art works for the ABC Radio's acoustic arts program, *The Listening Room*, and has published extensively on sound culture and digital media.

Phillip L. Ryan is a writer and artist, and founder of the 'Utopia Foundation' (1994).

Paul Thom is Dean of the Faculty of Arts at the Australian National University (ANU). From 1989 to 1997 he was Head of the Philosophy Department at ANU. He holds degrees from Sydney and Oxford Universities. His research areas are Aesthetics, Greek Philosophy, Logic, Metaphysics, and Theories of Interpretation. He has worked professionally as a harpsichordist and as an opera director.

Allen S. Weiss is author of *Perverse Desire and the Ambiguous Icon* (SUNY, 1994), *Phantasmic Radio* (Duke, 1995), *Unnatural Horizons: Paradox and Contradiction in Landscape Architecture* (Princeton Architectural Press, 1998), and editor of *Sade and the Narrative of Transgression* (Cambridge, 1995), *Experimental Sound & Radio* (The Drama Review, 1996), *Taste, Nostalgia* (Lusitania Press, 1997).

Authenticating The Real: Dawn on Red Lily Lagoon, 1948

Tony MacGregor

> SFX: The sound of a needle being placed into the groove of an old and worn 78rpm disc. A low level rumble, and the hiss and scratch of surface noise. And then the sound of birds—exotic whistles and cluckings, a cacophony of magpies, geese and plovers and a dozen species I've never heard before...
>
> —*Birdlife in Arnhem Land*, 1948

The recording lasts just over 3' 00". It is one of a set of early Australian Broadcasting Commission (now Australian Broadcasting Corporation) Sound Effects disks found buried in the ABC Radio Sound Effects library. A redundant effect, an archaic, almost arcane object, a relic from as far back as at least four generations of recording technology.

Birdlife in Arnhem Land is almost certainly the first environmental recording from that remote place to be broadcast, an artefact from the earliest days of extended field recording. It was offered to its audience not as illustration or background, but as thing in itself—as an experience, a sound picture of a remote and exotic locale.

I want to interrogate our audition of this sonically degraded, superseded sound object and suggest ways of listening that make it possible to hear across time the faint reverberations, the complex resonance of that morning fifty years ago when the writer/producer Colin Simpson and his companions rose before dawn and walked down to the billabong and began driving thousands of birds towards the recorder set up in its hide at the water's edge. I want to unpack the historical baggage that accompanies this scratchy audio artefact, and question what we hear. And I will argue that this recording is a souvenir from Paradise, a relic from before the Fall.

1

On 18 January 1949, the national service of the ABC broadcast a radio feature in its Walkabout series called *Expedition to Arnhem Land* by Colin Simpson.

Birdlife In Arnhem Land is taken from the many hours of recordings Simpson made in the course of the fortnight he and the PMG technician Ray Giles[1] spent at the Oenpelli base camp of the joint Commonwealth of Australia/National Geographic Society/Smithsonian Expedition. After his fortnight with the Arnhem Land Expedition, Simpson went on to Melville Island, where he recorded a Yoi, the Melville Islander corroboree, which formed the basis of another Walkabout feature called *Island of Yoi*, broadcast a fortnight before the Arnhem Land program. Simpson was to later write a best-selling book based these experiences, *Adam in Ochre*, published in 1951.

We have, then, three documents to work between: the raw recording, the feature program that incorporates the recording, and the book, which covers much of the same territory but differs significantly from the feature and in which he comments extensively upon the recording process. We can 'hear' Simpson's different voices—the voice of the independent writer and the voice of the State broadcaster—and it is possible to trace the lines of authority accorded to voice, sound and text. We can effectively triangulate this single recording and chart its course through the static of history.

In its publicity, the ABC describes *Expedition to Arnhem Land* as 'the authentic story of the Mountford Expedition'. The Walkabout series was established with the formation of the ABC's Features Unit in May 1947. The intention was to portray 'the life and history of important Australian towns and districts against the background of national development'.[2] The ABC was at pains to assure listeners 'that the greatest care was taken to see that every detail was authentic, the material gathered at first hand by the special writers concerned'.[3] Before moving to explore the varied meanings of 'authenticity' in this context, let's consider the program series in which this feature was broadcast.

'Walkabout' is a difficult term to approach in the 1990s. It's a word—an idea—that emerges out of the juncture of anthropology and popular culture with suspect credentials, a faint aroma of redneckery. In the 1940s and '50s it was in common usage. While describing the necessary peregrinations of Aborigines—to take part in ceremonial activity for instance—it carries with it the implication of unreliability, a feckless attitude toward work and settlement: 'walkabout' stands in contradistinction to civilised life. Aborigines on walkabout ceased to be stockmen or domestic help and became tribesmen. Frequently invoked in a negative sense, it also implies the recognition of cultural difference, the recognition by white Australia that there were things that Aboriginal people did—and *had* to do—that 'we' didn't understand. They were prepared to give up a job, reliable sources of food, the meagre comforts of the station settlement to go off and do mysterious things—sorry business, men's business, women's business. 'Walkabout', then, hinted at a deeper way of knowing the country and its workings. There is, I think, a clear sense that 'going walkabout' was seen as an expression of authentic Aboriginal culture—and therefore not fully explicable (and we shall return to this question of authenticity). In the vernacular, as applied to white Australia, the idea of 'going walkabout' has also acquired a set of seductive and subversive meanings: loading up the station wagon with swag and billy, suburban man and his family leaves the bitumen and heads off 'outback'; they return from this unstructured journey into the interior more knowledgeable, more at home with our country and with themselves. So, while there were numerous cartoons that depicted shifty blacks slinking back from 'walkabout', the name was also used as the title of the Australian Geographical Society's popular magazine and the Chauvel's best-selling account of their trip from Sydney to Darwin, and still resonates as the name of outback tour operators and airline special deals.

The ABC's Walkabout carries this ambivalent baggage. The portability and reliability of recording equipment in the immediate post-war years enabled the program maker to not simply get out of the studio (they had been doing that for years) but to venture forth into remote places with relative ease. The idea of reporting the richness and complexity of life in the 'wide brown land' obviously met with the Commission's sense of high national purpose, congruent with an invigorated sense of national development—especially of the remote and sparsely populated north—in the aftermath of the Pacific War.

But there is also, I suspect, a suggestion of the feckless in calling this roving features program 'Walkabout'. One of the implications of getting out and about is that we will hear the unruly voices of ordinary Australians talking about their extraordinary, ordinary lives. But, the Commission assures us, every detail is authentic: the risks of 'going Walkabout' could only be justified by its claim to authenticity. (Listeners could be assured, however, that not a lot of 'wild talk' would be allowed to leak out of the wire. After all, ABC announcers still wore evening dress, and speaking proper was all the go). Parcelled up with this dangerous suggestion of untamed authenticity is an ambiguous gesture toward the indigenous, partly a recuperation of the Aboriginal need to walk the land into being, and partly a new claim made on behalf of white Australia to share this ancient nomadic way of knowing. That we might 'go Walkabout' in the name of national development further complicates the picture.

You can hear all of these things at work in the opening sequence of *Expedition to Arnhem Land*: the mixture of self-importance, exoticism and cautious reassurance, and then from Charles Mountford, the insistence on the scientific purpose of the expedition and the solemn invocation of the Commonwealth Government. The announcer enters on the back of a pompous and extended orchestral fanfare which cross-fades with the sound of didgeridoo (possibly the first broadcast of this instrument). The announcer notes that this exotic music was recorded up in remote Arnhem land, and then enjoins his listeners to attend this authentic account of the 'joint Commonwealth and National Geographic Society Expedition' and 'what the scientists did', which is presented in this 'not-too-formal account'. The announcer throws to Simpson, who proceeds in a tone of weary seriousness (a tone at odds with the words he uses) to evoke beautifully the magical scene that greeted him at Oenpelli, before introducing a recording of an 'interview' with the expedition's Australian leader, C.P. Mountford. Asked to explain the purpose of the expedition, Mountford launches into a statement that is almost certainly read, in which he outlines the scientific brief of the expedition: to collect samples of the flora and fauna and to study the habits of the natives, and its explicit nature as a government-backed exercise.

2

'The greatest care was taken to see that every detail was authentic, the material gathered at first hand by the special writers concerned.'

Portable tape recorder in tow and notebook in hand, our special writer is finally on Walkabout. He is in the service of the Australian Broadcasting Commission, attached to an international scientific expedition, the composition of which is an expression of the new, postwar relationship with the United States. Every detail must be authentic. Clearly, this authenticity depends upon the presence of the special writer, a reliable witness, an author. What role then for the recording?

There is no single answer to the question; rather, a set of conflicted relationships between writing and sound recording, between writer and speaker, are present from the opening moments of Simpson's feature. Questions of authority, authorship and authenticity are raised constantly in moving between reading *Adam in Ochre* and listening to *Expedition to Arnhem Land*.

Before returning to questions of recording and writing, it is necessary to expand upon the idea of the authentic. One assumes the ABC has something like the dictionary definition in mind: 'Real, actual, genuine: original, first-hand; really proceeding from its stated source, author, painter, etc.'.[4]

Yet authenticity is a much more culturally determined idea. The question of indigenous authenticity, for instance, is one of Simpson's concerns, even though in the radio feature Aborigines are present only as 'wild sound'[5] leaking into the official discourse of the Expeditioneers. In the book, Aboriginal authenticity is the organising principle, and the activities of the expedition are largely a means toward a more ambitious pedagogic and personal end, that of telling an originary story for contemporary Australia: 'Not so much has been written about the northern tribes as, for instance, about the Arunta of the Centre; which is one reason for writing this book. Yet the Arnhem Lander can represent the prototype, the first man, the Adam of this land...'.[6] Here authenticity in the sense of the original is invoked, but by extension, so is the post-Edenic state, the Fall, the Fall into civilisation. But who has fallen from grace in Simpson's Eden? I do not wish to dwell too much on this question, but if (as we shall see) our recording *Birdlife in Arnhem Land* is in fact a souvenir from Paradise, the expulsion from Paradise cannot be ignored.

In the late 1940s, 'the Aboriginal problem' was subject to intense public discussion. Legislation was before State and Federal Parliaments to give Aborigines limited franchise. The practice of removing children from their mothers was being debated. Assimilation was Government policy, but exactly what this might entail was also being discussed in the press and the legislature. There was a strong interest in Aboriginal art and culture. In public discourse, a clear division emerged in the way Aborigines were imagined: on one hand there were the 'real Aborigines'—'full bloods' living more or less traditional lives in the remote north and centre of the country—and on the other, the 'half castes' who lived in the settled districts. One of the ironies of this cultural bifurcation is that popular opinion denied 'real' authentic Aborigines citizenship while acknowledging their cultural integrity and the right to control their destiny on their traditional lands, while the 'half castes'—the inauthentic Aborigines—might be granted full citizenship, but denied their aboriginality. (This was the position put by the Australian Aboriginal League).[7]

Simpson's take on this debate is complex. He begins by asking if the Aborigines have fallen from grace. Has their contact with white society diminished their originality? At first Simpson assumes this is the case, but his later experience makes him question his initial impressions:

> The old men Mountford brought back to the tent had been hoeing the mission's melon patch. They looked unimpressive, they looked dreadful in cast-offs of clothing and shapeless relics of felt hats. They sat down on the grass, folding themselves down in that slow and diffident way they have with white men, one wringing his nose out with his fingers, another coughing. I thought to myself, 'Nothing much can come of this'. I was judging by appearances, presuming that the old men had shed their validity as aborigines and put off their old culture because they had put on rags of white-man clothing and were taking hand-outs from the mission. It was these old men and others they mustered who, transformed with paint and fervour, gave us the unforgettable performance of the balnooknook [sacred drum] corroboree a few days later.[8]

In *Adam in Ochre* Simpson essays a number of ways of approaching Aboriginal culture and the so-called 'Aboriginal problem'. From this distance, his attitudes can appear contradictory—he can be patronising while asserting the cultural and intellectual equality of white and black Australians—but his underlying commitment is clearly to encourage his fellow citizens to recognise the diversity and complexity of Aboriginal culture, and to see the fundamental importance to Australian society of coming to terms with history.

In this context it is interesting to note that Simpson claims credit for bringing together the composer John Antill and the painter William Constable with the idea of having a ballet created. The resulting *Corroboree* was a disappointment to Simpson:

Through a lack of understanding and plain lack of knowledge, the choreographer completely missed the spirit of the real thing in a riot of baseless representationalism, full of incongruous and extraneous elements.[9]

To return to the Fall and the question of authenticity: the authentic being of the Arnhem Land Aborigines serves to remind us—the listener, the reader, the author—of the inauthentic nature of white, urban, civilised existence. Never stated explicitly, this confrontation with our own inauthentic nature—and the possibility of redemption—is the book's essential sub-text.

3

The notional loss of our authenticity—the corrosive nature of post-Enlightenment culture on our true being—is a recurrent philosophical theme, and Simpson was working at the very moment when existentialism, this century's most persuasive—or seductive—version of this theme, was rapidly finding audience in the intellectual life of the West. He was never Sartre; there is nowhere the suggestion that 'Hell is other people'. Nevertheless, Simpson's writing conveys a generalised sense of the inauthentic nature of contemporary being expressed in a sentimental, vernacular way which remains seductive today. 'All other people', to quote Lionel Trilling discussing Sartre,

> make the Hell of recognised and experienced inauthenticity. They make the inhabited nothingness of the modern world. They speak to us of our own condition; we are members one of another. Certain exemptions are made: the poor, the oppressed, the violent, the primitive.[10]

These were Simpson's subjects—he was to write two more books in the *Adam*[11] series, both on traditional cultures in Papua New Guinea, and another on the 'real' Bali.

I also want to consider Susan Stewart's discussion of the souvenir and its relationship to the desire for authenticity. She says:

> Within the development of culture under an exchange economy, the search for authentic experience, and correlatively, the search for the authentic object, become critical. As experience is increasingly mediated and abstracted, the lived relation of the body to the phenomenological world is replaced by a nostalgic myth of contact and presence.[12]

Simpson's introduction to the radio program evokes the idyllic setting in which he first encounters the expedition members: the lagoon with its water lilies, the sacred mountain behind; the natives fishing at one end, the naked scientists bathing at the other. It's a scene sketched with great economy and skill, and Charles Mountford's rehearsed banalities bring us down to earth with a thump. In the book, Simpson can tell the story his way, and he completes an extended version of the same introduction like this:

> In the lagoon at evening, when the last glow of the sun made satin of the water and the wind stood still, was the day's best hour. Down there at the big billabong mirroring Inyaluk, shared with the natives and the near birds, no one turned to hunt, there was a feeling of being part of a quest that was wider and *more real than anything you could seek for in a city*, and there was no sense of urgency in need or time. There was a balm and essence I have not felt before or since. Others felt it, too. I remember Bob Miller, the ichthyologist, standing out there in the quiet water the evening before he had to leave Oenpelli and return to America, saying, 'This I am going to miss a great deal...'.[13]

A tropical evening, the company of honest men and the companionship of unsullied natives: 'more real than anything you could seek for in a city...a quest...a balm and an essence'.

This is Eden both invoked and evoked, and at a time, as the *Sydney Morning Herald* noted, when in the popular imagination, Arnhem Land 'bore a sinister reputation and was shunned by whitemen except for a few buffalo hunters, traders, missionaries, patrol officers and anthropologists'.[14]

Critically, Simpson extends his projection of Aboriginal authenticity into the realm of cultural production, into art making. When talking about the hundreds of bark paintings that Mountford collected in Arnhem Land, Simpson notes:

> it never happened that a native said, if asked to do a bark painting, 'Not me, boss, I can't draw.' In a tribe every man was an artist, just as every man was a hunter. Art, to them, had never become the specialist activity of the few.[15]

This is one of the key tropes in the modern discourse of authenticity (largely the pre-occupation of writers and artists), and it presents a paradox: art, when consciously conceived of as such, manifests its inauthenticity, its artifice, and yet true art—authentic art—must needs be remind *us* of our inauthenticity. The role of art then is to make us aware—and ashamed—of our empty, false lives. Trilling again, here discussing Roquentin, the protagonist of Sartre's novel *Nausea*: 'When… at the end of his diary of queasy despair, [Roquentin] permits himself to entertain a single hope, it is that he may write a story which will be 'beautiful and hard as steel and make people ashamed of their existence'. Trilling goes on to say: 'The authentic work of art instructs in our own inauthenticity and adjures us to overcome it'.[16]

Simpson is equally romantic but more sentimental. Unquestionably he seeks to alter his (primarily) white, urban reader's way of seeing both Aborigines and him or herself. And *Adam in Ochre* recounts a personal journey which at least suggests the recuperation of an authentic being. Nor does Simpson shy from seeking to shame white Australia. One section of *Adam in Ochre* is a novella called *Kakadu Naked* which tells the story of 'Nabanja, man of the Kakadu people' and his children. It is a love story which turns into a tragedy, told from an Aboriginal perspective. It concludes with the careless debauching of a young Kakadu woman by a white adventurer. It depicts a truly nasty encounter between white and black Australia distinguished by hypocrisy and cruelty.

4

Let's return to *Expedition to Arnhem Land*.

In the book, Simpson makes clear both the personal impact of his journey and his central concern with coming to terms with the Aboriginal situation. How is this reconciled with his role as a Commission employee, a State functionary, out there reporting on an official Commonwealth-sponsored expedition? I think you can hear something of the conflict that Simpson negotiates in the shift in the tone of his voice between Simpson-in-the-field and Simpson-in-the-studio. The effect is no doubt accentuated by the slippage in playback and recording speeds: the light, easy voice of the man on walkabout, the altogether more solemn, deliberate tones of the pipe-smoking narrator on duty in the studio. Simpson's studio narration is economic, but his sense of poetry and his personal reflections are constrained by the imperative to recount 'what the scientists did'. And what the scientists did is by and large less than rivetting. Each interview adheres to much the same formula: description of task: 'I collect fish'; summary of findings: 'there are lots of fish'; and an anecdote: 'I found a funny fish'. On location, Simpson is enjoying himself, but also working to rule. He is interested, but the real work is going on in his head, and in his diary, finding its fullest expression in the nuanced complexity and descriptive richness of the book.

And so the question again: What role for the sound recording? The tape recorder had allowed the producer to roam far and wide, to talk to real people—to capture the authentic sounds of Australia—but the feature was still authored by writing, not by recording. In *Expedition to Arnhem Land*, we listen on the cusp between the authority of writing and the authenticity of (recorded) actuality, at a moment when the contemporary radio feature is being born. I want to us to listen more closely to the sound of Simpson in the studio—the inauthentic Simpson perhaps—before turning to *Birdlife in Arnhem Land*, and to further explore this question of the relationship between writing and recording.

On the radio, Simpson introduces his interview with the deputy leader of the expedition, the American archaeologist Dr Frank Sezler, by describing it as 'the liveliest of our recorded interviews'. When then cut to the field recording, Simpson describes Sezler entering the tent at the end of the working day, covered in dust, and emptying a haversack of found objects onto his work table. It's all done as 'live': 'here's Dr Frank Sezler now, he's covered in dust; he looks as black as his native helpers...he's emptying his bag of finds onto the table...[SFX: clattering stones...]...'. Then Simpson asks Sezler what he's been up to, and Sezler replies: 'wait a moment Colin, until I get this dust off...'. It all sounds bright and enthusiastic.

But to the contemporary listener there is something odd about this, the 'liveliest of our recorded interviews'. The quality that jars for our ears is that it's clearly rehearsed: you can imagine the scene—'first I'll describe you coming in, then you put down the knapsack, and I'll ask you what you've been doing', and so on. In some cases, as with Mountford's recitation of the expedition's history, Simpson's interview subjects read from prepared texts. I have no doubt that Simpson's reporting of the scenes is accurate, and the material he recorded proceeds from his inquiries. In effect, Simpson has simply chosen the best bits from his conversations with people, and asked his subjects to repeat them for the wire recorder. (The same stories appear in the book). Mostly Simpson treats the recorder as something like a typewriter, a tool with which the writer transcribes his rough notes, turning them into reportage for public consumption. Simpson does not appear to trust the recorder as an observing device in its own right, as something capable of hearing beyond his own listening, that he might possibly *work with the wire* in the same manner as he might rework his notes.

There is a curious sequence in *Adam in Ochre* which allows us to explore the ambivalent nature of the author's relationship to the sound recording—and to the recording machine itself. Simpson goes on a buffalo hunt, with a number of Aborigines, Len Hillier, a professional buffalo hunter employed by the Oenpelli mission, and Aub Dunkley, one of the white mission employees. The buffalo hunt doesn't make it into *Expedition to Arnhem Land*, but the episode as written is told almost exclusively through quotation from, and comment upon, the recordings Simpson and Giles made. It is a story about recording and radio as much as it is about buffalo hunting.

First, they set up to record the hunt:

> We went across a narrow stretch of plain into a clump of paperbarks that came out like a peninsula on a sea of green rice-grass. ...Ray would stay on the truck with the wire recorder...I picked a paperbark...and from its fork I could see right out over the plain where some buffaloes were already grazing. We ran the microphone lead through a few tree tops to the tree I was in. I looped the mike on to a limb where I could let it hang... A wind was blowing, so I tied a handkerchief over the front of

the mike, otherwise the wind comes in a low roar. Then I tested with Ray and, settling myself back in the fork of the paperbark, waited for the shoot-boys to come in sight with that good feeling of anticipated excitement. Maybe we'd get a recording that would have the listeners in the suburbs gripping the Genoa velvet of their lounge chairs. But it wasn't our day.[17]

The buffalo weren't to come crashing through the paperbarks, so Simpson is left with providing a running commentary from his view of the hunt taking place out on the plain. In the book, Simpson directly transcribes the recording, but inserts a number of observations which can be seen as Simpson the writer admonishing Simpson the speaker.

> Ah...over here...er...well, a shot buffalo is not down...he's charged at a horse...the horse jumps aside. The wounded buffalo stops, even from here he looks bullet-stricken and bewildered. The horseman rides away, just a calm canter, about fifty yards, looking over his shoulder at the bull, still standing there. Now the shooter has dismounted, he's on foot (*of course he's on foot, mug, if he's dismounted*). The shooter walks towards the buffalo and now the buffalo (*keep your voice down!*) walks toward him, head lowered and...his...the shooter's rifle goes up—and he drops the buffalo with a shot between the eyes. (*How the hell do you know at this distance whether it was between the eyes? Well where else... Get on with it! But there's nothing doing, except that the other buffaloes have got away*). The rest of the buffaloes are racing for the paperbarks on the right—they'll make the timber—while all the shooters are across on the left...okay Ray, cut, you can switch off now. Was I working too close to the mike again and how did it sound...bloody? I'm coming down now, you can tell me. Sorry you couldn't see it from where you are...[18]

At one level, Simpson is simply allowing us behind the scenes, unveiling the clunky machinery of recording and the frailties of the reporter. But it is a passage which also seeks to undermine the authority of the 'live' recording and Simpson's 'wild talk', his unwritten self. This spontaneous commentary may be authentic, true to the moment, but it lacks the authority of the written word, committed to paper after considered reflection.

5

There is an incident later in the buffalo hunt which perfectly captures Simpson's profound ambivalence about the function of the recorder as a source of authority, a moment when that which is unrecordable—unsayable—is able to be written, a neat illustration of the opposition between speech and writing. It also reveals the extent to which Simpson attributes to the recorder an element of agency, in much the same way we attribute agency to a gun in saying it 'goes off'. (It is also important here to consider broadcast speech—especially on the State broadcaster—as the speech of teachers, and the notion that Barthes explores in 'Writers, Teachers, Intellectuals', where he says '[T]he writer stands apart. Writing begins at the point where speech becomes impossible'.[19])

Back to our buffalo hunt.

Given the extreme heat, the shooters prefer to cripple rather than kill the buffalo outright. They then leave the animal lying there, in the heat and in pain, until they can come back to skin it—in some cases, overnight. The buffalo is finally killed just before skinning—it is easier to skin a freshly killed carcass, and there is no risk of the beast rotting in the heat—a rotten skin is of no value commercially. Simpson finds the practice repugnant, and determines to expose it as cruel:

> When we got back to the waterhole near the camp Aub superintended the washing of the hides. They were dragged off the truck and into the water and left there to soak off the mud and the blood, and then they would be liberally salted to keep them. I got Aub to explain that on to the recorder which was on the truck, working off two six-volt batteries.
>
> 'We'll go straight from there with a snap start,' I told Ray. I didn't like what I was going to do next, as I went ahead on [Ray's] nod.
>
> 'Mr Dunkley,' I said, 'have you lost any hides today in the heat?' I turned the mike to Aub.
>
> 'Yes, we've lost one that was left too long before skinning,' he said, coming into it like a child.
>
> I lowered the mike and told Ray to cut; I couldn't do it cold.
>
> 'Aub, I'm going to ask you about leaving them alive until the next day. You represent the mission out here...'. I looked at Len sitting in the truck.
>
> 'You can't ask him that,' Len said. There was no rancour in his voice.
>
> 'No,' I said. 'I think that'll do, Aub. Thanks.' I told Ray to finish. I felt grateful to Len. It was as though he had knocked up my rifle when I was going to blast a sitting bird.[20]

It's an interesting moment, and our inquiry might take off in any number of directions. Let's follow the hunting metaphors for a moment. What starts off as entrapment, with the intention of capturing wild talk ('coming into it like a child') suddenly takes on the character of an act of unsportsmanlike aggression: 'it was as though he had knocked up my rifle when I was a going to blast a sitting bird'. It is as if the act of recording Aub's unprepared answer parallels leaving the wounded buffalo out on the plain, an act of unnecessary cruelty. And yet Simpson the writer has little hesitation in giving us exactly the same information he could not bring himself to 'capture' on tape by interviewing Aub Dunkley.

WHY?

Issues of journalistic ethics aside, I think the answer lies in Simpson's recognition of the authenticating nature of the unmediated speech act, and his own belief in or commitment to the authority of writing. It is an appropriately complex moment—contradictory, intensely felt, revelatory. As I remarked before, Simpson may well express the existential malaise of modernity, but he is no Sartre or Camus. The Paradise of authenticity he evokes at the beginning of *Adam in Ochre* has its limits, nowhere more evident than when Simpson writes:

> ...pre-literate people are sickeningly insensitive to animal suffering, and the first thing expected of any mission is that it should counteract cruelty, not countenance it as a means to an end—the end, in this case, being to earn funds to carry on its work of Christianising.[21]

I think here we find a key to understanding Simpson's ambivalence toward the sound recorder. It is in the pre-literate moment, Simpson is saying, that man is at his most authentic, and most cruel. The writer can choose his words, but the tape recorder is insensible to desire; indiscriminate, immoral, it captures everything, unrestrained. It is a strangely primitive tool which the writer must keep continually in check lest it reveal the violence in Paradise—the violence of pre-literate speech, of utterance. This is the risk of 'going walkabout' with the recorder, that the unsayable will be said, promiscuously authenticating the real with no care for the civilising effect, the discipline, of the (written) Word.

While Simpson's abhorrence of what he perceives as cruelty delineates the limits of his romance of the real and original, it would be wrong to see Simpson as in some reactionary way resisting sound recording, as a kind of media Luddite. Instead, he is grappling with the problem of authorship in an emerging medium. Indeed, he continually reminds his reader that the writing of *Adam in Ochre* owes everything to the act of recording.

Simpson is also mindful of the way in which the recorder is fundamentally an extension of a larger cultural institution which in the immediate postwar years was directly implicated in the task of 'national development'. There is a wonderful celebratory passage in *Adam in Ochre* where Simpson looks 'back on the cavalcade of people I have seen carrying ABC recording equipment', which begins:

> I see the recorder-box and the label-gaudy Globite cases of mikes and vibrators and wires and spare parts being passed from an Indian taxi-driver in Singapore to a Dusan or a Murat carrier in North Borneo who puts some of it in a round bark basket called a *boongen* and hoists it on his back.

The recorder passes from hand to hand through Asia and across Australia, until finally 'A Canberra technician sets it up before the Prime Minister'.[22]

It's a neat summary of Simpson's ABC career—a series of journeys to exotic places, which ends in an audience with the Prime Minister. For all the opportunity to travel, Simpson worked for the ABC for only three years. He joined in 1947 to help establish the Features Department, and left in 1950. *Adam in Ochre* was published the following year.

'[A]ll speech is on the side of the Law,' writes Barthes. The speaker/teacher either accepts his role as Authority—speaking clearly—or attempts to subvert it by 'speaking badly'—correcting, adding, wavering. But in the end 'the choice is gloomy: conscientious functionary or free artist...'.[23] We might hear broadcast speech—radio talk—as both confirming and complicating Barthes' critique. The voices we hear can either be reading from prepared texts, or they can be extemporising. In either case, the voice is framed—authorised—by its institutional context—in this case the ABC. The Simpson we hear in *Expedition to Arnhem Land* and read about in *Adam in Ochre* is the writer negotiating the paradoxes of recording, but he is also attempting to reconcile his role as a broadcaster within an expressly pedagogic and nationalistic cultural institution, a role defined by speech. One of the paradoxes of the move from writing to extemporary speech which the Features Department initiates is that it in fact seeks to reverse the power relations sketched by Barthes: in letting Australians speak freely (more or less) the authority of the written talk is diminished. Australians talk back to the lecturer, albeit within a highly regulated context.

These are the paradoxes Simpson must negotiate in his attempt to record (in writing or sound) the authentic experience of his journey to Arnhem Land. Up at Oenpelli, Simpson is almost the free artist, the writer 'on walkabout' from the ABC, but the Pyrox wire recorder is both his excuse for being there, and the source of his authority as agent of the State. It has an almost living presence. Is Simpson accompanying the recorder, or the recorder accompanying Simpson?[24]

6

I have tried to locate Simpson in the midst of complex cultural and historical forces. We see and hear him negotiating competing discourses of authenticity and conflicting notions of authority, attempting to reconcile writing with speaking, and confronting the dilemma of Aboriginal existence in the Australia of 1948.

As is evident in his writing, all these problems engage him very personally. Yet this experience is largely inaudible in the radio program, heard only in the reluctance which I feel is evident in Simpson's voice as he reads his narration, which might be read as discomfort with his role in the nation-building functions of 'Walkabout'. (You can also hear in the studio presentation, on close listening, the sound of traffic on the street outside the studio. This sonic leakage of the 'outside' into the acoustic sanctum of the studio would be regarded as intolerable in contemporary practice, but in this context it has a strangely poignant effect, placing Simpson behind a desk in a banal Sydney office, far from the exotic doings of his freer, recorded self. It recalls the office-bound narrator of Patterson's 'Faces in the Street'.) Similarly in the field recordings, Simpson may be enjoying himself in his rehearsed interviews with the scientists, but he is not giving much away either. It is only in those brief moments when the recording breaks with the word and allows 'wild sound' to burst through that we even begin to approach the effect Simpson sought when he described the 'listeners in the suburbs gripping the Genoa velvet of their lounge chairs'. These are the moments when recording takes over from writing—those rare radiophonic moments when Simpson allows sound, not scientists, to speak.[25]

The extract from the recording *Birdlife in Arnhem Land* is one such moment. Why does Simpson include it? Superficially, it's consistent with the program's pedagogic intent, and it provides audible evidence of the exotic location. But it is certainly not intended to engender the virtual presence that attends contemporary environmental sound recording. Such recordings depend for their effect upon both high fidelity and extended durations.[26]

In introducing the recording in his radio program, Simpson, while offering a detailed description of the location and the mass of birds, is restrained, opening with the observation that 'The birdlife in Arnhem Land is amazing'. It gives no hints at the emotional importance he attaches to the experience, which he describes in great detail in 'The Morning of the Birds', a chapter close to the middle of his book.

One morning before dawn, Simpson sets off with four Aborigines toward the lagoon. The recording gear has already been set up in a hide at the water's edge the previous night:

> The babel of birds came to us before we reached the nearest edge of mile-long marshy lagoon. I have never seen such a sight as it was that morning. An empty stretch of water can be beautiful, but this was something beautifully alive. The multitude of birds across the expanse of water left few patches where they were not feeding or swimming or alighting or taking off. Yet, with all their movement, and all their cries and murmur vibrant in the air, there was serenity, as of a park pond made enormous, a sanctuary limited only by the flank of sandstone on our right and the far, tall trees of the paperbark belt. Veils of mist were rising and wreathing away. The sky was pearly and the far scarps of sandstone beyond the trees stood up like unsubstantial walls in the soft light that made them mauve. There was no flush of sunrise yet across the water…

After some trepidation about leeches and the possibility of encountering crocodiles, Simpson and the Aborigines enter the water and begin slowly driving birds to within range of the microphone.

> The sun was coming up now and the water was shining. The sun gave the birds shadows and reflections. I was nearly out in the centre of the lagoon then and, more than ever, the air was alive

with the sound. I waded on through the sunrise colours in the water, the birds rising before me, knowing that it was a morning that would be with me as long as I lived.

It was almost seven o'clock when I waded up to a little rocky islet, rolled a cigarette, and wrote some of it down...[I'm glad I did]...because the notes have fixed impressions that might have blurred. For all [the birds] that had been flushed to the upper reaches there were still thousands down the lagoon and on either side. The top end had been crowded with birds for the best part of an hour. Ray should have some good sound. It was time to go right up and create the final sound we hoped would make a fine climax.

As I started wading the last stretch there were necks up everywhere; the geese, talking, talking, talking—here was that man again. If I wanted photographs, and I did, this was the time to use the camera, or it would be too late. I took it out of its case, the little Nagel that fits in the palm of my hand, and waded on a few more yards. I was raising the camera to shoot when my right sandshoe went *slip* in the mud and as I saved myself from falling, the camera slipped out of my hand and plopped into the water. I whipped it straight up from the muddy bottom. I looked at it and the picture in front of me, a picture such as I shall never get again. Raising the dripping camera I looked at the picture through the viewer. Geese were rising in hundreds just in front of me, and the water was full of the reflections of geese flying. Knowing it was senseless to do so, I clicked the sodden shutter. I swore, but mechanically. The cursing chagrin I felt I should feel just wasn't there. The morning was too big for a thing like that to spoil.

To complete the sound picture, which was the important thing, I quickened my pace. The thousands of birds between me and the hide all began to take the air, flapping and honking and calling and crying. More than I had ever anticipated was the surge of sound as their wings beat the air, almost a thunder of sound, a noise like a great cacophonous aerial host, still mounting to a crescendo beyond any crescendo expected as all the flocks wheeled back over my head and the sky was gone in a rushing, breath-taking pattern of black and white.

When it was over I walked out through the ankle-deep shallows. The piping of the plovers at the edges and the little running snipe was like a twitter of sound underscoring a silence. I went up to the hide and Ray Giles came crawling out to meet me.

'Did you get it all mate?'

'All you'll ever want and more,' he said. 'Come and listen to a bit of it back. It's wonderful.'

It was, too, even if we say so ourselves. We played back enough of the recording to know it was all there. The takeoff was terrific.[27]

Compare that euphoric riff to his comment in the radio narration, where his joy at the crescendo of sound is reduced to 'toward the end of this recording you will hear hundreds of birds take off from the water'.

There are many things that could be said about the narrative Simpson weaves around the moment of this recording. We might ponder the fact that although his camera has been destroyed, he must complete the ritual of the snapshot. It might appear that the sound recording is not a reliable witness to dawn in Paradise. But we must also note that the whole sequence refers to, is articulated by and through, the act of recording: the reader is in the end reminded that she cannot hear what Ray Giles and Simpson hear 'off the wire': 'Come and listen...it's wonderful'.

The irony is that this recording—which the reader must imagine as 'real' in contradistinction to the description—in no way matches the grandeur of the experience evoked by Simpson's text. It is this fundamental inadequacy which defines this recording as souvenir, rather than as the presage, the pre-echo, of contemporary environmental sound recording and the acoustic ecology movement.

Susan Stewart argues that

> ...the souvenir must remain impoverished, and partial so that it can be supplemented by a narrative discourse, a narrative discourse which articulates the play of desire [without which] it would not function, that both attaches it to its origins and creates a myth with regard to those origins.[28]

In this instance, several 'narrative discourses' stitch this souvenir to its origins. (And clearly this presentation makes up one strand of this mythologising).

Notionally included to illustrate the prolific nature of the birdlife in Arnhem Land, the recording functions as a souvenir of Arnhem Land's prelapsarian state, but also of the impossibility of Simpson's return to that state, figuratively and literally.

In a radio program constructed almost entirely of kinds of writing, this sudden opening onto the natural world represented by *Birdlife in Arnhem Land* is the exception, the irruption. Its brief presence serves to subvert the carefully constructed discourse of scientific inquiry. Almost despite himself, Simpson has offered a souvenir of the real world to which the words—culture—can only refer. In this sense, it also momentarily resolves the dilemma of speaking on the radio for the writer: it blows away all speech. And in doing so, it becomes a souvenir of Simpson's journey with the ABC, authorised excursions into remote places, meeting real people, having authentic experiences far from his city desk, but always accompanied by the wire recorder. *Birdlife in Arnhem Land* is a souvenir of a moment when Simpson managed to step aside from Barthes 'gloomy choice—conscientious functionary or free artist'.[29]

Finally, I want to suggest that for the listener today, this fragile artefact is also a souvenir, around which I have attempted to weave my own version of originary myth. As a feature producer with the ABC, working fifty years after Colin Simpson helped establish the Features Unit, I hear *Birdlife in Arnhem Land* as a souvenir from the earliest days of the form. More poignantly, it is a souvenir from a moment when one Australian writer and broadcaster tried to imagine that white and indigenous Australians might share equally in Paradise.

1. Technical services for the fledgling national broadcaster were provided by the Post Master General's Department—precursor to Telecom—and a strict demarcation applied between the recordist and the writer/producer, which continued well into the 1970s.
2. ABC Annual Report, 1948.
3. ABC Annual Report, 1949.
4. And interestingly enough, the OED uses this example from the British Listener magazine: 'BBC1's Tenko was the most authentic representation to date of the Far East prisoner's life'—a nice coincidence given the fact that Simpson's first work for the ABC was a series of scripted features on the life of POWs in Borneo.
5. For a critical discussion of the idea of wild sound and its relationship to ideas of 'the real', see Virginia Madsen, 'The Call of the Wild', in *Uncertain Ground*, ed. Martin Thomas, Sydney: Power Publications, forthcoming.
6. Colin Simpson, *Adam in Ochre*, Sydney: Angus & Robertson, 1951, p. 7.

7. See 'Tribal Life Menaced', H. S. Groves, Secretary, Australian Aboriginal League, Letters to the Editor, *Sydney Morning Herald*, 8 September 1949, and 'Australia and the Aborigines', A. P. Elkin, *Sydney Morning Herald*, 29 January 1949.
8. Simpson, op. cit., p. 196.
9. ibid., pp. 6–7.
10. Lionel Trilling, *Sincerity and Authenticity*, London: Oxford University Press, 1972, p. 102.
11. *Adam in Plumes*; *Adam with Arrows*.
12. Susan Stewart, *On Longing*, Durham & London: Duke University Press, 1993, p. 133.
13. Simpson, op. cit., p. 10. My emphasis.
14. 'Expeditions Begin Assembling', *Sydney Morning Herald*, 26 February 1948.
15. Simpson, op. cit., p. 42.
16. Trilling, op. cit., p. 100.
17. Simpson, op. cit., p. 30.
18. Simpson, op. cit., p. 31.
19. Roland Barthes, 'Writers, Intellectuals, Teachers', in *Image, Music, Text*, trans. Stephen Heath, Oxford: Flamingo, 1984, p. 190.
20. Simpson, op. cit., p. 36.
21. ibid., p. 39.
22. ibid., p. 137.
23. Barthes, op. cit., p. 192.
24. In fact Simpson includes a description of the recorder, and its cost, in his extensive glossary to *Adam In Ochre*, a self-consciousness which is unimaginable in contemporary reportage.
25. The other key moment is a recording of the didjeridoo. This was the first time the sound of the didjeridoo was ever broadcast, and these recordings are also held in the ABC's Sound Effects Library. They merit a much longer discussion.
26. See Virginia Madsen, 'Notes Toward Sound Ecology in the Garden of Listening', in *Essays in Sound 2: Technophonia*, Sydney: Contemporary Sound Arts, 1995.
27. Simpson, op. cit., p. 70–73.
28. Stewart, op. cit., p. 136.
29. After his Adam series, Simpson went on to write popular guides to exotic cultures and difficult countries, roaming from Japan to the remote republics of the USSR. But his independence was provisional; he wrote a sponsored history of the AMPOL oil company, *Show Me A Mountain*, and between book projects worked in advertising.

The Psychology of Terra Nullius in Australian Composition

Carolyn Minchin

> We see them as their first ancestors coming in here illegally, sailing in here with a boat and sticking their flag up. Now, that's when the first divisions began. They say we are creating divisions today. That is when the first division began. They created it, and the problems that followed for the next two hundred and ten years. They created the problems for us and they turn around, the poor mixed up souls, and say we have the problem and they're trying to change it. You know, these poor people haven't dealt with their identity and where their roots are. So they're not at peace with themselves.
>
> —Wadjularbinna (Gungalidda, Gulf of Carpentaria),
> speaking at the Women's Constitutional Convention, January 30, 1998

> While the two groups are apart and walking different paths from one another, the Land is heavy, overlooked and unsung. But when beyond the dawn the people walk together the Land awakens and rejoices, the spirit flows and once more harmony and balance are possible in people.
>
> —Yiri, Aboriginal artist,
> Marai Yammuna (paintings of spirit), Lisarow, New South Wales

As Australians have struggled to establish an identity over the twentieth century, many of our composers—including Margaret Sutherland, Clive Douglas, James Penberthy, George Dreyfus and Peter Sculthorpe—have turned to Aboriginal culture for inspiration. The generation of the forties and fifties was strongly influenced by the 'Jindyworobak' movement, with the ideal of 'joining' Aboriginal and colonial culture.

While this music acknowledges a romanticised version of Aboriginal culture, it ignores the existence of Aboriginal law, cultural survival, traditional boundaries and protocol. I argue that in fact such music reflects the dominant culture of *terra nullius*, the legal fiction that Australia was settled as an unoccupied land. Henry Reynolds points out that once it became clear that the land was occupied and vigorously defended, this legal fiction was maintained by the assessment that no system of law existed amongst the indigenous peoples. What I refer to as the psychology of *terra nullius*—or the absence of Aboriginal people in the minds and popular culture of Australians—became further embedded in the national psyche with the expectation that Aborigines would eventually 'die out'.[1] Despite the fact that the Mabo judgement overturned *terra nullius* in regard to native title, the denial of Aboriginal sovereignty remains a part of the Australian legal system. The cultural ramifications of this are immense, in that Aboriginal culture is widely regarded as a national resource which may be used with impunity, rather than as a complex system of law to which we, the colonisers of this country, are also subject if we wish to engage with Aboriginal people.

The appropriation of Aboriginal culture by Australian composers has been studied in depth by various musicologists, with the main concern generally being the musical success of the appropriation.[2] This paper is not an attempt to assess the musical value of these works in Western terms, or to make moral judgements about the composers who were struggling to relate to Aboriginal culture within the confines of the colonial culture which surrounds us all—for the term 'post-colonial' can hardly be applied to Australia where recognition of Aboriginal people is just beginning to break through the extraordinary historical denial on which this country was founded. Rather, I look at the use of sound in terms of its relationship to Aboriginal law, and I hear these works as a reflection of the selective deafness of the colonial culture, and of our lack of ability to listen to Aboriginal people and to communicate musically with them.

The four works I have chosen to analyse—Alfred Hill's *Poor Fella Me,* John Antill's *Corroboree,* Moya Henderson's *Sacred Site* and Anne Boyd's *Kakan*—all stem from academically trained composers; I believe that the music of the academies bears a particular social and political responsibility in the history of this country. In 1994, Melbourne composer Jane Belfrage spoke of the double-edged nature of the institutionalisation of music at the Centenary celebration of the Melbourne University Conservatorium. Locating herself within its tradition, she interpreted the centenary as being

> at the same time a profound symbol of destruction of the musical traditions of the peoples of the Kulin nations... Musically speaking, the Conservatorium symbolises the usurpation of their soundscapes in the same way that their lands were usurped.[3]

Studying the works of early twentieth-century composers, I began to realise I was listening to the sound remnants of a holocaust in this country, and that unravelling these compositions reveals a history of attempted genocide and protectionism.

The works of Alfred and Mirrie Hill were the predominant representations of Aboriginal music over the first half of the twentieth century. Much of their Aboriginal-styled music was based on recordings brought back from an expedition to Central and Northern Australia by C. P. Mountford. In 1950 Alfred Hill said: 'There is enough material in these recordings to start an entirely Australian school of music, as different in idiom as Vaughan Williams and the English school from anything else. It's a gold mine'.[4]

Alfred Hill's most famous song based on Aboriginal music is entitled 'Poor Fella Me', and was published in 1949 by Chapel.[5] Words were by W. E. Harney and A. P. Elkin. Elkin, an anthropologist at The University of Sydney, was widely regarded at the time as an expert on Aboriginal affairs and was the architect of much of the government policy of the day, including the forced removal of children from their families. The song portrays an Aboriginal elder grieving for the loss of his land. The line 'Poor fellow me, My country it gave me all that I see' is scored in a chromatically descending chant to mimic traditional song, with a minor harmonic backing. Colonial dispossession, massacre and forced removal from land are coyly brushed over in the phrase 'Then came the day, I went away, Now I am grey, Poor fellow me'. 'Now I'm alone...spirit has flown' continues to pronounce the destruction of the culture. The harmonic language changes to a major key for the final section: 'So let me die, Peaceful I lie, Let my shade fly, Poor fellow me'.

The song finishes on a tone of happy, late-Victorian resolution: the passing of the black man has been duly acknowledged, the sun sets on the tribal past. The piece reflects the turn of the century assumption that 'full-blood' Aborigines would die out, and the responsibility of the missions was to 'smooth the dying pillow'.[6] Jenny Munro, of the Sydney Metropolitan Lands Council, identified the song as having likely been taken from a traditional chant of the Gurindji, the group whose extraordinary struggle for land, recorded in the Paul Kelly/Kev Carmody song 'From Little Things Big Things Grow',[7] tells a story of resistance and survival quite different from that penned by Elkin and Hill.

While Hill's work was evidently popular, John Antill's work *Corroboree* is hailed historically as Australia's first major successful composition based on Aboriginal music. The work was championed by ABC conductor Eugene Goossens and received many acclaimed performances, including tours overseas and adaptation as a ballet, over the late nineteen-forties and fifties and on into the mid-nineteen-eighties.[8] It was released as a complete recording by the Sydney Symphony Orchestra in 1977, conducted by John Lanchbery.

The work was inspired by a visit to the Aboriginal settlement at La Perouse, near Botany Bay, when Antill was a boy, where a version of traditional dance and chanting was performed for visitors, presumably as a means of survival for the local community.[9] He was deeply impressed by the music, and in his adult life spent years studying Aboriginal culture via anthropology and sound recordings before drawing on his memories and early sketches to create *Corroboree* in 1936. Written as a tribute to Aboriginal culture, the work was acclaimed by Fred Blanks in the *Sydney Morning Herald* in 1984 as 'a cultural landmark in two fields—the maturity of Australian composition and the recognition of Aboriginal artistic expression'.[10] The work is divided into six movements, each dominated by a particular totem.

> And so the 'corroboree' works up to its climax. First comes the raising of the Totems, then the grand procession of the Emblems. In the mass of howling, writhing bodies, the ballet ends on a scene of chaos and prostration.[11]

This sense of primitive chaos is clearly present in the score, which conveys a sense of mystery and fear far more expressive of the colonial mind than of 'Aboriginal artistic expression'.

The last movement, 'The Morning Star Dance', contains a bullroarer, which in the law of the regions in which it is used, is not an instrument for music and dance, but a call for men's business. This was included in the plot of the 1954 ballet version, when choreographer Beth Dean chose male initiation as the theme of the ballet for a gala performance for the Queen; 'When the bullroarer sounds, the women race away, holding their ears, and the boy knows his worst imaginings will soon be realised as he is thrown high above the men's heads'.[12]

The desecration involved in the inclusion of a bullroarer, and the public representation of secret men's business, can only be properly understood from an Aboriginal perspective. Further sacrilege was enacted at the 1950 Sydney performance, when 'the atmosphere was enhanced with the burning of gum leaves in large urns placed in the foyer',[13] an obvious reference to the traditional smoking ceremony which should only be performed with respect to proper protocol. Given the strict pass laws of the day, it is unlikely that any Aboriginal people were present at any of these performances to complain.[14] It is interesting to note that as a ballet, the work has dropped out of the repertoire in recent years—perhaps the thought of blacking up white dancers became too much even for Australian sensibilities. Despite the best intentions of the composer, the Antill orchestration still stands as a testimony, however, to the incredible distance which was maintained between Aboriginal and colonial cultures and to the lack of acknowledgment of Aboriginal law.

Jenny Munro responded to these works as follows:

> All they do is provide us with a type of cultural death every time they do this, you know. It's insulting to watch our music and our songlines abused in the way that white people think they can. They have no understanding of the high regard that we give to music, they have no understanding of the religious implications of the music, the story that comes across the land in the song...these people can't keep appropriating things that they have no understanding of, saying 'oh, I'm an expert in this area because I can so readily appropriate someone else's cultural material'. It just says a lot to me about how far this society's got to go to be a tolerant one.[15]

In the period since the 1967 referendum, where for the first time Aboriginal people were counted as citizens in their own right, there has been a burgeoning of Aboriginal music, and a number of non-indigenous musicians—such as Paul Kelly, Neil Murray and Sally Dastey of Tiddas—have emerged who have found ways to cross the cultural divide and express our common history musically. Art music, however, remains very much inside the colonial approach to music-making.

Moya Henderson's *Sacred Site* was commissioned to celebrate the anniversary of the Sydney Opera House in 1983. According to the program note,

> It blends white Australian and ancient Aboriginal cultures, and juxtaposes their most distinctive instruments: the organ and the didgeridoo. As the basis of this work Moya Henderson draws a parallel between the sacred sites of the Aborigines and the Opera House seen as the great icon of modern Australia. In conjunction with an organ part strongly echoing Aboriginal music, 'Sacred Site' utilises a recording of a didgeridoo, clapsticks, jaw harp, and emu eggs bounced on piano strings, all played by the composer.[16]

The piece begins with organ, ethereal-sounding didgeridoo, and rather insistent use of clapsticks. It portrays, variously, 'the Australian bush, a jaunty tram ride, a frenzied corroboree...an anguished lament, a mysterious and consolatory passage of 'Dreamtime' music, and a closing toccata of cathartic effect'.[17]

A powerful, dark and somewhat gothic-sounding work, to my ear it represents an uncomfortable clash of two worlds rather than a blending. My reading of this music is that it creates a disturbing sense of incongruity between the two worlds, where the foundations of the Opera House are undermined by an awareness of the bones of the older culture beneath it. Aboriginal culture, as it appears in this work, is subordinate to colonial power; the laws relating to use of the didgeridoo as men's business are conveniently ignored, and yet the memory of the older culture disturbs the comfort of the celebration of the contemporary Opera House.

Mary Coe's book *Windradyne: A Wiradjuri Koorie* contains a rare written account of Wiradjuri music and dance from an Aboriginal perspective during the time of martial law in the mid-eighteen-twenties.

> The women began to beat their possum skin drums and sing in a low rhythmic chant, the men began to dance, looking like skeletons in the light of the fire. Their complicated movements were accompanied by hitting their clubs, boomerangs, spears and shields. The crowd divided into parties and after a chorus of yells they rushed together in close mock battle. One division gave way and was

driven from the fields and chased into the darkness where the sounds of moans and groans and blows represented a massacre.[18]

The image of the 'frenzied corroboree' which recurs insistently in Australian composition may well be a poorly understood reflection of our own violent incursion upon Aboriginal people.

To return to the question of instrumentation, the meanings of clapsticks and didgeridoo in terms of Aboriginal law is not something I could come close to understanding—nor, as an outsider to the culture, is it my place to know or write about these meanings. However, I am aware that their use as musical instruments in the Western context of sound production is often deeply disturbing to people inside this system of law. The didgeridoo is widely recognised as men's business, certainly in the communities I associate with. That it is not recognised as such by many ethnomusicologists is, in my view, a reflection of the problem of Western epistemology. Western knowledge is based on asking questions and observation, and often false answers are obtained this way because both these acts are foreign and disrespectful to Aboriginal ways of transmitting knowledge. Historian Ann McGrath points out: 'Important cultural information was for those worthy, ready or appropriate to receive it'.[19] The problem is deeply embedded in our systems of teaching Aboriginal studies in universities, which is still dominated by non-indigenous academics, while the knowledge of Aboriginal people themselves goes unrecognised.

Anne Boyd's work *Kakan* (1984), scored for alto flute, marimba and piano, is described as being named after an Aboriginal myth concerning the origins of fire, quoted from Jennifer Isaacs book *Australian Dreaming*. Boyd states that '*Kakan* aims to give an impressionistic effect of Aboriginal music and the Australian outback viewed as it were from a distance, so that the subtle character of each blurs into a sense of sameness'.[20] It does not seek to emulate Aboriginal music, apart from the evocation of clapsticks in the third movement.[21]

Mudrooroo approaches the question of the translation of Aboriginal storytelling into myths in *Us Mob*:

> Oral literature, especially the genres termed 'Dreamtime stories', is too often relegated to the status of children's stories and hacked to pieces by collectors and editors who do not pause to think why they existed and what they signified... I would like to suggest that these so-called stories or myths were never primitive attempts to understand the universe, but were narratives which had encoded within them the divine sanction of law, the law itself and a commentary on how the law was to be enforced.[22]

Seen in this light, it is clear that there is a fundamental disrespect involved in the use of such material for composition titles or artistic inspiration.

Christine Morris, an academic in the field of Culture and Media Policy, and member of the Kombumerri and Munaljalai clans, advocates the recognition of traditional Law in dealing with cultural breaches and copyright disputes. Her work gives a new depth to questions of cross-cultural exchange:

> For once you have entered the Law of 'the other' you have taken something from that Law (this includes indigenous people who enter the white world). It is something which is beyond the grasp of your contemporaries, and makes you different from your contemporaries—for you now see the world in a more enhanced way. And this change of mindset can never be given back or erased from your mind. You have to sort out this Law, for it has a price which it will extract from you, whether you acknowledge it or not—*for it is not knowledge, it is a Law*.[23]

Clearly the Law that our forebears sought to extinguish still exists, and is still present for every Aboriginal person who practises it. Until this is recognised, our works as composers will continue to express a colonial mindset. Crucially, it is our ability to listen which holds the key to carrying us across this impasse. Philosopher of sound David Michael Levin talks about lack of listening as fundamental to the problem of colonial domination:

> Do white people really hear what the long-suffering Indians and blacks have to tell them about racial hatreds, colonial exploitation, and bureaucratic indifference? To what extent has our collective deafness itself been responsible for this misery and suffering?[24]

Australian musicologist Thérèse Radic takes Bruce Chatwin's novel *The Songlines* as the basis for her 1991 monograph *Whitening the Songlines*:

> We should understand what it is that we have been given [by our Western heritage] and then, politely, turn our faces to the hinterland. There, our tracks leading back behind us, and only unmarked earth between us, white and black can come face to face in mutual need to create new songlines. Each comes with a score, not to settle, but to sing—to sing up the country.[25]

But the ground between us is not unmarked. It is scarred from battle, with a long and painful history of relationship between the coloniser and the colonised. If we wish to communicate musically with Aboriginal people, then we need to come to terms with the sonic disturbances to both the landscape and cultural activities which have come about through our invasion of this land. And we need to come to terms with Aboriginal Law. For inclusion into this complex, ancient culture is not the prize of colonial victory. It is a privilege to be earned—waited for, listened for.

1. Henry Reynolds, *Aboriginal Sovereignty*, Sydney: Allen & Unwin, 1996, pp. x–xi.
2. See for example Deborah Crisp, 'The influence of Australian Aboriginal music on the music of contemporary composers', *Australian Aboriginal Music*, ed. Jennifer Isaacs, Sydney: Sydney Aboriginal Artists Agency, 1979.
3. Jane Belfrage, 'Applying Native Title to the Practice of Australian Music History: Beyond *Terra Nullius*'. Paper presented at the University of Melbourne Faculty of Music Centennial Conference, June 1995, available on file at the Sounds Australian library. For further reading see Jane Belfrage, *The Great Australian Silence: Knowing, Colonising and Gendering Acoustic Space,* MA Dissertation, La Trobe University, Melbourne, 1993.
4. John Mansfield Thomson, *A Distant Music,* Auckland: Oxford University Press, 1980, p. 225.
5. ibid., p. 207.
6. *Bringing Them Home: Report of the National Inquiry into the Separation of Aboriginal and Torres Strait Islander Children from Their Families*, Commonwealth of Australia, Sydney: Sterling Press, 1997, p. 28. (Available on the internet: www.austlii.edu.au/rsjlibrary/hreoc/stolen/)
7. Kev Carmody and Paul Kelly, Mushroom/White Records, 1991.
8. Beth Dean and Victor Carell, *Gentle Genius; A Life of John Antill*, Sydney: Arkona Press, 1987, p. 12.
9. ibid., p. 15.
10. ibid., p. 189.
11. Vincent Plush, program note to *Corroboree*, 1977. *Corroboree*, Symphonic Ballet by John Antill, ME Records.
12. Dean and Carell, op. cit., p. 132.
13. ibid., p. 109.
14. Movements of Aboriginal people were strictly controlled for most of this century. It is widely held that the pass laws and mission system of New South Wales and Queensland provided the models for the South African pass laws and homelands system.

15. Jenny Munro, Sydney Metropolitan Lands Council. Personal communication, 1997.
16. David Kinsela, program notes to *Organ Aurora,* Sydney Opera House, 1989.
17. ibid.
18. Mary Coe, *Windradyne, A Wiradjuri Koorie,* Canberra: Aboriginal Studies Press, 1989, p. 43.
19. Ann McGrath, ed., *Contested Ground; Australian Aborigines under the British Crown,* Sydney: Allen & Unwin, 1995, p. 381.
20. Program notes, *Strange Attractions,* Sydney Alpha Ensemble Live, ABC Classics, 1997.
21. ibid., Richard Toop.
22. Mudrooroo, *Us Mob: History, Culture, Struggle*, Sydney: Angus & Robertson, 1995, p. 94.
23. Christine Morris, 'Ethnographies and Indigenous Law', paper presented at *Urban Life, Urban Culture: Aboriginal/Indigenous Experiences Conference,* Goolangullia Centre, UWS Macarthur, 1997. My italics.
24. David Michael Levin, *The Listening Self*, London/New York: Routledge, 1989, p. 85.
25. Thérèse Radic, *Whitening The Songlines*, ASME Monograph Series, #1, ed. Martin Comte, 1991, p. 26.

Back to a Sonic Future

John Potts

Cultural hierarchies, including the hierarchy of the senses, are never static. As new media evolve, attaining dominance in their societies over other media, this hierarchy of the senses also changes. This is true in the transition from an oral culture to a literate one, from a literate culture to a mass media society, and from the electronic world of mass media to the more interactive processes of digital multimedia. Different media represent the world by different means, placing emphasis on a particular sense at the expense of others; we can expect that the emerging new media technologies will inflect the human sensorium in a new way—or, perhaps, in a way that comes closer to previous configurations.

In considering new media in this way, we should take literally the term 'multimedia': as a multiplicity of media, an assemblage of different media or versions of media, each with its own different mediation of reality, each with a specific engagement of the senses. Earlier forms of representation, then, have constituted 'multimedia' in their own way: none more so than those used in oral cultures, that is, prior to the technology of writing. The communal participation in ritual and storytelling comprised a highly interactive engagement of all the senses, with sound bearing the most important information. By comparison, reading—which engages only the visual sense—and television—relying on sound and vision—are meagre multimedia experiences. In the contemporary multimedia ensemble, sound is often an under-utilised element; yet the properties of digital audio cry out for a major role in the new media interface.

BACK TO THE TWENTIETH CENTURY

In general terms, the electronic media culture that developed in the twentieth century downplayed the role of sound in the sensory hierarchy. The camera, with its direct descent from technologies of vision developed in the Renaissance, has been at the centre of mass media entertainment; sound has been a secondary consideration, from most practitioners and most theorists alike. This direction of the human sensorium towards the visual is evident in the common vocabulary: 'viewers' of TV and film are 'glued to their screens'.

Exceptions to this tendency are the central role of music in youth culture, with its configuration of hearing and tactility more important than the visual aspect. In recent years, the techniques of digital audio—sampling, manipulating sources—have been foregrounded and celebrated in pop culture. Another consequence of digital audio has been its growing importance to Hollywood blockbusters. As narrative and characters have thinned, surround-sound digital soundtracks have thickened, becoming a key selling-point to lure filmgoers to theatres. But there can be no doubt that the visual sense still sits at the top of the hierarchy.

Is there a new hierarchy cultivated by new media, or even a fuller version of the old one? Which parts of multimedia engage which senses? A quick study of the standard multimedia formats—CD ROMs, websites—seems to confirm McLuhan's adage that old media become the content of new media, the way films became television content. The multimedia ensemble contains text (from print); graphics; still image (photography); moving image (video, film); and sound. Sound is last because that's the way, in most cases, it's treated: the last call on available memory; the last subject to be discussed at international electronic arts events. Also, in many cases, the multimedia experience of sound is limited, laborious, often of poor quality, tokenistic—in short, crude in its application, at least so far.

So what's new in new media, at least new enough to give reasonable grounds for all the fuss surrounding it? Interactivity is the crucial addition. This entails: increased user-choice (more than the choice of flicking between TV or radio channels, because the choice occurs within works); and non-linear usage, including hyper-text links (similar perhaps to flicking randomly around a print encyclopaedia, or even a magazine, with the difference that web links join sites at a continually expanding rate).

If we consider the form of the medium—that is, its technology and interface—we can conclude, ironically, that reading a book is the closest analogue, in many cases, to operating a CD ROM or website. The technology—keyboard, mouse, screen—is familiar office equipment, to be used by an individual.[1] The experience of attending exhibitions of such screen-and-mouse-based works usually entails peering over the shoulder of individual users hunched over their consoles—as if they were poring over a book or magazine. Such an experience, for those other than the fortunate individual user, is, need it be said, far from satisfying.

The defining difference, however, between new media and mass media relates to the level of interactivity. Despite the claims of active audience theories arguing for a participatory TV audience, mass media cultivates a passive audience, 'comfortable and relaxed', with pre-ordained, mostly mediocre content. New media, by contrast, encourages activity, curiosity, interaction with others, or with a developing site of discourse.

What of the multimedia hierarchy of the senses? The visual sense is dominant, multi-represented by graphics, still and moving images, and electronic text (the latter leading a revival of literacy after years of erosion effected by audio-visual media). Tactility is present through mouse, keyboard or other interface technology. As previously mentioned, audio is poorly represented in most multimedia enterprises.

A SOUND FUTURE?

Yet, sound has the potential to broaden the range of multimedia. The imaginative use of audio can heighten the intensity of a work's impact; it can also be deployed to break out of the individuated book-like user structure. This is due to sound's essential characteristics: it fills space; it is inherently communal. These characteristics were most fully expressed in pre-literate cultures: the crucial information was carried by sound in narration, music and ritual; audiences were communal with high interactivity levels (call and response patterns, active participation in dance and rituals). The other senses, including touch and smell, would have played supporting roles, making oral culture performative events multi-sensorial experiences. Extending Ong's notion of a 'secondary orality' constituted by electronic technology, a fuller use of the human sensorium may well emerge in a digital multimedia culture, with sound at the forefront.

There are several examples, in a variety of formats, of the way audio may assert its potential in the future. Austria's Kunstradio has instigated a number of live telematic radio/internet events such as *Family Auer* and *Radio The Ne(x)t Century*. These projects encourage collaborative input, collective authorship and the fusion of mass media (radio) with interactive media. Artists' sites functioning as expanding organisms of collected audio samples also exist, as well as live musical and sound art jamming in virtual space.

Because sound fills space and engages the bodies of all those in that space, digital audio can move interactive media away from individual, vision-based terminals. Bodies triggering sounds in space, in installation works, create a continually shifting soundscape. The sound space is a communal space defined by the sculpted sound. Two contrasting deployments of this approach have been made by the German group Knowbotic Research, and the British group Audiorom. Both groups construct large-scale interactive works, driven by digital audio but engaging other senses in a complementary manner, while allowing communal interface.

The 1996 work by Knowbotic Research, Anonymous Muttering, drew listeners inside a large apparatus ringed by a stroboscopic light system triggered by the digital sound source. This sound could itself be manipulated by participants handling a silicon membrane, and by on-line participants via their PCs: these multiple inputs created an indeterminate authorship of the sound. On-site participants used their tactile sense in contributing to the audio-visual felt wrapped around them; the sheer volume of the electronic noise, with its accompanying visual flash-track, made the experience an intensely physical one.

The sonic ferocity of this work, along with the uncertainty surrounding cause and effect, suggest a Modernist approach to interactivity on the part of Knowbotic Research. The installations by Audiorom, by contrast, are much more playful, with a postmodern incorporation into the interface of the pleasure derived from games. 1998 works such as Trigger Happy and Big Bevelled Button allow multiple users to shape sound by hand gestures and movements. In the case of Trigger Happy, up to eleven participants gather
at a round table, combining to compose a musical track by covering light sensors with their hands. Video images are simultaneously manipulated, but, as their name suggests, Audiorom place the emphasis on sound. Their other works similarly combine sound, vision and touch in continuous interplay, always co-authored by multiple users. The communal aspect of their works is made possible by the articulation of sound: all participants are aware of their contribution to the unfolding work because they occupy the same soundspace. This group interface has an immediate appeal as an alternative to the solitary interface of a screen-based point-and-click terminal.

Of course, it would be naive in the extreme to draw a simple parallel between contemporary digital practice, achieved by banks of technology, and pre-literate culture. The salient point remains, however, that different media engage different senses, with different effects. Although often hidden 'from view' in a predominantly visual culture, sound may well be foregrounded in a new media age.

1. Sean Cubitt makes this point in 'Online Sound and Virtual Architecture', ISEA96 Proceedings, ed. Roetto Michael, Rotterdam: ISEA96 Foundation, pp. 17–21.

Where are we now? Sound in Computer Interactives

Bronwyn Coupe

In discussing and reviewing computer-based interactives, the sound of the work is often ignored or sidelined. While this is not unusual practice in (visual) art debate, it is unfortunate in that it bypasses the most interesting aspect of many works. Sound, rather than just image, is coming to define the space of interactive multimedia. This is quite a turn-around in the Western tradition where the visual has been understood to be dominant in experiencing spatiality. However, especially as the place of interaction within or behind the screen becomes more abstract, the user of an interactive often finds that listening is the best way of orienting in a virtual world.

SEEING: VISUALITY, SPATIALITY AND SUBJECTIVITY

Vision has been the key to understanding, mastering and representing space in the West. The representation of space is also correlated with the production of the subject, the identity that we experience as our self. The psychoanalytic account of the formation of the subject, particularly Lacan's mirror stage, provides an influential account of how the subject is formed and how, mediated through the body, it recognises and operates in space.[1] The infant, who up to this point experiences its body as a fragmentary and poorly bounded field, finds its first identity in the visualisation of itself in the mirror.

It has been useful for film theory that the mirrored space in which the infant sees itself is not a real space, but a virtual space. The mirror stage thus provides an explanation for how visual representations are able to be recognised and psychically entered as real, inhabitable spaces. The impact of cinema then comes from the use of a contiguous relation to extend the material space of the viewer into the screen space.

In the (mis)recognition of the self in the virtual space of the mirror, the subject internalises an imaginary anatomy represented by the surface of the body. This psychical map of the body thus later allows for the possibility of remapping the body—allowing for prosthetic relationships. This is essential for harnessing the sense of touch in multimedia interfaces, for letting us exert our will in the screen world via a mouse. For both the child and the later adult, the visual sense comes to dominate oral, tactile and auditory sensations to produce a unified spatiality.

THE EMBODIED VOICE AND PRESENCE

However, subjectivity is very firmly grounded in at least one particular sound—that of the human voice. While subjectivity is established in the mirror stage through looking, we are also constructed as human through language. Listening and speech are fundamental to both meaning and to any relationship of self to other. The textual 'I', formed through relations with others, is grounded in the materiality of the physical body. We experience ourselves as speaking subjects and cannot help but ascribe the sound of another, even disembodied, human voice to a speaking subject. That is, we happily ascribe the disembodied voice with presence and a nominal space to inhabit.

Hence a particular spatiality, which is a kind of displacement, is created through phonographic, telephonic and radiophonic technologies. This telepresence is a familiar condition of presence bridging two places at one time.[2] The entirely imaginary spaces evoked can be at once intimate, literally in the ear, and distantly elsewhere, in the ether. The audio perspective of a microphone close to a speaking voice brings disembodied presences near, into the same room as us. Conversely, live radio broadcasts that mix different and even moving auditory perspectives produce a notion of 'being there'—
at the place of the event.

The CD ROM *You Don't Know Jack* is an exemplary evocation of this sense of 'being there'. This commercially produced CD ROM game is modelled on quiz shows that were first popularised by radio and which continue as cheaply produced television. *You Don't Know Jack* has a linear introduction which sets up a busy media studio where the crew, presenter and producer are finalising details for the 'show' in the countdown before it 'goes to air'. This aural hub of activity is represented by a range of actors' voices, pacy music and the words 'ON AIR' flashing in time to the countdown. The game progresses in this fashion with the sound of the presenter's voice, musical stings, the competitors' buzzers and an active studio audience constructing the 'live' space. Visual representation is reduced to text that floats, flashes and fades on and off the screen. The game is exciting, and involving. The sound and the haptic response of the player creates the virtual space of this very successful entertainment product.

VIRTUAL COMMUNITIES AND SOCIAL SPACE

You Don't Know Jack is unusual in its almost complete reliance on audio. However, many other multimedia works use voice to create a virtual relationship. The Canadian artist Luc Courchesne has been very successful in constructing imaginal spaces in which we can converse with an other.

Portrait One invites you to have a conversation with a rather mysterious 'woman', Marie. Marie is presented as head and shoulders in a dark box so that 'she' appears to float in the depth of a space. The sophisticated visual presentation still leaves you in no doubt as to the programmed nature of the encounter, but the voice is powerfully engaging. Marie speaks to you and you respond to her performed conversation. A slight pause and jumpcut in the video punctuates the exchange. The conversation may be blunt, flirtatious or philosophical; she may reply with a question or even terminate the conversation and turn away.

In Courchesne's more recent *Hall of Shadows*, four virtual characters talk to you and to each other. The virtual characters Paul, Alain, Jean and Gisele are each projected separately and at life size onto sheets of glass positioned in an inwardly looking circle. The audience is aware of both the individual character they may be interacting with and of the group as a whole. The voice of each of the characters is audible within the circle, and they address each other as well as the audience. In some instances a character may actually leave the screen in front of you to join another. The interplay constitutes a relation amongst members of a virtual community. Unlike everyday experiences of a virtual community, such as mixing in the packed public space of radio, or connecting with a distant friend on the telephone, the 'person' we are talking to is a computer construct.

SOUND, IMAGE AND THE FICTIONAL WORLD

Beyond the space of a relationship, many multimedia works want to take us on a journey or to a particular place. These works, like cinema, have a need to create an imaginary world and often use the same techniques to do so. Sound and image work together and with the sense of touch to produce technologically simulated virtual spaces.

MYST, the best selling and critically acclaimed CD ROM game, is a 'classic' of interactive multimedia in establishing a coherent spatiality or geography within the screen. Highly detailed but static images visually represent the five time zones in which the user can visit an island. The ambient sound constructs the space, scale, weather and atmosphere of these zones and specific spaces within them through a mix of music and looped, ambient sounds. The loops are cunningly constructed and use naturally occurring sound patterns to make continuous soundscapes that are not obviously or irritatingly repeated.

The interactive nature of the work means the movement through the virtual world is determined by the user, at least in so far as up to four options for direction are available. The user can 'cut' to a view of the 'place' in a direction indicated by the cursor. The user, educated in both the narrative of the quest and cinematic connection of screen space, chooses the cut and creates the scene over time.

Dyson has noted that in cinema the relation between image and sound is more 'hyperreal' than 'real'. The soundtrack of a film is the sound corresponding to the image track, not to an actual world.[3] The soundtrack is as manipulated as visual imagery, with elements of voice, music and other noises complementing, underlining or counterpointing the image track. And, in order to avoid confusion, ambient sounds are often reduced to clearly recognisable and locatable sound effects. The soundtrack, then, is a highly artificial representation of sound that corresponds to a visual representation of a space. Point-of-view of camera is often matched with acoustic perspective. This draws attention to the spatial, architectural qualities of audio and the movement of the body as a determinant of sound. *MYST* exploits cinematic methods effectively.

In moving across the island, with the eye directing the hand, the naturalistic sound plays a major role in constructing the 'where' of the screen space and marks the transition from one location to another. Relative volume emphasises the distance to visual features. Synchronised sound effects such as page turning and door opening accompany action. Replacing the entire mix of audio elements tells us we are in a 'new' environment. *MYST* uses standard narrative continuity with matching audio perspective to progress the user through the still frames of its island exteriors and architectural interiors.

By contrast, the audio conventions of documentary are applied to the exquisitely produced three-dimensional computer animation of Jon McCormack's *Turbulence*. McCormack's virtual worlds exemplify the realistic computer created image. Highly detailed image sequences resemble those nature documentaries that use stop motion and macro lenses to reveal, for example, the germination of a seed. McCormack's animations show his own 'type of life that exists only within the abstract pluriverse of computational space'.[4] One sequence shows a plain transformed by the growth of a forest of bizarre animal-plants. The extremely mobile 'camera' moves fluidly across a forest floor, where the wildly developing life springs up in the path of an animated tumbleweed. The 'camera' then climbs up a stem to look at the flower heads bursting open against a stormy sky.

The opulent (if synthesised) orchestral soundtrack enhances the hypernatural spectacle of McCormack's work and supports the myth of the work as a realistic documentation of another world. Low in the mix, sounds of thunder transform the imagery into landscape, even if we imagine that landscape to be microscopically enlarged.

SOUND AS NAVIGATION SIGNAL

Sound used as an alert has a long history—drums, bells and sirens call for attention and action. A similar operation of sound has been incorporated into the training of listeners who have grown up with television. The flow of programming is punctuated by repeated noises, changes in volume and other aural cuing devices that allow viewers to constantly monitor without watching. Music in film has also become a device for signalling that attention is required. Musical motifs become 'cues for reinvest[ing] attention in a spectacular effect...and begin to operate as markers in diegetic space'.[5] Consider the shark leitmotif from *Jaws*.

The use of simple tones or short musical phrases swiftly became obligatory as guides for the operation of personal computer application software. The iconic use of sound to signal actions is an important navigational device in computer-based work. The now ubiquitous 'clicking' sound associated with using a computer mouse is commonly incorporated into the recorded audio of the program. This click, as opposed to the sound mechanically produced by depressing the mouse, accompanies any simple action to communicate that the computer recognises the user has 'done' something. Chords tell us that something is starting, error beeps tell us we have done the wrong thing or are in the wrong place. These conventions contribute to a language of orthodox spatial representations of the screen, an architecture of the interface.

Chris Hales has extended the use of motif sound in interactive works. Hales' works can be described as interactive films where segments of moving images are linked intuitively by colour or symbolic images. In his work *Les Mystères du Chateau de D...* he makes complex and poetic use of portions of a concert by Wagner.[6] *Les Mystères du Chateau de D...* is a loose and suggestive series of linked cinematic scenes that describe an island, a mysterious chateau, and a character who is the owner of both. The user can slowly piece together the narrative, travel the island, enter the chateau and finally reveal the character of the owner. Each sequence consists of one or a number of shots of moving image accompanied by a musical score. Links are formed by images of light. A sequence will repeat until interaction triggers another sequence. The Wagner score, which is also a work based on motifs of light, loops in self-contained parts with the most frantic portion signalling the user when the interactive elements of the image are coming to the screen. Progression through the story is also linked to progression through the movements of the concert.

THE SPACE OFF-SCREEN

The CD ROM by Leon Cmielewski and Josephine Starrs, *User Unfriendly Interface*, uses a mixture of sound and image to alternately pull the user into, and then push them out of, the computer on which it is played. Its makers have chosen an aesthetic that values the obviously synthetic. The overall feel is anti-naturalistic. It presents a series of discontinuous, and often flat, graphical spaces that are linked and fleshed out through synthetic sound and the evocation of real or imaginary social spaces. Featured sounds rely on totally artificial 'conventions' for signification and it contains highly manipulated and unmistakably repeated looped sound.

The opening screen of *User Unfriendly Interface* shows a sneering man's face with the text 'Get Past the Door Bitch to Play'. The soundtrack here is a loop composed of some fairly ominous cello chords, glasses clinking and voices mumbling. The density and perspective of the sound suggests a crowded public space—presumably the 'club' that the text implies we are seeking entry to.

The visual depiction of location usually takes precedence over aurally represented location. If a specific directional sound is heard and not seen, it is assumed to be somewhere other than where we are looking. The sound of a voice playing at the same time that an animated dog occupies the screen is invariably read as a talking dog. However, a barking dog that is not sourced through the image on the screen immediately creates another space, literally 'off-screen'. So, at the start, this interactive sets the user up as outside of the action—the club is situated behind the door that the 'door bitch' is guarding, i.e., on the other side of the screen.

In many other parts of the interactive, the screen is simply a computer screen, a machine we use by entering text or clicking on buttons. It delivers images and sounds as we progress frame by frame by clicking on the 'arrow' button that has become the symbol for the command 'next'. This arrow itself refers to the arrow on a slide projector which also advances the frame. This metaphor demands no further spatial relationship between the 'frames' or connection between the audio grabs.

At one point of *User Unfriendly Interface* a single button is displayed on the screen labelled 'Don't click here'. When the button is clicked (the only option for the user) a man's voice says 'Don't click that'. The button splits into two—both with the same label. The voice of the 'door bitch' is the voice of the computer. However, the timbre of the voice, and the fact that the computer doesn't 'behave' as expected, positions the voice as human. Here a tension is set up— we find ourselves engaged with a computer construct that acts like a virtual person. This pulls us into the 'game', into the space of the screen, which is an imaginary space not necessarily constituted behind the glass of the monitor.

ANIMATED SOUND

The pesky buttons in *User Unfriendly Interface* finally turn into insects which scuttle off the screen, moving with a cute rattling, cheeping sound. The sound suggests the bugs are above the glass on the monitor. The sound is a standard trope of classical animation. The rattling of the legs of the bugs as they run away (possibly created by the drumming of fingers) is familiar from cartoons. While it is patently unreal we recognise it and understand that it is a sound signifying a comic movement of a small animal.

Martine Corompt's intriguing installation *Sorry* also borrows from cartoon sound. To interact with *Sorry* the user punches or stomps on one of a number of cute cartoon characters. To the comic sounds of 'thwack', 'thwonk', 'boing', or 'swoosh', interaction results in 'blows' to the head which progressively damage the character. The injuries sustained are represented in an abstracted, stylised fashion familiar to all comic readers: the Cupid's bow mouth transforming into a 'sad' wriggly line; a criss-cross of bandaids on the forehead; a train-track scar on the cheek and so on.

Finally the character is reduced to black and white, with a cross drawn over the closed eyes—which in 'toon land means death.

Corompt's work, like many animated 'shoot 'em up' games, depends on a sophisticated contextual reading of her basic visual and aural iconography. It requires a strong imaginative investment on the part of the participant. The essential element here is the relationship of apparent control, which is unique to interactive multimedia.

THE SPACE OF METAPHOR

Many artists' multimedia art works tend towards the creation of abstract spaces and use a variety of sound-based techniques to give dimension to spaces that are not necessarily visually or geographically coherent. Take for example *Mnemonic Notations*, an interactive that uses loaded but floating visual and aural fragments in an attempt to draw the user into an internal space. The image content of the work was originally based on thirteen individual paintings by Phillip George. Clicking on any area results in an arbitrary change to part of the image and the triggering of a sound. Elements associated with the spiritual combine in recurring patterns: religious icons such as crosses, runes and mandalas; natural and musical sounds including bells, chimes, chants, drums and didgeridoos, along with revolving wheels and pouring and running water.

Mnemonic Notations utilises the immersive quality of sound. It works a little like guided relaxation—a meditation with machine-assisted visualisation and a randomly generated chant ('Om Om Om on CD ROM'). The screen-space of *Mnemonic Notations* is one of multiple and infinitely dissolving layers confined by the edges of the screen. It is a plot which can be archaeologically investigated by digging down, rather than a spot linked left and right to other off-screen places. Images and sounds emerge out of the work as so many artefacts released from their electronic earth.

ART AND LIFE

In contemporary society, characterised by a plethora of media images and the ascendancy of the screen, new transformations of the subject have taken place. Mechanisms of identificationary scopophilia, developed in the nexus of shopping, mechanical transport and tourism, sustain the reality effect of cinema and television.[7] Sound recording technologies from the phonograph to the CD are capable of bringing the past into the present (including the very voices of the dead). The telephone allows us to be simultaneously in two time zones while conversing with a friend who is both spatially and temporally elsewhere/elsewhen to us. Everyday practices, such as walking out of a cold, dark night into the warm, bright day of a tropically-themed shopping mall, involve virtual experiences in real space, destabilising spatiality. Computers allow for the creation of simulations—screen spaces which are entirely unrelated to real spaces though often indistinguishable from them. All of these experiences blur the boundaries between real and virtual space and undermine expectations that a space will necessarily make geographic sense.

If a space doesn't have to conform to visually coherent locations then the possibilities for representing it increase. Interactive multimedia uses and has expanded the repertoire of techniques for representing space that it inherited from previous art and media. Commercial programs like *You Don't know Jack* and *MYST* make excellent use of the familiar tropes of radio and narrative cinema respectively. Interactive art works, such as Chris Hales' attenuated narratives, also connect screen spaces through the sometimes perverse logic of film continuity.

Alternately, works may present an arbitrary computer architecture traversed by buttons. Sound is important in giving some sense of spatial coherence. It can be used to gain our attention, convey instructions for use, or motivate the desire to 'look' in a particular direction. Audio may be used to employ a dramatic persona as tour guide or engage the subject in a narrative or social space. Even in less naturalistically conceived electronic spaces, iconic sound may provide the major cues to 'where' the user is in the work as well as indicating progress, stasis, or return in relation to the various sites within it.

The most tenuous links of visual metaphor may serve when audio is describing a path. Unstable and shifting spaces can be enjoyed when the listener is immersed in an aural environment. Sound is essential in delivering us to a zone elsewhere, somewhere between the 'inside' of the computer and the 'outside' of the user.

Which makes it a greater shame when the audio of multimedia works are poorly served in exhibition. The ability of users to enter the space of a work can be severely impeded when the sound is restricted to a single pair of tinny headphones or confused in a wash of competing sounds coming from nearby installations. Without the help of aural navigation, users can end up unable to answer the question: 'where are we now?'.

1. For an account of Lacan's notion of the mirror stage, see Elizabeth Grosz, *Space, time and perversion: the politics of bodies*, St Leonards: Allen & Unwin, 1995.
2. See Frances Dyson, 'Circuits of the Voice: From Cosmology to Telephony', in *Essays in Sound*, Sydney: Contemporary Sound Arts, 1992.
3. Frances Dyson, 'When Is the Ear Pierced? The Clashes of Sound, Technology and Cyberculture', in *Immersed in Technology: Art in Virtual Environments*, eds. M. A. Moser and W. D. MacLeod, Cambridge, Massachusetts: Massachusetts Institute of Technology, 1996.
4. Jon McCormack, 'Artist's Statement', in *Sequinz*, Australia: Artlink Australia in association with the National Association for the Visual Arts, 1996.
5. Sean Cubitt, 'Video Installation and the Neo-Classical Soundtrack', in *Essays in Sound #3: Diffractions*, Sydney: Contemporary Sound Arts, 1996.
6. Chris Hales, 'The Twelve Loveliest Things I Know', guest presentation to *The Language of Interactivity* conference, Sydney: The Australian Film Commission with Radiant Productions and CLiCK Interactive Magazine (c), http://www.click.com.au/afc.
7. For a detailed account, see Anne Friedberg, *Window Shopping: Cinema and the Postmodern*, Berkeley: University of California Press, 1993.

A Shock in the Ear: Re-Sounding the Body, Mapping the Space of Shock Aesthetics[1]

Norie Neumark

INTRODUCTION: THE EVENT AND ITS AFTERMATH

Shock is an event, but it is also an aftermath; it is a figure, and it is a formal device. Through sound these can overlap and reverberate so that the figure or metaphor of shock moves through the time and space after the event and into the body of the listener. My aim in my radiophonic work *Shock* was to map the aesthetics and kinaesthetics of the shock experience, historically, physically and psychically: from modernism to late or post modernism; from the attack of event to the decay of after-shock;[2] from the metaphor into the corporeal body. In this essay I will broadly consider that piece and the new media art project which reworked it as a CD ROM-based installation and CD ROM, *Shock in the Ear*.

To understand shock as an experience, it is useful to delineate its spatial character. The space of shock, whether physical, psychic and/or artistic, is the corporeal body, from its surface to its cells and nerves to its organised sensations and perceptions—the very space that sound pre-eminently can map. The space is also the space of time, the etymology of space being just that, the space of time. It is momentary and forever—intensive and extensive, stretching after, into, and before the very event; a moment of intensities and energies—a hot/cold moment—the cold sensation of dislocation and the warm melting of an everyday numbness. The shock experience rips the body out of its accustomed time and space and in so doing leaves its traces in the body's memory.

The event of shock is an opening—onto the body surface and into the tissues, cells and viscera; it opens the body itself to a heightened awareness and reorganised perceptions and sensations. To map this space is not a documentary realist exercise but rather an aesthetic gesture. For, as Susan Buck-Morss argues about aesthetics, the 'original field of aesthetics is not art but reality—corporeal, material nature'.[3]

> 'Aesthetics is born as a discourse of the body.' It is a form of cognition, achieved through taste, touch, hearing seeing smell—the whole corporeal sensorium.[4]

RADIOPHONIC SPACE AND CORPOREALITY

How to map this strange space of mixed sensations—and, beyond mapping, to experience it? Through radio and CD ROM sound—as media that literally enter the body and the imagination. Before turning to shock aesthetics and the new media, I need to linger in radiophonic space. I am concerned with radiophonic space, not only because it was important for the sound work that preceded the new media art work, but also because the CD ROM itself does not use movies or even still visuals of the people whose voices you hear—so many of the issues about 'disembodiment' are actually the same. Further, basing the new media art work on the radio piece and a radiophonic type of space meant that my approach to voice and subjectivity was very different from the approach in *cyberspatial* works.

The first thing I listen to in radiophonic space is corporeality, and the second, relatedly, is a space of memory. I realise that to say that radio/sound enters the body—and, further, is about the corporeal space of the body—contradicts a prevailing mapping of radio as a dead space of disembodied voices. However, as a radiomaker and listener, these metaphors have never fully addressed my experience or practice. What does disembodied mean? After all, any voice leaves a body to be heard by another; any speaking voice moves outside the speaker's body into that of the other, so the radiophonic voice is similar here. What is noticeably different, though, is that the listeners cannot see the body—so perhaps this notion of embodiment yet again amounts to a privileging of vision, since the loss of body in radio seems to be particularly the loss of *sight* of the body. As I said, in my new media art work, too, the literal image of the body is not there.

It seems to me that a more useful metaphor for understanding and working with both media is that of *dislocation* rather than of disembodiment. Listening to the radio voice, like the CD ROM voice, we are in a different physical space and time to that of the speaker. This, in a way, makes radiophony eminently available for the aesthetic shock effect of dislocation because it is dislocation which so aptly expresses the way in which different spaces and times seem to pass into each other during shock, and it is dislocation which has become an important part of shock aesthetics. In shock, and in shock aesthetics, we can sense a dislocated space and expanded time during which, or after which, new sensations and perceptions can flood in.

Of course there is also the important matter of the electronic mediation and reproduction and their reconfiguring of 'the body'. While mediation and reproduction obviously have effects on subjectivity, desire, and meaning, this is a complex question which I cannot go into here. However, I would suggest that to focus on *electronic* mediation tends to mask other mediations which are always already present, such as the way that the voice is mediated culturally and historically. Culture, sex, gender and history colour the voice, contour its performative capacities, leave imprints in its shape and depth—that is, they mediate 'the' voice, its accent, intonation, timbre, cadence, rhythm. And these mediations and their performances matter and are just as powerful as—and indeed underpin—the electronic effect.

In a way, like the 'expressive face' analysed by Buck-Morss, the voice is written by the body. It is marked by 'accents of intensity' and expresses a 'material awareness'. And it is a site of excess, running 'out of the control of conscious will or intellection'.[5] So it was not the disembodiment of the voice in radiophony and new media art that I heard and wanted to work with, but rather the opposite. These media invite me to explore and perform the voice because of the traces of embodiment they carry—which are all the clearer, in some sense, by not being obscured by as-if self-evident signs of vision. Indeed, in the CD ROM, I played with this even more, using different performances of the same text.

The second thing I want to say in relation to radiophonic space is that it is also a space of memory—the embodiment of memory, of memory in the body. At a more literal level, sounds can both carry memory and stimulate memory. In my interviews with people who had experienced shock, what emerged was not just that certain sounds were reminders that evoked the very experience which was mapped in their memory aurally as well as visually, but that the experience itself could have a certain aural quality. Further, radiophonic space is often *formally* constructed, through repetition, as a memory space: we hear something and then hear it again, but this time inflected by what has occurred in between. So it not only sounds different each time, but we *remember* the first hearing and (re)hear it too, anew—a sort of conscious/unconscious echo.

Sound itself has a lot in common with memory, combining evanescence, transience and chance with a materiality; i.e., sound is material and physical and sensual but it changes over time. Sound exists *in* time rather than *through* time; it is about duration rather than durability. It is also spatially as well as temporally contingent. So there is an *experiential*, sensual quality of both memory and sound that radio art plays on and with.[6]

SHOCK AESTHETICS AND RADIOPHONIC SPACE: MONTAGE, CUT-UP, THE CUT.

To turn from the general character of radiophonic space to its particular relation to the aesthetics of shock, I would like to look first at the importance of shock aesthetics, both as a practice and theory, in early modernism. For Walter Benjamin, shock was to do with historical changes in sensory perceptions. Shock became available to art because it was already available in everyday life, where time and space were being radically altered with industrial and technological development: life in the city as an unending series of shocks, acting like physical blows, a jostling crowd. Following life, film, too, provided a series of shocks; shifts in camera position, discontinuity of time and space, in and out, tempo, scale.[7] According to Benjamin,

> technology has subjected the human sensorium to a complex kind of training. There came a day when a new and urgent need for stimuli was met by the film. In a film, perception in the form of shocks was established as a formal principle. That which determines the rhythm of production on a conveyor belt is the basis of the rhythm of reception in the film.[8]

Shock aesthetics were thus, for Benjamin, particularly associated with film and montage. Shock-montage collided dissimilar fragments to shock an audience into a different mode of seeing, sensory perception, understanding, insight. Or it brought into focus unnoticed details of the familiar to break through the frozen deadness of everyday perception. It violently disrupted and re-ordered the physical world and its meanings, speaking to the psyche more than to rationality. Furthermore, it became a form of 'training' into new 'habits' of perception, a new 'psycho-physical complex'.[9]

In conventional radio, like film, montage has now been reduced to seamless editing, cut down to size, cut—the cut in conventional radio which tries to be imperceptible and intangible. This cut removes time and duration from our experience. It excises the
abnormal and carves out the normal and desirable. It habituates our ears and it constructs the boundaries of morality. Besides the editing of unwanted time and speech, there is the removal of offensive and unseemly body hair—I mean body bits and traces, matter, material. It is a technique of removing corporeality from the voice, the ums and erhs, the clicks, the breaths. However, I would not say that this results in a disembodied voice, even in its most extreme, everyday use, so much as an anorexic, anaesthetised, Ajaxed, Hollywood body. In particular, it removes the *alterity*, the otherness, which slaps us in the ear with an unassimilable difference.[10] It gives us not no-bodies but endless variation/repetition of the same old bodies.

Anaesthesia and surgery. The cut. The so-called 'cosmetic' procedure generally operates as entirely 'normal' and unquestioned, and is certainly itself normalising: it is aimed to produce a supposedly universally desired 'clean' sound—as if this were not an aesthetic/political/historical decision, but a technical, professional one. However, if you trace the historical role of obsession with cleanliness in constructing the emerging bourgeois subject—cleanliness as a way of distinguishing the bourgeois self from the dirty, messy, noisy, carnally excessive, sexually out-of-control working class and colonials—you may begin to wonder about the pleasures and urgency and political effects of the 'clean' sound.

The history of the obsession with cleanliness—an obsession which is very relevant to the dominant digital aesthetic—is explored by Peter Stallybrass and Allon White in *The Politics and Poetics of Transgression*.[11] They argue that the (English) bourgeois subject continually defined and redefined itself through the exclusion of what it marked out as low, as dirty, repulsive, noisy, contaminating; and that this very act of exclusion was constitutive of its identity. In this process, as the bourgeoisie constructed its 'respectable' and conventional body by withdrawing itself from the popular, it constructed the popular as object, *grotesque Otherness*, an otherness quite different from the subjectivity of alterity. In other words, according to Stallybrass and White, the bourgeoisie—in its manners and morality, through to its body, bearing, tastes and *sounds*—encoded a subliminal elitism and self-referentiality which constituted its historical being and subjectivity (while objectifying others). I would argue that this is the historical basis for the aesthetics of conventional radio which hears differences in voices and bodily sounds as unpleasant, resonant with unwanted class, race and sexual life.[12] To be excised—subject to surgical operations which require and produce an anaesthetic effect on the listener.

The same gesture that wields the surgical knife of the cosmetic edit on the radio voice, severing the nerves and cutting away the excess which traces alterity, also drains the life-blood out of montage in radiophonic space. This same gesture further operates to endlessly repeat anaesthetising hits of the moment of shock. So the shock aesthetics of an Eisenstein are very different from the shock anaesthetics we have come to know through Hollywood or most public and state broadcasting. Here shock has become stuck in a groove—locked at the moment of *impact*, looping, repeating, never moving on to the after-time and space.

Through its 'extraordinariness' and 'abnormality', shock anaesthetics underscores and reaffirms existing 'normal' perceptions rather than dislocating and disrupting them.[13] We stare at, thrilled and horrified (or turn away from, in a conditioned response, chilled and horrified) the same old wounds, rather than map their etchings through the body. We are shown the blood and the wound, the impact, the melodrama; we hear the screams and the crash. We have sensationalism—but do we have sensation? An extreme of sensationalism that underpins rather than undermines an extreme of rationalism, a refusal to feel, experience and *remember* intensities and energies. Are our senses altered or just jagged? Are we re-habituating ourselves to the late-modern world, or feeding a habit born in earlier modernism? the degrading repetition of drill,[14] not the experiential repetition of memory space? arming the body's defences against the very thing it 'represents'?

This would seem to be the anaesthetising workings of shock, the hard encrustation or reversal of shock aesthetics which Susan Buck-Morss analyses. It is a de-sensitising and re-education, a re-habituating of the body surface and viscera, a making dull and stupid of the body of the listener/viewer. It works either by numbing or by flooding the senses. 'Its goal is to numb the organism, to deaden the senses, to repress memory: the cognitive system of synaesthetics has become, rather, one of anaesthetics'.[15] This shock anaesthetics is characterised by a 'simultaneity of overstimulation and numbness...whereby aesthetics changes from a cognitive mode of being "in touch" with reality to a way of blocking out reality'. In this situation of 'crisis in perception', the aesthetic need is 'no longer a question of educating the crude ear to hear music, but of giving it back hearing'. So in order to 'shock' now we would need to melt the numbed perceptions of shock as scream and crash, to break through the anaesthetised perceptions of impact-fixation and experience the before/after moments.

SHOCK: A RADIOPHONIC AND DIGITAL RE-SOUNDING OF SHOCK AND SHOCK AESTHETICS.

In this context, I wanted to produce a radiophonic work about shock, from shock aesthetics to culture shock to electric shock. My interest was first sparked when I suffered shock myself after a car accident. It had a profound effect which I found difficult to convey, as I had no visible wounds and gashes. Perhaps it addled my brain but the connections between these various articulations of 'shock' became electrically clear. I wanted to explore the bodily space of shock which, as I have said, I believe to be the landscape of radio/sound.

Before starting, I thought that my formal use of shock would be montage but in fact, perhaps not surprisingly, this surfaced mainly in the historical section. Did I plan this or just remember it this way in the mix? I was struck in the ear by the voices of the story tellers. Story is not, or not just, the retelling of the event, but it is where the senses speak; it re-sounds with the voice, the voice of the experience. As Benjamin remarked:

> It is not the object of the story to convey a happening *per se*, which is the purpose of information; rather, it embeds it in the life of the storyteller in order to pass it on as experience to those listening. It thus bears the mark of the storyteller much as the earthen vessel bears the marks of the potter's hand.[16]

Listening to the embodiment of the shock experience—following the *durée* of shock in the storytellers' bodies through their voices, sometimes distant, sometimes frozen, often dislocated even now as they returned to that memory space—the after-moment of shock came to be what I wanted to express and have listeners experience. And the bodily etching of the memory was the space I wanted to sound out. So it was a mapping of bodily shock space experience rather than early modernist shock aesthetics or recent Hollywood that I sought. I worked with sounds that traced that space. Not so much the crash of glass at impact, but the sweeping of shards that mark and mark out a fragmented space. Not the scream, but the sucking-in of breath, deep into the body, along the nerve lines, into the tissues.

The question of shock and postmodernism became all the sharper when I moved into the computer realm of CD ROM. In one way, as I have discussed, shock aesthetics seem outmoded, out of their time, overdone or underdone. Yet the late-modernist era does re-sound with the early modernist obsession with technology as producing a new sense of time and space. The concern with speed (from theorists like Virilio to everyday users) recalls the Futurists' sense that speed was changing daily life, subjectivity, and art.

For me, one of the crucial questions was how to translate a sound work designed for radio to an interactive form. How to retrain the ear and the hand in the computer era in the way that cinema retrained the eye in the era of early modernism—to answer the need, thrown up by computer culture, to undo the already moribund habits of hand/eye/ear control? A question made all the more complex by the general failure so far of CD ROMs to have developed *genres* and forms in the way that radio art does, giving you a space, artistic and historical to work within, a body of works.

Whereas the bodily space that is so readily mapped by radio and radiophonic space can be so corporeal, what of cyberspace? The paltry presence of sound here is well known. And there is also (consequently) the common lament that the space it traces, deep cyberspace, is non-corporeal. Even 'shocking' cyberart seems often to *represent* the body rather than remember or evoke it, to display wounds rather than etch along their kinaesthetic, physical, memory pathways. This may be explained by the aesthetics that still seem techno-centred—driven by the machine possibilities rather than trying to decentre and de-fetishise them. Remembering Benjamin, his interest in technology was through film rather than being fixated on the camera *per se*—or the car or the airplane or the spectacle of war, the latter articulation of technology, politics and art being the one that animated the Fascists.[17]

Before finishing this essay with a discussion of my attempts to deal with all this, I want to say a bit more about the deep hole of cyberspace that my new media art works attempted to avoid—to play instead in the space around its edges, to map virtual space onto theatrical and corporeal space rather than plunge into cyberspace. I need to allude to the genealogy of cyberspace itself, to explain its lack of appeal to me, which is partly, and relatedly, at an aesthetic level.

Once upon a time there was *space*, the distant but alluring location of 'progress' and the 'future'. Space-age space was a nodal point, a construct of scientific space-age discourse as well as geographic/imperialist discourses. Like 'nature', in her time, it was figured as 'out there', to be observed and measured. Its enticing, defining characteristic was being unknown and therefore producing the desire to be known, explored, conquered. Culturally, in terms of desires and metaphors, this space-age space took over from nature and the colonies as the 'elsewhere'.

But in this once-upon-a-time story the future arrived and it began to look not awesome but awful as space filled up with space junk—a deadly oxymoronic development that threatened all the desire and fascination. So now the desire and fascination have regrouped their forces, transformed themselves and headed inwards (it's a convenient aspect of space that it can extend inwards as well as out). And so we have cyberspace—an inner space inviting entry and conquest. This cyberspace is the progeny not just of engineering/scientific space-age discourse but earlier philosophical discourses of space as well—ranging from the romantic, religious, metaphysical, to the phenomenological—which construct an apocalyptic, vertiginous, awesome, disorienting space. And, not surprisingly, the bodies that roam this space—the virtual bodies—are armoured by technology in the very way the futurists dreamed of: 'with a virtual body, one that can endure the shock of modernity without pain'.[18] And often with an aesthetics, an anaesthetics to match.

There can, however, be a different mapping of computer space, an elsewhere, which like radiophonic space can have room for alterity and aesthetics, rather than this anaesthetics. Buck-Morss:

> If we use this technological apparatus as an aid to sensory comprehension of the external world, rather than as a phantasmagoric, or narcissistic, escape from it, we see something very different.[19]

In this sense, or for these senses, I prefer such an elsewhere, a space where performance and corporeality replace or at least re-animate and sensitise the 'interactivity' of CD ROMland. My CD ROM project, *Shock in the Ear*, involved a two stage process, beginning with a physicalisation, through an installation, and moving on to a stand-alone CD ROM. The CD ROM was not intended to be a documentation space, documenting and re-presenting in an anaemic way the installation space, but rather to construct a virtual space inspired by the installation as an *experience* of movement in a physical theatrical space.

My concern was for the audience/user to experience the after-shock, the time of decay. The audience/user experiences this both in an indirect way through hearing stories from those who have been through it and directly through being themselves dislocated from their usual bearings in interactive cyberspace. Their accustomed location in computer space is one where they are emotionally and psychically immersed but physically and sensually distant as they carry out a quest or play a game, voyage into the future (into the machine) space or descend into a fact-laden encyclopaedic 'past' space. In *Shock in the Ear* they find themselves somewhere else.

The invitation is to an intense experience through their senses, especially hearing. The sorts of movements and perceptions that are provoked are disorienting, disrupting—'shocking'—to CD ROM aesthetics and kinaesthetics. The CD ROM-based installation created and operated in a theatrical space with various experience points/stations. By moving around the space and engaging with different objects (such as a telephone), people accessed a different aspect, sense and sensation of shock kinaesthetics and aesthetics. They also 'triggered' and experienced a different aural perspective as well as shifting and disrupting the flow of the sound material. The interactions did not just bring in new 'set' sounds but actually altered the sounds and their perspectives.

Sound in both versions of *Shock in the Ear* (installation and stand-alone CD ROM) includes voice (both performers and interviews), music, and sounds, all of which work in ways which are non-conventional (for CD ROMs). Music counterpoints as well as provides emotive/sensual effect and a sense of dis/location in time and space. Sounds evoke space and sensual responses more than operate as literal effects. Performance works as texture and rhythm as much as for content. Visuals are integral but not dominant (they were produced in response to the sound) and their character is intense and textural rather than realist and 3D. They invited a new kinaesthetic approach to interactive sound.

The aim is to go into the body of the audience/user, and sound is crucial here. It does not work as background or filler, or via short repeating loops, but physically to provide the shifts that are part of a shock experience. In short, *Shock in the Ear* is a sound-centred sensual and disruptive experience for the audience/user.

CONCLUSION

To conclude, briefly, let me just say that to translate a project from radiophonic space to CD ROMland is neither easy nor self-evident. Perhaps it is not a matter of translation or even transportation, but of re-sounding—seeking in both media the corporeal or experiential space which was once delineated by shock aesthetics and is still perhaps open to their impact.

I would like to thank Susan Dermody, Ross Gibson, Robyn Ravlich and Noel Sanders for their discussions about shock aesthetics. And the participants of the radiophonic work Shock *for their experiences/analyses.* Shock *is distributed, in an abridged form, in the U.S. by Helen Thorington and Regina Beyer, New Radio and Performing Arts, Inc., 120 Tysen Street, Staten Island, NY 10300; and in Australia by* The Listening Room, *ABC FM Radio, which commissioned the work.* Shock in the Ear, *the installation, was assisted by the Commonwealth Government through the Australia Council, its arts funding and advisory body. The CD ROM* was developed with the assistance of the Australian Film Commission. The assistance of the University of Technology, Sydney is also gratefully acknowledged. The CD ROM is available through n.neumark@uts.edu.au

1. This is an updated version of a paper delivered at SoundCulture 96 in San Francisco.
2. Shock was analysed in terms of 'attack and decay' by Noel Sanders, speaking in *Shock*, produced by Norie Neumark for *The Listening Room*, ABC Classic FM, March, 1995.
3. Susan Buck-Morss, 'Aesthetics and Anaesthetics: Walter Benjamin's Artwork Essay Reconsidered', in *New Formations*, No. 20, Summer 1993, p. 125.
4. Terry Eagelton, quoted by Buck-Morss, idem.
5. Buck-Morss, op. cit., p. 130, my italics. I would extend her argument to say that the 'expressive face' (as she describes it on p. 129) reflects, leaves its traces on the voice which emerges from it.
6. And not only is there an experiential quality to memory, there is a memory quality to experience. The space of experience is also the space of memory, as Benjamin argues, following Bergson. Walter Benjamin, *Charles Baudelaire: A Lyric Poet in the Era of High Capitalism,* trans. Harry Zohn, London: Verso, 1983, pp. 110–113.
7. See the discussion of Benjamin in Peter Wollen, 'Cinema/Americanism/The Robot', in *New Formations*, No. 8, Summer 1989, p. 21.
8. Benjamin, op. cit., p. 132.
9. Wollen, op. cit., p. 22; Bill Nichols, 'The Work of Art in the Age of Cybernetic Systems', in *Screen*, Vol. 29, No. 1, Winter 1988, pp. 24–26; Andreas Huyssen, *After the Great Divide: Modernism, Mass Culture, Postmodernism*, Bloomington: Indiana University Press, 1986, p. 14.
10. The concept of 'alterity' is developed by Emmanuel Levinas. Emmanuel Levinas, *Collected Philosophical Papers*, trans. Alphonso Lingis, Dordrecht: Martinus Nijhoff, 1987, pp. 39–44, xv–xvii. See also Elizabeth Grosz, 'The "People of the Book": Representation and Alterity in Emmanuel Levinas', in *Art and Text*, 26, 1987, pp. 32–34.
11. Peter Stallybrass and Allon White, *The Politics and Poetics of Transgression*, London: Methuen, 1986. See especially Chapter 3 and Conclusion.
12. And not just radio. Much the same holds for film sound, where the body is either not recorded or edited out—except, significantly, in the Horror genre!
13. Huyssen, op. cit., p. 15.
14. Benjamin, op. cit., p. 133.
15. Buck-Morss, op. cit., pp. 131–134.
16. Benjamin, op. cit., p. 113.
17. Alice Yaeger Kaplan, *Reproductions of Banality: Fascism, Literature, and French Intellectual Life*, Minneapolis: University of Minnesota Press, 1986, pp. 26–30. On Fascism, voice and sound see also pp. xix, 3–13.
18. Buck-Morss, op. cit., p. 139.
19. ibid., p. 142.

Metamorphoses

Nigel Helyer

One of the most striking features of an insect collection is its absolute silence, but a silence which conceals an inaudible resonance which issues from the conjunction of Macleay's obsessive and encyclopaedic collecting, and the general process of colonial 'clearing'.

By this I refer to both a literal, cultural and metaphorical silencing of the locale in terms of ecology and human culture—a silencing effected by the superimposition of alternative physical and cultural structures and by the substitution of plant and animal species.

From this perspective, the garden, more than the architectural structure of the house itself, constitutes the fundamental assault on the history and biological identity of the site—the domesticated corollary of such an assault is the Macleay insect collection.

It seems paradoxical that genuine interest in Natural History which drove the taxonomic obsessions nineteenth-century science to establish such a thoroughgoing system of species identification was so thoroughly modelled on the property relations of Industrial Capitalism: the exotic and the unfathomable *bought* to heel and delivered into servitude.

The act of collecting was an act which froze life-forms into miniature catacombs; the act of planting an English garden demanded the elimination of a much more varied and fragile ecology.

Such acts of substitution are a common trope throughout colonial histories, and usually go hand in hand with efforts to record that which is being disrupted. Ironically, such forms of ethnography or ethno-biology are a sure signal of real trouble for the object of study!

What might survive in the interstices of the relationship between the well- meaning interest of the insect collector and the environmental carnage that his act unintentionally signalled?

How can we re-imagine the possibility of re-establishing a natural voice within this idea of collecting and within the house itself?

A significant element in the colonial process of overlay is always carried within the apparently benign forms of cultural expression. That this house was musicalised and held a significant library provide a key counterpoint to the concept of re-sounding the original insect voice which is the task of the work *Metamorphoses*.

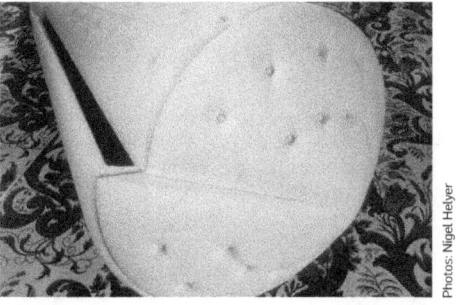

Photos: Nigel Helyer

Metamorphoses *(1997) was part of the* Artists in the House *exhibition series conceived and curated by Michael Goldberg, and was designed to provide a platform for the critique of the representations of history. The exhibition was held at Elizabeth Bay House, Sydney, which was designed in 1835 by John Verge for Alexander Macleay, a renowned entomologist, and his wife and six intelligent and lively daughters. It has been a 'museum' since 1977 as part of the Historic Houses trust and houses Macleay's insect collection.*

On Humming
Paul Thom

> Hum, sb.1. [Cogn. w. HUM v.1] 1. A low continuous sound made by a bee, etc., also by a spinning top, machinery in motion, etc. (Dist. from a buzz by not being sibilant.)
>
> —*Oxford English Dictionary*

The *Oxford English Dictionary* definition of the noun 'hum' might do for some purposes, but it's hardly suitable as a foundation for a systematic study of humming, a bombology. Such a study would need to be based on a clear account of what a hum is—an account that the dictionary doesn't provide. Having identified a hum as a type of sound, the dictionary goes on to do two things that will seem inessential, and therefore superfluous, to the bombologist.

First among these extras are the dictionary's *illustrations* of hummers—bees, tops and machinery. The bombologist, being a student of essences, may well regard these illustrations as gratuitous—salient not so much to the nature of the hum as to its distribution among living species, not so much to pure as to applied bombology. Says the bombologist: a hum may come from a bee; that is as it may be, surely a matter of contingency, not in the nature of the bee. The bombologist is right; even worse for the *OED*, the *actual* sound of the bee is arguably not a hum.

The *OED* also draws a distinction between hums and buzzes. The latter, we are told, are sibilant, produced in the way 'ss' or 'zz' is produced. Hums, by implication, are not produced in that way (but presumably are voiced labial sounds). But the original definition didn't tell us this. It only told us what a hum sounds like (its phenomenology), not how it is made (its aetiology). The bombologist will want to know whether a hum is defined by its sound, or its method of production, or a combination of these. It makes a difference, because some things have the phenomenology of the hum (phen-hum-enology) while lacking its aetiology. Let's resolve this by declaring that for bombological purposes a hum is understood to be a kind of sound. Whether the sounds made by particular beings, or the sounds produced by particular methods, are hums—these questions can be settled only by *listening*.

Humming is a kind of action, not a kind of sound. Aetiology has to be taken into account in determining whether a particular action is a case of humming. Humming is done with closed lips. So hums can be produced by beings for whom humming is not a possibility—
the humming top for instance. A hum's causal history does not include closed lips when it is the hum of a top. Equally, humming can be done otherwise than by producing a hum. For the sound made by humming is not necessarily low. The top singer in The Ink Spots, or the soloist in

Bachianas Brasileiras No. 5, hums without producing a hum. The hum is characteristically, but not invariably, produced by humming.

Two kinds of humming can be distinguished. When a hum possesses a melodic contour we have melodic humming, i.e. singing with closed lips. The production of a non-musical sound with closed lips we may term hm-ing. A familiar example is *Frontline's* Mike Moore's ambiguous non-verbal comment at the end of an interview.

Before embarking on a discussion of these kinds of humming, let's look briefly at hum(ming)s in nature.

> The hummingbird family, the Trochilidae, consists of 319 species grouped into 121 genera. This family of birds is restricted in distribution to the New World, where it ranges from Tierra del Fuego to Alaska and reaches its greatest abundance in the northern Andes.[1]

Birds of the family *Trochilidae* are known as humming birds because they make a humming sound by the rapid vibration of their wings. But humming birds do not hum. The humming sound they make appears to be merely a by-product of their wing-action, not itself serving any particular function.

And what of bees? Do they hum? Or do they buzz?

> The familiar buzzing of a flying bee is largely due to the passage of air through the thoracic spiracles.[2]

If the familiar sound of the bee is produced by the passage of air through small vents in the thorax then even if it sounds like—and therefore is—a hum, its *production* has more in common with buzzing than with humming. Unlike the hum-making of the humming bird, that of the bee has been thought, since the time of Aristotle, to be functional.

> At early dawn they make no noise, until some one particular bee makes a buzzing noise two or three times and thereby awakes the rest; hereupon they all fly in a body to work. By and by they return and at first are noisy; then the noise gradually decreases, until at last some one bee flies round about, making a buzzing noise, and apparently calling on the others to go to sleep; then all of a sudden there is silence.[3]

Various explanations have been offered for the hum-making of the 'trumpeter' bee.

> It has often been reported that fanning of the wings, accompanied by a characteristic buzzing sound, is initiated early each morning by one particular bumblebee in a colony. This has led to a fanciful story regarding the presence in the bumblebee community of a so-called 'trumpeter' or 'drummer' bee. The first reference to this behaviour was made in the late seventeenth century by the Dutch painter, J. Goedart (1700). Goedart described the activity of a bee which allegedly mounted the top of the comb at about seven o'clock each morning and for about fifteen minutes sounded a reveille, calling the other nest inhabitants to begin work... Later, von Buttel-Reepen (1903, 1907), LiePattersen (1906), Wagner (1907), Bischoff (1927), and many others, concluded that the behaviour of the trumpeter was merely connected with a need to ventilate the nest, and that the bee either fanned to expel accumulated carbon dioxide or disagreeable odours, or to lower nest temperature or humidity. Most writers have since treated the ventilation theory as a plausible explanation for the actions of the trumpeter, but Haas (1961) has produced a new interpretation. He rejects the ventilation theory since, in his experience with both large and small colonies, the trumpeter phenomenon can occur at low nest temperatures and also when air within the nest is fresh. Further,

he has shown that the action of the trumpeter occurs in response to light entering the nest; he believes it to be a 'light-alarm', which is connected with colony defence in that it alerts the guard bees.[4]

Besides the trumpeter phenomenon, bees have been observed making intermittent buzzes or hums during the so-called waggling dance, and this behaviour too has been hypothesised to be functional.

> The sound during the waggling movement consists of a series of short bursts of tone...that are produced by the flight muscles in the thorax. In one second there is a series of about thirty bursts; being about 250 Hertz (cycles per second), the frequency of vibration of these short individual tones conforms with the wingbeat frequency (Esch, 1961, 1964; Wenner, 1962). The bees that are in contact with the dancer...can perceive the sound and the waggling movements with their delicate sense of touch and thus are informed how far they need to fly.[5]

We turn now to humming proper, and to a brief characterisation of its first species, hm-ing. Hm-ing possesses a large expressive range, being capable of expressing mental states including hesitation, embarrassment, affectation, approbation, mild surprise, dissent, or dissatisfaction, depending on its precise phonetic contour and the context. Phonetically, hm-ing is quite distinct from ahem-ing, hmpf-ing, oo-ing, tsk-ing etc., but functionally there are considerable overlaps.

In the case of melodic humming, we should distinguish the mimetic from the non-mimetic variety: I have in mind a notion of mimesis as the imitation of an object by reproducing some of its features. (Mimesis should, of course, be relativised to particular features of a particular object since what is mimetic of one object, or of one set of features, may not be mimetic of another.) Distinguishable from mimesis is substitution: one object(ive) is substituted for another when that other is for some reason blocked and the former adopted in its stead as an approximation to it. Substitution, like mimesis, is an important feature of many types of humming.

Let's begin with non-mimetic melodic humming, and with the simplest case of melody—a monotone. Schizophrenic patients who suffer auditory hallucinations (hearing voices) report being able to control the voices by softly humming a monotone.

> Softly humming a single note significantly reduced auditory hallucinations (voices).[6]

The reason why humming works is unknown. Is it a *distraction* from the inner voices? Is it merely something that uses up *effort* that would otherwise be expended on the production or perception of the voices? Does it *over-ride* the voices? Green and Kinsbourne express doubts about all these explanations. The way we explain the humming is going to depend on the way we explain the auditory hallucination. If the latter is thought of as associated with subvocalisation that involves minute laryngeal movements, then it makes sense to think of the humming as a substitution for those movements.

Let's move to cases where someone hums a tune. It's reasonable in such cases to ask why there are no words. There may never have been any words of course, and the hummer may have just made the tune up; this is creative humming, and there is no suggestion here of either mimesis or substitution.

Another possibility is that, though there are words to the tune, the hummer has forgotten them. In the latter case humming is a substitution for singing the words. The original objective (singing the words) is blocked because of the singer's memory-lapse. Humming substitutes for singing the words: it is the closest the singer can get to the original objective under the circumstances. It is also mimetic of some of the singing's features (its purely musical features), but not of others; in particular, the humming is not mimetic of the currently blocked aspect of the singing, namely its lyrics.

Another kind of case occurs when a 'backing' group change from singing to humming in order to highlight the soloist's part. This too is a case of substitution, if we suppose open-mouthed singing is excluded because of their 'backing' role. And again, their humming isn't mimetic of the contextually salient feature of open-mouthed singing, even if it is mimetic of other features.

Non-mimetic melodic humming is written in to several pieces of music. When, in Mozart's *Die Zauberflöte,* Papageno's mouth is padlocked he hums the phrase:

Humming is again a substitution here, not (in salient respects) a mimesis. Open-mouthed singing is denied to Papageno, so all he can manage under the circumstances is to hum.

A celebrated example of composed humming is the Humming Chorus in Puccini's *Madama Butterfly*.

This chorus, directed to be sung offstage and *a bocca chiusa*, signifies the standing still of time as Butterfly waits up through the night for Pinkerton's return.

The Humming Chorus has been read as a nocturne (it is sung at night-time), and as a lullaby (the baby *does* go to sleep).[7] It has the stillness of a nocturne or a lullaby; but an eeriness underlies its serenity. This eeriness is picked up by another reading, according to which the off-stage chorus is imagined as sung by a kind of all-knowing Greek chorus whose wordlessness signifies the unspeakableness of the tragedy they know is about to break. The humming would then be a substitution for a full utterance, but of course not mimetic of one.

In the David Belasco play on which Puccini's opera is based, the scene corresponding to the Humming Chorus is done as a fifteen-minute actionless and wordless lighting change, separating the play's two halves. An off-stage Humming Chorus in an opera is an effective operatic analogue to an extended dumb-show in a play. What better way to show the standing still of time than by excluding the most vital elements in the theatre, action and language? In opera, the exclusion of language is only emphasised by having an off-stage wordless chorus. The humming here is a substitution, by the composer, of wordless for worded singing, the latter being excluded as too eventful for a scene in which time is supposed to stand still. It is not, in the relevant respect, mimetic of such singing.

We now turn to mimetic melodic humming; and let's begin by considering a case that combines aspects of the mimetic and the non-mimetic varieties. It's the case of Saul the obsessive hummer.[8] Saul himself saw his humming as a substitution for other vocal activity.

> Saul described himself as an obsessive hummer. He spent much of the time he was not with others humming to himself. At times he would hum aloud, while at other times he would 'hum in his mind'. This humming activity never interfered with his work and was seen instead as an activity that served to fill his free time when he had nothing else to do. 'Nothing else to do' referred only to activities that would compete with the humming in that they required talking or listening; thus, periods of time when he would be walking, traveling, eating, or writing were not at all exempt from humming.[9]

His hummed melodies were original to him. On the surface this humming would not seem to be mimetic of anything. Yet in Saul's mind it was indeed mimetic. What was significant to him about his melodies was their rise and fall, and these fluctuations of pitch seemed to him to be mimetic of some imagined drama whose only salient features were 'going up' and 'coming down'.

Two varieties of mimetic melodic humming can be distinguished, depending on whether the object imitated is absent or present.[10] Let's now suppose the object is absent. And let's begin again with the simplest possible melody, a monotone.

> Now then, the Udgitha is *Om*; *Om* is the Udgitha. And so, verily, the Udgitha is yonder sun, and it is *Om*, for it is continually sounding '*Om*'.[11]

The *Om* of the *Upanishads* is mimetic of an absent object. If *Om* is thought of as the sound made by the sun, then the chanting of this syllable is mimetic; and if it is also thought of as somehow *being* the sun, then its chanting is a substitution—one charged with magical powers of transformation.[12]

A more mundane example is provided by the familiar experience of music-lovers who find themselves humming or otherwise singing snatches of a recently heard piece of music. The music-lover *recalls* the absent melody by humming it.

There are instances in musical performance where humming is mimetic of something absent. In a passage towards the end of the Catalogue Aria in Mozart's *Don Giovanni* Leporello sings:

> *Purché porti la gonnella*   If she wears a petticoat,
> *voi sapete chel che fa!*   you know what he does!

On the word *fa* he repeats a figure three times.

The last repeat, in some performances, is hummed (though humming is not specified in the score). In Gregory Yurisich's 1993 recorded performance, with Roger Norrington conducting,[13] the humming is phrased in such a way as to imply a lewd gesture signifying what the petticoat-wearers 'do'.

This implied gesture seems addressed to the audience in the theatre; certainly Donna Elvira is not going to be sympathetic to it. It displays Leporello's envy of his master's successes with the ladies, and enlists a similar envy from the audience. Notice that the object of mimesis is here an action, not a sound. We can also take the humming as a substitution for that gesture, if we suppose that the gesture has been blocked, for reasons of propriety.[14]

There's another way in which the humming in the Catalogue Aria can be seen as mimetic of an absent object. This arises from the fact that the hummed phrase is a *repeat* and as such is a mimesis of its original. The Humming Chorus is also a reprise—a reprise of the scene in which Sharpless reads out Pinkerton's letter to Butterfly. The theme that is later to be hummed is here played by the violins accompanying Pinkerton's quoted words.

SHARPLESS:	'E forse Butterfly non mi rammenta più.'	'And perhaps Butterfly doesn't remember me any more.'
BUTTERFLY:	No lo rammento? —Suzuki, dillo tu. 'Non mi rammenta più.'	Doesn't remember him? —Suzuki, tell him. 'Doesn't remember me any more.'
SHARPLESS:	Pazienza! 'Se mi vuol bene ancor, se m'aspetta...'	Have patience. 'If she still loves me, if she expects me...'
BUTTERFLY:	Oh, le dolci parole! Tu, benedetta!	Oh, sweet words, bless you!
SHARPLESS:	'A voi mi raccomando perchè vogliate con circospezione prepararla...'	'I beg you, gently prepare her...'
BUTTERFLY:	Ritorna...	'He's coming back.'
SHARPLESS:	'...Al colpo.'	'...for the blow.'

Rich in intra-textual ironies, Puccini's score first states the to-be-reprised theme as a setting of the words 'He doesn't remember me'. With another irony, Butterfly's first response on seeing the letter is to take it from Sharpless and kiss it, singing *'Sulla bocca'* ('On my mouth'); the reprise of the 'letter' theme in the Humming Chorus is marked *'a bocca chiusa'*. As a reprise, the Humming Chorus is mimetic of the earlier theme; and the same applies to the humming in Villa-Lobos' *Bachianas Brasileiras No. 5*.

Villa-Lobos admired Puccini's Humming Chorus. In a review of a performance of *Madama Butterfly* he wrote 'the audience likes the chorus's improvised singing with the mouth shut'.[15] And the contour of the Aria in his *Bachianas Brasileiras No. 5* is similar to that of the Humming Chorus, at least at the beginning.

The Aria is in A-B-A form. Both A sections are wordless, the B section being a setting of a poem by Ruth Corrêa. According to Stokowski,[16] the poem evokes 'a mood of moonlight and slowly drifting clouds'. Other critics are more effusive.

> A wordless soprano muses lyrically around a long-breathed modinha-type melody, declaims forcefully on the almost painful beauty of a tropical twilight and then returns to semi-conscious contemplation.[17]

At its return, the soprano hums the main theme. The first phrase is hushed and serene, and the humming seems to express an innerness and a contented recollection.[18] But the second phrase suddenly soars, and here the humming seems to express a more intense inner joy. Humming can indeed be expressive of innerness. This expressiveness works by mimesis: the melody is 'hidden' within the mouth just as the inner self is hidden within the body. Humming is here over-determined, as both reprise and expression.

If the object of mimesis is present, it may or may not be a sound produced by the hummer. Suppose the latter. We sometimes hum along with music that we hear. And perhaps music would not be music (certainly not *musica humana*) if it could not be hummed along with, or more generally humanly shadowed in sound or movement. That is what we are dealing with here—a type of shadowing (and hence a type of mimesis). Other types of shadowing include dancing to the music, foot-tapping, finger-snapping, and generally grooving-along. Humming-along with the performer can be seen as a case of substitution, if we cast the listener as a performer *manqué*. But the listener who hums along can also be seen as an interpreter[19] who (in the manner of all interpreters) constructs a larger whole into which the interpreted object fits as a part, a part which—in this instance—is mimetic of the whole.

Finally, let's suppose that the object of mimesis is a sound actually produced by the hummer. Humming-along with one's own performance is a specially interesting case. It shares with other behaviours such as tongue-biting, teeth-grinding, grimacing, and certain types of grunting, the aspect of shadowing the musical performance. (Normally one is not conscious of these behaviours.) Besides its aspect of shadowing, this type of humming-along can (in different respects) be brought under the concept of substitution. One might conjecture the following construction.

Melodic humming-along—as well as behaviours from the GR-group (grinding, grimacing, grunting, etc.)—is a type of *behavioural integration*, whereby the agent makes a single whole of behaviours originating in diverse bodily systems. Contrasted with such integration are uncoordinated behaviour (in which unrelated behaviours issue from different bodily systems), but also abstracted behaviour (in which whole bodily systems seem to be suppressed into inaction—as with the 'stiff' musician whose only movements are those immediately demanded for the production of the music). This integration involves a shadowing—and thus a mimesis—of the central behaviour. But the circumstances of performance dictate that such shadowing not be too overt, as that would be considered offensive. (In performance as in everyday life there are standards of acceptability for shadowing: beyond a certain point, gesticulation accompanying speech is intolerable, and similarly with self-shadowing behaviours by performers.) So the shadowing has to be suppressed, at least to some extent. And this suppression turns mimesis into substitution.

Glenn Gould is a case in point. He hums loud and often in his recordings. His 1969 recording of the Bach Prelude in G minor from Book 1 of the *Well Tempered Clavier* establishes an aesthetic of contemplation, partly through the pianist's use of humming.[20] (Again humming expresses innerness.)

Gould's humming is spasmodic and off-key. He is particularly poor at managing the rising sixth in the prelude's theme and sometimes descends a third rather than risking the leap of a sixth. So unmusical is his humming that one is tempted to think it comes from another person who has somehow wandered into the studio. In any event, our construction of humming-along-with-one's-own-performance applies, except that Gould sometimes forgets to make the substitution that performatory propriety requires, and allows himself to break out in open singing.

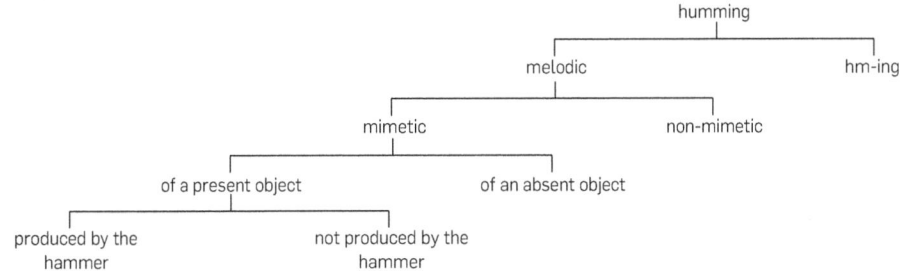

We have distinguished five species of humming, three involving mimesis; and we have encountered mimetic humming under the guises of expression, substitution, reprise, recall and shadowing. Hm.[21]

1. Karen A. Grant and Verne Grant, *Hummingbirds and their Flowers*, New York: Columbia University Press, 1968, p. 5.
2. D. V. Alford, *Bumblebees*, London: Davis-Poynter, 1975, p. 26.
3. Aristotle, *History of Animals*, Book 9, Chapter 40, 627a 25–28.
4. D. V. Alford, *Bumblebees*, op. cit., pp. 65–66.
5. Karl von Frisch, *Bees: their vision, chemical senses and language,* Ithaca: Cornell University Press, 1950; revised edition, 1971, p. 93f.
6. Michael Foster Green and Marcel Kinsbourne, 'Auditory hallucinations in schizophrenia—does humming help?', in *Biological Psychiatry*, 25, 1989, pp. 633–635.
7. Both readings are in Mosco Carner, *Puccini: a critical biography* 2nd ed., Duckworth, 1974, p. 396.
8. Samuel Juni, 'From the analysis of an obsessive hummer: theoretical and clinical implications', in *The Psychoanalytic Review*, 74, 1987, pp. 63–81; Samuel Juni and Bernard Katz, 'Theoretical and transferential debacles in analysis of humming; or, play it again Sam', in *The Psychoanalytic Review*, 77, 1990, pp. 235–244.

9. Samuel Juni, 'From the analysis of an obsessive hummer: theoretical and clinical implications', op. cit. p. 63.
10. It's unclear which variety Saul's humming belongs to.
11. *Chandogya Upanishad* 1.5.1. In *The Thirteen Principal Upanishads translated from the Sanskrit by Robert Ernest Hume*, Oxford: Oxford University Press, 1877, 2nd ed., 1937.
12. According to *Chandogya Upanishad* 1.4.4 it was by taking refuge in this sound that the gods became immortal.
13. EMI Classics, CDS 7 54859 2.
14. But compare Rolando Panerai's 1985 recording, with Rafael Kubelik conducting (RCA Classics, 7 4321-25284-2). Here the humming section seems more linguistic than gestural, expressing re-affirmation as if to say 'Yes, you heard me right'. Panerai's Leporello addresses himself to Donna Elvira, grimly confirming her view about the Don's behaviour. In Nicolai Ghiaurov's 1963 recording, conducted by Edward Downes (Belart 461 319-2), the humming is again linguistic rather than gestural, in this case suggesting that Leporello reflects on the Don's conquests with the thought 'How delicious!'.
15. L. M. Peppercorn, *Villa-Lobos*, Aldershot: Scolar Press, 1992, p. 64.
16. Liner notes to RCA Victor GD87831, Canteloube, *Songs of the Auvergne*, Villa-Lobos, *Bachianas Brasileiras No. 5*, Rachmaninoff, *Vocalise*—Anna Moffo, American Symphony Orchestra, Stokowski.
17. Simon Wright, *Villa-Lobos*, Oxford: Oxford University Press, 1992, p. 93.
18. Different types of innerness are found in the 'backing' humming of The Ink Spots, and the group backing Elvis Presley's version of 'Are You Lonesome Tonight'. Where the former can be blissful, the latter is wistful.
19. cf. Paul Thom, *For An Audience: a philosophy of the performing arts*, Philadelphia: Temple University Press, 1993, p. 196ff.
20. Sony SM2K 52603. By contrast, the vocal sounds Rudolph Serkin makes while playing the piano belong predominantly to the GR-group. They are reminiscent of the grunts of a tradesman plying his tools; they convey a sense of effort and of the involuntary ejaculations that accompany it. Serkin, when making these sounds, is no hummer.
21. Thanks to Kathleen Higgins for help with this project.

The Birds: The Triumph of Noise over Music[1]

Philip Brophy

ESTABLISHING SUBJECTIVE SOUND THROUGH ELECTRONIC TREATMENT

The opening sequence of *The Birds* serves as an entry to the non-musical, solely sonic domain of its soundtrack. High contrast visual abstractions of birds move across the frame, half-photographed, half-animated (Ub Iwerks, veteran cartoon director/producer, served as special photographic consultant on the film). Simultaneously, squeals and squawks attack the viewer's ears. These sounds have a birdlike quality about them, but it soon becomes apparent that the sounds are more alien than avian, more artificial than natural.

Produced by electronic music composers Remmi Gassman and Oskar Sala, the processing of the sounds utilises many stylistic traits established in the field of *musique concrète*. In this case, taped sounds of birds are altered in pitch, tone, duration and shape, then mixed into a multi-layered cacophony of screeches and flapping sounds in sync with the animated silhouettes of bird shapes. Having been cued to read a mimetic representation of 'birds' with the title *The Birds* we are propelled into experiencing a sensation of 'birdness'.

Does this difference between 'birds' and 'birdness' signify anything? In a story about birds whose behaviour defies ornithological precepts, the very concept of a bird comes into question. Thematically we can accept the birds' presence and actions as symbolic of an inexplicable terror, but only if a collapse of everything that defines a bird is visually and aurally apparent on the screen. We should hear and see birds while acknowledging that they are not like normal birds. The key solution provided by *The Birds* lies in presenting the birds from both objective and subjective viewpoints—identifying 'birds' (photographed/depicted/wrangled) versus sensing 'birdness' (animated/suggested/matted).

The title sequence is a distillation of the subjective impression of birds—of being caught by a flock of them as they swoop around you, pushing envelopes of air against your eardrums and flitting within your peripheral vision. You are not watching birds: you are being attacked by them. You are more aware of their presence—sonically and visually—than you are able to objectively hear and see them. Other factors come into play. In formal terms, there is a title sequence devoid of music and hence the emotional cues and stylistic cards conventionally employed to situate the viewer/auditor in a specific frame of mind. Technically, the frequencies of the sounds are harsh, sharply resonant and reverberant with clashing tones. No sweet trills and warbling melodies here (in part due to atonal composer Bernard Herrman operating as sound consultant for the film). Combined, the subjective viewpoint of attacking birds, the unconventional title sequence and the technical aural aspects work psychologically on the viewer/auditor to unnerve and unsettle: *these birds are after you.*

The title sequence fades to black as the bird noises reach a reverberant crescendo. This cross-fades with an unstylised sound of massed birds as the image of a flock circling over San Francisco's business district fades up on the screen. Car traffic and tram bells mingle with the birds in long shot, replacing the abstract/stylised/artificial sonorum of the title sequence with what one presumes will be the representational/realistic/natural make-up of the depicted fiction. Yet this simple cross-fade—this sleight-of-hand in the momentary black pause—perversely forecasts the collapse between objective illustration and subjective impression which will shape the film. At points the sounds of birds will be the symbolic conveyance of invisible terror; at moments their silence will mark their deathly presence. In short, all modes of audio-visual depiction exude dread as they carry the potential to be diametrically inverted. This is nothing short of a 'terror of illusion'—a specifically audio-visual illusion—central to *The Birds'* psychological horror.

PSYCHOLOGICAL AND SCOPIC MANIPULATION THROUGH NOISE AND SILENCE

The psycho-acoustic manipulations which characterise the narrative purpose of *The Birds* come into play immediately. The first scene set in the bird shop is a remarkably long one where slight plot and character information is imparted. Melanie (Tippi Hedren) orders a bird; she meets and plays a game on Mitch (Rod Taylor); he uncovers her pose as a saleslady; after a heated exchange she decides to buy him the birds he was after. This in itself appears to be a studied and drawn-out tease typical of director Alfred Hitchcock's approach: submitting trivial information to distract you from the true mechanisms of the story. Throughout this scene—one of many banal, domestic exchanges—a wall of bird noise blankets all dialogue, forcing the audience to selectively mask out the high frequency information of bird noise from the mid-range tones of the actors' voices. While one can readily perform this complex perceptual manoeuvre in reality, many films will selectively reduce the volume of background noise to privilege on-screen dialogue. The fact that *The Birds* refrains from this indicates that the noise level is deliberately maintained to build auditory stress within the viewer as a means of destabilisation. You are subtly yet fundamentally being introduced to the unsettled psychological state which will eventually befall all the characters of the film as they are terrorised by bird noise.

In contrast, the ensuing scene deploys unnerving passages of silence. When Melanie delivers the lovebirds to Mitch's apartment, the scene's exposition is disarming in its lack of spatio-temporal ellipses. Melanie enters the building, catches a lift and walks down a corridor, closely observed by a resident. A strange voyeuristic effect is distilled through his silent, pernicious monitoring of her every move as she carries the lovebirds in a cage. As he scrutinises her, we move with him in a tracking vacuum through the hotel's interior spaces. The plot remains immobile and silent, progressing nowhere and telling nothing. Just as bird noise has already been subliminally ear-marked to trigger anxiety whenever it recurs, so is extended silence now signposted as an aural appendage to telescoped viewpoints. A lack of sound will mean someone (or something) is watching.

Who/what is watching Melanie when she drives up to Bodago Bay in a string of plotless wide-shots? Hard cuts between loud and soft engine drones transpose us into the car, the bird cage, then back out to the undulating landscape. Perversely, we have been granted visual information (she rides in the car with the birds) only to be split away from it, thereby inducing a desire to be thrust back into the action. Like all voyeuristic vantage points—the hill top, the keyhole, the binocular glasses—frustration wells from seeing but not being there. Phenomenologically, one experiences sight at the expense of sound. Melanie's drive to Bodega Bay is an archetypal cinematic reconstruction of this crucial aspect of the voyeuristic effect, one that binds us, the film itself, and the birds. Only all three are capable of such telescoped viewpoints, and all three are perversely ensnared by *The Birds'* empty silence.

When Melanie hires a boat to cross the lake and surprise Mitch's sister with the lovebirds, a highly choreographed staging of voyeurism unfolds which formally melds audio-visual symmetry with spatio-temporal symmetry. Corresponding shifts in fields of vision and acoustic space occur as Melanie carries out her task:

1. motor noise	loud volume	Melanie sees Mitch
2. rowing/lapping water	soft volume	Melanie spies on Mitch
3. silence in house	absent volume	Neither sees the other
4. rowing/lapping water	soft volume	Mitch sees Melanie
5. motor noise	loud volume	Mitch spies on Melanie

With droll expectancy, the scene plays itself out, threading our voyeuristic pleasure into the game played by Melanie and Mitch. The major narrative purpose, though, is to rupture this dome of interaction with an inexplicable and unexpected force: the peck on Melanie's head by the seagull, sonically generated as a percussive incision into the sustained passages of sound and silence. This is the third governing effect of sound in *The Birds*—the sudden interruption of any low-key ambience with a violent pneumonic event. Once quiet builds, noise will collapse it.

The voyeuristic configuration of us/the film/the birds peaks at the climactic gas station explosion, helplessly witnessed by Melanie, Mitch and other diner patrons. The scene's perspective shifts with the advent of the explosion, transporting us to an aerial perspective—literally, a bird's-eye view. The microscopic melee below—a mere scar of flame and smoke on the landscape—emits a thin trail of screams, lifted and dispersed by the hollow sound of upward spiralling winds. Who is watching here? On cue to the questioning of this shot, floating birds creep into the frame from all sides, gently hovering and letting loose occasional uninterested squawks. These visually matted birds are those same birds from the title sequence. Again, they terrorise the frame they transgress: they artificially inhabit the illusionary realm of the cine-photo frame, and their cry conveys a similar disjuncture between normal and aberrant sound effects. Again, we are made complicit with the actions of the birds by enjoying an avian sensory perspective of telescopic vision and displaced, wind-strewn acoustics. Again, the poetics of an emptied sound field haunted only by slight wind instil the scene with pregnant yet unspecified dread.

ABSENT MUSIC AND THE AMORALISING OF DRAMA

There is much that is pregnant in *The Birds* due to a distribution of radical imbalances between the audio and image tracks. The highest degree of this is to be found in the absence of music. Save for a piano, a radio and some children singing (which all occur within the visual diegesis) there is not a single note of orchestrated music sounded during the entire film.

The soundtrack of *The Birds* is literally that: voices, sounds, atmospheres. No violins. It rejects all musical coding traditionally employed to inform us of how we should care/think/feel/project at any point in the film. The absence of music is a specific 'sound of silence' which greatly enhances *The Birds'* peculiarly perverse dramatic tone. Picture one of many silent Melanies locked into a seductive, gravitational sway with her birds as she navigates the winding road up to Bodega Bay. She resembles an entranced conductor orchestrating her droning car engine. No purpose. No reason. No emotion. No music.

Many such absences of music accrue, fusing Melanie's smooth composure, impassive face and impeccable style. In fact she becomes more 'inhuman' as the film progresses. It is hard to watch the scene where she plants the bird cage in Mitch's bay house without admiring how a woman in a fur coat and stilettos can row a boat across a lake and perform such a cunning task without messing a hair on her head. While the scene's aural dynamics refuse to choreograph changes in dramatic degree of the actions depicted, the absence of music instills this protracted scene with a haunting quality that brings into sharp relief every action, movement and gesture. Far from being cued to respond to changes in the tempo of the drama, we project dramatic build-up onto this empty soundtrack, willing her to get away with her trick and to get caught at the same time. Music cues conventionally moralise such incidents, enjoining us to empathise with a character. Remove the music and you effectively 'amoralise' the drama, displacing the viewer/auditor from controlled streams of empathy.

The birds themselves narratively thrive in non-musical silence. Rather than embodying or transmitting a superimposed musical logic which tags them as monstrous, malicious and maniacal, they speak in their own voice to their own kind. Their language is foreign, alien, avian, excluding us from the inner mechanisms of their motives and operations. In sync with a decultured slant on nature, these birds simply have no concept of the human. Accordingly, human musical codes do not apply. No *Jaws*-style orchestral throbbing portentously trumpets their arrival. As in their attack on the children playing Blind Man's Bluff at a birthday party, the birds orchestrate and enact a cacophony upon their arrival. Balloons burst, children scream, feathers flutter and beaks peck, all played against a continual delivery of bird squawks. In the absence of music, all sound becomes terror; gulls and children scream and screech alike.

A peculiar type of silencing occurs when Melanie waits for Cathy: a silencing through music. Most of the following incidents are covered by an irritating canon voiced by the lackadaisical tones of children singing in school:

1. Melanie enters the school room without disturbing the children's singing;
2. still directing the children's singing, X silently mouths a directive for Melanie to wait outside;
3. Melanie waits outside silently, listening to the children singing;
4. crows gather just as silently while the children continue singing;
5. Melanie observes a single crow's trajectory and sees it take its place with the massed crows in the children's playground;
6. Melanie opens her mouth in a silent scream;
7. Melanie moves back inside the school room and confers with X without the children hearing;
8. X tells the students to leave school as quietly as possible—without voicing the danger which could cause the children to panic and thereby disturb the crows.

This scene is no mere set-piece based on undercutting 'mood'. Tension is painstakingly created by juxtaposing the deadly delicacy of the situation with the harsh ringing of children's voices. Devoid of non-diegetic orchestral tones to put us on edge, the innate and unpolished humanness of their voices serves to offer them as fodder for the abject inhumanity of the silent crows. It is even as if they are ignorantly conjuring up more birds with each refrain. This silencing 'through' music is yet another return of the terror of illusion: the innocence of the singing child—long exploited as a penultimate trigger of humanness in audio-visual history—is here a retainer of fate more than a container of pathos.

FORMAL ORCHESTRATION OF BIRD NOISE

The title '*The Birds*' is simultaneously blunt and unspecific. It could be referring to any birds, some birds, all birds. It could indicate a group anywhere between two to two million. It could be aligned to species, family, genus. It eventually means every bird, and every bird potentially belongs to the dreadful mass of *The Birds*. As forecast by the *musique concrète* overture during the title/credit sequence, bird noise is circulated and distributed throughout the film following this logic. The highly orchestrated soundtrack expands and contracts with the flux between dense sound of massed birds and sonically isolated elements of single bird movement.

When the sparrows first invade Mitch's house, their entrance is announced by the insignificant tweeting of a single sparrow who seems to have aimlessly flown down the chimney. Melanie—by now accustomed to reading the ominous signs of silence and emptied sound fields—prompts Mitch, her voice instantly swallowed up in a wall of bird noise. This 'wall of noise' is more of a three-dimensional space which terrorises the empty domestic domain. As we move from shot to shot, not the slightest difference in acoustic perspective can be monitored. The mass screeching sounds the same in the centre of the room, on the floor, in any corner. The sheer density and volume of the multiplied frequencies becomes a total noise from which there is no escape; there is no alcove or pocket the noise does not occupy. Further, the sparrows occupy the totality of the audio-visual spectrum. Once again matted as an abstracted planar field movement over the actors, flailing their arms and cowering in terror, the sound of the birds obliterates all other space in the soundtrack.

A similar yet distinct orchestration is played out following a prolonged build-up as the school children try to sneak away from the crows. If one shuts one's eyes, one can distinctly hear aural layering reminiscent of the symphonic approach taken in many *musique concrète* compositions:

1. an envelope of low frequency rumble as the children break into a run
2. an envelope of low frequency rumble as the crows take flight
3. a sustained sheet of crow noise, highly reverberated and dispersed as they maintain a hovering cloud of terror over the frantically running children
4. within this sheet of crow noise, punctuated screams, wing flaps and distorted squalls
5. a dampening of the volume of this sheet of noise, reduced and muffled as Melanie and some children take refuge in a car with the windows wound up.

Just as the sparrows earlier are treated as a mass of sound, so too is the sheet of crow noise unbroken and undiluted. Rather than thinning out into individual crow sounds, the complete aural texture fades down in combined volume, suggesting that the existence of the birds is predicated on mass and not individual birds. A more complex and multi-layered sequence develops in the petrol station attack. It features a linear dramatic shape, starting low and building to a climax, then dying down. The aural dynamics of each of these components are crucial to the controlled deployment of the drama, enhancing and marking its rhythm, as well as temporising it by matching dramatic events with the dynamic shape of aural events:

1. sound of running petrol; series of near/far loud/soft perspectives; clear, light treble layer
2. shouts of people in diner; series of near/far loud/soft perspectives; mid-range density of sounds overlapping
3. sound of burning petrol; close-up puff and sustained noise; low gradual rumble
4. screams of diner patrons; muted/sharp choral effects; arrhythmic group of harsh mid-range incidents
5. scream of Melanie; solo event; clear and high-pitched
6. explosion; loud, single sonic event; sharp, quick envelope of noise followed by low sustained rumble
7. bird's-eye view; faint screams; hollow wind, distant rumble, occasional close-up bird calls.

Prior to Melanie becoming involved as a witness to the petrol station explosion, a key scene condenses the film's approaches to aural orchestration. When she is trapped inside the telephone booth, moments, incidents, spaces and occurrences are swirled and concatenated, with emphasis on perspectival shifts in the sounds of bird noise, human screams, running feet, gushing water, a car crash, smashing glass, and so on. The telephone booth's confines serve as a sensory-realignment chamber. Melanie sees everything through the glass, free from physical contact; she hears less but experiences increased physical sensation. Chaos surrounds her on all sides while water, gulls and fists hit the glass and create sonic booms inside her terrorised space. This is one of many ironic retributions against the voyeuristic characters of the film, and the telephone booth's sensory realignment is a typical inversion of normal audio-visual relationships. While such states can be suffered subjectively within a character's mind (and distorted/stylised sounds would represent this), Melanie must endure the terror at the hands (or wings) of forces outside of her own mind. Put another way, it is as if she is trapped in the mind of someone being terrorised by imaginary birds, and as such is a symbolic conduit for the means the film uses to psychologically unsettle and terrorise us.

THE DOMINANCE OF BIRD NOISE OVER THE HUMAN VOICE

By the film's midway point, the plot forces all characters to concede that there is something unusual about the behaviour of the birds. We too, as viewers/auditors, tread lightly as the film is brimful of harbingers of death. Most importantly, silence and sound become key markers of terror more so than the sight of a bird alone. This shifts our human perceptual sense of visual primacy into the auditory realm which for many animals is the primary field within which they assess danger. Sound without sight may be the ultimate terror for the human untrained in reading sonic signs, and *The Birds* preys upon the viewer/auditor by incessantly mismatching the two and exploiting the ultimately arbitrary representational codes which fix the two together.

In the opening pet shop scene, Melanie, Mitch and the saleslady have no problem talking over the bird noise. Perhaps the fact that the birds are caged subliminally gives the characters a sense of aural control over the situation: they believe and feel that they can make themselves heard. By the end of *The Birds*, however, many a character has been silenced—acoustically, figuratively, terminally. The collective chin-wagging which builds in the diner gives way to collective jaw-dropping in wake of the birds' devastating attack on the school and petrol station. The ornithologist talks too much: she is left half-framed in profile, stripped of the power of speech. The same events lead the concerned mother to hysterical accusations after she is powerless to silence the adults' inconsiderate chatter in ear-range of her children. Even the most humanised and domesticated birds—Cathy's lovebirds—just won't communicate with each other.

As Melanie witnesses the petrol station carnage, she is left speechless in a series of hysterical jump-cuts. She revives the voyeuristic effect of previous scenes, but this time her displacement from the action induces stress rather than pleasure. Her awareness of this accentuates her powerlessness: the jump-cuts represent the time that literally disappears as she realises there is not enough time to warn the man who is holding a lighted match while standing in a stream of petrol. A lag follows, after which she and the others scream out too late—screams which perversely attract his death by causing him to drop the lighted match after straining to hear their calls. Their cries are silenced by the gas pump detonation.

Silence reaches the zenith of terror in the Brenner household. After spending much time and energy fortifying all potential entrances into the domestic domain, the family lie in wait—obviously trapped like birds in a cage. An unnerving silence precedes the attack as everyone (us included) waits for something to happen. It does. The soft sound of a few birds merrily chirping cues the sonic assault which immediately follows. Sound now is at its most abstract and most deafening as electro-acoustic sheets of noise totally replace all lip-sync dialogue—visibly inaudible as Mitch gathers everyone into place. An equally inaudible hysteria ensues as no one knows where to go. This sense of alienation is intensified by numerous unmotivated camera angles which make the loungeroom space as alien to us as it is to the characters trying to take refuge there. As with the earlier sparrow attack, the soundtrack is devoured by bird noise—but here there is not a bird in sight. This is pure, unadulterated sound, recalling everything from Chinese water torture to Muzak, from sonar crowd control guns to industrial noise deafness. It is an apocalyptic decimation of personal space: relentless, invisible, deafening. Ironically, the first lip-sync dialogue heard as the birds leave (signalled by a decrease in the roar) is 'they've gone'. This scene demonstrates the extent to which the birds are represented both *as* sound and *by* sound.

After the cacophonic climax of the Brenner attack, Melanie cautiously checks the attic. All is still and quiet—until she unwittingly shines a torch on the massed birds roosted there like a cancer within the household. They swoop on her as she flails her arms desperately like someone trying to fly. Her cries for help slowly disintegrate into a field of whimpers, gasps and fluttering wings; she lapses into catatonia, recalling her stilted silent scream as she witnessed the petrol station incident. The soundtrack impassively documents the near-silence that ensues as her near-lifeless body is pecked at by near-noiseless birds. The silence truly is deafening here, because the birds know that they have her: they need no longer communicate to each other untranslated directives for procuring her body. She is now carrion; they need no clarion. The birds—hitherto named vaguely—reveal themselves to be psycho-genetic amalgams of carrion crows, desert vultures, scavenger gulls. They terrorise us from above with the sophistication and precision dreamed of in military aviation. They feed off our cadavers in disrespectful, piecemeal fashion. And in a fitful triumph of the sonic, they peck out our eyes. As we die and fade to black, so does the film's sun set, blurring the calm chattering of all those gathered birds into an agitated chorus that reverberates deep in the caves of the hollow sockets that were once our eyes.

CITED SOUNDTRACK INCIDENTS IN CHRONOLOGICAL ORDER

1. Bird sounds and images occupy the audio-visual screen during the title sequence.
2. Melanie converses with a saleslady in a bird store while loud bird noise continues unabated. Melanie meets Mitch and further dialogue develops over the bird noise.
3. Melanie delivers caged lovebirds to Mitch's apartment, and is followed by a neighbour.
4. Melanie travels in her car with the lovebirds from San Francisco to Bodega Bay.
5. Melanie takes a hired boat from the port to the back entrance of Mitch's house. She enters the house and delivers the lovebirds, then sneaks back to the boat and watches through binoculars as Mitch discovers the birds. She rows back to the port as he watches her through binoculars. He drives around the bay while she motors the boat to port. She is attacked by a gull as she and Mitch arrive together at the dock.
6. The children's birthday party is interrupted by a gull attack as Cathy plays Blind Man's Bluff. Balloons are burst and children are pecked.
7. A flock of sparrows suddenly invade the Brenner loungeroom and terrorise Melanie, Mitch, Cathy and Mrs Brenner.
8. Cathy and fellow classmates sing in class as Melanie waits for Cathy outside. Melanie smokes as they continue singing. She notices a single crow and discovers a flock gathered in the playground. She enters the school to warn the teacher, who then dismisses the children to exit quietly.
9. The children break into a run and disturb the crows. The crows attack the children as they run screaming. Melanie gathers Cathy and another girl into a car for protection.
10. Birds attack the petrol station and diner exterior. A pecked gas attendant falls and leaves petrol spilling downhill. The gathered diner patrons see the petrol trailing to a man standing near a gas pump. He lights a cigarette; they scream a warning to him; he drops the match on the spilt petrol and blows up the gas pumps. Seen from high above, the birds survey the disaster.
11. A variety of birds attack the Brenner residence from the outside while everyone remains locked inside the loungeroom. Mitch fortifies the barricades and repels attacks by gulls.
12. Melanie checks the attic and accidentally disturbs massed birds with her torch. They attack her and peck her to near-death as she falls into catatonia.
13. Melanie and the Brenners exit the house and leave Bodega Bay by car as the birds roost everywhere.

This material, originally presented as a lecture on The Birds' *soundtrack for the subject 'Film, Sound and Music', was devised by Philip Brophy and first run in the Communications Department at RMIT, Melbourne, in 1985. Since 1989 the subject has been run as the 'Soundtrack' subject in the Media Arts Course at RMIT. For information on the course contact: p.brophy@rmit.edu.au*

1. Excerpt from the in-progress text *Sonic Cinema* © 1996 Philip Brophy.

Further Monuments for a Critical History of Music, Sound Generation and Transmission

Phillip L. Ryan

> Composition is the sole definition of art.
>
> —Gilles Deleuze

The subsequent orientation is from 'Western civilisation' by date. Compositions are marked with an asterisk.

50,000,000	Cetacea return to the oceans.
6000 b.c.	Origin of the drum; (?) didgeridoo (didjeridu).
3000 b.c.	Harps and flutes in Egypt.
2700 b.c.	China: music, for harmony between the self and the universe.
n.d.	The god Apollo; pre-Homer—Orpheus tames the trees and beasts with his lyre. 'The Greek Miracle'...
850 b.c.	(c.): Homer relates how music stopped a haemorrhage in Ulysses.
800 b.c.	(c.): First notated music in Sumeria.
650 b.c.	(c.): First (Greek) composer, Arion.
600 b.c.	(c.): 'Music of the Spheres': Pythagoras.
	(c.): Lao-Tzu teaches that the art work can deafen the ear.
500 b.c.	(c.): *The Upanishads*—re: 'Mystical Auditions' (cf. yoga).

> Musical modes are nowhere altered without (changes in) the most important laws of the state.
>
> —Damon of Athens

320 b.c.	(c.): Aristotle's codification of the foundations of music theory. (spurious?) *Perl Thaumasion Akousmaton (On Marvellous Things Heard)*—Aristotle.
100 b.c.	*On Music*—Philodemus of Gadara.
50 b.c.	Chinese octave subdivided into sixty notes.
	(c.) Work of the Roman architect, Vitruvius, on acoustics, after Greece.
200	*Natya-Sastra*—Bharata (treatise on all aspects of Sanskrit theatre: music, poetics, general aesthetics, dance).
300	(c.): The organ (Byzantium): but cf., Greece, Ctesibius, 300 b.c.
500	*De Institutione Musica*—Boethius.

619	...formation of orchestras of hundreds of players in China.
900	(c.): *De Harmonica Institutione*—Hucbald.
1000	(c.): Work of Guido d'Arezzo.
1250	Invention of the 'Portatio', a small, portable organ.
	Sangitaratnakara—Shangadeva ('Ocean of Music and Dance').
1309	Plea for counterpoint by Marchettus of Padua.
1319	*Ars Novae Musicae*—Jean de Muris.
1325	*Ars Novae Musicae*—Philippe de Vitry.
1465	First printed music.
1477	*Liber de Arte Contrapuncti*—Johannes Tinctoris.
1500	(c.): Invention of the 'Viola Organista' (Leonardo da Vinci): n.b., Leonardo was left-handed, as was Ludwig van Beethoven...
	Western civilisation: book—*Utopia*—Thomas More, 1516.
1550	(c.): The Protestant, John Calvin, warns against voluptuous or disorderly music, Calvin attempting to assert ecclesiastical authority and supremacy at this time.
1555	*L'Antica Musica Ridotta alla Moderna Prattica*—Nicola Vicentino.
1581	*Dialogo della Musica Antica e della Moderna*—Vincenzo Galilei.
1582	Invention of 'Eine Symphonie' (a keyboard stringed instrument).
1598	Invention of the first musical clock: 'Turkish Organ' (Dallam).
	'The Italian Miracle' (Heirs-Gottfried Leibniz, Friedrich Schelling...).
...1600	'Modernity' (the 'old' and the 'new') involving 'repudiation' of the Renaissance (Europe)... 'Modern Art' (cf., Baudelaire, Manet) arises c. 1860: contested by such as Stéphane Mallarmé, and may be considered a personalism bequeathed by 'modernism'. The last should be distinguished from 'modernisation' (after the industrial revolution and enlightenment c. 1750 [Europe]), and 'modern civilisation' from 'industrial civilisation (secularisation, science, technology): the 'modern' is urbane, cosmopolitan; the 'industrial' generally 'historical'. 'Modernism' accommodates ideals and formal enquiry (or 'anti-tradition' and 'non-tradition', not necessarily respectively). The 'ultramodern' is untimely: 'progressive', 'elitist', not anti-democratic and has concern for 'prophylaxis' or the 'amodern', affirmation of the normal 'world' of everyday life and its achievements as they develop. Accommodating the 'amodern', the 'ultramodern' in turn accommodates the 'classical' impulse and learning without the 'neoclassicism' as at the beginning of 'modernism' (c. 1800, France) and strategically involves such as the 'futurist anti-tradition' of Apollinaire (c. 1910): 'New syntheses' may be achievable (in philosophy, art, music, and scientific discoveries might become transdisciplinary, interdisciplinary). Such defines a certain 'crisis' in the 'modern world' ('western'), as received. One might posit the 'ultramodern' as the way to see such through. The term 'Utopian' had become current by 1600, and the phrase 'new world' probably derives from the pamphlet (1505) by Amerigo Vespucci.
	Further reading: 1991—*Utopianism*—Krishan Kumar (U.K.)
	What one is postulating here is that the 'scene 2000' knows 'how' enough (technocracy) but is still struggling with 'what': for research...
1600	Mechanical Virginal.
1602	*Nuove Musiche*—Giulio Caccini.

Further Monuments for a Critical History of Music, Sound Generation and Transmission

1610	Invention of the 'Geigenwerck' (Hans Heyden: a keyboard stringed instrument).
1612	'On Music', in *Aurora*—Jacob Boehme.
1619	*Harmonices Mundi*—Johannes Kepler.
1620	(c.): 'Intermedia' productions.
1644	Invention of the first *digital* computer (Blaise Pascal).
1650	*Caturdandiprakasika* ('The Illuminator of the Four Pillars of Music').
1662	*The Harmony of the World*—John Heydon.
1673	*Phonurgia Nova*—Athansius Kircher.
1700	(c.): Leibniz states that music reflects a universal rhythm and mirrors a reality that is fundamentally mathematical.
1709	Invention of the 'Piano Forte' (Bartolomeo Cristofori).
	(c.): Joseph Sauveur suggests the term 'acoustics' ('harmonics').
1722	*Critica Musica*—John Mattheson.
1725	(c.): Work of Johann Sebastian Bach.
1729	*Medicina Musica*—R. Browne (cf., 'music therapy' generally).
1730	(c.): *Six sonatas for two violins—Comte de St-Germain.
1734	Invention of the first colour-organ (Louis-Bertrand Castel).
1740	(c.): Invention of the 'nail violin' (Johann Wilde).
1746	(c.): *Concerto for glass harmonica—Christoph Gluck.
1749	'Reflections on Antient and Modern Musick with the Application to the Cure of Diseases'—R. Brocklesby.
1750	(c.): Invention of 'Singing Birds' (mechanical birds in cages).
1770	Invention of the 'music box' in Switzerland.
1780	(c.): Visionary Architecture.
1787	*Blikke Fines Tonkunstlers in Die Musik Der Gelster*—Johann Von Dalberg.
1793	Debut of Niccolo Paganini.

Music is nothing other than the primordial (urbildiche) rhythm of nature and the universe itself.
—Friedrich Wilhelm Joseph von Schelling

1800	(c.): Beginning of 'avant-gardism' (music [later, other media] incl. the 'New German school'): 'ultramodern', distinct from 'modernism'. (c.): Invention of 'mechanical musicians' and 'musical watches'.
1802	*Die Akustik*—Ernst Chladni.
1810	(c.): Project: 'Times of Day' by Philipp Otto Runge (painting) and Ludwig Berger (music).
1817	Poetry: Two 'Fragments to Music'—Percy Bysshe Shelley.
1818	Invention of the 'physharmonica' (Anton Haeckl) leading to the 'seraphine' (John Green) and the 'harmonium' (1840—Alexander Debain).
1820	(c.): Friendship of Goethe and Mendelssohn.

> ...and like Lutes, touched by the skill of the enamoured wind, weave harmonies divine, yet ever new, from difference sweet, where discord cannot be.
>
> —Percy Bysshe Shelley

1825	(c.): Charles Wheatstone demonstrates that musical sound can be transmitted through metallic and glass rods.
1826	First determination of the velocity of sound in water, by C.-F. Sturm.
1829	Invention of the 'Componium' ('mechanical musicians').
1830	(c.): Work of Tyagaraja ('Gana-Marga' or 'Salvation through devotional music').
	(c.): *Symphony No. 4 'The Consecration of Sound'—Louis Spohr.
	(c.): *Project: 'Revolutionary Symphony'—Franz Liszt.
1834	Foundation of the '*Neue Zeitschrift fur Musik*' by Robert Schumann.
1835	Novel: *Nepenthe*—George Darley.
1837	'Duel' between Franz Liszt and Sigismond Thalberg.
	The 'Piano Eolien'.
1840	(c.): Work of Anthony Philip Heinrich (incl. a 'Barbecue Divertimento').
	Symphonie Funèbre et Triomphale—Hector Berlioz.

> Normal harps will sound beneath any hand; those of Aeolus only when the storm strikes them.
>
> —Karl Marx

1843	*Traité de l'Instrumentation et d'Orchestration Modernes*—Hector Berlioz.
1846	Invention of the saxophone (Antoine-Joseph Sax).
1848	Invention of the 'symphonic poem' by Franz Liszt.
1849	'Art and Revolution'—Richard Wagner.
	'The Artwork of the Future'—Richard Wagner.
1850	(c.): Development of player pianos.
	(c.): Work of Alkan.
1851	*Opera and Drama*—Richard Wagner.
	12 Etudes d'Execution Transcendente—Franz Liszt.
1853	*Piano Sonata—Franz Liszt.
1857	Invention of the 'phonautograph' (E. Scott de Martinville).
1861	Project: 'The History of the World in Sound and Picture' by Franz Liszt.
	(c.): Work (music) of Eduard von Hartmann, the philosopher of the 'unconscious' (after the German Romantics and such as Anton Mesmer).
1863	First use of the term 'musicology' ('*musikwissenshaft*') by F. Chrysander.
1866	Visible speech—Alexander Melville Bell (Père).
	*St John's Night on the Bare Mountain (original version)—Modeste Moussorgsky.

Further Monuments for a Critical History of Music, Sound Generation and Transmission

1868	Invention of the 'Typophone' (Victor Mustel).
1870	(c.): Work of Joachim Raff.
1872	Invention of the first *analog* computer (William Thomson, Kelvin).
	The Birth of Tragedy out of the Spirit of Music—Friedrich Nietzsche.
	Novel: *Erewhon*—Samuel Butler ('Hollow Statues Vibrating in the Wind with "unearthly chords" ').
1874	*Les Éléments d'Acoustique Musique…* —Victor Mahillon.
1875	(c.): Musical compositions of Friedrich Nietzsche.
1876	Opening of the Bayreuth Festival Theatre of Richard Wagner (Greek acoustics…).
	(c.): Invention of the 'Wagner Tuba' by Richard Wagner.
	(c.): Project: 'For a Symphony of Mourning for Those who had Fallen in the War', after 'Romeo and Juliet' (Gounod)—Richard Wagner.
	(c.): Aesthetics of David Sutter (musicology and mathematics).
1877	First cylinder recording (Thomas Edison).
1878	*Theory of Sound*—John Strutt, Rayleigh.
	First microphone (David Hughes).
1880	Invention of the 'polyphon' (a music box).
	The Power of Sound—Edmund Gurney (a psychologist).
	(c.): Physics of sound investigated by August Kundt.
	(c.): Papers on theories of colour music and instruments using gas and illumination by electricity of D. D. Jameson, Frederick Kastner and
	A. W. Rimington.
1882	First 'motion picture' (Etienne-Jules Marey).
1884	First television system (Paul Nipkow: cf., 1926—John Logie Baird).
1885	…Albert Einstein has learnt to play the violin…
1886	Invention of the 'celesta' (A. Mustel).
1887	Patent on a 'gramophone' by Emile Berliner (produced 1894).
	Death of Alexander Borodin, composer/scientist.
	Friedrich Nietzsche speaks for the music of Jacques Offenbach.
	Establishment of the 'mach number' by Ernest Mach: ratio of the velocity of an object to the velocity of sound.
1888	*Psyché*—Cesar Franck.
1889	First experimental school (Cecil Reddie, U.K.).
1890	*Tonpsychologie*—Carl Stumpf.
1891	(English) *The Beautiful in Music*—Eduard Hanslick.
1894	*Prélude à l'aprés-midi d'un Faune*—Claude Debussy.
	First phonograph factory (France: Charles and Emile Pathé).
1895	Concert on a colour-organ by A. W. Rimington.

1896	*Thus Spoke Zarathustra—Richard Strauss.
1897	Invention of the 'pianola' (E. S. Votey).
	*The Sorcerer's Apprentice—Paul Ducas.
1898	First magnetic recorder (Valdemar Poulsen).
1899	'Music and Staging'—Adolphe Appia.
	The unified 'astronautical vision' of Konstantin Tsiolkovsky... (actually, 'cosmonautical').
	...the non-Euclidean, non-Newtonian, non-Aristotelian...

THE TWENTIETH CENTURY: CONCERNING THE 'ULTRAMODERN', AND PLANETISATION...

1900	(c.): Choral dramas of Christian Ehrenfels.
	(c.): Research of the phenomenologist, Carl Stumpf, Berlin.
	The century is to see many individuals, groups and '-isms' in a vast 'laboratory' often approaching successful 'experiment'...: '-isms' denotes the aspect of an (art) movement that comprises its 'ideological' difference.
	'Experiment': as in science—practical intervention and not just 'experimental': 2000— approaching the planetary/cosmic, after such as Wilfred Desan, a phenomenologist. Permanent objecthood.
1905	Invention of the 'mandolin street piano'.
1906	Lecture: 'The Inner Nature of Music and the Experience of Tone'—Rudolf Steiner (cf., 'psychometrics'; also, his 'dramas').
	Work in electronics ('vacuum tube') of Lee de Forest.
1908	*Principles of Orchestration*—Nikolai Rimsky-Korsakov.
	*Poem of Ecstasy—Alexander Scriabin.
	The Music Drama of the Future—Rutland Boughton.
1910	Vienna: (c.): '*Klangfarbenmelodies*' and '*Sprechstimme*' theorised by Arnold Schoenberg. Harmonielehre (1911). Schoenberg thinks highly of Gustav Mahler.
	(c.): (n.d.) Dr Sigmund Freud reportedly enjoys Mozart's 'Don Giovanni': Music arouses recollections (and hence can be considered 'utopian' in the Marcusean sense [1977]).
	Colour music: The Art of Mobile Colour—A. W. Rimington.
1911	'*Manifesto Tecnico della Musica Futurista*'—Francesco Pratella.
1912	*The Yellow Sound*—Wassily Kandinsky. Also: *Cosmic Rays*.
	First use of 'tone clusters' in 'The Tides of Manauhaun' (piano) by Henry Cowell.
	**Gurrelieder*—Arnold Schoenberg.
1913	Poems: sounds—Wassily Kandinsky.
	First recording of a Beethoven symphony (No. 5: Arthur Nikisch).
	(c.): The Clown 'Grock' (a 'simpleton' amongst musical instruments).
	*Fragments from Apokalypsis—Anatol Liadov.
1914	(c.): Project: 'Mysterium'—Alexander Scriabin.

Further Monuments for a Critical History of Music, Sound Generation and Transmission

	Paper on 'colour-hearing' in the *British Journal of Psychology* (Vol. VII) by Charles Mayer. (cf., Olivier Messiaen's reported capacity for 'synaesthetic' hearing).
1916	(c.): Project: Opera—'The Fall of the House of Usher'—Claude Debussy.
	Work: With Hidden Noise—Marcel Duchamp.
	(c.): The 'English Renaissance' (esp. music).
	*The Planets—Gustav Holst.
1917	*The Philosophy of Modernism*—Cyril Scott.
1918	...Operational, active sonar (U.S. and England).
1919	First commercial radio broadcast.
1920	*Essays before a Sonata*—Charles Ives.
	(c.): Revolutionary Russia: Orchestras without conductors.
	Group: 'Les Six.'
1921	*The Rational and Social Foundations of Music*—Max Weber.
	(c.): Work of Julian Carrillo (incl. the '13th Tone').
	Invention of the vibraharp (vibraphone): first used in the opera 'Lulu' by Alan Berg (an opera distinctly 'feminist' and critical).
	Demonstration in New York of a colour-organ by Mary Hallock-Greenwalt.
1922	*Speech and Hearing*—Harvey Fletcher.
	Formation of the 'International Society for Contemporary Music'.
	First public performance (keyboard) of the 'Art of Light' of T. Wilfred.
	'Graphic Sound' (Moholy-Nagy, Avzaamov, Fischinger, etc.).
	3D film: Movies of the Future.
	'Symphonies Under the Stars' begins at the Hollywood Bowl, Hollywood.
1923	*For the Voice*—Vladimir Mayakovsky and El Lissitzky.
	'New Form in Music: Potentialities of the Phonograph'—Laszlo Moholy-Nagy.
	Film: *Diagonal Symphony*—Viking Eggeling.
	*The Creation of the World—Darius Milhaud.
	Das Geistige Wesen der Tonarten—Ernst Bindel.
1924	*The Pines of Rome—Ottorino Respighi (use of the gramophone).
	Invention of the 'spharaphon' (Jorg Mayer).

The age of musical renewal is proving to be also the age of experiments of a technical and rational kind. Thus form-oriented contemplation above all is closer to the musical will-to-the-unknown than is a psychology or even metaphysics, which apparently forces its object under the light of Romantic aesthetics time and again...modern music is returning to the 'direct factors'...the actual physics of musical notes...

—Ernst Bloch

Film *Metropolis* in production (Fritz Lang).

1925	(c.): Electrical sound recording.
	(c.): Work of Alban Berg.
	(c.): Use of the electrophonic instrument—'Croix Sonore'.
	'On the Mathematical and Dialectical Character in Music'—Ernst Bloch.
1926	(c.): Project: (to 1954) 'Universe' Symphony—Charles Ives.
	*Opera: The Angel of Peace—Siegfried Wagner.
	*Ballet Mècanique—George Antheil.
1927	Colour-music: The Art of Light—Adrian Klein.
	Beginning of the fifty year experiment of R. Buckminster Fuller.
	*Rise and Fall of the City of Mahagonny—Kurt Weill.
1928	First animated cartoon with music and voices (sound)(Walt Disney).
1929	The Masterpiece in Music—Heinrich Schenker.
	(c.): Project: The Astronomer—Edgard Varèse.
	(c.): Project: Espace—Edgard Varèse.
	Invention of the term 'science fiction' (Hugo Gernsback).
	(c.): Work of Alexander Zemlinsky.
	...An American in Paris (cf., Gershwin): A Frenchman in New York (cf., Milhaud)...
1930	**Utopian decade.**
	Invention of the 'Trautonium' (Friedrich Trautwein).
	*Begleitmusik zu Einer Lichtspielszene—Arnold Schoenberg.
	Phonographes et Musique Mècanique—Eugene Weiss.
	Eurythmics, Art and Education—Emile Jaques-Dalcroze.
	Spoken Music—Ernst Toch.
	(c.): Work of Dmitri Shostakovich, Nicolai Miaskovsky, Heitor Villa-Lobos.
	(c.): 'Gebrauchmusik' (Paul Hindemith); 'Gemeinschaftsmusik' (Hans Eisler). Theories of film music also of Eisler, and V. I. Pudovkin.
1931	Invention of the 'rangertone' (Richard Ranger).
	*Concertino for Trautonium and Strings—Paul Hindemith.
	*Opera: Pier Li Houien—Eugene Ysaye (in Wallon dialect).
1932	Invention of the 'electronde' (Martin Tausmann).
	Work: 'Object to be Destroyed' (Man Ray).
1933	Invention of the 'electrochord' (Vierling of Berlin).
	Film: The Sound ABC—Laszlo Moholy-Nagy.
	Music: Its Secret Influence Throughout the Ages—Cyril Scott.
1934	*Ecuatorial—Edgard Varèse.
1935	Free Composition—Heinrich Schenker.
	Invention of the 'partiturphone' (Jorg Mayer).
1936	Invention of the 'hellertion' (Bruno Helberger and Peter Lertes).

Further Monuments for a Critical History of Music, Sound Generation and Transmission

	Film: *Things to Come* (H. G. Wells; Music: Arthur Bliss).
	Group: 'La Jeune France'.
1937	*Mechanics, Molecular Physics, Heat, and Sound*, Robert Millikan, et. al., (n.b.: n.d. Military Sonic Engineering).
	Uber Neue Musik—Ernst Krenek.
	*Sonata for Two Pianos and Percussion—Bela Bartok.
	Film: *Lost Horizon* (music: Dmitri Tiomkin).
	'The Future of Music: Credo'—John Cage.

> Music is pure vibration, unity with the original source.
> —Wilhelm Reich

1938	Invention of the 'pianotron' (Selmer of London).
	'On the Fetish Character of Music and the Regression of Hearing'—Theodor W. Adorno.
1939	Invention of the 'electrone'.
	(c.): Project: '*L'Atlantida*'—Manuel de Falla.
	Supersonics: The Science of Inaudible Sounds—Robert Wood.
	New York—World's Fair: 'The World of Tomorrow' (incl. designs by Norman Bel Geddes).
1940	Invention of the electronically amplified piano (Walter Nernst).
	'Making Music Together'—Alfred Schutz (as a model of social communication).
	(c.): Work of Erich Korngold, Max Steiner (incl. films).
	(c.): Ultrasonics (from c. 1910): cf.: infrasonics.
	(c.): Work of Roger Sessions.
1943	*Opera: *Der Kaiser von Atlantis*—Viktor Ullmann.
1944	*Technique de Mon Langage Musical*—Olivier Messiaen.
1945	Paper: 'Extraterrestrial Relays'—Arthur C. Clarke. Also: The 'A-Bomb'.
1946	*Traite d'Harmonie Tonale, Atonale, et Totale*—Nicolay Obukhov.
	*Symphony No. 3—Aaron Copland.
	The Schillinger System of Musical Composition—Joseph Schillinger.
1947	*Étude pour Espace*—Edgard Varèse.
	*Concerto for Ondes Martenot and Orchestra—André Jolivet.
	First supersonic plane: n.b., 'Sonic Boom' (Concorde, 1976).
1948	'Therapeutic and Industrial Uses of Music'—Boris Soibelman.
	First 12-inch (30cm) vinyl record discs (U.S.).
	Proposal: stereoscopic television (John Logie Baird).
1949	*Genesis of a Music*—Harry Partch.
	Film: *Orpheus* (Jean Cocteau).
	'Fantasy' with music: *Atalanta—Gerald Hargreaves.

	Experiments re musical parameters of Olivier Messiaen (Neumes rythmiques, etc.).
	(c.): Work of Werner Meyer-Eppler on electronics and sound.
1950	**Atomic decade.**
	Work: Bugle of Peace—Bruno Munari.
	Olivier Messiaen is working on a treatise on rhythm.
	Norbert Wierner writes about 'Music-Box Automata' and cybernetics.
	(c.): Invention of a 'polyphonic trautonium' (Oskar Sala).
1951	*'Jami'* symphony—Kaikhosru Sorabji.
1952	(c.): *Electronic music of Vladimir Ussachevsky and Otto Luening.
	*Symphony No. 7—Serge Prokofiev.
	*Piano Sonata—Jean Barraqué.
	First 'live electronic music': Musica su due Dimensioni 1—Bruno Maderna.
1953	*The Psychoanalysis of Artistic Vision and Hearing*—Anton Ehrenzweig.
	Musique concrete: 'Orphée'—Pierre Henry.
	'Project for Music for Magnetic Tape' (John Cage, Morton Feldman, Earle Brown, Christian Wolff, David Tudor).
	First radio broadcast of rock 'n' roll: let's be selective here…
	(c.): George Pierce researches sound generation by bats and insects.
1954	*Der Ultraschall und Seine Anwendung in Wissenschaft Und Technik*—L. Bergmann.
	Le Marteau sans Maitre—Pierre Boulez.
	Martin Heidegger speaks of the 'Misled Wagner Cult' imposing an aura on Nietzsche… (n.b.: Nietzsche was left-handed). Also: the 'H-Bomb'.
1955	(c.): *Hybrid* computers…
	(c.): *'Musique concrete'* of Luc Ferrari, Bernard Parmegiani, Michel Philippot, Francois-Bernard Mache, André Bourcourechliev, etc.
	Journal: Die Reihe.
	La Procession Dans Verges—Edgard Varèse.
	Invention of the 'Olsen-Belar sound synthesizer'.
	Work: 'Meta-Mechanical Sound Relief 1 & 11'—Jean Tinguely.
1956	Videotape recorder (Ampex).
	Gesang der Junglinge—Karlheinz Stockhausen: a work enjoyed by
	Max Ernst, the anti-surrealist.
	Electronic score (Louis and Bebe Barron): Film: *Forbidden Planet*.
1957	First computer generation of sound (to 1963) by Max Mathews.
	First artificial satellite ('sputnik 1'): from c. 1870.
	*Illiac Suite—Lejaren Hiller.
1958	Stereophonic recording: from c. 1933. Also: Van Allen radiation belts.
	*Nirvana Symphony—Toshiro Mayuzumi.

*The Butterfly Lovers Violin Concerto—He Zhanhao/Chen Gang.

*Concert for piano and orchestra—John Cage.

*Atlantis—Morton Feldman.

First 'Happening' of Allan Kaprow (towards critique of the 'museum').

(c.): Work in information and aesthetic perception of Abraham Moles.

Unfulfilled Passion: writings on music 1910–1951—Massimo Bontempelli.

Listening in the Dark—Donald Griffin (on acoustic orientation).

(c.): Aleatorics, and the texts of Hans G. Helms.

Magazine: *Sonorama*.

1959   (c.): Writings on music by Theodor W. Adorno, and during the next decade. There are also writings on 'experimental music' by Abraham Moles, Lejaren Hiller. Heidegger on 'World War III'… (Jaspers discussed the 'bomb' in 1957…).

Differences—Luciano Berio.

Refrain—Karlheinz Stockhausen.

Space opera: *Aniara*—Karl-Birger Blomdahl.

Recording: 'Indeterminacy: New Aspect of Form in Instrumental & Electronic Music'—John Cage/David Tudor (in effect, a 'critique' of (musical) determinism with 'scientifico-poetic' ramifications').

1960   (c.): Work of Richard Maxfield, Jean Dubuffet (music), La Monte Young (on consonance after dissonance), Earle Brown.

(c.): Film music of Bernard Herrmann.

Intolleranza 1960—Luigi Nono.

(c.): Empirical sociology of music of Alphons Silbermann.

Experiments in Hearing—Georg von Bekesy.

(c.): Work of Nicolas Schoffer ('spatiodynamic kinetic sculptures' using 'sound machines': also, the idea of 'Festival of Participation').

Chronochromie—Olivier Messiaen.

Circles—Luciano Berio.

Atlantis (antiphonal symphony)—Henry Brant.

(c.): '*Hyperphonie*' (lettrism), sound poetry, work of Francois Dufrenne and Henri Chopin and Bernard Heidsieck; concrete art and poetry (Gomringer, Gerstner, Bill); neo-Dada, anti-music…, concept art.

(c.): Songs: 'Venus'; 'Blue Moon'; 'Fools Rush In'; 'Swinging High School', etc.

(c.): Andre Segovia warns about excessive use of electric guitars.

1961   Work: Box with a Sound of its Own Making—Robert Morris.

Sonic exchanges of dolphins are discovered (cf., the work, c., 1965, on psychoacoustics and interspecies communication, of Dr John Lilly).

Venetian Games—Witold Lutoslawski.

Atmospheres—Gyorgy Ligeti.

Future of Music: A Collective Composition—Gyorgy Ligeti.

	First 'Once' Festival (incl. the work of Robert Ashley).
1962	Invention of the 'harmonic tone generator' (James Beauchamp).
	*Sul Ponte di Hiroshima—Luigi Nono.
	*...an early version of 'Momente' by Karlheinz Stockhausen.
	'Telstar' (incl. a recorded piece of music).
1963	TV: Outer Limits (Music: Dominic Frontiere, Harry Lubin).
	(c.): Work of Milton Babbitt, Herbert Brun, Bruno Maderna.
	The Path to the New Music—Anton Webern (English ed.).
	An Anthology—ed. La Monte Young.
	Grundlagen der Musikalischen Reientechnik—Herbert Eimert.
	Architecture: Berlin, Philharmonie (Hans Scharoun): conductor: Herbert von Karajan.
1964	*In C—Terry Riley.
	Exhibition: For Eyes and Ears (New York; sound—Billy Kluver).
1965	(c.): Work of Christian Wolff, George Brecht, Giuseppe Chiari, Joe Jones, and many composers (worldwide) working with serialism and experiment (graphics: cf., Anestis Logothetis).
	Invention of the 'buchla synthesizer' (Donald Buchla).
	(c.): Experimental dance and electronic scores of Alwin Nikolais.
	Computer digitalisation of the sound of a trumpet by Jean-Claude Risset.
	...The 'End of the Orchestra' is on the horizon, after electronics...
	*'Sound Sculptures' of Harry Bertoia.
	(c.): 'World Soundscape Project' (R. Murray Schafer), 'Zaj' (Marco, Marchetti, Hidalgo): sculpture: 'The Ear' (Tomio Miki).
	Invention of the 'Synket' (Paul Ketoff).
	Work: 'Oracle' (Robert Rauschenberg).
	(c.): Music of Henri Dutilleux: art of Victor Vasarely.
	'Experiments' of The Beatles.
1966	'Technological Happening Room' (Wolfe Vostell).
	*De Natura Sonoris No. 1—Krzysztof Penderecki (No. 2 [1971]).
	Das Schriftbild der Neuen Musik—Erhard Karkoschka.
	*Life Music—Toshi Ichiyanagi: cf., The work of Toru Takemitsu, Yoji Yuasa.
	(c.): Work of Lowell Cross.
	(c.): Continuing work of Pierre Schaeffer.
	*'Infiltration-homogen' for grand piano—Joseph Beuys.
	Concrete/cinematographic novel Sweethearts—Emmett Williams.
	Magazine: Source (U.S.).
	(c.): Konrad Boehmer on 'Open Form'... ('pattern' not imposed on the 'primary process' but emergent).
	Journal: Electronic Music Review.

Further Monuments for a Critical History of Music, Sound Generation and Transmission

1968   Question: Is the use of the scores in *2001: A Space Odyssey* (film) acceptable aesthetically? Rather: an original score.

(c.): The Situationists (France) object to 'mere spectacle'.

Exhibition: *The Machine as Seen at the End of the Mechanical Age* (New York, M.O.M.A.).

(c.): 'Action Music' of Boguslaw Schaffer.

International Electronic Music Catalogue—Hugh Davies.

(c.): Investigation—'Black Light' and sound (Larry Austin).

Invention of the 'Shozyg I, II, III' (Hugh Davies).

Sinfonia—Luciano Berio.

Anaparastases—Jani Christou.

Armageddon—Henk Badings.

Schooltime Compositions—Cornelius Cardew.

(c.): Work of Gordon Mumma, Morton Subotnik.

The White Book of Total Art: Towards a Prospective Aesthetics—Pierre Restany.

1969   'The Scratch Orchestra: Draft Constitution'—Cornelius Cardew.

Notations—John Cage/Alison Knowles.

*Electronic Opera No. 1 (video)—Nam June Paik.

The Technology of Computer Music—Max Mathews.

1970   Anti-utopia.

(c.): All-night concerts of Terry Riley.

(c.): Quadraphonic recording.

(c.): Luc Ferrari wonders why anything should be composed at all.

*Third Planet from the Sun—Ramon Zupko.

(c.): Australia—work of Stanislaw Ostoja-Kotkowski, Keith Humble.

(c.): Works for synclavier by Jon Appleton.

Journal: *Musique en Jeu*.

Theoretical Fragments 1 on Experimental Music—Henri Pousseur.

(c.): Work of Alvin Lucier, Francois Bayle, Gottfried Koenig.

Teaching and Learning as Performing Arts—Robert Filliou.

*Scottish Symphony—Joseph Beuys/Henning Christensen.

(c.): 'Egg' synthesizer of Michael Manthey.

'Cultural Studies' of Marshall McLuhan, Jean Baudrillard.

La Prophetie Musicale dans l'Histoire de l'Humanité Precedée d'une Étude sur les Nombres et les Planètes dans leur Rapports avec la Musique.

—A. Roustit; preface by Olivier Messiaen

A comment: at about this time, the 'ultramodern' and 'postmodern' come to be confounded, with a certain 'iconoclasm' of the latter. Webern's discovery of 'equipotentiality' (cf., Karl Lashley, the psychologist) in musics may have contributed to the 'vision' of Bernd Alois Zimmermann for a complete space/time structural work using film, speech, electronic music, sound (after Wagner, Scriabin and the architect, Walter Gropius). 'Postmodernism' may be 'empty' (Baudrillard). Psychiatry and psychoanalysis were evolving disciplines from c. 1900–1970, non-punitive and helping to articulate the realities of nervous 'diseases' without 'politics' ('mental health' defined by the United Nations in 1946 as not the absence of infirmity but a state of complete well-being). Thus expressions can be communicative, communicable and unexpected: 'New'. Creativity is by definition 'free' of pathogenesis but may 'express' it. But, there is also a 'psychiatric' crisis or 'crisis' in psychiatry: with (c. 1970) 'anti-psychiatry', the judgement was made that certain music may be 'pathological'. However, this does not comprehend that the scope of much work is not expressed in individual works which may just be 'working' through whilst being original and intact: against 'psychiatropathy'. Stravinsky's 'oeuvre' was attacked by some whereas one may characterise it as 'circus novelty' (cf., the inventiveness of Mauricio Kagel): 'well-formed' and 'meaningful'... (against the phenomenon of 'schizography'). 'Repression' is 'failure of translation' and not necessarily political.

1971	*Invitation á l'Utopie*—Henri Pousseur.
	'New sound synthesis model' (Hiller/Ruiz).
	*Nature Study Notes—ed. Cornelius Cardew.
1972	*Musique, Sémantique, Société*—Henri Pousseur.
	Computer synthesis of sound of Barry Vercoe, John Chowning.
1973	Film: *Fantastic Planet* (Rene Laloux).
	*Einstein—Paul Dessau.
	*Rainforest—David Tudor.
	Architecture: Australia—Sydney Opera House (Jørn Utzon).
1974	*Writings about music*—Steve Reich.
	*Toneburst—David Tudor.
1975	*Mechanische Musikinstrumente und Musikautomaten*—W. Weiss-Strauffacher.
	(c.): Work with synthesizers of Isao Tomita, Jean Michel Jarre.
1976	*Listening and Voice: Phenomenology of Sound*—Don Ihde.
	Musik und Verstehen—W. Gramer.
	*Forest speech—David Tudor.

...bringing an end to repetition, transforming the world into an art form.

—Jacques Attali

	The 'internet' (but it has no 'centre': information, by itself, just 'wanders about').
1977	*Star-Child—George Crumb.
	*Figure in a Clearing—David Behrman.
	*Sirius—Karlheinz Stockhausen.
	Death of the conductor Leopold Stokowski.
1978	Work: Meta-harmonies—Jean Tinguely.

1980	(c.): Many synthesizers are available, and there has been developed 'ambient music' (cf., Brian Eno; Muzak...after Satie).
	Futuriste—Pierre Henry.
	(c.): Work of Alan Hovhaness, Lou Harrison.
	Explorations in the Geometry of Thinking—Peter Kotik.
	(c.): Film music of John Williams (U.S.).
	Digital Harmony: On the Complementarity of Music and Visual Art—John Whitney.
	(c.): 'Ocean acoustic tomography' developed.
1981	*Memoires de l'Ombre et du Son: Une Archéologie de l'Audio-Visuel*—Jacques Perrault.
	(c.): *Sea and Sky*—Stomu Yamash'ta.
	(c.): ...the 'traditionalism' of the work of Philip Glass.
	(c.): A 'new religiosity' in European music...; resort to tonality.
	Edition of *experimental music*—Michael Nyman: also, compositions.
	A Bibliography of Computer Music—Sandra Tjepkema.
1982	*The Idea of Absolute Music*—Carl Dahlhaus.
	Aesthetics of Music—Carl Dahlhaus.
	First 'compact disc' (Japan).
1983	'Virtual Environment Display' (later, 'Virtual Reality, c. 1990).
	'Composition and Utopia'—Henri Pousseur.
	(*On the Line*—Gilles Deleuze/Felix Guattari: ambiguously views 'avant-gardism' as of 'marginal groups': this may be the European experience, c. 1980, but this view may also be viewed ominously).
	Work: 'The Stravinsky Fountain' (Paris: Jean Tinguely and Niki de St. Phalle).
	'*La Musique dans la Société de Divertissement*'—Heinz-Klaus Metzger. (Metzger is editor, with Rainer Riehn, of the publication on music: *Text + Kritik*).
	Jean Baudrillard, author of, 'America' (Engl. 1988), comments that 'Utopia' has now entered the 'real': and 'here we are'... (but society is still primitive). The 'crisis' mentioned may entail a certain 'worklessness' inherited from the enlightenment (c. 1750–1800) and now conspicuous.
1984	*Messe*—Wolfgang von Schweinitz.
	The Postmodern Condition—Jean-Francois Lyotard.
1985	*Essays on the Philosophy of Music*—Ernst Bloch. Also 'Star Wars'.
	(c.): Work of John Adams, Rolf Gehlhaar.
	Ryoanji—John Cage.
	The Magic of the Tone and the Art of Music—Dane Rudhyar.
	Work: Surrounded Islands—Christo ('concrete utopia').
1986	*Orientations: Collected Writings*—Pierre Boulez.
	Music, Mysticism and Magic—Joscelyn Godwin.
1987	*La Ville d'en Haut*—Olivier Messiaen: The 'Sound Colours of Paradise'.

	The Philosophical Discourse of Modernity—Jürgen Habermas. (n.b. Martin Heidegger had expressed a willingness to learn about modern experimentalism in 1966 (Der Spiegel 1966).
1989	**La Lontananza Nostalgica Utopica Futura*—Luigi Nono.
	**Voyage Absolu des Unari vers Andromede*—Iannis Xenakis.
	'Music, Language and Modernity'—Andrew Bowle, in *The Problems of Modernity*, ed. A. Benjamin (U.K.).
	**Jade Palace Orchestra Dances*—Terry Riley.
	Cosmic Music—ed. Joscelyn Godwin.
	(c.): Europe—'techno'/'house music'/'dance music'...
1990	(c.): Women composers becoming more prominent (one may recall Fanny Mendelssohn, Clara Schumann).
	*Opera: New Year—Michael Tippett (...'Space Visitors from Nowhere Tomorrow').
	Towards a Cosmic Music—Karlheinz Stockhausen.
	Available: *Texte*, Vols. 1–6—Karlheinz Stockhausen.
	*The Heavens—Peter Schat.
	...'Avant-gardism' against 'radicalism': an unpursued perspective...
	Image: (information theory)—'This Island Earth'...: but, the soil?...: Heritage of the work of Joseph Beuys... Dr Jacques Lacan: 'He has always spoken against: "liberation"...'
	...Scriabin in New York: Korngold in Moscow...: new 'conservatism'.
1991	**Unforeseen events*—David Behrman: 'mutantrumpet' and computer (Experimental Intermedia Foundation, New York).
	...*'Neural Network'—David Tudor.
	...**Éclairs sur l'Audelà*—Olivier Messiaen.
	*June Buddhas—Terry Riley.
	(c.): Work of John Zorn (controlled improvisation), Alfred Schnittke.
1992	Australia: Publication: *Essays in Sound* by Contemporary Sound Arts, Sydney, initiated.
	Deaths of Olivier Messiaen, composer/teacher; and John Cage, whose 'oeuvre' includes the experimental involving the attempt to teach the excellence of existence. 'Big Bang' theory questioned (U.S.).
	Healing Sounds—Jonathan Goldman.
1993	*Harmony of the Spheres*—Joscelyn Godwin.
	*'...explosante-fixe...'—Pierre Boulez: after the work of 1972.
1994	**The Points of the Compass*—Mauricio Kagel.
	(c.): (re)investigation of 'sonoluminescence', and 'brownian noise'.
1995	(One Critique of 'Modernity': Introduction to Modernity—Henri Lefebvre [orig. 1962]).
	*City Life—Steve Reich.
	Seiji Ozawa forms his own orchestra; Simon Rattle on television...
	(c.): *'Metropolis' symphony—Michael Doherty.
	(c.): David Cope (U.S) and 'Experiments in Musical Imagination'

	(Stanford University).
1997	'Sonic Bloom' (Dan Carlson): for use with plants.
	The Mozart Effect—Don Campbell.
	...'Flicker Noise' investigated.
	—Acoustic Sensor:—'x-ray sound'—'swept frequency acoustic interferometry'.
	(c.): *Dream House: Seven Years of Sound and Light—La Monte Young/Marian Zazeela.
1998	Crisis: CD 'Utopia Banished' (group: Napalm Death), versus—CD 'It's Tomorrow Already' (group: Irresistible Force).
	From c. 1968: consideration of the creation of 'concept music' (Phillip L. Ryan), along with 'sonogeny' after 'terra-formation' and 'planetary engineering'.
2000	(c.): Rethinking nature and culture for tomorrow.
2008	...'cyberetics', 'psybernetics': protection and management of the brain...

Art is an imagined experience of total activity.

—R. G. Collingwood

Music is one among other means towards self-fulfilment, integration, self-actualisation, including the concept of 'play.

—Abraham Maslow

'The Music of the Future' (Cyril Scott, 1933): 'Psychically gifted composers will further set themselves the task of writing types of music creating thought-forms suited to specific moods or emotional states. With the vast array of musical resources available, they will be able to meet the needs of the most complex of modern psychology'.

...'unimaginable unity-song'...: however: ...tomorrow ever comes...

A NOTE OF MUSIC AND UTOPIA: LOST WORLDS, NEW FOUND LANDS

Artwork: 'Draw air...': ...the air of another planet (after Stefan George/Arnold Schoenberg).

Music, as projective (Feuerbach) or as 'object' (experiment), teaches appropriation. Recently, Jacques Derrida (1995) called such appropriation impossible, but he listens. What precisely is to be appropriated? Bach is original; Handel inspires conventionalism (Cyril Scott, 1933). The 'bland utopia' (Boulez, 1985) admits anything, and 'we' do not wish to be bland! There is presented absolute music (Bach), 'genius' (Beethoven), cosmic music (Stockhausen) and the other, from 'popular culture' especially after jazz (1917: the first jazz record) to the project of 'avant-gardism', sound art and sonics, 'expanded music'. 2000—the problematic presents that of the 'house' and the cosmos, and that of finding a way forward. Has the 'peak' (after Maslow) been reached? Luigi Nono expressed regret in 1989 at aspects of the 'future utopia'. Towards 'sonogeny' (after H. G. Wells, 1933) or the creation of sound environments, including a 'sound environment' (pun intended), after 'Happenings' (c. 1948–1970...), haiku theatre, events, assemblage: the proponence of an ultimate spontaneity or appropriation by those with 'personality', talent even genius (the last a 'problem' for education)—'no mere action will change the world' (Heidegger, 1954)? Some 'ends' have been proposed by composers involving 'world-views', including Rilke's (that art proposes the ultimate goal): *Staatstheater*—Maurico Kagel (1970); *Theatre Piece*—John Cage (1960); *Originale*—Karlheinz Stockhausen (1961); Pierre

Boulez does not compose very many works except, importantly, engagement expressed in a continuity of aesthetic (cf., Mallarmé and the 'work'). 'Semi-direct democracy' (Alvin Toffler, 1980 [the *Third Wave*], after the pessimism of *Future Shock* [1970])' 'direct electronic voting' (Buckminster Fuller)? 'Utopia', its concept however defined, presents the possibility of post-historical, plenitudinous finality (cf., Finalism after Bergson [1911, 1946]): a research project. 'Open World' (Bohr), 'Supranational' (Einstein), 'Open Society'(Bergson; critical of Popper): (against 'pop philosophy')—henceforth, after all is said and done, what is incontrovertible, no matter what means of expression and communication, style and (necessary) 'ideology' are utilised, the first and final foundation is *the whole*. 'Ultramodernity' turns out to be means only and it knows it. Research project: critique of Atlantis as figure of the 'crisis' (or 'critical zone') in and as 'culturalism' as distinct from 'living culture'.[1]

To organise a reading of the present statement towards a critical history of music and sound, it should be noted that:

1. Any 'piling up' of confusions precipitates 'collapse' or 'history'.
2. Genealogy and criticism restore originality.
3. 'History' is not memory.
4. Synthesis subsumes analysis: cf., the 'analog' and the 'digital' respectively.
5. Constitution is genesis which is also constituting.
6. Any object, e.g. a musical object, has both being and character (after Alexius Meinong).
7. Any object is impossible which is contradictory in its character so precluding its being. It is homeless.
8. Contradictions are inadequate concepts (after Georg Hegel) which should be 'worked through' (appreciation and dialectic): logicistic, psychologistic, ontologistic (after Edmund Husserl).
9. A 'world' qua 'world' = a 'non-being', sic 'means' (after Martin Heidegger). (As such, one can 'judge' something as being marvellous, intriguing, amazing, and so on—cerebral process is transcendental and not 'under the object').

As such, one can begin reading between the lines in addition to critical assessment. Reading (...appropriation) is at least 'metanoic'.

Part one of this paper appears in Essays in Sound #1, *1992.* —*Genealogy, 'History', Criticism: 'Natura Naturans...'*—

1. Further reading: *The Urban Revolution*, Henri Lefebvre, 1970.

Death's Murmur
Allen S. Weiss

'I am dead, and resuscitated with the bejewelled key to my last spiritual Casket'.[1] So writes Stéphane Mallarmé to his friend Théodore Aubanel on 16 July 1866, with the certainty that he has discovered the secret to his life work. It is a secret that stems from an impossible subject position, a paradoxical enunciatory act, a morbid ideal, a quasi-mystical affective structure, and a contradictory narrative sequence. This 'death' is more than mere metaphor, since for years Mallarmé had suffered from such a great a variety of psychic and physical symptoms, probably both real and hypochondriacal, that his condition escapes precise medical diagnosis: 'peculiar sterility', 'crushing powerlessness', 'I am sick in the head', 'real debasement', 'spleen', 'complete exhaustion', 'illness attacking the "saint of saints", the very brain', 'sterile despair', 'instants bordering on madness', 'hysterical crisis', 'cataleptic absence', 'disorder', 'total nullity', 'anxiety and conflict'.[2] The moment that he overcame those years of pain and crisis coincided with a metaphysical revelation that set the stage for the aesthetic underpinnings of his most profound and complex work.

In April 1866 Mallarmé plunged into, and returned from, the abyss. Writing on 14 May of that year to Henri Cazalis, he explains both the spiritual delicacy and the metaphysical megalomania of that condition:

> I admit, furthermore, but only to you, that I still need, so great was the damage to my triumph, to look at myself in this mirror in order to think, and that if it were not in front of the table where I write this letter to you, I would once again become Nothingness. This is to let you know that I am now impersonal, and no longer the Stéphane that you knew but rather an aptitude that the Spiritual Universe has to see itself and to develop, through what used to be me.[3]

Thus shall the universe find its identity in Mallarmé, in a moment of synthesis destined to produce the work which is the very image of this psychocosmic development. He will realise several years later that in order to succeed in this project he would have to 'relive the life of humanity from its infancy and coming to consciousness of itself',[4] a precursor to Nietzsche's famous claim that 'I am all the names in history'. It would seem that poetry and aesthetics had found yet another transpersonal model of inspiration, where the muse was to become Universal History. This extreme spiritual condition was certainly not without relation to the major totalising idealist philosophical statement of the epoch, Hegel's *Phenomenology of Mind*, the final chapter of which, 'Absolute Knowledge', ends with a verse adapted from Schiller's 'Die Freundschaft':

> The chalice of this realm of spirits
> Foams forth to God His own Infinitude.[5]

Henceforth, narcissism would be cosmic (or at least pantheistically worldly), and self-reflection could hardly avoid the incursions of contingency and history. Metaphysics would be nothing but the remains of madness in the face of a destabilising contingency; no longer theory, but the simulacrum of theory. As a prelude to Nietzsche, Mallarméan poetry as sublimated activity would be an ego defence against the last vestiges of theology. Yet poetry's manifestly desublimatory moment had not yet arrived—at least not in the French language.

The quasi-Hegelian, solipsistic explanation of Mallarmé's 'terrestrial apparition' received its poetic representation in four prose poems 'on the spiritual conception of Nothingness'.[6] Though henceforth inextricably linked to the Void, his crises would now serve as inspiration ('for I experience moments akin to the madness glimpsed in equilibrating ecstasy'[7]) rather than blockage, attested to by the fact that for years he had conceived of entitling one of his books *Somptuosité du Néant*.[8] This is a sumptuousness inherent in the very texture of his verse and prose, one which would in turn inspire several major trends in twentieth-century poetry and theory.

Georges Poulet, in the chapter of his *Etudes sur le temps humain* devoted to Mallarmé, understands the implications of this metaphysical and moral crisis as follows: 'But what is Nothingness? It is thought, all thought. There is not one of our ideas that is not a lie, there is not one of our dreams that is not a nonreality'.[9] Poulet would seem to be misled by the generalities of his own phenomenological limits, perhaps exacerbated by a contemporary Sartreanism derived from *Being and Nothingness*. For as shall become apparent: (1) the ultimate personal enunciation of death, 'I am dead', is an impossible thought; (2) nothingness has a very specific signification for Mallarmé, directly related to worldly contingence and the fleetingness of perceptual presence; (3) nothingness is thus a precondition both for his thought and his poetry.

*

At the moment of his revelation, Mallarmé writes: 'Unfortunately, while excavating verse to this point, I have encountered two abysses, which drive me to despair. One is Nothingness…the other void that I found is that of my chest'.[10] As the basis of both his existence and his poetry, the different voids—inner and outer, body and world—will often textually appear as equivocal, articulated by that central Mallarméan metaphor, the fold (*le pli*). What might have become an insurmountable ontological doublebind will be sublimated into a renewal of French syntax and poetics. The polysemic valence of the term hinges on the abyss separating life and death, such that the fold reconstitutes the rich and ambivalent space of the tomb—specifically, Mallarmé's long deferred but often meditated upon grave, where the inner and outer voids shall finally converge.

Following Maurice Blanchot, Roland Barthes characterised the writing of Mallarmé as follows: 'This art has the very structure of suicide: within it silence is a homogeneous poetic time that wedges the word between two layers and makes it burst, less like the scrap of a cryptogram than like a light, a void, a murder, a freedom'.[11] Mallarmé's art is conceived of as a cryptogram, the writing of the crypt: hidden, covered, invisible, latent, occult, secret, private, unavowed, hidden by dissembling.[12] Nothing less than consideration of all of these nuances at each and every instant of Mallarmé's poetry can suffice as an overture to his writing.

The fold hides nothing, enfolds itself, and veils anything whatsoever. As image (polyvalent and disseminant as it may be), the fold proves to be the metaphor, model and paradigm of the void, of nothingness. It is the subtle insinuation (and never eruption) of nothingness in the world, the mind, the text. For Mallarmé, the fold is equivalent to a textual tomb, the transcendent origin of all rhetoric, the innate *telos* of every poetic enunciation. According to Jean-Pierre Richard, the polysemy of this term is central to Mallarmé's poetics; he writes here in a particularly Bachelardian mode:

> The Mallarméan figure of the *fold*, for example, permits us to join the erotic to the sensible, then to the reflexive, the metaphysical, the literary: the fold is simultaneously sex, leaf, mirror, book, and tomb, all of them realities that it brings together in a certain special dream of intimacy.[13]

Yet the link between the fold and the void would seem to take ontological, if not always poetic, precedence in this metaphoric sequence, as the fold is precisely the site of the void that confronted Mallarmé both within and without. It ambiguously assumes both a decentring function of fluctuation and a recentring movement of reflexion—unlike the mirror, which operates as a sign of the impossible adequation of image and object, of word and thing. Appearances of the fold manifest a perpetual ontological slippage in contrast to any possible mimetic, symbolic or metaphysical operation of resemblance or representation.

The ambiguity between inner and outer voids would seem to function psychologically for Mallarmé as an ego defence against the idea of his own, definitive death. Yet its textual role relates more specifically to that cognitive and emotive interference known as chance, the vagaries of which will increasingly haunt the author until his final work, 'Un coup de dés', where the aleatory will finally be reckoned with. For if chance disrupts meaning and creativity, it is nevertheless a perpetual sign of life. Mallarmé himself states, in 'Le livre, instrument spirituel', that: 'The folding is, in regard to the large printed page, an almost religious index, which is not as striking as its piling up, in thickness, offering the minuscule tomb, most certainly, of the soul'.[14] Tome, tomb: this would be to poetically locate the soul immediately within the book as monument, such that literary life eternally bears its morbid counterpart at its very depths. This notion is an integral part of the 'crisis of verse' which was the subject of one of Mallarmé's central theoretical statements, where he recognises a *fin de siècle* crisis in poetry characterised by 'a disquietude of the veil in the temple with its significant folds and its tear'.[15] This was, certainly, a crisis he helped create, precisely thanks to the very use of the metaphor he used to signify it, the fold, which alternately caressed and tortured the French language to new structural and intellectual limits.

A continuous, stylised and indefinite folding is already apparent in the complexities of Mallarmé's syntactic convolutions (not unrelated to Wagnerian chromaticism): the elongated sentences, as if folding over on themselves clause after clause, lead to suspension, evanescence, absence, and rupture within both subject and object. Yet unlike so much modernist poetry inspired by Mallarmé, a faultless if tortuous syntax is never belied; it is contorted and knotted, yet 'proper' usage is never surpassed. Syntax always remains, as Mallarmé insists, the 'pivot of intelligibility', even as it leads to that supreme site of nonsense, death.[16] The fold, whiteness, silence, nothingness, the tomb, the void: these are the figures—or perhaps we should rather say immaterialities, or nullities, or imponderabilities, or intangibilities—that circumscribe the Mallarméan text and subject. For isn't noise the epitome of life and absolute silence the sign of death? As Jean-Pierre Richard explains, regarding Mallarmé's discovery of the void while writing the 'Ouverture ancienne':

It would therefore be necessary to closely analyse all the movements of style—the multiplications of appositions, cascades of genitives, doublings of terms, the dizzying use of semantic inversions or ambiguities, all of which transform the Mallarméan sentence into a sort of calculated chasm.[17]

Witness the second verse of the famed 'sonnet in -yx', where the abyss is named:

Sur les crédences, au salon vide: nul ptyx,	On the credenzas, in the empty sitting room: no ptyx,
Aboli bibelot d'inanité sonore,	Abolished bibelot of sonorous inanity,
(Car le Maître est allé puiser des pleurs au Styx	(For the Master has gone to draw from the tears of the Styx
Avec ce seul objet dont le Néant s'honore.)[18]	With this sole object by which Nothingness is honoured.)

The 'ptyx' (nonsense in French; 'fold' in Greek) rhymes and resonates with the river that separates the world from the underworld and the beyond, the *outre-tombe* which is the topos of death. Whether the ptyx be the fold in general, or the involuted seashell—precisely the *bibelot* that evokes the *inanité sonore* of both the sublime sound of the sea (another, sonorous, void) and of the improbable sound of the word 'ptyx'—it is, in any case, present through its intuited absence, in an empty room, honorific of Nothingness. Absent because the Master is dead, already across the river Styx. There is little doubt, though much ambiguity, of the relation between Mallarmé and the Master.

*

The existence of the abyss is twofold: as nothingness (unlocalisable and ever absent, as manifested in each and every person's death, traditionally mediated by theology) and in the chest (localisable and omnipresent, prone to malady and decay). About the external void, nothing may be said except by metaphor, analogy, allegory or dialectical contradiction. About the inner void, to the contrary, there exists a wealth of information, for, in the great mythical lineage of the West, the breath is the seat of the soul, and the lungs are the origin of the breath. On the biological level, it is estimated that there are between three and four hundred million alveoli (the microscopic sacs which are the site of the respiratory exchange of gases, leading oxygen to the bloodstream) in each person's lungs, so that this organ would be the ultimate set of folds, with a surface area of approximately one hundred square metres, over fifty times the average surface area of the skin. Breath and blood are corporeally linked such that, as Nietzsche insists in *Thus Spoke Zarathustra*, the soul is indeed something of the body.

Poetry, like life, is a matter of breath, as Gaston Bachelard explains throughout *L'air et les songes*. In the chapter oxymoronically entitled 'La déclamation muette', he states:

> The *poetic breath*, before being a metaphor, is a reality that can be found in the life of the poem, if one wishes to learn the lessons of the *aerial material imagination*. If more attention were placed on *poetic exuberance*, on all forms of the pleasure of speaking, softly, quickly, crying, murmuring, psalmodising...an incredible plurality of poetic breaths would be discovered.[19]

The poet is appropriately characterised by the famed definitions of man as a *tuyau sonore* (sonorous pipe) and a *roseau pensant* (thinking reed), such that even silence becomes a positive, meaningful function of breath:

> It is then truly the breath that speaks, it is the breath that is then the first phenomenon of the being's silence. Listening to this silent breath, hardly speaking, one well understands how different it is from the taciturn silence of pinched lips.[20]

Here commences the reign of breathed silence, the infinite domain of an 'open silence', which indeed has its own poets and its own poetic structures. One of the marks of modernism in poetry is the shift in the constitution of lyricism: from a descriptive model in which the musical, melodic aspect is pre-eminent, to a categorical model in which broader architectonic, performative and phatic functions reign. It is significant that this shift is in part structurally based on the advent of silence within poetry, as this silence permits both typographic expansion and free, polymorphic forms of versification (including the prose poem, which in fact constitutes the major part of Mallarmé's poetic *oeuvre*)—not to speak of its increasing role in new paradigms of subjectivity. In turn, the influence of this new form of poetic musication will transform the course of avant-garde music at mid-twentieth century.

But if there indeed exists silent poetry, poets of silence and a poetics of silence, there is certainly also a pathology of silence and breath. On 8 September 1898 Mallarmé—who during his lifetime experienced numerous episodes of laryngitis which caused him to lose his voice—suffered increasingly from that malady that had again troubled him for several days. The violent attempts to breathe exhausted him, and he feared that he would soon die. He thus asked his wife to burn his manuscripts, since, as he then explained, 'The terrible spasm of suffocation I just suffered could recommence during the night and overcome me'.[21] His premonition was correct, as the next morning, just as his doctor again began to examine his throat, the laryngeal spasms recommenced, he could not breathe at all, and died on the spot. The cause of his death was pronounced as a 'spasm of the larynx'.

In *Le Souffle coupé: Respirer et écrire*, François-Bernard Michel explains the existential significance of the symptoms of asthma. Asthma usually manifests itself as a nocturnal crisis, of mixed somatic and psychic origin, caused by the inflammation and consequent constriction of the bronchial tubes: 'This crisis mimes, in a dramatic and repetitive manner, DEATH BY SUFFOCATION'.[22] Asthma is thus one of the most anxiety-producing diseases, as the incapacity to breathe evokes the immediate spectre of the most horrible death. Hippocrates already noted that this crisis takes the form of a cataclysm, a veritable tragedy, a morbid classical drama with its well-ordered stages of augmentation, crisis and decline. He understood that the asthmatic crisis constitutes the resolution of a conflict: its cathartic finale leads the suffering protagonist towards a cure.[23] Asthma entails the blockage of breath, whence the impossibility of speaking: it is the symptom of an inadmissible pain that literally can not be stated, and thus signifies something that is to remain ineffable. What in other conditions may be expressed by the scream, as so poignantly and violently stressed by Artaud and Bataille, the asthmatic expresses by a choking silence that metaphorises the most horrifying and crushing solitude of death. It transforms breath into a death rattle. The asthmatic crisis paradoxically brings the sufferer to the verge of death so as not to die, so as not to go mad, so as not to commit suicide. Literally speaking, asthma is *mortification*: it is thus the expression of an unexpressible tragedy, the stigmata of a veritable refusal of communication, the impossibility of admitting a profound inner conflict.[24] François-Bernard Michel cites Pierre Gazaix on the topic, explaining that the asthmatic is rarely mentally ill, since the symptom is used precisely to avoid neurosis and psychosis:

> The destructive phantasms that would turn him into a neurotic, a madman or a pervert, are staged in his body and maintain the possibility of communicating through its symptom. By means of the symptom he can seduce, attack, instil guilt, castrate, idealise, punish, pervert; he can punish himself, valorise himself, project himself; he can take power or submit, he can obey or disobey; he exists.[25]

Thus the asthmatic symptom constitutes a rudimentary language, the very sign of an insufficiency—on the anxious border of an active, morbid silence or aphasia—with its whistlings, wheezings, gaspings, moanings, and stifled cries often approximating a death rattle.

Its equivocation and polysemy make it a symptom of prime value for the poetic imagination and praxis, the pathological trace of a veritable epistemological shift. Paul Valéry well understood this mode of expressing the ineffable and corporeally situated its origin, as stated in a section of his *Cahiers* entitled 'Ineffable': 'There exist no words to express certain states, just as the horse has no hands to hold a pen... So certain organs, whose function is not to do so, are obliged to receive these powerless efforts of *expression*, of *expulsion*. The heart and the breath are altered'.[26] Thus we find, in relation to Mallarmé's expression of the two voids, that one void in turn expresses the other, that the breathless emptiness of the chest is a prime existential signifier of the unutterable, unnameable, nonsensical void of Nothingness. Yet it is not as psychopathological symptom—coherent as it may be with Mallarmé's own physical and metaphysical crisis—but rather as poetic allegory, that this corporeal expression of the ineffable pertains to modern poetics and aesthetics.

*

'I am dead'. This enunciation, existentially impossible as it may be, has a history, both literary and otherwise. Soon after his crisis, in the letter where he wrote of the two voids which oriented his soul, Mallarmé also spoke of the vast efforts of writing 'Hérodiade', as well as of the need for three or four more years to complete the poem: 'I will have finally made what I dream of as a Poem—worthy of Poe and unsurpassed by his own'. (*J'aurai enfin fait ce que je rêve être un Poëme—digne de Poë et que les siens ne surpasseront pas.*)[27] It is difficult for an Anglophone reader not to note the Francophonic addition of the diacritical marks to Poe's name, corresponding to the still current orthography of the word '*poëme*'—a usage that Mallarmé significantly commenced at about the same time he wrote this letter—such that *Poë* would seem to be an epitome of *Poësie*.

In response to a survey taken a quarter of a century later, Mallarmé explains the motives of his profound and continued interest in Poe. Most tellingly, he writes: 'The intellectual armature of the poem is dissimulated and remains—takes place—in the space that isolates the stanzas and amidst the white of the paper: a significative silence that is no less beautiful to compose than the verse'.[28] Yet this silence—writerly and white, composed and intellectual—would seem to dissimulate yet another silence—corporeal and dark, morbid and harrowing—at the core of Poe's work. For Mallarmé was certainly cognizant of Poe's story 'The Facts in the Case of M. Valdemar' through Baudelaire's translation of it in *Histoires extraordinaires* as 'La Vérité sur le cas de M. Valdemar'. This is the tale of a man dying of phthisis (pulmonary tuberculosis, commonly known as consumption, a highly stigmatised disease of that epoch, and, not coincidentally, the cause of death of Poe's young wife) who is mesmerised by a friend in order to see whether death can be arrested. It is interesting to note that a medical definition of the period characterises the disease as follows: 'By pulmonary phthisis is understood a disease of the lungs which is characterised by progressive consolidation of the pulmonary texture, and by the subsequent softening and disintegration of the consolidated tissue'.[29] Compare the description of the patient in Poe's tale: 'The left lung had been for eighteen months in a semi-osseous or cartilaginous state, and was, of course, entirely useless for all purposes of vitality. The right, in its upper portion, was also partially, if not thoroughly, ossified, while the lower region was merely a mass of purulent tubercles, running one into another'.[30] It would be a mistake simply to classify this tale as one of complete fantasy or Gothic horror—just as it was a mistake for readers of the period, especially those who claimed to be partisans of mesmerism, to believe in its actuality (as they also did of Poe's other tale on the topic, 'Mesmeric Revelation').

Summoned to Valdemar's deathbed, the narrator proceeds to mesmerise (hypnotise) the patient in the state of *articulo mortis*, such that, in a description which doubtlessly fascinated Mallarmé (as well as Derrida and Barthes a century later), 'the skin generally assumed a cadaverous hue, resembling not so much parchment as white paper'. From this point on, the only words that Valdemar manages to offer in response to his being questioned about his condition, whether he feels pain and whether he is sleeping, move from constatation to contradiction: 'Yes;—asleep now. Do not wake me!—let me die so!'; 'No pain—I am dying!'; 'Yes; still asleep—dying!'; 'Yes;—no; I *have been* sleeping—and now—now—*I am dead*'. The experiment is continued for seven months, and, as the mesmerist at last decides that the time has come to end the episode of arrested death, Valdemar is finally asked his wishes on the matter. His response, his very last words, are declaimed in the same voice in which he had earlier responded: 'harsh, broken and hollow...the hideous whole is indescribable, for the simple reason that no similar sounds have ever jarred upon the ear of humanity'. They are: 'For God's sake!—quick!—quick!—put me to sleep—or, quick!—waken me!—quick—*I say to you that I am dead!*'. The tales ends:

> As I rapidly made the mesmeric passes, amid ejaculations of 'dead! dead!' absolutely *bursting* from the tongue and not from the lips of the sufferer, his whole frame at once—within the space of a single minute, or less, shrunk—crumbled—absolutely *rotted* away beneath my hands. Upon the bed, before that whole company, there lay a nearly liquid mass of loathsome—of detestable putrescence.

In 'Analyse textuelle d'un conte d'Edgar Poe', Roland Barthes explains the profound meaning of this impossible enunciation:

> The saying 'I am dead' is an exploded taboo. Now, if the symbolic is the field of neurosis, the return of the letter, which implies the foreclosure of the symbol, opens up the space of psychosis: at this point of the story, all symbol ceases, all neurosis too, and psychosis enters into the text through the spectacular foreclosure of the signifier: the *extraordinariness* of Poe is certainly that of madness.[31]

The 'I am dead' of both Mallarmé and Valdemar instantiates a paradoxical, indeed impossible, enunciation. Does it signify dying, or death, or death-in-life, or life-in-death, or life-after-death? Like the final sensations of the beating of the heart in Poe's 'The Tell-Tale Heart'—where there exists a narrative equivocation as to whether the terrifying, guilt-evoking sound of the beating heart is that of the murdered man, of the murderer, or merely a figment of the murderer's imagination—the voice of Valdemar arises from an ambiguous subject position, unidentifiably dead or alive.

In any case, such 'madness' is precisely what Mallarmé *poetically* and *asthmatically* avoided or surmounted. Whence the ambiguous, mortal significance of the asthmatic's crisis, as well as the profound linguistic conundrum of Valdemar's enunciations and Mallarmé's poetry. Barthes, again, explains:

> ...whence the fright and terror: there is a gaping contradiction between Death and Language; the contrary of Life is not Death (this is a stereotype): it is language. It is undecidable if Valdemar is living or dead; what is certain is that he speaks, without it being possible to ascribe his words to Death or Life.[32]

Yet there is a further impossibility involved in the tale of this inconceivable enunciation, one that operates on the phonetic level. Indeed, the narrator himself claims that it would be madness to try and describe what he is about to recount. Madness of the narrator, or of Valdemar? There is a manifest contradiction involved in the description of the tonality of the voice itself in relation to its manner of production. The narrator describes the intonation of the voice as if it came 'from a vast distance, or from some deep cavern within the earth', and, all the while conscious of the very incomprehensibility of his description, he remarks how that voice impressed him as 'gelatinous or glutinous matters impress the sense of touch'. Given this description, one might well imagine this speech as emanating from the 'caverns' of the belly or chest; but this is not the case. The veracity of these descriptions is, in fact, quite improbable, as the actual source of the sound is simply 'a strong vibratory motion' of the tongue, which later 'quivered, or rather rolled violently in the mouth', within 'distended and motionless jaws' which remain rigid to the end. Yet the vibratory tongue alone would be incapable of rendering the bilabials, labiodentals, alveolars, velars, and the sundry vowels of Valdemar's enunciations. As Anthony Burgess suggests in the title of his book on linguistics, speech exists thanks to 'a mouthful of air'—precisely what Valdemar cannot summon from his ossified, dead, airless lungs. Here, the symbolic function of breath itself is that of a *memento mori*. Barthes suggests that 'the voice in preparation is not dental, external civilised...but internal, visceral, muscular...the voice of death arises from the thick, internal muscular magma, from the *depths*'.[33] Were his voice to have come from a cavern, as Poe's text and Barthes' analysis misleadingly suggest, it would be that of the chest. But this is not the case, for the narrator tells us that Valdemar showed 'not the faintest sign of vitality', that 'the mirror no longer afforded evidence of respiration', and that 'the only real indication, indeed, of the mesmeric influence, was now found in the vibratory movement of the tongue'. The words of Valdemar bespeak a double impossibility: they are conceptually impossible enunciations, appropriately declaimed by a phonetically impossible voice. Indeed, this is not a question of life or death, but of language—precisely the drama to which Mallarmé wished to reduce the world.

*

Mallarmé was instrumental in one of the great aesthetic inventions of perverse and profound whiteness. In his comments, in 'Mimique', on Paul Margueritte's *Pierrot Assassin de sa femme*, we find a telling evocation: 'the mute soliloquy which, with all his soul, the white phantom spoke with his face and gestures, like a page not yet written'.[34] This phantom, white as a 'page not yet written'—which parallels Pierrot's 'cadaverous face', as well as Valdemar's skin with its 'cadaverous hue, resembling not so much parchment as white paper'—constitutes the crux of Derrida's critique, in 'La double séance', of Jean-Pierre Richard's reading of Mallarmé in *L'univers imaginaire de Mallarmé*, and motivates a principal statement of the notion of *dissémination*. The debate between Richard and Derrida is well documented, as is the critique of deconstruction, both regarding literary hermeneutics in general and more specifically Mallarmé. Rather than rehearse these familiar issues, I wish to suggest a different *use* of dissemination, a different manner of contextualising its effects—in the spirit of reading Derrida according to Mallarmé— within this narrow investigation of one aspect of the origin of modernist poetry and the precursors of sound art. In such an account, Derrida's hermeneutic hypercriticism, itself owing much to Mallarmé's syntax, encounters the abyss.

Derrida criticises the inherently phenomenological, hermeneutic and dialectical thematism in Richard's analysis, citing the sensible, reflexive and metaphysical implications of Richard's position, as exemplified by the already-cited consideration: 'the fold is simultaneously sex, leaf, mirror, book, and tomb, all of them realities that it brings together in a certain special dream of intimacy'.³⁵ Where Richard sees in 'whiteness' and 'folds' the richness of a 'particularly fecund or exuberant plurivalence',³⁶ Derrida argues for a singular textual poverty, a non-theme, a non-sense; not a polysemic field, but the inscription of a perpetual supplementarity, ruled neither by metaphor nor metonymy; not the transcendental origin of a series, but a mode of textual spacing.

> ...the white, that hymen, always re-marks itself as disappearance, erasure, non-sense. Finitude then becomes infinitude, according to a non-Hegelian identity: by an interruption that suspends the equation of mark and sense, the 'white' marks each white (this one plus every other), virginity, frigidity, snow, veil, swan's wing, froth, paper, etc., *plus* the white that permits the mark, by assuring the space of reception and production. This 'last' white (as well as that 'first' white) exists neither before nor after the series.³⁷

The fold (like whiteness) does not metaphorically mark reflexivity or coincidence with self, since it exists simultaneously and equivocally as inside and outside. Unlike Richard, who confines Mallarmé to an intimist, Symbolist, neo-Hegelian aesthetic, Derrida opens Mallarmé to an infinite dehiscence, dissemination, spacing, temporalisation.³⁸ This disseminative procedure is homologous with Mallarmé's own, for Mallarmé was, indeed, the author of the infamous notion in 'Quant au livre' that, 'Everything in the world exists in order to end up in a book'.³⁹

Yet in Mallarmé's procedure, which borders on the aesthetic limit of art-for-art's-sake, what cannot be totally sublated is death. For death is the ultimate nonsense, that which reifies the intentional meaning of the text by destroying the tacit significance of the writer's body. Derrida writes as if the body had no memory, as if voice had no body, as if writing necessitated no writer, as if a corporeal semiology were not possible. Furthermore, the allegory that drives Derrida's text must not be forgotten: tickled to death by Pierrot, Colombine dies laughing, breathless. This death is protected by a vast textual regress, as if protecting the reader, or Derrida, from the abyss apparent in the ceaseless folding over of whiteness upon whiteness—beyond all perceptual and conceptual horizons—that marks Mallarmé's texts and Pierrot's face.⁴⁰ This is an abyss, an empty *mise-en-abîme*, that Derrida textualises (or that textualises Derrida!), he who never dares to settle on the teleological impact of its terrible reality: death. This textual prophylaxis is dense. Derrida reads Mallarmé's 'Mimique' such that the simile of the white phantom, 'like a page not yet written', is taken paradigmatically (and nearly literally), thus subsuming any possible corporeal or historical reference into the (Derridean) textual system: first of all, Mallarmé probably didn't see the performance to which *Pierrot Assassin de sa Femme* refers, and he might not even have read the specific version of the publication in which the descriptive 'Notice' appeared; furthermore, Colombine is not visible and her death is never evidenced, since both victim and assassin are mimed by Pierrot—there is, most tellingly, no *corpus delicti*; and finally, after all, what is being considered is only a mime. For Derrida, all bodies constitute *corpora vilia*, to be inexorably reduced to the book.

Parallel to Pierrot's symbolic doubling and splitting into self and other, we must remember Mallarmé's need to gaze at himself in the mirror in order to exist. It is as if the mirror image were to enact an adequation of enunciation with existence, where the silent gaze in the mirror, or the tortured yet stifled laughter of the mime—each indicative of an artist split by specular ecstasy—would suffice to bridge the gap between perception and object, word and image, desire and satiety, life and death, being and nothingness. The image in the mirror doesn't breathe or see; the reflected seer, though, can easily fog over the specular image. Death exists, unnameable, somewhere in the abyss; or rather, it *is* the abyss. Is 'Mimique', standing in for the rest of Mallarmé's project, about loss of breath, or loss of death?

One might compare the appearance of the mime in the poem written by Ligeia (in Poe's tale of the same name), which ends with the affirmation,

> That the play is the tragedy, 'Man',
> And its hero, the conqueror Worm.

The silence, whiteness and cruelty of Mallarmé's mime may be compared with the universal destiny of Poe's mime, recited to Ligeia on her deathbed by her beloved:

> But see, amid the mimic rout
>   A crawling shape intrude!
> A blood-red thing that writhes from out
>   The scenic solitude!
> It writhes!—it writhes!—with mortal pangs
>   The mimes become its food,
> And the seraphs sob at vermin fangs
>   In human gore imbued.

The morbid self-reflection of this narrative construction is parallel to that of *Pierrot Assassin de sa Femme*, where the textual circuit of Pierrot-Colombine parallels that of Ligeia and her beloved, inexorably articulated by death. By enacting the other's death, one temporises in relation to one's own demise—a teleology of bad faith if ever there was one. Yet where Mallarmé seeks the universal soul, Poe sees the mortal body.

In *L'air et les songes*, Gaston Bachelard reminds us of Charles Nodier's attempt—in his *Examen critique des Dictionnaires de la langue française* (1828)—to create what he termed a *mimologism*. Sounding like a classic eighteenth-century *fou littéraire*, Nodier suggests the possibility of founding an etymology based on the observable functions of the vocal organs, a sort of active phonetics. As Bachelard explains: 'He seeks there a "mimologism", that is to say, the totality of the buccal and respiratory conditions that must be revealed by a physiognomic imitation of the *speaking face*'.[41] Surface effects are interpreted in relation to corporeal depths, where internal organs are granted a foundational role in the generation of linguistic meaning. The Mallarmé/Derrida '*mimique*' reveals the silent gestural and facial postures of the mime in an abyss of future signification; to the contrary, the Nodier/Bachelard '*mimologisme*' entails the imitation of the human voice, in order to seek a meaning grounded in the body. Following Nodier, Bachelard proposes such an etymology of the word '*âme*' (soul), concluding:

> Let us live the word like we live it when we swear to love 'with all our soul', to love 'to our last breath'. Let us live it by 'breathing' it. It will then appear to us as a *mimologism of total expiration*... In order to express the word soul (*âme*) from the depths of the imagination, the breath must offer its last reserve... Our soul, in this imaginary life of the breath, is always our *last sigh*. It is a bit of the soul that rejoins a universal soul.[42]

While such a 'mimologism of total expiration' precisely describes the schizoid simulacrum of a soul within Pierrot's murder scene, the 'soul that rejoins a universal soul' also describes the soul of the narrator of *Igitur*: 'You, expired mathematicians—me, projected absolute. Must end in Infinity. Simply word and gesture'.[43] It would also seem to indicate the Mallarmé who has suffered certain absolutely necessary developments so that 'the Universe finds, in this self, its identity',[44] and who also exclaims, in a somewhat more metaphorical, albeit still Hegelian, rhetoric, 'I worked infinitely this summer, first of all on myself, by creating, in the most beautiful synthesis, a world of which I am the God'.⁴⁵ Could we then believe that there may be an effective deduction or intuition of the words, breath and soul of the mimed Pierrot? Or is this scenario rather a precursor to Nietzsche's notion that the role of the mask in tragedy is to cover other masks, beneath which there is nothing but the abyss, as is the case in Poe's 'The Masque of the Red Death'?

Though Derrida would certainly argue for the sublation of the world within the text, he would hardly maintain the primacy of a God's eye point of view. The ambiguity or paradox inherent in Mallarmé's position does not end there. At the very moment that Mallarmé began his investigations into linguistics—which entailed both a study of epistemology (René Descartes' *Discours de la méthode*), and of physiology (Thomas Huxley's 1866 treatise, *Lessons in Elementary Physiology*)⁴⁶—he wrote, in an oft-cited letter: 'You are right, but a science book can't be simple enough for me, who easily places the larynx in the brain'.⁴⁷ This confusion of the locus of speech and thought is not just a modest joke on Mallarmé's part: it bespeaks a radical introversion of signifier and signified within the intelligible elocutionary act. It is precisely here that we discover what may be termed the *antinomy of pure poetry* in Mallarmé's work, that is: the irreducible difference between poetic voice and written verse; the fact that lyricism is based on rhetorical musication, but that a certain poetic lyricism demands silent reading; and the fact that 'inspiration' is simultaneously a matter of the interiority of the 'soul' as breath *and* its fixation in the work as exteriority, where the total distance from breath instantiates the text as tomb, as monument. Consider the following citation from 'Crise de vers', which inaugurated a certain inclination of modernist poetry toward both silent reading and unpronounceable textual experimentation (however contrary to Mallarmé's own classically based forms and syntax this influence may have turned out to be):

> The pure work implies the elocutionary disappearance of the poet, who cedes the initiative to words, by the shock of their mobilised unequalness; they are lit up by reciprocal reflections like a virtual trail of fire in gems, replacing the perceptible respiration of the ancient lyrical breath or the personal enthusiastic direction of the sentence.⁴⁸

This radical statement contradicts his continual need, to which all verse must submit, of 'suffering the oral trial or confronting diction as a mode of exterior presentation and to find high and in the crowd its plausible echo'.⁴⁹ The antinomy between elocutionary disappearance and oral trial proffers the antinomy that guides the seemingly paradoxical loss of voice in one marginal but crucial trend of nineteenth-century lyrical poetry, with huge consequences for subsequent modernism.

It is generally conceded that some time in 1863 Mallarmé abandoned the *baudelairisme* that guided his early efforts, exemplified by the poem 'Les fenêtres', which opens with a vision of 'the banal whiteness of the curtains' in a hospital as a sign of the illness, perhaps of splenetic origin, that is at the core of the poem.⁵⁰ Georges Poulet characterises this poem as 'authentically Mallarméan because ultra-Baudelairean'.⁵¹ As Mallarmé himself stated that same year, 'You are right, the spleen has nearly left me, and my poetry arises on its debris, enriched by its cruel and solitary hues, but luminous'.⁵² At that moment, Mallarmé effected a *tabula rasa* concerning his own anxiety of influence vis-à-vis Baudelaire, setting the stage for the psychic crisis which would bring him in direct contact with the void, with nothingness, with death. Here, the white page, screen, veil and mask function variously as either abysmal ground or psychic screen. Mallarmé's Hegelianism expressed the form of this crisis, not a means to its resolution. Poetics would no longer be determined by the thoughts of a God speaking to itself, but rather—as Nodier-

Bachelard might interpret Pierrot—by an interlocutor's paradoxically silent voicings of Mallarmé's words. Henceforth, aesthetic possibility exists for the reader, as suggested in the epigraph to *Igitur*: 'This Tale is addressed to the reader's Intelligence that, itself, stages the things'.[53] This aesthetic, later appropriated by Marcel Duchamp, has ramifications still being played out. Anxiety—of influence, of madness, of death—is exteriorised and projected into the work, besetting the reader with its morbid effects. Is this the scenarisation that modernism would desire for its paradigmatic instance?

*

Concerning the publication of one of Armand Renaud's books, Mallarmé wrote: 'I will not tell you anything today of its beauty; of that amorous blood that courses in its verse as in the arteries of a god'.[54] What is particularly telling is that in the manuscript, the word *vers* is written over the word *veines*. It might be said that this lapsus allegorises Derrida's hermeneutic excess, which is precisely to transmogrify *veines* into *vers*, body into text. Reading Derrida according to Mallarmé, an epistemological corrective might be to provide a corresponding, albeit antithetical, consideration of the corporeal substrate to the text. As Mallarmé explains:

> I tried to no longer think of the head, and in a desperate effort, I tightened all my nerves (of the pectus) in the manner to produce a vibration (keeping the thought on which I was then working, which became the subject of this vibration, or an impression)—and in this manner I sketched out an entire, long dreamt of poem. Since then, I told myself, in the hours of necessary synthesis, 'I will work with the heart', and I sense my heart (without a doubt my entire life is borne along by it); and, with the rest of my body, except for the hand that writes and the heart that lives, forgotten, my sketch is made—makes itself.[55]

Writing as vibration; thought as corporeal; nerves as origin. Perhaps the most extremely visceral, indeed erotic, moment in all of Mallarmé, where veins burst into verse, is in 'L'Après-Midi d'un Faune':

Tu sais, ma passion, que, pourpre et déjà mûre,	You know, my passion, that, purple and already ripe,
Chaque grenade éclate et d'abeilles murmure;	Each pomegranate bursts and bees murmur;
Et notre sang, épris de qui le va saisir,	And our blood, burning for those who shall seize it,
Coule pour tout l'essaim éternel du désir.[56]	Flows for the entire eternal swarm of desire.

It is precisely the dehiscence of the pomegranate that metaphorises shed blood as a sign of desire, of the unstated side of Eros: death. The redness of Mallarmé's pomegranate and veins, the flesh of his verse, are an integral part of these considerations of lyrical breath and breathlessness, where an underlying whiteness is always stained by the corporeal redness indicative of the violence, hermeneutic and otherwise, inherent in the gesture of reading.
As Mallarmé writes: 'The virgin folding-up of the book, again, offers itself up to a sacrifice which bloodied the red edge of ancient tomes; the introduction of a weapon, or paperknife, in order to establish the taking of possession'.[57]

'Death's Murmur' is derived from the manuscript of a forthcoming book, Breathless: Disembodiment, Sound Recording, and Transformations in Lyrical Nostalgia.

1. Stéphane Mallarmé, *Correspondance*, Paris: Gallimard/Folio, 1995, p. 312.
2. Cited in Michel Pierssens, *The Power of Babel: A Study of Logophilia*, trans. Carl R. Lovitt, London: Routledge & Kegan Paul, 1980, p. 5.
3. Mallarmé, *Correspondance*, p. 343.
4. ibid., letter to Henri Cazalis of 18 or 19 February 1869, p. 425.
5. G. W. F. Hegel, *The Phenomenology of Mind* (1807), trans. James Baillie, London: George Allen & Unwin, 1966, p. 808.
6. Mallarmé, *Correspondance*, letter to Henri Cazalis of 14 May 1867, p. 343.
7. ibid., letter to Eugène Lefébure of 3 May 1868, p. 384.
8. ibid., letter to Henri Cazalis of 3 April 1870, p. 470.
9. Georges Poulet, *Etudes sur le temps humain*, Paris: Plon, 1952, p. 323.
10. Mallarmé, *Correspondance*, letter of 28 April 1866 to Henri Cazalis, pp. 297–298.
11. Roland Barthes, 'Le degré zéro de l'écriture' (1953), in *Oeuvres complètes*, Vol. I, Paris: Le Seuil, 1993, p. 179.
12. Definition from entry *crypt* in *Webster's Third New International Dictionary,* Chicago: G. & C. Merriam, Co., 1966, Vol. I, p. 548.
13. Jean-Pierre Richard, *L'univers imaginaire de Mallarmé*, Paris: Le Seuil, 1961, p. 28.
14. Mallarmé, 'Le livre, instrument spirituel' (1895), in *Oeuvres complètes*, eds. Henri Mondor and G. Jean-Aubry, Paris: Gallimard/Pléiade, 1945, p. 379.
15. Mallarmé, 'Crise de vers' (1886-1892-1896), *Oeuvres complètes*, p. 360.
16. Mallarmé, 'Quant au livre' (1895), *Oeuvres complètes*, p. 385.
17. Richard, op. cit., p. 72.
18. Mallarmé, 'Plusieurs sonnets', *Oeuvres complètes*, p. 68.
19. Gaston Bachelard, *L'air et les songes: Essai sur l'imagination du mouvement*, Paris, José Corti, 1943, p. 271.
20. ibid., p. 274.
21. Cited in Gérard Macé, 'Mallarmé, mort en miroir', *La Nouvelle Revue Française # 321* (1979), p. 90.
22. François-Bernard Michel, *Le Souffle coupé: Respirer et écrire*, Paris: Gallimard, 1984, p. 7. For a very different account of elliptical, and thus silent, writing, see Allen S. Weiss, 'Impossible Sovereignty', in *The Aesthetics of Excess*, Albany: State University of New York Press, 1989, pp. 12–28.
23. Michel, ibid., pp. 197–198.
24. ibid., p. 195.
25. Pierre Gazeix, 'Aspects psychologiques de l'asthme', *Médicine actuelle*, Vol. 8, No. 4 (1981), pp. 131–133; cited in Michel, p. 209.
26. Paul Valéry, *Cahiers*, Vol. 2, Paris: Gallimard/Pléiade, 1974, p. 362; cited in Michel, p. 53.
27. Mallarmé, *Correspondance*, letter of 28 April 1866 to Cazalis, p. 297.
28. Mallarmé, 'Sur Poë', *Oeuvres complètes*, p. 872. It might be noted that in French 'blank verse' is '*vers blanc*'.
29. Thomas Henry Green, *An introduction to pathology and morbid anatomy* (1871), cited in *The Compact Edition of the Oxford English Dictionary*, Vol. II, Oxford: Oxford University Press, 1971, p. 2160.
30. Edgar Allan Poe, 'The Facts in the Case of M. Valdemar', in *The Complete Tales and Poems of Edgar Allan Poe*, New York: Random House/Modern Library, 1938, pp. 96–103, *passim*. All subsequent quotations are from this edition.
31. Roland Barthes, 'Analyse textuelle d'un conte d'Edgar Poe' (1973), in *Oeuvres complètes*, Vol. II, Paris: Le Seuil, 1994, p. 1671.
32. ibid., p. 1669.
33. ibid., p. 1668.
34. Mallarmé, 'Mimique' (1886), *Oeuvres complètes*, p. 510.
35. Richard, op. cit., pp. 27–28; cited in Jacques Derrida, 'La double séance', in *La dissémination*, Paris: Le Seuil, 1972, p. 281.

36. Derrida, ibid., p. 282.
37. ibid., p. 285.
38. ibid., p. 303.
39. Mallarmé, 'Quant au livre', p. 378.
40. ibid., p. 297.
41. Bachelard, op. cit., p. 272.
42. ibid., p. 273.
43. Mallarmé, 'Igitur ou La folie d'Elbehnon', in *Oeuvres complètes*, p. 436.
44. Mallarmé, *Correspondance*, letter of 14 May 1867 to Henri Cazalis, p. 343.
45. ibid., letter of 20 December 1866 to Armand Renaud, p. 335.
46. ibid., letter of 31 December 1869 to Henri Cazalis, pp. 456–458.
47. ibid., p. 472.
48. Mallarmé, 'Crise de vers', *Oeuvres complètes*, p. 366.
49. Mallarmé, 'Notes, 1895', *Oeuvres complètes*, p. 855.
50. Mallarmé, 'Les fenêtres', *Oeuvres complètes*, p. 32.
51. Poulet, op. cit., p. 305.
52. Mallarmé, *Correspondance*, letter to Frédéric Mistral of 31 December 1863, p. 275.
53. Mallarmé, *Igitur*, p.433.
54. Mallarmé, *Correspondance*, letter of 20 December 1863 to Armand Renaud, p. 155.
55. ibid., letter of 27 May 1867 to Eugène Lefébure, p. 354.
56. Mallarmé, *Oeuvres complètes*, p. 52.
57. Mallarmé, 'Le livre, instrument spirituel', *Oeuvres complètes*, p. 381.

The Moon in Front of the Window: Reflections on the radio of Kaye Mortley[1]

Virginia Madsen

She says: 'I work in two different ways. Sometimes I record myself and sometimes I don't record myself. When I don't record myself, I work with either someone I know very well, or someone I don't know at all. I'm speaking here about outdoor recordings'.[2]

Kaye Mortley travels with a microphone; 'I like to catch some of the sound of the place, wander around with a tape recorder'. The places she records, 'cuts', and later rebuilds—often much later when they have acquired a degree of strangeness—are made for radio and the mysteries which still reside in radiophonic transmission.

Mortley's life work in radio appears to be part of a long and slowly unravelling project. 'I do listen to everything I record but it's not punctual. I just keep recording and recording and cut it up as if it were paper. I keep very small bits, so it's actually the editing rather than the microphone.'

Kaye Mortley began working in radio at the ABC in Australia at a time in the early seventies when the radio drama and features department was looking for ideas beyond the familiar and overly authoritative BBC role model. How had she come to the radio? 'Almost by chance', she says, and elaborates no further. Later she adds, 'I think it has something more to do with writing and when I was a very small child I thought I'd like to write. I used to write things. I still do'.

There are texts in Kaye's work—fragments finely sculpted, the concrete drifting towards fiction. There are 'floating memories of texts' and single words that billow, opening out like a sail.

Here one senses the materiality of time, as expressed by the movement of sound in a bounded space, the marks of a journey felt in small vibrations, between reality and fiction. Voice and sound are woven into exquisitely rendered radio films, immersive 'acoustical universes' and, more recently, the series she calls 'transparent documentaries'. The work lies in the tradition of minimalism with its respect for the purity of forms. Although cool in temperament (the opposite of McLuhan's 'hot' radio) the work is never totally detached. Often Mortley records for hours and hours, listening and forgetting, filling old boxes with tapes, working always with time and the spaces time inhabits. The work is subtle, surprising the listener with a hard-edged, gritty quality that seems to emanate directly from reality itself.

In the era of the sound bite, radio with this kind of temperament is rare. It is close to what we most often call documentary, but Mortley's work is more akin to poetry than document; a poetry of the real found in ordinary places, overheard, translated, on the way to somewhere else. Here the ordinary reveals its strangeness and space is heard to be haunted by memory and desire.

For Mortley, the very tape used—and digital tape, she believes, is no cleaner or more pure in this regard—is marked with time and the memories of its first listener. It is a ruin, covered by the strata of lost civilisations, promising 'some perfect archaeological object at the bottom'. This is what happens when you work with recordings, touched by memory and desire.

'Every piece of tape I deal with is so overlaid with every moment I've touched it. It's very strange. It's overloaded with a million memories, so it ceases to be the actual sound. It's a little as though the material were building its own archaeology. It begins in a pristine, virgin state and you listen to it once and all you can remember is what happened when you recorded it. Then you listen to it again and it's already overloaded with the memories of what happened the first time you listened to it. Each time you work on it, something else falls on top.'

Mortley calls this the *couche renversé* of the tape—an upside-down layer of another civilisation, a reversed archaeology. 'Then you start working on it, and battling with the tape, and it becomes something else. You get to the point where there are so many layers that it has become nothing. It's ceased to be a sound film or sound postcard and has become something else. The tape then no longer feels the same way. It becomes objectified in a sense, and I know I can only deal with a piece of tape when it's completely separate from me, from this construct of time. At this point I begin to use it.'

In our interview at her home and workspace in Paris, Kaye says she is drawn to record places which 'have a sort of delimitation to the space; otherwise, I feel, it could be...endless...'. These 'closed spaces' open out to the listener like little universes whose particular sounds and silences go towards the sustaining of time.

'Sometimes they have a wall around them, or they're called "Paris", or a shearing shed, or a concentration camp, or St Lucia's Day. It could be the space between you and me, an interview...'

In this space of only sound, 'voices' emerge from the darkness, giving time density and durability, the *durée* referred to by Bergson—something like a resonance, something still, like memory.

Here are memories of absence or transience, the awkwardness of the microphone, or its blindness, residues of surface noise and silences beyond translation: *Stopover Bangkok, Under Madrid, Do You Remember Jogjakarta?, Images of Yrkalla...* [3]

A place is also a marking of time in this body of work (time is a space) and there are places built just for time, where time idles and gathers. There are small and sometimes invisible monuments for the consciousness of time which is remembered but not always understood:

- *It's the Day's—Lucy's*.[4] (The place: Sweden. December 13. St Lucia's Day, day of the longest night, and the brightest flame. Text, Interview, Genesis and Revelation.)

- *2146 Stones...2146 Places*.[5] (An architecture of ordinary, yet extraordinarily textured, voices from the seven linguistic regions of Germany, made with German radio and 'set against the banality of everyday life'.[6] A recitation of names—the still unnameable, burning beneath the cobblestones. After Jochen Gerz's 'invisible monument'[7] in Saarbrucken Square, Germany.)

Mortley has been described as a 'documentarian', but this is not a term I'd use to speak of her work which, as she says, must 'glide toward fiction'. She is a 'writer in sound'; one of radio's few genuine *auteurs*.

Kaye makes programs about places she knows, and does not know. 'It's to do with knowing and not knowing', she says. 'I always felt I was a foreigner wherever I was.' In a sense all of her programs are foreigner's programs: 'Because I think that even if you're there for your whole life you don't know it. So everything is a pretext for something, I think. Most of my radio pieces are a pretext for a state of mind, a state of feeling'.

Kaye left Australia a long time ago and began to work in this very particular, and perhaps arcane, space carved from this still quite young medium, the radio.

In this precarious space, the silences become as important as words. (How to translate them with elegance?) These silences, these little or long spaces, can so easily be filled in, be buried by the accretion of words and questions.

Kaye's speech is filled with such 'empty' moments, as are her own 'writings on tape'. She says: 'It's where the listener can write himself into the tape, which is why a lot of my programs seem very empty'.

Silence is as important as sound, as dense or as empty... The work gravitates towards these kind of time-spaces—or places where there can be little '*creux de vie*', as she calls them, little pockets of life—where the silences act as a centrifuge for the pirouette of words.

We think silence doesn't exist, except in the negative, as death. But there is the *durée* of places of silence, little hollows in time which draw silence in towards them.

She says: 'I think what remains are distances, you know.'

I hear myself asking: 'Do you consciously feel you have a project with radio or is it something more...intuitive, accidental?'

'Always there are things which touch me very deeply, but I have to let them go a certain distance, like the tape I was talking about before, until I feel I'm not just doing them about myself; they can belong to everyone. There is that famous line of Rimbaud's: "I is always an other". "I" has to become an other before you can work on it.'

If Kaye's programs give silence a density—something unimaginable in information media—they also explore the complex universe of what is left unsaid, the gaps and resonances around words which always reveal too much or too little. The work opens a space in which we can sense small nerve-end fractures in the self-contained worlds we so often build around us. Kaye calls this, after Nathalie Sarraute, 'conversation and subconversation, text and subtext'. *Tropismes*.[8]

'I have said sometimes that what interests me most is a sort of change of emotional state in the perception of the listener. It's very pretentious to say it like that, but I think what is interesting is when something happens—when something topples over and you feel or perceive something for which there are possibly no words. In French you say, "*Il y a un ange qui passe*", and this is when an angel goes by. For instance, when everyone is quiet for a second at a table: everyone has been talking and then suddenly they are quiet. An angel has passed by and there is some slight perception which cannot be verbalised, only perceived acoustically, but which touches the whole state of being of the person. And this is made possible by radio work. I think that is what is most interesting for me in the work.'

Kaye's project in radio has very little to do with journalism or the contemporary obsession with information. In the mass media, information appears like an expanding universe, an infinity of stars appearing everywhere at once, shooting outwards from us at the speed of light. A swarm of journalists runs close behind.

We are never in one place long enough, nor find the silences in which to idle in dead time. What remains are distances without density, collapsed into one another by the collective *trompe l'œil* of the media.

What you notice in particular about Mortley's programs is the absence of the interviewer, or at least the absence of certain familiar questions. 'I find it very hard to ask people questions. I don't ask people questions which they don't want to answer. I ask people questions which I think they're going to answer and then I don't ask so many. I feel if you have enough time with people and the climate is sufficiently right, they will end up saying something for you along the lines of that which interested you in the first place.'

The microphone here is not transparent, and yet it can reveal the question as well as the answer, opening up the space between them. Paradoxically, then, Mortley's subject is often the questions (or their absence) and the very particular ecologies opened up by the apparently 'transparent' microphone. 'My project', she affirms, 'has got nothing to do with information.'

Could it be a space in which you might not ask questions?

'Maybe', she replies, and then returns to the subject of writing which concerns her most. 'I was attracted to radio by the (Kaye breaks the word into fragments) e-phem-er-al-ity...the fact that something could be very highly worked and very highly written onto a tape, then disappear and only leave its trace in the mind of the hearer. The idea of doing something quite invisible which literally passes in the air; that pleased me very much. And that this could happen outside the circuit of actual writing.'

In the days when Kaye began to write, the publishing circuit was mostly out of reach to young Australian would-be writers. Surprising as it may seem now, State radio became a place for limited experimentation. By the early seventies the BBC hold on 'good' production values and the 'well-made' was increasingly under attack. After May '68 some young producers turned to the revolts in Europe for inspiration, the desire there to unlock the studios, opening their 'dead' air to the breath of the world. With new, more portable recording technology, and an increasing disrespect for formulaic professionalism, producers like Mortley became interested in the world beyond the studio and its limited repertoire of sound effects. Mortley in particular became interested in exploring sonic actuality and its ability to metamorphose in the mind of the listener, to glide towards fiction.[9]

In October 1969 Radio France opened its studio doors to the experiment known as *L'Atelier de Création Radiophonique*, literally the workshop for radiophonic creation. (Kaye now produces regularly for the Atelier).

Founded by René Farabet and Alain Trutat, this *atelier* was something new in the history of French radio and artistic traditions. In the wake of student revolts, and because of more profound changes in public perception, a space was offered (of the long *durée*) to explore what radio might be, what it could become. Of course there had already been some experiments such as Antonin Artaud's 1947 *Pour en Finir avec le Jugement de Dieu* (To Have Done With the Judgement of God), an extraordinary piece of radiophonic performance and heresy which had never in fact left the French studio mausoleum. A dead letter awaiting transmission, the subject of a profound censorship.[10]

Farabet was 'given' nearly three hours of time to do with as he pleased—to excavate the time-spaces of radio, and take microphones outside into the light and into the noise. Kaye Mortley very quickly discovered the Atelier: 'When I was twenty-one I went to Europe and I was plunged into a bath of European activity, where I stayed a long time and didn't come back to Australia...'. She continues to be one of the Atelier's principal protagonists, producing often long, immersive pieces which do not merely represent worlds in sound, but connect more intimately with the listener, opening the space to a kind of freedom.

I say: 'I can't hear pigeons anymore without thinking of your *Ailles, Entre Elles* (Wings, Between Women) program'.[11]

And she says, almost laughing, 'I can't hear pigeons the same way either'.

I ask her if, in her own work, there is a strong connection with the work of the Atelier—this spatial openness, and 'the emptiness' she described before. Is there something like the same attitude?

'Maybe.'

I say: 'With the Atelier there is for me an idea of a research process going on, unwinding; but the workshop is also akin to the laboratory and the developing room. One goes outside to the world, listens, records, becomes immersed in the life there, but then returns to a kind of darkroom where something both physical and metaphysical can occur'.

'The immersion process, perhaps...' She is remembering something. 'What interested me [with the Atelier] was that someone could be so completely immersed in the material, so completely one with the material; that the material could, on the one hand, be itself, and, on the other, express what the author wanted to say... There is the *cinéma d'auteur* and the *radio d'auteur*.'

We are speaking about the author, yet in another part of the tape Kaye is awkward with these terms. When I suggest that the work she is doing might be art she counters: 'I have a problem with words like writer or artist or things which are almost words of praise'.

'Words of transcendence?'

'Transcendence, yes. I think you just do things you see, so maybe I just wished to avoid all these other circuits... I'm not sure that the first vocation of radio, even of works that are put under the label of radio art, is to be art, what one calls "art". Jochen Gerz always says "if you write in the context of writers you're called a writer, if you write in the context of artists, it's called art, you're an artist". And radio programs are not made for museums: radio programs are made for broadcasting companies, and there's a little difference. Logically, the "other" is always present because the work is destined to the other who is making this possible. In a sense this is true of the artwork. It can hang in a museum because someone has decided to hang it there, but if no one goes to see it it's still an art work.'

'Is there a problem with this lack of a history in radio, of markers, of *repères*? You can feel very alone.'

'It would be useful if there were more markers; the idea of a community or some literature. But then again, the whole nature of radio work is ephemeral and, in a sense, maybe it's appropriate, even though it's a completely awful situation—but maybe this is written into the nature of radio work.'

'Samuel Beckett, who also moved to France and worked outside his mother tongue, talked about the "dark space of the radio". He was one of the few writers who tried to make something particular with radio, in radio. He was not in the habit of translating other forms into radio, trying to translate them "for" radio. Does that notion of his, of the "dark space", have any resonance for you?'

'Dark space? Because you don't see it?'

There is a silence. I'm not wishing to be the journalist here.

'Blind space. It's a blind space'.

(At this interval, while we wait for each other to hold on to the idea, I hear a train coming into a platform, and, far off, the muddy phantom sounds of Paris and car wheels and walled-in voices, and some uncertain whistling hovering above the apartments.)

'I don't think I think like that. I don't have many references, but Beckett isn't one of them.'

'What references do you have?'

'I have very few.'

We laugh.

'Are there any references?'

'As regards radio I don't think I have any, not really. But in a sense, I suppose, Nathalie Sarraute—who also did quite a lot of radio pieces in the sixties—she would be one of my references. Her idea of "*tropisme*", where something unnameable happens or is said, and the person feels something which she absolutely cannot explain. It might be embarrassment, it might be anything. She constructs this all in words, on the page... So it's very good for radio. This tiny thing happens and everything is changed: I find that very interesting. I also find very interesting the fact that she says, "for me, there have been no wars". No anything. She just works in this headspace. It's not an internal monologue: it's something else which she calls text and subtext, conversation and subconversation.'

Like most things, this began some time ago. And in another place.[12]

This is a sort of reference. It's not directly a reference but otherwise I think my references are, oh, to a certain number of Fluxus artists whose work is very open and who dealt with image and text or things like that...'

'And', I say, 'the transient moment.'

'...and the transient moment, and the work which crosses the life and the life which crosses the work. They, for me, are things which are fundamental. And a certain turning the back on...' There is a silence; '...not just on information, but "knowledge"—on academia, things which you can find in books. And calling up that which the work invokes from the person'.

'In a sense', I say, 'you make very modest gestures. Do you continue to do these things, as you once said to me about your work, because of *la beauté du geste*, the beauty of the gesture?'

'*La beauté du geste*, yes.'

'Is that part of the Fluxus idea also?'

'It's a little more cynical.'

She laughs.

'Do the thing for the thing's sake, yes?'

'It's maybe because you can't do anything else.'

'You seem to be after a pure gesture?'

'I don't know.'

'And there's something Zen in this too.'

'Oh yes, it's fairly Zen. I wrote a paper recently in which I compare the detachment required of a radio producer to that of a Zen monk. Because, as you know, there is a great deal of work that goes into a radio program, a great deal of time invested in it. Maybe no one will speak to you about the radio program, and you have to be prepared for this. All the *tractations*[13] have to have been done between you and the work. So the attitude is already one of extreme detachment— and, in a sense, a radio program has absolutely no necessity except the sort of necessity of the moon in front of the window which is the subject of a lot of Bashō's poetry. It just happens to be there and you make of it whatever necessity you wish—but there is probably no other real necessity, is there?'

We both smile. The tape finds a space in which to gather silence.

She adds, 'Except necessity in the philosophical sense of that without which you cannot exist, *sans quoi tu ne peux pas vivre*... You could live without a radio program'.

1. Kaye Mortley won the prize for Best European Radio Documentary at the 1998 *Prix Europa* in Berlin for *Struthof: the French camp*, a documentary about a French concentration camp.
2. Interview with Mortley, Paris, 1994. All interview quotations of Mortley are from this same recording.

3. Produced for ABC Radio's *The Listening Room*.
4. Broadcast ABC Radio (ABCFM), *The Listening Room*, December 12, 1994. Co-production Australia/Sweden.
5. Broadcast ABC Radio (ABCFM), *The Listening Room*, March 23, 1998. First made for German National Radio, 1995. Original duration: two hours and twenty minutes.
6. In a letter to the author from Kaye Mortley, December 26, 1995.
7. *2146 Steine: Mahnmal gegen Rassismus, Saarbrucken (2146 Stones: Monument against Racism, Saarbrucken),* Jochen Gerz, 1990. For the work, Gerz and his students removed 2146 cobblestones from a square in Germany, engraved each with the name of one of the 2146 Jewish cemeteries existing in pre-Third Reich Germany, and then replaced them facing downwards. To mark this place a small sign was erected: 'Invisible Monument Square'.
8. *Tropismes* was the title of Sarraute's 1939 book. She continued to use the term to describe the little turnings and metamorphoses (from the word 'trope') which occurred in the atmosphere created by conversation and subconversation, the furtive or fleeting moments which often went unnoticed but could be given density by the silences between words. Such moments could reveal 'other worlds', 'trembling and sometimes fearful', or 'innumerable little crimes'. *Le Petit Robert Dictionnaire des Noms Propres*, Paris: Dictionnaires Le Robert, 1994, p. 1872. (Author's translation.)
9. Mortley had spent some of this time in France working on her Doctorate. In 1974 she returned to Australia and began work in the ABC Radio Drama Department. She entered a production milieu undergoing profound and 'historic' change. In 1971, for example, ABC Radio Head of Drama, Richard Connolly, had visited the *Atelier de Création Radiophonique* at Radio France as part of a Churchill Scholarship (specifically to investigate such new and exploratory models in radio). His report and ideas on the radio there had a profound influence on the work of Mortley and others. Connolly's research in Europe also led to the establishment of a new space 'of the long durée' on Sunday Night Radio 2, where producers like Mortley were given the chance to make a new kind of 'auteur radio', to experiment along the lines of the Atelier in France and the Neu Hörspiel in Germany. Strong links were made with experimental programs in Europe and producers began to meet regularly to discuss this work. The Atelier continues to exert a strong influence in the audio arts both in Europe and Australia. Source: Roz Cheney, ABC Radio Head of Audio Arts, interview with the author, 1998.
10. Artaud's radiophonic final statement, *Pour en Finir avec le Jugement de Dieu*, was finally broadcast on the Atelier de Création Radiophonique by René Farabet in 1973, some twenty-five years after it was scheduled and then banned for broadcast on Radio France. Farabet has called it 'perhaps the first very great program in radio terms; a monster in the landscape of radiophonic history'. It is ironic that Artaud, too, was seeking to escape the confines, as he then saw them, of literature, of the prison of the text. Radio, he imagined, could be a laboratory for discovering a way to talk to the audience, not as a State mass—this was the prison developed by mass radio then—but from and to a position of solitude. According to Farabet, this was remarkable for its time. It was an idea later taken up by Farabet and in fact became part of the ethos of the Atelier. (René Farabet, interview with the author, ABC Radio, 1996.)
11. *Atelier de Création Radiophonique*, 1994, Radio France. Over two hours in length, the program opens a sonic window onto the world of two old women living in Paris, alone in their small apartment, living and dying with their hundreds of pigeons. This is a 'transparent documentary', perhaps, or as Mortley says in the interview, 'a closed world that existed so strongly that I felt I could hardly touch it. You had to pretend that you hadn't touched it, you couldn't perform too many tricks in this world. Instead you had to enhance the world, and let it be. I just sat there for hours while they talked and they forgot I was there'.
12. *The Sea is to the East then All Around*, ABC Radio (ABCFM), *The Listening Room*, 1989.
13. A French word meaning negotiations, bargaining. There is a sense of 'shadiness' to such dealings.

The Sound of the Crowd Watching

John Conomos

> Above all our royalty is to be reverenced, and if you begin to poke about it you cannot reverence it. Its mystery is its life. We must not let in daylight upon magic.
>
> —Walter Bagehot

> *God, how the corpse's blood is sad in the depth of sound.*
>
> —Music-hall song cited in Georges Bataille, *W.C.*

> A vast crowd marches on Buckingham Palace screaming 'BUGGER THE QUEEN!'
>
> —William Burroughs

> The crowd is no longer content with pious promises and conditionals. It wants to experience for itself the strongest possible feeling of its own animal force and passion and, as means to this end, it will use whatever social pretexts and demands offer themselves.
>
> —Elias Canetti

How do we talk about the death and funeral of Diana, Princess of Wales, without resorting to the familiar constraints, excesses and tropes of academic writing and/or popular tabloid journalism? How do we even negotiate the shifting complexities of Diana's life apropos of class, audience, culture, emotion, gender and nation in a manner that can adequately capture the public engagement with the Diana phenomenon in all of its dynamic transformations since her marriage to Charles in 1981? What are the various narrative forms that have constructed the popular understandings of Diana's life and death in and around the House of Windsor for the best part of nearly two decades? We speak of Diana's life as a fractured fairytale or as a cautionary, tragic soap; an intricate cultural narrative of glamour, fame and wealth, and, at the same time, marital unhappiness—eating disorders and almost 'autistic' shyness—lending itself to gossip, jokes and conspiracy speculation. What exactly are the implications of trying to see beyond this regurgitated Diana, the People's Princess, the global hologram or CNN icon, and the huntress-hunted of paparazzi media culture?

For one thing, Diana during her life and after, Diana as a mutating 'sign of the times' media event with her swirling, contradictory meanings, has contributed to a radical questioning of the Queen's hegemony in contemporary Britain. Arguably, as we witnessed on numerous TV talk shows, in tabloid newspapers and magazines, and in academic discourse, the republican debate took on a certain urgency as a consequence of Diana's death and funeral. Kerb-side interviews with constitutional scholars examining Diana's possible impact on the constitution and the monarchy became a common if surreal spectacle in front of Buckingham Palace. Within that one week, the people of England were compelled by the enormous mythic power of Diana's death to construct new frameworks of interpretation, to make cultural and psychic sense of their mutual loss in their everyday lives. This meant examining themselves, their positions as subjects, and the established signifiers of their monarchy. It also meant that the Queen was forced to make numerous concessions to the people. Specifically, observe how, due to public outcry, the Royal family (contra protocol) finally allowed the flag at Buckingham Palace to fly at half-mast. Also note how the Queen, the Queen Mother, Prince Phillip and others reluctantly choreographed their movements during the funeral itself. Television cameras also intensely scrutinised Charles' interactions with his own sons. Indeed, the public pressured the Queen to make the funeral a TV broadcast, to lengthen the funeral route and to generally accept the idea of her subjects becoming citizens—articulate, assertive participants in, Beth Edington reminds us, not a 'nation-as-Establishment', but rather, a 'nation-as-the-people'.[1]

Let us put aside for the moment the compelling issues salient to the questioning of the monarchy, and focus on the sonic architectonics of Diana's televised funeral. I will examine the funeral as a sonic event in terms of what might be called Bataillean 'aural rupture': the sounds of the grieving, anonymous crowd that greet Diana's casket, carried on a gun-carriage and draped in the British flag as it is conveyed to Westminster Abbey. Georges Bataille's libidinal materialism is a radical critique of Western idealism, humanity, religion, morality and sovereignty, a heterogeneous philosophy of profligate expenditure and self-annihilation which undoes the 'restricted' economy of the hegemonic social order.[2] It takes on acute resonance in these animalistic cries of mourning from London's streets. I am interested in the complex acoustic tension between the first, barely audible utterances of interiority from a hitherto silent crowd—cries which mark, in Bataillean terms, the abject, automutilation and loss—and the socio-cultural exteriority of the crowd as a material representation of changing sensibilities in British public culture. These public vocalisations of ritualistic mourning are, I would argue, an expression of vertigo related to a rapidly unfolding dialectic of questioning resistance, precipitated by Diana's death, to an archaic British monarchy.

But the aurality of the public event began well before the funeral. The massive deluge of media coverage of Diana's life intensified after her Ballardian end with her Muslim lover Dodi in the Parisian road tunnel carnage. The poignancy of her demise is heightened by the fact that we were shown, repeatedly, silent surveillance video footage of Diana leaving the Ritz Hotel a few minutes before the fatal accident. This footage—together with the initial mute Sky News coverage of the King's Troops and the Welsh Guard escorting Diana's body along her private avenue—anticipates the eerie silence of the public funeral parade, punctuated by vocalisations of grief and other sporadic sounds. Further, what we hear from the volatile, kinetic crowd contrasts with the more subdued tone of the Griersonian voice-over commentary: it is as if Diana herself is engaged in talking to her mourners. Given that, as Allen S. Weiss notes, sound recording was invented to preserve the human voice as frozen speech from beyond the grave, the disembodied commentary here has rich, spectral connotations.[3]

An invisible bell chimes as Diana's body is escorted along her private avenue, presaging a further chime as her body leaves the avenue's gate. We hear the hooves of the King's Troops' horses—clip-clop, clip-clop—as they pull the gun-carriage through the streets. Yet silence, as Kitzinger rightly points out, is the operative sound of Diana's TV funeral.[4] But if we increase the volume of our Sky News telecast we can hear numerous nondiegetic sounds—chthonian expressions of the end of the human—emanating from somewhere nearby the commentator narrating the mournful spectacle.

In a fleeting moment, there along the avenue, a male voice erupts in uncontrolled sobbing, initially reminiscent of orgiastic laughter from a Buñuel movie (perhaps it belongs to one of Diana's male staff members lined up to pay their final respects). Next we hear the ecstatic cries of the crowd when it finally sees Diana's body coming into High Street: first, deep sobbing female voices, anonymous, grief-stricken, barely human, like animals caught in traps screaming into the void of Bataillean bestiality, unreason, and inner violence: 'Diana, we love you, we love you, Diana...'. Then, another anonymous voice, this time male, desperate, drunk with grief and resignation: 'Bye, Diana'.

Sonically, we have entered Bataille's realm of the 'formless', where zero is immense: the endpoint of the human 'where the universe is like a spider or spit'.[5] The crowd, in all of its grieving anonymity, is experiencing devastating loss in a world without Diana's comforting telegenic aura. These crushing cries of despair sum up, in Canetti's monumental study *Crowds and Power* (1960), the crowd's burning imperative, as Helen Grace recently interpreted it, to incorporate the dead into itself.[6] It is as if, via these disturbing expressions of desperation, excess and negation, the crowd is engaged in reworking ideas about nationhood, citizenry, emotion and ritual; and although it is drawing a long bow to argue that it is involved in a revolutionary project to subvert the royal family, its actions nevertheless echo a long and complex history of crowd dynamics in art and politics. In slapstick comedy, dadaist film, and situationist art, during the tumultuous political events of Europe in the '20s and '30s, more lately in Tianenmen Square in 1989, at the fall of the Berlin Wall, in Moscow in 1991, etc., crowds have featured as the paradigmatic forces for change at significant aesthetic, cultural and historical junctures.[7]

To encounter these staggering lamentations as Bataillean ecstatic moments is also to venture into the wilds of Bataille's total expenditure without return. These voices motivate us to locate their anonymous sources. Thus, we are faced with a substantial dilemma, if we subscribe to Metz's claim to understand our aural world we are obliged to find the source of the sound we are phenomenologically experiencing.[8] As Weiss puts it: 'We seek that realm where the voice reaches beyond its body, beyond the shadow of its corporeal origins, to become a radically original sonic object'.[9] But at Diana's funeral we hear undifferentiated cries from the crowd. We can't, in Metzian terms, clearly identify who exactly is responsible for these voices. This incapacity to define the voices' sources intensifies their Bataillean contours as aural motifs of devastating loss.

Another sound featured significantly: the crowd sporadically applauds throughout the funeral procession. The most critical manifestation of this phenomenon takes place at the conclusion of Diana's brother's stirring eulogy in the Abbey. A rolling thunder of anti-Royal sentiment, sparked by Earl Spencer's overtly critical references to Diana's treatment at the hands of 'the firm', erupts in the park where the crowd watched on large video screens, and spills into the cavernous space of the Abbey. The formerly silent, bereaved audience of celebrities and politicians joins somewhat hesitantly in. Aurally, the applause is ambiguous: is it born of mourning, protest and/or fandom? In the simulacral economy of the televised event, a spiralling sonic chiasm gathers between the video screens, the mourning public, the interiority of the Abbey and the vast, global exteriority of televisual space.

The ecstatic wretchedness of the first vocal utterances from the waiting crowd in High Street, Kensington is a sonic index of the Diana media phenomenon. The funeral telecast is, literally, a resonant public performance which will be remembered, culturally and sonically, as a watershed local and global mass media experience. Cloaked in silence and pierced by cries, the shared audiovisual event of Diana's funeral, central to the rapidly changing nexus between the British monarchy and its citizenry, will become part of global collective memory.

This is a shorter version of a paper which addresses the sonic architectonics of Princess Diana's funeral in the context of the monarchy/republic debate. Many thanks to Angela Bucci for her Diana videotape.

1. See Beth Edington, 'Nation', in *Screen*, Vol. 39, No. 1, Spring 1998, pp. 79, 80.
2. See Bataille, *Visions of Excess: Selected Writings 1927–1939*, ed. Allan Stoekl, Minneapolis: University of Minnesota Press, 1985.
3. Allen S. Weiss, *Perverse Desire and the Ambiguous Icon*, Albany: State University of New York Press, p. 141.
4. Jenny Kitzinger, 'Image', in *Screen*, Vol. 39, No. 1, Spring 1998, p. 78.
5. Bataille, 'Formless', op. cit., p. 31.
6. Helen Grace, 'Introduction: The Lamenting Crowd', in *Re:Public, Planet Diana*, Kingswood: Research Centre in Intercommunal Studies, University of Western Sydney, 1998, p. 2. I am indebted to this invaluable anthology of seminar proceedings on Diana as a popular global media event, and, particularly, Grace's suggestive reading of Canetti apropos of Diana's mourning crowd.
7. Grace, ibid., p. 1.
8. Christian Metz, 'Aural Objects', in *Film Sound: Theory and Practice*, eds. Elizabeth Weis and John Belton, New York: Columbia University Press, 1985, pp. 155–156.
9. Weiss, op. cit., p. 138.

Measuring Sound Art

Densil Cabrera

Sound theory, like many contemporary disciplines, freely draws from other fields including physical and psychological acoustics. Principles and anecdotes from these fields serve to illustrate sound theory's essentially philosophical agenda, and may be brought to bear in one of its more specific functions: the exploration of ideas around sound art. Although such borrowings enter a speculative discourse, the original disciplines remain thoroughly empirical. If these empirical disciplines provide useful concepts in the context of sound theory, then might they not also have some limited use in their own right for the study of sound art?

Just as sound theory exhibits an occasional interest in the acoustical sciences, certain forms of sound art draw inspiration from these fields, explicitly applying acoustical and psychoacoustical devices. Alternatively, an artist might be unconcerned by acoustical considerations but may nevertheless produce a piece that can be well understood in acoustical terms. One relatively homogenous form of sound art that is heavily engaged in physical acoustics involves works that are based on acoustical resonance. For such a piece, an artist finds or constructs a resonating acoustical system and presents it to the public as an installation or recording. Many artists have worked in this way, including Ros Bandt,[1] Garlo,[2] Alan Lamb,[3] Annea Lockwood,[4] Alvin Lucier,[5] Mins Minssen,[6] Gordon Monahan,[7] Bruce Odland and Sam Auinger,[8] Paul Panhuysen and Johan Goedhart,[9] Minoru Sato and Toshiya Tsunoda,[10] Dan Senn,[11] and Roger Winfield.[12] Here, the acoustical phenomenon of resonance may be expressed in a number of ways: as an inner-space (contrasted to the visual space of superficial exteriors); as a partly stable system which, after sustained drone-like periods, will swell into a much more complex sound; as a harmonic or anharmonic frequency structure depending on the type of resonating system; as a particular set of strong frequencies; or as an almost overwhelming filter through which an environment or process is heard.

While these issues of physical acoustics might be of considerable interest, they are only indirectly related to the perception of the work. They are probably of greatest importance when the artist emphasises them in associated text. By contrast, the phenomena described by psychoacoustics deal directly with the perception of sound, and should be of greater general value in the study of these pieces. But in what sense are these pieces 'psychoacoustical'—or more precisely, in what sense are they especially suited to psychoacoustical analysis? Psychoacoustics studies low level auditory perception and cognition. At best it will be of secondary use in art forms where the emphasis is on high-level coding of sound such as in language, symbolic musical structures, or the sampling of cultural artefacts. The resonating sound art referred to here is comparatively lacking in such high-level auditory codings and is concerned largely with concrete sound.

A second more pragmatic reason why these works are suited to psychoacoustical analysis is that their sound is simple. Psychoacoustics is an incomplete science, and the modelling of fine temporal detail of rapidly varying sound is one of its most difficult problems both in terms of the computational resources required to apply existing models and the adequacy of these models. Models of steady-state, regular, or slowly evolving sound are more developed and easier to apply, and are well suited to the slowly evolving sounds of sustained resonance.

Computational models of loudness,[13] aspects of pitch,[14] sharpness (or brightness),[15] roughness,[16] dissonance,[17] and spatial aspects of sound are among those available to the current day researcher. The form, availability, applicability and accuracy of these models varies widely. They all take a number of physical sound measurements as input from which a psychoacoustical quality is calculated. For instance, the model of loudness depends not only on the physical sound intensity but also on its frequency content (both position on the frequency scale and bandwidth), and thus loudness is given in sones rather than decibels. This model reflects the fact that a broadband noise is much louder than a single tone of the same decibel level. Similarly, modelling of pitch is much more complex than frequency analysis and involves masking (making some physical frequencies inaudible) and virtual pitches (pitches that do not necessarily correspond to frequencies present in the sound). As pitch is a multidimensional percept, measures of higher level aspects of pitch have been developed, including those of 'multiplicity' (the average number of audible pitches), and tonalness (the extent to which the sound is tone-like).[18] Sharpness is largely determined by the relative amount of high frequency content in the sound, and to a lesser extent by its overall loudness. Roughness is determined by rapid fluctuations in the sound (at a rate around 70Hz), but its accurate computation is intensive and was not available to the author at the time of writing. Dissonance is a form of roughness, but models exist based on tonal components close in frequency (rather than fluctuations in the sound envelope), and it is therefore rather simple to calculate. Spatial aspects of sound are both subtle and difficult to quantify. Lateralisation is related to the sound level and phase at the two ears, and a full computational model requires large resources. Auditory spaciousness, which is the sense of sound surrounding the listener, might also be modelled (based on interaural cross-correlations), although that has not been attempted by this author.[19]

Basic measurements such as these can also be analysed as they change in time, allowing sound to be characterised as static, swelling or decaying, changing pitch, and in many other ways. Statistical functions may also be used to characterise the sound over time. Hence these tools can produce many more sound measurements that are relatively close to perceptually salient qualities.

A finding that one piece is louder or rougher than another on its own gives no great insights into the pieces or the art form. This type of measurement gains value when it is related to a person's experience of listening to the sound or to material such as the artist's writings. Introspective listening tests are the simplest experimental approach to studying the experience of listening. In such a test, many listening subjects comment in a predetermined format on sound stimuli which could be examples of resonating sound art. While it is possible to ask the subjects to reflect upon the loudness or roughness of the sounds, it is probably more important to gather data on qualities that cannot be approximated by standard models. Thus subjective evaluation of the sound and emotion evoked or represented by the sound can be statistically related to the output of psychoacoustical models.

It can be argued that this type of testing might produce considerable distortion. Many of the pieces under consideration are installations, and the isolation of the recorded sound from the original context is a dilution of the work. Nevertheless, the artists released these works to the public as audio recordings, so it is justifiable to analyse them as such. The subjects' act of introspection and the communication of their thoughts is not part of the normal listening process, so there is a question of the effect of this added self-consciousness. The communication process itself may be difficult and imprecise. Alternatives, such as physiological tests, offer only crude measures, the meaning of which may be obscure. The physical environment of some tests—where a computer presents the sound over headphones and gathers responses, and where many stimuli of short duration are assessed in succession—also differs substantially from a normal listening situation. Quantitative analysis is, by necessity, reductionist, and subtleties of meaning are lost when complex human responses are reduced to numbers. Compromise is inevitable in experiment design of this type.

AN EXPERIMENTAL APPROACH

In research currently being undertaken by the author, three introspective listening tests have been completed. The first investigated responses to samples of room resonance which was generated in a manner similar to Alvin Lucier's process of *I am Sitting in a Room*, and is described in detail elsewhere.[20] The second experiment is briefly described here as an illustration of the application of psychoacoustics to the analysis of sound art. Some of the limitations of this experiment are addressed by the third one.

Fifty-three samples of twenty seconds' duration were arbitrarily selected from twenty-seven published recordings of resonating sound art. Works by Bandt, Garlo, Lamb, Lucier, Monahan, Odland and Auinger, Panhuysen and Goedhart, Senn, and Winfield were represented.[21] Most of these sounds were quite static, although some (particularly the aeolian works) fluctuated a little. The experiment was conducted on a computer,[22] and the subject wore high quality headphones.[23] The relative sound levels of the stimuli were maintained from the original recordings. For each sound stimulus, the computer presented the subject with three evaluation scales and two emotion scales (see Figure 1). The evaluation scales sought to distinguish general, intellectual and sensory evaluations. The emotion scales sought only to record the most basic of emotional responses: emotional arousal and emotional valence (expressed as displeasure/pleasure).[24] While these bipolar scales were continuous, text categorising seven discrete sections of each scale appeared in a box above it and changed with the position of the slider. Twenty-seven of the fifty-three sound stimuli were assessed four times while the remainder were assessed just once. There were eleven subjects, nine of whom had extensive experience in sound art, music or sound production.

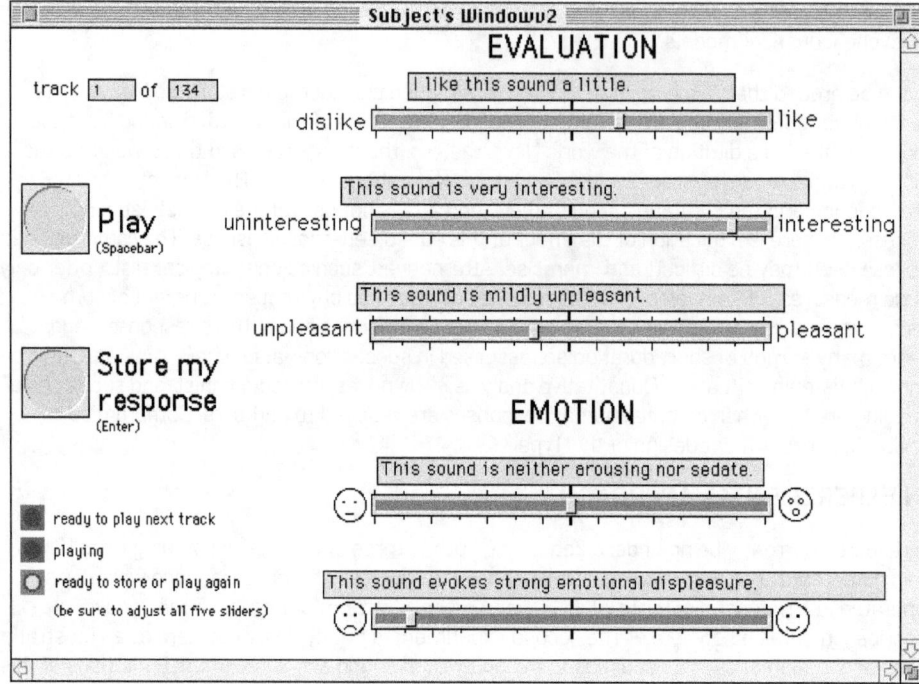

Figure 1. Experiment interface with examples of slider positions.

The resulting subjective responses showed that overall the stimuli were mildly interesting (average = .16, where -1 and +1 represent extremely uninteresting and interesting respectively), and evoked mild emotional displeasure or negative valence (-.16). The other three scales had averages closer to 0.

Together the two emotion scales—Arousal and Valence—can represent a wide range of emotion that can be visualised in the two-dimensional emotion space of the left-hand chart in Figure 2.[25] The upper right-hand quadrant contains aroused emotions with positive valence such as joy and exuberance. Likewise the lower right-hand quadrant includes calmness and serenity; the lower left-hand quadrant includes gloom and depression; while the upper left-hand quadrant includes alarm and distress. Stronger emotions are further from the centre. When the sound stimuli of the experiment are charted in this way, evoked emotion is seen to vary overwhelmingly along a line extending between distress and calm: the emotional response is largely one-dimensional. The sine tone-like stimuli of Lucier and Senn are the main ones to significantly encroach into the negative arousal and negative valence quadrant, and no stimuli are in the positive arousal and positive valence quadrant.

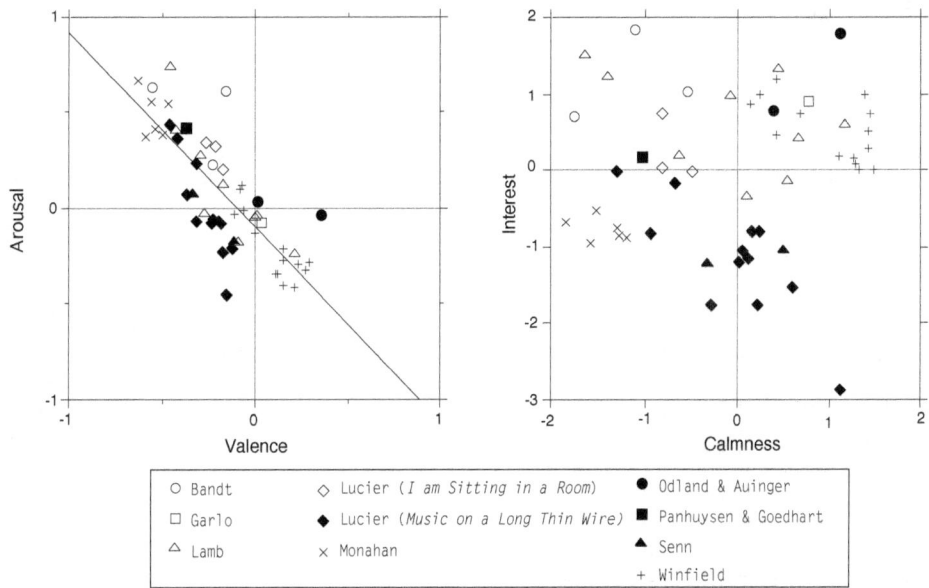

Figure 2. The position of the sound stimuli in a two-dimensional emotion space (left); and Calmness versus Interest (right), both separated by artist.

A factor analysis of the five response scales found that they were used in just two ways. The first factor (accounting for .69 of variance) will be called 'Calmness' and was formed by the following scale weightings: Like .58; Interesting .00; Pleasant .89; Arousal -.96; Valence .93. Here, the sensory aspect of evaluation (Pleasant) is associated with both of the emotion scales; as pleasantness increases, Arousal decreases and Valence increases. The second factor (accounting for .28 of variance) will be called 'Interest', and is essentially the same as the Interesting scale. It had the following weightings: Like .84; Interesting .99; Pleasant .49; Arousal .15; Valence .38. Together these factors account for nearly all of the variance (.97), indicating that Calmness and Interest are the only subjective responses detected by the five scales when all stimuli are considered. In the right-hand chart of Figure 2 where the results for the two factors Calmness and Interest are plotted against each other, the samples of each artist tend to form clusters, characterising the works' emotional and evaluative qualities.

The sound samples were analysed in many ways including for time-varying loudness, sharpness, dissonance, and aspects of pitch, as outlined earlier. Overall loudness, sharpness, and dissonance were positively mutually correlated and were negatively correlated to Calmness (for loudness, $r=-.79$, $P<.0001$). Overall measures of pitch (pure and complex tonalness, and multiplicity) were also positively mutually correlated but had no significant correlations to either factor. The standard deviations of loudness and sharpness had a logarithmic relation to Interest (for sharpness, $r=.74$, $P<.0001$). Thus Interest was partly predicted by the amount of variation in the sound sample while Calmness was predicted by quietness, dullness and consonance. These two results are far from surprising, but it is interesting that the pitch measurements, which appeared to be reasonable, were unrelated to the two types of subjective response.

DISCUSSION

Consistent evaluation and emotion qualities were elicited by the sound stimuli suggesting that such qualities might also be attributed to the original full recordings. Thus each piece was characterised for Calmness and Interest. Some people find it difficult to imagine that 'found sounds' (which many of these recordings were) can represent emotions. Others would consider emotion to be of little relevance to an abstract experimental art form. These results (as well as results of the author's other experiments) show that listeners attribute emotions to such sounds with a fair degree of consistency. One question that remains is how these emotional responses reflect the perception of the artwork in the broader aesthetic and cultural context.

It is conceivable that the use of numerical analysis techniques might permit the construction of broad predictive models of perception (although such models are heavily limited by factors such as the type of listeners, the range of sounds, and the listening context). Such a model raises complex questions of the extent to which predictions reflect 'innate', cultural, and contextual responses which only very extensive research would succeed in separating. Resonating sound art is possibly less contentious in this respect as the artist's contribution to the sound is largely at arm's length.

One of the main problems with this experiment is that it gives a greatly reduced representation of the subjective response. A subsequent experiment sought to address this by retaining the five scales, but emphasising freely written responses to the open questions: 'Describe the sound'; 'What emotions does the sound evoke or represent?'; 'What imagery does the sound suggest?'; and 'What do you like or dislike about the sound?'. This experiment was conducted on the listener's own stereo system at their leisure and had just twelve sound samples of three minutes' duration. The quantitative results of the two experiments are well matched and many concepts such as 'anticipation', 'artificiality', 'metallic', 'immersion', 'little or no emotion' and 'little or no imagery' were extracted and quantified from the open responses. Nevertheless, even the three minute samples fail to provide the prolonged meditative context in which many of these works are envisaged, and further work may address that issue.

This methodology assumes that concrete sound is an important aspect of the art work, and that the sound retains meaning when presented in a relatively arbitrary context. There is a sort of paradox in applying this type of study to these art works where the artist's concern is largely with the broad production process rather than with the specific sound outcomes, so that, to an extent, the sound may be incidental. Psychoacoustical analysis is concerned with the surface of listening, hence with the most widely available and immediate experience of the art work. In Nattiez's terminology, the listening tests fall into the category of 'external esthetics', while the psychoacoustical models might be called 'empirical inductive esthetics'.[26] Even if the nature of the poietic process is somewhat unusual, the sound recording remains as a stable trace, and the experience of listening may be studied without dwelling on its initial conception.

In personal communications to the author, Lucier and Lamb both described listening experiences beyond the concrete. Lucier commented on the sense of anticipation created by simple and slow processes which may be more important than the actual sound. Lamb described an imaginary music provoked by the sound of his wire recordings. If such experiences are generalisable, they will be reflected in the subjective responses of an appropriately designed listening test, but may not have any particular relation to psychoacoustical modelling of the sound.

More conventional analyses of sound art—where one reviewer responds to a work—are at least as much dependent on the reviewer as on the work in question. Here, the reviewer has the advantage of being highly informed of the work's cultural context. The experimental approach—where the limited responses of multiple 'reviewers' are combined—has the potential to give a more stable and immediate assessment of the work, can be reinforced by psychoacoustical measurements, and does not preclude the additional application of speculative analysis.

The author is thankful to the listeners who voluntarily participated in the experiment described in this paper, and to Simon Hayman, Alvin Lucier and Alan Lamb for their comments and criticisms. The research was conducted under an Australian Postgraduate Award and a Department of Architectural and Design Science Supplementary Scholarship.

1. Ros Bandt, *Mungo, The Listening Room: Beta*, ABC Music, 1994.
2. Garlo, *Vent de Guitares*, CIP/Audio, 1994.
3. Alan Lamb, *Primal Image*, Dorobo, 1995; *Journeys on the Winds of Time*, Austral Voices, New Albion Records, 1990.
4. Annea Lockwood, *The Glass World*, ¿What Next? Recordings, 1977.
5. Alvin Lucier, *Music on a Long Thin Wire*, Lovely Music, 1992; *I am Sitting in a Room*, Lovely Music, 1990.
6. Mins Minssen, *Aeolsharfen*, Fundmbules Records, 1994; *Windharfen*, Fundmbules Records, 1995.
7. Gordon Monahan, *Long Aeolian Piano, Speaker Swinging*, self-published LP, 1987; *Documentations 1986-95*, self-published video, 1995.
8. Bruce Odland and Sam Auinger, *O+A Resonance*, O+A, 1995.
9. Paul Panhuysen and Johan Goedhart, *Requiem, Long String Installations*, Apollo Records, 1986.
10. Minoru Sato and Toshiya Tsunoda, *Ful*, Selektion, 1996.
11. Dan Senn, *Hands Off (Shmoos Harp), Flutter Moths*, Newsense Intermedium, 1993.
12. Roger Winfield, *Windsongs*, Saydisc Records, 1991.
13. Brian C. J. Moore, Brian R. Glasberg and Thomas Baer, 'A Model for the Prediction of Thresholds, Loudness, and Partial Loudness', in *Journal of the Audio Engineering Society*, Vol. 45, No. 4, April 1997, pp. 224–240; Erbart Zwicker and Bertram Scharf, 'A Model of Loudness Summation', in *Psychological Review*, Vol. 72, 1965, pp. 3–26.
14. Ernst Terhardt, Gerhard Stoll and Manfred Seewann, 'Algorithm for Extraction of Pitch and Pitch Salience from Complex Tonal Signals', in *Journal of the Acoustical Society of America*, Vol. 71, No. 3, 1982, pp. 679–688; E. Terhardt, G. Stoll and M. Seewann, 'Pitch of Complex Signals According to Virtual-pitch Theory: Tests, Examples, and Predictions', in *Journal of the Acoustical Society of America*, Vol. 71, No. 3, 1982, pp. 671–678.
15. Erbhart Zwicker and Hugo Fastl, *Psychoacoustics: Facts and Models*, Heidelberg: Springer-Verlag, 1990, pp. 215–221; W. Aures, 'Berechnungsvefahren für den sensorischen Wohlklang beliebiger Schallsignale', *Acustica*, Vol. 59, 1985, pp. 130–141.
16. Peter Daniel and R. Weber, 'Psychoacoustical Roughness: Implementation of an Optimized Model', *Acustica/Acta Acustica*, Vol. 83, 1997, pp. 113–123.
17. William Hutchinson and Leon Knopoff, 'The Acoustic Component of Western Consonance', in *Interface*, Vol. 7, 1978, pp. 1–29; William Sethares, 'Local Consonance and the Relationship between Timbre and Scale', in *Journal of the Acoustical Society of America*, Vol. 94, 1993, pp. 1218–1228; William Sethares, *Tuning, Timbre, Spectrum, Scale*, London: Springer-Verlag, 1998.
18. Richard Parncutt, *Harmony: A Psychoacoustical Approach*, Berlin: Springer-Verlag, 1989.

19. Jens Blauert, *Spatial Hearing*, Cambridge MA: The MIT Press, 1997, pp. 348–358.
20. Densil Cabrera, 'Resonating Sound Art and the Aesthetics of Room Resonance', in *Convergence*, Vol. 3, No. 4, Winter 1997, pp. 108–137.
21. Ros Bandt, *Mungo* (3 samples); Garlo, *Vent de Guitares No.7* (1 sample); Alan Lamb, *Primal Image* and *Journeys on the Winds of Time* (9 samples); Alvin Lucier, *Music on a Long Thin Wire* (12 samples) and *I am Sitting in a Room* (3 samples); Gordon Monahan, *Long Aeolian Piano* (6 samples); Bruce Odland and Sam Auinger, *O+A Resonance* (2 samples: tracks 3 and 5); Paul Panhuysen and Johan Goedhart, *Requiem* (1 sample); Dan Senn, *Hands Off (Shmoos Harp)* (2 samples); Roger Winfield, *Windsongs* (14 samples). The number of samples was determined by the number and length of relevant tracks.
22. The program was written in Opcode Max 3.0 on a Power Macintosh computer.
23. AKG K1000, using an AKG BAP1000 stereo to binaural converter.
24. James Russel, 'A Circumplex Model of Affect', in *Journal of Personality and Social Psychology*, Vol. 39, No. 6, 1980, pp. 1161–1178.
25. James Russel, op. cit., and 'Pancultural Aspects of Human Conceptual Organization of Emotions', in *Journal of Personality and Social Psychology*, Vol. 45, No. 6, 1983, pp. 1281–1288.
26. Jean-Jacques Nattiez, *Music and Discourse*, Princeton: Princeton University Press, 1990.

www.ingramcontent.com/pod-product-compliance
Lightning Source LLC
Chambersburg PA
CBHW060505300426
44112CB00017B/2553